10/99

D1227448

Racism

Key Concepts in Critical Theory

Series Editor
Roger S. Gottlieb

JUSTICE
Edited by Milton Fisk

GENDER
Edited by Carol C. Gould

DEMOCRACY
Edited by Philip Green

RACISM
Edited by Leonard Harris

ECOLOGY
Edited by Carolyn Merchant

EXPLOITATION
Edited by Kai Nielsen and Robert Ware

ALIENATION AND SOCIAL CRITICISM
Edited by Richard Schmitt and Thomas E. Moody

Key Concepts in Critical Theory

Racism

EDITED BY LEONARD HARRIS

Humanity
Books

an imprint of Prometheus Books
59 John Glenn Drive, Amherst, New York 14228-2197

Published 1999 by Humanity Books, an imprint of Prometheus Books

03 02 01 00 99   5 4 3 2 1

Library of Congress Cataloging-in-Publication Data

Racism / edited by Leonard Harris.
        p.   cm. — (Key concepts in critical theory)
    Includes bibliographical references and index.
    ISBN 1–57392–639–6 (pbk.)
    1. Racism. I. Harris, Leonard, 1948–   II. Series.
HT1521.R3414   1999
305.8—dc21   97–24857
                                                                            CIP

Printed in the United States of America on acid-free paper

Dedication

I AM INDEBTED TO the fellowship, counsel, love, and support of Carolyn Johnson, J. Evertt Green, Lucius Outlaw, Judith Green, Blanche Radford-Curry, William McBride, James Williams, Greg Moses, Patricia Knox, Jeffrey E. Letzkus, Vernon J. Williams Jr., Carl Briscoe, Kube Sherron Jones, Sherii Hill, Daphne Thompson, Darryl Scrivens, Carol Black, Chris Sowe, Rita Hillman, Jason Hill, and the next generation, Jamila R. Harris, Jarrard L. Harris, L. Nawatu Harris, and Jade Renee Harris.

Contents

PART I: OBJECTIVE REALISM

7

Objectivist Explanations of Racism

PART II: CONSTRUCTIVE REALISM

Constructivist Explanations of Racism

PART III: REASON, RACE, AND MORALITY

PART IV: POSTSCRIPT

Acknowledgments

ACKNOWLEDGMENT IS MADE TO the parties below for generously granting permission to reproduce the following works.

Ruth Benedict, "Racism: The *ism* of the Modern World," "Why Then Race Prejudice," in *Race and Racism* (New York: Routledge, 1942), pp. 1–13, 141–65; reprinted with permission of Viking Penguin.

Pierre van den Berghe, "Ethnicity as Kin Selection," in *The Ethnic Phenomenon* (New York: Elsevier Publishing Co., 1981), pp. 18–22, 24–36; reprinted with permission of Greenwood Publishing Group, Inc.

Albert G. Mosley, "Negritude, Nationalism, and Nativism: Racists or Racialists?" in *African Philosophy: Selected Readings* (Englewood Cliffs, N.J.: Prentice Hall, 1995), pp. 216–34; reprinted with permission of the author.

Joel Kotkin, "The Making of Global Tribes," in *Tribes: How Race, Religion, and Identity Determine Success in the New Global Economy* (New York: Random House, 1993), pp. 14–35; © 1992 by Joel Kotkin; reprinted with permission of Random House, Inc.

John Rex, "Racism, Institutionalized and Otherwise," in *Race and Ethnicity* (Buckingham, U.K.: Open University Press, 1986), pp. 99–118; reprinted with permission of Open University Press and author.

D. A. Washbrook, "Ethnicity and Racialism in Colonial Indian Society," in Robert Ross, ed., *Racism and Colonialism* (The Hague: Martinus Nijhoff Publishers, 1982), pp. 143–81; reprinted with permission of Kluwer Academic Publishers.

Etienne Balibar, "Class Racism," in Etienne Balibar and Immanuel Wallerstein, *Race, Nation, and Class* (London: Verso Press, 1991), pp. 204–16; © La Découverte, 1988; reprinted with permission of Éditions La Découverte.

Alain L. Locke, "The Contribution of Race to Culture," *The Student World* 23 (1930): 349–53; reprinted by permission of Moorland-Spingarn Research Center, Howard University.

Colette Guillaumin, "Race and Nature: The System of Marks," *Feminist Issues* 8, no. 2 (Fall 1988): 26–43; © 1988 by Colette Guillaumin; reprinted with permission of Transaction Publishers; all rights reserved.

Martin Barker, "Biology and the New Racism," in *The New Racism* (Westport, Ct.: University Publications of America, an imprint of Greenwood Publishing Group, Inc., 1981), pp. 12–29; © 1981 by University Publications of America; reprinted with permission of Greenwood Publishing Group, Inc.

Claudia Card, "On Race, Racism, and Ethnicity," in Linda A. Bell and David Blumenfeld, eds., *Overcoming Racism and Sexism* (Lanham, Md.: Rowman & Littlefield, 1995), pp. 141–52; reprinted with permission of Rowman & Littlefield.

K. Anthony Appiah, "Why There Are No Races," in K. Anthony Appiah and Amy Gutmann, *Color Conscious: The Political Morality of Race* (Princeton: Princeton University Press, 1996); reprinted with permission of Princeton University Press.

Paula Rothenberg, "The Construction, Deconstruction, and Reconstruction of Difference," *Hypatia: A Journal of Feminist Philosophy* 5, no. I (Spring 1990): 42–57; © 1990 by Paula Rothenberg; reprinted with permission of *Hypatia* and the author.

Pierre-André Taguieff, "L'identité nationale saisie par les logiques de racisation: Aspects, figures et problèmes du racisme différentialiste," *Mots/Les langages du politique* 12 (March 1986): 91–128; translated for this edition by Bernard Pony; reprinted with permission of Presses de Sciences Po.

Antonio Sérgio Alfredo Guimarães, "Racism and Anti-Racism in Brazil," in Benjamin P. Bowser, ed., *Racism and Anti-Racism in World Perspective* (Thousand Oaks, Calif.: Sage Publications, 1995), pp. 208–26; reprinted with permission of Sage Publications, Inc.

George M. Fredrickson, "Reflections on the Comparative History and Sociology of Racism," in American Studies in Southern Africa: Symposium Proceedings; © 1993 by United States Information Service; reprinted with permission of author.

Lewis R. Gordon, "Antiblack Racism and Ontology," in *Bad Faith and Anti-Black Racism* (Atlantic Highlands, N.J.: Humanities Press, 1995), pp. 130–37; reprinted with permission of Humanities Press International, Inc.

Gerald Torres, "Critical Race Theory: The Decline of the Universalist Ideal and the Hope of Plural Justice—Some Observations and Questions of an Emerging Phenomenon," *Minnesota Law Review* 75, no. 993 (1991): 993–1007; reprinted with permission of University of Minnesota Law School.

David Theo Goldberg, "Racism and Rationality: The Need for a New Critique," *Philosophy of the Social Sciences* 20, no. 3 (September 1990): 317–48; © 1990 by Sage Publications, reprinted with permission of Sage Publications, Inc.

Jorge L. A. Garcia, "The Heart of Racism," *Journal of Social Philosophy* (forthcoming); reprinted with permission of the Journal of Social Philosophy and the author.

Series Editor's Preface

THE VISION OF A rational, just, and fulfilling social life, present in Western thought from the time of the Judaic prophets and Plato's *Republic*, has since the French Revolution been embodied in systematic critical theories whose adherents seek a fundamental political, economic, and cultural transformation of society.

These critical theories—varieties of Marxism, socialism, anarchism, feminism, gay/lesbian liberation, ecological perspectives, discourses by anti-racist, anti-imperialist, and national liberation movements, and utopian/critical strains of religious communities—have a common bond that separates them from liberal and conservative thought. They are joined by the goal of sweeping social change; the rejection of existing patterns of authority, power, and privilege; and a desire to include within the realms of recognition and respect the previously marginalized and oppressed.

Yet each tradition of Critical Theory also has its distinct features: specific concerns, programs, and locations within a geometry of difference and critique. Because of their intellectual specificity and the conflicts among the different social groups they represent, these theories have often been at odds with one another, differing over basic questions concerning the ultimate cause and best response to injustice, the dynamics of social change, and the optimum structure of a liberated society, as well as the identity of the social agent who will direct the revolutionary change and in whose interests the revolutionary change will be made.

In struggling against what is to some extent a common enemy, in overlapping and (at times) allying in the pursuit of radical social change, critical theories to a great extent share a common conceptual vocabulary. It is the purpose of

15

this series to explore that vocabulary, revealing what is common and what is distinct, in the broad spectrum of radical perspectives.

For instance, although both Marxists and feminists may use the word "exploitation," it is not clear that they really are describing the same phenomenon. In the Marxist paradigm the concept identifies the surplus labor appropriated by the capitalist as a result of the wage-labor relation. Feminists have used the same term to refer as well to the unequal amounts of housework, emotional nurturance, and child raising performed by women in the nuclear family. We see some similarity in the notion of group inequality (capitalists/workers, husbands/wives) and of unequal exchange. But we also see critical differences: a previously "public" concept. extended to the private realm; one first centered in the economy of goods now moved into the life of emotional relations. Or, for another example, when deep ecologists speak of "alienation" they may be exposing the contradictory and destructive relations of humans to nature. For socialists and anarchists, by contrast, "alienation" basically refers only to relations among human beings. Here we find a profound contrast between what is and is not included in the basic arena of politically significant relationships.

What can we learn from exploring the various ways different radical perspectives utilize the same terminology?

Most important, we see that these key concepts have histories, and that the theories of which they are a part and the social movements whose spirit they embody take shape through a process of political struggle as well as of intellectual reflection. As a corollary, we can note that the creative tension and dissonance among the different uses of these concepts stem not only from the endless play of textual interpretation (the different understandings of classic texts, attempts to refute counterexamples or remove inconsistencies, rereadings of history, reactions to new theories), but also from the continual movement of social groups. Oppression, domination, resistance, passion, and hope are crystallized here. The feminist expansion of the concept of exploitation could only grow out of the women's movement. The rejection of a purely anthropocentric (human-centered, solely humanistic) interpretation of alienation is a fruit of people's resistance to civilization's lethal treatment of the biosphere.

Finally, in my own view at least, surveys of the differing applications of these key concepts of Critical Theory provide compelling reasons to see how complementary, rather than exclusive, the many radical perspectives are. Shaped by history and embodying the spirit of the radical movements that created them, these varying applications each have in them some of the truth we need in order to face the darkness of the current social world and the ominous threats to the earth.

ROGER S. GOTTLIEB

Introduction

RACISTS BELIEVE THAT THE human family is divided into stable racial categories of superior and inferior kinds from birth. For racists, groups have properties which cause unique behaviors or traits. Invidious distinctions between groups are justified, for a racist, because of alleged unique features endogenous to inferior races. Invidious distinctions include attributing character virtues such as honesty, thrift, or courage to one group while denying that members of another group have or can have such virtues. To describe a situation as racist is to describe racially motivated predicaments of segregation, discrimination, and exclusion. Ideas about race in such cases are the criteria for deciding, *prima facia*, personal character virtues, group membership, rights, and privileges. The above descriptions and propositions, taken together, provide a definition of racism.

Definitions provide descriptions and propositions useful for categorizing situations and beliefs. Definitions always included subtle value judgments. Most persons now consider, for example, the idea that some persons are inferior and others superior as empirically wrong and morally misguided. With these ideas as features of the definition of racism, the definition is compatible with popular value judgments. Concepts, however, have roles different from definitions.

A concept, as distinct from a definition, can tell us explicitly what a word *should* mean. Concepts provide guidance on how to judge and decide controversial cases. Whether races exist, for example, is controversial. A concept of racism will guide us in deciding if the belief in the existence of races is morally misguided. It would be appropriate to judge the population census of most countries as racist if a belief in race, and an associated practice, is considered racist. The 1990 United States census, for example used white, black, Hispanic origin, Native American, and Asian as racial categories. There were also 42 ethnic,

17

national, and language categories. Nearly every country that uses race as a category for its census uses its own unique definitions. The U.S. census is morally misguided if the use of race is racist. Countries that do not use race-based census categories, such as the Netherlands or China, would not be considered directly racializing their populations. However, if a concept held that races do exist, that terms should or do pick out objective facts, and that races are a feature of objective reality, then race-based censuses are not necessarily racist.

Morally, the more condemnable features of any form of racism, greater than race-based censuses, are the miseries, degradations, insults, stereotypes, pains, and life-destructive exclusions suffered by victims. Whether these miseries are significantly sustained with the aid of a socially constructed view of race or for reasons having little to do with a socially constructed view of race is often decided by what view of explanation our concept of racism supports. Social ideas are of secondary importance if we believe that natural and objective social entities substantively cause events. Social ideas of race would be, in effect, a subterfuge for substantive natural and objective social entities or forces such as classes or status group interests. If, however, we believe that all social groups are ultimately forms of language categories or social ideas, then racial ideations may be considered substantive forces. The idea that natural or objective groups exist and cause events, independent of whether we have corresponding language categories or social ideas, is not supported by the above constructivist view of racism. The nature of what is considered morally misguided and what practices influence race-based miseries, consequently, influence our concept of racism.

What actually exists is "real." If we believe that what is real exists objectively, that is, independently of social ideas, this belief is "objectivist." The following are the basic features of this approach.

OBJECTIVIST
—believes that there are facts about the human world independent of contingent cultural or social ideas
—can believe that there are groups, such as races, which exist independent of cultural or social ideas (races may be considered natural, caused by human biologies, intrinsic to human anthropological nature, based on inherent psychological traits, etc.)
—can consider racial groups as objective causal agents, that is, race causes groups to exist
—can argue that the uses of racial categories are justified because they refer to objective realities

If we believe that what is real exists either (1) completely as a function of consciousness (phenomenalism or idealism) or (2) that what exists is absolutely contingent on consciousness defining, categorizing, and socially conceiving 'a thing as existing, then we are "constructivist." The following are the basic features of this approach.

CONSTRUCTIVIST
—believes that facts about the human world are absolutely dependent on contingent cultural or social ideas
—does not believe that groups exist independent of cultural or social ideas
(races are not considered natural, caused by human biologies, intrinsic to
human anthropological nature, or based on inherent psychological traits, but
are in some way a function of consciousness or cannot be said to exist
without conceptual categorization)
—can believe that races are constructed causal agents (unnatural, without any
basis in biologies, strictly contingent on self- descriptions, culturally specific,
a feature of malleable social psychologies, defined by social relations of
ethnic or national character, etc., and thereby cause events to occur or are
strongly correlated to particular sorts of events)
—believes that the use of racial categories is never justified because they refer
to objective realities; but, justified—only if they serve some special social or
psychological role

Objectivism and constructivism are based on radically opposing philosophies that support irreconcilable concepts of racism.[1] If only one person existed,
that person, for objectivists, would have inherent properties independent of his
consciousness—one of which could be race. That is, he would have natural or
empirical properties that invariably create some universal human features. The
one existing person would have such properties even if that one person did not
believe she possessed any one or all of the properties. Objectivism, which is
sometimes termed essentialism or realism, has been used in gender studies. One
author defines objectivism in the following way: "In simplest terms, essentialists
[objectivist] think that the categories of sexual orientation (e.g., heterosexual,
homosexual and bisexual) are appropriate categories to apply to individuals . . .
there are objective, intrinsic, culture—independent facts about a person's sexual
orientation."[2] Analogously, an objectivist can believe that racial categories apply
to individuals or she can believe that racial categories describe real existing races
although any given person may be an anomaly.

Groups can exist, for an objectivist, as natural entities.[3] It is not simply that
the existence of groups is a heuristically useful assumption to explain behavior or
that groups are imagined identities; rather, for the objectivist, an ontologically
and morally meaningful claim is made when one believes that groups exist, have
properties, and cause behavior. Races, consequently, can exist as natural entities
divided into categories that together shape the human family—categories endogenous to our being independent of cultural, historical, or ideological contin-
gencies, regardless of existential, pragmatic, or rational choices made by anyone
or any group. Biological traits, geographies, relations of material forces, consciousness, intrinsic psychological traits, or some combination thereof, for example, can be thought to cause the behavior of objective and enduring entities.

An objectivist can believe that the term "race" does not refer to an objective entity; or, for that matter, an objectivist can believe that social groups are constructions. In addition, an objectivist may not believe that groups exist. Nevertheless, an objectivist must believe in external reality, the possibility of group existence, and the possibility that the agency of such groups is relatively independent of contingent social ideas.

Constructivists deny that races can exist as natural or objective entities. They often deny that groups act as culturally independent causal agents. The world mind, ideology, spirit, phenomenon, consciousness, constructed entities refracting on individuals, or some combination thereof, may define social realities for constructivists. For the constructivist, races can be socially defined groups that do not correspond to biologies, natures, or intrinsic psychological traits independent of contingent cultural ideas. For these persons, defining or categorizing groups as racial is at best a conceptually useful descriptive device that stands for socially defined and constructed categories—none of which are imbedded in objective, enduring reality.

If there were only one person in the world, and that person did not believe he was a member of a race with racial properties, then, for constructivists, races would not exist. Constructivists can argue that terms like "race" refer to social entities, but the entities in question would be social constructions.

Some constructivists believe that racial identities should be promoted (especially by oppressed groups as a way of creating cohesion and protecting their interests); others deny this.[4] What such authors often share is the belief that race is constructed.

Imagine that two authors disagree over whether or not a situation is racist. Their disagreement is exacerbated if they provide different causes for the miseries associated with the situation. Even if the two authors agree that "miseries" exist, their explanation of why they exist and whether or not they should be understood as "suffering" or "hardship" is contingent on their pictures of reality. What is considered as "suffering" because of racism—rather than "hardship" due to normal competition between breeding populations or hardships caused by misguided forms of group identity creating needless discrimination—might be a feature of contestation between the two authors. The status of the miseries—as hardship or as suffering—and thereby what our moral attitudes should be is affected by the explanation of what exists.

Imagine, in addition, that the two authors disagree over whether or not race is a natural feature of humanity. If race is considered to be one natural way groups maintain cohesion and transfer wealth across generations, the social trait of kin altruism as a source for racial nepotism may not be considered especially reprehensible. However, if race is considered strictly a constructed form of cohesion, instantiated by the reprehensible beliefs of dominant groups, by the consequence of reprehensible class conflict, and/or by failed strategies of racial cohesion for self-protection by subordinate groups, then kin altruism as a source for racial nepotism may carry strong moral approbation. Whether or not a situation is racist, and what our moral attitude should be toward that situation, is thus contingent on the application of conflicting explanations—kin altruism or the consequence of reprehensible class conflict.

There are certainly numerous views that might have features of objectivism and constructivism but do not fit neatly under either designation. Moreover, numerous accounts of racism may be intended as descriptions but not offer any view of social or natural causes. My designation of views as either objectivist or constructionist is intended to provide a way of understanding what any conception of racism must address: whether or not races exist, what attitude we should have toward races, how to explain the influence of objective or socially constructed racial groups, how to define racism, and some indication of how to judge controversial cases. Any conception that does not address the basic notions embedded in the objectivist and constructionist dichotomy would be seriously lacking.

The views of objectivists and constructivists may well converge or diverge on a host of issues. This anthology, however, is concerned with providing a heuristic way of categorizing irreconcilable approaches and introducing the link among conceptions, explanations, and moral issues. The distinction between objectivism and constructivism guides the organization of the anthology.

There is an important distinction, noticed by Ruth Benedict, Robert Merton, St. Clair Drake, and others: racist theories and forms of racial prejudice radically differ. Racist theories are accounts that purport to tell us about the whole of human existence, differentiation, origin, and telos. Prejudice is a crude form of differentiation. Racist theories are a product of the modern world. This anthology is limited to concepts of modern racism. Thus, it does not address the deeply religious or mythological antecedents to modern racism. The anthology focuses on complex notions about the existence of differentiations that are theoretically understood as racial.

The anthology avoids issues of color prejudice and ethnocentrism except in relation to race. It takes a special argument, for example, to show that prejudice against foreign nationals in Peru is motivated by racial antipathy, because it must be shown that the foreign nationals are seen as a race and that it is the racial factor which plays some substantive motivating role. However, it takes no special argument to show that the United States, Canada, South Africa, Austria, or New Zealand divide their populations, and the population of the world, into definitive racial categories. job applications, special education programs sponsored by the government, voting districts, applications for bank loans, as well as the census for these countries begin with "white" and then follow with an array of other racial groups, such as, black, Asian Pacific Islander, Hispanic non-white, or native. Persons applying for citizenship in these countries are asked to volunteer a racial self-designation. How race is defined and what categories exist differ in each country, although sharing numerous overlaps. We may debate the motivation for categorizing the world in this way, but we need no special argument to see that race is the factor defining the population. Color and ethnicity are significantly different variables in this regard. A physically black Egyptian or Israeli, for example, can be self-identified as white for American legal documents. Color does not dictate race in such cases. Tremendous color prejudice exists in India between different castes, but whether and in what cases this is racial requires a special argument. The Welsh were once considered a separate race from the English, while suffering racial prejudice in Europe; but in Australia or South Africa, their ethnic race was subsumed tinder the rubric of white. Although, in the United States, Japanese nationals are considered one nationality, undistinguished by race, among the Japanese various groups are categorized as ethnically racial. Indians in South Africa may be far darker than the race known as "coloured"; Hutus and Tutsis may be of the same black complexion, but differences in height, language, and culture are used by them to identify each other as different races. By focusing strictly on race and on works that have been concerned primarily, but nor exclusively, with countries that have well-defined racial distinctions, the anthology hopes to provide a reasonable picture of major competing theories between objectivism and constructivism.

The objectivism section of the anthology begins with a work by Ruth Benedict and the constructivism section begins with a work by Alain L. Locke. It is arguable that both authors, to some degree, believed that races exist as biological kinds. It is certain that both were dedicated activists as anti-racists and joined forces to help promote crosscultural dialogue, especially when Benedict was Chair of the Committee on Intercultural Education which, along with the Progressive Education Association, held meetings that resulted in the massive 825-page anthology edited by Bernard J. Stem and Alain L. Locke, *When Peoples Meet: A Study in Race and Culture Contacts* (1942).[5] Yet they each represent different orientations. Locke marks this difference definitively in his 1916 lecture series, *Race Contacts*.[6] Locke is critical of the approach to race initially developed by Franz Boas but subsequently refined, developed, and altered by Benedict. The dividing line between objectivist and constructivist involves the status of reality.

The objective realism section introduces the many orientations that shape the family of objectivist views. These views hold in common that races exist and that there is an objective, anthropological, or biological basis for racial divisions. Each author, however, represents a different orientation within the objectivist tradition.

A rich introduction to the world of racist beliefs from different cultures and historical periods is provided by Ruth Benedict in "Racism: The *ism* of the Modern World." Benedict exposes the disjunctions among race, language, culture, and many other misguided associations white arguing for the malleability of groups. Racial isolation or purity, for Benedict, is an unlikely reality, but Benedict considers races as anthropological types. Benedict thus combines the idea that race is objectively real (racialism) and the view that we often create misguided stereotypes. Benedict, noted for her anthropological work and relativism, proceeds, in relation to race, as an objectivist. Benedict reveals both an objectivist approach to morally demeaning stereotypes and an account of racism.

Ruth Benedict's "Why Then Race Prejudice?" exemplifies explanations that rely on a variety of motives, social structures, and psychological traits. The idea that there are underlying, misguided motives for racial prejudices provides a race-relations approach to explanation; that is, an approach that takes racial categories to be relatively stable and accounts for prejudice in terms of inappropriate relations.

Pierre L. van den Berghe, in "Ethnicity as Kin Selection," describes the major tenets of those who view race as a natural social function based on evolutionary imperatives. Ethnicity and race (socially defined) can be understood, for van den Berghe, as extensions and attenuated forms of kin selection. Ethnocentrism and racism are horrible social features, which can be eradicated, because one feature of the human is its ability to change. However, fitness and adaptation are important features of explanations for the existence and function of racial conflicts-conflicts that should not be reduced, for van den Berghe, to class or status conflicts.

Albert G. Mosley, in "Negritude, Nationalism, and Nativism: Racists or Racialists?" contends that races exist as biological and historical groups, and thus that racialism is not, contrary to Jean-Paul Sartre and K. Anthony Appiah, a form of racism. Mosley uses the works of Negritude authors and noted African American authors to defend this view.

Philip Kircher notes that one motivation for discarding the concept of race is to under-mine racism, in "Race, Ethnicity, Biology, Culture." This eliminativism approach to combating racism, although laudable, fails, for Kircher, to recognize the subtle ways that divisions into races have biological and important social significance as objective variables in human evolution.

The section on objectivist explanations of racism concentrates on the existence or function of races and racial identities, when the author considers races as anthropological or biological entities in some important way matching social differentiations. Explaining how groups function is crucial in defining what moral attitudes we should have and in what way, if any, we should consider races as real. Each author represents a different approach within the objectivist tradition.

Joel Kotkin's "Tribes" considers race and ethnicity as a subcategory or trope of tribe. The tribe has the effective reality of a race, that is, ancestry, heredity, breeding population, and close-knit community. Successful tribes, for Kotkin, have cultural capital (attitudes toward work and saving, beliefs about their historical roles, traditions of group commitment and identity, etc.). Tribes are not defined with the simplistic definitions of race popular in some countries, such as white, black, and Asian. Rather, Kotkin understands tribes as groups with fairly well-defined forms of social cohesion—race being a trope in the pantheon of markers for tribal identity—an objectively verifiable cohesion that has caused historically measurable change.

John Rex's "Racism, Institutionalized and Otherwise" explains racism and ways of ending racism by focusing on institutional variables. Rex considers the way explanations of social structures, particularly the way social entities such as race or class influence possible solution approaches. Rex argues for concentrating on structures, Stich as laws and policies, rather than relying on accounts that use logics of social entities to explain racism and recommend solutions.

D. A. Washbrook's "Ethnicity and Racialism in Colonial Indian Society" defines race in ideological terms; its main characteristic is "that of legitimating social inequality by reference to qualities inherent in different ascriptive communities." This approach avoids a definition strictured by biological considerations, cultural-boundary markers, religious views, and categories popular in such countries as South Africa and the United States. Washbrook explains race and racism through class structures and social stratifications. Thus Washbrook offers a picture, informed by Marxist views, that objective, material conditions play a crucial role in why social phenomenon have sustaining power. His view is enlivened by an argument about the role of national, ethnic, and racial formations as revolutionary sources.

Etienne Balibar, in "Class Racism," locates race and racism as features of nationalism. Balibar, also a Marxist, considers racism as a consequence of, made possible by, and sustained and exacerbated by class conflict. Balibar, however, believes in a reciprocal determinism, a mutual causal influence between nationalism and racism, ethnocentricity and racism, and the crucially important element of class racism. Rather than ask how objective class conditions cause racial conflict, Balibar queries how racism situates class conflicts.

The section on constructive realism introduces authors who believe races are fundamentally social constructions, the consequence of contingent ideas about what groups exist. It is possible, for an author in this section, to deny that groups exist, or could possibly exist, as independent causal agents. Each author represents a different approach within the constructivist tradition.

Alain L. Locke's "The Contribution of Race to Culture," unlike Ruth Benedict's view, contends that races do not exist except as value collectives. In addition, unlike Benedict, Locke argues that the racial sense of group interest has made a contribution, under certain conditions, to culture, and that groups suffering from prejudice are justified in holding on to this cohesion. Locke does not believe in the possibility that groups may exist as independent causal agents; they exist as groups or populations bound together by paradoxes and feelings of proprietorship and pride. He argues for an internationalism achieved through partisanship.

Colette Guillaumin criticizes the idea that races are natural groups in "Race and Nature." Guillaumin interrogates some ideas presupposed by the concept of nature and their relation to race, suggesting that races are a matter of social relations and cannot be imagined outside this context.

In "Biology and the New Racism," Martin Barker raises critical issues regarding ethology and sociobiological claims that racism and the belief in natural kin altruism are objective or intrinsic causes of group cohesion. Such cohesion would be a source of racial exclusivity. Barker seeks to show the links between politics and such views of human nature.

Claudia Card, in "On Race, Racism, and Ethnicity," queries the relationship between race and ethnicity. The works of W. E. B. Du Bois, Marilyn Frye, and Maria Lugones are used to discuss interrelated themes especially concerning the asymmetry between race and ethnicity and the significance of heritage.

K. Anthony Appiah, in "Why There Are No Races," contends that neither a referential concept of race (the term describes an objective reality) nor an ideational concept of race (race is based on socially constructed ideas) is warranted. Appiah's argument rejects the idea of race and its connection to culture.

The section on constructivist explanations of racism presents articles that explain the function of racial identities, by authors who consider races as fundamentally socially created entities. Constructivist authors may share many views with objectivists. However, they differ over whether or not race can exist independent of social ideas and racial groups can be said to be objective agents.

Paula Rothenberg's "The Construction, Deconstruction, and Reconstruction of Difference" considers how oppressors and oppressed create difference, and the import of assigning value to difference. Explaining and describing notions of difference rooted in nature, as well as notions rooted in ideas of moral deficiencies, as sources for creating artificial difference is an important feature of Rothenberg's argument. In addition, Rothenberg cites parallels involving colonialism and sexism to argue for moral sensitivity to difference.

Pierre-André Taguieff's "National Identity Framed in the Logics of Racialization" argues for vigilance against differentialist racism, a form not rooted in biological or anthropological claims but often making cultural differences surreptitiously essential. Taguieff analyzes individualism and collective identities. The arbitrary, and politically and morally motivated formation of, and freezing of, identities as absolutes and idols provides a way of seeing difference as ideological—but without a reduction to universalist structures.

Antonio S. A. Guimarães reconstitutes the idea of race as a floating signifier, in "Racism and Anti-Racism in Brazil," especially in the context of the meaning of color and race in Brazil. The mix of color nuances in racial formations makes the invisibility of racial discourse in a racialized context particularly troubling. Guimarães contends that "there is no absolute, metahistorical concept of race or racism."

George M. Fredrickson's "Reflections on the Comparative History and Sociology of Racism" defines racism as a form of ethnocentricity. Fredrickson, rather than use a race-relations paradigm in which groups are understood to compete for scarce resources, considers the pursuit of status as a crucial variable effecting an appropriate historical account of racism.

The section "Reason, Race, and Morality" concerns moral issues in the context of considering racism a concrete feature of socio-psychological malady. The works in this section also take account of the ontological status of races, but directly offer unique attitudes and moral approaches. The issues focus narrowly on how we are to understand the relationship among reason, race, and morality.

Lewis Gordon's "Antiblack Racism and Ontology" considers racism as a form of existentialist bad faith, that is, an effort to evade facing ambiguity and contingency. He presents various social and psychological dimensions of why persons feel responsible for their condition, and the difficulties of accepting group identity, as ontologically existing identities.

"Critical Race Theory" by Gerald Torres proposes the possibility of plural forms of morality and justice. Rather than a singular definition of racism, critical race theory approaches law and social rules as having webs of meaning and interpretations.

David T. Goldberg, in "Racism and Rationality," challenges definitions of racism that suggest it is necessarily irrational. Goldberg addresses the moral import of viewing racism in some respects as irrational.

Jorge L. A. Garcia's "The Heart of Racism" offers a conception of racism for descriptive, valuative, and moral purposes. Garcia rejects important conceptions of racism, including Ruth Benedict's, and offers one that takes seriously virtues and their import for descriptions and practical social policy.

The Postscript "What, Then, Is Racism?" argues for a moderate objectivism. This approach rejects the idea that races objectively exist, yet considers other groups as objectively real. Moderate objectivism prefers explanations that consider groups to be universal and invariant human features and objective causal or influential forces. This approach insists, however, that racial identities are socially created. It understands racism as a form of oppression which subjugates universal human potentials.

LEONARD HARRIS

NOTES

1. See, for examples of irreconcilable positions, Donald N. Levine, *Visions of the Sociological Tradition* (Chicago: University of Chicago Press, 1995); Vernon J. Williams Jr., *Rethinking Race* (Kentucky: University Press of Kentucky, 1996).

2. Edward Stein, *Forms of Desire: Sexual Orientation and the Social Constructionist Controversy* (New York: Routledge, 1992), pp. 4–5. I use "objectivism" where Stein uses essentialism and others use realism. I prefer objectivism because it allows me to emphasize that which is external to human will and that which exists. A scholar may or may not believe that that which is external and exists is in any way essential. An objectivist of this sort is necessarily a realist.

I avoid the realist vs. anti-realist distinction. According to Bas van Fraasen, *The Scientific Image* (Oxford: Oxford University Press, 1980), a realist aims to give "a literally true story of what the world is like" and the anti-realist aims to provide "theories that are empirically adequate" which yield truths about observables or socially agreed paradigmatic entities. This distinction concerns how we treat our stories, as true pictures of the world or as adequate presentations. However, both can conceptually agree that there is an objective world, whether or not our observation, adequately picture that world. The way I explicate objectivism and constructivism, the focus is on irreconcilable views about what exists and how what exists is to be explicated. Both approaches, consequently, consider themselves to be offering views about what is real.

3. An excellent example of this is Charles K. Warriner, "Groups Are Real: A Reaffirmation," *American Sociological Review* 21 (October 1956): 549–54.

4. See, for a discussion of this, Linda Martin Alcott, "Philosophy and Racial Identity," *Radical Philosophy* 75 (1996): 514. Also see K. Anthony Appiah and Amy Gutmann, Color Conscious (Princeton: Princeton University Press, 1996); and Richard Delgado, ed., *Critical Race Theory* (Philadelphia: Temple University Press, 1995).

5. Alain L. Locke and Bernard J. Stern, eds., *When Peoples Meet: A Study in Race and Culture Contact* (New York: Hinds, Hayden & Eldredge, Inc., 1942).

6. Alain L. Locke, *Race Contacts* (Washington, D.C.: Howard University Press, 1992).

Part I.
Objective Realism

1. Racism: The *ism* of the Modern World
Ruth Benedict

AS EARLY AS THE late 1880s a French pro-Aryan, Vacher de Lapouge, wrote: "I am convinced that in the next century millions will cut each other's throats because of 1 or 2 degrees more or less of cephalic index." On the surface it appears a fantastic reason for world wars, and it was certainly a reason new under the sun. Was he right? What could it mean? The cephalic index is the quotient of the greatest breadth of the head divided by its length, and some tribes and peoples over the world run to high indices and some to low. Narrow heads are found among uncivilized primitives and among powerful and cultivated Western Europeans; broad heads are too. Neither the narrow heads of the whole world nor the broad heads stack up to show any obvious monopoly of glorious destiny or any corner on ability or virtue. Even in any one European nation or in America, men of achievement have been some of them narrow-headed and some broad-headed. What could it mean that "millions will cut each other's throats" because of the shape of the top of their skulls?

In the long history of the world men have given many reasons for killing each other in war: envy of another people's good bottom land or of their herds, ambition of chiefs and kings, different religious beliefs, high spirits, revenge. But in all these wars the skulls of the victims on both sides were generally too similar to be distinguished. Nor had the war leaders incited their followers against their enemies by referring to the shapes of their heads. They might call them the heathen, the barbarians, the heretics, the slayers of women and children, but never our enemy Cephalic Index 82.

It was left for high European civilization to advance such a reason for war and persecution and to invoke it in practice. In other words, racism is a creation of our own time. It is a new way of separating the sheep from the goats. The old parable in the New Testament separated mankind as individuals: on the one hand those who had done good, and on the other those who had done evil. The new way divides them by hereditary bodily characteristics—shape of the head, skin color, nose form, hair texture, color of the eyes—and those who have certain hallmarks are known by these signs to be weaklings and incapable of civilization, and those with the opposite are the hope of the world. Racism is the new Calvinism, which asserts that one group has the stigmata of superiority and the other has those of inferiority. According to racism, we know our enemies not by their aggressions against us, not by their creed or language, not even by their possessing wealth we want to take, but by noting their hereditary anatomy. For the leopard cannot change his spots, and by these you know he is a leopard.

For the individual, therefore, racism means that damnation or salvation in this world is determined at conception; an individual's good life cannot tip the balance in his favor and he cannot live a bad life if his physical type is the right sort. By virtue of birth alone each member of the "race" is high caste and rightly claims his place in the sun at the expense of men of other "races." He need not base his pride upon personal achievement nor upon virtue; he was born high caste.

From this postulate, racism makes also an assertion about race: that the "good" anatomical hallmarks are the monopoly of a pure race which has always throughout history manifested its glorious destiny. The racialists have rewritten history to provide the scion of such a race with a long and glamorous group ancestry as gratifying as an individual coat of arms, and they assure him that the strength and vigor of his race are immutable and guaranteed by the laws of Nature. He must, however, guard this pure blood from contamination by that of lesser breeds, lest degeneration follow and his race lose its supremacy. All over the world for the last generation, this doctrine has been invoked in every possible kind of conflict: sometimes national, between peoples as racially similar as the French and Germans; sometimes across the color line, as in Western fears of the Yellow Peril; sometimes in class conflicts, as in France; sometimes in conflicts between immigrants who arrived a little earlier and those who came a little later, as in America. It has become a bedlam.

Where all people claim to be tallest, not all can be right. In this matter of races, can the sciences to which they all appeal judge among the babel of contradictory claims and award the decision? Or is it a matter of false premises and bastard science? It is essential, if we are to live in this modern world, that we should understand racism and be able to judge its arguments. We must know the facts first of race, and then of this doctrine that has made use of them. For racism is an *ism* to which everyone in the world today is exposed; for or against, we must take sides. And the history of the future will differ according to the decision which we make.

WHAT THEY SAY

In this there is nothing new: that when a philosopher cannot account for anything in any other manner, he boldly ascribes it to an occult quality in some race. (Walter Bagehot, *Physics and Politics*. London: George Routledge & Sons Ltd., 1948)

The white race [today read *Nordics*] originally possessed the monopoly of beauty, intelligence, and strength. By its union with other varieties [read *Alpines, Mediterraneans*] hybrids were created, which were beautiful without strength, strong without intelligence, or if intelligent, both weak and ugly. (Arthur de Gobineau, *Essay on the Inequality of Human Races*. Translated by Adrian Collins. London: William Heinemann, 1915, p. 209.)

List of physical characteristics of the genuine Teuton:

The great radiant heavenly eyes, the golden hair, the gigantic stature, the symmetrical muscular development, the lengthened skull (which an ever-active brain, tortured by longing, had changed from the round lines of animal contentedness and extended towards the front), the lofty countenance, required by an elevated spiritual life as the seat of its expression. (Houston Stewart Chamberlain, *The Foundations of the Nineteenth Century*. London: John Lane, 1910, Vol. 1.)

What racists say of their own race:

Judgment, truthfulness, and energy always distinguish the Nordic man. He feels a strong urge toward truth and justice. . . . Passion in the usual meaning of the rousing of the senses or the heightening of the sexual life has little meaning for him. . . . He is never without a certain knightliness. (Hans F. K. Gunther, *The Racial Elements of European History*. Translated from the second German edition by G. C. Wheeler. London: Methuen & Co., 1927, pp. 51, 52.)

In mental gifts the Nordic race marches in the van of mankind. (Baur Fischer, and Lenz, *Human Heredity*. Translated by Eden and Cedar Paul. London: Allen & Unwin, 1931, p. 655.)

What racists say of other groups:

Many intellectuals are trying to help the Jews with the ancient phrase, "The Jew is also a man." Yes, he is a man, but what sort of a man? The flea is also an animal! (Goebbels, reported in *Time*, July 8, 1935, p. 21.)

If non-Nordics are more closely allied to monkeys and apes than to Nordics, why is it possible for them to mate with Nordics and not with apes? The answer is this: it has not been proved that non-Nordics cannot mate with apes. (Herman Gauch, *New Foundations for Research into Social Race Problems.* Berlin, 1933. Cited by J. Gunther, *The Nation*, February 5, 1935.)

People who live in glass houses:

Opinions about our ancestors

FIRST CENTURY B.C.: Do not obtain your slaves from Britain because they are so stupid and so utterly incapable of being taught that they are not fit to form a part of the household of Athens. (Cicero to Atticus.)

ELEVENTH CENTURY A.D.: Races north of the Pyrenees are of cold temperament and never reach maturity; they are of great stature and of a white colour. But they lack all sharpness of wit and penetration of intellect. (Saīd of Toledo (a Moorish savant), quoted in Lancelot Thomas Hogben, *Genetic Principles in Medicine and Social Service.* London: Williams & Norgate, 1931, p. 213.)

🐜   🐜   🐜

WHY THEN RACE PREJUDICE?

AS WE HAVE SEEN, all scientific knowledge of race contradicts the idea that human progress has been the work of one race alone or can safety be entrusted to a program of racial hygiene in the future. No great civilization has been the work of a pure race, and neither history nor psychology, biology nor anthropology can render decisions about the future destiny of any present human breed. Racism has been a travesty of scientific knowledge and has served consistently as special pleading for the supremacy of any group, either class or nation, to which the pleader himself belonged and in whose permanent place in the sun he desired to believe.

Why then does racism have such social importance in our times? No discussion of race and racism can be complete without raising this problem; it is the really burning question, for upon our answer depend the measures we can trust to bring about a cure.

In answering this question we do not need to depend on fine-spun theories of self-communings; history has given the Answers many times. We need only to obtain a little perspective. We have seen that racist dogmas, as they are stated today, are modern. But they express an old human obsession and only the "reasons why" have been altered. This old human obsession is that my group is uniquely valuable, and if it is weakened all valuable things will perish. It were better, therefore, that a million perish than that one jot or tittle of that unique value should be lost. It becomes my divine mission to extirpate the challenger in whatever field.

The fields change, however. When one field has been won and tolerance and cooperativeness established in what was before an armed camp, we look back upon the episode as an example of human aberration. We think we are different and feel that progress has really been achieved—until other generations arise to look back upon us and decide that we have only shifted mutual intolerance to another area of life. For centuries the battlefield was religion. The Inquisition was not pure barbarism; it was the claim to unique value worked out with all its implications in a field where today we are willing to follow the precept of live and let live. We cannot see racism in perspective without reviewing the occasions and consequences of this earlier arrogance. The fact that it is in the field of religion instead of in the field of race is a reflection of the times; from every other point of view, religious persecutions and racial persecutions duplicate one another. Their proponents claimed similar sacred missions; they killed and looted and temporarily enriched themselves. From the standpoint of history, both set up false fronts that served political purposes; they destroyed brilliant civilizations. In that one matter in which they differ, religion as over against race, the earlier persecution was at least as justified as the latter. The medieval world, convinced that man's existence was an infinitesimal episode in his everlasting life, thought it was common humanity to kill the Anti-christ that would lead thousands of souls to damnation. Today we judge this a fallacy, but we must not underestimate the worthy motives of those who believed that they alone had received the divine command; they were not actuated solely by arrogance but by their duty to keep the world faithful to the word of God and to ensure salvation to as many souls as possible. In many churchmen this must have been a worthy emotion, just as today we recognize that patriotism or pride of class is a worthy emotion. However, the judgment of history is that, when either of these worthy emotions is carried into a campaign of extermination of all who belong in other camps, the exterminators suffer with the exterminated and the result is social tragedy.

It was so in the Inquisition. Between 1200 and 1250, the Roman Church was at the apex of its political and temporal power, and these were the great years of the Inquisition. Heresy-hunting was, like Jew-baiting in this decade in Germany, an eruption of minority persecution. It held out the same shortrange advantages to the persecutors; it could be used as a front for political purposes; the confiscation of the victims' property enriched the persecutors; and the campaign of hate distracted attention from real issues. The real issues, as they appear in the perspective of history, were two: the first was the issue of freedom of conscience, a freedom which all the tortures of the Inquisition were powerless to uproot and which eventually triumphed in spite of bishops and of kings; the second was the worldliness, and in some cases the corruption, of the Catholic clergy of the period. Even in the highest Council of the Church itself this had been for some time a grave issue, and under Hildebrand (Gregory the Great) and the monk Bernard of Clairvaux there had been valiant efforts toward reform. The times, however, were not auspicious, and the heretics took up the cry of licentiousness against the Church. In stamping out the heretics, the Church embarked upon a campaign of extirpation that absorbed the attention of the faithful and postponed reform in its own ranks.

As a front for political purposes the Inquisition was used in southern France to break the opposition to the growing power of the Capetian kings, and in Florence its terrible severities under Fra Ruggieri crushed also the Ghibelline revolt. wherever the Inquisition flourished—in France, in Italy, and in Spain—it made common cause with power politics. The full extent of this common cause depended upon the practice of confiscating the heretics' property. The Inquisition is linked in popular thought with the burning of heretics and the use of torture to obtain confessions, but the confiscation of property was sociologically more important. Originally such property confiscated by the Inquisition belonged not to the Church but to kings and secular rulers; the right of the Papacy, and hence of the Inquisitors, to a share of these riches was not accepted until almost 1250, and the lion's share went always to secular authorities. Heresy-hunting was profitable, and all those who sought riches and power eagerly took advantage of the opportunity, masking their satisfactions behind the dogma that the heretics were guilty of treason against the Almighty.

The most celebrated campaign of the Inquisition "in the name of God" was against the heretics of southern France in the first half of the thirteenth century. These heretics were known as the Albigenses, and their home in Provence was a region on which the Roman Church had a comparatively slight hold. In those days Provence had little in common with northern France, and her barons were not vassals of the French king. The house of Toulouse in southern France had had an especially brilliant history. For two centuries its court had been famous for its love of art and literature, for its wealth and gallantry, and it had established its sovereignty throughout half of Provence. Its cities were the most wealthy and independent in all of France, and their culture was greatly influenced by interchange of goods and ideas with the Saracens of Palestine and the Moors of Spain—cultures in many ways more enlightened than any others in the Western World at that time.

The heresy of the Albigenses was one of the many medieval cults of Manichaeism, which taught the strictest asceticism in order that man might free himself from original evil. Manichaean cosmology was an all-embracing dualism of good and evil, of light and darkness, and only by eating the light contained in plants and by eschewing the darkness in meat, only by eliminating the darkness of sensual acts, could righteousness be achieved. "Finished" ascetics, as in many Oriental religions, became divinities and objects of worship to the laity.

The dualism of these heresies was simple to grasp and offered an explanation of the evils of the world which had a strong appeal in those troubled times. But we know little of the teachings of the Albigensian sect; most of our knowledge is of their protest against the corruption of the contemporary clergy of the Church. Though Provence lay between great Catholic strongholds to the south and to the north, within its territories the Church was weak; the roots of Provençal culture were not in Rome. The rising burgher class in the towns especially espoused the heresy, and the growing independence of this class made the threat increasingly serious to the Church, which was then at the height of its temporal power. The Papacy ordered the faithful clergy of northern France to preach a campaign of extermination against heretical Provence, and the crusade became one of the most implacable of religious wars. Its conclusion established the Capetian kings of northern France as monarchs in Provence after mass executions had decimated the independent burghers of the cities and had destroyed the civilization that had flourished in southern France. The burning of heretics continued for a hundred years, and at last the cult was exterminated.

The Inquisition did not survive into the modern period, but religious persecution did. One of the longest and most disastrous of these conflicts occurred in sixteenth- and seventeenth-century France. French Protestants of that time were called Huguenots; by the middle of the sixteenth century they had grown greatly in numbers. Like the Albigensian heretics, they were mainly prosperous bourgeois, and the bourgeois of the sixteenth century were opposed to concentration of power in the hands of the French kings. The bloody wars of a generation (1562–1593) were fought in the name of religion, but they masked a conflict which was in great part economic and political. When the Huguenots finally succeeded in having their leader crowned king of France as Henry IV in 1598, the Edict of Nantes proclaimed full civil rights for the Protestants without withdrawing these from the Catholics. It was a signal victory. The law of the land now guaranteed religious and political freedom, but, as has happened before and since that time, the conflict continued. The Crown was Catholic and the Catholic clergy never accepted the Edict of Nantes. Cardinal Richelieu was the greatest power in France; he was both Cardinal and member of the royal council. His domestic policy was to concentrate power in the hands of the king, and to this the Huguenots were opposed. Therefore, his internal policy was dominated by his ruthless opposition to the Huguenots, whom he could persecute in the name of religion. Louis XLV, after the death of Richelieu, exercised these royal powers to the full; his dream of absolute monarchy could be realized only if the Huguenots were removed. He carried on a legal persecution, discriminating against them in the exercise of their religion and their civil rights, and the terrible *dragonnades* used torture to compel their acceptance of the "king's religion." It was then, in 1685, that Louis XIV revoked the Edict of Nantes, declaring it was now unnecessary since all his subjects were Catholics. The Protestants emigrated or were sent to the galleys. His act left Louis absolute monarch and enriched his coffers with the expropriated wealth of the Huguenots. It also bled France of more than 400,000 of its inhabitants, intelligent and courageous people who enriched with their abilities the countries which received them.

The Albigensian crusade and the expulsion of the Huguenots are only two high spots in the long story of the suppression of minority groups before the rise of racism.

This suppression of minorities has been continued in the persecutions and nationalistic wars of the twentieth century. In the thirteenth century and in the sixteenth, as in the world today, new economic and social necessities were starting new ferments. Groups arose which opposed some aspect of the old order. The party in power answered by using torment, death, and confiscation of property. Parties in power can always do this, but in the eyes of history these suppressions have purchased an empty triumph. The great period of the Inquisition marked the downwardturning point in the temporal power of the Church no less than the ruin of Provençal civilization, and the Huguenot expulsion gave France only the disastrous and temporary splendor of the reign of Louis XIV. "After me the deluge." Persecution stopped neither the growing demand for freedom of conscience nor the rise of the bourgeoisie.

For a theory of racism there are two conclusions to be drawn from the whole matter. The first is that, in order to understand race persecution, we do not need to investigate race; we need to investigate *persecution*. Persecution was an old, old story before racism was thought of. Social change is inevitable, and it is always fought by those whose ties are to the old order. These ties may be economic or they may tie religious, as in medieval Europe, or those of social affiliation, as with Roman patricians. Those who have these ties will consciously or unconsciously ferret out reasons for believing that their group is supremely valuable and that the new claimants threaten the achievements of civilization. They will raise a cry of rights of inheritance or divine right of kings or religious orthodoxy or racial purity or manifest destiny. These cries reflect the temporary conditions of the moment, and all the efforts of the slogan-makers need not convince us that any one of them is based on eternal verities. The battle-cries of Nordicism belong with "Keep Cool with Coolidge" and "He Kept Us Out of War" of American presidential campaigns, and with slight changes in social necessities they will be as evanescent. All slogans are useful in the degree to which they express the faiths and discontents of the hour. Religious varieties were politically useful in eras and regions which had powerful religious interests; when these were overshadowed by secular privileges and when cleavages along religious lines became less important, religious slogans no longer justified the persecution of minorities as they had in earlier days.

Racial slogans serve the same purpose in the present century that religious slogans served before—that is, they are used to justify persecution in the interests of some class or nation. This racial slogan is peculiarly congenial to our times. Science is a word to conjure with in this century; unfortunately it is often used to conjure. It is not racism alone that has turned to so-called science for its arguments. A manufacturer of cosmetics conducted, not long ago, an investigation of various advertisements of his wares. He found that the two words which had most sales-appeal were "immediately" and "scientific." Every rouge, every face powder must claim a "scientific" uniqueness, and by this ballyhoo millions are impressed. It was the same with fake medicines, with drug-store drinks, and with health foods until it became necessary to defend the public by federal supervision of manufacturers' claims. The slogan of "science" will sell most things today, and it sells persecution as easily as it sells rouge. The scientist repeatedly points out that the advertised rouge is indistinguishable from others, or even that he has found it especially harmful in a laboratory test; he points out that no race has a monopoly of abilities or of virtues, and that, as science, the racists' claims have no validity. For the scientist, science is a body of knowledge; he resents its use as a body of magic. But he knows that *scientific* is the word our civilization conjures with—in no matter what cause.

The choice of racial slogans to justify conflict is rooted in still another manner in the conditions of the modern age. Racial reasons for persecution are convenient just because, in Western civilization today, so many different breeds live in close contact with one another. The racist cries are raised not because those who raise them have any claim to belong to pure races, but because they do not; in other words, because today several ethnic groups occupy one city or one state, or states that share in one civilization are engaged in nationalistic wars. Hence comes the paradox that has been so often pointed out: that it is the most mongrel peoples of the world who raise the war cry of racial purity. From the point of view of race, this makes nonsense, but from the point of view of persecution, it is inevitable. No group raises battle cries against people whose existence is of no moment to it; for conflict to arise, there must first be contact. Racial slogans arose, therefore, in Europe in class and national conflicts. The old religious slogans for persecution had lost their hold, and the racists evolved in their stead a bastard version of contemporary science. Racism remains, in the eyes of history, however, merely another instance of the persecution of minorities for the advantage of those in power.

Once we have recognized that race conflict is only the justification of the persecution that is popular at the moment, the strangest paradox in all racist theory becomes clear. The racists have over and over again derived race prejudice from a race repulsion instinctive in mankind, and historians and biologists and anthropologists have as repetitiously pointed out that such a theory is impossible in view of the universal mixture of races. "Why, if nature abhors race-crossing, does she do so much of it?"[1] But repulsion to intermarriage accompanies any conflict of two groups, however the groups may be defined. They need not be racial. The patricians of Rome recoiled from marriage with plebeians in the same way, the Catholics of France from marriage with the Huguenots. It is not that man has a set of instincts which make only his own race sexually attractive, but that in-groups are unwilling to give status to the outsider. They do not want to share prerogatives with him. If this in-group is defined racially, as Anglo-Saxons have defined it in their contact with native peoples of the world, their desire to maintain the in-group will bring about selective mating in marriage, but it notoriously does not prevent mating outside of marriage. The great numbers of halfcastes in India and mulattoes in America are testimony to the fact that the antipathy is not instinctive aversion to members of another race.

Those theorists also who have explained race prejudice by visible racial differences are similarly confused. They have said that race prejudice is caused by obvious and striking contrasts in face and color. They are, however, mistaking a momentary feature of persecution for a causal one. There was no differentiating skin color or nose shape in a Huguenot or in the Albigensian victims of the Inquisition. On the other side of the picture, poverty sets groups as visibly apart as the color of their hair or the shape of their heads. Groups may be set apart by any number of things besides race—by whether they go to Mass or by whether they drop their *h*'s. Members of a primitive tribe have been known to kill at sight members of a neighboring tribe of the same race and language because they felt that the way they carried their burden baskets was an insult to human beings. Not the fact of "visibility" of skin color but the fact that racial characteristics are transmitted over so many generations makes racial prejudice a new problem in the world. A man can stop going to Mass or a Huguenot king take the sacrament because "Paris is worth a Mass," or the heroine of *Pygmalion* learn to enunciate her mother tongue in the Oxford fashion, but too dark a Negro cannot "pass" and not even his children's children may be born light enough to do so. This is a problem of relative permanence of distinctions, not specifically of "visibility." In the long course of history, persecution has been now more, now less intense; but these variations do not correlate with the presence or absence of racial visibility.

Mistaken explanations of the nature of race prejudice are of minor importance so long as they are concerned with theoretical points like instinctive antipathies or the role of racial visibility. There is a far more important issue. The fact that to understand race conflict we need fundamentally to understand *conflict*, and not *race*, means something much more drastic. It means that all the deepseated causes of conflict in any group or between groups are involved in any outbreak of race prejudice. Race will be cried up today in a situation where formerly religion would have been cried up. If civilized men expect to end prejudice—whether religious or racial—they will have to remedy major social abuses, in no way connected with religion or race, to the common advantage. Whatever reduces conflict, curtails irresponsible power, and allows people to obtain a decent livelihood will reduce race conflict. Nothing less will accomplish the task.

For the friction is not primarily racial. We all know what the galling frictions are in the world today: nationalistic rivalries, desperate defense of the status quo by the haves, desperate attacks by the have-nots, poverty, unemployment, and war. Desperate men easily seize upon some scapegoat to sacrifice to their unhappiness; it is a kind of magic by which they feel for the moment that they have laid the misery that has been tormenting them. In this they are actively encouraged by their rulers and exploiters, who like to see them occupied with this violence, and fear that if it were denied them they might demand something more difficult. So Hitler, when his armament program cut consumers' goods and increased hours of work and lowered real wages, exhorted the nation in 1938 to believe that Germany's defeat in 1919 had been due to Jewry, and encouraged racial riots. And this served two purposes: it gave an undernourished people an outlet harmless to the government, and it allowed the government treasury to appropriate to itself the wealth of the Jews.

In this sequence of events, the Third Reich is but following a long series of precedents in European anti-Semitism. During the Middle Ages, persecutions of the Jews, like all medieval persecutions, were religious rather than racial. Intermarriage between Jews and Gentiles was condemned, nor as a racist measure but in the same manner as marriages between Catholics and heretics were condemned. The pogroms of the time of the Crusades were carried out by stay-at-home mobs imitating the Crusaders in avenging the death of Christ; the mobs killed Jews, the Crusaders fought the Arabs and Turks. The link between Jews and Turks was not racial; in the period of the Crusades the two were equated because the first had crucified Christ and the second owned his tomb. Nor were persecutions other than those set in motion by the Crusaders directed toward eliminating a racial breed; apostate Jews purchased safety. A renegade Jew denounced or concealed his religion, not his race. The Popes and rulers favorable to the Jews promulgated laws directing that "they should not be baptized by force, constrained to observe Christian festivals nor to wear badges." Even tip to the World War, some important racists advocated, as the cure for conflict, not extinction of the Jewish race but a racial merger. This was especially true of the great nationalist historian Treitschke, who was one of Germany's foremost advocates of racist salvation at the turn of this century.

As racist persecutions replaced religious persecutions in Europe, however, the inferiority of the Jew became that of *race*. By the 1880s, a tidal wave of pogroms and persecutions swept over large parts of Europe. To the people it everywhere appeared that the bourgeoisie were in the saddle, and the Jews, owing to earlier segregation in city ghettos and to restrictions against land-owning, were all bourgeoisie. They were hated for this reason, and persecution was reinforced by the old tradition of religious animosity against the Jews. Racial anti-Semitism was all too easy to arouse. In Germany in the 1880s, an anti-Semitic demagogue of evil repute was cynically encouraged by members of the

Conservative Party in order to strengthen with his following their opposition to the Social Democrats; synagogues were burned and violence against the Jews went unpunished. The charge of Jewish ritual murder was revived. In France, the anti-Semitic movement came to a climax in the 1890s with the famous Dreyfus affair. It marks probably the climax of prewar anti-Semitism in Europe. The reactionary party was most strongly represented in the Army, and the "framing" of a prominent Jewish staff officer, Captain Alfred Dreyfus, and his conviction of treason on forged evidence were the occasion for a year-long conflict that rocked the nation. To the honor of France, the plot was laid bare, Dreyfus was exonerated, and it was shown that those who were really guilty of the treason had attempted to hide themselves behind a Jew because of popular anti-Semitism.

The more closely one studies European anti-Semitism in its modern racial guise, the less it appears that the conflict is racial; it is the old problem of unequal citizenship rights. Whenever one group, whether industrial workers or a religious sect or a racial group, is discriminated against before the law or in equal claims to life, liberty, and jobs, there will always be powerful interests to capitalize this fact and to divert violence from those responsible for these conditions into channels where it is relatively safe to allow. In the case of the Jews, we inherit from the old era of religious persecution all the necessary shibboleths of hate, and these are easily turned to account in a new setting. In addition there is exceptional profit; unlike most discriminated-against minorities, the Jews often provide rich contraband and are therefore marked objects for persecution to a poverty-stricken government or populace.

The cure for anti-Semitism, therefore, logically lies, as in all minority conflicts, in the extension to all men of full citizenship rights and of full opportunity to make good in any field. There would have been no Dreyfus case if certain traitors had not felt that a framed Jew would be found guilty by the courts. There would have been no nationwide pogroms in Germany in 1938 if all those who took part in them had known the state would hold them accountable. It is not only for the sake of the persecuted that the full rights of minorities need to be maintained. The minorities may be only martyrs, but the persecutors revert to savagery. If we are unwilling or unable to pay the price of equality in human rights, we, the persecutors, suffer brutalization in ourselves whenever we fall into the trap set for us.

The case of the Negro since the Civil War in America points the same social lesson. The only trustworthy objective in any color-line program is the ultimate elimination of legal, educational, economic, and social discriminations. The fact that such elimination is not accepted even as an ultimate objective in most parts of the South is due to the persistence of slave-owner attitudes, on the one hand, and, on the other, to the degrading conditions under which great numbers of Negroes have lived in the United States. Granted that great numbers of Negroes are not ready for full citizenship, the social conditions which perpetuate their poverty and ignorance must be remedied before anyone can judge what kind of citizens they might be in other, more favorable circumstances. To be able to live a decent life and be respected for it, without being subjected to a blanket damnation that one's personal life cannot remove, is a human right, the granting of which would have immense social repercussions.

In periods and places where social institutions have made this possible for the Negro in the New World, the results have been incomparably better than those in the United States since the Civil War. Lord Bryce, an excellent observer, said of Brazil: "Brazil is the one country in the world, besides the Portuguese colonies on the east and west coasts of Africa, in which a fusion of the European and African races is proceeding unchecked by law or custom. The doctrines of human equality and human solidarity have here their perfect work. The work is so far satisfactory that there is little or no class friction. The white man does not lynch or maltreat the Negro; indeed I have never heard of a lynching anywhere in South America except occasionally as part of a political convulsion. The Negro is not accused of insolence and does not seem to develop any more criminality than naturally belongs to any ignorant population with loose notions of morality and property. What ultimate effect the intermixture of blood will have on the European element in Brazil I will not venture to predict. If one may judge from a few remarkable cases it will not necessarily reduce the intellectual standard."[2]

Such conditions were possible in Brazil only because of the extreme lack of racial discrimination which the Portuguese everywhere showed in their post-Columbian colonization; with the growing influence of non-Portuguese cultures in modern Brazil, the Negro has to some extent suffered. With growing discrimination against his race, the usual effects have followed, small though these consequences are in Brazil in comparison with the United States. But while discrimination was at a minimum, the social results were good.

To minimize racial persecution, therefore, it is necessary to minimize conditions which lead to persecution; it is not necessary to minimize race. Race is not in itself the source of the conflict. Conflict arises whenever any group—in this case, a race—is forged into a class by discriminations practiced against it; the race then becomes a minority which is denied rights to protection before the law, rights to livelihood and to participation in the common life. The social problem does not differ whether such a group is racially distinguished or whether it is not; in either case the healthy social objective is to do away with minority discriminations.

We are so far from doing this in the modern world that it is likely to seem a program impossible of achievement. Even so, this is not the total program for a world free of race conflict. It is not enough merely to legislate human rights for the minorities. The majorities also—the persecutors—must have solid basis for confidence in their own opportunity to live in security and decency. Otherwise, whatever the laws, whatever the guarantees, they will find out a victim and sacrifice him as a scapegoat to their despair. Everything that is done in any nation to eliminate unemployment, to raise the standard of living, to ensure civil liberties, is a step in the elimination of race conflict. Whatever is done to fasten fear upon the people of a nation, to humiliate individuals, to abrogate civil liberties, to deny coveted opportunities, breeds increased conflict. Men have not, for all their progress in civilization, outgrown the hen-yard; a hen who is pecked at by a cock attacks not the cock, but a weaker hen; this weaker hen attacks a still weaker, and so on down to the last chicken. Man, too, has his "pecking order," and those who have been victims, even though they belong to the "superior race," will require victims.

The truth of the matter is that these two aspects of a program for preventing the ravages of racism—democratic opportunity for the privileged and for the underprivileged—cannot be separated from one another: they are web and woof. One of the great political advantages of racist slogans is that the under-privileged may use them. Therefore the unemployed and the low-income groups can vent, through this alleged racist "superiority," the hatred that is engendered by their fear and insecurity. Studies in America have many times shown that anti-Semitism is strongest among low-income groups and that the high peaks of racial persecution have coincided with the low troughs of depression periods. While America raises Negro standards of living, of health, and of education in the South, therefore, it is necessary also to raise the standards of the southern poor whites. Until we have "made democracy work" so that the nation's full manpower is drafted for its common benefit, racist persecution will continue in America. Until housing and conditions of labor are raised above the needlessly low standards which prevail in many sections of the country, scapegoats of some sort will be sacrificed to poverty. Until the regulation of industry has enforced the practice of social responsibility, there will be exploitation of the most helpless racial groups, and this will be justified by racist denunciations.

Hard-boiled economists and statesmen recognize today the shortsightedness of policies which allow such conditions to continue and to become intensified. Those who fight to perpetuate them are repeating the errors of the Albigensian crusade and the Huguenot expulsion; they are gaining a false and temporary advantage at the expense of their own permanent welfare. National prosperity, however thin you cut it, has two surfaces: ability to sell means ability to buy; employment means production. Whatever groups battle with each other, under conditions of modern industry and finance, the most important condition of either one's getting more is that the other shall also get more. Since their conflict is truly suicidal, it is necessary for the benefit of the contestants themselves that farsighted regulations should be imposed on both parties.

In the last decade we have grown to recognize much more fully the responsibility that rests on the state for achieving satisfactory national conditions, and from the standpoint of history it is likely that this role of the state will in the long run be extended rather than curtailed. A democratic state, when it lives up to its minimum definition at all, is the one institution which represents all the parts of the body politic. It can propose for itself programs which will eventually benefit the whole body. It is hard to see how this responsibility for the whole can be taken today except by the national government, and in the past decade state regulation has increased, national treasuries all over the Western world have been opened for the relief of the unemployed, and compulsory old-age insurance is in operation in many nations. These and other national undertakings can be used to minimize economic discrimination. Equality in the matter of civil liberties is closely bound up with such programs, and so long as civil liberties are made more, rather than less, equal for different groups, there is no historical reason for fearing the increased role of the state. For the true goal in any program for a better America is that all men may be able to live so that self-respect is possible and so that they may have confidence that prosperity will spread its benefits widely over the population.

The cultural anthropologist has the best reason in the world to know that conflict is eliminated only as men work together for common benefits and obtain them in common. In most of the tribes the anthropologist knows, he can study side by side two different codes of ethics: one is that of openhanded hospitality and liberality and sharing, along with condemnation of aggressions like stealing and murder; the other is death at sight, torture, and the exaltation of robbery. The first code a man applies to those whose economic and social activities benefit him; these form an in-group within which none but moral reprobates are penalized. No matter who is successful in the hunt, the whole in-group benefits; any special skills any man may possess are an asset to the group as a whole. The priests conduct ceremonies for the good of the tribe and for common advantages like increase of plants and animals; warriors defend the little group against predatory outsiders. The second code a man applies to tribes with whom his tribe makes no common cause. No activities of theirs feed or house or bless or defend him. They are outside the pale. It is only a question of whether he kills his enemies first or they kill him.

The in-group code of ethics arises, however, only as the institutions of a society provide for shared advantages. When increase of food supply is not a common benefit, but something one man must get at the expense of another; when supernatural power is not used for general blessings, like rain, which falls on all, but for charms to use for personal ends against a neighbor; when legal or economic or political institutions put one man at the mercy of his neighbors, persecution develops. The gain or loss of all men is no longer my own gain or loss, and the tribe is no longer a unit within which in-group ethics operate. The persecution that develops is most often sorcery. Sorcery is a very evil thing, and when society does not officially punish it the victim has no redress. Unchecked sorcery societies are like modern nations with Ogpus and Gestapos, and they act out in deeds Hitler's dictum: "We need hatred, hatred, and then more hatred."

In-group ethics is therefore a reflection of the fact that all members share in their tribal enterprises and do actually profit from one another's activities. In-group mutual support is as native to the human race as out-group hostility; it is not something precarious and achieved only by isolated individuals at the end of a long social evolution. It arose long before the higher ethical religions with their teachings of altruism and duty. It occurs automatically whenever the social order makes it advantageous. It is at home among the lowest savages, and the one essential contribution modern civilization has made has been to enlarge the size of the in-group. In this there has been incomparable progress. Millions today recognize their common cause as citizens of a great nation, or as members of a party, or as financiers, or as workers, whereas in past history some little territory might be divided into a dozen hostile groups recognizing no common bonds. Today the increasing complexity of the processes of production, the ease of transportation, the interdependence of financial systems have brought it about that people in the remotest part of civilization suffer from, catastrophe in another part.

The very progress of civilization, therefore, has laid the foundation for a vast extension of in-group mutual dependency and mutual support. Mankind has not yet adjusted its institutions to the real requirements of the world it has created, and this cultural tag today threatens the very bases of international life. Many serious students of human affairs have been driven to despair. The world of our fathers, they conclude, has been destroyed because it tried to ignore the real facts of human nature; it tried to impose a peaceful social order on a predatory animal. The lesson we should learn from recent events, they say, is that man is by nature a beast of prey who will always tear and rend his weaker neighbors; we must recognize that wars and racial persecutions are inevitable in human destiny. To the anthropologist such a counsel of despair is demonstrably false. In-group ethics are as "innate" as out-group ethics, *but they occur only when certain social conditions are fulfilled.* We cannot get in-group ethics without meeting those conditions. In our own country this means that a better America will be one which benefits not some groups alone but all citizens; so long as there is starvation and joblessness in the midst of abundance we are inviting the deluge. To avert it, we must "strongly resolve" that all men shall have the basic opportunity to work and to earn a living wage, that education and health and decent shelter shall be available to all, that, regardless of race, creed, or color, civil liberties shall be protected.

The elimination of race conflict is a task of social engineering. But what of education? It is often said that our school systems must make themselves responsible for ending race prejudice, and attempts have been made to achieve tolerance by special instruction. This is of great importance, but we should be quite clear about the limits of its effectiveness; otherwise, in the end we shall cry that we were betrayed because it has not succeeded. All education, whether of children or of adults, is important and necessary because it makes for an enlightened mind and for unbiased impulses. These are essential because without them discriminations may not be done away with at all and barriers to opportunity may never be thrown down. But good impulses are socially effective only when they have accomplished these results. "Hell is paved with good intentions"—intentions which were blindly regarded as ends in themselves and nor as mere preliminaries. This is a platitude, but one which is often forgotten in discussions of the role of our schools in racial matters. If we are to make good use of the great powers of education in combating racism, two goals should be kept clearly distinct. On the one hand, it is desirable to teach, in the regular social studies, the facts of race and of the share of different races in our civilization. On the other hand, it is necessary to hold up ideals of a functioning democracy; it is necessary to help children to understand the mutual interdependence of different groups; it is necessary to encourage comparison of our social conditions with conditions which are better than ours as well as with those that are worse. It is necessary that they should be taught to think of unsatisfactory conditions not as inescapable facts of nature, but as ones which with effort can be done away with. Only through such education can school instruction lay the basis for the amelioration of race conflict. We cannot trust to teaching them about the glories of Chinese civilization or the scientific achievements of the Jews. That is worth doing, but if we leave it at that and expect them to become racially tolerant we have deceived ourselves. The fatal flaw in most arguments which would leave to the schools the elimination of race conflict is that they propose education *instead* of social engineering. Nothing but hypocrisy can come of such a program.

The program that will avail against racism is called today "making democracy work." Insofar as it is achieved in America, it will produce the kind of behavior it has always produced in a mutually supporting-group. Change, we must recognize, is always difficult and produces dislocations. But if we know the direction in which we must move, we can resolve to pay the necessary costs of change. The Arabians have a proverb: " 'What will you have?' said the Prophet, 'take it and pay for it.' " We must pay for a democracy that works, but, fortunately in this case, we can reassure ourselves with the knowledge that, even in financial accounting, government investment in rehousing and rebuilding America, in soil conservation, in health and education, and in increasing the nation's purchasing power through insurance benefits pay their own way with handsome returns. A price is exacted also for a social order like Nazi Germany, and that price, in lowered standards of living, in brutalization, in denial of human rights, in sabotage of science and the intellectual life, is higher than any costs of democracy. In persecuting victims, the Nazis were themselves victimized.

Our Founding Fathers believed that a nation could be administered without creating victims. It is for us to prove that they were not mistaken.

What They Say

In the gain or loss of one race all the rest have equal share. (James Russell Lowell in *The Crisis*.)

There is no irrepressible conflict between Oriental and Western civilizations. On the contrary, they are complementary to each other, not necessarily competitive. (Paul Samuel Reinsch, *Intellectual and Political Currents in the Far East*. London: Constable & Co., 19.11, p. 35.)

Every effort of the Negro to move, to raise and improve his social status, rather than his condition, has invariably met with opposition, aroused prejudice, and stimulated racial animosities. Race prejudice, so conceived, is merely an elementary expression of conservatism. (R. E. Park, "Bases of Race Prejudice," *Annals of the American Academy* CXL [Nov. 1928], p. 13.)

Race thus has a profound social significance. . . . It is made the symbol of cultural status and thus serves to justify the exploitation of the weaker group with the inevitable political and cultural consequences. Being a symbol of cultural status it serves automatically to classify individuals, and so to retard their advance by limiting their freedom and determining the cultural values to which they have access. (E. B. Reuter, *American Race Problem*. New York: T Y. Crowell Co., 1927, p. 34.)

The philosophical implication of race-thinking is that by offering us the mystery of heredity as an explanation, it diverts our attention from the social and intellectual factors that make up personality. (Jacques Barzun, *Race: A Study in Modern Superstition*. London: Methuen & Co., 1938, p. 282.)

For the combating of racism before it sinks its ugly fangs deep in our body politic, the scientist has a special responsibility. Only he can clean out the falsities which have been masquerading under the name of science in our colleges, our high schools, and our public prints. Only he can show how groundless are the claims that one race, one nation, or one class has any God-given right to rule. (Henry A. Wallace, U.S. Secretary of Agriculture, in an address delivered at the World's Fair, New York, October 14, 1939.)

Anti-alien campaigns of whatever nature are a sickening travesty of Americanism. We can contribute nothing of more value to a sick world than proof that men and women of different racial origins can get along together peaceably and democratically. Go far enough back and we are all aliens. (*New York Times*, Editorial, December 7, 1939.)

NOTES

1. W. E. Castle, "Biology and Social Consequences of Race-Crossing," *American Journal of Physical Anthropology* IX (1926), pp. 145–46.

2. James Bryce, *South America, Observations and Impressions*. London, Macmillan & Co., 1912, pp. 477, 480.

2. Ethnicity as Kin Selection: The Biology of Nepotism

Pierre L. van den Berghe

THE NOTION THAT ETHNICITY has something to do with kinship or "blood" is not new. Indeed, descent seems to be, implicitly and very often explicitly, the essential element of the definition of those groups of "significant others" that go under a wide variety of labels: tribe, band, horde, deme, ethnic group, race, nation, and nationality. This is clearly the case in the Western tradition, where the ideology of nationalism is replete with the rhetoric of kinship: fellow ethnics refer to each other as brothers and sisters; soldiers are said to die for the *mère patrie* or the *Vaterland*, depending on the gender ascribed by language to the collective parent; mystical notions of blood are said to be shared by members of one nation and to differentiate them from other groups.

True, the legacy of two world wars and of virulent racism in Nazi Germany somewhat dampened nationalist fervor in some intellectual circles in Europe and America during the 1950s and early 1960s. No sooner did intellectuals pronounce nationalism dead or dying in the "advanced" industrial countries, however, than it resurfaced within long-established states in the form of multitudinous movements for regional autonomy, ethnic separatism, racial pride, cultural identity, and the like.

Nor is the irrepressible nature of ethnic sentiments a uniquely Western perversion. The most common origin myth of "primitive" societies ascribes the birth of the nation to an ancestral couple, divinely created or descended.

In the simplest form of the myth, the ancestral couple is thought of as the

Pierre L. van den Berghe, "Ethnicity as Kin Selection: The Biology of Nepotism," *The Ethnic Phenomenon*. New York: Elsevier Publishing Com, 1981, pp. 15–36, reprinted with the permission of Greenwood Publishing Group, Inc.

progenitors of the entire society. In stratified societies, the royal family often attempts to monopolize divine ancestry, but then it quickly makes up for it by claiming paternity over its subjects.

For the followers of the monotheistic religions of Judaism, Christianity, and Islam, the Book of Genesis serves as origin myth, and Adam and Eve as the ancestral couple. More specifically, Muslims and Jews see themselves as descendants of Abraham. Those groups have now become so large and so diverse that these putative ancestors are no longer very meaningful to many contemporary followers of these religions, but the biblical origin myths are in fact quite similar to those of other traditions. For example, the Yoruba of southwestern Nigeria place their own origin (which, in typical ethnocentric manner, they identify with the origin of mankind) in their sacred city of the Ile Ife. The earth was created at Ile Ife by Oduduwa, one of the main divinities of the Yoruba pantheon, on instructions from Olorun the supreme deity. Oduduwa came down to the earth he created, sired 16 sons who became the founders of the various Yoruba kingdoms and the ancestors of all the Yoruba people.[1]

The Navajo, an indigenous American group inhabiting the southwestern United States, have a complex myth in which Changing Woman, the principal figure among the supernatural Holy People, was magically impregnated by the rays of the Sun and by water from a waterfall and gave birth to twin sons, Hero Twins, who first dwelt with their father, the Sun. Holy People later descended to earth, where they created Earth Surface People, the ancestors of the Navajos, and taught them culture, that is, the Navajo way of life.[2]

The Pathan, stateless agriculturalists and pastoralists of Afghanistan and Pakistan, clearly define their ethnicity in terms of descent in patrilineal line from a common ancestor, Qais, who lived some 20 to 25 generations ago and was a contemporary of Prophet Mohammed, from whom he embraced the Muslim faith. A Pathan is thus a descendant of Qais in the male line who is Muslim and conforms to Pathan customs.[3]

Even a large, centralized state like Japan has a traditional nationalist myth whereby all Japanese are descended from the same common ancestor, of whom the Imperial Family represent the line of direct descent, and all the other families of Japan represent collateral branches formed by younger sons of earlier generations. The entire nation is, thus, one single vast lineage.[4] In the words of a Hozumi Nobushige, a Japanese writing in 1898, "The Emperor embodies the Spirit of the Original Ancestor of our race. . . . In submitting to the Emperor of a line which has persisted through the ages, we subjects are submitting to the Spirit of the Joint Parent of our Race, the Ancestor of our ancestors."[5] This "blood ideology," as Hayashida called it, has been the essential defining element of Japanese nationhood for centuries.[6]

Examples could be multiplied, but these few illustrations from widely scattered parts of the world will suffice. Ethnicity is common descent, either real or putative, but, even when putative, the myth has to be validated by several generations of common historical experience.

When most of the world's "traditional" societies became incorporated in the colonial empires of European or neo-European countries, ideologues and social scientists of both right and left believed that ethnic sentiments would become increasingly vestigial, and that "modernity" (or "socialist internationalism" in the communist societies) would engulf petty particularisms, giving rise to ever wider and more rational bases of solidarity based on market forces, proletarian consciousness, Third World brotherhood, or whatever.

Few, if any, of these expectations came to pass. When imperial rule was securely established, it often managed to suppress emergent nationalisms by violence, but no sooner did these imperial systems collapse in the aftermath of war or revolution than did ethnic sentiments burst forth. Ironically, the only large empire to have emerged relatively intact from the post-imperial turmoil of the two world wars is that of the Czars. Even the new successor states to the European colonial empires have been rent by ethnic dissidence: Nigeria, Zaïre, India, Pakistan, and Malaysia—to name but a few. Nor were the smaller imperial systems spared the threat of ethnic separatism when the traditional system of rule collapsed, as witnessed by the events of the 1970s in Ethiopia and Iran. Even centuries of centralized despotism cannot suppress ethnic sentiment.

The position that ethnicity is a deeply rooted affiliation is often labeled "primordialist" in social science. Articulated by Max Weber and later by Geertz (1967a) and Shils (1957), the primordialist position was under severe attack in the 1950s and 1960s, when most social scientists treated ethnicity as one affiliation among many—highly changeable and responsive to circumstances.[7] The Marxists viewed ethnicity as an epiphenomenon, a remnant of precapitalist modes of production, a false consciousness masking class interests, a mystification of ruling classes to prevent the growth of class consciousness.[8] To functionalists and other non-Marxists, ethnicity was also a premodern phenomenon, a residue of particularism and ascription incompatible with the trend toward achievement, universalism, and nationality supposedly exhibited by industrial societies (Deutsch, 1966).[9]

All the bad things said of ethnicity were of course ascribed *a fortiori* to race. Sentiments of group belonging, based on physical attributes, were held to be even more wrong-headed and heinous than group membership based upon cultural attributes, such as language, religion, and other customs—the usual diacritica of ethnicity (Comas, 1972; Glazer, 1975; Gossett, 1963; Hofstadter, 1959; Leo Kuper, 1975; Lévi-Strauss, 1952; van den Berghe, 1965).[10] Only recently, with the revival of ethnicity, is the "primordialist" position once more being stated (Francis, 1976; Keyes, 1976).[11]

The conventional primordialist position on ethnicity was vulnerable on two scores:

1. It generally stopped at asserting the fundamental nature of ethnic sentiment without suggesting any explanation of why that should be the case.
   As a theoretical underpinning, the primordialists had nothing better to
   fall back on than the nebulous, romantic, indeed sometimes racist ideologies of nationalists to which the primordialists pointed as illustrations
   of their contention. What kind of mysterious and suspicious force was
   this "voice of the blood" that moved people to tribalism, racism, and
   ethnic intolerance?
2. If ethnicity was primordial, then was it not also ineluctable and
   immutable? Yet, patently, ethnic sentiments waxed and waned according
   to circumstances. Ethnicity could be consciously manipulated for personal
   gain. Ethnic boundaries between groups are sometimes quite fluid. Smaller
   groups often merge into larger ones and vice-versa. New ethnic groups
   constantly arise and disappear, and individuals may choose to assert ethnic
   identities or not as their interests or fancies dictate. How is all this circumstantial fluidity reconcilable with the primordialist position?

In contrast to the primordialist view of ethnicity, there came to be formulated the "instrumentalist" or "circumstantialist" position that held ethnicity to
be something manipulable, variable, situationally expressed, subjectively
defined, and only one possible type of affiliation among many."[12] One of the
leading exponents of this position is Fredrik Barth, who in his classical introduction to *Ethnic Groups and Boundaries* (1969) explicitly defines ethnicity in
subjective terms.[13] Ethnicity is whatever the natives say it is. It is the natives'
perceptions of reality that create and define ethnic boundaries and ethnic relations. It just happens that the Pathans whom Barth studied so extensively define
their ethnicity in terms of descent from a common ancestor; that ethnographic
fact does not invalidate Barth's position. Indeed, nothing can, if the analytical
categories used in social science must always be defined by the natives, who, in
turn, are by definition always right! The problem for those of us who try to formulate scientific propositions is that natives do not always agree with each
other, even *within* cultures, and that therefore a science of human behavior
based exclusively on native opinion tends to be shaky.

As most controversies based on a simple-minded antimony, the primordialist-
instrumentalist debate serves little purpose other than to help Ph.D. candidates
organize their examination answers. It is one of the main aims of this book to show
that both positions are correct, although not necessarily in the way the protagonists envisaged, and that the two views complement each other. We shall see that
ethnicity is indeed situationally variable, according to a multiplicity of ecological
conditions.[14] We shall examine the many ways in which ethnicity is manipulated
in power relationships.[15] Before I turn to the ecology and politics of ethnicity, and
thereby vindicate the instrumentalists, however, a theoretical basis for the pri-

mordialist position must be developed. Briefly, I suggest that there now exists a theoretical paradigm of great scope and explanatory power—evolutionary biology—that sheds a new light on phenomena of ethnocentrism and racism. In so doing, I am fully cognizant of the protest that such an endeavor will elicit.

My basic argument is quite simple: ethnic and racial sentiments are extension of kinship sentiments. Ethnocentrism and racism are thus extended forms of nepotism—the propensity to favor kin over non-kin. There exists a general behavioral predisposition, in our species as in many others, to react favorably toward other organisms to the extent that these organisms are biologically related to the actor. The closer the relationship is, the stronger the preferential behavior.

Why should parents sacrifice themselves for their children? Why do uncles employ nephews rather than strangers in their business? Why do inheritance laws provide for passing property on along lines of kinship? Why, in short, do people, and indeed other animals as well, behave nepotistically? To many, these questions appear so intuitively obvious as to require no explanation. We favor kin because they *are* kin. This is no answer, of course, but a mere restatement of the problem. Besides, we do not *always* favor kin. Profligate sons are sometimes disinherited, incompetent nephews not hired, and so on. Yet, on the whole, we are nepotists, and when we are not it is for some good reason. Nepotism, we intuitively feel, is the natural order of things. Where we feel nepotism would interfere with efficiency, equity, or some other goals, we institute explicit safeguards against it, and even then we expect it to creep in again surreptitiously.

But why? A convincing answer was hinted at by the British biologists R. A. Fisher (1958, first published in 1930) and J. B. S. Haldane (1932) but elaborated on only about 15 years ago by W. D. Hamilton (1964) and J. Maynard Smith (1964).[16] The theorem of "altruism," "kin selection," or "inclusive fitness," as biologists often refer to nepotism, was increasingly discovered to be the keystone of animal sociality. Soon, a theoretical synthesis of population genetics, ecosystem theory, and ethology gave birth to the new discipline of "sociobiology" as E. O. Wilson labeled it in his magisterial compendium on animal behavior (1975, ably summarized in Barash, 1977).[17]

The problem that posed itself to biologists was the seemingly self-sacrificial behavior of some animals under some conditions, for example, the emission of alarm calls to warn conspecifics, the mimicking of injuries to distract predators, or seeming restraints on reproduction under adverse ecological conditions. Wynne-Edwards (1962) answered the problem in terms of group selection.[18] Altruists behave in such a way for the good of their social group; groups that produce altruists have a competitive advantage over those that do not. However, there is one big drawback to the group selectionist argument. Altruism, by biological definition, is behavior that enhances the fitness (i.e., the reproductive success) of others at the cost of reducing the fitness of the altruist. If the altruists do indeed reduce their fitness by behaving altruistically, then genes fostering altruism would be selected against. How can an animal population sustain altruistic genes that reduce the reproductive success of their carriers through enhanced predation, induced sterility (as in the worker castes of social insects), or some other cause?

The answer is so disarmingly simple and convincing that even WynneEdwards has recently recanted his group selectionist argument. Seeming altruism is, in fact, the ultimate in genetic selfishness. Beneficent behavior is the product of a simple fitness calculus (presumably an unconscious one in most animals, though often a partially conscious one in humans) that takes two factors into account: the cost–benefit ratio of the transaction between altruist and recipient, and the coefficient of relatedness, r, between altruist and recipient. Simply put, an altruistic transaction can be expected if, and only if, the cost–benefit ratio of the transaction is smaller than the coefficient of relatedness between the two actors.

The coefficient of relatedness between any two organisms is the proportion of genes they share through common descent. It can range from a value of one (for organisms that reproduce asexually, e.g., through cell division) to zero (between unrelated organisms). In sexually reproducing organisms, parents and offspring and full siblings share one-half of their genes; half-siblings, grandparents and grandchildren, uncles-aunts, and nephews-nieces share one-fourth; first cousins, one-eighth, and so on.

Reproduction, in the last analysis, is passing on one's genes. This can be done directly through one's own reproduction or indirectly through the reproduction of related organisms. The fitness of an organism is, by definition, its reproductive success. The *inclusive* fitness of an organism is the slim of its own reproductive success plus that of related organisms discounted for their coefficient of relatedness. Thus, it takes two children to reproduce the genetic equivalent of ego; but the same effect can be achieved through four nephews or eight first cousins.

As brilliantly argued by Richard Dawkins (1976), the ultimate unit of replication is the gene, not the organism.[19] Bodies are, in Dawkins's words, mere mortal and expendable "survival machines" for potentially immortal genes. Such genes, therefore, as predispose their carrying organisms to behave nepotistically will be selected for, because, by favoring nepotism, they enhance their own replication. Nepotistic organisms foster the fitness of relatives who have a high probability of carrying the same gene or genes for nepotism. Nepotism genes, therefore, will spread faster than genes that program their carriers to care only for their own direct survival and reproduction—genes, for instance, that would program organisms to eat their siblings when hungry. This phenomenon of fostering inclusive fitness through *kin selection* or nepotism has been conclusively shown (mostly by studies of social insects but also, increasingly, of vertebrates) to be the basis of much animal sociality (E. O. Wilson, 1975; Daly and Wilson, 1978).[20]

Animal societies, from social insects to higher vertebrates, are held together primarily by cooperating kin who thereby enhance each other's fitness. This seeming "altruism" is thus the ultimate genic selfishness of maximizing one's *inclusive* fitness. An individual will only behave "altruistically" (i.e., in such a way as to reduce its own direct fitness) if, by doing so, the increment of fitness of a relative more than makes up for the loss to ego. For instance, my full sister shares half of her genes with me; she must, therefore, get more than twice as much out of my beneficent act to her than what that act costs me. For a half-sister or a niece, who only shares one-fourth of her genes with me, the benefit–cost ratio of the transaction would have to be better than four to one—and so on, according to the coefficient of relatedness between giver and receiver. The biological golden rule is "give unto others as they are related unto you."

The applicability of the kin selection paradigm to humans has been hotly debated. While anthropologists and other social scientists can hardly deny that all known human societies are organized on the basis of kinship and marriage, forming relatively stable reproductive units called families and exhibiting preferential behavior toward relatives, a number of them continue to argue nevertheless that kinship and marriage for humans are purely cultural concepts showing only fortuitous resemblance to anything biological (Sahlins, 1976; Schneider, 1968).[21] Elsewhere, I have attempted to refute that line of argument. While man is in some important respects different from other species, while man has an enormous capacity to adapt through learning, and while most of human behavior is indeed patterned (but not single-handedly determined) by a culture transmitted through symbolic language, man nevertheless remains an animal who shares many features of the mating and reproductive system with that of other mammals.[22] Rapidly accumulating evidence shows how applicable the kin selection paradigm is to humans (Chagnon and Irons, 1979; Daly and Wilson, 1978; Greene, 1978; Hartung, 1976; Shepher, 1980).[23]

Relatedness is a relative matter. Kinship might be schematized as a series of concentric circles around ego, each circle representing a degree of relatedness (Schema I). In the smallest circles are small numbers of highly related ($r = \frac{1}{2}$ or $\frac{1}{4}$) individuals. As the circles become larger, so does the number of persons involved, but r becomes smaller $\frac{1}{8}$, $\frac{1}{16}$, $\frac{1}{32}$, and so on), and therefore the intensity of kin selection rapidly declines.

In theory, we could have a wide-open network of such overlapping egocentered kinship circles, with no particular clustering. At the limit, all of humanity would consist of one vast, undifferentiated surface of overlapping concentric circles with no cluster or boundaries between them. This condition would be produced by what population biologists call *panmixia*—that is, random mating. Panmixia never happens in humans, nor in other animals, for a very simple reason: if nothing else, space exerts a passive restraint on who mates with whom. Sheer physical propinquity determines who has sexual access to whom. Geographical barriers, such as mountain ranges, bodies of water, deserts, and the like isolate animal populations from each other, and create breeding boundaries between them that can and often do lead to speciation or subspeciation.

SCHEMA I. Ego-centered map of kin selection.

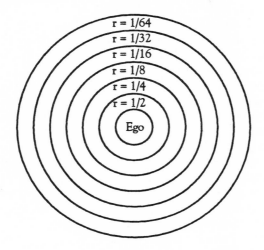

In humans, however, the story does not stop there. In addition to the purely physical impediments of distance, topography, and so on, human groups create cultural prescriptions and proscriptions concerning their mating systems. There is not a single known human group that lacks them and that even approximates panmixia. Rules specify whom one may, may not, should, or must marry. These rules and practices are almost invariably of a twofold nature. Certain individuals or members of some kin groups (such as lineages and class) *cannot* intermarry, while a wider group constitutes the people who are normally expected to mate and marry.

Indeed, nearly all of the small-scale, stateless human societies are groups ranging from a couple of hundred to a few thousand people, defined almost entirely by ties of descent and marriage. These breeding populations are internally divided into smaller kin groups that swap daughters and sisters for spouses between the men (Lévi-Strauss, 1969).[24] Elsewhere (van den Berghe, 1979a), I have dealt at length with human kinship and marriage systems and shown how closely they conform to the sociobiological paradigm. The relevance of all this to ethnicity is that the primeval model of the human ethnic group is, in fact, the breeding population of a few hundred individuals, the structure of which we have just sketched. This is what the anthropologists used to call the "tribe"—a group characterized by internal peace, preferential endogamy, and common ancestry (real or putative).

At this point, I would like to introduce the neologism *ethny* for "ethnic group." "Ethnic group" is clumsy and "tribe" has many different connotations— several pejorative. The French and Spanish cognates *ethnie* and *etnia* are already in common usage, and it is time to start using such a convenient term in English as well. The ideology usually referred to as "ethnocentrism" might then be more parsimoniously called *ethnism*. An ethny can be represented, as in Schema II, as a cluster of overlapping, ego-centered, concentric kin circles, encompassed within an ethnic boundary. The ethnic boundary is represented by a dotted line, since it is seldom completely closed. More typically, there is some migration, principally of women, among groups.

If the society in question has a rule of unilineal descent, either patrilineal or matrilineal, then the ethny may also be represented, as in Schema III, as internally divided into non-overlapping unilineal descent groups (clans) that exchange women. In fact, the vast majority of the stateless, tropical horticultural ists and pastoralists, and a considerable number of the preindustrial state societies, have unilineal descent and clan exogamy, often combined with preferential cross-cousin marriage. This is not the place to expand on the organizational advantages of this common system, as I have done so elsewhere.[25] Most of the remaining hunting and gathering societies have bilateral descent and a much less structured system of exchanging women, but, even in these less structured systems, which were presumably also characteristic of earlier phases of human social evolution, the ethny is also a breeding population of limited size (typically a few hundred), most of whose members are related to each other.

There are, of course, exceptions. Some women are captured from neighboring ethnies. Conquest and peaceful migration periodically mix populations, and new-

SCHEMA II. Kinship map of the prototypical ethny.

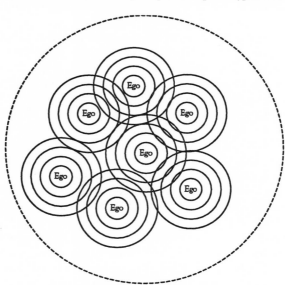

Ethnic Boundary

comers may be fictively related by adoption. It is very difficult and quite exceptional, however, for an ethny to form if the core of the group is not made up of
people who know themselves to be related to each other by a double network of
ties of descent and marriage. Ethnicity is thus defined in the last analysis by
common descent. Descent by itself, however, would leave the ethny unbounded,
for, by going back enough, all living things are related to each other. *Ethnic
boundaries* are created *socially* by *preferential endogamy* and physically by *territoriality*. Territoriality and endogamy are, of course, mutually reinforcing, for
without physical propinquity people can hardly meet and mate, and, conversely,
successful reproduction, with all the lavish parental investment it requires for
humans, favors territorialized kin groups. The prototypical ethny is thus a
descent group bounded socially by inbreeding and spatially by territory.

SCHEMA III. Clan exogamy in unilineal descent ethnies.

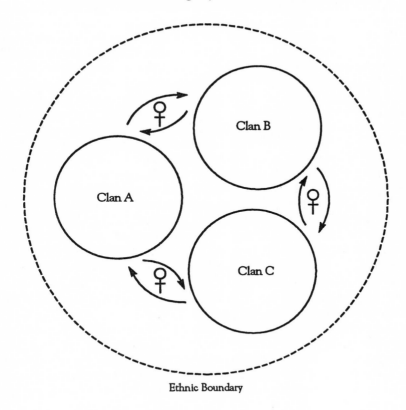

Ethnic Boundary

Until the last few thousand years, such groups were of limited size as witnessed by many surviving "primitive" societies. The natural ethny in which hominids evolved for several thousand millennia probably did not exceed a couple of hundred individuals at the most. Evidence for this is the great mental and emotional strain on the human brain to "know" more than a few hundred individuals. We can recognize by sight many thousands, but our ability to associate complex personalities with faces and to make reliable enough predictions about people's behavior to render interaction sufficiently unstrained is quite limited. Urban life constantly strains these physiological limits, and when we must constantly interact with a larger and rapidly changing cast of characters the very nature of the interaction changes drastically, as has been repeatedly noted by social scientists and others. There are many fundamental differences between what the German sociologists called *Gemeinschaft* (the small-scale, intimate, face-to-face group of a few hundred people, or the prototypical ethny in my terms) and *Gesellschaft* (the large, anomic, impersonal society characteristic of the industrial age).

We have evolved, I am arguing, the kind of brain to deal with smallscale, *Gemeinschaft*-type groups, the prototype of which is the ethny, the "we-group," the "in-group" of intimates who think of each other as an *extended family*. Beyond that kind and size of group, the strain of having to deal with people we do not know well enough, and therefore cannot trust, is of such a nature as to alter radically the very nature of the interaction. In the larger world, we expect ruthless self-interest and cheating to be rampant and to be constrained principally by the coercive power of the state. Furthermore, our brain, which in other respects is a stupefyingly complex instrument, rebels at "knowing" intimately more than a few hundred people at the limit. If we try to exceed an upper limit of, say, 500, we either have to slough off old acquaintances to allow new ones, or we simply fake familiarity and conviviality beyond our emotional and intellectual capabilities.

The primordial ethny is thus an extended family; indeed, the ethny represents the outer limits of that inbred group of near or distant kinsmen whom one knows as intimates and whom therefore one can trust. One intuitively expects fellow ethnics to behave at least somewhat benevolently toward one because of kin selection, reinforced by reciprocity. The shared genes predispose toward beneficence; the daily interdependence reinforces that kin selection. Fellow ethnics are, in the deepest sense, "our people."

This prototype of the small, endogamous, kin-related ethny is, of course, importantly modified in practice, especially in the larger societies that have arisen since the development of agriculture some 10,000 years ago, of large states some 5,000 years ago, and most recently of the industrial revolution 200 years ago. So far, we have merely sketched the evolutionary scenario of the ethny. Now we must fill in the picture by introducing the qualifications.

Ethnic endogamy is seldom strict and prescriptive. Generally, it is merely preferential and, most important, asymmetrical by sex. The double standard of sexual morality that is so apparent in many aspects of our behavior and so readily understandable in terms of the biology of asymmetrical parental investment is also glaringly present in the application of ethnic endogamy.[26] Much of the abundant literature on ethnicity and sex has been psychoanalytically oriented, invoking elaborate theories of frustration-aggression, sadomasochism, repression of libidinal urges, and attraction of forbidden fruits (Adorno, 1950; Bastide, 1950; Freyre, 1964; Mannoni, 1964; Lillian Smith, 1963; Stember, 1976).[27] The sociobiological paradigm provides a much simpler explanation. In nearly all species, the female is the scarce reproductive resource for the male rather than vice-versa. There are fewer females available for insemination than males ready to inseminate. Eggs are big, few, and therefore costly; sperms are small, abundant, and therefore cheap. Since females invest much more in the reproductive process than males, they maximize their fitness by being choosy about their mating partners. They seek to pick the best possible mates in terms of generic qualities and resources they have to offer. The male, on the other hand, maximizes his fitness by being promiscuous and by outcompeting his rivals in access to reproductive females.

Seen in that light, the ethny is a corporation of related men seeking to enhance each others' fitness by retaining a monopoly of sexual access to the women of their own group. This, however, does not preclude men from further enhancing their reproductive success by making the most of every opportunity to inseminate women from other groups. In fact, the whole history of ethnic relations powerfully confirms this interpretation. Men jealously "protect" "their" women from men of other groups, deeply resenting ethnic exogamy on the part of women, while at the same time seeking access to women from other groups. In ethnically stratified societies, this double standard takes the form of polygamy of the dominant-group men, with subordinategroup women becoming secondary wives and concubines. Where several ethnies live side by side in an unstratified system, the groups constantly raid each other for women.

This sexual asymmetry of endogamy has, of course, one important consequence—namely, that no ethny is a completely closed breeding system. The circulation of women between ethnies continuously brings in fresh blood. One may then look at ethnic relations from the point of view of the circulation of women, and arrive at the following formulation. *Within the ethny*, a group of related men peaceably exchange kinswomen for wives among themselves. After the system has been in operation for several generations, the wives are also related to their husbands; frequently, they are preferentially cousins, in fact. This leads to a certain degree of inbreeding that is ill the greater as the ethny is small.

Between ethnies, men use power and violence to secure access to women from other groups, and this reduces the level of inbreeding. When the ethnies in presence are equally matched, male competition for foreign women takes the form of inter-ethnic raids. After an ethnic hierarchy has been established, sub-ordinate-group men lose all or part of their control of "their" women, and their reproductive success is curtailed, while upper-group men are polygynous and incorporate subordinate-group women. An ethnic hierarchy, therefore, gener-ally results in a reduced fitness for subordinate-group males. The classical sce-nario for conquest is to rape the women and kill, castrate, or enslave the men.

Asymmetry of reproductive strategies for males and females has another important corollary for ethnic relations. In a situation of ethnic hierarchy, ethnic solidarity between men and women is undermined. The men of the sub-ordinate group are always the losers and therefore have a reproductive interest in overthrowing the system. The women of the subordinate group, however, fre-quently have the option of being reproductively successful with dominant-group males. Indeed, even where forced into relationships with dominant males, they must cooperate in the interest of their children. We shall return to that impor-tant point when we examine slavery systems.

Descent, I asserted, is the central feature of ethnicity. Yet it is clear that, in many cases, the common descent ascribed to an ethny is fictive. In fact, in most cases it is at least *partly* fictive. If such is the case, does not the fictive or puta-tive character of kinship invalidate the sociobiological argument presented here? I think not. Ethnicity, I suggested, is extended kinship. Even in restricted kinship, descent is sometimes a fiction. In most societies, some children are adopted or are not the offspring of their supposed fathers. Nevertheless, these exceptions do not invalidate the general proposition that human kinship sys-tems reflect biological relatedness. Some anthropologists have argued against this proposition (Sahlins, 1976; Schneider, 1968), but they must strain the data beyond credibility to defend their position.[28] A number of anthropologists have argued convincingly against the purely cultural-determinist view of human kin-ship (Fortes, 1969; Fox, 1967).[29] In a recent book, I have attempted to demon-strate how closely human systems of kinship and marriage fit expectations derived from the sociobiological paradigm.[30]

If kinship in the most restricted circle of the nuclear family is sometimes a biological fiction, it is little wonder that the greatly extended kind of kinship implicit in ethnicity should often be putative. The larger the ethny, the more likely this is. Clearly, for 50 million Frenchmen or 100 million Japanese, any common kinship that they may share is highly diluted, and known to be so. Sim-ilarly, when 25 million Afro-Americans call each other "brothers" and "sisters," they know that they are greatly extending the meaning of these terms. The enormous ethnies, running into millions of members, that characterize industrial societies are limiting cases, far removed from the evolutionary prototype of a few hundred people that we have been talking about.

Yet—and this is what begs explanation—the fiction of kinship, even in modern industrial societies, has to be sufficiently credible for ethnic solidarity to be effective. One cannot create an instant ethny by creating a myth. The myth has to be rooted in historical reality to be accepted. Ethnicity can be *manipulated* but *not manufactured*. Unless ethnicity is rooted in generations of shared historical experience, it cannot be created *ex nihilo*. Many attempts to adopt universalistic criteria of ethnicity based on legal citizenship or acquisition of educational qualifications, for instance, failed. Such was French assimilation policy in her colonies. No amount of proclamation of *Algérie française* made it so. Léopold Senghor, that masterful craftsman of the French language, ended up extolling *négritude* (in French!) and becoming the president of independent Sénégal. The Algerian *pieds noirs* were reincorporated into the French ethny despite five or six generations of African experience, while Muslim Algerians with French citizenship find acceptance difficult even after two or more generations of residence in France. Examples could be multiplied of nonacceptance, by industrial as well as Third World societies, of groups perceived as being of different genetic origin, despite their acquisition of dominant-group culture and language: Koreans in Japan, Afro-Americans in the United States, Jews in Europe, overseas Chinese and East Indians in Asia, Africa, and the Caribbean.

If myths of ethnicity must be credible, what tests of ethnicity are used to decide on their credibility? What criteria do people use to decide whether an individual is a fellow ethnic or not? In the small-scale societies typical of our species until a few thousand years ago, the simple test of acquaintance based on previous association sufficed in most circumstances. We share with other higher vertebrates, such as dogs and monkeys, the ability to recognize individuals and to carry faces in our memories for long periods of time. Occasionally a person kidnapped by another group early in life might face the problem of establishing his filiation with his group of origin, but, in most cases, in societies of a few hundred people the test of membership is straightforward enough: the person belongs if he is known to belong; he does not belong either if he is known not to belong or if he is not known to belong.

Obviously, the larger the society gets, the more difficult the problem of ascertaining membership becomes. Already in "primitive" societies that run into tens of thousands, membership is no longer always established *prima facie*; it must be proven. At that level the test is generally genealogical: the unknown individual claims membership through filiation with known members. Kinship, that is, is explicitly used to establish ethnicity. Australian aborigines are said to have been able to do so across the face of the continent, but this is an extreme case. Usually, tracing filiation only works in groups of moderate size (a few thousand) and spatial dispersal (a few hundred square kilometers).

Where societies run into hundreds of thousands or even millions of members, and cover vast stretches of territory, the situation becomes complicated. Ethnicity can no longer be so easily ascertained and, therefore, it can be faked. If ethnism is a way of maximizing fitness through extended nepotism, then a clever animal like man can be expected to fake common ethnicity for gain. Con games in which individuals gain "undeserved" advantage by exaggerating or counterfeiting a relationship to their victims thrive in largescale societies that lack the easy controls of recognition and intimacy found in small societies. Ethnicity is one of these manipulable relationships. At the same time, there are occasions where ethnicity has to be established quickly, where one literally shoots first and asks questions later. How, then, can one establish ethnicity quickly and reliably and also keep cheats under control? What features will be chosen as *ethnic markers*?

There are many possibilities, trending to fall into three main categories of traits. The three are not mutually exclusive, and their respective effectiveness varies greatly according to circumstances.

First, one can pick a genetically transmitted phenotype, such as skin pigmentation, stature (as with the Tuzi of Rwanda and Burundi), hair texture, facial features, or some such "racial" characteristic. Groups that are socially defined by genetic phenotypes are called "races," and societies that put emphasis on biological traits to differentiate groups within it can be called "racist."

Second, one can rely on a man-made ethnic uniform. Members of one's group are identified by bodily mutilations and/or adornments carried as visible badges of group belonging. These markers range from clothing and headgear to body painting, tattooing, circumcision, tooth filing, and sundry mutilations of the lips, nose, and earlobes.

Third, the test can be behavioral. Ethnicity is determined by speech, demeanor, manners, esoteric lore, or some other proof of competence in a behavioral repertoire characteristic of the group.

A brief review of the three classes of ethnic markers is useful at this point, for each has a different set of properties and of structural consequences. Race would seem the most obvious solution to the problem of ethnic recognition, especially if there is a biological basis for the extended nepotism that we are discussing. Does it not stand to reason that genetically inheritable phenotypes are the most reliable markers of ethnicity, if by ethnicity one means, in the last analysis, genetic relatedness? Would not one, therefore, expect racism to be universal? The answer to the first question, a theoretical one, is "yes," and to the second, an empirical question, "no."

However, before proceeding, I must clarify a common confusion about the term "race." The word has been used in several distinct meanings, *inter alia* as a synonym for nation or ethny, (e.g., "the French race"), as a biological subspecies or inbred population (e.g., "the Chihuahua or Cocker Spaniel race"), and as a synonym for species (e.g., "the human race"). None of these meanings is implied here. Where relatively inbred subgroups of the human species are meant, we will speak of "populations" in the genetic sense. What is meant by "race" here is a *social* label attributed to groups of people in particular societies at particular times, on the basis of inherited phenotypical characteristics. If phenotypic criteria are socially used to categorize groups (usually, if not always, invidiously), then races are said to exist in that society, and the ideology supporting that classification and its social consequences is called racism.[31]

It is also important to stress that phenotypes chosen for social relevance, while often clearly visible markers of genetic origin, are typically biologically trivial in terms of fitness, abilities, aptitudes, and temperament—indeed, anything of social consequence. To suggest that the sociobiological theory presented here is racist in the sense that I have just defined it is nonsensical. Our theory says nothing about racial differences between human groups—much less about any invidious ranking between them. On the contrary, it stresses a common biological propensity, not only of all humans but also of all social animals, to favor kin over non-kin, a propensity that gets translated into ethnism and sometimes (but only sometimes) into racism.

Having said this, there is no denying that, even though humans share the overwhelmingly greater part of their genetic material with each other (and indeed with other closely related organisms such as the great apes), the relatively small proportion of their gene loci that is multiallelic produces a wide range of individual variation and a smaller, but not negligible, amount of group variation. Human populations are strikingly different from each other in the distribution of some genes, and at least some of these differences have had adaptive significance during some periods of human evolution under certain environmental conditions. For instance, tropical populations of Africa and South India show a much higher incidence of the recessive gene for sickle cell anemia, an allele that, though highly deleterious in homozygous form, confers a measure of immunity to malaria to its heterozygous carriers.

Similarly, there is a close association between the distribution of a gene causing lactose intolerance in adults and the presence or absence of cattle. The lactose-intolerance gene is virtually absent from the gene pool of East African pastoralists but common in other parts of Africa where the tse-tse fly makes the raising of cattle nearly impossible. The several genes that regulate the amount of melanin in the skin are also distributed in a way that shows a close correspondence with climatic conditions. Through skin pigmentation, the amount of absorption of sunlight is regulated: some is needed because of the essential vitamin D, but too much is carcinogenic. Therefore, there is a direct correlation between skin pigmentation and latitude, or at least there was until the mass migrations that accompanied European slave trade and colonialism.

Some human groups are characterized by the significantly higher incidence of some deleterious genes for which no adaptive significance can be found. Examples are Tay-Sachs syndrome, a form of genetic idiocy found ten times more often among Askenazic Jews than among Gentiles and Sephardic Jews; and the relatively high frequency of hemophilia (a sex-linked recessive gene on the X chromosome) among the descendants of Queen Victoria, who in the early 20th century populated the royal houses of Europe from Spain to Russia.[32] Such phenomena are attributable to what geneticists call the "founder effect" (i.e., the effect of a prolific ancestor) and the resultant "genetic drift" in the gene pool of his or her descendants.

In these cases, however, the incidence of these harmful genes tends to be low, even in the populations where it occurs most frequently. For instance, one Askenazic Jew out of 25 is a carrier of the recessive Tay-Sachs gene, compared to one in 400 among Gentiles. Genetic differences between populations are thus generally a matter of relative frequency of alleles, not of absolute differences.

There is no denying the reality of genetic differences in frequencies of alleles between human groups. None of these differences, however, has yet been shown to bear any functional relationship with the *social* attribution of racial characteristics in any human society nor with the relative positions of dominance and subordination of racial groups in any society. There is nothing, either in the study of human genetics or in sociobiological theory, to support any social order or ideology, to vindicate or challenge the position of any group, or to buttress or attack any ethical premise or philosophical system. Human genetics and the presence or absence of racial distinctions in human societies are two almost totally discrete orders of phenomena. The only tenuous connection between them is that some human groups, under conditions to be specified presently, sometimes use genetically transmitted phenotypes as badges of membership in social groups. The *socially ascribed* significance of these genetic markers can be enormous, but it bears no intrinsic relationship to their biological, evolutionary significance. Humans use phenotypic characteristics first and foremost as probabilistic markers of common descent.

Now, let us return to the problem of the presence or absence of racism in human societies. With our contemporary knowledge of human genetics, we categorically exclude parenthood on the basis of a single nonmatching allele, and, conversely, we can establish kinship beyond reasonable doubt by matching individuals on a multiplicity of alleles of known frequency distribution in certain populations. In practice, however, most people are not geneticists, and, indeed, until less than a century ago, people had only the vaguest notions of how characteristics were inherited. The outcome is that, while in many, perhaps most, human societies, tests of physical resemblance are used to assess probability of kinship and, by extension, ethnicity, these tests are seldom the only ones or even the main ones that are relied upon, at least as far as establishing ethnic membership is concerned.

The reason for this seeming paradox is apparent enough. At the rudimentary level of folk genetics, racial phenotypes are often very poor indicators of group membership, because neighboring populations typically maintain a sufficient rate of migration to create genetic gradients, such that *intragroup* variation on specific loci is much greater than *intergroup* variation. In short, neighboring populations—the very ones that are concerned about maintaining and defending ethnic boundaries—typically look very much like each other. Phenotype is useful to distinguish individuals within groups but not to distinguish between groups. Let us take the example of eye and hair color in Europe. There is a gradient from south to north of increasing frequency of the recessive alleles for blue eyes and blond hair. A Greek army fighting in Finland might make reasonably effective use of these genetic traits as markers of ethnicity—but not in the far more likely circumstance of having to fight Albanians or Turks. Similarly, skin color might be used by a Moroccan army crossing the Sahara, but not between Moroccans and Algerians, or Ghaneans and Togolese. The most crucial ethnic boundaries most of the time are those between groups competing for scarce resources in the same general vicinity. Those are precisely the circumstances under which racial distinctions are most useless.

One can therefore expect racism to appear only where long-distance immigration has suddenly put in presence substantial numbers of people whose physical appearance is different enough as to make genetic phenotype a reliable basis for distinguishing between groups. People must migrate across genetic gradients before their physical appearance can be used as a reliable basis of inferring group membership. Under such unusual conditions, people often develop what Hoetinck, in the Caribbean context, has called a "somatic norm image," that is, some mental picture of what members of their own and of other groups look like.[33] Even then, however, miscegenation, which typically accompanies conquest and slavery, often blurs racial distinctions within two or three generations. The migration must not only be across large distances, but it must also be rapid and massive enough to make race a useful marker of genetic relatedness between groups. Such conditions have been exceptional in human history, until the colonial expansion of Europe in the past 500 years. If racism is to continue over several generations, it must be buttressed by severe barriers against miscegenation, a rare situation found in only a few countries such as South Africa and the United States.[34]

For these reasons, racism, as the primary basis for group distinctions, has been the exception rather than the rule. Racism is not a Western, much less a capitalist, monopoly. For example, when the tall Hamitic Tuzi conquered shorter Bantu speakers to the south, they invented their own brand of racism (more specifically, "heightism") to buttress their domination of the Rwanda and Burundi kingdoms.[35] But there, too, the reason was the same as for the development of Western racism in the wake of European colonial expansion: long-distance migration across a wide genetic gradient—in this case, in body stature. In short, racism can be expected to develop and thrive where genetically inherited phenotypes are the easiest, most visible, and most reliable predictors of group membership. When phenotypes lose these properties through intermixture of groups, cultural criteria typically supplant racial criteria of group membership. This happened, for instance, throughout the Spanish American colonies that began as a racial *casta* system (indeed, the word "caste" comes from the Spanish-Portuguese term) and gradually evolved as societies stratified by class and ethnic criteria and only minimally by phenotype.[36]

The theory presented here accounts better for the appearance and disappearance of racism in various times and places than competing theories that attribute racism either to ideological factors [e.g., Tannenbaum (1947) on the differences between Protestantism and Catholicism and their respective legal traditions in the Western Hemisphere] or to the capitalist mode of production [e.g., numerous writers of Marxist disposition such as Cox (1948) and Simons and Simons (1969)].[37] More than anything else, it is long-distance migration over genetic gradients that creates racism; conversely, miscegenation attenuates it. And miscegenation almost invariably occurs because racism as such does little to inhibit it. Dominant-group men, whether racist or not, are seldom reluctant to maximize their fitness with subordinate-group women. It takes extraordinary measures of physical segregation, such as long existed in South Africa and the United States, to preserve a racial caste system. Racism is the exception rather than the rule in intergroup relations, and racially based systems are peculiarly conflict-ridden and unstable. Attempts at maintaining them often result in cataclysmic bloodshed [see Leo Kuper's (1977) study of revolution in Algeria, Zanzibar, Rwanda, and Burundi; the Haitian revolution; and the mounting crisis in Southern Africa].[38] I shall return to the special case of race later in this book, especially when I deal with racial slavery systems.

Both the second and the third categories of cultural markers are manmade and cultural, but the second is visual and artifactual, while the third is behavioral. The two types of marker are often used conjointly, as multiple tests of ethnicity. If we turn first to what I have called the "ethnic uniform" type of marker, it has the advantage of providing a visible and therefore rapid clue of group membership. This is quite useful in combat or contest situations, for example, as witnessed by the widespread use of uniforms by armies, sport teams, and the like. Then the premium is on easy, quick detection at a distance. A drawback of many of these easily visible clues provided by headgear, clothing, plumage, body paint, and the like is that they can be faked. A system of ethnic recognition based solely on these would be widely open to cheating, and indeed cheating does occur as when opposing armies try to infiltrate each other by donning their opponents' uniforms. The sanctions against such cheating, incidentally, are often exceptionally severe, such as immediate execution when, normally, simple capture would be expected.

Ethnic markers based on bodily mutilations, such as facial tattoos, tooth filing, circumcision, nose, lip, and ear piercing, and the like are not easily reversible, but they are often not so striking and can only be identified at close quarters.

Finally, there are behavioral ethnic markers, which are among the most reliable and hence commonly used. They have the advantage of being difficult to fake, because the performance criteria are often of considerable subtlety and intricacy, but they require skill and time in being applied and hence do not satisfy the criteria of ease and immediacy. Behavioral criteria may include styles of body movement, gesturing, eating, or greeting etiquette and the like, but language holds pride of place among them. The way people speak places them more accurately and reliably than almost any other behavioral trait. Language and dialect can be learned, of course, but the ability to learn a foreign tongue without a detectable accent drops sharply around puberty. Therefore, speech quality is a reliable (and difficult to fake) test of what group an individual has been raised in. Moreover, acquisition of foreign speech is extremely difficult except through prolonged contact with native speakers, another safety feature of the linguistic test.

Although language is a relatively subtle test, certain easily detectable phonemes give the foreigner away. A classical historical episode concerns the massacre of French troops by Flemings in the city of Brugge (or Bruges as the French say) in 1302. The Flemings wanted to kill the French army of occupation in their beds without raising the alarm, so the problem was how to identify Frenchmen quickly and reliably, in the dark, in order to slaughter them without fuss. The solution was to make them repeat a short Flemish phrase, "schilde en de vriend," ("shield and friend") that contained phonemes unpronounceable to native speakers of French. History books tell us that the stratagem was devastatingly successful. (As the son of a Flemish Belgian father and a French mother, going to a French-medium Belgian school in Brussels, I distinctly remember the disturbing ambivalence that this gruesome bit of Belgian history left me with. It was by no means clear to me on which side I was.)

Besides the difficult-to-fake properties of language that make it a good test of ethnicity, language can also be used quickly to transmit simple esoteric information, such as passwords that are also easy tests of membership. In addition, language is a powerful vehicle for emotional communication. Not surprisingly, therefore, language is inextricably linked with ethnicity. An ethny frequently defines itself, at least in part, as a speech community: its particular speech is laden with emotional qualities and valued much beyond its efficacy as a means of communication. Second languages, or *linguae francae* adopted later in life for purposes of interethnic communication, can convey complex messages accurately and can become perfectly serviceable media for a wide range of practical purposes such as trade, formal education, technology, and so on. However, they are usually bereft of the multiplicity of emotional connotations that are largely restricted to one's "mother- tongue."

The first language learned in infancy is intimately associated with a whole register of emotions first experienced with close kinsmen, and, therefore, these affective qualities of kinship become associated with language and rub off onto other members of the speech community. The spontaneous joy of hearing one's mother-tongue spoken when surrounded by strangers is probably a universal human experience. It is experienced even after a long exile. One may become quite proficient in a foreign language yet still fail to enjoy and experience it at the gut emotional level. People often report, for instance, that they can only enjoy singing or poetry in their mother-tongue. Language learning is the universal human experience of early childhood through which full human sociality is achieved, and through which one becomes integrated in a kinship network. It is little wonder, therefore, that language is the supreme test of ethnicity. Fellow ethnics are those whose speech is sufficiently like one's own to allow for the unhindered communication of the entire range of human emotions and messages. Other languages are learned for the sake of instrumental convenience; the mother-tongue is spoken for the sheer joy of it. It is probably this fundamental difference in the speaking of first versus second languages that, more than any single factor, makes for the profound qualitative difference between intraethnic and interethnic relations. The mother-tongue is the language of kinship. Every other tongue is a mere convenience between strangers.

Let us summarize the argument so far. Humans, like other social animals, are biologically selected to be nepotistic because, by favoring kin, they maximize their inclusive fitness. Until the last few thousand years, hominids interacted in relatively small groups of a few score to a couple of hundred individuals, who tended to mate with each other and, therefore, to form rather tightly knit groups of close and distant kinsmen. Physical boundaries of territory and social boundaries of inbreeding separated these small human societies from each other. Within the group, there was a large measure of peace and cooperation between kinsmen and in-laws (frequently both kinds of relationship overlapped). Relations between groups were characterized at best by mistrust and avoidance—but frequently by open conflict over scarce resources. These solidary groups were, in fact, primordial ethnies.

Such was the evolutionary origin of ethnicity: an extended kin group. With the progressive growth in the size of human societies, the boundaries of the ethny became wider; the bonds of kinship were correspondingly diluted, and indeed sometimes became fictive, and ethnicity became increasingly manipulated and perverted to other ends, including domination and exploitation. The urge, however, to continue to define a collectivity larger than the immediate circle of kinsmen on the basis of biological descent continues to be present even in the most industrialized mass societies of today. A wide variety of ethnic markers define such collectivities of descent, but their choice is not capricious. Those markers will be stressed that are, in fact, objectively reliable predictors of common descent, given the environment in which the discriminating group finds itself. Sometimes, but rather rarely, race is the paramount criterion; more commonly, cultural characteristics, especially language, do a much better job of defining ethnic boundaries.

So far, we have suggested the *raison d'être* of ethnicity—the reason for its persistence and for its seeming imperviousness to rationality. Ethnic (and racial) sentiments often seem irrational because they have an underlying driving force of their own, which is ultimately the blunt, purposeless natural selection of genes that are reproductively successful. Genes favoring nepotistic behavior have a selective advantage. It does not matter whether their carrying organisms are aware of being nepotistic or even that they consciously know their relatives. Organisms must only behave *as if they knew*. It happens that, in humans, they often know in a conscious way, though they are sometimes mistaken.

The phenomenon of ethnicity in humans, however, is not in principle different from the phenomenon of boundary maintenance between animal societies. Other animals maintain clear boundaries between themselves and other species, most importantly barriers to matings between closely related species that are the very mechanism making for speciation in the first instance.[39] But humans are not even unique in maintaining societal boundaries *within* the species. Thousands of species of eusocial insects keep different colonies of the same species quite distinct from each other, often using pheromones (smell signals) to recognize each other.[40] Among mammals, man included, the boundaries between societies are, on the whole much *less* rigid than among the eusocial insects, but, nevertheless, societal boundaries between groups of conspecifics are clearly marked and defended.

We conventionally restrict the meaning of ethnicity to humans, but we would not be unduly extending the meaning of the term by applying it to troops of macaques, prides of lions, or packs of wolves. These other animal societies too are held together by kin selection and must compete with other societies of conspecifics for scarce resources.[41] In principle, the problems of boundary maintenance are the same for humans and other animals, despite the vastly greater order of complexity of human societies.

Like many other species, man too lives in an environment that includes other societies of his species. Interethnic relations, therefore, must be analyzed not only within the genetic context of kin selection but also, and equally important, within an ecological context.[42]

NOTES

1. William Bascom, *The Yoruba of Southwestern Nigeria*. (New York: Holt, Reinhart and Winston, 1969).

2. Clyde Kluckhohn and Dorthea Leighton, *The Navaho*, (Cambridge, MA: Harvard University Press, 1958).

3. Fredrik Barth, "Ecologic Relationships of Ethnic Groups in Swat, Northern Pakistan," *American Anthropologist* 58: 1079–89, 1956; *Political Leadership among the Swat Pathans* (London: London School of Economics; Monographs on Social Anthropology, No. 19, 1959).

4. Ronald P. Dore, *City Life in Japan*, Berkeley: University of California Press, 1958.

5. Ibid., p. 94.

6. Cullen Tadao Hayashida, "Identity, Race and the Blood Ideology of Japan" Seattle: University of Washington Ph.D. dissertation, 1976.

7. Edward Shils, "Primordial, Personal, Sacred, and Civil Ties" *British Journal of Sociology*, (1959) 8: 130–45; Max Weber, *Economy and Society* (New York: Bedminister, 1968).

8. Oliver C. Cox, *Caste, Class and Race* (Garden City NY: Doubleday, 1948); *Race Relations, Elements and Social Dynamics* (Detroit: Wayne State University Press, 1976).

9. Karl W. Deutsch, *Nationalism and Social Communication* (Cambridge, MA: MIT Press, 1966).

10. Claude Lévi-Strauss, *The Race Question In Modern Science* (Paris: UNESCO 1952). Leo Kuper, ed., *Race, Science and Society* (Paris UNESCO 1975). Nathan Glazer, and Daniel P. Moynihan, eds., *Ethnicity: Theory and Experience* (Cambridge: Harvard University Press, 1975). Thomas Gossett, *Race: The History of an Idea in America* (Dallas: Southern Methodist University Press, 1963). Richard Hofstadter, *Social Darwinism in American Thought* (New York: Braziller, 1959). Juan Comas, *Razas y Racismo* (Mexico: SepSetentas, 1972). Pierre L. van den Berghe, *South Africa: A Study in Conflict* (Middletown, CT: Wesleyan University Press, 1965).

11. E. K. Francis, *Interethnic Relations* (New York: Elsevier, 1976). Charles F. Keys, "Towards a New Foundation of the Concept of Ethnic Group," *Ethnicity* 3, no. 3 (1976): 202–13.

12 Paul Brass, *Language, Religion and Politics in North India* (New York: Cambridge University Press, 1974).

13. Fredrik Barth, ed., *Ethnic Groups and Boundaries* (Boston: Little Brown, 1969).

14. Pierre L. van den Berge, *The Ethnic Phenomenon* (New York: Elsevier, 1981).

15. Maynard J. Smith, *Models in Ecology* (London: Cambridge University Press, 1964). R. A. Fisher, *The Genetical Theory of Natural Selection* (New York: Dover Press, 1958). J. B. S. Haldane, *The Causes Evolution* (New York: Longmans, Green, 1932). W. D. Hamilton, "The Genetical Evolution of Social Behavior," *Journal of Theoretical Biology* 7 (1964): 1–52.

16. John Maynard Smith, "Group Selection and Kin Selection," *Nature* 201 (1964): 1145–47.

17. Edward O. Wilson, *Sociobiology: The New Synthesis* (Cambridge, MA: Harvard University Press, 1975). David Barash, *Sociobiology and Behavior* (New York: Elsevier, 1977).

18. V. C. Wynne-Edwards, *Animal Dispersion in Relation to Social Behavior* (Edinburgh: Oliver and Boyd, 1962).

19. Richard Dawkins, *The Selfish Gene*. (London: Oxford University Press, 1976).

20. Edward O. Wilson, *Sociobiology: The New Synthesis* (Cambridge, MA: Harvard University Press, 1975). *Human Nature* (Cambridge, MA: Harvard University Press, 1978).

21. David M. Schneider, *American Kinship* (Englewood Cliffs, N.J.: Prentice Hall, 1968). Marshall Sahlins, *The Use and Abuse of Biology* (Ann Arbor: University of Michigan Press, 1979).

22. Pierre L. van den Berghe, *Human Family Systems: An Evolutionary View* (New York: Elsevier, 1979). Pierre L. van den Berghe and David Barash, "Inclusive Fitness and Human Family Structure," *American Anthropologist* 79 (4): 809–23.

23. Martin Daly and Margo Wilson, *Sex, Evolution and Behavior* (North Scituate, MA: Duxbury Press, 1978). Joseph Shepher, *Incest: The Biosocial View* (Boston: Garland, 1981). Napoleon A. Chagnon and Paul E. Bugos, "Kin Selection and Conflict: An Analysis of a Yanomamo Ax Flight," in Napoleon A. Chagnon and William Irons (eds.), *Evolutionary Biology and Human Social Behavior* (North Scituate, MA: Duxbury). John Hartung, "On Natural Selection and the Inheritance of Wealth," *Current Anthropology* 17 (4) (1976): 607–22. Penelope Greene, "Promiscuity, Paternity and Culture," *American Ethnologist* 5 (1978): 151–59.

24. Claude Lévi-Strauss, *The Elementary Structures of Kinship* (Boston: Beacon Press, 1969).

25. van den Berghe and Barash, "Inclusive Fitness and Human Family Structure."

26. Robert L. Trivers, "Parental Investment and Sexual Selection," in B. Campbell (ed.),

Sexual Selection and the Descent of Man (Chicago: Aldine, 1972). Martin Daly and Margo Wilson, *Sex, Evolution and Behavior* (North Scituate, MA: Duxbury Press, 1978).

27. T. W. Adorno, *et al.*, *The Authoritarian Personality* (New York: Harper, 1950). O. Mannoni, *Prospero and Caliban* (New York: Praeger, 1964). Roger Bastide, *Sociologie et psychanalyse* (Paris: Presses Universitaires de France, 1950). *African Civilizations in the New World* (London: C. Hurst, 1971). Lilian Smith, *Killer of the Dream* (New York: Anchor, 1963). Charles Herbert Stember, *Sexual Racism* (New York: Elsevier, 1976). Gilberto Freyre, *The Masters and the Slaves* (New York: Knopf, 1964).

28. David M. Schneider, *American Kinship* (Englewood Cliffs, N.J.: Prentice Hall, 1968). Marshall Sahlins, *The Use and Abuse of Biology* (Ann Arbor : University of Michigan Press, 1976).

29. Meyer Forres, *Kinship and the Social Order* (Chicago: Aldine, 1969). Robin Fox, *Kinship and Marriage*. (Harmondsworth: Penguin, 1967).

30. van den Berghe and Barash, "Inclusive Fitness and Human Family Structure."

31. Pierre L. van den Berghe, *Race and Racism: A Comparative Sociology* (New York: Wiley, 1967).

32. Gerald James Stine, *Biosocial Genetics* (New York: Macmillan, 1977).

33. H. Hoetinck, *Caribbean Race Relations* (London: Macmillan, 1967).

34. Pierre L. van den Berghe, *Race and Racism: A Comparative Sociology* (New York: Wiley, 1967).

35. Jacques J. Maquet, *Ruanda* (Bruxelles: Elsevier, 1957). *The Premise of Inequality in Ruanda* (London: Oxford University Press, 1961).

36. Pierre L. van den Berghe, *Race and Racism: A Comparative Sociology*.

37. H. J. Simons, and R. E. Simon, *Class and Colour in South Africa, 1850–1950* Baltimore: Penguin, 1969. Frank Tannenbaum, *Slave and Citizen* (New York: Knopf, 1947).

38. Oliver C. Cox, *Caste, Class and Race*. Leo Kuper, *The Pity of It All* (Minneapolis: University of Minneapolis Press, 1977).

39. Ernst Mayr, *Animal Species and Evolution* (Cambridge: Belknap Press, 1963).

40. Edward O. Wilson, *The Insect Societies* (Cambridge, MA: Harvard University Press, 1971).

41. Edward O. Wilson, *Sociobiology: The New Synthesis* (Cambridge, MA: Harvard University Press, 1975). van den Berghe, *The Ethnic Phenomenon*.

42. van den Berghe, *The Ethnic Phenomenon*, chapter 3.

3. Negritude, Nationalism, and Nativism: Racists or Racialists?

Albert G. Mosley

IN HIS BOOK *In My Father's House: Africa in the Philosophy of Culture* (1992), Kwame Anthony Appiah defines "racialism" as the belief that all the members of a particular race "share certain traits and tendencies with each other that they do not share with members of any other race. These traits and tendencies characteristic of a race constitute, on the racialist view, a sort of racial essence . . . [which] accounts for more than the visible morphological characteristics—skin color, hair type, facial features . . ." (p. 13). Appiah denies that racialism itself is dangerous: "Provided positive moral qualities are distributed across races, each can be respected, can have its 'separate but equal' place."

While racism presupposes, with racialism, the selective distribution of traits by race, it differs from racialism in that it attributes the most valuable personal and social qualities to one race while limiting the presence of valuable social traits in other races. Racism thus establishes a hierarchy of qualities, reflecting a hierarchy of races. Racialism, on the other hand, denies that any one set of qualities is absolutely superior, or that any one race is superior to all others. Appiah aptly summarizes the "Africa for the African" position of Du Bois, Blyden, and Crummell as "the acceptance of difference along with a claim that each group has its part to play, that the white and the Negro races are related not as superior to inferior but as complementaries; the Negro message is, with the white one, part of the message of humankind" (p. 24).

Similar views were held by the founders of Negritude, Leopold Senghor and

Albert G. Mosley, "Negritude, Nationalism, and Nativism: Racists or Racialists?" in *African Philosophy: Selected Readings*. Englewood Cliffs, N.J.: Prentice Hall, 1995, pp. 216–34, reprinted with the permission of Albert G. Mosley.

Aimé Césaire. Initially both attributed the differences between African and European cultures to the influence of race. But while Senghor maintained a belief in a biological basis for the peculiar orientation attributed to African culture, Césaire altered his views and came to hold that Negritude was not biologically but historically determined:

> I do not in the slightest believe in biological permanence, but I believe in culture. My Negritude has a ground. It is a fact that there is a black culture: it is historical; there is nothing biological about it. (Arnold, 1981, p. 37)

While maintaining the importance of art and poetry as an antidote to logic and science, Césaire accounted for the orientation of blacks toward the arts as an adaptation of Africans to the historical conditions imposed by the slave trade, slavery, colonialism, and segregation.

Du Bois's concept of race likewise evolved from a biological to a socio-historical form. Thus, in 1947 Du Bois seemed quite clear about his notion of race: the Negro race is all those forced to bear the insult of being slaves or the descendants of slaves during the industrial revolution of Western Europe. Du Bois writes:

> Since the fifteenth century these ancestors of mine and their descendants have had a common history; have suffered a common disaster and have one long memory. The actual ties of heritage between the individuals of this group vary . . . . But . . . the real essence of this kinship is its social heritage of slavery; and this heritage binds together not simply the children of Africa, but extends through yellow Asia and into the South Seas. It is this unity that draws me to Africa. (Appiah, p. 41; *Dusk of Dawn*, pp. 116–17)

And in *The Crisis* (December 1947) Du Bois writes:

> The so called American Negro group . . . while it is in no sense absolutely set off physically from its fellow Americans, has nevertheless a strong, hereditary cultural unity born of slavery, of common suffering, prolonged proscription, and curtailment of political and civil rights. Prolonged policies of segregation and discrimination have involuntarily welded the mass almost into a nation within a nation.

Appiah acknowledges that Du Bois changed his view of race from a biologically based to a culturally based conception, but he nonetheless considers this insufficient to avoid a basic flaw. As such, Appiah asserts that the passage from *Dusk of Dawn* "seduces us into error" by substituting a socio-historical conception of race for a biological one. This, for Appiah, "is simply to bury the biological conception below the surface, nor to transcend it" (Appiah, 1992, p. 41).

Appiah characterizes the views of these African nationalists as Sartre had characterized Negritude—as forms of anti-racist racism. In order to defend labeling Senghor, Blyden, Crummell, and Du Bois as racists, Appiah proposes a distinction between what he calls "extrinsic" and "intrinsic" racism. Extrinsic racism associates valuable social traits with membership in a particular race. To illustrate, being a member of the white race would be conceived of as causally determining whether one would be a bearer of certain superior qualities (such as analytical intelligence). *Intrinsic racism*, on the other hand, makes no necessary association between being a member of a particular race and having certain valuable social qualities. For the intrinsic racist, the very fact that one is of a particular race gives one preferential advantages, just as a human being is granted preferential advantages over non-human beings.

Appiah argues that nationalists were "intrinsic racists" because they considered Africans to be more like members of a family than like bearers of similar traits. The fact that a particular individual, b, is a member of B's family *ipso facto* gives b preferential access to B's wealth over individuals who are not members of B's family, independently of whether b has any superior traits or not. In response, I would like to argue that Appiah's concept of "intrinsic racism" is a bogus concept because, as he has characterized it, "intrinsic racism" is not a form of racism at all.

The intrinsic racist views other members of his/her race as members of the same family, and, on that basis alone, irrespective of talent or merit, gives the "family member" preferential treatment over members of other "families" (or "races"). Thus, the preferential treatment of a member of one's own family over a nonfamily member need not be based on the belief that members of one's own family are superior to members of other families. Preferential treatment of a member of one's own family could as well be based on a moral duty of gratitude or a prudential rule favoring reciprocal altruism between (alleged) relatives. But there need be no assumption that members of one's own family are superior to members of other families.

But, as we have seen, the assumption of superiority is central to the definition of a racist. As such, Appiah's notion of intrinsic racism is not a form of racism at all. Nor is it a form of racialism, as it contains no suggestion that valuable social qualities are selectively distributed between groups. Preferential treatment for a member of a particular family requires no assumptions that the individual is the bearer of certain traits associated with that family. On the other hand, Crummell, Blyden, Du Bois, and Senghor were racialists because they did believe that the African harbored special talents which made possible certain contributions to world civilization that only the African could provide.

Despite whatever weaknesses racialism might harbor, one of the primary concerns of African nationalism and Negritude was to deny racist claims of superiority even as they acknowledged claims of racial differences. Racialism attempted to acknowledge racially determined differences while divesting those differences of any implication of absolute superiority or inferiority. To characterize the Negritude and African Nationalist movements as racist, as Appiah does, is to accuse them of an error they were designed to oppose. To do this using the notion of intrinsic racism amounts to an attempt to rewrite history by selectively redefining its central concepts. I believe Appiah is seriously in error in characterizing Senghor, Césaire, Crummell, Blyden, and Du Bois as racists. They espoused a form of racialism, not racism.

This is not to say, however, that racialism is itself without error. A commonly cited weakness of racialism is the suggestion that racial type is a necessary or sufficient condition for the display of certain behavioral and social traits. To say that being a member of race X is sufficient for having (the potential for) trait x does not preclude race Y and race Z from also having (the potential for) trait x. Both racism and racialism require viewing race as a necessary condition for possessing (the potential for) certain traits, in order to achieve selective distribution of traits by race.

To illustrate, if being a member of the Caucasian race were considered a necessary condition for being intelligent/analytical, then, while all Caucasians need not be intelligent/analytical, all intelligent/analytical type persons would have to be Caucasian. Similar comments apply if Negritude is interpreted in this way. As J. O. Sodipo points out, if the racialism of Negritude is taken literally, then Wordsworth and the romantic poets of Europe must be regarded as Africans. And, indeed, this is a conclusion accepted by both Senghor and Gobineau.

From Césaire we learn that it is no accident that Senghor's views seem so close to Gobineau's. In an interview in 1967, Césaire says this about the influence of Gobineau on himself and Senghor:

> Yes, we read Gobineau, Senghor and I. It was essentially to refute him, since he was the great French theoretician of racism. But at the same time, I must admit, Senghor liked him a great deal. His liking was understandable; he was grateful to Gobineau for saying: "Art is black." The Black is an artist. If there are artists in Western civilization, it is because there are nonetheless a few drops of Negro blood in them. Consequently the attitude toward Gobineau was very ambivalent. (Arnold, 1981, p. 41)

One way of avoiding this difficulty is to view the association between race and social traits in statistical rather than categorical terms. This involves viewing race X as displaying a significantly higher frequency of the occurrence of trait x, rather than as being the exclusive bearer of trait x. Thus, to use the typical traits cited by racists and racialists, a population with a higher proportion of Africans might show a higher proportion of artists, musicians, and athletes; while a population with a higher proportion of Europeans might show a higher proportion of scientists, mathematicians, and engineers. Nonetheless, many

Africans might be scientists, mathematicians, and engineers and many Europeans might be artists, musicians, and athletes.

Racialism affirms that certain kinds of social behavior are selectively linked to certain races, and explains this link in terms of causal connections. But, of course, correlation does not necessarily imply causation. Should such a correlation between racial type and behavioral type exist, it might nonetheless be purely coincidental, a mere artifact of chance. Or the correlation might be the result of some further cause, perhaps of a religious, economic, or other socio-historical nature.

To illustrate, the association between members of the African race and the display of an aesthetic orientation could be explained by reference to the systematic exclusion of Africans from the development of analytic skills and their confinement to opportunities in the "arts." Likewise, the higher frequency of the display of analytic skills among Europeans could be explained by the preferential treatment accorded Europeans for opportunities to develop such skills. On the other hand, if the frequency of x is a defining characteristic of race X, then the relationship between race X and trait x is stipulative rather than causal: race X just is that race in which x occurs with a higher frequency than in other races. Certainly, then, race X might display a disproportionate frequency of behavior x, without race itself being a cause of that behavior.

Despite these caveats, the possibility of a selective distribution of behavioral traits causally determined by race cannot be ruled out as impossible. The fact of such, were it established, could be used to justify a racist orientation, on the assumption that certain selectively distributed traits were inherently superior to other selectively distributed traits. But this is certainly not the position of the African nationalists we have reviewed, nor of the principal advocates of Negritude.

Appiah's error in characterizing nationalism and Negritude as racist is compounded by his misguided critique of a basic assumption of both racism and racialism. This critique calls into question the very existence of races, and hence the differential distribution of traits between races. Appiah denies the possibility of developing an adequate conception of "race," and urges that we "transcend" such usage altogether.

One of the reasons Appiah cites for rejecting the concept of race altogether is the dilemma that the offspring of two different races would be equally of both races or a hybrid that was a member of neither parent race. But it is not clear why this in itself is reason to reject racial classifications. The existence of cases that do not fit an accepted taxonomic schema has never, in itself, been a sufficient reason for rejecting that schema. More concretely, the fact that there might be more mongrels than purebreds is no argument against the existence of different breeds of dogs.

Indeed, a good model of a racialist schema would be the case of breeds of dog (see Smith, 1975). While each breed may be superior to other breeds in certain respects, no breed is superior to all other breeds in all respects. And, though it might be typical of breed X that it exhibit trait x, this might be neither a necessary nor a sufficient condition for a particular individual's being a member of that breed. Though the offspring of two distinct breeds might itself be a member of neither, it might still be possible to account for some of the mongrel's behavior/morphology by reference to the behavior/morphology of its immediate progenitors—to traits distinctive of the breed of its parents. Thus, pit-bulls (dalmatians) have traits that are distinctive to their breed, and while we might not want to say that having a pit-bull (dalmatian) parent is sufficient to cause a particular dog to be aggressive (white with black spots), we might explain its aggressiveness (being white with black spots) by pointing out that the dog is the immediate progeny of a breed that is typically aggressive (white with black spots).

To the extent that we accept the existence of different breeds of domesticated dog, I see no reason to deny the existence of different races of human beings. All that is necessary in either case is that a population (race or breed) be genetically isolated and that the frequency of certain traits be selected for.

Theodosius Dobzhansky (*Mankind Evolving*) defined races as "Mendelian populations which differ in the incidence of some genetic variants in their gene pools" (p. 239), and illustrated the concept in terms of different races of the fruitfly *Drosophila* that had adapted to different elevations of the Sierra Nevada mountains of California. Differences between races are not determined by distinguishing individuals with different traits into correspondingly different classes. Rather, racial differences apply only at the level of the population, in terms of the relative frequency of traits between populations. "Mankind," he writes, "is a polytypic species composed of a cluster of races, Mendelian populations with more or less different gene pools" (p. 232).

Usually the traits used to distinguish different races of mankind are the visible morphological ones such as skin color, eye color, hair type, nose and lip shape, and so forth. But such traits are not always the most important ones in distinguishing races, and recent research in human biology has used a number of traits that can only be discerned by instrumental analysis but which provide more reliable indicators. Appiah is aware of such developments and uses the genetically determined propensity to produce certain protein types to reach the following conclusion:

> The chances of two people who are both "Caucasoid" differing in genetic constitution at one site on a given chromosome are about 14.3 percent, while, for any two people taken at. random from the human population, they are about 14.8 percent. (Appiah, 1992, p. 36)

In other words, two individuals chosen at random from two different races have only a 0.5 percent greater probability of differing in the kinds of proteins they produce than two individuals chosen at random from within the same race. His general point is that, because variations within a race are almost as great as variations between different races, divisions between races are based on differences so minuscule as to be insignificant.

In a footnote to this discussion, Appiah scarcely veils his bias and selective use of data:

> These figures come from Nei and Roychoudhury, "Genetic Relationship and Evolution of Human Races." I have used figures derived from looking at proteins, not blood groups, since they claim these are likely to be more reliable. I have chosen a measure of "racial" biological difference that makes it look spectacularly small, but I would not wish to imply that it is not the case, as these authors say, that "genetic differentiation is real and generally statistically highly significant" (41). I would dispute their claim that their work shows there is a biological basis for the classification of human races: what it shows is that human populations differ in their distributions of genes. That is a biological fact. The objection to using this fact as a basis of a system of classification is that far too many people don't fit into just one category that can be so defined. (p. 196)

One marvels at Appiah's verbal sophistry, for as Dobzhansky has pointed out, races are just populations within a species that differ in their distributions of gene frequencies. Nei and Roychoudhury use both protein and bloodgroup data to conclude that "the genetic differentiation of human races is of the same order of magnitude as that found in local races of other organisms" (p. 41), and that "the races of each of Caucasoid, Asian, Mongoloid, and Negroid form a separate cluster" (p. 40). That there are many individuals that do not clearly fit into one race or another is never an issue.

While Nei and Roychoudhury acknowledge that interracial genic variation is small when compared with intraracial genic variation, they stress that "the genetic differentiation is real and generally statistically highly significant." At the same time, they warn that two populations that look alike (for example, Australian aborigines and South African Bushmen) might nevertheless be strikingly dissimilar in terms of protein and blood-type frequencies. Thus, "genetic distance between populations is not always correlated with morphological difference" (Nei and Roychoudhury, 1983, p. 41). To return to our previous analogy, just because a dog looks like a dalmatian doesn't mean that it really is one. But it also does not mean that there are no dalmatians.

The claim that concepts of race have a biological legitimacy is not meant to suggest that current concepts of race are based primarily on biological considerations. Indeed, the conceptions of race institutionalized by slavery and colonization were designed primarily around socioeconomic considerations. The conception of an African as any individual with at least one traceable African ancestor (the "one-drop rule") is absurd as a means of differentiating distinct biological groups. It is like claiming that having one traceable dalmatian progenitor made a dog a dalmatian. But such a rule did make sense in a society in which the most valuable form of property was in the form of human beings held as slaves.

The one-drop rule definition of the African race was devised to support the establishment and maintenance of slavery and segregation. Whereas in the rest of the Americas, slavery was replenished by new imports from Africa, in the United States the primary means of replenishing slaves was by birth. Rules stipulating that only Africans could be treated as property, that any person who had at least one traceable African ancestor was of the African race, and that the child of a slave was a slave were critical to the program of replenishing slaves by birth and maintaining the exploitation of freed slaves.

> Freedmen's status was not an end to the process of marginalization but merely the end of one phase of that marginalization, slavery, which itself had several stages. Freedmen's status began a new phase, but the ex-slave was still a marginal person. (Patterson, 1982, p. 249)

It is in this context that the current conception of the African or Negro or black race evolved. And, while such a conception may make little biological sense, it makes perfect sense seen as a historical means of establishing and maintaining European supremacy (Patterson, 1982, p. 176).

It is in such a historical context that Du Bois was considered an African, even though he was the product of a mixed father and a mixed mother. Clearly, the conception of race he lived was not a purely biological one, for biologically he was as much European as African (and perhaps more so). But Du Bois did not attempt to evade identification as an African, and deftly used the intellectual tools of his time to transform the view of the African as intrinsically inferior to the European.

In contrast, Appiah wishes to divest the world of the concept of race by denying that the notion plays any constructive part in dealing with the problems Africa faces. Further, since African Americans (such as Blyden and Du Bois) conceived of their relationship to Africa primarily in terms of their belonging to the same race, he considers that relationship to be as tenuous and infertile as the concept of race upon which it is built.

Appiah holds that Africans and African Americans have experienced different degrees of involvement with European cultural values, and so have been affected by European expansionism in very different ways. The vast majority of Africans, he argues, experienced European expansionism only tangentially, at the periphery of their lives. Only those Africans sent to be educated in the West approximated the degree of alienation experienced by slaves and their progeny.

The European conceived of the African as "the other," the opposite to the domineering and analytical bent of Europe; and Negritude enshrined this view of the African as a virtue, the natural antidote to European militarism and will-to-dominance. Appiah believes that African nationalists, because most have been influenced by African Americans, have accepted such a romanticized view of the African, a valorization of the European other.

In the field of literature, the claim to Africa's uniqueness is presented under the guise of Nativism: the view that African literature must take a peculiarly African form. Of course, for Appiah, this is merely a tacit acceptance of the European stereotype of the African while reversing its value. The nationalist/negritudist/nativist conception of the African remains that provided by the European.

Some nativists (e.g., Okot p'Bitek, Mazisi Kunene, Robert Mungoshi) have advocated writing in traditional African languages in order to recreate the values implicit in traditional life. But Appiah believes this offers tittle hope, because, he argues, our very conception of traditional African ways is shaped by the European reconstruction of African traditional life. Appiah illustrates his point with a case he should know best, that of his own group, the Ashanti.

For Appiah, what we know of the laws and customs of traditional Ashanti is best summarized in Rattray's book *Ashanti Law and Constitution*. But clearly, Rattray brought to his study of the Ashanti European assumptions which became embedded within his description of traditional Ashanti law and customs. This means that the nativist, in accepting such views of traditional life, is unwittingly adopting a European view of traditional African life.

During the rigors of the slave trade and colonialism, Europeans created chieftainships and tribal allegiances where none had existed before. More often than not, the traditional chiefs were chosen not by Africans but by Europeans, to represent Africans to Europeans, to the ultimate advantage of Europeans. In other words, the traditional chiefdoms recognized by Europeans were often as much a creation of the European as of the African. Rattray's book is supposed to describe the traditional world of the Ashanti, but it is as much a reflection of Europe's effect on Africa as it is of an Africa unadulterated with European cultural impositions. Thus, while nativists may want to go back to tradition, Appiah argues that the only tradition they have to go back to is the tradition as reconstructed by Europeans.

Appiah holds that the very idea that there should be a literature that is peculiarly African is a Western idea. He considers the conceptual progenitor of nativists and African nationalists to be Herder, who held that every race had an essence that was expressed through its literature. But for Appiah, the nativist attempt to realize such a form of literature is doomed to failure, much as the attempt to find a good witch is doomed. As there are no witches, the search for a good one is quixotic and self-abortive. And as there are no races, the nationalist quest for a racially determined culture can never be completed.

For Appiah, both the racialist and the nativist inherit their orientations from a European perspective in which a racial essence is manifested in the form of its nation-state and in the form of its literature. For this reason, Appiah considers African nationalism to be just as wrongheaded as European racism. Because nativists use European concepts of race to justify their rejection of European racism, Appiah is able to charge that "few things are less native than nativism" (p. 60). Nativism, he argues, is the continuation of a European problematic. It never escapes Western categories. "The cultural nationalists are blind that their nativist demands inhabit a western architecture."

> The very notion of Pan Africanism was founded on the notion of the African, which itself was developed, not on the basis of any genuine commonality between them, but on the basis of the European concept of the African. The very category of the Negro is a European concept, invented by the European so as to justify his domination of them. The very course of African Nationalism has been to make real the imaginary identities to which Europe has subjected us. (Appiah, 1992, p. 62)

Because African nationalists, nativists, and negritudists have defended their position by reference to the doctrines of Herder, Appiah assumes that they have no other basis for such views. We are left with the suggestion that African nationalists and nativists have no orientation except that derived from European influences. But this view must certainly be rejected. There is no reason to believe that traditional intellectuals such as Ogotomeli of the Dogon (*Conversations with Ogotomeli*), the Luo sages interviewed by Odera Oruka of Kenya, the Yoruba Babalowa interrogated by Hallen and Sodipo of Nigeria, and the Akan Onyansafo interviewed by Kwame Gyekye of Ghana were inaccessible to African nativists.

The Kenyan philosopher, H. Odera Onika, has coined the term "philosophical sagacity" to describe the result of traditional intellectuals reflecting on African traditional beliefs. Such individuals are not only wise in the customs and beliefs of their people, they are also wise in assessing the efficacy of such practices and beliefs. Oruka cites his father as such a sage, and in his book *Sage Philosophy* (1990) provides interviews with many other such individuals.

Barry Hallen and John Sodipo (1986) have also engaged in extensive interviews with the onisegun sages of Nigeria. In so doing, they uncover a critical, empirical epistemological orientation that is seldom attributed to traditional cultures. They conclude (p. 84) that "the conceptual systems of alien languages —including those of so-called traditional cultures—have implicit in them alternative epistemological, metaphysical, moral, etc., systems that are of philosophical interest in their own right." To illustrate, they provide a comparative investigation of "witchcraft" and its closest yoruba equivalent, "aje." But there is no reason to believe that their interest in this subject is merely the projection of a European phenomenon onto traditional African beliefs.

It is likewise with Appiah's countryman and fellow Akan, Kwame Gyekye. Gyekye's position is that the tendency to think deeply about certain kinds of questions is a universal human propensity, and is the source of all philosophical ideas. The task of the professionally trained African philosopher is to lift ideas expressed on such questions from their cultural context and critically develop them. He writes:

> Regarding the difficulty of getting at indigenous ideas in the light of Africa's historical contact with Christianity and Islam, I wish to say that in Akan, as indeed in every African community, there are certain individuals who are steeped in the traditional lore. These individuals are regarded as wise persons in their own right. They stand out in their own communities and command the respect and esteem of their townsfolk. A researcher who goes to any Akan town or village would invariably be directed to such individuals; they are generally tradition bound in their intellectual and general outlooks. Some of them have had no formal education at all. (Gyekye, 1987, p. 53)

In his book *An Essay on African Philosophical Thought—The Akan Conceptual Scheme*, Gyekye cites the medium-priest Kwaku Mframa, the elder Nana Boafo-Ansah, and other indigenous sources regarding traditional Akan beliefs about personal identity, the relationship between religion and ethics, the relationship between free will and responsibility, the nature of time and causality, and so forth.

Oruka, Sodipo and Hallen, and Gyekye see themselves as initiating dialogues which incorporate the analytical training of the professional philosopher with the critical reflections of the traditional sage. In such dialogues, it does not follow that European concepts must necessarily exert the dominant influence. African philosophers need not deny their Western training, nor need they depend on it as the only guide for their intellectual life.

Similar comments hold true for African literature. While the concept of "the African" has emerged as a result of historical processes over the last few centuries, its contingent beginnings do not make it any less real than our concepts of pit-bulls and parking lights. They are all social constructs that are appropriate only within a given socio-historical context. Abiola Irele has coined the term "African Imagination" to reflect "the expression of Africans and people of African descent arising out of these historical determinations":

> Despite the disproportionate attention paid to literature by Africans in the European languages, the primary area of what I've called the African imagination is represented by the body of literature produced by, within, and for the traditional societies and indigenous cultures of Africa. This literature forms an essential part of what is generally considered the oral tradition in Africa. (Irele, 1990, p. 53)

These comments apply no less to Africans in the diaspora as to Africans on the continent. Henry Louis Gates, in *The Signifying Monkey*, identifies a tradition of interpretation and reinterpretation that is an essential element in African American music and literature. If we were to adopt Appiah's orientation, this feature of African American culture would be interpreted as but one of many adaptations of European hermeneutics. To his credit, Gates's accomplishment was to demonstrate in "signifying" a hermeneutical principle of African origins that had maintained itself despite the rigors of slavery, colonization, and segregation.

Gates shows that the signifying monkey of African American oral literature is the cultural progeny of the trickster gods of West Africa. He argues that the tradition of interpretation and reinterpretation, exemplified by the Yoruba deity Esuelegbara, maintained its vitality among "traditional intellectuals" in the New World—individuals who maintained a connection with the vital cultural life of their communities. This would include storytellers, musicians, artists, and religious leaders—just those people who survived not by a wholesale adoption of the European cultural tradition, but by syncretizing it with African cultural memes.

It is not clear why Appiah would want to deny African intellectuals independent access to endogenous African beliefs and practices. But clearly, his views are not shared by many leading African and African-American philosophers and literary critics. Appiah makes much of the African intellectual's use of European languages and concepts in order to reject European hegemony. But as I have shown, using the concept of race to oppose racism does not make one a racist. Likewise, using European concepts to reject European cultural imperialism does not make one wholly Eurocentric. To the contrary, the creative accommodation of indigenous African traditions to modern, Western-derived forms reflects a characteristic feature of its orally based literature (Irele, 1990, p. 54; Gates, 1988, Chaps. 2, 3).

I have tried to show in this essay: (1) that contrary to Sartre and Appiah's claims, Senghor and Du Bois—with Crummell, Blyden, and Césaire—opposed racism, not with another form of racism but with racialism; (2) that though racialist claims may in many cases be in error, such claims are not nonsensical; (3) that the concept of race has both a biological and historical legitimacy; and (4) that African nativism (in both philosophical and nonphilosophical literature) is not necessarily a self-contradictory enterprise driven by European conceptions of African traditional culture. In all, I hope to have shown that Appiah's treatment of nativism, nationalism, and Negritude is seriously flawed.

References

Appiah, Kwame Anthony. 1992. *In My Father's House: Africa in the Philosophy of Culture*. New York: Oxford University Press.

Arnold, A. James. 1981. *Modernism and Negritude—The Poetry and Poetics of Aimé Césaire*. Cambridge, MA: Harvard University Press.

Bernal, Martin. 1987. *Black Athena*. New Brunswick, N.J.: Rutgers University Press.

Biddiss, Michael D. 1970. *Father of Racist Ideology—The Social and Political Thought of Count Gobineau*. New York: Weybright & Talley.

Campbell, Colin. 1987. *The Romantic Ethic and the Spirit of Consumerism*. Malden, MA: Blackwell.

Dobzhansky, Theodosius. 1962. *Mankind Evolving*. New York: Bantam Press.

Du Bois, W. E. B. 1940. *Dusk of Dawn*. New York: Harcourt, Brace, and Co.

———. 1947. *The Crisis* (December).

Frederickson, George. 1971. *The Black Image in the White Mind*. Wesleyan University Press.

Gates, Henry. 1988. *The Signifying Monkey*. New York: Oxford University Press.

Griaule, Marcel. 1965. *Conversations with Ogotemmeli*. Oxford, England: Oxford University Press.

Hallen, B., and J. O. Sodipo. 1986. *Knowledge, Belief, and Witchcraft*. London: Ethnographica Press.

Irele, Abiola. 1990. "The African Imagination." *Research in African Literatures, Special Issue on Critical Theory and African Literature* 21, no. 1 (Spring).

Lewontin, R. C., Steven Rose, and Leon Kamin. 1984. *Not In Our Genes*. New York: Pantheon.

Nei, Masatoshi, and A. K. Roychoudhury. "Genetic Relationship and Evolution of Human Races." *Evolutionary Biology* 14: 1–56

H. Odera Oruka. 1990. *Sage Philosophy*. New York: E. J. Brill.

———. 1983. "Philosophical Sagacity in African Philosophy." *The International Philosophical Quarterly* 23, no. 4 (December).

Reed, John, and Clive Wake, eds. 1965. *Senghor Prose & Poetry*. New York: Oxford University Press.

Sodipo, John. 1980. "Some Philosophical Aspects of the African Historical Experience." In Dr. Claude Sumner, ed., *African Philosophy*. Addis Ababa: Chamber Printing House.

Smith, Anthony. 1975. *The Human Pedigree*. George Allen & Unwin.

Williamson, Joel. 1984. *The Crucible of Race—Black White Relations in the American South since Emancipation*. New York: Oxford University Press.

4. Race, Ethnicity, Biology, Culture[1]
Philip Kitcher

I

DURING RECENT DECADES, A number of prominent anthropologists have defended *eliminativism about race*, arguing that the notion of race, as applied to our own species, is of no biological significance (Montagu, 1964; Livingstone, 1962; Marks, 1994; see also Diamond, 1994, for the perspective of an evolutionary biologist). One obvious motivation for discarding the concept of race is that it might provide the most effective way of undermining racism. Ironically, as I shall try to show later in this essay, important postracialist projects may require us to probe the connections between biology and race more deeply, to arrive at a clearer understanding of the concept of ethnicity, and to undertake empirical investigations of the connections between biological and social notions.[2]

However, whether or not eliminativism about race would achieve that goal, the first question concerns the truth of the thesis that races have no biological significance. Eliminativists have made two important points that should be recognized from the beginning. First, the phenotypic characters used to demarcate races—for example, the three "major races," Caucasian, African, and Asian—neither have any intrinsic significance nor have been shown to correlate with characteristics of intrinsic significance. Second, although generic and phenotypic studies have shown that certain alleles, dispositions to disease, and phenotypes occur at different frequencies in different racial groups, intraracial diversity is far more pronounced than interracial diversity. This latter point remains unchallenged. Painstaking research on human phenotypic variation has disclosed that, even with respect to the most evident marker of racial difference, skin color, there are profound differences within races (see Lewontin, 1982, p. 115). Moreover, the growing mass of data on human genetic variation down to the minutest details of DNA sequence makes it plain that so-called races differ only in the frequencies with which various alleles are found, often in complicated and bewildering ways (see Molnar, 1992; Cavalli-Sforza, 1994). Jared Diamond has made the point vivid by considering the ways in which various choices of genetic characteristics would subvert our standard racial classifications (1994).

But if the facts of intraracial diversity are widely accepted, the idea that there are no correlations between familiar phenotypic differences and more significant traits remains controversial. Users of the notion of race have often maintained that the physical traits used to demarcate the different races are correlated with "mental" and "temperamental" differences. Nobody has been more forthright than the American champion of Mendelism, the early eugenicist Charles B. Davenport, who gave stark expression to the principal ideas in an essay, "The Mingling of Races."

> Not only physical traits, like eye color, skin color, body build and such characters as stature, color and form of the hair, proportions of facial features and many others are inherited in race-crosses but also mental traits. This is a matter which is often denied, but the application of methods of mental measuring seem to have produced indubitable proof that the general intelligence and specific mental capacities have a basis and vary in the different races of mankind. Thus it has been shown, by standard mental tests, that the negro adolescent gained lower scores than white adolescents and this when the test is made quite independent of special training or language differences and also when the children tested have a similar amount of schooling. (Davenport, 1930, p. 557)

What goes for brains goes for character. Davenport explained:

> Common observation shows that the emotional output of different peoples is very different. We note that the North American Indian is little given to emotional expression. On the other hand, the African negro expresses his emotions copiously. In Europe the Scotch Highlanders are characterized by a prevailingly somber tendency, while the South Italians are characterized by lightness of spirit. (p. 558)

But there are even differences in instinct. Davenport continued:

> It is welt known that most of the races of Europe are fairly stable and domestic, engaged in agriculture or industry. However, from eastern Europe and western Asia have come forth races of mankind with a strong tendency to wander over the face of the earth. Such are the Gypsies which have run through Europe and America and such are some nomadic peoples who are scattered across the face

of Asia and Northern Africa and who even before the time of Livingstone had penetrated into the heart of Equatorial Africa. Now the instinct to wander, or nomadism, is one that has an hereditary basis. This has been worked out in some detail by the author and the results of his investigation have, so far, not been disproved. (pp. 558–59)

Plus ça change. Sixty years after these passages were written, we find contemporary authors adverting to the same themes as if the critiques of intermediate decades did not exist. Robert Herrnstein and Charles Murray confidently assert that IQ tests are free of cultural bias and that the 15-point gap between the means of Caucasians and African Americans points to genetic differences (Herrnstein and Murray, 1994). J. Philippe Rushton suggests that the major races have different reproductive strategies that reflect temperamental differences (Rushton, 1994). True, Davenport's marvelously looney idea about genes for nomadism seems to have vanished, but it is remarkable how many of his claims are resurrected, more apologetically, by those who feel that the world should know the true facts about racial differences.

This is not the place to engage in a full critique of the recent revivals of Davenportism. Suffice it to say that many of the old charges have not been satisfactorily answered. Herrnstein and Murray make crucial assumptions in arriving at estimates of heritability, and they put the notion of heritability to work in ways that have been attacked as inappropriate for over two decades (see Block and Dworkin, 1972; Lewontin, 1974; the best diagnosis I have seen of the errors in Herrnstein and Murray's much-criticized 1994 work is offered by Block [1996]). What we need to know about the genetic basis of intelligence are the shapes of the relevant norms of reaction,[3] and heritability estimates, even if correct, cannot enlighten us about these. Moreover, if we make some concessions, for the sake of argument, about the significance of IQ measures, there are interesting facts from the history of intelligence testing that point toward a quite different moral. One of the most noteworthy features of the data on which Davenport relied (the Army data from World War I) is the demonstration of a correlation between performance on the tests and quality of schooling (reflected in the differences between those educated in Northern and Southern schools; see Gould, 1981). Two groups once stigmatized for their "low" intelligence, the Jews and the Irish, currently perform better than members of other Caucasian groups. At the same time, data from Northern Ireland show that the mean score among Catholics is about 15 points below that of Protestants (see Block, 1996). It is tempting to think that if differences in scores show anything at all, they reveal that people belonging to a group that is socially and economically disadvantaged often do significantly worse than the more fortunate members of the population. Rushton's work is equally insensitive to well-known criticisms. Since the mid-1980s, many scholars interested in the evolution of human behavior have learned to moderate their claims to avoid the excesses of what I have called "pop sociobiology" (see Kitcher, 1985). Rushton writes as though there were no need for caution, investing anatomical and physiological differences with immense significance by spinning evolutionary scenarios that consistently ignore the possibility of alternative, more mundane, explanations.

So I begin from the position that the phenotypic characters used to pick out races neither have intrinsic significance nor are correlated with characteristics that are significant, and that intraracial variation is far greater than interracial variation. Does this mean that eliminativism is correct? I shall argue that it does not, and that, however admirably motivated, eliminativist approaches have failed to recognize more subtle ways in which divisions into races *might* have biological significance.[4] Further, in the light of this argument, I shall explore some of the ways in which concepts of race figure in social discussions, indicating questions that would have to be resolved if the practice of discarding racial divisions were to lead to desirable conclusions. We should all be worried by the thought that retaining concepts of race will foster racism—but my goal is to show that these should not be our only concerns.

II

It is helpful to begin an exploration of the biological significance of the concept of race by contrasting the uses that biologists make of this notion (and related notions) and those that figure in our social interactions. To fix ideas about the biological uses, we can turn to any of a number of standard examples that have been treated in contemporary neo-Darwinism. Dobzhansky's classic discussion (Dobzhansky, 1970, pp. 270ff) introduces three major illustrations: variant color patterns in the Asiatic beetle *Harmonia axyridis*, chromosomal races in *Drosophila pseudoobscura*, and shell coloring and patterning in the snail *Cepaea nemoralis*. Each of these instances involves a species with internal differentiation of groups. In the first and third examples, the groups are marked by readily identifiable phenotypic differences; in the second, the differences are solely at the chromosomal level. Underlying the phenotypic differences are differences in genes, while the chromosomal differences rest on heritable variations in the arrangement of genes. So, in all instances, the differences among members of the same species are heritable.

According to the neo-Darwinian synthesis, a species consists of a cluster of populations reproductively compatible with one another but reproductively isolated from other populations (see Mayr, 1942; Mayr, 1963, and many subsequent works by Mayr). The notion of reproductive isolation, often misunderstood, rests on the idea that some organisms have a dispositional property: were they to be in the same place at the same time, they would not normally mate with one another. I shall explore the nuances of this complex idea shortly. First, however, let us note that the various groups of beetles, flies, and snails are not reproductively isolated from their conspecifics. Despite the heritable differences among the groups, they remain reproductively compatible. However, the genetic differences among the groups persist from generation to generation, so there are factors that prevent genetic homogenization. In some cases, there are selective pressures that tell against intergroup hybrids, in others geographical isolation. But whether the blurring of genetic differences is blocked by natural selection or by physical separation, the different groups appear to be taking the first steps toward speciation. They are "*species in statu nascendi.*"[5]

There are three features of these examples that will be important in understanding a possible biological basis for racial concepts: the presence of phenotypic differences, the heritability of these differences, and the incipient reproductive isolation. All three deserve scrutiny, and will prove more problematic than might initially appear. First, however, it is worth contrasting, the biologist's demarcation of races with contexts in which the concept of race is employed in social discourse.

Some talk of race is overtly racist, and examples are too familiar to warrant recalling them explicitly. Yet there are other usages that might seem more benign, cases in which the concept of race fulfills a function in raising important problems. Consider discussions of the desirability of transracial adoption. In a society in which there is a practice of characterizing a majority race and a minority race, the adoption of a minority child by two majority parents might be opposed on the grounds that the child will be deprived of important parts of her racial identity.[6] The opposition recognizes, quite correctly, that in our species, genetic inheritance is one mode of transmission across the generations, accompanied by a different system in which items of culture are passed on. A particular style of cultural inheritance or, perhaps, a cluster of styles, regularly accompanies certain biological features; indeed, the division of the society into races on biological grounds maps onto a division into ethnic groups, ethnicities, marked out by alternative systems of cultural transmission. Because races are relatively broad categories, the mapping is hardly one–one.[7] Instead, the picture is of a cluster of related ethnicities, each more closely related to one another than with elements in the cluster associated with a different race. The picture reveals that at the basis of the opposition is the idea that the child will have an ethnicity that is at odds with her race. I shall later want to look at the notion of ethnicity introduced informally here, and at the assumption that it is desirable for ethnicity and race to be in harmony with one another.

For the moment, however, I simply want to place at the center of discussion the four elements whose interconnections I intend to explore: race, ethnicity, biology, culture. I want to review the ways in which a concept of race might be developed compatible with our present biological understanding, to explore the consequences of replacing the apparently biological concept of race with a social notion of ethnicity, and to ask if the social concept can play the role we intend for it without some biological notion lurking in the background. My strategy will be the inverse of one that is common in discussions of race. Rather than starting with our current conceptions of race, with all the baggage they carry, I want to ask how biologists employ the notion of race, and how we might regard our own species in similar fashion.[8] As I have already indicated, I believe that debates about the appropriate character of a postracialist society will he more sharply focused if we have information about the empirical issues which my probing of the notions of race and ethnicity will bring to the fore, specifically questions about the relationships between patterns of biological transmission and patterns of cultural transmission. It is also worth remarking, at the outset, that the notion of race I shall employ is minimalist: its ideas about racial division are far more modest than those to which defenders of race typically allude, and, as I have been at pains to argue in Section I, I concur in the eliminativist critique of the traditional views about the differences among races. indeed, I am inclined to think that, if nothing corresponds to the notion of race I reconstruct, then eliminativists are quite right to maintain that no biological notion of race can be salvaged.

III

So much by way of introduction. Let me now begin more slowly and more carefully. If we propose to divide the human species into races, we offer a set of subsets, not necessarily exhaustive, that constitute the *pure races*. "Pure" here is shorthand, *and the usage of this term should carry no connotation of superiority*. "Pure races" might just as well be called "completely inbred lineages" (except that the phrase is cumbersome), for that is what they will turn out to be.

A necessary condition on any concept of race is the following:

(RI) A racial division consists of a set of subsets of the species *Homo sapiens*. These subsets are the pure races. Individuals who do not belong to any pure race are of mixed race.

Now, there are all sorts of ways of dividing our species up that would by no means count as racial divisions. Suppose we considered subsets that marked out people according to income distribution, running speed, or average levels of ingestion of caffeine. One obvious reason why this kind of division is a non-starter as a partition into races is that the characteristics that would identify the pure races are not heritable. Ruling out such proposals is very easy: we can simply impose a requirement of reproductive closure.

(R2) With respect to any racial division, the pure races are closed under reproduction. That is, the offspring of parents both of whom are of race R are also of race R.

Existing concepts of race honor (R2) but do not satisfy the converse principle

(R3) With respect to any racial division, all ancestors of any member of a pure race belong to that race. The parents of an individual of race R are of race R.

Socially disadvantaged races consist of a pure core together with people any of whose ancestors belongs to that core. Madison Grant's chillingly racist pronouncement that one parent from an "inferior race" consigns the offspring to that race has become a cornerstone of American notions of race, and Naomi Zack has insightfully explored the consequences of this presupposition (Zack, 1993; for the reference to Grant, see p. 100).

Racial divisions need not embody the idea that "inferior" races expand by "tainting" their "superiors." It is possible to proceed symmetrically, honoring both (R2) and (R3), and counting offspring of parents from different pure races as being of mixed race.[9] However, even if both requirements are imposed, there are any number of divisions of *Homo sapiens* that do not constitute what we would intuitively think of as racial divisions. Consider, for example, division by eye color. If we were to partition people as blue-eyed or brown-eyed, this would fall afoul of reproductive closure—brown-eyed heterozygotes can have blue-eyed children—but this difficulty can easily be overcome. Let one pure race consist of people homozygous for the dominant (brown-eyed) allele, the other of people homozygous for the recessive (blue-eyed) allele; heterozygotes will be of mixed race. (R2) is now satisfied, for, disregarding mutation, mating between two people both homozygous for the same allele will only yield offspring also homozygous for that allele. However, we have not yet secured satisfaction of (R3). To assure that, it is necessary to prune the pure races, eliminating people who have any heterozygous ancestors. That can readily be achieved if we proceed recursively, identifying *founder populations* and the lineages to which they give rise.

Let us therefore fix a time in human prehistory, the *time of racial origination*. The set of human beings existing at this time will be divided by identifying the founder population of recessive homozygotes, the founder population of dominant homozygotes, and the residue (the heterozygotes). The first generation of the blue-eyed pure race is the founding population of recessive homozygotes; the $n + 1$st generation of the blue-eyed pure race consists of the offspring of matings between parents each of whom belongs to the nth generation of the blue-eyed pure race (or to some earlier generation). The pure races picked out in this way satisfy both (R2) and (R3), but "racial divisions" of this kind are of little significance. Part of the reason is surely that the overwhelming majority of the species would be counted as of mixed race, and many of these people would be both genetically and phenotypically identical (as far as eye color is concerned) to members of one of the pure races.

So while (R1)–(R3) pick out important features of the concepts of race which we employ, they are by no means sufficient to reveal what is distinctive about racial divisions. Nevertheless, the construction that shows how to prune populations of homozygotes so as to satisfy (R3) is helpful, for it makes explicit the idea of a historical lineage within which inbreeding occurs. I take this to be essential to any biologically significant racial concept: instead of trying to draw racial divisions on the basis of traits of the contemporary population, it is necessary to consider patterns of descent. *The concept of race is a historical concept.*[10]

However, while a certain type of history is necessary for racial division, it is not sufficient. Whether or not we demand some special genetic feature in the founding population, it is possible to satisfy (R2) and (R3) by choosing a time of origination, splitting the temporal segment of the species at the time of origination into founding populations, and identifying the successor generation of a pure race as the offspring produced by matings between members of earlier generations of that race. We can pick times of origination as we please, gerrymandering founder populations as we fancy, but none of this will be of the slightest biological significance unless two further conditions are met: (1) the members of the pure races thus characterized have some distinctive phenotypic or genetic properties; (2) the residual mixedrace population is relatively small, at least during most of the generations between the time of origination and the present.

It is important to recognize, from the start, that the idea of a pure race is an idealization (and, once again, the notion of idealization should carry no connotations of special goodness). Just as meteorologists analyze the complexities of the weather by producing charts with lines marking "fronts," so it is possible to understand the messy facts of human reproduction and biological transmission by looking for approximations to historical lineages that are completely inbred. The descent of contemporary people might show any number of patterns. Our species might have been completely panmictic from a time in the distant past (*panmictic* populations are those in which each member of one sex has an equal probability of mating and reproducing with each member of the opposite sex). Or, at the other extreme, inbreeding might have been so tight that, for generations, brothers have only mated with sisters. The concept of a pure race that I have described will be a useful notion in charting human reproduction across the generations, if there are groups that persist for long periods during which they are *mostly* inbred. Such groups will contain a number of families, and, at any given time, most of the families in a group will be interbreeding with other families in the group, and, for each family in the group, most of its history will be one in which family members interbreed with other families in the group.

This is the relevant sense in which the notion of a pure race might idealize (or approximate) actual mating patterns.

At this point it should be apparent how notions related to that of reproductive isolation enter the picture. For the residual mixed-race population to be small, interbreeding among the pure races has to be infrequent. Moreover, if this is the case, then the possibility of maintaining distinctive genetic properties for the pure races will be greatly enhanced.[11] Even if the initial differences between founder populations at the time of origination are small, if descendants of those populations face different selection pressures, and if they mate almost invariably with one another, it is possible that, after many generations, the pure races will have different distributions of genes and of allelic combinations.

At this point, we can begin to see how the racial concepts we actually employ might be generated.[12] Racial divisions start with the idea of a division of the species into founder populations (not necessarily contemporaneous), which generate pure races in the recursive way described. Through most subsequent generations, interbreeding between the pure races is low, initially, at least, because of geographical separation and limited dispersal. Thus we arrive at the idea that the phenotypic or genetic features taken to mark out particular races— skin color, physiognomy, distribution of blood types or of alleles conferring susceptibility to various diseases—gain their significance because lineages have differentiated in the absence of reproductive contact. But none of this would have the slightest importance, or interest, if geographical union produced a thoroughly panmictic population. The fact that lineages which have been geographically separated in the past have distinctive characteristics has no biological significance unless, when current populations in different lineages are brought together, there is an incipient form of reproductive isolation. If men and women with very different genealogies breed freely, then the separation of their ancestors is of no enduring biological significance.

The notion of reproductive isolation is frequently misunderstood. Clusters of populations are reproductively isolated from one another just in case, where populations in different clusters are in geographical contact, they interbreed only at low rates. The tendency in much nonspecialist thinking is to suppose that reproductive isolation requires the impossibility of mating under any conditions. But this is far too strong a demand: many species will interbreed when their natural environments are disrupted, as witnessed by the numerous instances of hybridization in captivity. Nor is it reasonable to demand that members of different species never mate in the wild. Naturalists know numerous instances of *hybrid zones*, regions within which two species meet and produce hybrids. In some cases, the hybrids are sterile, in others fertile; there are examples of hybrid species in frogs—and possibly even in chimpanzees. (For valuable discussions of hybrid zones, see Littlejohn and Watson, 1985, and Barton and Hewitt, 1985). What is crucial for preserving species distinctness is that the hybrid zones remain stable, so that genes from one species do not flow to the other. Stability of hybrid zones rests on the greater propensity of conspecifics to mate with one another than with a member of another species.

Hybrid zones typically occur at the edge of a species range. Here, members of the species seeking potential mates only encounter conspecifics at low density. If they are more likely to meet an organism from a closely related species, the lower propensity for mating with a member of the alien species may be overwhelmed by the greater frequency with which aliens appear. If we associate with each organism in a species a probability that that organism will mate with a conspecific, given that it mates at all, then that probability will vary from 1 (or a number infinitesimally close to 1) to a significantly lower number in those regions where conspecifics are rare.

Underlying this distribution of probabilities may be a species-wide propensity to favor conspecifics as mates. That propensity, in its turn, rests on the traits of the organisms that make them disinclined to interbreed, the so-called *isolating mechanisms*. Isolating mechanisms are of many types, ranging from incompatibility of genitalia, inability of sperm to fuse with ova, low survival probabilities for the embryo, through differences in time of activity or in microhabitat that keep the species separated, to complex behavioral differences. Some species of *Drosophila*, for example, are kept apart through subtle differences in the ritual behavior that precedes normal mating: males who perform a slightly deviant sequence of movements are only accepted as mates *in extremis*. Caribbean species of the lizard genus *Anolis* occupy the same area, but are differentiated in terms of habitat: one species is primarily found in the crowns of trees, another on the trunks, yet another on the ground around the trunks.

So far I have characterized reproductive isolation in terms of differences in mating probabilities, focusing on the probability that an organism will mate with a conspecific, given that it mates at all. However, it is also possible that mating within the species has a more fine-grained structure, so that the probabilities of mating with conspecifics with distinct phenotypic traits are different. So, for example, the species may divide into a number of groups with characteristic phenotypes, such that the probability of any group member mating with a member of the same group, if it mates at all, is very high, while the probability of mating with a member of another group, if it mates at all, is correspondingly low. If this occurs when the groups are in geographical contact with one another, then we can think of the groups as reproductively isolated *to some degree*, with the degree varying with (a) the probability of within-group mating and (b) the extent of the geographical contact. In the extreme case, in which the groups are thoroughly and completely geographically mixed within the range of the species, so that organisms are just as likely to encounter members of alien groups as they are to meet members of their own group, and in which the probability of mating out falls to the level that is usual for species within the interior of their range (i.e., little more than 0), then the groups have become distinct species. But long before the extremes are reached, the differences between inbreeding and outbreeding rates may be sufficient to preserve the genetic differences that underlie the distinct phenotypes—or, at least, substantially to retard the erosion of those differences.

If there is a workable biological conception of race, then it must, I believe, honor (R1)–(R3), employ the historical construction in terms of founder populations and inbred lineages, and, finally, demand that, when the races are brought together, the differences in intraracial and interracial mating probabilities be sufficiently large to sustain the distinctive traits that mark the races (which must, presumably, lie, at least in part, in terms of phenotypes, since organisms have no direct access to one another's genes). Now, it is evidently possible for groups with distinctive phenotypic traits that have been geographically separated for many generations to form a completely panmictic population when they are reunited—so that the intergroup mating probability is exactly the intragroup probability. If this should occur, and there are m pure races occurring at frequencies n_i, at the time of geographic union, then, after k generations, the frequency of the ith pure race would be expected to be n_i^{2k}. The significance of this point is that, if we contemplate an initial situation with two races in frequencies 0.9 and 0.1, then, after 10 generations the expected frequency of the majority pure race would be around 10^{-47}. If the distribution is less extreme, or if there are more races, pure races disappear even more rapidly.

IV

Let me now use the rather abstract and general approach I have been developing to consider the possible biological foundation for a division of our species into races. If my analysis is correct, then the core of any biological notion of race should be that phenotypic differences have been fashioned and sustained through the transmission of genes through lineages initiated by founding populations that were geographically separated, and that the distinct phenotypes are currently maintained when people from different races are brought together through the existence of incipient isolating mechanisms that have developed during the period of geographical separation. Part of this presupposition is probably correct. There surely were geographically separated populations that would serve as founder populations for making some facial divisions—although it is not clear to me that this can provide anything other than a coarse-grained division, picking out the "major races."

In fact, the patterns of gene flow in the history of our species are complicated. Eliminativists insist on the connection of sub-Saharan African populations to northern African populations; these, in turn, to Middle-Eastern Arab populations, and so forth; much has been made of the flow of genes across central Europe. However, such linkages do not ensure that extreme populations are linked in ways that make them part of the same evolutionary unit at all levels. Studies of the history of marriage in southern England and in Italy testify to an amazing proximity of spouses, even comparatively recently (Brierly, 1970; Cavalli-Sforza, 1969). It is not hard to show that if interbreeding is relatively tightly confined, then populations separated by large distances (at the opposite edges of a continent, say) are effectively independent with respect to the genetics of microevolutionary change. In effect, some populations—the Arabs of Mediterranean Egypt and the indigenous peoples of southern Africa, or Norwegians and Greeks—have not exchanged genes to any significant degree. The phenomenon is analogous to that of so-called ring species, illustrated in species of gulls around the north pole or snakes in Texas (Mayr, 1970): two species whose ranges join and which do not interbreed are connected by a chain of populations, each of which interbreeds with its neighbor. Just as biologists recognize two distinct species in such instances, so too they might view two populations that only interbreed to a very limited degree as constituting races, despite the fact that they occur at opposite ends of a transcontinental cline (a sequence of populations along which there is genetic variation in a particular direction, so that, while adjacent populations may be quite similar, differences in the extremes are quite pronounced).

So the first part of the presupposition—the commitment to a history of reproductive separation—strikes me as correct, at least for some ensembles of populations. In particular, the United States is currently home to many groups who represent the latest stages of lineages that have not exchanged genes for a very long time. What about the second part, the thesis that when the populations come together they still do not exchange genes at high frequency? Here, firm data are hard to find, and the picture that emerges from statistics and anecdotes is by no means uniform. Some groups, when reunited, interbreed more readily than do others. However, if the incomplete studies I have managed to track down are reliable, they do show that rates of interbreeding between some groups are very low. In particular, some groups of people designated as "black" only mate infrequently with other groups designated as "white."

At this point it is worth being very explicit about what I am claiming. In reconstructing the notion of race, I have suggested that groups are racially separated if certain facts about reproduction obtain: this shows the *possibility* of a biological notion of race. Specifically, if the "blacks" and "whites" in a particular region at a particular time reproduce together at a relatively low rate, then we can say that there is an incipient racial division between those groups at that place and at that time; if the rate of interreproduction remains low across a period, then we can talk about two races in that region. Since I can only appeal to indications of relatively low rates of mating between American "blacks" and American "whites," not to firm data, systematically collected over significant periods, I can only suggest, tentatively, that this division may answer to the notion I have reconstructed. I am, however, inclined to believe that this is likely to be one of the best (if not the best) examples of a racial division (although, here, as elsewhere, empirical research could prove me wrong).

Data on rates of interracial marriage are surprisingly hard to come by. I have not been able to obtain reliable recent figures. However, the picture from the 1970 U.S. Census figures shows the following distribution for black-white marriages:

		Race of Wife	
		White	Black
Race of Husband	White	99.7	0.7
	Black	0.1	99.2

Approval of interracial marriage apparently doubled between 1968 and 1978 (20 to 36 percent), although a recent poll (1994) has indicated that 20 percent of the American population still favor laws against miscegenation (earlier data derived from Porterfield, 1984).

Studies of other forms of intermarriage paint a different picture. It is reliably estimated that up to 50 percent of the marriages of Japanese people in the continental United States are with non-Japanese spouses (although by no means with non-Asian spouses—see Tinker, 1984). The picture of interracial marriage in Hawaii is far more complex (see Schwertfeger, 1984):

	Groom's Ancestry					
Bride's Ancestry	Ca	Ha	Ch	Fi	Ja	Ot.
Caucasian	517	230	36	86	79	52
Hawaiian and part-Hawaiian	177	515	20	121	94	72
Chinese	138	163	311	41	296	51
Filipino	114	159	26	584	69	48
Japanese	56	70	59	30	761	25
Other	201	18.5	.21	69	127	397

The "short version" of the recent survey of patterns of sexual behavior in the United States is very clear about the tendency to avoid interracial relationships.

> Almost as forbidden [as homosexuality] is interracial dating. The pressure to choose someone of your own race can begin as soon as teenagers start to date, and often sustains patterns of overt racism.
>
> That social pressure against interracial dating becomes greater the closer a couple comes to marrying. (Michael *et al.*, 1994, p. 57)

Interestingly, when the authors follow up these claims with several anecdotes about interracial couples who are cut off from their families and about the anger directed at people whose romantic friendships cross racial lines, the examples they choose all involve blacks and Caucasians (pp. 58–59). The more technical version explores various preferences for kinds of similarities in sexual partners, suggesting that even casual relationships across racial lines occur at low rates (see Laumann *et al.*, 1994, pp. 254–66; the data on the infrequency of Asian-Hispanic sexual relationships are particularly striking).

These sources clearly suggest that the second part of the presupposition for biologically significant racial divisions is partially satisfied. The United States consists of an ensemble of populations, some of which have been geographically separated before being brought into proximity with one another. Between some pairs of these populations, most notably between African Americans and Caucasians, the frequency of intermarriage is low, suggesting that these populations are behaving as separate units from an evolutionary and, perhaps, ecological standpoint. Emphatically, this does not mean that racial divisions can be drawn across the entire species, that the divisions into inbred populations that hold locally necessarily apply globally; my minimalist notion of race allows for the possibility that, within one geographic locale (say the United States, or even something narrower like the rural Midwest), two groups are racially divided, even though elsewhere they are not. The possibility of racial division which I am suggesting is specific to a broader group, an ensemble of populations that are present in a particular geographical region. Nor, even locally, need it honor all the traditional racial divisions. Although the evidence does appear to indicate a significant mating barrier between whites and blacks, the statistics about intermarriage between European Americans and Asian Americans (from at least some national backgrounds) tells a quite different story.

But why make such a fuss about intermarriage (or interbreeding)? If one grants, as I have done, that the phenotypic differences between groups are not significant and that intragroup variation swamps intergroup variation, why not let the race concept go? To answer these questions, it is helpful to adopt a conceit proposed by E. O. Wilson (1975), and recently taken up by Rushton. Imagine a Martian naturalist visiting earth for the first time and observing our species. What infraspecific divisions, if any, would the Martian draw? Rushton announces confidently that they would spot three geographical "races" with quite different body types. But simply noticing the phenotypic variation in height, bone thickness, skin color, or whatever should not inspire the Martians to divide our species into races—Rushton's Martians (and probably Rushton himself) make a mistake against which Ernst Mayr has inveighed for so long that it has become part of the standard equipment of any field naturalist concerned to identify the species in a particular area. Only the uninformed rush in and divide sexually reproducing organisms according to the differences which strike them, the outsiders, as salient. To repeat what is, perhaps, obvious: the notion of race I have been developing is not morphological, concerned with such features as skin color or physiognomy, but focused on patterns of reproduction; morphology plays a role only if morphological differences prove relevant to reproductive choices. In this, I am as much at odds with Rushton and others who deploy traditional notions of race as are the eliminativists who deny the biological significance of race entirely.

Taxonomic divisions should be grounded in distinctions that the organisms themselves make, in the propensities for mating and reproduction. Mayr named his conception of species "biological," both because it was founded on something of central importance to biology, the reproduction of organisms, and because patterns of reproduction reflect characteristics that matter to the organisms. So, a Mayrian Martian, looking at our species, would attend, above all, to the facets of our reproductive behavior, noting not simply the phenotypic differences but seeing that in some locales, like the United States, those phenotypic differences correlate quite strikingly with mating patterns. To return from our fantasy and state the moral more soberly, intermarriage statistics are crucial because those statistics (poor though they are) are proxies for what is biologically crucial in making taxonomic divisions.[13]

At this point it is important to confront an important objection. Many eliminativists have responded to the idea of articulating concepts of race along the lines I have proposed by suggesting that there are not significant intraspecific differences in gene flow, so that, despite the partial evidence from the incomplete statistics I have quoted, the presupposition for biologically important racial divisions is not satisfied. Two kinds of considerations prompt this line of response: (1) the familiar judgment that contemporary American "blacks" have some Caucasian ancestry, and, conversely, that many American "whites" have some African ancestry (see Zack, 1993, for elaboration of the point); (2) the suggestion that, if there are indeed large differences in frequency between intraracial and interracial mating, this is a temporary phenomenon that is unlikely to produce biological effects.[14] I shall take up each point in turn.

In rough outline, what we know of the history of sexual relations in America between people of European descent and people of African descent suggests that there have been two main periods during which such relations were relatively common. First, in the early colonies, particularly in Virginia, indentured servants from Europe and Africans (either slaves or servants) flouted the strictures against sexual liaisons. Later, in the plantation South, there is no doubt that white men from slaveholding families often treated female slaves as sexual property. Since the offspring of these unions were counted as "black" (under the notorious "one-drop" rule), many "blacks" had one parent of European descent. The sexual relations between these "blacks" and others, some of whom also had European ancestors, spread genes from the "white" population into the "black" population. In similar fashion, those blacks with enough "European" features to pass as "white" sometimes married people of purely European ancestry, so that the genetic mixing went in both directions. (For a lucid account of this story, see Davis, 1991.)

If we now attempt to apply the concept of race I have developed to this history, there are two options: we can take the races to be ancient, setting the time of origination during the period of geographical separation, or we can suppose that the process of race formation begins at the time of Reconstruction. The first alternative appears to be blocked by the existence of two periods of substantial gene flow, and I think that it is the recognition of this fact that motivates sophisticated versions of eliminativism. In fact, however, matters are not so simple. For, in the first place, nobody has proposed that the probability that children born to people of African descent resulted from a union with a person of European descent was ever close to the probability that such children would result from a union with a person of African descent: neither the relations between indentured servants and Africans nor the exploitation of black women by white slaveowners ever came close to attaining the frequency of within-group unions. Second, from a purely biological point of view, it would be natural to redescribe the history by identifying two periods during which the proximity of people from two groups produced hybrid descendants, with the majority of these hybrids being assigned to one of the groups.[15] After these two periods were over, groups with somewhat modified gene pools (more extensively modified in the case of the blacks, only slightly modified in the case of the whites) once again engaged in cross-group unions, only at low rates. Even though the history does not strictly correspond to the requirements I have laid down for racial divisions, we might see it as an approximation to the idealized notion of separated, predominantly inbred lineages, disturbed only by two anomalous episodes in which the races are reshaped. From that perspective, the second episode, with its exploitation of black women, would not be viewed as the benign breaking down of interracial barriers, but as the coercive restructuring of the minority race.[16]

The second alternative would be to abandon the idea that the races are old, and emphasize the low rates of interracial union during the past century (see Davis, 1991, pp. 71–72). This, of course, would be to invite the charge that such barriers are only temporary and thus of no significance for understanding human genetics and evolution. In response, it is worth noting two points. First, in introducing the biological species concept, Mayr insisted on a "non-dimensional" version: populations at a given place at a given time belong to different species if they are not exchanging genes. In exactly parallel fashion, we could recognize "non-dimensional" races, groups at a particular place at a particular time that are not exchanging genes at substantial rates.[17] Second, and more important, I see no reason to conclude from the history that there has ever been a time at which people of African descent and people of European descent, with ample opportunities for mate choice, freely chose members of the other group at rates close to those with which they selected members of their own group. (I emphatically do not rejoice in this idea, but it does seem to represent our species' sexual past.) If that is so, then the incidents during which intergroup unions have been relatively common are the anomalies, and we should not think that the current tow rates are a temporary phenomenon that will lack biological implications.

I conclude, tentatively, that we can use the concept of race I have articulated to identify at least some divisions among contemporary Americans. This conclusion is tentative because further information about the history and current state of sexual unions in the American population (most pertinently those unions that produce children) might reveal a much greater rate of mixing than my account could allow.[18]

At this stage, there are a number of obvious questions both about the details of the approach I have adopted and about the division of our species into races. In the interests of making the position as clear as possible, it seems worth offering brief replies.

1. Does this minimalist notion of race restore the status quo by yielding traditional racial divisions? Although the evidence on patterns of reproduction is highly incomplete, it seems very likely that the view that there are three major races (Caucasian, African, Asian) will survive, if at all, only in highly qualified form. The statistics I have cited indicate that it is possible that there should be a division between Africans and Caucasians within the United States (although this might not hold elsewhere in the world), and that it is unlikely that there will be a division between Asians and Caucasians that will hold across the United States (although there might be more local divisions of this kind). I have given no grounds for even the most tentative opinion on the issue of whether there will be a division between Asians and Africans.

2. How do divisions by race interact with divisions by social class? There are two interesting issues about the interconnections of race and class. The first is whether the account I have given can always distinguish class divisions from racial divisions. In England immediately after the Norman conquest, for example, it seems possible that the population divided into two classes, an affluent class of landowners (often Norman) and a class of peasants (virtually all Saxon), and that these were reproductively disconnected. On the account I have given, these classes could be viewed as races, and we could describe the situation as one in which the English aristocracy was fashioned from the restructuring of a Norman population by the admixture of some (wealthy) Saxons. More generally, any situation in which there is limited intercourse (primarily sexual) among different classes could be viewed as one in which those classes function as different races (a judgment, interestingly enough, that members of the classes may express, albeit often with a different conception of race in mind). Interestingly, the institution of the *droit de seigneur* may have undermined any such racial division.

Second, just as a racial division may hold only in a particular locale, so too it may also obtain only within a particular social class. Consider the possibility that middle-class American "blacks" and "whites" are far more likely to reproduce together than are their working-class counterparts (a possibility that would invert the likely situation in the original colonies). Under these circumstances, there would be a class-relative racial division between Africans and Caucasians.

3. *Aren't the notions of reproductive disconnection and of the endurance of races both matters of degree?* Yes. I have talked, vaguely, of populations exchanging genes at relatively low rates And of divisions as enduring. Behind these vague remarks stand precise figures, as yet unknown, about the rates at which different groups interbreed over a number of generations. The same vagueness infects biological usage of subspecific (and even higher-order) taxonomic categories, and it is easy for there to be unclear cases. Surely, however, if we were to discover that the population divided into As and Bs, that As interbred with Bs with probability 0.01, that Bs interbred with As with probability 0.03, and that these figures remained relatively stable (showing some fluctuations but never rising far above the values given) for a century and a half, then we could talk of a division into two races. Now, the actual data on patterns of reproduction may be nowhere near so dramatic, and we may end up by having to understand reproduction and biological descent by introducing explicitly degreed concepts. This could be done, for example, by measuring the *strength* of racial separation by the ratio of the probability of mating within to the probability of mating out, and by measuring the *endurance* of a racial division by the number of generations through which it persisted. Relations between groups could then be indexed by their endurance at or above a given strength: so we might discover that the African-Caucasian split relative to a geographic location (and perhaps to a class) had endured at a strength of 20 for six generations. Development of such degreed notions is straightforward, and I shall not pursue it here. It is sufficient to note that some of the questions about the relationship between biological and cultural transmission could be raised by employing such concepts.

4. *What is the relationship between my position and eliminativism?* Even though my approach and conclusions are at odds with eliminativism, I continue to share the fundamental points that eliminativists have made against older, typological, racial concepts: the characters that divide races (in my sense) are not significant, and the intraracial variation is greater than the interracial variation. What I deny is the eliminativists' insistence that racial divisions correspond to nothing in nature: I maintain that they correspond to patterns of mating, although I concede that empirical facts about such patterns could show that they are adequately charted only by using explicitly degreed concepts. However, even though I oppose the thesis that races are purely social constructions, there is a deeper sense in which I want to accept, and even to take further, this theme in eliminativism. When we look behind the patterns of mating at the underlying

causes, we see just the kinds of factors that eliminativists emphasize. I shall explore this theme in the next section.

V

Given that members of some pairs of groups do not engage in sexual relations at a very high rate, why does this occur? I can imagine all kinds of biological stories about our greater propensity for mating with members of our own race than for mating with members of different races. Perhaps our species has evolved "genes for xenophobia," and the statistics represent the impact of these genes. Maybe, we should take a cue from Patrick Bateson's beautiful experiments on mating, preferences in Japanese quail, which show that the birds have a degree of attraction that is low for very close relatives, low for their most unrelated conspecifics, and that peaks at second cousins (see Bateson, 1980, 1982). It is all too easy to lapse into pop sociobiology, either postulating genes and selective pressures to suit our fancy or extrapolating wildly from meticulous animal studies.

But there is, I believe, a much more obvious explanation of the differences in mating propensity. Isolating mechanisms may be very subtle, depending on the nuances of an organism's responses to the behavior of others. *Drosophila*, recall, are very sensitive to the movements of potential mates. Furthermore, even when members of two species occur in the same region, they may be separated by differences in times of activity or in their microhabitats. Combining these points, it is not difficult to sketch an explanation of the reduced probability of mating between whites and blacks that accords with a host of familiar facts. Black people and white people may traverse the same terrain—the streets of the same city—every day without much significant contact. So long as whites and blacks live in different areas, work and pursue recreation in different places, geographical contact between the races is only superficial (recall the *Anolis* lizards of the Caribbean). Moreover, even when contact does occur, the people who meet may not provide one another with the right signals: from the tiniest gestures to ways of expressing ideas, expectations may easily be defeated.

In fact, a single dominant theme runs through the literature on the difficulties of interracial marriage. Successful relationships must surmount a barrier built up from local attitudes to the history of racial interactions. Oversimplifying enormously, that barrier is constructed in three stages. At the first stage is the history of colonialism, slavery, decades of injustice, and the perpetuation of economic and social inequalities in the present. This produces, at the second stage, attitudes of fear and resentment in families who see a relative contemplating an interracial marriage. The third stage consists in the recognition, by the protagonists, of the attitudes of their families, and their growing awareness that they may be cut off from those they love and that their children may grow up without any extended family whatsoever. Whether or not other forms of cultural signalling operate at earlier stages, so that people from different races are rarely initially drawn to one another, for those who find themselves attracted to members of different races, the barrier I have described is frequently acknowledged as the crucial obstacle to marriage. Interracial couples almost invariably mention this barrier and the ways in which they have overcome it.

The sources of the low rate of black-white mating lie ultimately, I suggest, in the history of slavery and colonialism, and, more proximally, in socioeconomic inequities. The *current* economic inequalities make significant contact between blacks and whites unlikely, and the past history of economic differences, with the social consequences of past exploitation and attempts at suppressing black culture, erect barriers that are hard to remove. The eliminativist emphasis on the role of social causes in the construction of race is thus not entirely misguided: at risk of solecism, we might say that races are *both* socially constructed and biologically real. Biological reality intrudes in the objective facts of patterns of reproduction, specifically in the greater propensity for mating with other "blacks" (or other "whites" respectively); the social construction lies in the fact that these propensities themselves have complex social causes.

To understand this apparently paradoxical view, we should recognize that there are three distinct views one might take about the biological significance of racial divisions. The two that have figured largely in twentieth-century debate are, on the one hand, that there are biologically significant divisions between races (e.g., between whites and blacks), and, on the other, that there are no such significant divisions and that the concept of race is an illegitimate social construct that should be discarded. In my judgment, this opposition intertwines a number of separate issues. First, if there is, as I have claimed, significant difference between the probability of intraracial mating and the probability of interracial mating, then the phenotypic and genetic characteristics that distinguish racial groups can be sustained, and, at a micro-evolutionary level, races are behaving as separate evolutionary units. Thus, if the empirical facts are as I have taken them to be, eliminativism with respect to the concept of race, while an attractive position, cannot be upheld—although it might be noted that traditional racial divisions might be no more biologically significant than other divisions with the structure I have identified. However, while, in the case of other species, the development of incipient isolating mechanisms during a period of geographical isolation might be conceived as a purely biological phenomenon, resulting from the increase in frequency of alleles that dispose organisms not to mate with members of the other group, I see no grounds for any such explanation for the different mating propensities in races of *Homo sapiens*. Here, the account of the separation of (say) blacks from whites seems to be purely cultural, a matter of the patterns of behavior that have been transmitted across the generations through modes of *non-genetic* inheritance, as well as the accidents (many of them tragic and disastrous) of the relations among the two groups. Hence, while the concept of human races may have biological significance, in the sense that there are differences in gene frequencies which can be preserved because of low probabilities of interracial mating, the explanation of the mating preferences may have no biological significance. Races may *quite literally* be social constructs, in that our patterns of acculturation maintain the genetic distinctiveness of different racial groups.

I do not have any definitive refutation of the hardline sociobiologist who insists that our propensities for mating within racial groups are caused by our genes and not by differences in culture and history. There is no evidence in favor of any such view and, as I have noted, plenty of familiar phenomena that suggest the third option I have sketched. In the remainder of this essay, I want to explore the implications of that "mixed" approach to concepts of human race. I shall start with a closely connected notion, that of ethnicity.

VI

The core of the view that there are ethnic groups is that distinct sets of cultural items, including lore, habits of interpersonal interaction, self-conceptions, and behavior, are transmitted across the generations by a process akin to biological inheritance. In recent years, careful studies of cultural transmission (Cavalli-Sforza and Feldman, 1982; Boyd and Richardson, 1985) have revealed both similarities and differences with the process in which genes are passed on. Plainly cultural inheritance can involve more than two "parents," and some of the "parents" may even belong to the same biological generation as their "offspring." Nonetheless, there are enough common features to enable us to pick out cultural lineages with the same formal structure previously discerned in races. Thus we can introduce a concept of *ethnicity* meeting the following conditions:

E1 An ethnic division consists in a division of *Homo sapiens* into nonoverlapping subsets. These subsets are the pure ethnicities. Individuals who do not belong to any of the subsets are of mixed ethnicity.

E2 Pure ethnicities are closed under cultural transmission. That is, the cultural "offspring" of "parents" all of whom are of ethnicity E are of ethnicity E.

E3 All cultural "ancestors" of any member of any pure ethnicity are of that ethnicity. If someone is of ethnicity E, then all their cultural "parents" are of ethnicity E.

However, if these conditions are to be realized in a world in which different cultures collide, it will be important to impose restrictions on cultural parentage. Liberal definitions of "parent" would allow anyone who transmitted any item to another person to count as a cultural parent—so that attendance in a classroom taught by someone of a different ethnic heritage would automatically disqualify a child from belonging to a pure ethnicity. I shall tolerate considerable vagueness in deciding how to resolve this problem, proposing that cultural "parents" be those who are responsible for the dominant items of the offspring's culture, where this should be taken to consist of those facets of lore, habits, conceptions, and behavior that are both central to the person's life and distinct from parallel items in the rival surrounding cultures. Roughly, the idea is that cultural parents transmit something that is important for the people they influence and play a role that could not have been filled by others from a different culture.

A second important modification that might be made is to recognize lines of cultural descent with respect to particular areas of human life: so we might focus on the transmission of religious beliefs and practices, musical tastes, food preferences, and so forth. Looking at the lines of descent generated in these various areas, we might discover that they were importantly different, that it was impossible to assign people to single "ethnicities," but that all of us belong to a variety of cultural lineages, some of which might match biological lineages while others were quite distinct. Alternatively, we might find that whatever field of human life we considered, the division into cultural lineages always produced the same divisions, in which case we would be justified in speaking about a single ethnicity to which a person belonged. We could then go on to ask the question of the relations between ethnicities so defined, and races.

Assuming that we obtained consistent lines of cultural transmission across different areas of human life, we could construct ethnicities by considering lines of cultural descent from founder populations, supposing, as before, that the $n + 1$st generation of the ethnicity consists of all those whose cultural parents belong either to the nth generation or are one another, and who have at least one cultural parent in the nth generation (these complications are needed to circumvent the problem of within generation cultural transmission). As in the case of races, if ethnicities are to be important they should be able to maintain themselves when they come into contact. So we should demand that genuine ethnicities have mechanisms of partial cultural isolation. Even in a multicultural society, the chief influences on new generations should not be thoroughly mixed. This criterion might be formulated by demanding that only a small percentage of offspring have cultural parents from different ethnicities, or by requiring that for almost all offspring the set of cultural parents has a very large majority from a single ethnicity.

The main thought behind the approach I have taken to the concept of race is that the two systems typically harmonize—indeed, that they reinforce one

another. On the biological level, interracial mating is limited through the differences in the cultural items acquired by members of different races, that is,
because different ethnicities belong to different races. On the cultural level, patterns of culture are preserved because culture is usually primarily transmitted by
parents and other family members (who may also influence the receptivity to
other potential cultural parents), who belong to the same race and share the
same ethnicity. One particular consequence that I have emphasized above is
that past racism shapes the attitudes of people today, in particular their attitudes
to sexual union, and that this can maintain patterns of mating that are skewed
toward one's own group.

The picture I have been assuming allows for the possibility that each race
might correspond to many different ethnicities, although it suggests that the
transmission of culture through any of these ethnicities serves to lower the probability that someone will marry a person of a different race. One way to question
this assumption (already noted above) is to break down the notion that ethnicities are holistic entities that come one to a person. Just as eliminativists about
race argue for the appreciation of human diversity without supposing a discrete
system of divisions, so it might be suggested that cultural transmission affects all
of us in slightly different—or very different—ways, and that ethnic boundaries
are blurred. Further, following my oversimplified analysis of the causes of
propensities for not mating out, it might seem possible to detach the general feature of many systems of cultural transmission that creates the incipient barrier
to interracial marriage from the more specific characteristics of ethnicities. To
put the point concretely, perhaps a society-wide readjustment of economic and
social relationships among black people and white people would undercut both
the fears and the resentments, leading to a situation in which, while certain distinctive cultures (religious traditions, styles of music and of literature) were
retained within lines of cultural descent, the barriers to interracial marriage were
substantially weakened. If the family of the white fiancée of the young black
man no longer worries that she will be plunged into poverty, and if black women
no longer see the black man as a scarce resource in a world in which few black
men come to manhood with auspicious prospects, then whether or not differences in other forms of culture (ranging from tastes in food through styles of
socializing to appreciation of forms of art and entertainment) are lessened, the
pressures against interracial marriage may be substantially released. Hence it
would not be necessary that cultural transmission *as a whole* become more
mixed, but simply that certain background elements that affect part of every
system of cultural transmission be changed.

We currently know too little about exactly how to reconstruct ethnicities
and how to apply the reconstruction to understand their bearing on people's
decisions and actions (for example on their decisions about whom to marry). In
proposing a fairly abstract account of ethnicities, I presuppose a particular appa-

ratus which seems promising in coming to terms with systems of cultural transmission. It may turn out that this proposal fails at any number of levels: (1) the quasi-Mendelian formalism in terms of transmission of discrete items of culture is just inadequate to the phenomenon of cultural transmission; (2) when that formalism is applied it may reveal a parallel situation to that found in the case of conventional racial divisions, to wit that minority ethnicities are "mixed" whereas majority ethnicities are "pure"; (3) the mapping from ethnicity to race may not be many–one; and (4) detachable elements within the system of cultural transmission and/or common features which shape all such systems within the society (e.g., background economic and social inequalities) may play a dominant role in certain kinds of decisions and actions (e.g., decisions about marriage). All of these points need detailed exploration. Here I intend only to raise what I take to be important neglected questions about ethnicity and its connection with race, and to consider the consequence of *fallible* assumptions. Thus I do not wish to claim that it is plainly impossible to detach those features of cultural transmission that lower probabilities of interracial marriage from other parts of the system of cultural transmission.[19]

VII

I now want to explore the connections between race and ethnicity in a bit more detail, by considering how biological races and ethnic identities might both break down.

Suppose, first, that cultural transmission were to become much more heterogeneous, so that children became influenced by the ideas, habits, and lore of what now count as many distinct ethnicities. If my conjecture about the mechanisms underlying the differences in probabilities of intraracial and interracial mating is correct, then the more multicultural society might exhibit an increased frequency of interracial mating. This increased frequency would, in its turn, be likely to generate an increase in the proportion of children of mixed ethnicity. Perhaps that mixture, in its turn, would continue to erode the (partial) isolating mechanisms among races. We can envisage a spiral toward a point at which the divisions by race and by ethnicity both disappear.

All this is speculative, and the interface between biology and culture is a region in which speculations should be taken with great caution. Nonetheless, I think it is worth considering the consequences of this speculation, asking, in particular, whether it points to a constraint on our future social practices.

I began by considering what I characterized as a relatively benign social use of the concept of race, envisaging serious discussion of the desirability of trans-racial adoption. One important question to ask is whether the issues can properly be framed in terms of ethnicities—is the significant question whether trans-*ethnic* adoption is desirable? At first sight, this appears to be quite wrong. The child's ethnicity is not already defined at birth (or at the early age at which she is adopted): her ethnicity will be identified through the cultural influences that impinge upon her, and there is no issue of *violating* an ethnic identity she already has. Supposing we assume that the cultural milieu into which she will be pitched through adoption will be rich, whereas, if she is left where she is, she will have to struggle simply to survive, there would seem to be no reasons for opposing the adoption.

Now, there seem to me to be two important ways of undermining this argument, one that attends to the consequences at the level of the entire population (or species) and the other that makes explicit use of the concept of race. The most forceful way to express the first is to envisage a situation in which there are two ethnicities, E_1 and E_2. Suppose that children born to parents of one of these ethnicities, E_1 say, routinely experience various forms of deprivation, that they have little chance of benefitting from the richness of the culture, that, in many instances, biological parents simply lack resources to provide their children with access to significant parts of the culture, that with high frequency those children are simply left to rot. The alternative ethnicity, E_2 by contrast, is well-endowed, and children reared by people in that ethnicity are assured physical well-being and security as well as a rich cultural milieu. Acting in the interests of the children, well-meaning social planners allow the adoption of a large proportion of children from the economically disadvantaged ethnicity, so that the cultural traditions of that ethnicity are weakened and finally disappear. They reason, quite understandably, that issues of survival may swamp considerations of cultural transmission.

Conservationists are property concerned about the extinction of biological species. We should probably be even more worried by the thought that major cultural traditions might vanish: diversity enriches our lives. However, for each individual, it may be better if that individual belongs to the dominant ethnicity. Hence a social policy directed toward individuals may bring about a situation in which valuable cultural traditions are lost.

An obvious remedy, roughly realized in contemporary treatments of Native American ethnicities, is to "protect" cultural traditions that are in danger of disappearing either by enhancing the benefits of remaining within that ethnicity or, more likely, by offering to people of a particular racial group only limited opportunities for transferring to the dominant ethnicity. What I want to note is that, once again, the concept of race, and the ideal of harmony between race and ethnicity, figures here. The strategy of preserving a culture threatened with extinction is not implemented by proceeding in race-blind fashion, so that biological ancestry is irrelevant to who undertakes to continue the ethnic traditions. Genealogy is felt to make a difference: people should preserve "their" culture.

The second way of questioning trans-racial adoption makes explicit use of the concept of race, and tries to defend the principle that ethnicity and race should be in harmony. As I pointed out at the beginning, the phenotypic and genetic differences among racial groups for which we have any evidence are trivial. Nevertheless, those differences, particularly the differences in skin pigmentation and physiognomy, have come to be taken as markers that signal membership in distinct clusters of ethnicities. In societies which make the biological mistake of overestimating the significance of variations in trivial aspects of the phenotype, and the moral mistake of showing at least sporadic intolerance toward the ethnicities associated with certain biological markers, a person's manifest biological traits will make a difference to the way in which she is treated. Thus, even if she comes to think of herself as part of the dominant ethnic group, if she has the phenotype associated with another ethnicity, it is likely that she will be treated, at least periodically, as if she were not a full member of the ethnic group with which she identifies. Nor will she have available to her the strategies for coping with the repudiation of the culture assigned to her which have been passed on in the ethnicity associated with her phenotype. So the simple argument for the harmony between race and ethnicity emphasizes the idea that the biological and moral mistakes of the past live on in the present, and that, in a society that has not completely freed itself from racism, mismatch between race and ethnicity will leave people rootless and defenseless.

This argument allows for the possibility of a future in which tolerance for alternative cultures is so widespread that insignificant phenotypic markers lose their significance in our social interactions. Harmony between race and ethnicity is valuable only because it serves instrumental purposes in societies with residues of racism. Yet it may well be thought that this does not uncover the deep motivation for insisting on the match. Other things being equal, we may feel that individuals should identify with the culture of their biological ancestors, that they should sympathize with the pains and struggles of great-great-grandparents whom they know only as dim figures in a shadowy past. Or, to put it more negatively, that failure to carry on the culture of one's genealogy is a kind of betrayal. I want to conclude by scrutinizing this idea.

On grounds of promoting cultural diversity, as I have remarked, it is important that some group of people should continue the lore and customs of each ethnicity—including the one of my biological ancestors. But why should it fall to me to continue those traditions? Why should I not pick and choose, identifying with bits and pieces of cultures that are quite alien to the practices of my forebears? After all, cultural inheritance, unlike biological inheritance, is multiparental, and it would be possible for each of us to make cultural linkages with all sorts of people and traditions, weaving their contributions together into idiosyncratic patterns.[20] We can envisage, and perhaps educational reformers are already envisaging, a multicultural society in which we are all ethnic hybrids. What exactly would that society have lost?

Moved by a biological analogy, we can appreciate the possibility that cultural mixing would quickly destroy the distinctive contributions of pure ethnicities, ultimately arriving at a state of relative cultural homogeneity. When populations that have been geographically, but not reproductively, isolated are brought together to form a thoroughly panmictic unit, the range of phenotypic variation may quite dramatically decrease. Setting on one side arguments from the intrinsic value of cultural diversity, there is a very different style of consideration that develops the thought that our biological ancestors should have a special role in our identification of who we are. Perhaps we have a natural tendency to identify with our biological parents, so that we take pleasure in developing a sense of values that accords with theirs and feel pain when we are at odds with their customs and ideals. A society which made a radical divorce between ethnicity and biological ancestry would thus rub against the grain of human nature.

Like most claims about the relationship between biology and culture, this seems to me to be pure speculation. It is possible that people are "hardwired" to feel this special cultural kinship with their biological ancestors. It is also possible that our sense of identification with our biological forebears expresses a pattern of socialization common to all, or most, societies, a pattern that may itself be part of the legacy of racism and xenophobia. We simply don't know if ethnic roots have to be biological roots to make us happy.

Of course, the consequences of the two assumptions are quite different. If the propensity to identify with our biological parents would develop in us across the entire range of social environments that we might contrive (or, more exactly, the entire range in which people would flourish), then we can expect ethnicities to remain relatively pure, to be in harmony with divisions into races, and for the practices of dividing people by race and by ethnicity to reinforce one another in the fashion I suggested earlier. It would not inevitably follow that we were committed to a racist society, for the appreciation of difference might not be associated with the idea that distinct groups have distinct worth. Nevertheless, there are surely grounds for concern that, either because of cognitive or moral limitations, people would, in practice, think of their own culture not as one among many but as the best.

By contrast, if our descendants could fashion their own eclectic mixes of culture without violating any sense of identification with ancestors, then we can envisage a future in which the concepts of race and ethnicity both become irrelevant. Cultural hybridization could be so promiscuous that we would simply recognize the different cultural identities of all individuals, and, as I suggested earlier, it is likely that the breakdown of ethnicities would promote mating between people now identified as belonging to different races, thus undercutting what I have exposed as the biological significance of racial divisions. Perhaps in this imaginary society the inability to demarcate clear groups would promote greater tolerance or even a celebration of human diversity.

Something like this vision is what moves eliminativists. They worry that it is not enough to insist on the equality of races, and they propose that the most thorough way to combat racism is to discard the outworn concept of race. To this end, they contend that the concept of race lacks biological significance. I have been arguing that this is wrong, and that the interconnections between biological and cultural concepts are intricate. Those interconnections raise numerous empirical and moral questions that must be addressed if we are to decide if the vision of a society that abandons practices of racial division is either realizable or desirable.

NOTES

1. I owe an enormous amount to many people who have helped me with this project. My colleagues Jim Moore and David Woodruff gave me excellent advice about issues in anthropology and evolutionary biology (they should not, of course, be blamed for my errors). The first version of this essay was written for a wonderful conference on concepts of race and racism, organized by Jorge Garcia at Rutgers University in the fall of 1994. The high standard of the discussion at that conference and the combination of incisiveness and open-mindedness among the people with whom I interacted were a vivid reminder of how productive philosophical exchange can be. I am grateful to Lorenzo Simpson for his extremely thoughtful comments which have helped me reshape much of my raw material. The comments of David Goldberg, Leonard Harris, John Ladd, Howard McGary, Michele Moody-Adams, Lucius Outlaw, Ken Taylor, and Gregory Trianosky-Stilwell have also been valuable. I am particularly indebted to conversations with Anthony Appiah, Amy Gutmann, Michael Hardimon, and Naomi Zack. Finally, I would like to thank Michael Hardimon for some wonderfully constructive comments on the penultimate draft and Leonard Harris for his encouragement, as well as for his invitation to contribute to this volume.

2. This should become clear in Section VII. See, in particular, the remarks about Anthony Appiah's postracialist project in n20.

3. The norm of reaction of a trait is the function that, for given genotypes, maps constellations of environmental variables onto phenotype. It is most conveniently represented as a graph showing the variation of phenotype with environment. Fundamental points about the importance of norms of reaction are made in (Lewontin, 1974). I attempt to articulate those points and defend the notion of a norm of reaction against recent criticisms (including some from Lewontin himself) in (Kitcher, forthcoming).

4. It is well to acknowledge, from the beginning, that the conceptual clarification I try to offer here should be viewed as a prelude to empirical investigations. Throughout the essay I shall appeal to the partial findings that are currently available. However, my main purpose is to pose precise questions whose answers ought to be employed in tackling the tricky moral and social issues that surround the notions of race and ethnicity.

5. The phrases is Dobzhansky's.

6. Later in this essay (Section VII) I shall indicate why I believe we need a biological notion to understand this example.

7. I shall elaborate this point at some length below, where I try to articulate the intuitive concept of ethnicity that is often employed in social discussions.

8. Caution is needed here. Many biologists are driven to avoid the notion of race because they are mindful of the harm that the concept has done in its application to *Homo sapiens*. Others are moved by the difficulties of any kind of intraspecific taxonomic category (lucidly pointed out in Wilson and Brown, 1953). Yet, under many different names, the idea of intraspecific divisions lingers

in ecological and evolutionary studies, where biologists recognize stocks, strains, breeds, evolutionarily stable units, geographical races, morphs, and so forth. Without commitment to the general applicability of an intraspecific category, it is possible to maintain that, with respect to particular species, a division of the species into biologically significant subunits is profitable. This kind of local pragmatism, which seems to me to permeate contemporary biological practice, provides the basis for my explorations here.

9. The best argument for eliminativism is that if this requirement is honored, virtually the entire species will turn out to be of mixed race. I shall consider this argument in some detail below.

10. However, it is worth noting explicitly that the time of origination can be chosen to suit the purposes of the investigation, and there is no reason to think that this time must always be in the very distant past. As I shall point out below, the claim that racialization is now occurring in America might turn out to be defensible.

11. Or distinctive frequencies of particular alleles. Note that it does not matter whether or not the genetic (or phenotypic) differences are important or trivial. The concepts of race characterized here have no commitment to the racist doctrines repudiated in Section I—just as Dobzhansky's use of a concept of race for nonhuman species made no claim that the variant characters maintained in the races of snails, flies, and beetles were particularly important.

12. Note that it is an empirical question whether the notion of race I am reconstructing will pick out any racial divisions at all, and, if it does, whether it will pick out (for example) the "big three." In the next section, I shall make some tentative claims about the racial divisions I think most likely.

13. For present purposes I ignore all kinds of complexities about how to draw species divisions. I have argued elsewhere for the need for a plurality of species concepts (see Kitcher, 1984), but my pluralism is quite compatible with recognizing the role that reproductive patterns play in making taxonomic divisions among sexually reproducing organisms. The approach of the text is also consistent both with Mayr's more negative approach ("look at which organisms *don't* interbreed") and the more recent attention paid to positive cues ("materecognition systems").

14. In conversation Naomi Zack has made a forceful case for (1), and, in the original discussion at Rutgers, Michele Moody-Adams independently gave a lucid presentation of the same point. A number of people referred me to a seminal essay by Adrian Piper (Piper, 1993), in which she summarizes the biological and anthropological sources for (1) (see her footnote 27). In public and private exchanges at Rutgers, both Anthony Appiah and Amy Gutmann argued for (2). I am grateful to all these people for pressing the case so well.

15. It is worth noting that the first episode, the intergroup unions in Virginia, looks very like the standard situation for hybridization among nonhuman animals. Individuals at the limits of their ranges sometimes have little chance of mating with conspecifics, and mate with a member of a closely related species. We could regard the two populations of servants in the colonies as cut off from the main body of the groups from which they came, partly by geographical, partly by social causes.

16. It is, I think, peculiar that eliminativists, who are surely moved by repugnance at the horrible things that have been done in the name of racial purity, should think that the breakdown of the notion of race is due to the fact that Southern white men were often prepared to rape black women or bribe them into sexual unions.

17. Starting with the non-dimensional notion, we could then build up the full notion of race, which I have explicitly taken to be a historical notion, by considering intervals of times at each of which the groups under study count as nondimensional races. This procedure raises the obvious question: How long must the reproductive disconnection last for the lineages to count as separate races? I shall come to terms with this, and other questions that turn on the difficulties of degreed notions, at the end of this section.

18. A recent report in the *New York Times* (July 4, 1996) suggests that rates of interracial marriage, especially those involving black women and white men, are on the increase. But the report has two interesting aspects. First, this seems to be a trend among middle-class people (and, as I shall

suggest below, economic and class factors loom large in the maintenance of racial divisions). Second, a hypothesis about the cause suggests that young educated black women greatly outnumber young educated black men, so that their choices of mates are limited unless they accept white men as potential partners. If this is correct, then the situation would again be analogous to that of members of nonhuman populations at the limits of the species range.

It is also worth noting that there is a significant amount of black-Hispanic mating as well as a significant amount of Hispanic-white mating, so that Hispanics could serve as a "bridge" population between the two groups (this point was made in the discussion at Rutgers by Gregory Trianosky-Stilwett). Only in the light of much more extensive knowledge will we be able to discover if the resulting population structure is more like that of an effectively panmictic population or the case of "ring races."

19. It is worth noting that evidence for (4) might be derived from study of patterns of mating among indentured servants, both black and white, in pre-revolutionary Virginia. If the population of servants showed a far higher rate of interbreeding than is now found between African Americans and Caucasians, an obvious explanation would be that economic disparities and the history of injustice have played a major role in the dramatic lowering of the rate of intermarriage.

20. This prospect is defended with great eloquence by Anthony Appiah (1996). Appiah uses eliminativism about race as a steppingstone to recommending a future in which the contributions of all cultures are available to everyone. In my judgment, the points for which he wants to argue can be clarified by probing the connections between race and ethnicity in ways I have begun here. Indeed, many of the issues that divide Appiah from his critics seem to me to require empirical exploration of issues posed in Section VI: we need to know just how lines of biological descent and cultural descent interact with one another. Even if Appiah were to view my earlier reconstruction of the concept of race as mistaken, I think he would still have to confront questions about patterns of mating and biological inheritance and how these affect and are affected by cultural transmission, for precisely those questions are pertinent to the kinds of futures he imagines. Those who oppose his "liberal cosmopolitanism" often seem to he making different assumptions about the answers to those questions, and I think it important to identify the empirical issues and try to resolve them.

REFERENCES

Appiah. 1996.

Barton, N. H., and G. M. Hewitt. 1985. "Analysis of Hybrid Zones." *Annual Review of Ecology and Systematics* 16: 113–48.

Bateson, P. P. G. 1980. "Optimal Outbreeding and the Development of Sexual Preferences in Japanese Quail." *Zeitschrift für Tierpsychologie* 53: 231–44.

———. 1982. "Preferences for Cousins in Japanese Quail." *Nature* 295: 236–37.

Bloc, N. J. 1996. Review of *The Bell Curve* (Herrnstein and Murray, 1994), *Cognition*.

Block. N. J., and G. Dworkin. 1972. "IQ, Heritability, and Inequality." *Philosophy and Public Affairs*.

Boyd, R., and P. Richardson. 1985. *Culture and the Evolutionary Process*. Chicago: University of Chicago Press.

Brierly, J. K. 1970. *A Natural History of Man*. Madison, N.J.: Fairleigh Dickinson University Press.

Cavalli-Sforza, L. L. 1969. "Genetic Drift in an Italian Population." In *Readings from Scientific American: Biological Anthropology*. New York: Freeman.

———. 1994. *The History and Geography of Human Genes*. Princeton: Princeton University Press.

Cavalli-Sforza, L. L., and M. Feldman. 1982. *Cultural Transmission: A Quantitative Approach*. Princeton: Princeton University Press.

Davenport, C. B. 1930. "The Mingling of Races." In E.V. Cowdry, ed., *Human Biology and Racial Welfare*. Originally published by Paul B. Hoeber, Inc., reprinted College Park, Md.: McGrath Publishing Company.

Davis, F. J. 1991. *Who Is Black?* University Park: Pennsylvania State University Press.

Diamond, I. 1994. "Race without Color." *Discover* 15, no. 11: 82–89.

Dobzhansky, T. 1970. *Genetics of the Evolutionary Process*. New York: Columbia University Press.

Gould, S. J. 1981. *The Mismeasure of Man*. New York: Norton.

Herrnstein, R., and C. Murray. 1994. *The Bell Curve*. New York: The Free Press.

Kitcher, P. 1984. "Species." *Philosophy of Science* 51: 308–33.

———. 1985. *Vaulting Ambition: Sociobiology and the Quest for Human Nature*. Cambridge, MA: MIT Press.

Laumann, E. O., et al. 1994. *The Social Organization of Sexuality*. Chicago: University of Chicago Press.

Lewontin, R. C. 1974. "The Analysis of Variance and the Analysis of Causes." Reprinted in N. J. Block and G. Dworkin, eds., *The IQ Controversy*. New York: Pantheon, pp. 179–93.

———. 1982 *Human Diversity*. San Francisco: Freeman.

Littlejohn, M. J., and Watson, G. F. 1995 "Hybrid Zones and Homogamy in Australian Frogs." *Annual Review of Ecology and Systematics* 16: 85–112.

Livingstone, F. B. 1962. "On the Nonexistence of Human Races." In A. Montagu, ed., *The Concept of Race*. New York: Free Press.

Marks, J. 1994. "Patterns of Human Biodiversity," unpublished manuscript.

Mayr, E. 1942. *Systematics and the Origin of Species*. New York: Columbia University Press.

———. 1963. *Animal Species and Evolution*. Cambridge, MA: Harvard University Press.

———. 1970. *Populations, Species, and Evolution*. Cambridge, MA: Harvard University Press.

Michael, R. T., et al. 1994. *Sex in America*. Boston: Little, Brown.

Molnar, S. 1992. *Human Variation*. Englewood Cliffs, N.J.: Prentice-Hall.

Montagu, A. 1964. *The Concept of Race*. New York: Free Press.

Piper, A. 1993. "Two Kinds of Discrimination." *Yale Journal of Criticism* 6: 25–74.

Porterfield, E. 1984. *Black and White Mixed Marriages*. Chicago: Nelson-Hall.

Rushton, J-P. 1994. *Race, Evolution, and Behavior*. New Brunswick, N.J.: Transaction.

Wilson, E. O., and Brown, W. L. 1953. "The Subspecies Concept and Its Taxonomic Application." *Systematic Zoology* 2: 97–111.

———. 1975 *Sociobiology: The New Synthesis*. Cambridge, MA: Harvard University Press.

Zack, N. 1993. *Race and Mixed Race*. Philadelphia: Temple University Press.

Objectivist Explanations of Racism

5. The Making of Global Tribes
Joel Kotkin

THERE IS NO HINT of grandeur, no shining corporate logo, no edifice of modern art outside the imposing nineteenth-century mansion on Faubourg Saint Honoré. The stuffy, carpeted interior, with antique clocks and pictures, exudes more the hushed, reverently preserved atmosphere of a museum than the manic bustle of a worldwide financial empire.

Alone, in an office lined with books and photos, Edmond Rothschild sits nervously, pondering his far-flung concerns. Today the baron, whose title is a holdover from an epoch when his family dominated the finances of the aristocracies of Europe, seems in ill humor, agitated by the political turmoil in Yugoslavia, Argentina's chronic debt, and rising religious fanaticism in the Middle East, among other global problems.

A man born to wealth, Rothschild could well have lived without confronting such problems, not to mention the preoccupations of his chairmanship of over a dozen financial firms spanning from the West Indies to Tel Aviv, including the family's sprawling Paris-based Compagnie Financière.[1] Yet, like generations before him, he believes that being a Rothschild means choosing not to live comfortably from the accumulations of the past.

This, perhaps more than anything else, sets the Rothschilds apart from other wealthy families of the nineteenth and early twentieth centuries who long ago faded into relative obscurity. Though they possessed all the accoutrements of the landed gentry, the Rothschilds rarely opted to lose themselves in the good life. They chose instead to accumulate capital and invest:

Joel Kotkin, "The Making of Global Tribes," *Tribes*. New York: Random House, 1993, pp. 14–35, reprinted with the permission of Random House Publishing Co.

We are different for a simple reason. Many families disappear in one generation because they don't realize that whatever they had, you must have discipline and that you have to work whether you like it or not. Otherwise why not become a drug addict or a drunk.

It's very simple. Discipline. I received it from my mother and my father and hopefully my son is going to give it to his children. It's the discipline of tradition.[2]

For the Rothschilds, however, the "discipline of tradition" meant something quite different from merely the noblesse oblige that has been the creed of the best wealthy Europeans since the ascendancy of capitalism. They did not suffer the hangover of Medieval ideals about the piety of poverty—or the supposed wickedness of profit seeking.[3] Indeed, when Nathan Rothschild, the founder of the British house, was asked in the 1830s whether he wished his children to be as capitalistic as himself, he responded: "I wish them to give mind, and soul, and body, and everything to business; that is the way to be happy."[4]

Within less than a century, this ethos primed an ascendancy so great that Baron James Rothschild, the Paris-based son of Frankfurt coin dealer Mayer Amschel, stood, in popular accounts of the time, as "the absolute monarch of the financial world," with the power to determine the fiscal fare of nations. By the 1840s the family, in the estimation of Austria's Prince Metternich, possessed more influence over the affairs of France than any foreign government, save that of its arch-rival, Great Britain.[5]

But the Rothschilds did not live purely by a capitalist ethos, what German Chancellor Otto von Bismarck disparagingly referred to as their "absurd desire to leave to each of their children as much as they themselves inherited."[6] No single-minded worship of money in itself, Edmond Rothschild insists, would have maintained a family tradition against the temptation to fully assimilate over the generations. Along with love of business, the Rothschilds remain united by another, larger vocation, one extending beyond business, family, and even nation—the vocation of being Jews. As his cousin David Rothschild, who heads up a family merchant bank not far from the squat estate on Faubourg Saint Antoine, puts it: "Judaism creates the cement—the Jewish family has the tradition of solidarity."[7]

THE WORLD AS STAGE

At a time when global economics is often perceived in the abstract, defined by cold statistics and computer-driven models, it might seem odd, even anachronistic, to speak of "the discipline of tradition" and ethnic "solidarity" as critical elements in understanding the ways of commerce. Yet the history of modern capitalism has been shaped largely by the progress of such global tribes, dispersed groups held together by a common culture.

The power of global tribes derives from their successful coalescing of two principles that, in classic liberal thought, have been separated: an intrinsic "tribal" sense of a unique historical and ethnic identity and the ability to adapt to a cosmopolitan global economy. In this respect, the Jews present the archetypical, but hardly the only, example of a global tribe. Over the past four centuries the dynamics of various global diasporas (from the Greek, meaning a scattering) have shaped the world economy, from the great ascendancy of the British and their descendants in the seventeenth century to the recent growth in influence of the Asiatic global tribes, principally the Chinese, Japanese, and Indians. Other smaller but influential groupings—such as Armenians, Cubans, and Palestinians—also represent what Wesleyan University's Khachig Toloyan calls "transnational groups," often combining homelands with colonies dispersed around the world.[8]

These dispersed ethnic groups have exercised a disproportionate influence on the growth patterns of nations, cities, and regions. On this level, the continuous interaction of capitalism with dispersed ethnic groups—not just the staid history of financial flows or the heroic stories of nation builders—constitutes one of the critical elements in the evolution of the global economy. As the economist Joseph Schumpeter observed:

> A process [such as] railroadization, or the electrification of the world transcends the boundaries of individual countries in such a way as to be more truly described as one world-wide process than as the sum of distinct national ones. Capitalism itself is, both in the economic and the sociological sense, essentially one process, with the whole earth as its stage.[9]

In this process, global tribes represent a critical dynamic element—the historical protagonist—on the world economic stage. Where they appear, new combinations of technology, industry, and culture flourish. When they leave, by choice or through compulsion, the commercial lifeblood, more often than not, runs dry; to the countries that subsequently receive them come the blessings of new ideas, technologies, and intelligence. "Every advance of culture," noted economist Carl Bucher, "commences with a new period of wandering."[10]

At the onset of transnational commerce, even before the emergence of the Jews as traders, the Phoenicians, arguably the world's first global tribe, served as key transmitters of culture, technology, and products across the ancient world. These "bedouins of the sea" not only sold products from remote places such as Britain, with its tin deposits, or silver-rich Spain, they also brought the art of mining to the Greeks.[11] As advisers to rulers in Babylon, Ashur, Persepolis, and

Thebes,[12] they helped marry technology and resources from India and interior Africa with those of classical antiquity.[13]

In the ensuing centuries, other largely commercial empires, perhaps most prominently the Portuguese[14] and the Dutch, also played important economic roles, developing trade and political spheres of influence from Europe to the furthest reaches of Africa, Asia, and the Americas. Yet no global tribe in history has endured longer than the Jews. Forerunner of all other global tribes, from the British to the modern Asian diasporas, the Jews developed a unique set of attitudes toward themselves and the world. In a pattern seen today most noticeably with the Japanese or the Chinese, the Jews maintained a ferocious loyalty to their own identity even as their power reached its fullest expression through dispersion. Mormon historian Spencer Palmer has observed:

> A sense of *insularity* that the Japanese and the Jews nurtured was *combined with openness to the outside world*. This has made the Jews and the Japanese very conservative, but at the same time very innovative.[15]

Serving as middlemen, traders, and arbitrageurs of information and products on a global basis, much like today's Japanese, they appeared in most of the major cities of the known world, representing, in Oswald Spengler's somewhat derogatory phrase, "a new kind of nomad cohering unstably in fluid masses, the parasitical city-dweller. . . ."[16] Yet for their host countries these "nomads" became indispensable not only as traders but as transmitters and translators of knowledge among at least three major cultures—Christian, Arabic, and Indian.[17] Indeed, according to at least one medieval account, it was a Jewish scholar, sent to India by an Arabic ruler, who brought back the Indian numerical inscriptions thereafter widely known as "arabic" letters.[18]

In Spain, first under the Moors and later under the Christian kings, Jews rose to intellectual heights perhaps unequaled in modern times. But with the expulsion of 1492, as Spanish social critic Angel Gavinet has observed, Spain emptied itself of much of its scientifically curious population. The Ottoman sultan, who received much of this gifted population, with its cadre of cartographers, swordsmiths, and metallurgists, was astounded by his good fortune. "And you call this man, the King of Spain, a politically wise King, he who impoverishes his kingdom to enrich ours?" asked Bejazet II, whose descendants would use Jewish physicians extensively over the next several centuries.[19] "I receive the Jews with open arms."[20]

Later these same Jews from Spain and Portugal would play critical roles in the emergence of new world cities, such as Amsterdam, London, and, eventually, New York. Meanwhile the Hispanic peninsula, after a century of rapid conquests, fell into a long period of decline.

When the Jews left their ghettos and entered European society, even sympathetic observers supposed that the Jews would lose their separate identity. In the early 1830s, for instance, the poet Heinrich Heine, a German-Jewish apostate, foresaw the inevitable assimilation of Jews in France as the "witty acid" of rationalism demolished all traces of ethnic identification.[21] Similar views were held by Karl Marx, son of a Jewish convert to Christianity, who believed that in the struggle for a socialist rational universe all such ethnic distinctions would fade away, replaced by the overarching imperatives of class.[22]

Others, particularly among the Anglo-American elite, saw the Jews as a hopelessly backward people, largely incapable of adjusting to the new demands of advanced capitalist societies. One prominent academic, H. H. Godard, director of research at a school for mentally impaired children in New Jersey, in 1913 found over four out of every five Jewish immigrants to be "feebleminded." Godard and others of his time wondered if the best use for the Jews would be to employ them at tasks requiring an "immense amount of drudgery" that would be unacceptable to more advanced and intelligent races.[23]

Yet rather than causing the Jews to be overwhelmed by modernity or to lose their sense of identity, the encounter with the new conditions of advanced societies generally stimulated the Jews' progress. To some extent, notes Jewish religious scholar Jacob Neusner, the tribe's tradition of "systematic skepticism"—particularly in Talmudic reasoning—proved fortuitous in aiding its adjustment to the emerging technological order.[24] Once animated by the Western liberal and scientific spirit, no ethnic group anywhere in the world likely has produced so many gifted intellectuals per capita, whether in the sciences, the arts, or technology. As early as 1934, Jews, most of them Europeans, constituted the third largest group of recipients of Nobel Prizes, behind only the *countries* of Germany and France.[25] Later the Jewish intelligentsia shifted largely to North America, where by 1983 fully one-quarter of America's Nobel Prize winners were Jews.[26]

Even the depredations of Nazism failed to blunt their growth. Since the Holocaust, in fact, Jewish influence has reached levels unprecedented in their history; in virtually every society where they are represented in any significant number—from the Americas to South Africa and Europe[27]—their levels of educational achievement and occupational and economic status remain far above the national averages.[28] By the 1990s, in virtually every country of their dispersion they have achieved significant global influence in critical fields as varied as entertainment, fashion, communications, and finance.

THE BRITISH TRIBE: SHAPERS OF MODERNITY

Yet, if the Jews remain the prototype of the global tribe, the most important and enduring diaspora has been that originating in the British Isles. Although in the

Middle Ages they remained, in Lewis Mumford's phrase, "one of the backward countries of Europe,"[29] by the seventeenth and eighteenth centuries the British increasingly emerged as the primary force in the emerging global economy.

As with the Jews, much of the British genius stemmed from adapting to changing conditions and from an openness to acquiring skills from other cultures. And like the Japanese earlier in this century, they borrowed shamelessly the best techniques from France, Germany, or Asia for everything from shipbuilding to the construction of waterworks and spinning mills and land-clearance schemes.[30] As Defoe remarked, perhaps a bit unfairly, the British improved everything and invented nothing.[31]

In America, these innovative and inquiring traits became even further developed, primarily in New England. There, amidst the virgin forest, the migration of well-educated Puritans, as Max Weber later pointed out, brought an unprecedented explosion of "mass intellectualism" as well as "the rational spirit, the rationalization of the conduct of life in general and the rationalist economic ethos."[32] Later on, American industrialists—like their British—forebears spared little expense to garner technical and scientific knowledge from any source, most notably Great Britain itself.

Weber suggested that such acquisitive attitudes found their roots in the Calvinistic faith of the British and their progeny. Today, the epitome of this mentality can perhaps be found among the Mormons, a spin-off of radical British Protestantism, who in their institutions and faith have made even more explicit the connection between religion, on one hand, and education, science, and technology, on the other. "The Glory of God," explains the Mormon *Doctrine and Covenant*, "is intelligence."[33]

Driven by such attitudes, the British tribe ultimately developed most of what has come to be the basis of modern industrial, scientific, and technological process. Between 1750 and 1950, the two primary English-speaking nations, the United Kingdom and the United States, according to one detailed survey, accounted for nearly three out of every five major inventions, discoveries, and innovations in the world.[34]

As the world's first fully industrialized nation, Britain in particular carved out a unique hegemonic role in the developing world economy. Flush with the profits from its precocious technological leap, British financiers and industrialists—including the descendants of emigrants such as the Rothschilds—dominated the flow of capital throughout the world, financing, among other things, the emergence of eventual rivals for global dominance, including Japan, Germany, and Russia.[35]

But the most important edge for the expansion of the British tribe, and its culture, lay in the mass migration of English-speaking people. No other major competing European nation sent nearly as many of its native sons abroad; by 1700, for instance, over 400,000 British had left for North America, compared to only 27,000 Frenchmen. By that dare, Britons and their descendants totaled twice the number of expatriates represented by the peninsular Spaniards and Creoles, although their migration to the "new world" had begun a century earlier.[36]

Indeed, between 1832 and 1932 the British Isles accounted for over one-third of all European emigration, twice as much as any other country, the vast majority going to the United States and Britain's vast colonial possessions."[37] As no group before them, the British extended their diaspora—which includes the culturally distinct but English-speaking Irish—through the entire breadth of the known world, from North America and India to Africa and Oceania, everywhere carrying their technology and ways of doing business. By the mid-nineteenth century, British firms were constructing irrigation canals and railroads from India to Patagonia. In Asia, they established many of the great commercial centers such as Hong Kong, Bombay, Singapore, and Calcutta.[38]

Linked together by language, culture, and traditions of political economy, the descendants of Britain forged the largest cultural and economic diaspora in world history. Even as other Europeans—notably Germans and Italians—started to emigrate in large numbers to the new lands of settlement, nearly four in five found themselves forced to adjust to a country either under direct British control or, like the United States, an English-speaking former colony.[39]

Only the Great British tribe combined mass immigration with political and cultural dominance over the lands of settlement, in the process creating a mass global business and political culture never before seen in history. As early as the mid-nineteenth century, enthusiasts, including some espousing various theories of an inherent Anglo-Saxon racial supremacy, envisioned these various offshoots of Britain as part of a single global entity destined to rule the world. Charles Wentworth Dilke, a prominent purveyor of this idea, wrote in his 1868 polemic *Greater Britain*:

> There are men who say that Britain in her age will claim the Great England across the seas. They fail to see that she has done more than found plantations of her own—that she has imposed her institutions upon the offshoots of Germany, of Scandinavia, of Spain. Through America, England is speaking to the world.[40]

The power of this unique connection between the various offshoots of home islands helped sustain the cultural, financial, and political influence of Great Britain long after its decline from the pinnacle of global power. Through its diaspora, and most particularly the United States, the British tribe has created most of the critical standards—in everything from the world language to political economy, science and basic business practice—for the contemporary global economy.

Over the past half century, numerous attempts have been made to overcome these standards. European fascism, Arab petrodollars, communism, and, most recently, Islamic fundamentalism attempted to erect alternative systems of value, but none have come close to eclipsing those established by the progeny of Britain.

FROM NATIVES TO GLOBAL TRIBES

Yet the triumph of the Anglo-American system does not guarantee the continuing preeminence of its racial progenitors. In contrast to other groups who sought to create their own separate standards, the emerging Asian global tribes—the Japanese, the Chinese, and the Indians—chose instead to exploit the technologies and use the pathways established by the British diaspora. Now, with the center of economic dynamism shifting from Europe to Asia, these emerging global tribes are powerfully positioned for future expansion.

This reflects a major shift in the history of world capitalism. Until the mid-twentieth century, most Asians, with the possible exception of the Japanese, were relegated to the periphery of the world economy, serving largely as petty brokers or middlemen, with the central commanding heights belonging almost exclusively to Europeans. As Jean-Paul Sartre noted in 1966:

> Not so very long ago earth numbered two thousand million inhabitants: five hundred million men and one thousand five hundred million natives.[41]

The transition of the Indians, Chinese, and Japanese from the status of "natives" to that of global tribes stems largely from the fact that, like the Jews and Anglo-Saxons of earlier times, they have developed a strong, ethnically based, morally anchored form of capitalism. Today, the rationalistic capitalism developed by the Anglo-American diaspora has lost its grip on its ethical moorings, in particular, its intrinsic belief in family and self-help and the need for continuous self-improvement. Instead those virtues seem more evident today among the Asiatic global tribes. Indeed, in one critical measurement of capitalist vitality—investment as percentage of GDP—East Asia by 1990 led all regions of the world, investing in domestic industry at a rate 25 percent higher than America or Europe.[42]

The rise of globalized Asian tribes has had two crucial outstanding preconditions: the emergence of a comprehensively transnational economy and huge leaps in communication and transportation technology. The development of a world economy under British and later Anglo-American hegemony provided the critical infrastructure and, ultimately, the scientific and technological knowledge underpinning the expansion of Indians and Chinese into other regions of the world. Indeed, even as colonial rule devastated the patterns of life in India and elsewhere in Asia, European science and technology also slowly reawakened the slumbering technical, scientific, and industrial potential of the primary Asian ethnic groups. In the face of the obvious exploitation that took place in China and India, historian Tony Smith notes:

> These admittedly negative factors must . . . nevertheless be weighed against the transfer of technology and capital that association with the world market brought these lands and that there is no reason to think they would have developed on their own. In fact, one of the persistent myths propagated by southern nationalists and Marxists is that European and North American economic expansion inevitably occurred in a fashion detrimental to the economic well-being of the peoples on the periphery.[43]

It was under the British flag, first and foremost, that Indians—ranging from "semi-slaves" on tropical farms to government clerks and merchants—first gained a permanent foothold in Africa and the China coast.[44] Those in closest contact with the Europeans, such as the Parsis in the region around Bombay, quickly adopted the new technology and developed their own global trading network under British protection.[45] Ultimately British attempts to encourage science and technology[46] led to the founding of new schools and colleges, creating in the process a large cadre of technically competent Indians.

Similarly, the Chinese followed the British flag from Hong Kong to Malaysia and Singapore. They came initially as coolies, as petty merchants, and skilled artisans, first establishing themselves at the root of newly developing economies, then subsequently moving on to California and Hawaii. It was these Chinese, operating in areas fully integrated into the world economy, who were most directly exposed to the full force of European and American business; quickly they grasped the value of acquiring their technology, science, and organizational principles.[47]

Later on, Japanese traders, moving along trade routes developed largely by the Anglo-Americans, branched aggressively into diverse markets from the Americas to Southeast Asia. Writing in the late nineteenth century, Marx described Japan as a backward feudal society, much like Britain before its rise, offering "a truer picture of the European Middle Ages than all our history books."[48] Yet, faced with the sudden realization of their enormous technological backwardness, the Japanese after the Meiji Restoration of 1868 launched a modernization drive on a scale unprecedented in the non-European world. Students were dispatched to all the leading centers of Western technology, while at the same time new institutions of learning at home accelerated the creation of a local technical elite. Within five years of its founding in 1872, Tokyo's engineering college—today the Tokyo Institute of Technology—had become the largest technological university in the world.[49]

Yet, despite these efforts, until the latter part of the twentieth century

Anglo-Americans and other Europeans dominated the financial, transportation, and communication infrastructure. But as international business expanded—by the 1980s growing more than twice the rate of global GNP[50]—the gap between Asia and the American-European world began to dissipate, creating a more equal relationship between the two largest economic regions.

Sparked initially by American aid, investment, and technology, Southeast Asia by the 1970s clearly emerged as the world's fastest growing economic region, growing at an average of two to three times the older industrial economies. Equally important, Asia's population between 1950 and 1990 jumped to roughly half the world's total, while the share of Europe and North America combined slipped by nearly one-third, to under 15 percent of humanity.[51] This development played to the basic strengths of the Asian tribes, who long had focused more of their efforts on the area, as opposed to the Europeans and Americans, who have primarily been interested in each other's regions. By the late 1980s, both Japanese-owned and Chinese-owned firms were investing twice as much as firms from the United States in rapidly growing nations such as Thailand, Indonesia, and Malaysia.[52]

At the same time, the rapid improvements in communication and transportation technology accelerated the development of the key Asian tribes. In the past, dispersed peoples like the Jews were forced to operate on the basis of only infrequent, and often unreliable, contact. A sunk ship, or a road closed by bandits, could interrupt the critical flow of information among the various tribal centers. Today instantaneous communications link dispersed groups with an ease unimaginable to the scattered traders of the past. Between 1980 and 1989, for example, the volume of phone traffic across international lines increased more than 400 percent in the United States,[53] while the cost of transcontinental calls has been dropping roughly fivefold per decade.[54]

Moreover, since the end of the Second World War, Asian tribal links have been further enhanced by the creation of a comprehensive global air transport system. Because the real cost of air travel has dropped—by roughly 50 percent—since 1950,[55] the opportunities for regular contact among dispersed groups have exploded. Between 1978 and 1988, the number of passengers transported by plane more than doubled, and by the year 2000 is expected to more than double once again, with the highest rates of growth expected in the Pacific region.[56]

These developments have helped create a world where dispersed Asians, rather than being culturally isolated, can now find in most major world cities easy access to everything from Asian-language broadcasts and newspapers to shops selling videotapes in Japanese, Mandarin, or Hindi. The "little Tokyos," "little Punjabs," or Chinatowns of the late twentieth century are more than merely quaint reproductions of ethnic villages; increasingly, they are transplanted portions of transnational world cities, complete with modern telecommunications linkages to other key tribal outposts. The trip from Taipei to Monterey Park, California, therefore now resembles little more than a commute across different parts of the same Chinese world city.

These new technologies also have facilitated the successful globalization of traditional, highly consensual Asian business forms, from the Japanese *keiretsu* to the Indian joint-family companies to Chinese family networks. Certainly Asian entrepreneurs felt themselves compelled to study Western science, learn the basics of Anglo-Saxon business practices, gain fluency in English or French, don the coat and tie. As the old south Indian proverb puts it: "if you put on the garb of a dog, you must bark like one."[57] Yet, through the use of fax machines, telephones, and direct computer linkups, Asian firms have managed to maintain, in a way never before possible, their traditional forms without dissipating their competitive advantage.

The new technology has been particularly critical in allowing for the outward expansion of Asian family-owned businesses. At the family-owned Chung Cheong Group, faxes and frequent air connections allow for the monitoring of literally dozens of businesses scattered from Los Angeles to Thailand without the need for a central control system or a formal board of directors. Using the new technology, decisions can be made between Hong Kong and Zurich more reliably than in the 1920s, for example, when the group's patriarch relied on the often unreliable telegraph service from Canton to Hong Kong. Members of the clan even keep up on family gossip through a regular newsletter called "The Chungs' Times," faxed regularly from Los Angeles to family members dispersed globally.[58]

The emergence of the new Asian global tribes, with their philosophies and ways of doing business, marks a new epoch in the history of capitalism. Peoples who were once remotely distant to each other suddenly find themselves face-to-face in the marketplace, the stock exchange, the labor market. Indeed, a nineteenth-century English or American entrepreneur, transported to our times, would be struck by nothing so much as the leading role played in the affairs of London or New York by Japanese, Chinese, Indians, and Arabs. Where once the only strangers were the Jews, today there are other Rothschilds of differing complexions operating along networks far vaster than just a few nations in western and central Europe.

THE VOCATION OF UNIQUENESS

Yet it is their enduring sense of group identification and global linkages, far more than their dispersion or the extensiveness of their business empires, that most clearly distinguishes global tribes from other migrating populations. In other migrating groups—such as Italians or Germans—the acquisition of skills and intelligence has meant a quick assimilation into the cultures, and even the elites, of their adopted countries. For global tribes, this process of assimilation tends to be slower, less sure, and attenuated by the continued tug of old affinities and memories.

For many global tribes, depredations visited upon them by others have created particularly acute attachments among scattered members of the group, something most clearly seen in ties among diaspora Jews and Israel due to the Holocaust.[59] Similarly, the cohesion of Armenians worldwide developed through their centuries-long struggle against Muslim invaders who conquered and persecuted them, culminating in the infamous Turkish genocide after World War I. Memory of this genocide is so intense that even everyday articles left over from that era—dishes, photographs, clothing—are treated with reverence. A priest at a recent Armenian service, reports author Jenny Phillips, compared the handling of one such relic, a torn pair of child's trousers, to "touching the robe of the Lord."[60]

Like the Jews, Armenians worldwide consider themselves essentially one people, albeit living in numerous different countries. It was natural, then, that when the former Soviet Republic of Armenia declared its independence it received immediate support from its large diaspora community, even recruiting as its foreign minister a 32-year-old native of Los Angeles whose father, a professor at UCLA, had insisted on speaking Armenian at home and instructing his son in his people's traditions.[61]

Khachig Toloyan, editor of *Diaspora: A Journal of Transnational Studies*, himself an Armenian-American brought tip in Syria, Lebanon, and Egypt, suggests that diaspora groups such as his, or the Jews, are fundamentally different from other emigrant peoples in that

> [they] have kept alive in their consciousness [themselves] as something in their host country; and that [they] either hope to go back to the homeland or care enough about it to try to interact with it in some way. For example, Italian-Americans are *only* an ethnic community, not a diaspora; they don't particularly worry about the cultural and political life in Italy, or about Argentineans of Italian descent. Armenian-Americans are an ethnic community but we're more than that. . . .[62]

For global tribes, such transnational group loyalties constitute a critical distinguishing characteristic, what Jewish philosopher Martin Buber once called a "vocation of uniqueness."[63] In many cases, this "uniqueness" is built around an elaborate mythology of origin, which serves to provide a common link between all members of the group. Armenians such as Toloyan, for instance, trace their lineage to a common mythological ancestor, Haig, and later to a series of kingdoms that were among the first to espouse Christianity and even experience an apparition of Christ.[64]

Like the Armenians, other global tribes possess a similarly shared sense of tribal lineage and mythology.[65] For Indians, their origination myths derive from the ancient stories of the Vedas, "the first Bible of the Hindus"[66]; the legends associated with the rise of the first "Yellow Emperor" serve as the mythological basis for the unique sense of venerable and noble beginnings of the Chinese[67]; the Japanese concept of the "divine" origin of their land and the Yamato race underlies a particularly well-developed sense of their tribal uniqueness.[68]

Origin myths can even include those borrowed from others. In the case of the British, much of the mythology of uniqueness—including the myth of King Arthur and the Holy Grail—draws on themes derived from the Jewish Holy Land.[69] Perhaps more important, Old Testament stories dominated the ideology and imagination of the Puritans, who, historian Barbara Tuchman observes, "were the self-chosen inheritors of Abraham's covenant with God, the reembodied saints of Israel, the 'battle axe of the lord.' "[70] Later on, at the height of empire, this messianic urge was expressed in poet Rudyard Kipling's concept of "the White Man's Burden," with the British divinely chosen to bring religion and civilization to the nonwhite masses.

This same sense of mission developed early as well in Britain's North American colonies. The Puritans, notably, envisioned themselves as builders of "the new Jerusalem." Today Anglo-American messianism is reflected by Mormonism, North America's fastest growing major religion. Although initially consisting overwhelmingly of English and other North European immigrants, the Mormons trace their origins from Hebrews who allegedly migrated to North America. Not coincidentally, when they escaped their persecutors to their haven near the Great Salt Lake, they named their theological center Zion, after the Jewish homeland.

For the archetypical global tribe, the Jews, the descent myth—beginning with the story of the patriarch Abraham and his progeny—has had peculiar significance. For the Jews, the Old Testament, as the German philosopher Friedrich Nietzsche noted, was more than a religious text; it was a national epic.[71] Nietzsche, who despite his later usurpation by the Nazis despised anti-Semitism, saw the Jews' adherence to their biblical legacy not as religious piety but as a demonstration of "the toughest life-will that has ever existed in any people on earth."[73]

The force of this "life-will" became noticeable early in the history of the dispersion. In the period after the conquests of Alexander, as the cultures of other peoples faded before the brilliance of Hellenistic civilization, the Jews, even those speaking the language and enjoying the culture of the Greeks, remained, in the phrase of classical historian Michael Grant, "not only unassimilated, but unassimilable."[73]

Even then, the links between scattered Jewish communities remained remarkably strong. The Israel restored by the Maccabees—much like the modern state founded in 1947—depended heavily upon aid from more affluent Jews from the diaspora, then largely concentrated in Alexandria and Babylon.[74] The ties forged by this "vocation of uniqueness" may help to explain why the Jews, virtually alone among the peoples conquered by Rome, continued to struggle against their imperial masters for over two centuries after the initial conquest,[75] including some Jews living in the diaspora communities.[76]

And even after the loss of their homeland to the Romans, the scattered Jewish communities retained their unique identity, to the wonderment and frequently the annoyance of other peoples. Mass conversions, often at the threat of death,[77] reduced their numbers to a pitiable fraction of their former population, yet the surviving remnants kept their covenant with their ancient religious traditions[78] as well as their sense of obligation to other Jews.

With the homeland lost, preservation of "the vocation of uniqueness" quickly became a struggle, particularly in the increasingly intolerant environment of early Christian Europe. To preserve the economic self-sufficiency of Jewish families, the holding of slaves was denounced as onerous.[79] The preference, wherever possible, was for hiring other members of the tribe as free laborers. "He who increases the number of his slaves increases sin and iniquity in the world," wrote the Spanish sage Maimonides, "whereas the man who employs poor Jews in his household increases merits and religious deeds."[80]

This sensibility of self-help helped the medieval and early modern European Jewish communities survive such natural disasters as the Black Death. A combination of ritual sanitary injunctions and the practice of providing professional medical care to the impoverished sick, known as *Bikur Holim* ("visiting the sick"), helped quarantine the tiny communities across Europe from devastation.

But perhaps the most remarkable feature of this self-help was that it extended beyond local communities. In 1627, when Dutch Jews learned through the Venice ghetto about the depredations on the small community in Jerusalem, they arranged payment to the local Turkish despot to mitigate "the great calamity and misery" of their distant brethren. Similar efforts were made by Italian and Dutch Jews on behalf of Jewish captives in the central European cities of Prague, Budapest, and Belgrade.[81]

When Jews began to achieve a greater measure of economic power, they were not loath to use it for the protection of even the most distant branches of the tribe.[82] In 1904 and 1905, on the eve of the Russo-Japanese War, the New York investment bank of Kuhn, Loeb,[83] led by its German-born president, Jacob H. Schiff, extended a critical series of loans to Japan as a means of taking revenge for the anti-Semitic outrages of the Czarist regime.[84]

As Jews began their first mass migrations from Russia, the tradition of self-help brought critical assistance to newcomers from the already established communities, particularly in Britain, France, Germany, and the United States. In 1914, there were over 514 different Jewish benevolent societies in the United States alone, providing everything from insurance and burial plots to summer camps for children.[85]

And when Alain de Rothschild, descendant of the great French Baron James de Rothschild, died in 1982, the shopkeepers of the poorest Jewish district in Paris—largely immigrants from North Africa who had benefited from his philanthropy—closed their doors for an hour in mourning.[86] Leon Masliah, director of the Consistoire General of the French Jewish communities, who himself emigrated from Tunisia in 1961, recalls:

> When we came, we had help with money, with housing, with the synagogue. We had a whole administration dedicated to our people. When a Jew comes to France, he knows where to go, where to worship. I am a North African—I know what *fraternité* really means. It means people waiting for you at the airport.[87]

Perhaps more important, newly arriving Jews, whether in France or America, developed their communities by building their own, largely self-contained economy. Following Maimonides's advice, Jews tended to hire as well as buy from their own community. In early twentieth-century New York, notes author Irving Howe, Jews went to their own doctors, butchers, dry goods dealers, shoe stores, coalmen, and grocers; both their apartments and their places of employment were owned largely by fellow Jews.[88]

But perhaps nothing reflects the remarkable bonding of the Jewish tribe more than the establishment and successful maintenance of the state of Israel. The revived Jewish state was conceived, financed, and led from the diaspora. Virtually all the great names of Jewish business—Rothschild, Kadoorie, and Warburg, among others—contributed to the building of the state.[89]

During crises, the diaspora's support for Israel has often taken dramatic forms. In the initial struggle for the establishment of the state, French Jews, with the tacit support of their government, helped provide training facilities for thousands of young Jewish military recruits streaming in from Europe, Canada, and the United States.[90] In 1967, at the onset of the Six Day War, over ten thousand American Jews volunteered for service in Israel.[91]

By 1990, contributions of Jews abroad, particularly from the United States—as well as American government support, secured largely through their political influence—accounted for as much as 12 percent of Israel's total GDP.[92] Similarly, diaspora Jews have applied much of the political pressure and financial wherewithal behind the massive exodus of their landsmen from the collapsing former Soviet Union, most of whom had little previous knowledge of their heritage.

This ethos of self-help, with all of its occasional flaws and excesses, characterizes virtually all the ascendant global tribes, from the Chinese and Japanese to the Indians, Armenians, and Palestinians—some of whom at times express a desire to model their organizational and communal ethos around a Jewish template. "What we need is something like the United Jewish Appeal for Palestinians," explains Paul Ajlouny, the New York–based publisher of the Jerusalem Palestinian newspaper *El Fajr*. "Be together like the Jews. That should be our goal."[93]

As Ajlouny suggests, group survival, particularly in dispersion, relies on a combination of factors: group self-help, a strong ethnic sense of identity, and a powerful ethos of self-preservation. The conscious cultivation of ties based on enduring feelings of family, ethics, and ethnic solidarity has been a consistent element in the education of young Palestinians, in Detroit or San Francisco as well as in Middle Eastern centers such as Amman, Tunis, or Nablus.

Similarly, each of the major dispersed Asiatic groups has established elaborate systems of educational institutions, religious centers, and social clubs. Japanese *salarimen* abroad support a worldwide network of schools, Buddhist temples, and associations designed to maintain their identity in far-off countries. Members of the overseas Chinese communities, even after generations in diaspora, maintain membership in clan and regional groups whose origins tie on the mainland.[94] Indians abroad have established cultural and religious institutions so they can keep their *man* (heart) in India even as they place their *dhan* (wealth) in Britain and their *tan* (body) in a third country such as one in Asia or Africa.[95]

Like the Asian tribes, the Jews also have retained their own communal educational and cultural institutions. An estimated 50 percent or more of American Jews send their children to an ethnic school, and over three-quarters of young men undergo the traditional bar mitzvah ceremony.[96] In contrast, counterpart systems promoting specifically Italian or German language, culture, and history largely have disappeared in most major countries of their immigration. Even among intermarried couples—roughly half of all Jews now marry outside the tribe—a large majority claimed that most of their friends were Jews and two-thirds observed at least some family religious rituals.[97]

Even as the world economy becomes ever more intertwined, Jews and other global tribes may find these ancient linkages still a powerful asset, as they have been for generations. Nothing on the disorderly horizon that suggests the struggle for economic survival will become any less brutal or difficult in the years ahead, with family groups, multinational corporations, and state enterprises battling for dominance across the global economic landscape. In such an environment, the medieval Arab historian Ibn Khaldun once noted, a powerful sense of belonging constitutes perhaps the most essential element for survival. "Only tribes held together by group feeling," he noted, "can live in a desert."[98]

NOTES

1. From biography provided by M. de Rothschild to the author.
2. Interview with author.

3. Rabbi Alexander Feinslaver, *The Talmud for Today* (New York: St. Martin's Press, 1980), p. 71.

4. Richard Davis, *The English Rothschilds* (Glasgow: Collins Publishers, 1983), p. 82.

5. Ignatius Balla, *The Romance of the Rothschilds* (London: Eveleigh Nash, 1913), pp. 146–47.

6. Frederic Morton, *The Rothschilds: A Family Portrait* (New York: Atheneum, 1962), p. 219.

7. Interview with author.

8. "Diaspora," *AIM*, April 1991, p. 28.

9. Brinley Thomas, *Migration and Urban Development: A Reappraisal of British and American Long Cycles* (London: Methuen, 1972), p. 2.

10. Robert Ezra Park, *Race and Culture* (New York: The Free Press, 1950), p. 346.

11. W. H. G. Armytage, *A Social History of Engineering* (London: Faber and Faber, 1961), p. 22.

12. Gerhard Herm, *The Phoenicians: The Purple Empire of the Ancient World*, trans. Caroline Hiller (New York: William Morrow, 1975), p. 14.

13. Philip D. Curtin, *Cross-Cultural Trade in World History* (Cambridge, Eng.: Cambridge University Press, 1984), pp. 66–67.

14. C. R. Boxer, *Race Relations in the Portuguese Colonial Empire: 1415–1825* (Oxford, Eng.: Clarendon, 1963), p. 3.

15. Dr. Spencer J. Palmer, "The Japanese and the Jews: Two Peoples That Have Surprised the World," paper delivered at the Kennedy Center, Brigham Young University, February 27, 1986.

16. Oswald Spengler, *The Decline of the West* (New York: Knopf, 1928), p. 32.

17. Eliyahu Ashtor, *The Jews and the Mediterranean Economy, 10th–15th Centuries* (London: Variorum Reprints, 1983), pp. 89–91.

18. Cecil Roth, *The Jewish Contribution to Civilization* (London: Macmillan, 1938), pp. 169–70.

19. Thomas Sowell, "Cultural Diversity: A World View," lecture presented at the American Enterprise Institute's Annual Policy Conference, December 5, 1990, p. 9.

20. Mauricio Hatchwell Toledano, "History of Sepharad," unpublished paper, pp. 2–9.

21. Balla, *The Romance of the Rothschilds*, p. 170.

22. Karl Marx, *A World Without Jews*, trans. Dagobert Runes (New York: Philosophical Library, 1959), pp. 42–49.

23. Stephen J. Gould, "Science and Jewish Immigration," *Natural History*, December 1980, p. 16.

24. Ibid., p. 8.

25. Roth, *The Jewish Contribution*, p. 173.

26. Abraham Korman, *The Outsiders: Jews and Corporate America* (Lexington, MA: Lexington Books, 1988), p. 113.

27. Chart provided by Sergio DellaPergola. "Jewish and General Populations in Selected Countries According to Education, 1957–1987" (Jerusalem: The Institute of Contemporary Jewry, The Hebrew University, 1983 and 1988).

28. Chart provided by Sergio DellaPergola. "Jewish Population and Total, According to Country and Occupation, 1960–1980" (Jerusalem: The Institute of Contemporary Jewry, The Hebrew University, 1983 and 1988).

29. Lewis Mumford, *Technics and Civilization* (New York: Harcourt Brace, 1934), p. 152.

30. Ibid.

31. R. H. Tawney, *Religion and the Rise of Capitalism* (London: Hazell, Watson and Viney, 1926), p. 205.

32. Max Weber, *General Economic History* (New York: The Free Press, 1950), pp. 352–69.

33. Jacob Neusner, "The Glory of God Is Intelligence: Four Lectures on the Role of Intellect in Judaism," vol. 3, *The Religious Studies Monograph Series* (Salt Lake City: Brigham Young University, Bookcraft Inc., 1979), p. xviii.

34. Mark Casson, "Changes in the Level and Structure of International Production: The Last Hundred Years," in *The Growth of International Business*, John H. Dunning, ed. (London: George Allen and Unwin, 1983), p. 106.

35. Herbert Feis, *Europe: The World's Banker, 1870–1914* (Clifton, N.J.: Kelley, 1974), p. 23.

36. Bernard Bailyn, *Voyagers to the West* (New York: Vintage, 1988), pp. 24–25.

37. Brinley Thomas, *International Migration and Economic Development* (Paris: UNESCO, 1961), p. 32.

38. Rhoads Murphey, *The Outsiders: The Western Experience in India and China* (Ann Arbor: University of Michigan Press, 1977), pp. 18–22.

39. Thomas, *International Migration and Economic Development*.

40. Louis L. Snyder, *Macronationalisms: A History of Pan-movements* (Westport, CT: Greenwood Press, 1984), pp. 96–97.

41. Sartre quoted in Frantz Fanon, *The Wretched of the Earth* (New York: Grove Press, 1966), p. 7.

42. "Economic and Financial Indicators," *The Economist*, September 29, 1990, p. 114.

43. Tony Smith, *The Patterns of Imperialism: The United States, Great Britain, and the Late-Industrializing World Since 1815* (Cambridge, Eng: Cambridge University Press, 1981), p. 57.

44. M. C. Madhavan, "Indian Emigrants: Numbers, Characteristics and Economic Impact," *Population and Development Review*, Vol. 11, no. 3, September 1985, p. 460; Murphey, *The Outsiders*, p. 101.

45. Noboru Tabe, *Indian Entrepreneurs at the Crossroads* (Tokyo: Institute of Developing Economies, 1970), pp. 8-13.

46. Dharma Kumar, *The Cambridge Economic History of India. Vol II: 1757–1970* (New Delhi: Cambridge University Press, 1982), p. 565.

47. Murphey, *The Outsiders*, pp. 17–18.

48. Karl Marx, *Capital* (New York: Vintage, 1977), vol. 1, p. 878, note 3.

49. Armytage, *A Social History of Engineering*, pp. 233–34.

50. "World Trade Survey," *The Economist*, September 2, 1990, p. 7.

51. "Future Shocklet," *The Economist*, September 22, 1990; "Survey: Asia's Emerging Economies," *The Economist*, November 16, 1991, p. 1; "World Population, By Region," *The Economist*, April 11, 1992, p. 107.

52. F. Gerard Adams, "Economic Performance and Prospects: South East Asia and Latin America," in *Perspectives on the Pacific Basin Economy*, eds. Takao Fukichi and Mitsuhiro Kagami (Tokyo: Institute of Developing Economies, 1990), p. 32.

53. "Price of Speech," *The Economist*, July 6, 1991, p. 16.

54. *The Economist*, July 20, 1991.

55. *The Economist*, July 20, 1991.

56. "Viewpoint," paid advertisement by Commerzbank; "Air Transport: Deregulation Will Stimulate Growth," *The Economist*, October 20, 1990, p. 82. The statistics are based on estimates by the International Civil Aviation Association.

57. Milton Singer, *When a Great Tradition Modernizes* (New York: Praeger, 1972), p. 317.

58. Interview with author.

59. Highlights of CJF 1990 National Survey, published by Council of Jews Federation, New York, pp. 56–58. Nearly three-quarters of American Jews, including a considerable majority of the third generation, consider themselves closely attached to Israel.

60. Jenny Phillips, *Symbols, Myth and Rhetoric: The Politics of Culture in an Armenian-American Population* (New York: AMS Press, 1989), pp. 2–3.

61. Mathis Chazanov, "Job Springs from Ethnic Roots," *Los Angeles Times*, November 3, 1991.

62. Interview in "Diaspora," *AIM*, April 1991, p. 29.

63. Arthur Hertzberg, ed., *The Zionist Idea* (New York: Doubleday, 1959), p. 455.

64. Phillips, *Symbol, Myth and Rhetoric*, pp. 39–43.

65. Morton H. Fried, *The Notion of Tribe* (Menlo Park, Calif.: Cummings Publishing, 1975), p. 7.

66. Percival Spear, *India: A Modern History* (Ann Arbor: University of Michigan, 1961), p. 33.

67. Lynn Pan, *Sons of the Yellow Emperor: A History of the Chinese Diaspora* (Boston: Little, Brown, 1990), p. 10.

68. John W. Dower, *War Without Mercy: Race and Power in the Pacific War* (New York: Pantheon, pp. 215–25.

69. Barbara Tuchman, *Bible and Sword* (New York: Ballantine, 1984), pp. 1–21.

70. Ibid., pp. 121–22.

71. Friedrich Nietzsche, *The Birth of Tragedy and the Genealogy of Morals*, trans. Francis Golffing (Garden City, N.Y.: Doubleday Anchor edition, 1956), p. 281.

72. Walter Kaufmann, *Nietzsche: Philosopher, Psychologist, Anti-Christ* (New York: Vintage, 1958), p. 339.

73. Michael Grant, *From Alexander to Cleopatra: The Hellenistic World*, p. 75.

74. Michael Grant, *The Jews in the Roman World* (New York: Scribners, 1973), p. 30.

75. Hyam Maccoby, *Revolution in Judea* (New York: Taplinger, 1980), p. 53.

76. Martin Gilbert, *The Jewish History Atlas*, 3rd ed. (Jerusalem: Steinmatzky Press, 1975), p. 75.

77. Ibid., pp. 19–21.

78. Grant, *The Jews in the Roman World*, pp. 289–90.

79. Nachum Gross, Sato W. Baron, Arcadius Kahan, *et al.*, *The Economic History of the Jews* (New York: Schocken Books, 1975), p. 22. The authors cite an old proverb: "He who buys a Hebrew slave acquires a master unto himself."

80. Ibid., p. 52.

81. Jonathan I. Israel, *European Jewry in the Age of Mercantilism*, 2d ed. (New York: Oxford University Press, 1989), pp. 202–205.

82. Josef Kastein, *History and Destiny of the Jews*, trans. Huntley Paterson (New York: Viking Press, 1933), pp. 404–405; Elkan Nathan Adler, *London* (Philadelphia: Jewish Publication Society of America, 1930), pp. 172–74, 218–20; Anka Muhlstein, *Baron James: Rise of the French Rothschilds* (New York: Vendome Press, 1982), p. 65.

83. David Kranzler, *Japanese, Jews and Missionaries* (New York: Yeshiva University Press, 1976), pp. 174–76.

84. Jacques Attali, *A Man of Influence: Sir Siegmund Warburg*, trans. Barbara Ellis (London: Weidenfeld and Nicolson, 1986), pp. 54–56.

85. Mark Rosentraub and Delbert Taebel, "Jewish Enterprise in Transition: From Collective Self-help to Orthodox Capitalism," in *Self-Help in Urban America*, Scott Cummings, ed. (Port Washington, N.Y.: National University Publications, 1980), pp. 194–97.

86. Muhlstein, *Baron James*, p. 216.

87. Interview with author.

88. Irving Howe, *World of Our Fathers* (New York: Harcourt Brace Jovanovich, 1976), pp. 163–64.

89. Dennis A. Leventhal, *The Jewish Community of Hong Kong*, rev. ed. (Jewish Publication Society of Hong Kong, 1988), p. 9; Attali, *A Man of Influence*, pp. 120–22; Morton, *The Rothschilds*, p. 286.

90. Vicki Tamir, *Bulgaria and Her Jews: The History of a Dubious Symbiosis* (New York: Yeshiva University Press, 1979), p. 229.

91. Arthur Hertzberg, *The Jews in America: Four Centuries of an Uneasy Encounter* (New York: Touchstone Books, 1989), p. 373.

92. Joel Bainerman, "Cut Off Aid to Israel and Watch It Thrive," *The Wall Street Journal*, July 23, 1991.

93. Interview with author.

94. Henny Sender, "Inside the Overseas Chinese Network," *Institutional Investor*, August 1991, p. 30.

95. Michael Twaddle, "Was the Expulsion Inevitable?" in *Expulsion of a Minority: Essays on Ugandan Asians*, ed. Michael Twaddle (London: University of London, 1975), p. 13.

96. American Immigration Institute, July-August 1990, "Melting Pot Still Works," in *Focus on Immigration*, p. 6; U. O. Schmelz and Sergio DellaPergola, "Basic Trends in Jewish Demography," *Jewish Sociology Papers* (New York: American Jewish Committee, 1988), pp. 17–24; "WASP Children Are Waning," *American Demographics*, May 1991, p. 21.

97. Steven M. Cohen, *American Assimilation or Jewish Revival?* (Bloomington: Indiana University Press, 1988), p. 180.

98. Hamid Mowlana, *Global Information and World Communication: New Frontiers* (New York: Longmans, 1986), p. 175.

6. Racism, Institutionalized and Otherwise

John Rex

ACTION, LANGUAGE, AND RACE

THE THIRD PART OF the definition of a race relations situation given in chapter 3 of *Race and Ethnicity*, emphasizes the importance of the ideological justification of social structures. It was said there that a differentiating feature of race relations situations was that they were justified by powerful groups "in terms of some sort of deterministic theory (usually a biological or genetic one) which suggested that the position of the different categories could not be other than it was." We now have to consider whether argument about such theoretical or ideological justification can be thought of as having a curative role and whether the injustices inherent in racial conflict, discrimination, exploitation, and oppression can be put right or overcome by an exposure and rejection of theories.

The Marxian answer to this question, which would also be given by many non-Marxist sociologists, is that "it is not the consciousness of men that determines their existence, but their social existence that determines their consciousness" (Marx, 1962). Before we can accept this, however, we must consider more closely what is meant by "social existence." More complex answers to this question are suggested by the work of Pareto and by the American phenomenologists, Berger and Luckmann.

Pareto (1963) assumes that much of our social action is of a non-logical

John Rex, "Racism, Institutionalized and Otherwise," in *Race and Ethnicity*. Buckingham, U.K.: Open University Press, 1986, pp. 99–118, reprinted with permission of Open University Press and the author.

kind. We do not first set out our goals and then choose the scientifically appropriate means for attaining them as we would do in logical action thus:

Setting of goal—Development of theory—Choice of Appropriate MeansAction

Rather we begin with certain sentiments requiring expression, and at the same time as we act we offer a verbal account of that act, called a residue. The model of such action is

The residue is never a rational or logical theory, although we often seek subsequently to rationalize it in terms of another verbal utterance, which Pareto calls a "derivation." In fact, as we study actions we often have to start with these "derivations." It is when we analyze these into their variable and constant parts that we discover the residues. There is almost no limit to the variety of the rationalizations or derivations we may offer, but underlying them are certain repeated non-logical theories. Economics is the theory of logical action but sociology deals with these nonlogical theories or alternative logics.

The implication of Pareto's theory for the study of race relations is that instead of assuming that consciousness determines action, we should assume that individuals engage in interaction with other individuals or quasi-groups for reasons to do with conflict, exploitation, and oppression, and in the course of so doing give an account of their action. Our task is to see through the rationalizations and to discover the constants which determine such action. There is no need to follow Pareto in his account of the constant part of theories, the residues. He speaks of the residues of combination, of the persistence of aggregates, of the manifestation of sentiments through external acts, residues of sociability, residues of the integrity of the individual, and sexual residues. Those relating to the persistence of aggregates and the integrity of the individual would probably be most relevant to race and ethnic relations. It would probably be better, however, if we were merely to posit basic processes of human need fulfillment which underlie the actions rationalized by derivations.

Pareto's approach appears to downgrade the importance of theory compared with those who see all behavior as determined by theory. But he also upgrades it by pointing out that verbalizations and theorization go along with behavior. There is no pure social existence without theorization of some sort. Human action may therefore be observed and classified on two levels. One deals with actual behavior, the other with the verbal justification of that behavior. Racialist behavior like any other goes along with racist theory.

Pareto's conception of the unity of theory and practice, however, is somewhat distorted and peculiar in that it is especially concerned to differentiate economic and non-economic behavior. Of greater relevance to our argument is the work of the phenomenological and symbolic interactionist schools, who have recognized that social existence involves, as Weber put it, one actor orienting his conduct to another, and that this in turn is only possible if these two actors share the same intersubjective world.

We create such an intersubjective world by agreeing to attach labels to our experience. In so doing we make the claim that they are in some sense the same experiences which other people have had, and we also connect them with other experiences of our own, in that meanings do not stand by themselves but have definite relations to each other. If I say that I am seeing a chair, I am saying that I am having an experience which is similar to some of your experiences, but also different and related to other experiences of yours and mine, which I describe as seeing a table. In using language about the physical world, therefore, we must already hold implicit shared theories about the world and how it works.

In ordinary speech, however, this is far from being simply a cognitive business. At this level no distinction is made between saying something exists and giving advice or instruction on how it is to be treated, or saying whether it is good or beautiful or sacred. Thus a Christian who learns to use the word "cross" or "communion" does not simply learn to attach a particular label to a particular thing. He acquires a knowledge of the appropriate attitudes to these symbols and in so doing acquires not simply a scientific but a moral and religious education.

In our own Western culture, of course, we have sought to distinguish the question "What is this object?" from all questions about aesthetic or moral qualities. There is a set of procedures we call "science" by which we arrive at a picture of the world that is more relevant for a number of purposes, especially for the purposes of controlling that world. But this is not the only possible or even the most relevant picture. We do not make chemical analyses of the substances used in a religious sacrament in order to understand the sacraments better. Nor are we helped in appreciating a picture by a geometrical analysis of its form. There is more to life than science can tell us.

If, however, it is true that our language is loaded with aesthetic and moral meanings so far as objects in the physical world are concerned, how much more true must it be in the case of social objects. Here we rarely distinguish between the question "What is this?" and "How should I feel and act toward this?" The goal of Positivism has been to eliminate this confusion both for scientific purposes and in everyday life (Lundberg, 1939; Chase, 1938), but it is not a goal which has been or is likely to be realized.

In any case, it is not clear what a scientific way of looking at and labeling social objects would be like. We might seek to replace the observation "this is a Jew" or "this is a Negro" with a statement that "this is a human being" in order to eliminate the moral and political overtones of the terms "Jew" and "Negro," but we would nonetheless be making implicit reference to some other moral and political code which asserts that the universal qualities of men are more important than their differences. Not surprisingly, therefore, there is no known society in which social actors are not categorized in terms much narrower than "human being," and these categorizations imply a set of moral duties and a form of social organization.

The simplest form of categorization of social objects is seen in systems of kinship terminology. Such a terminology constitutes a primitive society's own sociology. Unlike a system of personal names, the system of kinship terms brings into being a group structure. It makes clear what rights and duties any individual has not merely vis-à-vis ego but in relation to every other individual.

There will, however, be individuals to whom ego cannot relate in terms of kinship terminology. Some of these will be grouped in classificatory groups such as clans. The position of an individual in one group vis-à-vis an individual in another group will follow from the relationship which any individual in the one group is held to have with an individual in the other. A social system based upon a normative consensus may be built up in this way, often involving totemic classes. What differentiates such a system from the sort of system we have discussed in previous chapters dealing with composite societies is that the system of rights and duties which it implies is a means of achieving a division of labor, through which overall group ends can be attained. There is no question of the group which is singled out in this way becoming the target of hostile policies. This may be the case with people who fall right outside of the tribe or its constituent classes, in which case there may be parallels with race relations problems depending on whether the groups are in conflict with one another over resources. But the outside in such a system may be simply an individual for whom it is impossible to define rights and duties rather than an outright enemy.

In many cases which Barth considers in his account of ethnic boundaries, even the relations of these larger groups may be complementary. They may occupy separate ecological niches, they may have separate political territories, or they may perform complementary economic roles. But where such complementarity does not exist, groups of outsiders or enemies may be defined, and very often they will be defined, not simply for cognitive purposes, but in such a way as to mobilize specific attitudes toward them. Thus a Spanish historian refers to American Indians as "lazy and vicious, melancholic, cowardly and in general a tying and shiftless people" (Hanke, 1959). Similarly Van Riebeck, the first Governor of the Cape Colony, refers to the Hottentots as "stupid, dull stinking people" (de Kiewier, 1948).

Such statements, which are the normal stuff of intergroup relations in colonial circumstances, are clearly not simply intellectual responses. Instead of saying "this type of person is my competitor for resources and in attempting to realize my goals I have to stop him attaining his," the individual makes the much simpler response "these people are evil." Such statements have the characteristics of Pareto's residues. They are not deductions from some higher theory. Along with acts which they accompany, they are themselves forms of aggression. Once this is understood, the problem of "curing racism" becomes not one of correcting theory on the abstract level, but of dealing with these basic acts of aggression. Of course, one will find that reasons of all kinds are adduced in support of these basic verbal acts of aggression—theological, biological, historical, and cultural—but the use of these reasons as justification is precisely what Pareto meant when he referred to derivations based on verbal proofs. Faced with this sort of data, the real problem is to look for the "constant part" or "residue" which underlies the "derivation." Here the residue is simply a verbal act of aggression rather than any of the subtle alternative logics to which Pareto refers.

THE PROBLEMATIC OF RACISM

It is important to understand that in recent years the most common approach of sociologists and politicians to resisting racism and racialism has not been based on the kind of analysis above. Nor has the whole sociology of race relations. Rather, sociologists have seen themselves as having the task of finding tendencies to racism largely on the level of theory and proposing ways in which it might be cured, with little serious discussion taking place about the relationship between theories and social structure. This is evident in the way in which the problem of race relations was discussed in relation in Nazi Germany, in relation to South Africa, in the United States and, more recently, in Britain.

In the case of Nazi Germany, the central problem is the extermination of seven million Jews. The usual explanation is that it was the consequence of racism on the part of the Nazi leaders and party members. They were thought to have falsely claimed that the Jews were a race and that their racial characteristics included tendencies toward various sorts of political behavior, ranging from capitalist exploitation to communist subversion. In its most developed form, Nazi doctrine was based upon a false theory of physical anthropology which suggested that "Aryans" were a superior race. The way to prevent the recurrence of genocide in the future, therefore, was seen as lying in the correction of these false beliefs, both at the highest level of biological theory and at the level of popular beliefs. What is not usually discussed is the nature of the social structure of Germany and the place of the Jews within it. This is by no means to suggest that the theory followed from the structure because it gave a correct account of it. It does suggest, however, that it is worth considering whether there were strains in the German social structure which made the occurrence of scapegoating likely, and whether the social and economic position of the Jews as well as their distinctive appearance made them suitable candidates for scapegoating as a group. An enquiry along these lines would start with an analysis of structure and, on the empirical level, would study the behavior of individuals pursuing hostile courses of action against the Jews. The Republic of South Africa occupies a similar place in the international political conscience of the world today to that occupied by Nazi Germany in the 1930s. The South African nationalists are seen as believing in racist theories, often backed by fundamentalist religion, about the inferiority of the black races. This is seen as being of the essence of what is called the doctrine of "apartheid." In this case, there is a greater understanding among sociologists of the structural basis of race relations, but the popular view which still informs many sociological investigations is that the structure of South African society follows from the racist theory of apartheid.

Thinking in the United States was influenced after the 1939–45 war by refugee scholars who explained the phenomenon of racism in terms of personality variables like authoritarianism. At that time very little was said about the relevance of the theory of race relations for blacks. Myrdal, called on as an outsider to investigate the so called Negro problem, however, saw it as representing a dilemma on the part of white America, which was committed by its constitution to principles of equality, but which in practice tolerated segregation and racial domination (Myrdal, 1944). In the wake of political changes in the 1950s and black resistance in the 1960s, America became much more committed to rooting out "racism." It was then discovered, however, that very often discrimination and disadvantage among blacks was not the result of intentional policies or of psychological racism among those who discriminated. This led to the adoption of the problematic concept of "institutional racism," which will be discussed below.

Finally, Britain began to face race relations problems with the settlement of about one million immigrants from the Indian subcontinent, from the Caribbean, and from East Africa. The adoption of racially selective immigration controls after the arrival of the bulk of the male workers in this population then produced a crisis of conscience. The government was assailed by its critics for having made concessions to "racism" by adopting a "racist" immigration policy, and the government itself drew attention to the dangers of racism in the support for the more extreme policies of Enoch Powell, the Conservative Member of Parliament, and of neo-Nazi groups like the National Front. Eventually the policy of anti-racism became widespread and attempts were made to develop educational policies which would eliminate even unconscious racism among gatekeepers in the social services and in society at large.

Given the approach of this author, racism was to be expected in all of the cases mentioned. The Jews were the chosen scapegoat of a Nazi government facing economic and political crises. "Racism" in South Africa was the inevitable accompaniment of a situation in which white employers exploited black labor. In the United States there was not only the historical legacy of a slave-plantation society, but black migrants from that society were seeking to compete for employment and housing with white Americans and white immigrants in the North. Finally, in Britain, there was a legacy of a colonial society in which the colonized people were regarded as inferior, and an industrial and social structure in which socially mobile whites had abandoned jobs and other social positions and black workers were brought in to fill these positions. The problems were not those which arose from racism on either the psychological or the theoretical level, but questions of social structure and inequality. Curing racism would require either that the inequalities in these societies should be eliminated or else that policies should be developed to ensure that racial and ethnic difference were not used as a basis for assigning men and women to unequal positions.

PSYCHOLOGICAL EXPLANATIONS OF "RACISM"

Undoubtedly, the more influential theory in the study of race relations in the 1950s was that which sought to explain racist behavior as due to tensions within the personality system. This was originally developed by a team of psychologists. Although most of them were of empiricist and positivist background, they became associated with a leading member of the Frankfurt School of Critical Theory, T. W. Adorno (Adorno *et al.*, 1950).

The Frankfurt School had been forced to modify its own version of Marxist theory because it had seemed too rationalistic. German workers simply did nor behave as they might have been expected to do in the light of rationalistic theories of behavior. To explain the discrepancies, the school had recruited the psychoanalyst Erich Fromm, who was eventually to give his own account of psychologically disturbed behavior in his *Escape From Freedom* (see M. Jay, 1973; E. Fromm, 1942). According to this account, it was characteristic of the modern age that it present human beings with a possibility of freedom of which they were terrified because they had been inadequately socialized. The individual fleeing from being alone with himself sought escape through sick personal relations of a sadistic or masochistic kind, through retreating into work, or through dependence upon a political or religious leader.

The last of these notions was independently investigated by Adorno and his colleagues. They suggested that there was a type of personality that scored highly on the so called F-scale, which measured willingness to submit to a form of rigid authority, coupled with aggression against those who reject this authority. Such individuals look at the world in a tough-minded way, have a paranoid fear of outsiders, and tend to think in dichotomous terms. People who scored highly on this scale were likely to be anti-Semitic and to show prejudice toward blacks and outgroups of all kinds. They were also likely to be individuals who had had a strict family upbringing or adhered to fundamentalist religious beliefs.

Although this theory exercised great influence in America, it was subject to a number of difficulties. One was that both left- and right-wing authoritarians, although they held rigid beliefs, were not necessarily prejudiced against minorities.

The central difficulty about the Authoritarian Personality School, however, was that the number of people in most populations who had high scores on the F-scale was usually small, and "racism" was often a form of majority behavior. It explained why people who became Nazis were racist and even why racialist policies were adopted when a minority of Nazis exercised power. What it could not explain was the racist thinking and the racialist practice of majorities among ruling groups. This certainly seemed to be the problem in countries like South Africa.

Another and simpler version of Freudian theory was developed by John Dollard and his colleagues. According to this theory, serious frustration leads quite naturally to aggressive behavior against the frustrator. If, however, the frustrator is in a position where he cannot be attacked, the aggression will be stored up and eventually directed against a more suitable target (i.e., someone or some group which is unable to protect itself against aggression, Dollard et al., 1939). Dollard used this explanation to explain white behavior in the Deep South (Dollard, 1957).

There may well be some value in this type of explanation in that it would explain why an individual should act aggressively against competitors. It is not easy to see, however, why we should apply it more to a ruling group like the whites of the Deep South rather than to those whom they ruled and oppressed and frustrated. In fact, the theory of frustration and aggression would serve best to explain the aggression of oppressed groups rising in revolt.

RACISM AND THE SOCIOLOGY OF KNOWLEDGE

Talcott Parsons has suggested that the sciences of social action involve reference to three systems, the social system, the personality system, and the cultural system (Parsons and Shils, 1962). The explanation of racist thinking and racialist behavior which we have just been discussing involves the second of these. Another possibility, however, is that what happens on the social level is at least in part determined by what happens on the cultural level. Individuals might be perfectly sane and undisturbed on the personality level and yet be forced to act through a particular language or culture which they have inherited. This is a matter we have discussed earlier in this chapter. The very words we use to label social objects have meanings which are related to other meanings and which have an effective as well as a cognitive content. We may through a process of education displace this cultural inheritance by putting another in its place. We might, for example, eliminate the use of the term "Jew" or "black" in its current meaning and see that its implications have to do with universally shared rights of man. What we cannot do is to eliminate culture and meaning systems altogether.

There is no reason why we should not admit that part of the total source of racist belief and racialist practice is to be found in the personality and the culture systems. This can be dealt with by those opposing racism, by curing or isolating those with disturbed personalities, and by modifying culturally transmitted belief systems in a universalist direction. There does remain, however, the possibility that the problems arise within the *social* system itself and that they are only supported by tendencies on the personality and cultural system levels. It is to this we must now turn, emphasizing especially the problem of what has come to be called, following political and ideological events in the United States, "institutional racism."

THE PROBLEM OF INSTITUTIONAL RACISM

It should not come as a surprise that the social system has its own dynamic independent of the personality and cultural system. It was the study of this system that Talcott Parsons chose to make his own specialism (Parsons, 1937 and 1950). True, much of his attention was devoted to normative controls which relate to the culture system, but these controls were concerned with ordering a process of interaction which turned as much as anything on the power relations of the parties. It is still the case that the study of the social system as such involves above all the power relations which exist between individuals, groups, and quasi-groups and categories. When we say that an explanation is structural rather than psychological or cultural, we refer to pure social relations of this kind.

Before we turn to the specific theoretical development known as the problem of institutional racism, which is deeply concerned with social interaction as such, we must clear up a terminological confusion. This concerns the use of the terms racism and racialism. Conscious that there was a certain amount of confusion between the malign affects of bodies of ideas, on the one hand, and actual actions or practices, on the other, a number of British sociologists (Banton, 1969) suggested that we should use the term racism to refer to theories only and racialism to refer to the putting of those ideas into practice. Others suggested that we should use the term racialism to refer to practice without any suggestions that such practices were necessarily related to theory at all.

There were difficulties about getting this terminology adopted, however. Popular usage of the term racism was indiscriminate, and this usage increased as conflict in Britain and the United States deepened; many sociologists stuck to or adopted the use of the single term "racism"; and several other languages, including especially French, had only one term.

Sociology, however, has ideological and political competitors whose speeches and writings are so influential that it is difficult for sociologists to ignore them and to insist upon pure academic discourse. If their work is to have any influence on public debate, they are bound to take up the terminology of the ideologies and politicians, even if in so doing they seek to use it with greater precision. This was certainly the case when American sociologists in the late sixties and early seventies had to respond to the use of the term "institutional racism" as it was used by the black American student teacher, Stokeley Carmichael (Carmichael and Hamilton, 1967).

One can easily see why the term came to be used at a particular historical conjuncture. In 1954, the *Brown vs. Board of Education* decision had brought to fruition a process of attempting to use law to rectify the condition of black Americans. Subsequently, civil rights programs had been instituted to outlaw discrimination in a wide variety of spheres, and poverty programs to ensure that white and black poor alike achieved a minimum of welfare. But now it seemed that even though racism was under attack and racial discrimination of an overt sort was being outlawed, black people were still finding themselves at the bottom of the heap. Thus it was argued that even if government was not in the hands of racists, and deliberate racial discrimination was outlawed, the very institutions which were normal to the functioning of American society were producing consequences which were disadvantageous to blacks and represented a kind of "institutional racism."

Even though it is easy to understand how such a concept evolved, it is still possible to recognize that it was full of ambiguity. There would seem to be at least four meanings which could be attributed to it as follows:

(1) Although institutions are not governed by "psychological" racists or by believers in racist theory, they may be subject to unconscious racism.
(2) Discrimination on racial grounds exists but is difficult to prove. The most important proof of its existence, however, is in the outcome in terms of black or minority disadvantage.
(3) The reasons why blacks do badly out of ordinary market processes are hard to understand and their outcome difficult to rectify except by intervening in market processes to ensure that some blacks do well.
(4) Discrimination on racial grounds does not exist, but the important fact is that the disadvantaged poor suffer and that a high proportion of the black population are to be found among the disadvantaged poor.

We now need to look at each of these different interpretations in turn.

(1) Unconscious Racism

Very relevant to this question is the distinction we have drawn between "psychological" racism and racism which is inherent in the belief system of a society. The first of these, however, is not what those who speak of institutionalized racism are referring to. It is in a very literal sense unconscious behavior having to do with the defense mechanisms of the personality system. But this overt behavior which is to be found in "psychological" racists is recognized as racist and is precisely the sort of behavior which the theorists of "institutional racism" mean to exclude, as important.

Much more important is the racism inherent in the belief system of a society. Here actions are taken on the basis of commonsense reasoning, using commonsense knowledge of the world. Even in a society committed to universalism and equality of opportunity, such commonsense knowledge is marked by the use of stereotypes of minority individuals which are derogatory to them or which place them in questionable settings. This is inevitably the case with commonsense knowledge in a society with a history of war and imperialist involvement. Even liberal culture in such a society is impregnated with what are in effect racist and paternalist assumptions, as Wellman (1977) in the United States and Dummett (1973) in Great Britain have shown.

Central to plans for combating institutional racism is the proposal to reeducate social gatekeepers and the public at large through courses in "ethnic or racial awareness" following lines suggested by Katz in the United States (1978). Such courses, if they are successful, must do nothing less than question the received assumptions of commonsense language, and, indeed, must propose a wholly new social language. The task is on a par with ridding our language of "sexist" assumptions.

More than this, however, it is necessary to institutionalize the new language. It must be shown that it is not an artificial language but one which authoritative figures in our society wish to see spoken. The relative success of such training in the United States has to do with this. There, as a result of civil rights programs, the United States government, from the President downward, had become publicly committed (as when President Johnson used the words of the Civil Rights song "We shall overcome") to ensuring equality for blacks in American society. In these circumstances it made sense to tell, say, policemen or schoolteachers that they were required to learn And think in a new language. Acceptance of this new language was reinforced, moreover, by professional rewards in terms of posts and increments. It is much more difficult to imagine such training programs being successful when they do not have central government backing as well as the backing of the press. Thus in Britain in the early 1980s, professional race relations workers were attempting to mount such courses but were seen a politicizing the professions in an undesirable way, because what they were trying to do ran counter to the dominant political culture fostered by politicians and the national media.

It is perhaps too early to say how far programs of this kind are likely to be successful. Their mere existence is indicative of the existence of anti-racist forces in a society, and shows that we need not accept that we are totally entrapped in the language we inherit. But it clearly does require a very strong commitment of a society to universalism if normal language and thinking are to be changed.

(2) DISADVANTAGE AND DISCRIMINATION

The term "disadvantage" came into general use in the United States and Britain in the 1960s. It was used, however, in two quite different ways. According to the first, acts of discrimination by specific individuals existed, but it was difficult to prove except that in the outcome certain groups were shown to be systematically disadvantaged. According to the second, it was unknown whether or not discrimination was occurring, but in any case it did not matter, because other things could be done to correct the disadvantage which was evident in the outcome. We are concerned with the first usage in this section.

I find it useful to illustrate what is involved here by an example. In Britain in the 1960s there was a debate about the allocation of publicly built and owned houses for rent. Only rarely were there specific rules saying that black people should not be offered these tenancies. In the event, however, one found that black people were seriously underrepresented among those who obtained such houses. Their disadvantage was a clear indication that some kind of concealed discrimination was going on. Therefore, the conclusion to be drawn was not simply that disadvantage was a fact and that the position of blacks could be improved by dealing with disadvantage as such, but the renewed efforts had to be made to disclose the kinds of discrimination which were occurring.

Very important in this regard was the fact of indirect discrimination. In the example given, there were no rules against giving houses to blacks, but there were rules against considering applications from those who had recently arrived in the local authority area. There were also rules about overcrowding, which prevented the allocation of houses to large families. The first of these sets of rules especially, but the second to some extent, had the *effect* of preventing the allocation of houses to black families. The problem then was one of indirect discrimination. Quite essential to fighting institutional racism was the task of combating such indirect discrimination. This was different in that it always seemed possible to offer as a defense against the charge of indirect discrimination a claim that a rule was necessary on other, non-racial grounds.

In the British case, laws were passed which dealt with this problem. According to the 1976 Race Relations Act, "A person discriminates against another" if

> he applies to that other a requirement or condition which he applies equally to persons not of the same racial group as that other, but (1) which is such that the proportion of persons of the same racial group as that other who can comply with it is considerably smaller than the proportion of persons not of that racial group who can comply with it and (2) which he cannot show to be justifiable irrespective of the colour, race, nationality or ethnic or racial origin of the person to whom it is applied and (3) which is to the detriment of that other because he cannot comply with it. (HMSO, 1976)

The enforcement of such a law, however, stilt required its implementation by courts and tribunals and this was likely to be a difficult process.

(3) DISADVANTAGE AND POSITIVE DISCRIMINATION

The alternative view of disadvantage is that it is not necessarily caused by discrimination at all, or, if it is, such discrimination can be corrected at a later stage.

The normal processes of allocation in a complex society are through market or through formal bureaucratic systems operating according to the rules of format justice. Under such systems black people may be shown to do less well than whites. They may get inferior jobs and inferior houses and do less well in the selective processes within the education system. In these circumstances, what is proposed is not any interference with the market or with allocation processes or with exams, but simply a wholesale bending of the rules so that a definite percentage outcome is achieved for blacks.

It is surprising that the highest development of this policy should have been in the United States, where the market and the system of formal justice might be thought of as having a near sacred quality. It is, therefore, a sign of how seriously the fight against institutional discrimination was taken that what amounted to a wholly new principle of social organization was adopted.

It was not intended, however, that such a system of predetermined outcomes should become a permanent feature of the society. The logic behind it may be called a "logic of role models." According to Gunnar Myrdal (1944), progress or otherwise in race relations matters followed a cumulative principle. If discrimination led to the appearance of poor, dirty, incapable people, there would be more discrimination because the people involved were poor, dirty, and incapable. *Per contra*, if some individuals in the minority group were shown to be rich, clean, and successful, discrimination would become more difficult, and others in the minority group would emulate the rich, clean, and successful. Eventually the whole process would therefore be self-sustaining. It was only necessary in the first place to establish the positions of the few by what came to be called positive discrimination, or affirmative action.

Such positive discrimination and affirmative action could take a variety of forms. It might simply monitor the percentages of a minority who attained particular positions and consider what training might be necessary for a percentage, equal to that of the minority in the population at large, to be attained. But it might at the other extreme simply promote the incompetent in order to increase numbers of the minority in positions of authority and prestige. It is because the latter policy has been adopted, or because it has been thought to have been adopted, that there has been a backlash in the dominant group against such policies. The argument of those involved in the backlash is that "these people have been given equal rights and have still not been successful; so they are now asking for more than their share."

(4) DISADVANTAGE AND THE DENIAL OF DISCRIMINATION

One possible interpretation of Stokely Carmichael's argument was not that discrimination had to be fought, in that there needed to be positive discrimination on behalf of those in the minority who suffered disadvantage, but that there was no problem other than that of disadvantage as such. It was a particularly popular argument with radicals and socialists, for whom the primary problem was one of class rather than race or ethnicity. The condition of the blacks was simply a dramatic proof of the tendency of the capitalist society to produce inequality.

Such an argument was also popular in England, when for a long time the civil servants responsible for the various social service ministries had been influenced by Fabianism. It was their habit to intervene on behalf of the poor and the disadvantaged among the native working class, and the condition of the blacks was one with which they thought themselves familiar.

Throughout the 1960s and the 1970s, the problem of racial disadvantage was seen as part of the general problem of disadvantage. The National Committee for Commonwealth Immigrants responded to allegations of discrimination in the housing field with a pamphlet entitled "Areas of Special Housing Need" (1967). In policies developed for disadvantaged schools, immigrant needs were not particularly singled out. Indeed, the *presence* of immigrants was one of the *criteria* selected for declaring that a particular school was disadvantaged. The Urban Programme was set up to offer aid to the urban disadvantaged as such, and the Community Development Programmes which followed were concerned with the needs of all inner-city residents. The Department of Health and Social Security sponsored studies of cumulative disadvantage as such rather than the particular cumulative disadvantage of black minorities. The Department of Education, asked to set up a center for the study of minority problems in education, decided instead to create a Centre for the Study of Educational Disadvantage (Rex and Tomlinson, 1979). Finally, the White Paper Policy for the Inner Cities (HMSO, 1977), although it was widely thought of as being a policy for dealing with minorities, actually went out of its way to insist that it was not concerned with racial discrimination but solely with the problem of the disadvantaged poor in the inner city, arguing that any help given to this group must benefit the minorities. During this time it should also be said that other measures were adopted which were specifically directed at combating racial discrimination, but they were on the whole weakly applied until the urban disturbances of 1981, after which it was widely acknowledged that the disadvantage experienced by minorities required separate measures from those concerned with erasing disadvantage as such.

CURING A SOCIETY'S "RACISM"

Summarizing the experience referred to in the previous section, we may say that the attempt to eliminate institutional racism has led to confused policies which have as yet failed to achieve their objectives. We end this chapter, then, by considering some of the ways in which a society might deal with racialist practice and racism, institutionalized and otherwise, if it really decides to do so.

The qualification "if it really decides to do so" is important, because it would seem unlikely that any complex modern society would eliminate all the practices and ideas which are grouped together under the headings "racism" and "racialism." All thinking about social objects in such a society requires the use of what Schutz called typifications (1967), and when there is group conflict such typifications very easily become derogatory stereotypes. Why, then, if racial along with other forms of stereotyping is normal in any functioning society, should it be the case that the member of any society should seek to eliminate it?

Clearly it would be absurd to suggest its elimination in those societies in which rights are apportioned directly or indirectly on a racial basis. One could not deracialize South African society, for example, without it ceasing to be South African society, because rights to the franchise, to jobs, to education, and to housing are allocated there on a racial basis. The myth is that rights are given equally but separately to Coloureds and Indians, and that blacks are only treated differently because they are immigrants from the Homelands. In fact, separate facilities are, as the *Brown vs. Board of Education* judgment argued, inherently unequal, and the classification of blacks as immigrants is a massive act of indirect discrimination.

The same kind of indirect discrimination, of course, exists in any society which classified a part of its working population as "guestworkers," as is the case in West Germany, and so far as that part of the population is concerned government policies are racialist.

What can happen in such societies is the punishment of acts of aggression, including verbal acts of aggression, against minorities. This is the first and most elementary development of policy in a society which wishes to deracialize itself.

Coming back to the question of why any society should wish to deracialize itself, however, all that can be said is that there are societies which are so committed. The United States is one, so is post-revolutionary France, and so in a different way is the Soviet Union. The Constitution of the United States formally commits that country to equality of opportunity regardless of race; the French Revolution was fought on the basis of the slogan "Liberty, Equality, and Fraternity"; and in the Soviet Union a revolutionary government exists which is committed to the Dictatorship of the Proletariat (not the white Proletariat or part of the Proletariat).

The situation in Britain is somewhat different. There is no written constitution, and before 1948 all those who lived in the British Empire were British protected persons. What had to be worked out after that date was what rights British subjects migrating to the metropolis were to have as compared with the metropolitan population. In approaching this question, each of the political parties paid formal allegiance to a universalist ideology; the Conservatives to the notion of equality among the Queen's subjects, the Liberal Party to equality before the law, and the Labour Party to the brotherhood of man.

One can with some justification be cynical about the extent to which these universalist ideologies actually influenced behavior, and I have shown how, in the British case, ideologists gave way to doctrines of expediency in all cases (see Rex and Tomlinson, 1979). Nonetheless, it is a sociological fact that such ideologies exist and that an argument can be held in all such societies against the continuance of racialist practice. It may even be that such developments are to be expected in any modern industrial society. If this is the case, then the arguments we have been discussing in this chapter are to be seen not as moral arguments in the abstract but as part of the factual social process.

The very first implications of such arguments is that ethnic populations should be protected against physical attack and derogatory abuse. This will in large part depend upon the behavior of the police and the media. So far as the police are concerned, they cannot be a law unto themselves. They must not harass any section of the population and they must give due protection to all sections of the population. These things will only occur if the policing policy of the society is governed by its overall political objectives, but such a situation is difficult to achieve since the police are employed to exercise legitimate force, and the control of the use of that force is a subtle and taxing task.

With regard to derogatory abuse, it is necessary that a law against group libel should be rigorously enforced, and the media themselves would have to be subject to a code of practice. These things again are difficult to achieve when the media are not subject to government control. What is wanted, however, is a situation in which there is a sufficient impetus for anti-racism for it to be natural for a free press and free broadcasting to express such sentiments, rather than, as is often the case, more popular newspapers and programs allowing themselves to be used to foster authoritarianism and antiminority sentiment.

The next radical task must be the reform of language. This is necessary because language always carries the legacy of the past, and the language in use would not necessarily be adapted to anti-racism. The renewal of language would be a prime task of racial awareness training. On the other hand, it should be recognized that language cannot be deracialized *in vacuo*. Its reform must go along with a simultaneous reform of racialist practices. Unless it does, the proposed new linguistic usage will be as artificial and irrelevant as Sunday School lessons often are to normal healthy children.

The most crucial aspect of a deracializing policy, however, will lie in the elimination of discriminatory practices. The debate about positive discrimination is often misleading about this. It seems to be saying that there is no actual discrimination and the minorities are still behind. Therefore, it is argued, they must be given extra rights. If positive discrimination is not to produce a backlash, it must not appear in this light. It is necessary that positive action should be taken to prevent discrimination in the first place, and if this is unsuccessful, its consequences must be corrected. Policies on these lines would give no moral justification for a backlash.

Finally, there is the question of breaking Myrdal's vicious cumulative cycle through the provision of new role models. There is no doubt that accumulation cycle of this kind does operate. What should be questioned, however, is the notion that the provision of role models can be achieved by the desperate means of promoting the unqualified and the incompetent. What can be done, if it is shown that there are insufficient minority representatives through the monitoring of percentages attaining or employed at different levels, is to provide training to ensure that *qualified* minority candidates are available. That may, in turn, imply pushing the process further back to ensure that sufficient minority candidates emerge from the schools of qualification. A qualified majority candidate cannot have a grievance at a delay in his appointment if his qualification was gained without fair competition from minority people.

CONCLUSION

Racist thinking and racialist practice are a natural part of advanced industrial societies and they are difficult to eliminate. Many of the proposals for eliminating them are all too facile, and the policies to which they lead are likely to be forced and to lead to a backlash. Nonetheless, there are universalistic elements in the political culture of all such societies, and it is reasonable that systematic anti-racist and anti-racialist policies should be argued for. Despite present failures, there is at least some reason to suppose that in the long run they will be carried through, particularly when the minorities themselves find ways of exercising political power.

In the long run, the guarantee of anti-racist policies will, in fact, depend upon the political power of the minorities, but even before then it is possible to envisage a society becoming committed to anti-racism. It can only do this, however, if such policies are backed unambiguously by the highest political authority. It is when there is doubt about commitment at the top that all of the policies which we have discussed here are put in jeopardy.

REFERENCES

Adorno, Theodor, *et al.* 1950. *The Authoritarian Personality.* New York: Harper and Row.

Banton, Michael. 1969. *Race relations.* London: Tavistock.

———. 1970. "The Idea of Race" in Zubaida, Sami, ed. (1970), *Race and Racialism.* London: Tavistock.

———. 1983. *Racial and Ethnic Competition.* Cambridge: Cambridge University Press.

Barth, Frederick. 1959. *Political Leadership among the Swat Pathans.* London: London School of Economics Monographs on Social Anthropology, No. 19.

———. 1969. *Ethnic Groups and Boundaries.* London: Allen and Unwin.

Berger, Peter, and Luckmann, Thomas (1967) *The Social Construction of Reality.* London: Allen Lane.

Blau, Peter Michael 1964. *Exchange and Power in Social Life.* New York: Wiley.

Bonacich, Edna. 1973. "A Theory of Middlemen Minorities," *American Sociological Review* 38.

———. 1980. "Class Approaches to Ethnicity and Race," *Insurgent Sociologist* 10, no. 2.

Brenner, Robert 1979. "The Origins of Capitalist Development—A Critique of Neo-Smithian Marxism," *New Left Review*, no. 104.

Carmichael, Stokely, and Charles V. Hamilton. 1968. *Black Power—The Politics of Liberation in America.* Cape, London.

Chase, Stuart. 1938. *The Tyranny of Words.* London: Methuen.

Cohen, Abner, ed. 1974. *Urban Ethnicity.* London: Tavistock.

Cohen, Yehudi. 1969. "Social Boundary Systems," *Current Anthropology* 10.

Cox, Oliver Cromwell. 1970. *Caste, Class and Race.* New York: Monthly Review Press.

de Kiewiet. 1948. *A History of South Africa—Social and Economic.* London: Oxford University Press.

Devereux, Edward C. 1961. "Parsons' Sociological Theory." In *The Social Theories of Talcott Parsons,* ed. M. Black. Prentice Hill, New York.

Doeringer, Peter, and Michael Piore. 1971. *Internal Labour Markets and Manpower Analysis.* Lexington, Mass.: Health.

Dollard, John. 1957. *Caste and Class in a Southern Town.* New York: Doubleday.

Dollard, John. *et al.* 1939. *Frustration and Aggression.* New Haven: Yale University Press.

Dummett, Ann 1973. *A Portrait of British Racism.* Hammondsworth: Penguin Books.

Durkheim, Emile. 1915. *The Elementary Forms of Religious Life.* London: Allen and Unwin.

———. 1938. *The Rules of Sociological Method.* Chicago: University of Chicago Press.

———. 1952. *Suicide.* London: Routledge and Kegan Paul.

———. 1974. *The Division of Labour in Society.* Glencoe, Ill.: Free Press.

Ekeh, Peter. 1979. *Social Exchange Theory—The Two Traditions.* London: Heinemann.

Elkins, Stanley. 1959. *Slavery—A Problem in American Institutional and Intellectual Life,* Chicago: University of Chicago Press.

Fanon, Frantz. 1952. *Black Skins, White Masks.* New York: Grove Press.

———. 1965. *The Wretched of the Earth.* London: MacGibbon and Kee.

Fletcher, Ronald. 1957. *The Family and Marriage in Britain—An Analysis and Moral Assessment.* Harmondsworth: Penguin Books.

Frank, Andre Gunder. 1967. *Capitalism and Underdevelopment in Latin America.* New York: Monthly Review Press.

Freyre, Gilberto. 1963. *The Mansions and the Shanties—The Making of Modern Brazil.* New York: Alfred Knopf.

Fromm, Eric. 1942. *The Fear of Freedom.* London: Routledge and Kegan Paul.

Furnivall, John Sydenham. 1939. *Netherlands India—A Study of Plural Economy.* Cambridge: Cambridge University Press.

————. 1968. *Colonial Policy and Practice*. Cambridge: Cambridge University Press.

Geertz, Clifford. 1963. *Old Societies and New States—The Quest for Modernity in Asia and Africa*. Glencoe, Ill.: Free Press.

Gordon, Milton M. 1978. *Human Nature, Class and Ethnicity*. New York: Oxford University Press.

Hall, Stuart. 1980. "Race Articulation and Societies Structured in Dominance." In UNESCO *Sociological Theories of Race and Colonialism*, UNESCO.

Hanke, Lewis. 1959. *Aristotle and the American Indians—A Study in Race Prejudice in the Modern World*. New York: Hollis and Carter.

Hechter, Michael. 1983. *The Micro Foundations of Macro Sociology*. Philadelphia: Temple University Press.

Hiernaux, Jean. 1965. "Introduction—The Moscow Expert Meeting," *International Social Science Journal* 17, no. 1.

Homans, George. 1961. *Social Behaviour*. New York: Harcourt Brace World.

HMSO. 1976. *Race Relations Act 1976*, Chapter 74.

————. 1977. *Policy for the Inner Cities*, Cmd 6845.

Jay, Martin. 1973. *The Dialetical Imagination—A History of the Frankfurt School and the Institute of Social Research*. London: Heinemann.

Katz, Judy. 1978. *White Awareness Handbook for Anti-Racist Training*. Norman: University of Oklahoma Press.

Levy, Marion. 1952. *The Structure of Society*. Princeton: Princeton University Press.

Lipset Seymour, Martin. 1960. *Political Man*. London: Heinemann.

Lundberg, George. 1939. *Foundations of Sociology*. New York: MacMillan.

Malinowski, Bronislaw. 1944. *A Scientific Theory of Culture*. Chapel Hill: University of North Carolina Press.

Marshall, Thomas Humphrey. 1950. *Citizenship and Social Clays and Other Essays*. Cambridge: Cambridge University Press.

Marx, Karl. 1957. "Theses on Feuerbach." In Karl Marx and Frederick Engels, *On Religion*. Moscow: Foreign Languages Publishing House.

————. 1961. *Capital*. Moscow: Foreign Languages Publishing House.

Marx, Karl, and Friedrich Engels. 1962a. "The Communist Manifesto." In *Karl Marx and Friedrich Engels Selected Works*, Vol. 1. Moscow: Foreign Languages Publishing House.

Marx, Karl. 1962b. "Address to the Communist League." In *Karl Marx and Friedrich Engels Selected Works*, Vol. 1. Moscow: Foreign Languages Publishing House.

————. 1962c. "Preface to the Critique of Political Economy." In *Karl Marx and Friedrich Engels Selected Works*, Vol. 1. Moscow: Foreign Languages Publishing House.

————. 1962d. *The Poverty of Philosophy*. Moscow: Foreign Languages Publishing House.

————. 1967. "Toward the Critique of the Hegelian Philosophy of Law: Introduction." In Lloyd D. Easton, and Kurt H. Guddatt, *Writings of the Young Marx on Philosophy and Society*. New York: Anchor Books.

Mason, David, and John Rex, eds. 1986. *Theories of Ethnic and Race Relations*. Cambridge: Cambridge University Press.

Montagu, Ashley. 1972. *Statement on Race*. Oxford: Oxford University Press.

Myrdal, Gunnar. 1944. *An American Dilemma*. New York: Harper Bros.

————. 1964. *Challenge to Affluence*. London: Macmillan.

National Committee for Commonwealth Immigrants. 1967. *Areas of Special Housing Needs*. London.

Pareto, Vilfredo. 1963. *The Mind and Society—A Treatise on Sociology*, 4 Vols. New York: Dover Books.

Parsons, Talcott. 1949. *The Structure of Social Action*. Glencoe, Ill: Free Press.

————. 1952. *The Social System*. London: Tavistock.

Parson, Talcott, and Edward Shils, eds. 1962. *Towards a General Theory of Action*. New York: Harper and Row.

Parsons, Talcott, Robert Bales, and Edward Shils. 1953. *Working Papers in the Theory of Action.* Glencoe, Ill.: Free Press.

Rex, John. 1961. *Key Problems of Sociological Theory.* London: Routledge and Kegan Paul.

———. 1973. *Race Colonialism and the City.* London: Routledge and Kegan Paul.

———. 1983. *Race Relations in Sociological Theory.* London: Weidenfeld and Nicolson, 1970. 2d rev. ed., London: Routledge and Kegan Paul.

———. 1985. "Neo-Kantianism Methodological Individualism and Michael Banton," *Ethnic and Racial Studies* 8, no. 3.

———. 1986. "Race and Ethnicity." In *Introducing Sociology,* ed. P. Worsley. New edition. Harmondsworth: Penguin Books.

Rex, John, and Robert Moore. 1967. *Race, Community and Conflict.* London: Oxford University Press.

Rex, John, and Sally Tomlinson. 1979. *Colonial Immigrants in a British City.* London: Routledge and Kegan Paul.

Schelsky, Helmut. 1957. *Soziologische Bemerkungen zur Rolle der Schule in Unserer Geseltschefruer Fassung.* Unpublished paper quoted by Ralf Dahrendorf, *Class and Class Conflict in Industrial Society.* London: Routledge and Kegan Paul.

Schermerhorn, Richard. 1970. *Comparative Ethnic Relations—A Framework for Theory and Research.* New York: Random House.

Schutz, Alfred. 1967. *The Phenomenology of the Social World.* Evanston, Ill.: Northwestern University Press.

Smith, David. 1967. *Racial Disadvantage in Britain.* Harmondsworth: Penguin Books.

Smith, Michael Garfield. 1965. "The Plural Society in the British West Indies." Berkeley: University of California Press.

———. 1974. *Corporations and Society.* London: Duckworth.

Smith, Michael Garfield, and Leo Kuper, eds. 1969. *Pluralism in Africa.* Berkeley: University of California Press.

Sorel, Georges. 1961. *Reflections on Violence.* London: Collier-MacMillan.

Sumner, William Graham. 1959. *Folkways.* New York: Ginn, 1906; Dover Publications 1959.

Tinker, Hugh. 1974. *A New System of Slavery—The Export of Indian Labour Overseas 1830–1920.* Oxford: Oxford University Press.

Tonnies, Ferdinand. 1967. *Community and Society,* translated by Charles P. Loonis. New York: Harper and Row.

Van den Berghe, Pierre Louis. 1978. *Race and Racism—A Comparative Perspective.* New York: Wiley.

Wallerstein, Immanuel. 1974. *The Modern World System.* New York: Academic Press.

Wallman, Sandra. 1979. "The Boundaries of Race. Processes of Ethnicity in England." In *Man,* no. 13, pp. 200–17.

———. 1986. "The Application of Anthropological Theory to the Study of Boundary Processes." In David Mason and John Rex, *Theories of Ethnic and Race Relations.* Cambridge: Cambridge University Press.

Warner, W. Lloyd. 1936. "American Class and Caste," *American Journal of Sociology* 17 (September): 234–47.

Warner, William Lloyd, and Paul S. Lunt. 1947. *The Social System of a Modern Community.* New Haven: Yale University Press.

Weber, Max. 1930. *The Protestant Ethic and the Spirit of Capitalism.* London: George Allen and Unwin.

———. 1962. *General Economic History.* New York: Collier Books.

———. 1968. *Economy and Society.* 3 Volumes. New York: Bedminster Press.

———. 1976. *The Agrarian Sociology of Ancient Civilization.* London: New Left Books.

Wellman, David T. 1977. *Portraits of White Racism.* London: Cambridge University Press.

7. Ethnicity and Racialism in Colonial Indian Society
D. A. Washbrook

I

DURING THE LATER NINETEENTH century, Indian political activity exploded in many new and different directions. One of these was the politics of ethnicity and race. The political stage became filled with groups and associations, defined by reference to common features of caste or religion or vernacular culture, each battling for political rights and/or social status in relation to one another.[1] Sometimes, indeed most often, such movements claimed to be responding to perceived oppressions which they sought to escape either by promoting equality within a continuing ethnically "plural" social order or by pursuing autonomy through territorial separation. Movements of these types I shall term "ethnic." Occasionally, however, aims were rather different and centered on the attempt by one group to legitimate claims to political dominance or superior social status over others. Movements of this type I shall term "racialist." From this period, ethnic and racialist movements have come to establish a permanent place in the politics of India. In this chapter, I shall attempt to explore their origin and character and to assess their significance in the society which emerged in 1947 from the colonial experience.

As any historian who ventures into the sociology of ethnicity and race soon discovers, he is entering a theoretical minefield. Debates about the primary def-

D. A. Washbrook, "Ethnicity and Racialism in Colonial Indian Society," in Robert Ross, ed., *Racism and Colonialism*. The Hague: Martinus Nijhoff Publishers, 1982, 143–181, reprinted with the permission of Kluwer Academic Publishers.

inition of concepts continue to rage, and no usage which he adopts can be entirely uncontroversial. Perhaps the most enduring of conflicts has come over whether race and ethnicity are better understood in terms of the information provided by specific sets of ideas or of the imperatives generated by general social functions.[2] In brief, should "racialism" be seen as a cultural phenomenon, reflecting beliefs about the social implications of genes, or as a sociological phenomenon, representing a type of ascriptive social stratification? Of course, put this way, it could be argued that the conflict is artificial and that any adequate concept would require adequate "cultural" and "sociological" specifications. Indeed, only in the crudest caricatures of each other do cultural definitions not imply theories about social functions and vice versa. But the question of emphasis is important, for, depending upon where it is placed, analysis may be pushed back to rest upon the assumptions of very different methodological traditions. Conceptualization from a sense of cultural priority tends to lead toward neo-Idealist (Parsonian, liberal, or bourgeois) sociology and an understanding of modern history rooted in the paradigm of "modernization." Conceptualization from a sociological priority points toward the Positivist tradition and, these days especially, the Marxian discourse.[3]

The definitions adopted here, while recognizing the significance of cultural specificities, arise from the Positivist side of this divide and reflect the author's location within the Marxian discourse. Lack of space and the author's greater interest in the particularities of Indian history than the universalities of sociological theory prevent him attempting an adequate defense of this location (although at present it might be felt that it was a continued reliance on bourgeois theory and the concept of modernization which needed the defense).[4] Space also prevents a discussion of the point within the wide Marxian discourse from which the following remarks are made. But it is hoped that enough will appear implicit in his formulations for this position to be picked up. All he can do is to make his own usages as clear as possible.

First, he takes the concept of ethnicity to refer to the division of society into a number of separate organic communities. Membership of these communities is ascriptive, and each is held to encompass the entire social identity and political interest of its members. Rights in the "whole" society are defined in relation to prior membership of the specific community. The precise criteria of ascription used to define the community may be various—language, religion or caste—and do not matter, for the primary characteristic of the concept is only ascriptive social division. Second, he takes racialism to refer not merely to the division but to the stratification of society along the lines of ascriptive community. The concept of racialism is an extension of that of ethnicity and implies a ladder of rank by reference to which communities can be placed in an order of superiority and inferiority. The ranking scheme justifies and explains differential and deferential patterns of right and obligation in the whole society. Once again (and in contrast to "cultural" definitions), the specific criteria of ranking may be various—hierarchical theories of cultural development or notions of a divine order or theories of biogenetic social determination (whether "scientific" or "superstitious"). It does not matter-here whether "the race" is conceived as a biological or cultural entity,[5] nor whether it is defined on the information of nineteenth-century Western social science or on that of non-Western religious beliefs.[6] The defining characteristic is that of legitimating social inequality by reference to qualities inherent in different ascriptive communities.

II

In order to explain the upsurge of ethnic and racialist sentiment in the politics of the later colonial decades, it is necessary first to appreciate the role of such sentiments in the pre-colonial context. Sociological opinion on this question is deeply divided. At one extreme stand the analysis by Max Weber, who saw a strong component of ethnicity in the social differentiation imposed by the traditional caste system, and the work of the American race sociologists of the 1930s and 1940s, who assumed in caste a concept to describe race stratification in their own country.[7] At the other extreme stand the more recent analyses by Louis Dumont and Stephen Barnett, who explicitly deny that the classic Hindu theory of varna, which informed the caste system, reflects an ethnic or racial scheme of reckoning and evaluation.[8] (And in between there lies a host of varying and often confusing formulations concerning the traditionality of ethnic and racialist "casteism.") As Dumont's revisionism seems at present to hold the field, it may be most useful to focus upon it.[9] Dumont argues that varna theory is based upon a holistic, integrative, and hierarchical vision of society. This vision, or ideal, is holistic because it incorporates all the different castes into membership of a single, whole community; it is integrative because it conceives them as mutually interdependent rather than competitive; and it is hierarchical because it possesses a ladder of status ranking. The key to understanding it lies in the dichotomy of the Pure-Impure, which represents a consensual value accepted by all and defining their membership of the community. Purity is possessed and achieved not only through genetic inheritance but also, and very importantly, through style of life. Castes represent social groupings differentiated by their lifestyle in relation to the universal norm of purity, which provides each with a distinctive "code for conduct." The system necessarily imposes interdependence, for no caste can maintain the relative purity of its code for conduct without others to perform code-breaking acts of impurity for it; and it implies hierarchy, for the codes of some castes contain less impurity than those of others. But the rationale of rank does not reflect differential access to or possession of

political power. Looked at this way, castes cannot be seen as ethnic groups: neither are they founded upon beliefs about their cultural (still less genetic)
autonomy nor are their relationships competitive. Equally, the caste system
cannot be seen as one of racial stratification: its categories of evaluation refer as
much to ways of behaving as to modes of being, and, in any event, differentiation within it derives from a commonly held value system, not from the exercise
of power and domination by one ascriptive grouping over others.

Dumont's principal arguments pertain to relations within the Hindu community, the community of the relatively pure-impure. But what of relations outside, especially with untouchables and Muslims? The question of untouchability
is complicated both by the fact that the concept is defined by total lack of purity
(which may imply non-membership of the respectable community of the pure)
and that Sanskritic scripture frequently associates it with "blackness" (in a way
which may imply a racialist connection between inherited appearance and
social status). Dumont's own discussion is perhaps not satisfactory even in his
own terms,[10] but Stephen Barnett has developed the logic of Dumont's inquiries
more fully. He argues that, even in relation to untouchability, inferiority was
seen more as a product of polluting activities than polluted being: it was more a
matter of "code" than of bodily "substance."[11] With regard to attitudes on the
significance of the Hindu-Muslim divide, we possess very little work. But it has
been popular to assume that this relationship was not perceived in ethnic or
racial terms. Paul Brass, for example, has argued that Hindu-Muslim conflict in
North India from the late nineteenth century arose out of the conditions of
"social mobilization" developing at the time.[12] This would imply that, prior to
these conditions, the two communities did not confront each other in ethnic
competition or racial struggle for dominance.

If we turn from sociological conceptualization to the social history of the
two centuries before the colonial conquest, much evidence can be found to support these interpretations of "traditional" ideology. The weakness of the ethnic
component in caste identity, for example, is well seen in the practices of dominant land-controlling castes such as the Rajput of the North and the Nair of the
Southwest. Both seem to have absorbed easily into their ranks new families and
lineages which had come to possess the resources necessary for the exercise of
rural power and were prepared to accept their respective lifestyles and symbols
of prestige as those legitimating power.[13] This openness bespeaks less an ideology
of tight ethnic corporateness than one in which caste was seen to demarcate per-
meable status categories defined around particular codes of behavior. Further
evidence of the mutability of caste rank and of its relationship to properties of
"doing" can be noted in the widely differing effective statuses which local groups
of the same caste "mega-category" could come to possess.[14] In South India, the
Padayachi of North Arcot were generally regarded as members of a prestigious
caste but those of Tanjore were held scarcely to be "clean"; the Shanar of

Southern Tinnevelly were deeply polluted but those of Kumbakonam were bordering on Vaishya status. Behind these variations lay sharp differences in lifestyle (with obvious purity connotations): North Arcot Padayachis were landowners but Tanjore Padayachis laborers; Southern Tinnevelly Shanars were involved in toddy-tapping but Kumbakonam "Nadars" were merchant-traders.[15]

If these features make the caste hierarchy appear closer to a hierarchy of "orders" or "estates" than of ethnicities and races, the structure of temple festivals, religious melas, and so forth can be taken to illustrate how the scheme of order was founded in values consensus. On these occasions, differential caste rankings were publicly paraded in contexts incorporating the entire Hindu community and indicating a universal acceptance of the ladder of rank. Each order was allocated its own place and its own rights of participation in the celebration. While indeed (and *pace* certain versions of modernization theory) there is overwhelming evidence of social competition in "tradition," it was not generally expressed in terms or rivalry between the different orders (the different ranks of caste). Rather, as Stephen Barnett has argued, its conventional manifestation was in the rivalry or small, discrete family and kin groups for membership of association with more prestigious ranks.[16] The ranks themselves did not compete and the criteria of rank were not in contention. One central exception to this would seem the great South Indian division of Left Hand–Right Hand. Violent conflicts over the status to be accorded to these two clusters of castes racked South Indian political life for centuries and very much concerned the criteria of social evaluation. Debates about the nature and origin of this division have been long and remain as yet inadequately resolved. But although, as we shall see, the phenomenon in some regards suggests ethnic competition, it may be worth pointing out here that in others it does not. In the port cities of the seventeenth and eighteenth centuries, where Left-Right strife was especially chronic, membership of the two "factions" was far too unstable and flexible to fit an "ethnic" interpretation. Discrete caste groupings sometimes supported one side and sometimes the other; in certain cases the women of a caste affiliated with one Hand and their menfolk with the other; in other cases, members of castes not actually involved in the confrontation (such as Brahmins) played active organizing roles.[17] Whatever its ultimate character, Left-Right conflict did not accurately demarcate the conflict of two ascriptive communities.

The history of Hindu-Muslim relations at this time also provides much material to sustain the case that ethnic and racialist sentiments, if they existed at all, were of limited scope in traditional society. The Mughal Empire seldom presented itself explicitly as a Muslim conquest state and, indeed, relied heavily on Hindu symbols of authority to legitimate its power. Behind this paradox may be seen the inability of orthodox Islamic political theory to accommodate a state independent of the Caliph. The empire also drew Hindu landed and "service" elite groups into its governing institutions and generated a distinctive "Mughlai" ruling cultural style which bonded them together with its Muslim servants.[18] At a more popular level, many Islamic ideas and symbols penetrated North Indian religious practice and belief, helped by the eclecticism of Hinduism at the point of folk culture. There was here no clear, unequivocal confrontation between rival religious ethnicities.

Importantly, however, although it is possible to select discrete empirical facts from history to support this interpretation, it is no less possible to find others which challenge it. If, for example, it is true that dominant rural castes absorbed powerful outsiders in a way which questions their nature as groupings founded upon a common heritage, it is no less true that these same castes maintained origin myths and legends, which suggest that they did take part of their character from perceptions of a common cultural, or even genetic, inheritance. Emphasis on this inheritance would give them an identity historically separate from that of the rest of society and provide an obvious basis for ethnic consciousness. That this emphasis existed is plain enough in the extent to which newcomers had to indulge in elaborate fictions in order to lay claim to the common ancestry.[19] Equally, the praxes of the past do not entirely justify the neat distinction made by Dumont and Barnett between "doing" and "being" (between code and substance). While indeed the polluting qualities of lifestyle had a major impact on caste status, it is unclear that a change in lifestyle could ever fully compensate for a demeaned inheritance of "substance" or association with demeaned groups. North Arcot Padayachis, for example, might live as "purely" as their Vellata landlord neighbors, but they never had quite the same status; Kumbakonam Nadars might live to Vaishya standards, but they were never fully accorded this status in temple rituals. The taint of their ancestry and associations held them back in a manner which is explicable only in terms of theories which evaluate and rank social groups on the qualities of their "substance."

Moreover, it could not be said that pre-colonial society lacked all instances in which ethnic- and race-like conflicts between castes developed. In urban contexts, for example, artisan and mercantile groups frequently became embattled over the standards of evaluation used to determine their relative status. Down the Southeast coast, the rivalry between Komatis and Beri Chetties was notorious and manifested itself in periodic confrontations between these "communities" for honorific precedence. Such rivalries could extend beyond discrete caste groupings to fill out the framework of Left-Right division. As Burton Stein has argued (and whatever the incidental complications caused on the fringes by the shifting of allegiances, the sexual division of labor and factional strife), both sides contained a hard core composed over centuries of the same castes.[20] Many elements in their self-definition, which arose out of their long-term conflict, are suggestive of an ethnic communalism. In certain parts of the countryside, too, lines of ascriptive caste affiliation could demarcate lines of communalist conflict. In areas of North India, where conquering Rajput warriors encountered entrenched resistance from Jat settlements, battle was joined not only over the simple possession of dominion but over the relative value to be assigned to the separate lifestyles and traditions embodied in the opposing forces. Jat beliefs in the worthiness of work on the land and in "independence" stood juxtaposed to the martial and luxury-orientated values of the Rajput. The reassertion of Jar authority in eighteenth-century Punjab saw not only the replacement of one warrior group by another, but an important change in the nature of the state.[21] Jat-Rajput rivalry betimes took the form of a communal confrontation replete with ethnic and racial stereotypes. On a much more limited scale, so did Brahmin-Kammala conflict in Southeast India. Here, the issue was the supposed replacement of Kammalas (artisans) by Brahmins in the offices of village government following warrior conquests of the fourteenth century.[22] Kammalas maintained a tradition of resistance to, and criticism of, Brahmin authority, which served to define the two as rival communities separated by historical origin and present values.

These outbreaks of ethnic competition in caste relations inevitably extended themselves into "racialist" forms of struggle. As Dumont argues, the caste categories of the varna scheme, in their *locus classicus* of apolitical, holistic Hindu social theory, may not outline a system of race stratification. But suppose those categories are relocated in different social theories which assume ethnicity and deal with the question of political power? The case then seems entirely altered, for the caste hierarchy now represents a scheme for the sub- and super-ordination of ascriptivety defined communities under and over each other. Differential and deferential political liberties and social rights are determined by membership of the ascriptive caste community. The tendency for some social groups to define themselves in caste ethnic terms, and for issues of caste identity to intrude into the political arena, made the "racialization" of the caste system a possibility—and an occasional reality—in "tradition." When Right and Left competed for honors and Jar and Rajput fought for the land, they were struggling to establish the superiority/dominance of their community over another. The caste system, when invoked in these contexts, was being used as the tool of a racialist theory of legitimation.

On the Hindu-Muslim front, also, all was by no means as smooth as we first pictured it. On the Hindu side, resistance to Muslim rulership sometimes could involve religious mobilization. The Vijayanager Empire, which stood against the Deccani Sultanates, for example, consciously developed the symbols of Hindu kingship to provide itself with political legitimacy, internal authority, and external definition.[23] Much later, Sivaji adopted the same symbols to identify his rebellion against the Mughal Empire. On the Muslim side, rulers such as Aurangzeb and Tipu Sultan enforced Koranic discrimination against infidels and Kaffirs and presented their states as conquests for Islam. Equally, the tong-term preference of the Mughals for administrators drawn from international Islam may be seen not only as a prudent device to prevent the build-up of local particularism but also as an attempt to preserve a distinctively Islamic element in the character of the regime. However conflated and interpenetrated Hindu and Muslim cultures may have become, especially in North India, there remained a level at which the two were separate and potentially conflictual. Occasionally, this conflict was brought to the surface of political life.

The position we have reached on the question of "traditional" ethnic and racialist sentiments, then, is distinctly ambiguous. On the one hand, it would appear that society was not structured around principles of competing ethnicity or racial domination; but on the other, it would seem that such forms of competition and domination could emerge and sometimes did realize themselves in the social structure. To make sense of this paradox, it may be useful to look at some post-Dumont developments in the study of Hindu ideology and at some other aspects of Indian cultural history. Recently, Marriott and Inden have claimed to detect beneath the surface of Hindu social theory a fundamental set of beliefs concerning the relationship of man and nature. They regard this relationship to be essentially monistic, with society and nature being seen as interpenetrating and continuous.[24] This monism is most obvious in the concept of pollution, where relationship to various biological substances determines purity of lifestyle and hence social status. The substances held relevant to pollution, however, are conveyed not only through contact with "outside" objects and people but also through inherited blood. Seen in this light, the central dichotomy which Dumont and Barnett use to illustrate the non-ethnic/non-racialist character of traditional Hindu ideology begins to collapse. The separation of caste as code for conduct and caste as bodily substance is clearly difficult to maintain if, in fact, pollution is judged in relation to both criteria simultaneously. Within the monistic theory of Marriott and Inden, it would seem necessary to classify the caste system as one which certainly contains the qualities of the system of hierarchy outlined by Dumont, but which also and inseparably contains the qualities of a system of ethnic polarities and race stratification. Monistic concepts blur the meaning of the distinction.

In addition to the implications of monistic theory, the paradox can be further clarified by reference to the character of certain "non-Hindu" beliefs which also informed the social context. Hindu varna theory was by no means the only ideological system available to society. Dumont himself recognizes the existence of a parallel set of categories (of Artha) which evaluated status in terms of the possession of power and territorial domination. It is his contention that this alternative system was structurally subordinate to that of Dharma, of the pure-impure dichotomy.[25] However, it is unclear how this structural notion is to be translated into historical concept or how this subordination can be demonstrated. That beliefs drawn from the theory of varna informed and helped to mold Indian social life through the centuries may readily be conceded. That this constancy, or persistence, represents "encompassment" or domination of the culture is another, more difficult matter. It would be problematic in the extreme when considering cultural history to leave out of account, or relegate to a level of inconsequence, the information available to social actors from other sources and traditions. Of these, perhaps the most important with regard to ethnicity and racialism was the legacy of the "tribal" past. The social structure of many parts of rural India bore the imprint of settlement, colonization, and conquest by tribal groupings, affiliated through the principles of clan and lineage. Access to land, land revenue, and command over labor were functions of membership of a corporate group defined by genealogy.[26] Admittedly, in post-conquest and colonization situations of economic development and growing social plurality, where the influence of varna theory became strong, the significance of genealogy tended to weaken and become formalistic. As we have seen, scarcely disguised fictions allowed new groups to be absorbed into the Rajput and Nair communities of descent. But the very need for fiction is indicative of the residual importance attached to ancestry in defining the community and of a continuing relationship between blood, social status, and political power. The clearest example of the "tribal" imperative on social organization may be found among the Jats, on whose heterodoxy to classical Hindu norms even Dumont has remarked.[27] But tribalistic principles underlie social structure much beyond the Punjab. Recently, for example, Burton Stein has noted their presence even in the "core" areas of Southeastern civilization.[28]

A second influence promoting ethnic or racialist conceptions of society can be traced to certain aspects of Islamic ideology. Most obviously, the application of theocratic principles in this most plural of religious contexts would make religious affiliation the test of civil rights and turn society into a battlefield between religious communities competing for political dominance. That an association existed in North India between Islam and access to political power may be seen in the extent to which Hindu elite groups were drawn toward Mughlai culture and to which Islamization provided an alternative model to Sanskritization for groups seeking to assert claims to higher status based upon improved codes for conduct. At least indirectly, the ideology of Artha also played a part in informing racialist attitudes. If territorial domination determined social status, and if that dominion were organized around principles of clan and lineage, then society appeared as a system of stratification, based upon differential access to power, in which the ascriptive criteria of blood and descent determined membership of the top stratum.

In the society of the two centuries or so before the colonial conquest, then, there existed a number of cultural strands which could be drawn upon to provide ethnic or racialist interpretations of society. But, of course, there also existed a number which led to very different conclusions and systems of social evaluation. The next question must be contextual: Under what circumstances were the different strands woven into the social fabric? Briefly, the rise of ethnic and racial sentiment appears a characteristic response to certain types of political and economic instability.[29] Both the Jat-Rajput and Brahmin-Kammala cases, for example, represented post-conquest situations in which the conquerors, clearly distinctive cultural styles, had failed to make their positions fully effective at the level of the relations of production. Residual layers of Jat power and autonomy, even in areas where Rajputs dominated the state, survived in strong peasant corporations which controlled agricultural production. Tight artisanal organizations, based upon the preservation of rare skills, gave Kammalas the foundations of an independence in the economy. From these defensible (and defended) platforms, both were able to mount resistance to the new order being imposed upon them and to maintain a critique which questioned the value of the conquerors' cultural distinctions. Unresolved political tensions, or contradictions, also can be seen to lie behind Left-Right divisions in South India. Burton Stein has identified the emergence of these juxtaposed groupings with deep-seated changes in the political structure from Chola times. The political authority assumed by dominant agrarian groups was subject to challenge from the rise of independent artisan and mercantile communities. Vacuums, as much as conflict, in political power also were capable of mobilizing society along the lines of ethnic competition. The hierarchical Hindu honors system was integrated under the power of "the king," who, indeed, received his religious legitimacy in part from his function in maintaining the social order implied by varna theory.[30] But suppose no king existed or had sufficient power to arbitrate disputes about the proper position of groups within this order? The result would tend to be conflict between caste-defined groups, which could harden into ethnic confrontations. In the European-ruled port cities of the seventeenth and eighteenth centuries, the failure of alien political rulers to operate the honors system satisfactorily, or at all consistently, can be seen to lie behind the near-continuous caste strife.

Economic pressures also created quakes in the social structure. The basic organization of the market was monopolistic, and considerations of caste and religious status were significant in determining access to privilege. Changes in the distribution of patronage, competition in trade from newly arriving immigrant groups, and changes in the locus of economic activity all could provoke social conflicts expressed in the language of ethnic rivalry. Arjun Appadurai, for example, has traced the Left-Right riots of Madras city in the seventeenth century to a struggle between leading merchants for East India Company contracts.[31] The frequency of conflict between different caste and religious sections of the South Indian weaving class at this time also is indicative of the economic imperative.

The generality of this ethnic response to political and economic change reveals a crucial structural feature of precolonial society. Not merely the relations of territorial domination but also those of production tended to be penetrated by and organized around principles of kinship. Position in the labor market was in many ways ascriptively determined by membership of a corporate kinship body, which took responsibility for the preservation and transmission of skills, for the maintenance of craft and more general social discipline, and for the provision of welfare. In any given local context, such kin-corporations carried specific and recognizable caste or religious designations from which they derived their effective status. Doubtless in stable politico-economic conditions, this society of corporations could be integrated into a broader structure. The specialization of skills promoted functional interdependence; the consensual values beneath varna theory implicitly articulated a social hierarchy. But if the politico-economic framework were subject to sudden pressure, or collapsed, the nexus holding the corporations together looks weak indeed. In any struggle to protect or advance political and economic position, the likely participants would be discrete corporate groupings. And, given that their public identities were described in caste and religious terms, their friction would likely generate the heat of ethnic conflict. Indian society was constructed in a way which made it fragile to the imperatives of change. Local social integrations were easily disturbed and, should they start to break up, there was a strong probability that they would break into competing "ethnic" pieces based upon the ascriptive ties of kinship, caste, and religion.

III

To return to our central problem, can the late colonial explosion of ethnic and racialist politics be understood simply as the generalization of this structural proclivity in response to the conditions of change and instability created by colonial rule? Was the explosion essentially "traditional" in character? There is much to support such an argument, and presently we shall have to turn to the nature of the colonial impact. But before doing so, it may be worth noting that there were qualitatively new elements in the ideology of ethnicity and racialism of this later period—elements which make it difficult to treat mobilization solely as a lineal continuity. One aspect of this novelty was that several of the principal categories of traditional ethnicity lost their significance while others, meaningless before, appeared. In South India, the great Left-Right division ceased to be central and was replaced by divisions along the axes of vernacular culture and Brahmin-non-Brahmin. A second was that, to some degree, demands for equality crept into the disputes between ethnic communities. The older conflicts always reflected demands for differential status and power in a social order which was assumed to be hierarchical (or stratified). Disputes concerned honors, rights to territorial dominion, monopoly positions in the market. Now there occasionally appeared demands for equal treatment between communities and for free access to the market economy. Third, the "fissionary" logic which had underlain the definition of the older (especially caste) identities was joined by a new "fusionary" logic. Whereas previously caste groups had sought to define themselves "minimally" on the basis of the narrow particularities of kinship, residence, occupation, etc., and to differentiate themselves from others bearing the same caste title but of lower-status particularities, now they began to seek "maximal" definition of their community. Castes, at least through their formal associations, opened their doors to all claiming the least affiliation.[32] Fourth and most importantly, the implicit class component in ethnic identity started to disappear. Traditional ethnic and class identities were extremely difficult to separate. When South Indians told "Komati" jokes, they assumed the Komati to be a (greedy) money-lender; when they told naughty children "Kallar" stories, they assumed the Kallar to be a thief (which the term means). On Burton Stein's analysis, behind the Left-Right division there lay a juxtaposition of agrarian and mercantile/artisan class interest.[33] The newer conceptions of caste (and religious and vernacular) ethnicity divorced identity from any specific class context and defined "the community" in terms (of descent, historical ancestry, common culture) which made class irrelevant.

As Dumont and Barnett argue, these novel features are to be associated with the irruption of a "modernistic" ideology predicated on the values of equality and individualism.[34] Indeed, so strongly do they argue this that they make these values central to their definition of any concept of ethnicity or racialism. While appreciating the significance of the break between tradition and modernity seen from their structuralist perspective, nonetheless such definitions may be historically obfuscating. On the one hand, they provide no adequate concepts to describe the caste and communalist conflicts which we noted in tradition and whose very existence both authors appear to overlook or treat as inconsequential; on the other, they create difficulties in explaining the relativities and specificities of change. They posit an absolute dichotomy between tradition and modernity which allows the particular nature of the past no role in determining the particular forms of "the present."[35] It is an old criticism, but not even the social structures of the modern Western world can be analyzed satisfactorily on the assumption that they have been redrawn on a blank sheet over the last hundred years. But before considering the relationships between past and present involved in this case, it may be necessary first to look rather more closely at the character of this modern ideology. While an extrapolation from the values of individualism and equality to theories of ethnicity and racialism may be possible, it is not inevitable. International socialism and atomistic free-market capitalism, in which ethnic criteria are irrelevant, represent ideologies no less deducible from the same modern base. What was there about the historical condition of modern ideology as it reached India, which encouraged sociological theorizing to follow ethnic or racialist lines?

Any answer to this question must turn to the culture of the British rulers.[36] From at least the middle of the nineteenth century if not earlier, British histor-ical and sociological accounts of Indian society tended to converge on pluralistic theories. Indian society was seen to consist of an almost endless series of cultur-ally distinct communities, demarcated along lines of caste, religion, and language. Her history was written in terms of the over, lapping and collision of these eth-nicities. Dr. Caldwell, for example, saw the South Indian Brahmin–non-Brahmin divide as the product of an Aryan (Brahmin) conquest and subordination of the Dravidian (non-Brahmin) peoples. Edgar Thurston's celebrated *Castes and Tribes of Southern India* mapped out the thousands of differences in custom and belief in South Indian society and appended a community label to each. India appeared to contain a vast plurality of culturally distinct groupings.

Nor was it only through concepts of ethnicity that the British perceived Indian society: it was also through concepts of race stratification. These various commu-nities were capable of being ranked on the basis of their supposedly inherent attrib-utes. The "martial" races of the Rajputs and Muslims of the North were seen to hold their premier positions in rural society by right of blood and ancestry, which gave them special (fighting) qualities. They came to enjoy much economic protection from the Raj.[37] The "criminal" tribes of South India, by contrast, were regarded as inherently deviant and became subject to increasing restriction on their civil liber-ties through laws which reflected apartheid-like discrimination.[38] The British expe-rience of Indian society was mediated through systems of reckoning and evaluation which centered on the implications of ethnicity and race.

To explain this, we can look, of course, at the background of domestic British culture. A crucial legacy of the era of liberal nationalism in Western Europe was the concept of "a people" as a distinctive, unified social community defined by possession of a common culture. Coming to India, with its array of minute symbolic distinctions and immense heterogeneity of languages, sects, and customs, it is not difficult to conceive how British sociologists would see in these differences the origins or makings of many different "peoples." Equally, the development of Social Darwinism and the emergence of the science of eugenics clearly influenced the way in which the British explained Indian social stratifi-cation to themselves. Yet reference to these general intellectual backgrounds may not of itself be very adequate. In Britain, theories of ethnicity and race were but one part of a much broader sociological culture and their significance was subject to much debate and disputation. In India, however, they stood supreme and virtually unchallenged as representing obvious social scientific truths. They lay at the core of the hegemonic ideology of the Raj.

Ultimately, it is very difficult to dissociate the significance of ethnicity and race in the British sociology of India from the imperatives of the colonial situa-tion. These theoretical assumptions simultaneously legitimated imperialism and dissipated opposition to it. Race theories provided a ready explanation and justification of Indian subjugation in terms of white superiority. The extent to which such theories informed British policy may be seen both in the vagrancy laws, which permitted the deportation of whites whose deviant behavior undermined "the mystique" of their race, and in the resistance of the Indian Civil Service to power-sharing with Indians lest the "English" character of the administration be diluted.[39] As applied internally to Indian society, race theories also served to show up multiple divisions which were held to deny Indians the status of a people, or *volk*, founded upon common "stock," and hence to deny them the political rights which contemporary liberal-nationalist beliefs imputed to such a *volk*. This divisive function was further served by theories of ethnicity. It can be seen most clearly in the writings of Sir Reginald Craddock, whose critique of Inthan nationalism was based on the premise that India contained "not one but sixty nations," each culturally distinct from the others.[40] A sociology of multiple ethnicity sustained imperialism on the "umpire" analogy, positing the need for an independent arbiter to regulate the affairs of these naturally conflicting communities.

The usefulness of these theories to the Raj, however, raises the question of how they came to be accepted and "internalized" by Indians themselves. They helped to keep India a colonial dependency, yet they gained a wide following among the subject population, especially within the emergent Western-educated intelligentsia. The many movements which sought to mobilize society along the lines of "modernistic" ethnicity were uniformly led by members of this intelligentsia. Indeed, the Oxford University could be said to bear prime responsibility for modern casteism in South India for a large number of early caste activists were its graduates.[41] The concept of "culture-change" is very problematic, and we may not get far toward understanding it with the notions of "culture contact" and "diffusion" which modernization theory offers us. The former rests on the vacuous and improbable assumption that one culture changes "osmotically" simply by coming into contact with another; the latter is elitist, presupposing an innate superiority in the new, modern culture which obliges those who receive it to accept it.[42] We need to consider more carefully (indeed at all) the mechanisms to exchange. One of these might be seen in the status of tile social sciences at the time. In Britain, sociology was seen less as a reflective and critical discipline than as a branch of the natural sciences, capable of discovering universal laws and truths. Its methodology (and the relative methodological consensus) gave its pronouncements a finality and authority which could not be assailed at the level of value-bias. This made it difficult to attack, and left Indians poorly placed to develop an alternative sociology which could lay claim to the same scientific status. Second, in a perverse sense the authoritative nature of the sociological discipline fitted with certain aspects of the Hindu philosophical tradition. In classical debate, the status of an argument frequently was evaluated in terms of the status of the authority proposing it rather than of its own coherence or rationality. What was true was what the best authority said was true. Who could deny the truth emanating from a source whose massive authority was manifested not only in the efficacy of its science but in its contemporary world dominion? And third, there were several "elective affinities" between the concepts of this colonial modernity and those of Indian tradition. At a superficial level, labels tended to overlap. Whatever immense differences there may be in the meaning of "caste" to a modern as opposed to a traditional sociological theory, they are blurred by the use of a common term. Indians found many familiar reference points in the language of the new social science. At a deeper level, however, there were also points at which concepts themselves partially merged. The belief in a continuum between nature and society, which informed Hindu monism, had a strong parallel in the assumptions which underlay Social Darwinist and, more explicitly, eugenicist thought. There were major differences in the precise understandings of society reachable from these various positions. (For a start, Hindu monism saw bodily substance as transmutable.) But a traditional Hindu intellectual might not have found great difficulty in appreciating the analysis of leading members of the British medical profession who, during the birth-control controversy of the 1930s, rationalized the domestic British class structure in terms of a model of genetic differentiation.[43] The character of Hindu intellectual tradition made Indian society very vulnerable to the penetration of British colonial sociology and facilitated the internalization of the latter's conceptual norms.

But, of course, this process of cultural transfer was wrought not only in an abstract realm of ideas but also in the concrete realm of social and political relationships in which the intelligentsia lived. In part, modern ethnic and racialist theories arose as a by-product of resistance to the colonial power. The British frequently gave to the different categories of Indian ethnicity a particular evaluation. In seeking to reject the specificities of this value-weighting, Indian society inadvertently could come to admit the principles on which it was made. In Bengal, for example, imperial ideology denied to the loose cluster of Hindu upper castes known as the bhadralogh the status of a "martial" race and imbued them with a congenital effeteness which made them unfit to rule themselves or, and inextricably, the Muslim peasant masses in the east of the province.[44] In reacting to this, not only was a much sharper sense of cultural distinction and common identity forged within the bhadralogh (with many features peculiar to upper-caste culture becoming codefined with Bengali culture), but British race theory was inverted and thereby accepted in principle. Patriots of the new Bengal sought to assert a martial spirit which would give them the rights and dignity of independence. Through guerrilla activities and, later, quasi-military political organizations, they challenged the Raj from the premise of its own concepts. Indeed, the influence of Western race theory reached full extent when Subash Chandra Bose attempted to take militant Bengal into an alliance with the Axis powers during the Second World War.[45] Another means by which colonial resistance promoted internal communalism was through the corollaries of cultural revivalism. A widespread response to imperial assertions of the superiority of the Western scientific and/or Christian traditions was a counter-assertion of the virtues of various Indian traditions. But while these revivalist/reform movements may have been intended originally as critiques of the alien West, they also might have the side effect of implicitly criticizing or threatening alternative Indian traditions. If, for example, the Arya Samaj were initially a reaction to Christianity, its conversion ethic soon came to have implications for Indian Islam.[46] If South Indian Brahmin varnashramadharma were originally aimed at Western secularism, it soon came to have implications for the status of non-Brahmins.[47] The pluralism of the Indian cultural inheritance (which is not to say that, by the nineteenth century, India was a plural society) made the revivalist response to the Raj dangerously divisive and even provided evidence for a post hoc confirmation of British sociological analysis and prediction.

But popular though it has become in the post-independence climate to see the Indian experience under colonialism exclusively in terms of resistance, it would be very partial indeed to dismiss the subtler means, through compromise and coalescence, through which British and Indian history were interwoven. In many ways, the penchant of the intelligentsia for ethnic and racialist social theories reflected pursuit of their own more limited aspirations and ambitions in the context of a historically given set of opportunities. First, those who were committed more to promoting a fundamental change in the structure of Indian society than a narrow political excision of the British ruling power frequently found it necessary to approach and work with and through the existing institutions of the Raj. State power was essential to any effective program aimed at widening opportunities for education, improving the status of women, or abolishing what were held to be reprehensible social practices. It was a paradox of the colonial situation that often the most radical proponents of social reform were forced into the most moderate or even mendicant postures in relation to the Raj (and vice versa).[48] The state power which the radicals sought to engage, however, was already organized on the information provided by British sociology. The apparatus of law and administration was designed, in part at least, on principles necessary to governing a plurality of ethnicities and races. In matters of personal civil law, for example, Indians were subject to different rules (and hence possessed different rights) depending on the ascriptive community to which they were assigned.[49] In engaging this apparatus, for whatever purpose, the intelligentsia found itself obliged to move society along the lines of imputed ethnicity and thus to mobilize and make real that ethnicity. When Sir C. Sankara Nair tried to attack the principles of polyandrous sambadarn unions in Keralan society, what he actually achieved was a Nair Marriage Act which gave statutory definition to the concept of a distinctive Nair caste community and ethnic identity.

A second means by which the intelligentsia became trapped in the conceptual categories of the Raj was through its power to structure their class and career interests. As education slowly expanded beyond the confines of a narrow high-caste elite, and as competition for access to colleges and post-graduate employment rose, so the internal struggle for "place" within the intelligentsia intensified. The colonial state mediated in this struggle by increasingly organizing the "competition of the talents," the market for merit, around categories of imputed ethnicity. The distribution of educational patronage, the design of recruitment policies for the civil service (one of the principal sources of employment among the Western educated), and career status in the professions all reflected criteria of ethnic evaluation. In early twentieth-century South India, the "life chances" of an educated man increased dramatically if he were a non-Brahmin rather than a Brahmin;[50] in North India at various times, depending on the shifts in British policy, there was an immediate importance in being Muslim or Hindu. In many ways, the simple pursuit of a living pushed members of the intelligentsia into acting out a social theory predicated on ethnic pluralism.

And third, appeals to ethnic identity helped certain sections of the intelligentsia to overcome their otherwise great estrangement from the mass of Indian society. Once more, in the post-independence climate, it has become fashionable (for members of the contemporary intelligentsia) to challenge the existence of this estrangement which was cited by the British as a reason for discounting the nationalist movement. It may be important, however, to distinguish sociological from political arguments. There are many ways in which the late-colonial intelligentsia can be seen as differentiated from the rest of society. Culturally, they tended to be drawn from the status (if not power) elites of the old social structure and, via the process of Western education, to be influenced by the "alien" ideology of modernity. In class terms, they were orientated toward rentier landownership, state service, and ideologies of capitalist industrialization and modernization which not merely differentiated but juxtaposed their interests to those of a small-holding, craft-based, and subsistence-concerned society. By any standards but those of a blind bourgeois nationalism, they faced problems in establishing bases for popular communication and political leadership. Yet it was such a position of leadership which they sought, or at least which was imposed upon them. It may be going too far to understand this position in the frankly Machiavellian terms implied by Karl Deutsch's model of "social mobilization," which Paul Brass recently has adapted to the Indian context.[51] Here, the emphasis is placed heavily on their own personal interests in maintaining or extending their political power and privileged status in a changing situation. It may be fairer to see their political role arising necessarily from the imperatives of the colonial context. This was an essentially bureaucratic state in which the process of political representation centered on the mechanisms of petition and agitation. For petitional politics to function, it is necessary that rulers understand the objectives being pursued. The authoritarian and alien character of the

Raj meant that this "understanding" had to be achieved in terms of its own language and concepts, which made the Western-educated crucial mediators. At the same time, for agitation to be effective it had to demonstrate large popular involvement. This in turn necessitated communication outside the intelligentsia itself.[52] The colonial political structure both promoted the leadership of the Western-educated and required them to seek popular mandates. But, given their estrangement, how could these mandates be obtained? At this point, the analysis of Brass (and its recent elaborations by Robin Jeffrey and Margueritte Barnett)[53] becomes useful in showing how the atavistic and multivocal properties of ethnic symbols served as potential rallying points for forces drawn from many different sources. They got over the communications gap in ways which were unique and not available to other symbols of class or secular loyalty. Indeed, ultimately they came to affect even the principles of nationalist mobilization, which would seem to stand against them. As G. Pandey has shown (or implied), the mass popularization of the Indian National Congress in North India was coincidental with its shift toward Hindu communalism.[54]

IV

Can, then, the politicization of ethnicity and race be understood as the product of the impact of modern ideology and its diffusion to society? This certainly appears the current orthodoxy of interpretation, with the means of diffusion being seen, variously, in the spread of education and the communications revolution, in urbanization and social differentiation, in political modernization and social mobilization.[55] But grave problems become apparent when the movements and organizations of ethnic mobilization are subjected to close scrutiny. In the first place, the assumed dominance of the modern conception of ethnicity, with its relationship to the values of individualism and equality, is very questionable. Whenever an ethnic association or movement is broken open, it almost always tends to reveal lines of deep internal division over its social definition and precise objectives.[56] While, to a degree, such cleavages may be put down to personal rivalries and factional strife, they were frequently also indicative of a more fundamental conflict in which "modernistic" and "traditionalistic" aims stood juxtaposed. The modern conception of caste ethnicity, for example, was inclined to promote programs which centered on the abrogation of internal status differentials, the elimination of Sanskritic status symbols (which implied deference to other, purer "communities"), and the reform of "irrational" (un-Western) social practices. The traditional conception, by contrast, produced programs for greater Sanskritization, which implied continuing deference to the Brahmin-dominated social hierarchy and a rejection of the value of equality. These divergent principles were regularly in conflict—as, for example, over whether a caste should seek classification as "depressed" to gain benefits from the stare or pursue "elevation" to a higher varna. And often they achieved practical compromise only at the expense of all logicas when caste conferences endorsed simultaneously a range of contradictory proposals. Some analysts have sought to reconcile these tensions through the supposition that Sanskritization was relevant only to the early phases of mobilization and modernization only to the later. But such nice dichotomies hardly fit the facts.[57] The two strands were (and are) cotemporal in the same movements over long periods, and plainly demonstrate that an acceptance, or even awareness, of modern ideology was never a condition of participation in the late-colonial politics of ethnic mobilization.

Second, and to go farther, it does not seem to have been the modern ideological elements in these movements which actually drew the greatest popular response. Occasionally, for example, Indian political leaders influenced or captured the state apparatus and bent it to serve their own modernizing aspirations. But what then is most noticeable is the extreme slowness and apathy with which the bulk of society responded to the opportunities won for them or in their name. The Nair Marriage Act, which we noted earlier, was passed in 1885 under the influence of a reformist group of the Western-educated to permit those members of the caste who wished it to register their marriages and thus opt out of the sambadam system. Forty years later, there had not been a single registration under the Act. Similarly, the reserved employment opportunities won by, or given to, South Indian non-Brahmin leaders in the 1910s and 1920s neither reflected nor immediately produced a revolution in society. Indeed, by 1927, after six years of non-Brahmin justice Party government, there was a higher proportion of Brahmins in the Madras bureaucracy than there had been before."[58] Insufficient numbers of non-Brahmins had come forward to take up the reservations. In these circumstances, the popular followings which occasionally gathered to the symbols of Nair and non-Brahmin ethnicity can hardly have been drawn by the modern elements of social reform and career opportunity in the programs of their leaders.

And third, and the corollary of this, when ethnic movements did gain major followings and achieve political significance, it was usually in response to appeals more meaningful in the terms of traditional ideology. Issues directly related to the Hindu honors system, such as those concerning temple entry and ritual status, brought South Indian caste associations their greatest popularity and fanned most fiercely the flames of caste conflict.[59] Also in South India, the only groups from which the non-Brahmin movement drew a significant cultural response were those of high Sat-Sudra status, who had long maintained an independent religious tradition, parallel to that of Brahmanic Hinduism, which they now mobilized for criticism.[60] Again, the appeal of Pakistan expanded beyond a narrow regional elite to the Muslim "masses" only when it managed to catch the imagination of the extremely traditionalistic local priesthood and peasantry of

Punjab and East Bengal.[61] In many ways, it was less the diffusion of a modern than the disturbance of a traditional ideology that took the politics of ethnicity and race out of the libraries of the Western-educated and onto the streets.

Whence flowed the forces behind this disturbed and increasingly conflictual tradition and why were they manifested particularly in the intensification of ethnic rivalries? Earlier, we suggested that the pre-colonial social structure possessed a strong propensity to crack along the fissures of competitive ethnicity in response to conditions of political and economic instability. The imperatives to change imposed by the rise of colonial rule made such conditions endemic. First, the problems faced by the British in their early port settlements, of relating their government to the honors system which articulated the social hierarchy, deepened as their political hegemony extended. At one level, they attempted to build the Raj as a modern secular state. They counterposed to the principles of the pre-existing social structure a set of laws and institutions based upon notions of contractual obligation rather than status-derived privilege;[62] and they withdrew the state from "interference" in matters of indigenous culture and religion. Both of these developments had grave consequences for stability. The first undermined the position of traditional authorities, while the second divorced the new possessors of political power from the function of maintaining the social structure through its established ritual forms. Both were, in context, revolutionary and generated a response of ethnic conflict. The new legal and administrative systems raised questions about the legitimacy of dominant caste groups to an apparently ascriptive control of land and power. The policy of withdrawal created a vacuum in authority within which ritual disputes could be neither contained nor settled.[63] But at another level, and as if to compound the confusions already caused, the British did indeed "interfere" in matters religious and cultural, and counterpose to their own modern secular institutions a further set predicated on a distorted notion of tradition. Responsibility for overseeing religiously based personal law and for arbitrating a limited range of religio-cultural disputes was passed to the law courts. These, notoriously, tried to rule through a strict application of scriptural injunctions and a rigid interpretation of custom.[64] They attempted to hold the society of the colonial era to the norms of the Vedic age and the past "since time immemorial" (or rather to what nineteenth-century Anglo-Indian jurists conceived those norms to be). Especially in the evaluation of social status, they removed a flexibility which previously had existed through a system of arbitration which relied heavily on unwritten rules and ad hoc and customary tribunals. The new rigidities made extremely difficult the adjustment of caste status to change in lifestyle, which was implicit in the "code for conduct" component of varna theory. The membership, customs, and rights of a caste were now fixed in perpetuity and prescribed by statute or recoverable precedent. Reaction to the novel obstructions posed to social mobility by the law and administration lay behind many a caste mobilization from the later nineteenth century.

The economic implications of colonialism were even more disruptive of the social structure and no less inclined to provoke ethnic responses. The modern, contractual elements in the law and administration, of course, had their counterparts in attempts to break open the economy to the principles of individualistic competitive capitalism. The impact of such principles on a market oriented toward monopoly forms and organized around corporations of kinship and caste could be devastating. A rational reaction was to seek to defend the bases of subsistence by strengthening the social institutions which surrounded and protected them. Attempts to cartelize the market along lines described by the old corporations produced conflicts which were led toward ethnic forms by the ascriptive nature of the corporations. Strife became especially noticeable among artisan and weaving groups, whose general economic space was in any event being squeezed. Moreover, the economic impact of colonialism was no more unilineally modern than its institutional impact. Just as the law contained its own contradictions between a contractually based public side and a personal side founded upon notions of a frozen tradition, so the market also came to be split between principles of free competition and principles of monopoly. The British regularly interfered to create conditions which favored or protected certain interests at the expense of others. While the defense of their own home country's interests would seem the most obvious example of this, it also extended to particular sections of Indian society. Often the groups enjoying preference were defined by the British in ethnic terms, as when the Punjab Land Alienation Act took a list of Hindu urban castes out of legitimate involvement in the land market. State intervention on these lines helped further to structure competition in the market around ascriptive social categories.

Colonial rule also promoted long-term changes in the class structure, which had obvious effects on ethnic relations. A continuing theme in the social history of the period is the drift of wealth and power away from the warrior/aristocracies and rentier/gentries and toward urban mercantile and rich peasant groups. Once more, given the mediating role played by kinship and caste in the organization of the relations of production, it was inevitable that the conflicts which were generated by this drift should be expressed, at least in part, in the terms of ethnicity. In Upper India, for example, the symbols of Sanskritic Hinduism, which had long been buried in the mercantile Vaishya communities and submerged beneath the power of the Mughal Empire, were asserted against the authority of Mughlai culture as wealthy townsmen began to challenge the position of the old gentry.[65] In the South, it was more the symbols of a caste than a religious ethnicity which were mobilized when low-status mercantile groups, such as the Nadars, put pressure on erstwhile dominant agrarian groups, such as the Maravars.[66] In the context of such confrontations, too, traditionalistic theories of ethnicity could be pushed a long way toward theories of race. Behind the growth of Hindu-Muslim conflict in East Bengal lay the growth of class tensions between a rising and predominantly Muslim upper tenantry and a declining, predominantly high-caste Hindu landed gentry.[67] The class underpinnings of bhadralogh authority were fast collapsing in diminishing rent rolls, increasing criticism from below, and, perhaps as a last straw, shrinking access to the state as a result of British policies of discrimination. Faced with these extreme pressures, it may not be surprising that bhadralogh political culture should have been moved toward a martial race theory. Racialist forms of legitimation continued to provide a means of justifying claims to social leadership and power when all else was crumbling away. If society were evaluated in terms of the qualities of inherited blood and cultural tradition, the awkward facts of relative poverty and loss of state power could be overlooked and the bhadralogh might yet preserve their social preeminence.

In many ways, then, the stronger drive toward the politics of ethnicity and race seems to have come less from the force of a diffusing "modernity," revolutionizing the ideology and forms of society, than from a recalcitrant and resistant tradition. Nor should this be very surprising, for, when compared with the empirical record, an interpretation of Indian social history as the fulfilling of the prophesies of modernization theory leaves much to be desired. By 1947, how far had society become "Anglicized, secularized, modernized,"[68] its value-base moved to individualism, achievement-orientation, and equality? How far had the modernization of the economy gone by way of industrialization, urbanization, the competition of the talents, and rapid social mobility? How widespread was literacy and access to the communications revolution? A history which concentrated exclusively on the significance of these indices could but be the history of a small elite, masquerading as the history of the whole society. Nor would it necessarily be a very adequate history even of the elite. Much of the significance attached to these indices derives from sociological theories of the most dubious status, whose explanations oscillate between the vacuous and mechanistic.[69] Much of the movement detected in them derives from a peculiar view of an Indian past which had no communications systems, towns, industry, or physical and social mobility. However, it is arguable that Indian society possessed more of these characteristics of modernity (especially industry and urbanization) before 1800 than in 1900. Moreover, the whole "modernizing" history of India assumes the colonial state to have been a prime agent of the process. But what precisely was modernizing about a state which allied itself with the feudality and peasantry against a rising national bourgeoisie, inhibited (if it did not prevent) industrialization, sought to restrict as much as to expand access to Western education, and tried to freeze the traditional norms of society? Even if the Raj did generate certain modernizing imperatives, it would be a simplistic and eclectic history indeed which isolated those alone and overlooked the counter-imperatives and contradictions which went with them.

But if India's "positive" social history was not one of smooth and progressive modernization, is it then better seen as one of "negative" reactions to the threat of modernization? Did tradition (or pre-capitalist social forms) rise up to block, divert, or overrun the advance of modernity (or capitalism)? Recent trends in Indian historical interpretation, which focus closely on "protest" movements, convey this impression. But it may be just as partial as its linear opposite. The surges of traditional or pre-capitalist consciousness which marked the politics of the later nineteenth and twentieth centuries had a habit of drawing sustenance from relationships with modern/capitalist ideas and institutions. Tenants protesting against their landlords looked for protection simultaneously to a golden age of harmonious paternalism and to the contractual rights given them by the British courts.[70] Punjabi and East Bengali Muslim peasants, rising in defense of Islam, carried themselves into a movement making the modernistic demand for a territorial state. In South India, the most vociferous grain-rioters and preachers of the moral economy came from the areas where grain production had been marketized longest and to the highest degree.[71] In effect, the neat juxtapositions of tradition/modernity, pre-capitalism/capitalism, repeatedly break down in the context of Indian history. These supposed opposites stood in relationships of mutual reinforcement, and most of the institutions of society reflected this contradiction. We need concepts of a different design to capture the processes of the Indian past, and these can come only from a more adequate theory of class relations and colonialism than we presently possess. Obviously, any attempt to develop this theory lies much beyond the scope of this chapter,[72] but a small step toward it might be made by considering a problem in the relations of ethnicity. As we have seen, ethnic movements frequently were internally conflictual over their precise value-basis and the goals which it should set. Yet this conflict never meant that the protagonists would desert the movement, give tip the politics of ethnicity and race. That remained a fixed point for them all. But why should tradition and modernity flow together in this curious way? To emphasize the significance of this confluence and demonstrate the scope of its problematic, what brought the Westernized secularist Jinnah together with the priesthood and peasantry of Punjab and East Bengal? What made the self-proclaimed atheist and communist E. V. Ramaswami Naicker enter a non-Brahmin alliance with the feudal magnate, the Maharaja of Bobbili?[73] It is difficult to conceive of greater political polarities than these.

There seem two possible approaches to the problem. The first is to assume that the symbols of ethnicity of themselves attracted a "primordial" species of loyalty, which subordinated all other political and ideological interests. But this may not get us very far. On the one hand, the Indian context contained a huge variety of ethnic symbols derived from caste, religion, and language. Sometimes mobilization took place around one, sometimes another. The concept of primordial loyalty possesses no means of explaining the shifts. On the other, it is clear that political mobilization was not tied exclusively to ethnicity. Class movements also developed, and the most significant mobilization of all (the Indian National Congress) formally pursued secular goals.[74]

The second and more promising approach, as seen by Paul Brass, is to examine the specificities of "the political process" for clues to the political attractiveness of the ethnicity. Brass's own formulation of this process, however, may not be satisfactory. As we have seen, he relies on a reworking of Deutsch's "social mobilization" thesis. But this requires the assumption of a greater degree of modernization than can be demonstrated for the case, at least in the colonial era, and places too large a stress on elite manipulation. The problems thrown up by the application of this thesis can be seen in many areas. Robin Jeffrey, for example, has used it to argue that the rise of the South Indian non-Brahmin movement at the time of the First World War resulted from the forces of political (particularly democratic) modernization, which created the need for political symbols around which to organize. The non-Brahmin symbol, with its multivocal properties, was peculiarly convenient.[75] But the democratic electorate for whose benefit this symbol appeared consisted of barely 2 percent of the population, half of whom did not vote; many of the followers of the symbol were not involved in formal institutional politics; the political process was dominated by an unrepresentative foreign bureaucracy, and political relations (especially those around the non-Brahmin symbol) were strongly influenced by traditionalistic concerns of patronage and patrimonialism.[76] Equally, there are theoretical difficulties in explaining the role assigned to "power" in the thesis. Ethnic symbols are held to be convenient symbols of mobilization, but mobilization for what end? Sometimes, it seems mobilization simply for the end of achieving power. However, unless assumptions of a general power mania can be grounded in some wider sociological or psychological theory, this cannot represent more than an ad hoc explanation. Sometimes, indeed most often, the implications point to the seizure or maintenance of power by a manipulative elite for its own personal ends. But while this may offer insight into why the elite favor these symbols, it provides little into why the "masses" should be so foolish as to follow them. Moreover, the reliance of the thesis on a bland concept of "modernization" obscures two central contradictions in the politics of ethnicity. First, by assuming tradition to be dying away or inert, it misses the conflict between traditionalistic and modernistic ideologies and objectives, which we have seen to be central to Indian ethnic movements. And second, by assuming a homogeneity of all "modern" ideologies, it misses the conflict between different "modern" programs (socialism and capitalism), which also was contained in certain of these movements. The significance of these contradictions, however, is that they reduce the politics of ethnicity to a zero-sum game. By mobilizing along ethnic lines, in concert with many of their wider "ideological" opponents, Indian political actors made it virtually impossible for themselves to achieve any major social objective, to use power once won to effect a restructuring of society. For, of course, the instant that these movements gain access to power, they necessarily fall apart into their inherent class and cultural divisions which contradict one another's goals. But why then should they ever come together in the first place?

A more satisfactory explanation might be found in the relations of the state. In a seminal article, P. Schmitter developed the concept of "state corporatism" to show how the state could play an active role in the organization and manufacture, as well as resolution, of the conflict between interest groups in the political arena.[77] He contrasted this concept with that of "social corporatism" (or pluralism), in which the interest groups are taken to be generated out of "given" values and market situations in society. There is much in the concept of state pluralism which can be applied fruitfully to the Indian case. Already we have seen how, in matters of the law, the market for talent, and the market for land, the Raj structured identities before state tribunals, and the social categories through which "legitimate" competition took place, around the principles of ascriptive ethnicity. In fact, its use of ethnic categories went much farther, providing the basic information on which it operated its general systems of resource distribution and conflict arbitration. Ascriptive ethnic identity determined differential status with regard to many forms of state patronage, from land grants to school fees to famine relief to income tax liability; it affected rights in the credit, commodity, and labor, as well as land, markets; it even carried implications for the criminal law. Moreover, from the later nineteenth century, the Raj presided over a revolution in the character of its own government, which proceeded simultaneously through a devolution of power and a great expansion in competence. "Representative" tribunals of various kinds slowly took over many of the functions of administration and arbitration while the state sought a deeper control and regulation of civil society. Categories of ethnicity again played a large part in this revolution: through seat reservations and nominations, they affected access to these tribunals and, through growing political manipulation of the market, they influenced access to work and capital.[78]

Viewed in the light of these developments, several of the paradoxes of ethnic politics begin to become reconcilable. Whatever the variety of its value-orientations and goals, Indian society was impelled to organize on the lines of ascriptive ethnicity when it sought to engage the power of the state. The state recognized and responded to appeals coming from ethnic constituencies. That the ends for which this power was to be used were various and often in implicit conflict was not a matter of immediate consequence and, anyway, was obscured by the intervening state apparatus. The same caste association, reflecting the different interests within it, could ask for and receive simultaneously reclassification in the census to a higher varna status and inclusion in the Grant-in-Aid code as a depressed community. The point was, that to get anything, an appeal needed to be launched from an ethnic constituency, and this drew the many opposites into the same nominal organization, imposed a degree of cohesion upon them, and made the struggle to give their movement a coherent social purpose a post hoc problem after the decision to establish it had been taken. This need was especially pressing because not only was the Raj peculiarly sensitive to issues of ethnicity, it was extremely insensitive to issues raised upon other principles of affiliation, such as those of class. In South India, for example, the Madras government never developed a program to help "the landless," but it occasionally produced land resettlement schemes for "pariahs"; it never offered aid to "the poor" but it provided scholarships and cheap education for "depressed castes"; it never designed special electorates or seat reservations for the interests of "labor" but it did for Muslims, Nadars, Christians, Harijans, and many others. The transactional, constitutional, or reformist side of colonial politics was very much conducted in the vocabulary of a sociology of ethnicity, and all those who were concerned with this side had to learn the appropriate terminology or see their interests overlooked and jeopardized. Ethnic forms of political mobilization were obliged to act as the surrogates and agencies of many wider mobilizations.

Adequately to relate the politicization of ethnicity and race to the evolution of the Indian state would require a theoretically adequate treatment of that state. The scope of this chapter no more permits an attempt to provide such a treatment than it did of class and colonialism, of which this could be but a part. However, briefly, there are several reasons why the Raj might be regarded as having an especially important role in influencing the forms of political competition and conflict. First, there was its inheritance. The British took over a political system which was strongly state-centered in both theory and practice. The recognition and arbitration of rulers was highly significant in the effective legitimation of social status. Admittedly, the Hindu king was circumscribed by the need to protect the proper and pre-existing order of society. But he was permitted to change the position of groups and individuals within it, and, ultimately, his authority was important in holding it together. On the more practical side, regimes such as the Mughal Empire maintained monopoly controls and claimed the right to levy a limitless taxation. While doubtless only a small proportion of the profits of monopolies and the land revenue actually reached its treasury, its influence over who precisely enjoyed the rest (through farms, licenses, and zamindari rights) was considerable. State and political authorities also were leading investors in economic development. The prior location of state power (predicated ultimately on the organization of warfare) deeply affected positions in the local class structure. Second, although the imperatives of competitive capitalism forced it to dismantle part of this system, the Raj never abandoned it entirely and, indeed, faced other imperatives which demanded its development. The need to service British interests, for example, kept monopoly controls central to the economy. Strategic concerns and the role imposed by India's situation as an agricultural producer for world markets necessitated state-sponsored programs of infrastructural investment in railways and irrigation works. Most importantly (and significantly for ethnicity), the parlous political situation of the Raj made active state-interventionism the only response to the growth of social conflict.[79] The Raj was exceptionally poorly placed to cope with the turmoil thrown up by the pressures of social change. Its masters kept it in too great a penury to spend its way out of trouble by improving welfare and the level of material benefits in society. They also laid a prior imperial claim on its army, which prevented it from relying on simple policies of domestic coercion. Moreover, the imperial-national contradiction made relations with its most obvious social allies, the Indian bourgeoisie, exceptionally difficult. In the context of rising class tensions from the later nineteenth century, the colonial state intervened increasingly in the marketplace. It tried to cool the heat of competition by apportioning "fair" rights and rewards to the contending parties through its legal and bureaucratic instruments. Not only did this expand its presence in and relevance to Indian society, but it provided a great impetus to the ethnic imperative, for its instruments were especially tuned to the ethnic note.

Certainly, the history of ethnic politicization is much clarified in the context of the history of the colonial state. The chronology of mobilization, for example, fits closely with that of state development and interventionism. The origins of the South Indian non-Brahmin movement are hard to separate from the concerns of the Madras government to counter what it perceived as a Brahmin-led nationalist (and private conspiratorial) threat. Its leading civil servants were trying to restructure the bureaucracy and educational system to aid the cause of a non-Brahmin community for some years before that community demonstrated an ethnic political consciousness.[80] Equally, the role of state relations in the making of the greatest ethnic movement of the epoch, the crusade for Pakistan, was preponderant. Until 1942/43, the Muslim League was able to make little impact on the majority provinces of Bengal and Punjab, whose support was essential to its credibility. Regionalist party governments were still serving satisfactorily many of the interests which it courted. It was only after these governments collapsed, under the pressures of nationalist resurgence and wartime dislocation, and after discussions on the future constitution of postwar India began to point toward nationalist conclusions, that the league succeeded in spreading the message of separatism and in drawing the majorities to the green flag of Islam.[81] A crisis, real or imagined, in the structure of the state provided the final link in the chain to Pakistan.

V

The rise of ethnic and racialist politics, then, may best be understood in the context of the political process developing under colonial rule, whose character was crystallized in and reinforced by the structure of the state. Viewed in this way, however, two problems emerge which become crucial in the analysis of the post-colonial period. First, if these politics were an essential part of the previous historical process, why was their logic not taken much farther at independence? Why was India not fully "Balkanized" after 1947 into a series of autarchic, ethnically based nation-states, or deeply federated according to such principles, or even given a constitution which closely reflected the "plural" status of her society? Yet, with the exception of Pakistan, a case unique both in its significance to the Raj and in the underlying strength of its symbolism, none of these developments took place. India emerged from the British Empire as a secular nation-state based upon territorial principles and with a centrally biased constitution. While, indeed, the forces of vernacular ethnicity have helped to reshape her system of regional government, that system is quintessentially subordinate to the power of the center. The politics of ethnicity have been remarkably ineffective in directing the course of modern Indian history. It is, however, this very ineffectiveness which gives rise to the second problem. Why do these politics still persist at all? If the logic of political development since independence has been toward secularism and territorial integration, why do movements reflecting particularist ethnic sentiments continue to operate and to vociferate apparently hopeless demands?

Some light can be thrown on the first problem by looking at the inconsistencies and inherent contradictions of ethnic movements as primary principles of mobilization. In the first place, if ever one wanted a case from which to challenge Ernest Gellner's belief in the necessary association of language with ethnicity, it would be this one.[82] As we have seen, religion and caste, as much as language, provided the symbols of ethnicity. Clearly, this created major practical difficulties, for every individual was potentially open to mobilization along several different lines of affiliation simultaneously, was implicitly the member of several different ethnic communities at once.[83] A close examination of the politics of ethnicity shows rapid and kaleidoscopic changes in "identity," as betimes one set of symbols became critical and contentious and betimes another. In these circumstances, it was very difficult for ethnic movements to provide themselves with a stable, long-term following. The unique success of Islam perhaps derives from the degree to which lines of linguistic, religious, and lifestyle differentiation converged upon it, although even here its political appeal varied greatly over relatively short stretches of time.[84] A second problem was posed by the lack of correspondence between ethnicity and discrete territory. The strongest political sanction available to ethnic movements, that of "withdrawal" into their own state, was available only to very few. Indeed, it was less seen to be available than forced on the Pakistan movement which, while it always proclaimed territorial ambitions, originally designed them in a way which made nonsense of the ethnic principle and which served more the purposes of gaining special privileges in a still-united pan-Indian state. The logic of territory has perhaps had most to do with the greater spread of the politics of vernacular ethnicity since independence, for it offers a stronger bargaining counter against the center.[85]

Yet the ineffectiveness of ethnic movements may lie in causes deeper than these. To see them, it is necessary first to correct an error of parallax, which has crept into this discussion from the nature of its subject matter. In selecting the phenomena of ethnicity and racialism and sifting through Indian history solely to locate their origins, it is inevitable that we should have given the impression that all the developments of the past led toward them, that all the roads of history converged on their conclusions. This impression, of course, would be quite false, and we have tried to hint at least that other historical themes were unfolding beside these. The politics of race and ethnicity, in effect, were but part of, and were set in the context of, a much greater whole. In examining this whole, it is possible to see a range of distinct disadvantages in or limitations to the politics of ethnicity in comparison to other available models of mobilization. The most obvious of these limitations lay in doing battle with the Raj. The pluralist theory of society was a valuable aid to the maintenance of imperial rule, and while Indian political activity which was informed by it could bring a range of benefits within the colonial system, it was in a very weak position to break that system. Indian nationalism always contained, and its leadership always tried to preserve, a strong emphasis on territorial and secular principles of social identity and political loyalty. From the 1930s, when the final struggle with the Raj was joined in earnest and began to take precedence (and itself to determine) the more restricted competition of domestic politics, the nationalist leadership moved to the center of the political stage. Their principles bound the colonized society together in ways which were crucially necessary, and they both organized and negotiated India's final independence. On the other side, too, the Raj was given reason to question a total devotion to pluralistic premises. These were most useful in the situation of a distant, enervate authority ruling over a stagnant society, for they broke up and neutralized the bases of opposition. But for a state forced into an active role in a more dynamic society, they could carry awkward implications and, particularly, raise contradictions with the class and bureaucratic requirements of rule. In North India, for example, the British had partially rested their regime on the greater territorial landlords, whose authority was coming to be undermined by the growth of class tensions. These tensions were especially open to ethnic expression and forms of political mobilization, for the Islamic or Islamized culture of the landed magnates distinguished them visibly from their more demotic and folk Hindu tenantry. The preservation of landlord authority now started to conflict with the premises of Hindu-Muslim divide-and-rule. In the 1920s and 1930s, the British tried to develop a more secular, class-based system of government through the Legislative Council, while, perversely, it was the forces of nationalism which mingled ethnic with class protest.[86] At a much less significant level, pluralist principles of representation and the needs of "good government" came into conflict in South India. By the mid-1920s, the British discovered that were the non-Brahmin Justice Party allowed to "communalize" appointments, as had first been intended, they would have had to face the new, deepening, and more expert tasks of administration, which were being imposed upon them, with a civil service consisting increasingly of semi-literates and ministerial placemen.[87] Few of the communalist promises of the justice Party government were, or were allowed to be, fulfilled. As India's national class and state structures evolved toward independence, the principles of ethnic affiliation within them came into increasing conflict with alternative principles of statecraft and nation-building. It was by no means a foregone conclusion that they would be deferred to in preference to these others.

Indeed, that this was an unlikely conclusion can be seen by probing further into some of these contradictions. As noted by Dumont, the modern ideology of ethnicity is predicated on the value of equality. This is expressed not only in appeals for a social equality between ethnicities, but also in the corollary to the proposition that the individual's social identity is founded in his ethnicity, which is that all members of the same ethnic group share a common identity and therefore are equal. The egalitarian implications of modern ethnic ideology make it a very radical social philosophy. It was no coincidence or mere opportunism, for example, that E. V. Ramaswami Naicker should have taken his non-Brahmin Self-Respect movement to Moscow and toward communism. Fully extrapolated, the logic of the modern ideology of ethnicity leads to social revolution—albeit one rather more in keeping with Hitler's than Lenin's vision. This logic inextricably entwined the history of ethnicity with that of class, and, in the world of Indian political praxis, it was always going to be extremely difficult to generate the former's revolutionary potential out of the latter's context. On the one hand, appeals to social equality met resistance from the more traditionalistic conceptions of, particularly, caste ethnicity, which were located in the kin- and craft-based organization of the continuing, if distressed, "petit" economy. On the other, and even more significantly, they met resistance from the inegalitarian logic which arises out of the "free" capitalist system and legitimates the social differentiation of class. The development of Indian class relations under colonialism was very complex and we cannot discuss it at length here. But it would be possible to argue that an important theme was the emergence of a dominant class alliance under bourgeois direction.[88] While this alliance was born of growing conflict with other groups, it was not yet under severe stress. Indeed, it was being consolidated as the imperial-national contradiction within the bourgeoisie was progressively resolved, or at least moved to a different plane. In short, the class history of the period made it "unripe" for revolution and extinguished the possibilities of radical change from the ethnic as much as the class perspective. Ethnic movements and associations remained critically reliant on the patronage and support of members of the dominant class alliance, whose self-preservation instincts ensured that their programs were moderated. It was again not opportunism but an acknowledgement of harsh realities that led E. V. Ramaswami Naicker back from Moscow to the Bobbili palace and an electoral pact in 1937 with the conservative Justice Party. Except by attaching himself to the bandwagon of one or other of the dominant class parties, there was no way that his movement could hold any political importance.

The processes of class formation in the late-colonial period, however, can be seen to have done more than limit the radical component in ethnic ideology. They also circumscribed the extent to which its more malleable liberal components could be built into the institutions of the "new" society. At least at the heights of the state and economy, the Raj had imposed systems which operated on unitary territorial principles. These set the framework within which the struggle for independence took place. They also set the framework of institutions within which Indian class relations evolved. As, with the expansion and devolution of government and the beginnings of industrialization, these "haute" systems became more penetrative, so they increasingly helped to determine the distribution of wealth and power in society. Membership of the "All-India" Congress party came to be necessary for effective participation in the state; influence over national policies of protection, subsidy, and labor repression, important for success in the marketplace. There were strong imperatives toward territorial integration at work on the dominant class sections of the emergent national society (if not on all sections, as "integrationist" modernization theories assume). Contrariwise, of course, there were also strong imperatives against weakening the forces of territorial integration. What could ethnic principles of political federation or even autonomy offer to the dominant bourgeoisie to compare to the security of a central umbrella of coercive force, the rewards of a large protected market, and the weight lent to international bargaining strength by size? Ethnic movements, resting on liberal social principles and appealing to a bourgeois following, were obliged to subordinate their aspirations (however tacitly) to the premise of continuing territorial unity or risk compromising their leading members' class interests. The logic of this subordination can be seen in two enduring features of Indian political behavior. First, there seems a strong propensity for the leaders of ethnic movements to sell out their principles as soon as they break into the corridors of power and for movements to moderate their own demands as they get nearer to the apparatus of power. The strength of the Tamil separatist demand, for example, appears to move in an inverse direction to the success of Dravidian parties in constitutional politics.[89] And second, there seems a strong propensity for ethnicity to reach its most extreme manifestation in racialist social theories only among those groups who have no future in the dominant class structure. If ideologies which focus closely on the significance of sub-national ethnicity make territorial integration difficult, those which hypothesize racialism make it impossible. In these, there is no basis for transregional relationships to develop by means other than political domination, which the historical processes through which the Indian nation was built rule out. It is very striking that the Bengali bhadralogh's lurch toward racialism had its counterpart in their progressive alienation from the Gandhian Congress and the mainstream of the national movement.[90] And that this too had its counterpart in their declining position in the Bengali class structure. The forces of national and class history ran against the prestige and privilege of high-caste landed gentries. Their racialism may have represented a legitimate protest against the times, but it was the protest of dead men passing into political insignificance.

But if integrationist themes dominate the development of modern Indian society, why do fissiparous ethnic themes continue to persist and, more than this, strongly to influence the forms in which political competition takes place? At the subordinate levels of the political system, the symbols of regional, religious, and caste ethnicity play an important role even though, when transposed to the national arena, their meaning is wont to become obscure. Part of the answer perhaps may lie in the extent to which, for all its utilitarian value, a national identity based largely on the claims of territory is aesthetically unsatisfying. It can give the relations of society no legitimacy in a theory of organic unity. Attendant upon the processes of nation-formation have been recurring attempts to give the Indian identity a firmer cultural base, most obviously through association with the symbols of the Hindi language and Hindu religion. But the historical parochialism of these symbols makes them problematic agents of unification. The more vigorously they are manipulated, the more vehement become the reactions to them and the stronger the juxtaposition of sub-national ethnicities. In Tamil India, for example, the Hindi language seems to be seen more as the symbol of northern domination than as that of national unity. The secular logic that brought India to independence left an important vacuum, which is filled by a continuing dialogue between her many cultural traditions.

Another part of the answer, however, may lie in the concept of state corporatism, which is as relevant to the republican as to the colonial context. A crucial feature of the constitutional or legitimate political process is the way that "particularist" interests mobilize themselves to compete for rewards and favors from the institutions of the state. These interests are manifested in many forms—as pressure groups cohering around specific issues and as geographically defined local constituencies. The role of the state in this process is to be seen in the extent to which its own design elicits such particularistic responses. The executive agencies of government enjoy a wide measure of discretion in the allocation of patronage. They do not treat individuals as anonymous atoms, each of whose claim on the state is inherently equal and to be adjudicated against standards of merit and efficiency. Rather, they distribute quotas, ranks, and protection in the marketplace, and so on to individuals as members of prior social categories with differential rights and privileges. These categories form obvious nodal points around which pressure groups can gather. Similarly, local government systems tend to operate by allocating block grants, licensing powers, and the like to lower-level, geographically defined, "self-governing" institutions which administer their immediate distribution. What this means, however, is that these lower geographic units are placed in competition with one another for resources from the state and impelled toward a local particularist identification of their interests. Of course, neither pressure group nor locality particularism need engage ethnic affiliations, but a number of factors make this a likely outcome. The state frequently designs social categories/pressure groups around ethnic criteria. The geographic divisions separating competing localities often overlie lines of potential ethnic differentiation (reflected in old, dominant-caste territories, sectarian religious centers, areas of linguistic peculiarity, etc.). Moreover, the tendency is encouraged by a further aspect of the political process. Pressure groups and local administrative institutions gain much of their weight from their role in vote-gathering and -banking. If "government" flows down the political system from above, democratic power flows up it from electoral constituencies beneath. But how is this power to be organized, consolidated, and projected? A strong incentive exists to maximize the public support on which pressure groups and local interests can call, and the symbols of ethnicity are especially advantageous agencies of popular mobilization and group solidarity. They obscure points of possible class conflict and, as "social mobilization" theorists have seen, possess multivocal properties and sentimental attachments which are capable of drawing support from the widely spread corners of an otherwise much differentiated society. The way that republican India structures her systems of government guarantees a continuing undertow of ethnic politics.[91]

But recognition of this political logic creates a further problem. Why should a state whose historical struggle to freedom and dominant institutions so heavily emphasize the virtues of national integration and territorial identity function in a manner which seems to promote disintegration and sub-national ethnic identity? The colonial rationale for a pluralist sociology ended in 1947. What presently informs the republic's adoption of these same assumptions? The answer perhaps might be seen in the difficulties and dangers to the existing territorial state, and the class interests which it enshrines, of attempting to realize the ideal of national integration and, reciprocally, in the practical advantages which accrue to the regime from the maintenance of internally competing ethnicities and particularisms. The lack of uncontentious points of cultural reference cuts the republic off from the easiest means of developing, or imposing, a meaningful and uniform national identity. It also shifts the focus of any desirable identity onto strictly secular criteria. It may be, indeed logically it ought to be, that a secular, territorial national identity is capable of arising, or at least generalizing itself, only on the social facts of effective national integration and secularization.[92] But if this is so, then there lies the Indian rub. It is hard to see how, in the context of the international and social contradictions of capital, India ever is to produce these transforming social facts. Integration and secularization are parts of the ideal-typical program of modernization. They require the equality (or at least potential equality) of individuals, an open-market society, the protection of secular freedoms, and so forth. Unless these requirements are met, the individual's life-chances will continue to be bound up with a host of particularistic institutions (of family, ascriptive corporation, parochial organization, etc.) which protect and determine his welfare, career opportunities, and so on. Yet the costs in social overhead capital necessary to bring these facts into existence are enormous. They require a huge expansion in the institutions of the state, to equalize life-chances by providing equality of access to education, welfare, and the like, and a "perfection" of the communications, specialization, and articulation of the marketplace. They demand a modernizing transformation of the economy. No such transformation has attended India's history since independence nor, given her reliance on capitalist processes and specific situation in the world of capital, can it reasonably be expected in the foreseeable future (even if it were accepted that the dynamic of capitalist development made the notional properties of the "modern" society fully realizable, which is highly arguable). In effect, the condition and situation of Indian society turn the generalization of the secular territorial national identity into an improbable dream.

In the light of this improbability, those who remain committed to the values implicit in the dream may better protect their position by seeking to subordinate and neutralize the forces of ethnicity than by trying forthrightly to oppose and destroy them. What the territorial principles of the republican regime are most vulnerable to are general critiques from the premises of cultural nationalism and territorially coherent pressures for withdrawal. The structure of the state can be seen, paradoxically, to inhibit both of those developments precisely by granting a limited recognition and legitimacy to ethnic principles of affiliation. First, by offering special and particular grants of patronage and protection, the national center encourages ethnicities to compete against one another rather than itself. It provides the favors which ethnic pressure groups pursue, and stands as a potential friend to them all. But to get these necessarily scarce favors, these groups must mobilize against their rivals. The tactic prevents the groups from merging their particularistic interests into general principles of criticism. Its efficacy is well seen in the history of Southern India, which witnessed two major vernacular mobilizations among the Tamils and Telugus at almost the same time. Yet the conflicts between the two, for appropriate territory and patronage from the center, far outweighed any tendency for them to move together. Second, by recognizing and supporting widely various criteria of ethnic identity (caste, locality, religion, and language), the center ensures that many different foci of loyalty converge on the same social field and makes difficult the construction of large-scale territorial solidarities. Through policies which promote internal divisiveness, the territorial secular state can keep itself out of and above the fray of ethnic politics. Indeed, it can do more and stand as the independent arbiter between the claims of rival ethnicities, whose members perceive themselves to have more to fear from one another than from it.

The logic of class relations also can be seen to promote this partial and contradictory solution. First, it is arguable that the personal material interest of members of the dominant class alliance, which holds the national regime, inhibits them from pursuing the realization of the secular national ideal. At present, they enjoy the benefits (of access to monopolies, subsidies, governing institutions, etc.) which flow from possession of the state apparatus. Were society to be effectively secularized and modernized, switched to a value-base in individualism and equality, one consequence would be a great increase in competition in the marketplace and political arena. But this in turn would place an increasing strain on their personal positions of dominance. It is very noticeable that a utilitarian willingness to take advantage of the national government has never implied a reciprocal willingness to accept the secular ideals on which it formally stands. But second, and more importantly, the imperatives of general dominant class interest also sustain sub-national ethnicity. As the British discovered in the last decades of their regime, sociological pluralism can be as useful in dissipating and controlling class as nationalist threats. On the one hand, it breaks up lines of potential cohesion and divides subordinate classes against themselves. On the other, it organizes society into cross-class categories which give subgroups with interests or position in the dominant class alliance leadership roles and authority over their weaker brethren.[93] The radical component in the ideology of ethnicity is thus moderated. In the Indian context, the class functions played by the relations of ethnicity may be especially significant to the development of capitalism. If one accepts the argument that the progress of capitalism in Third World societies faces peculiar and severe problems, is unlikely in the short term to produce a general increase in material benefits to offset the effects of its social disruption, and is likely to involve an exceptional degree of coercion and brutality, then the political means of coping with class resistance lie at the center of the process and prospects of capital itself. The propagation of sub-national ethnicities is, for India, one of the most advantageous means.

For this very reason, however, it may also provide an advantageous point of attack on that capitalism. The interpretation offered in the last few paragraphs leans heavily on Marxist functionalist formulations. These, seeing the role played by its divisiveness in maintaining the class and state structures, are inclined to write off ethnic consciousness as lacking in political potential. But this may reflect an analytical confusion: that because ethnicity may be used as a control mechanism by the dominant institutions, it has its origins in and is simply imposed by those institutions. On our wider arguments, this does not follow. We have tried to show that the tendency toward ethnic politics also arose from certain features of the social structure and, further, that it could express demands for radical change. Traditional ethnicity might emerge as a protest and reaction against pressures on the corporate organization of the relations of production. The egalitarian component in modern ethnic ideology might draw in revolutionary aspirations. A history of class conflict and change lies behind that of ethnic politicization. Indeed, it is only by virtue of the fact that ethnic movements and organizations contain radical "material" and are related to class issues that they can be, or need to be, used as instruments of control at all. But such instruments are two-edged weapons, and, should they be turned back on their current masters, the political implications could be immense. Cultural nationalist campaigns, for example, could weaken the center of the territorial state and greatly limit its coercive umbrella, which, at present, represses the possibilities of radical movements taking place in any one region. Equally, a greater emphasis on the egalitarian ideals implicit in modern ethnicity would open out vast contradictions in the structure of the state. The extent to which the state recognizes ethnic appeals allows them to be brought inside its own regulating systems. Once there, however, the demand for effective equality would confront the class partialities of the regime. The demand could not be met from the class premises of the state, whose legitimating ideology would then stand clearly contradicted by its reality. Given the importance and yet ambiguity of ethnicity to the maintenance of the dominant class alliance and its state, its evocation as part of a radical program seems one of the most promising of all revolutionary tactics.

Whether or not the tactic comes to be used, of course, is another matter. The Indian Left, whether from doctrinal purism or post-colonial nationalist atavism, has shown a great disdain for the politics of ethnicity and a great reverence for the territorial principle. By most standards, its history over the last thirty years also has been one of dismal failure. In contrast, the star of political parties such as the D.M.K.(s), offering an American-style populism tied to ethnic symbolism, has been in the ascendant. But however the future develops, it is hard not to feel that changing configurations around the nexus between class and ethnicity will play a very large part in it.

NOTES

1. To illustrate the profusion: in South India between 1900 and 1930, there were important movements to found a Telugu-speaking province, to improve the position of many separate castes (Nadars, Komatis, Veltalas, etc.) and of non-Brahmins generally, to further the causes of Christianity and Islam, and to promote several forms of Hindu revival (Theosophy, Saiva Siddhanta, Vamashramadharma, etc.).

2. For a discussion of this point, see J. Rex, *Race, Colonialism and the City* (London, 1973).

3. It need perhaps hardly be said that these lines of demarcation are rough and ready at best.

But they gain some force in the Indian context, where a long debate has continued over whether the study of India necessitates a particular Indian sociology, reflecting the uniqueness of Indian culture, or whether it can be pursued through the concepts of universalist theories. This author obviously leans toward the second view. See *Contributions to Indian Sociology* 3 and 4 (1959 and 1960).

4. See R. Bendix, "Tradition and Modernity Reconsidered," *Comparative Studies in Society and History* 9 (1967); D. Tipps, "Modernization Theory and the Study of National Societies," ibid. 17 (1975); L. E. Shiner, "Tradition/Modernity: an Ideal Type Gone Astray," ibid. 17 (1975); J. Gusfield, "Tradition and Modernity: Misplaced Polarities," *American Journal of Sociology* 73 (1967); H. Alavi, "Peasant Classes and Primordial Loyalties," *Journal of Peasant Studies* 1 (1973); M. Hechter, *Internal Colonialism* (London, 1975), Chap. 2. It is singularly unfortunate that, in spite of this tide of critical literature, the bulk of writing on ethnicity and racialism in India has proceeded as if it did not exist and as if the theory of modernization in particular represented an obvious scientific truth. One of the differences between the following account and the main lines of interpretation in the conventional literature is that the former does not rest on a view of India's social history derived from the theory of modernization.

5. Since the Holocaust, this distinction has become important in bourgeois political theory, which legitimates the claims to rights and identity of communities defined by a common culture but not by common genes. But it represents a dichotomy which is difficult to apply historically, for it is unclear that, before the 1930s, many social actors were sensitive to its implications. Popular conceptions of "stock," "people," "vok" etc., tended to assume some species of connections between genes and culture. Moreover, it may not represent a dichotomy of much practical significance. The South African state appears recently to have moved from an ideology of genetic to one of cultural discrimination without turning its world upside down.

6. The argument for a narrow definition of racism on the basis of information from certain Western social scientific theories is made by M. Banton, *The Idea of Race* (London, 1977); and criticized in Rex, Race.

7. M. Weber, *The Religion of India*, trans. H. H. Gerth and D. Martindale (New York, 1958); J. Dollard, *Caste and Class in a Southern Town* (New York, 1940).

8. L. Dumont, *Homo Hierarchicus* (London, 1970); and S. Barnett, "Identity Choice and Caste Ideology in Contemporary South India," in *The New Wind: Changing Identities in South Asia*, ed. K. David (The Hague, 1977).

9. The following reprise of Dumont's argument may appear awkward, but this results from its being strained through our own concepts of ethnicity and racialism, which do not come from his neo-Idealist perspective.

10. Dumont argues that untouchability does not represent racialism, because it is based upon an evaluation of "purity" nor the lineage of "blood." But his own evidence shows that lineage is a consideration in assessing purity; and, besides, what racialist ideology does not assess the significance of "blood" inheritance against a wider standard (of congenital intelligence, *volk* genius, etc.)? Dumont, *Homo*, Chaps. 3 and 10.

11. Barnett, "Identity Choice."

12. See P. Brass, *Language, Religion and Politics in North India* (Cambridge, 1974); also his "Elite Groups, Symbol Manipulation and Ethnic Identity among the Muslims of South Asia," in *Political Identity in South Asia*, ed. M. Yapp and D. Taylor (London, 1979).

13. See R. Fox, *Kin, Clan, Raja and Ride* (Berkeley, 1971); and the review by C. J. Baker of R. Jeffrey, *The Decline of Nayar Dominance* (Brighton, 1976), in *Modern Asian Studies* 11 (1977).

14. For a discussion of the geographic and spatial dimensions of caste, see J. Manor, "The Evolution of Political Arenas and Units of Social Organisation," in *Dimensions of Change in India*, ed. M. N. Srinivas (New Delhi, 1976).

15. See my "The Development of Caste Organisation in South India," in *South India: Political Institutions and Political Change*, ed. C. J. Baker and D. A. Washbrook (New Delhi, 1975); also R. Hardgrave, *The Nadars of Tamilnad* (Berkeley, 1969).

16. Barnett, "Identity Choice"; also, "Approaches to Change in Caste Ideology in South India," in *Essays on South India*, ed. B. Stein (Honolulu, 1975); for a discussion of the temple-related honors system, see A. Appadurai and C. Appadurai Breckenridge, "The South Indian Temple," *Contributions to Indian Sociology* 10 (1976).

17. See B. Stein, *Peasant State and Society in Medieval South India* (New Delhi, 1980), Chap. 5; A. Appadurai, "Right and Left Hand Castes in South India," *Indian Economic and Social History Review* 11 (1974); and P. Roche, "Caste and the British Merchant Government in Madras 1639–1749," ibid. 12 (1975).

18. See F. C. R. Robinson, *Separatism among Indian Muslims* (Cambridge, 1974); and C. A. Bayly, *The Local Roots of Indian Politics* (Oxford, 1975).

19. See Fox, *Kin, Clan*.

20. Stein, *Peasant State*, Chaps. 5 and 8; also B. Beck, "The Left-Right Division in South Indian Society," *Journal of Asian Studies* 29 (1970).

21. See M. Pradhan, *The Political System of the Jats of Northern India* (Oxford, 1966); T. Kessinger, *Vilyatpur 1848–1968* (Berkeley, 1974), Chap. 1; and J. Pettigrew, *Robber Noblemen* (London, 1975).

22. R. E. Frykenberg, *Guntur District 1788–1848* (Oxford, 1965), Chap. 1; see collection on the Kammalas in the Sir Walter Elliott manuscripts, India Office Library, London.

23. See Stein, *Peasant State*, Chap. 8.

24. M. Marriott and R. Inden, "Caste Systems," in *Encyclopaedia Britannica*, 15th ed., Vol. 3; also R. Inden and R. Nicholas, *Kinship in Bengali Culture* (Chicago, 1977).

25. Dumont, *Homo*, Chap. 3.

26. See Fox, *Kin, Clan*; F. G. Bailey, *Tribe, Caste and Nation* (Oxford, 1960); and Kessinger, *Vilyatpur*.

27. Kessinger, *Vilyatpur*, Chap. 1; and Dumont, *Homo*, Chap. 7.

28. Stein, *Peasant State*, Chaps. 2–4.

29. S. B. Kaufmann, "Popular Christianity, Caste and Hindu Society in South India," unpublished Ph.D. dissertation (University of Cambridge, 1980).

30. See B. Stein, ed., *South Indian Temples: An Analytical Study* (New Delhi, 1978).

31. Appadurai, "Left and Right."

32. Fox, *Kin, Clan*; Hardgrave, *Nadars*; and my "The Development."

33. Stein, *Peasant State*, Chap. 5.

34. Dumont, *Homo*, Introduction; and Barnett, "Identity Choice."

35. This critique is made most clearly in S. and L. Rudolph, *The Modernity of Tradition* (Chicago, 1967), although whether the Rudolphs' own formulation of the relationship between past and present is successful is another, more questionable matter. See R. Fox, "The Avatars of Indian Research," *Comparative Studies in Society and History* 13 (1971).

36. B. S. Cohn, "The Census, Social Structure and Objectification in South Asia," paper read at Second European Conference on South Asia, Copenhagen, 1970; L. Carroll, "Colonial Perceptions of Indian Society and the Emergence of Caste(s) Associations," *Journal of Asian Studies* 37 (1978).

37. C. Dewey, "The British Army and the Society of Punjab," unpublished conference paper (University of Leicester, 1977).

38. The Criminal Tribes legislation, which developed from the early twentieth century, involved compulsory fingerprinting and restrictions on mobility.

39. See my *The Emergence of Provincial Politics* (Cambridge, 1976), Chaps. 1 and 5; and D. Arnold, "European Orphans and Vagrants in India in the Nineteenth Century," *Journal of Imperial and Commonwealth History* 7 (1979).

40. R. Craddock, *The Dilemma in India* (London, 1929).

41. P. T. Rajan, N. G. Ranga, K. Koti Reddi, *et al.*

42. See Hechter, *Internal Colonialism*, Chap. 2.

43. I am grateful to Dr. J. Winter of Pembroke College, Cambridge, for drawing my attention to this debate.

44. See A. Seal, *The Emergence of Indian Nationalism* (Cambridge, 1968), Chap. 4.

45. For discussions of Bengali politics, although not quite in these terms, see J. Broomfield, *Elite Politics in a Plural Society* (Berkeley, 1969); and L. Gordon, *Bengal: the Nationalist Movement 1876–1940* (New York, 1974).

46. K. Jones, "Communalism in the Punjab," *Journal of Asian Studies* 28 (1969).

47. M. Barnett, *The Politics of Cultural Nationalism* (Princeton, 1977), Chap. 2.

48. For a proper appreciation of the radical content of "Moderate" thought, see B. R. Nanda, *Gokhale: The Indian Moderates and the British Raj* (Princeton, 1977).

49. See J. Derrett, *Religion, Law and the State in India* (London, 1968).

50. For example, Sir C. Sanakaran Nair was chosen from among other qualified candidates for a High Court judgeship, "because he is not a Brahmin." See my *Emergence*, Chap. 6.

51. Brass, *Language* and "Elite Groups."

52. This thesis is developed in my *Emergence*, Chaps. 5–7.

53. M. Barnett, Cultural Nationalism; and R. Jeffrey, "A Note on Anti- Brahminism," Indian *Economic and Social History Review* 14 (1977).

54. G. Pandey, *The Ascendancy of the Congress in Utter Pradesh, 1926–34* (New Delhi, 1978), Chap. 5.

55. As in M. Barnett, *Cultural Nationalism*; S. Barnett, "Approaches" and "Identity Change"; Jeffrey, "A Note" and "The Decline"; Brass, *Language*; Yapp and Taylor, *Political Identity*; and J. Manor, D. Arnold, and R. Jeffrey, "Political Mobilization and Social Change," *Indian Economic and Social History Review* 13 (1977).

56. See L. Carroll, "Ideological Factions in a Caste(s) Association," *South Asia* 1 (1978).

57. L. Carroll, "Caste, Social Change and the Social Scientist," *Journal of Asian Studies* 35 (1975).

58. See my *Emergence*, Chap. 6.

59. These issues often have been seen as the result of modernization (Jeffrey, *The Decline*; Hardgrave, Nadars, *et al.*). But it is problematic what is qualitatively "modern" about the desire to improve one's status in the hierarchic Hindu honors and varna systems. See Kaufmann, "Popular Christianity."

60. Saiva Siddhanta.

61. Paul Brass has associated the support for Muslim separatism with conditions of "social mobilisation" (Brass, *Language*). For refutations and critiques, see F. C. R. Robinson, "Nation Formation," *Journal of Commonwealth and Comparative Politics* 15 (1977), and his "Islam and Muslim Separatism," in Yapp and Taylor, *Political Identity*; D. Gilmartin, "Religious Leadership and the Pakistan Movement in the Punjab," *Modern Asian Studies* 13 (1979); and I. Talbot, "The 1946 Punjab Election," *Modern Asian Studies* 14 (1980).

62. B. S. Cohn, "From Indian Status to British Contract," *Journal of Economic History* 21 (1961).

63. See, e.g., C. Breckenridge Appadurai, "From Protector to Litigant," *Indian Economic and Social History Review* 14 (1977).

64. Derrett, *Religion*; Rudolph and Rudolph, *Modernity*; also see my "The Law, State and Society in Colonial India," *Modern Asian Studies*, forthcoming.

65. Robinson, *Separatism*; and Bayly, *Local Roots*.

66. Hardgrave, *Nadars*.

67. R. and R. Ray, "Zamindars and Jotedars in Bengal," *Modern Asian Studies* 9 (1975); Seal, *The Emergence*, Chap. 2; and G. Johnson, "Bengal 1904–1908," and J. Gallagher, "Congress in Decline," in *Locality, Province and Nation*, ed. J. Gallagher et at. (Cambridge, 1973).

68. These are the principal themes which R. Jeffrey has claimed to see unfolding in Indian history to 1908. Jeffrey, *Decline*, p. xiv.

69. For a classic critique, see A. G. Frank. "The Sociology of Development and the Underdevelopment of Sociology," in *Latin America*, ed. A. O. Frank (New York, 1969).

70. See, e.g., P. J. Musgrave, "Landlords and Lords of the Land," *Modern Asian Studies* 6 (1972).

71. This point is not noted in D. Arnold, "Looting, Grain Riots and Government Policy in South India," *Past and Present* 84 (1979).

72. Some very tentative steps are taken in my "Law."

73. "F. V. R." led the Self-Respect wing of the non-Brahmin (later Dravidian) movement.

74. For a critique of "primordiality," see Brass, "Elite Groups."

75. Jeffrey, "Anti-Brahminism. "

76. See my *Emergence*, Chap. 7; also C. J. Baker, *The Politics of South India 1919–1937* (Cambridge, 1976), Chaps. 1 and 2.

77. P. Schmitter, "Still the Century of Corporatism."' *Review of Politics* 36 (1974).

78. These points are elaborated in my Emergence, Chap. 6; "Caste Organisation"; and "Law."

79. See my "Law."

80. See my *Emergence*, Chap. 6.

81. See Talbot, "Punjab Election."

82. E. Gellner, *Thought and Change* (London, 1964).

83. These problems are explored in S. Barnett, "Identity Choice."

84. See Robinson, *Separatism*.

85. See R. Gopal, *Linguistic Affairs of India* (London, 1966).

86. Robinson, *Separatism*, Chap. 9.

87. Baker, *The Politics*, Chap. 1.

88. See P. Patnaik, "Imperialism and the Growth of Indian Capitalism," in *Studies in the Theory of Imperialism*, ed. R. Owen and B. Sutcliffe (London, 1972).

89. See M. Barnett, *Cultural Nationalism*.

90. L. Gordon, Bengal, Chap. 9; and Gallagher, "Congress."

91. For discussions of caste ethnicity in the political process, see R. Kothari, ed., *Caste in Indian Politics* (New Delhi, 1970).

92. Hechter, *Internal Colonialism*, Chap. 2.

93. See J. Mencher, *Agriculture and Social Structure in Tamil Nadu* (Durham, 1978), Chap. 10.

8. Class Racism
Etienne Balibar

ACADEMIC ANALYSES OF RACISM, though according chief importance to the study
of racist theories, nonetheless argue that "sociological" racism is a popular phenomenon. Given this supposition, the development of racism within the
working class (which, to committed socialists and communists, seems counter to
the natural order of things) comes to be seen as the effect of a tendency allegedly
inherent in the masses. Institutional racism finds itself projected into the very
construction of that psycho-sociological category that is "the masses." We must
therefore attempt to analyze the process of displacement which, moving from
classes to masses, presents these latter both as the privileged *subjects* of racism
and its favored *objects*.

Can one say that a social class, by its situation and its ideology (not to mention its identity), is predisposed to racist attitudes and behavior? This question
has mainly been debated in connection with the rise of Nazism, first specula-
tively and then later by taking various empirical indicators.[1] The result is quite
paradoxical, since there is hardly a social class on which suspicion has not fallen,
though a marked predilection has been shown for the "petty bourgeoisie." But
this is a notoriously ambiguous concept, which is more an expression of the apo-
rias of a class analysis conceived as a dividing up of the population into mutually exclusive slices. As with every question of origins in which a political charge
is concealed, it makes sense to turn the question around: not to took for the
foundations of the racism which invades everyday life (or the movement which
provides the vehicle for it) in the nature of the petty bourgeoisie, but to attempt

---

Etienne Balibar, "Class Racism," *Race, Nation, and Class*. New York: Verso, 1991, pp. 204–16,
reprinted with the permission of Éditions La Découverte.

to understand how the development of racism causes a "petty bourgeois" mass to emerge out of a diversity of material situations. For the misconceived question of the class bases of racism we shall thus substitute a more crucial and complex question, which that former question is in part intended to mask: that of the relations between racism, as a supplement to nationalism, and the irreducibility of class conflict in society. We shall find it necessary to ask how the development of racism displaces class conflict, or, rather, in what way class conflict is always already transformed by a social relation in which there is an inbuilt tendency to racism; and also, conversely, how the fact that the nationalist alternative to the class struggle specifically takes the form of racism may be considered as the index of the irreconcilable character of that struggle. This does not, of course, mean that it is not crucial to examine how, in a given conjuncture, the class conditions [la condition de classe] (made up of the material conditions of existence and labor, though also of ideological traditions and practical relationships to politics) determine the effects of racism in society: the frequency and forms of the "acting out" of racism, the discourse which expresses it, and the membership of organized racist movements.

The traces of a constant overdetermination of racism by the class struggle are as universally detectable in its history as the nationalist determination, and everywhere they are connected with the core of meaning of its phantasies and practices. This suffices to demonstrate that we are dealing here with a determination that is much more concrete and decisive than the generalities dear to the sociologists of "modernity." It is wholly inadequate to see racism (or the nationalism-racism dyad) either as one of the paradoxical expressions of the individualism or egalitarianism which are supposed to characterize modern societies (following the old dichotomy of "closed," "hierarchical" societies and "open," "mobile" societies) or a defensive reaction against that individualism, seen as expressing nostalgia for a social order based on the existence of a "community."[2] Individualism only exists in the concrete forms of market competition (including the competition between labor powers) in unstable equilibrium with association between individuals under the constraints of the class struggle. Egalitarianism only exists in the contradictory forms of political democracy (where that democracy exists), the "welfare state" (where that exists), the polarization of conditions of existence, cultural segregation, and reformist or revolutionary utopias. It is these determinations, and not mere anthropological figures, which confer an "economic" dimension upon racism.

Nevertheless, the heterogeneity of the historical forms of the relationship between racism and the class struggle poses a problem. This ranges from the way in which anti-Semitism developed into a bogus "anti-capitalism," around the theme of "Jewish money," to the way in which racial stigma and class hatred are combined today in the category of immigration. Each of these configurations is irreducible (as are the corresponding conjunctures), which make it impossible to define any simple relationship of "expression" (or, equally, of substitution) between racism and class struggle.

In the manipulation of anti-Semitism as an anti-capitalist delusion, which chiefly occurred between 1870 and 1945 (which is, we should note, the key period of confrontation between the European bourgeois states and organized proletarian internationalism), we find not only the designation of a scapegoat as an object of proletarian revolt, the exploitation of divisions within the proletariat, and the projective representation of the ills of an abstract social system through the imaginary personification of those who control it (even though this mechanism is essential to the functioning of racism).[3] We also find the "fusion" of the two historical narratives, which are capable of acting as metaphors for each other: on the one hand, the narrative of the formation of nations at the expense of the lost unity of "Christian Europe" and, on the other, that of the conflict between national independence and the internationalization of capitalist economic relations, which brought with it the attendant threat of an internationalization of the class struggle. This is why the Jew, as an internally excluded element common to all nations but also, negatively, by virtue of the theological hatred to which he is subject, as witness to the love that is supposed to unite the "Christian peoples," may, in the imaginary, be identified with the "cosmopolitanism of capital" which threatens the national independence of every country while at the same time re-activating the trace of the lost unity.[4]

The figure is quite different when anti-immigrant racism achieves a maximum of identification between class situation and ethnic origin (the real bases for which have always existed in the interregional, international or intercontinental mobility of the working class; this has at times been a mass phenomenon, at times residual, but it has never been eliminated and is one of the specifically proletarian characteristics of its condition). Racism combines this identification with a deliberate confusion of antagonistic social functions: thus the themes of the "invasion" of French society by North Africans or of immigration being responsible for unemployment are connected with the theme of the money of the oil sheikhs who are buying up "our" businesses, "our" housing stock or "our" seaside resorts. And this partly explains why the Algerians, Tunisians, or Moroccans have to be referred to generically as "Arab" (not to mention the fact that this signifier, which functions as a veritable "switch word," also connects together these themes and those of terrorism, Islam, and so on). Other configurations should not, however, be forgotten, including those which are the product of an inversion of terms: for example, the theme of the "proletarian nation," which was perhaps invented in the 1920s by Japanese nationalism[5] and was destined to play a crucial role in the crystallization of Nazism, which cannot be left out of consideration when one looks at the ways in which it has recently reappeared.

The complexity of these configurations also explains why it is impossible to hold purely and simply to the idea of racism *being used* against "class consciousness" (as though this latter would necessarily emerge naturally from the class condition, *unless* it were blocked, misappropriated, or denatured by racism), whereas we accept as an indispensable working hypothesis that "class" and "race" constitute the two antinomic poles of a permanent dialectic, which is at the heart of modern representations of history. Moreover, we suspect that the instrumentalist, conspiracy-theory visions of racism within the labor movement or among its theorists (we know what high price was to be paid for these: it is tremendously to the credit of Wilhelm Reich that he was one of the first to foresee this), along with the mechanistic visions which see in racism, the "reflection" of a particular class condition, have also largely the function of denying the presence of nationalism in the working class and its organizations or, in other words, denying the internal conflict between nationalism and class ideology on which the mass struggle against racism (as well as the revolutionary struggle against capitalism) depends. It is the evolution of this internal conflict I should like to illustrate by discussing here some historical aspects of "class racism."

Several historians of racism (Léon Poliakov, Michèle Duchet and Madeleine Rebérioux, Colette Guillaumin, Eric Williams on modern slavery, and others) have laid emphasis upon the fact that the modern notion of race, insofar as it is invested in a discourse of contempt and discrimination and serves to split humanity up into a "superhumanity" and a "sub-humanity," did not initially have a national (or ethnic) but a class signification, or rather (since the point is to represent the inequality of social classes as inequalities of nature) a caste signification.[6] From this point of view, it has a twofold origin: first, in the aristocratic representation of the hereditary nobility as a superior "race" (that is, in fact, the mythic narrative by which an aristocracy, whose domination is already coming under threat, assures itself of the legitimacy of its political privileges and idealizes the dubious continuity of its genealogy); and second, in the slave owners' representation of those populations subject to the slave trade as inferior "races," ever predestined for servitude and incapable of producing an autonomous civilization. Hence the discourse of blood, skin color, and cross-breeding. It is only retrospectively that the notion of race was "ethnicized," so that it could be integrated into the nationalist complex, the jumping-off point for its successive subsequent metamorphoses. Thus it is clear that, from the very outset, racist representations of history stand in relation to the class struggle. But this fact only takes on its full significance if we examine the way in which the notion of race has evolved, and the impact of nationalism upon it from the earliest figures of "class racism" onward—in other words, if we examine its political determination.

The aristocracy did not initially conceive and present itself in terms of the category of race: this is a discourse which developed at a late stage,[7] the function of which is clearly defensive (as can be seen from the example of France with the myth of "blue blood" and the "Frankish" or "Germanic" origin of the hereditary nobility), and which developed when the absolute monarchy centralized the state at the expense of the feudal lords and began to "create" within its bosom a new administrative and financial aristocracy which was bourgeois in origin, thus marking a decisive step in the formation of the nation-state. Even more interesting is the case of Spain in the Classical Age, as analyzed by Poliakov: the persecution of the Jews after the *Reconquista*, one of the indispensable mechanisms in the establishment of Catholicism as state religion, is also the trace of the "multinational" culture against which Hispanization (or rather Castilianization) was carried out. It is therefore intimately linked to the formation of this prototype of European nationalism. Yet it took on an even more ambivalent meaning when it gave rise to the "statutes of the purity of the blood" (*limpieza de sangre*), which the whole discourse of European and American racism was to inherit: a product of the disavowal of the original interbreeding with the Moors and the Jews, the hereditary definition of the *raza* (and the corresponding procedures for establishing who could be accorded a certificate of purity) serves in effect both to isolate an internal aristocracy and to confer upon the whole of the "Spanish people" a fictive nobility, to make it a "people of masters" at the point when, by terror, genocide, slavery, and enforced Christianization, it was conquering and dominating the largest of the colonial empires. In this exemplary line of development, class racism was already transformed into nationalist racism, though it did not, in the process, disappear.[8]

What is, however, much more decisive for the matter in hand is the overturning of values we see occurring from the first half of the nineteenth century onwards. Aristocratic racism (the prototype of what analysts today call "self-referential racism," which begins by elevating the group which controls the discourse to the status of a race—hence the importance of its imperialist legacy in the colonial context: however lowly their origins and no matter how vulgar their interests or their manners, the British in India and the French in Africa would all see themselves as members of a modern nobility) is already indirectly related to the primitive accumulation of capital, if only by its function in the colonizing nations. The industrial revolution, at the same time as it creates specifically capitalist relations of production, gives rise to the *new racism* of the bourgeois era (historically speaking, the first "neoracism"): the one which has as its target the *proletariat* in its dual status as exploited population (one might even say super-exploited, before the beginnings of the social state) and politically threatening population.

Louis Chevalier has described the relevant network of significations in derail.[9] It is at this point, with regard to the "race of laborers," that the notion of race becomes detached from its historico-theological connotations to enter the field of equivalences between sociology, psychology, imaginary biology, and the pathology of the "social body." The reader will recognize here the obsessive themes of police/detective, medical, and philanthropic literature, and hence of literature in general (of which it is one of the fundamental dramatic mechanisms and one of the political keys of social realism"). For the first time those aspects typical of every procedure of racialization of a social group, right down to our own day, are condensed in a single discourse: material and spiritual poverty, criminality, congenital vice (alcoholism, drugs), physical and moral defects, dirtiness, sexual promiscuity, and the specific diseases which threaten humanity with "degeneracy." And there is a characteristic oscillation in the presentation of these themes: either the workers themselves constitute a degenerate race or it is their presence and contact with them, or indeed their condition itself, which constitute a crucible of degeneracy for the race of citizens and nationals. Through these themes, there forms the phantasmatic equation of "laboring classes" with "dangerous classes," the fusion of a socioeconomic category with an anthropological and moral category, which will serve to underpin all the variants of sociobiological (and also psychiatric) determinism, by taking psuedoscientific credentials from the Darwinian theory of evolution, comparative anatomy, and crowd psychology, but particularly by becoming invested in a tightly knit network of institutions of social surveillance and control.[10]

Now, this class racism is indissociable from fundamental historical processes, which have developed unequally right down to the present day. I can only mention these briefly here. First, class racism is connected with a political problem that is crucial for the constitution of the nation-state. The "bourgeois revolutions"—and in particular the French Revolution, by its radical juridical egalitarianism—had raised the question of the political rights of the masses in an irreversible manner. This was to be the object of one and a half centuries of social struggles. The idea of a *difference in nature* between individuals had become juridically and morally contradictory, if not inconceivable. It was, however, politically indispensable, so long as the "dangerous classes" (who posed a threat to the established social order, properly, and the power of the "elites") had to be excluded by force and by legal means from political "competence" and confined to the margins of the polity—as long, that is, as it was important to *deny them citizenship* by showing, and by being oneself persuaded, that they constitutionally "lacked" the qualities of fully fledged or normal humanity. Two anthropologies clashed here: that of equality of birth and that of a hereditary inequality which made it possible to re-naturalize social antagonisms.

Now, this operation was overdetermined from the start by national ideology. Disraeli[11] (who showed himself, elsewhere, to be a surprising imperialist theorist of the "superiority of the Jews" over the Anglo-Saxon "superior race" itself) admirably summed this tip when he explained that the problem of contemporary states was the tendency for a single social formation to split into "two nations." In so doing, he indicated the path which might be taken by the dominant classes when confronted with the progressive organization of the class struggle: first divide the mass of the "poor" (in particular by according the qualities of national authenticity, sound health, morality, and racial integrity, which were precisely the opposite of the industrial pathology, to the peasants and the "traditional" artisans); then progressively displace the markers of dangerousness and heredity from the "laboring classes" as a whole onto foreigners, and in particular immigrants and colonial subjects, at the same time as the introduction of universal suffrage is moving the boundary line between "citizens" and "subjects" to the frontiers of nationality. In this process, however, there was always a characteristic lag between what was supposed to happen and the actual situation (even in countries like France, where the national population was not institutionally segregated and was subject to no original apartheid, except if one extends one's purview to take in the whole of the imperial territory): class racism against the popular classes continued to exist (and, at the same time, these classes remained particularly susceptible to racial stigmatization, and remained extremely ambivalent in their attitude toward racism). Which brings us to another permanent aspect of class racism.

I am referring to what must properly be called the *institutional racialization of manual labor*. It would be easy to find distant origins for this, origins as old as class society itself. In this regard, there is no significant difference between the way contempt for work and the manual worker was expressed among the philosophical elites of slaveowning Greece and the way a man like Taylor could, in 1909, describe the natural predisposition of certain individuals for the exhausting, dirty, repetitive tasks which required physical strength but no intelligence or initiative (the "man of the type of the ox" of the *Principles of Scientific Management*: paradoxically, an inveterate propensity for "systematic soldiering" is also attributed to this same man: this is why he needs a "man to stand over him" before he can work in conformity with his nature).[12] However, the industrial revolution and capitalist wage labor here effect a displacement. What is now the object of contempt—and in turn fuels fears—is no longer manual labor pure and simple (we shall, by contrast, see this theoretically idealized—in the context of paternalistic, archaizing ideologies—in the form of "craft work"), but *mechanized* physical work, which has become "the appendage of the machine" and therefore subject to a violence that is, both physical and symbolic without immediate precedent (which we know, moreover, does not disappear with the new phases of the industrial revolution, but is rather perpetuated both in "modernized" and "intellectualized" forms—as well as in "archaic" forms in a great many sectors of production).

This process modifies the status of the human body (the human status of the body): it creates *body-men*, men whose body is a machine-body, that is fragmented and dominated and used to perform one isolable function or gesture, being both destroyed in its integrity *and* fetishized, atrophied *and* hypertrophied in its "useful" organs. Like all violence, this is inseparable from a resistance and also from a sense of guilt. The quantity of "normal" work can only be recognized and extracted from the worker's body retrospectively, once its limits have been fixed by struggle: the rule is overexploitation, the tendential destruction of the organism (which will be metaphorized as degeneracy) and, at the very least, excess in the repression of the intellectual functions involved in work. This is an unbearable process for the worker, but one which is no more "acceptable," without ideological and phantasmatic elaboration, for the worker's masters: the fact that there are body-men means that there are *men without bodies*. That the body-men are men with fragmented and mutilated bodies (if only by their "Separation" from intelligence) means that the individuals of each of these types have to be equipped with a *superbody*, and that sport and ostentatious virility have to be developed, if the threat hanging over the human race is to be fended off.[13]

Only this historical situation, these specific social relations, makes it possible fully to understand the process of aesthericization (and therefore of sexualization, in fetishist mode) of the body which characterizes all the variants of modern racism, by giving rise either to the stigmatization of the "physical marks" of racial inferiority or to the idealization of the "human type" of the superior race. They cast light upon the true meaning of the recourse to biology in the history of racist theories, which has nothing whatever to do with the influence of scientific discoveries but is, rather, a metaphor for—and an idealization of—the somatic phantasm. Academic biology, and many other theoretical discourses, can fulfill this function, provided they are articulated to the visibility of the body, its ways of being and behaving, its limbs and its emblematic organs. We should here, in accordance with the hypotheses formulated elsewhere regarding neo-racism and its link with the recent ways in which intellectual labor has been broken down into isolated operations, extend the investigation by describing the "somatizarion" of intellectual capacities, and hence their racialization, a process visible everywhere—from the instrumentalization of IQ to the aestheticizarion of the executive as decision maker, intellectual, and athlete.[14]

But there is yet another determining aspect in the constitution of class racism. The working class is a population that is both heterogeneous and fluctuating, its "boundaries" being by definition imprecise, since they depend on ceaseless transformations of the labor process and movements of capital. Unlike aristocratic castes, or even the leading fractions of the bourgeoisie, it is not a social caste. What class racism (and, *a fortiori*, nationalist class racism, as in the case of immigrants) tends to produce is, however, the equivalent of a caste closure at least for one part of the working class. More precisely, it is maximum possible closure where social mobility is concerned, combined with maximum possible openness as regards the flows of proletarianization.

Let us put things another way. The logic of capitalist accumulation involves *two* contradictory aspects here: on the one hand, mobilizing or permanently destabilizing the conditions of life and work, in such a way as to ensure competition on the labor market, draw new labor power continually from the "industrial reserve army," and maintain a relative over-population; on the other hand, stabilizing collectivities of workers over long periods (over several generations), to "educate" them for work and "bond" them to companies (and also to bring into play the mechanism of correspondence between a paternalist political hegemony and a worker familialism). On the one hand, class condition, which relates purely to the wage relation, has nothing to do with antecedents or descendants; ultimately, even the notion of class belonging is devoid of any practical meaning; all that counts is class situation, *hic et nunc*. On the other hand, at least a section of the workers have to be the sons of workers, a *social heredity* has to be created.[15] But with this, in practice, the capacities for resistance and organization also increase.

It was in response to these contradictory demands that the demographic and immigration policies and policies of urban segregation, which were set in place both by employers and the state from the middle of the nineteenth century onwards—policies which D. Bertaux has termed *anthroponomic* practices[16]—were born. These have two sides to them: a paternalistic aspect (itself closely connected to nationalist propaganda) and a disciplinary aspect, an aspect of "social warfare" against the savage masses and an aspect of "civilizing" (in all senses of the term) these same masses. This dual nature we can still see perfectly illustrated today in the combined social and police approach to the "suburbs" and "ghettos." It is not by chance that the current racist complex grafts itself on to the "population problem" (with its series of connotations: birth rate, depopulation and overpopulation, "interbreeding," urbanization, social housing, public health, unemployment) and focuses preferentially on the question of the *second generation* of what are here improperly called immigrants, with the object of finding out whether they will carry on as the previous generation (the immigrant workers properly so-called)—the danger being that they will develop a much greater degree of social combativeness, combining class demands with cultural demands; or whether they will add to the number of "declassed" individuals, occupying an unstable position between sub proletarianization and "exit" from the working class. This is the main issue for class racism, both for the dominant class and for the popular classes themselves: to mark with generic signs populations which are collectively destined for capitalist exploitation—or which have to be held in reserve for it—at the very moment when the economic process is tearing them away from the direct control of the system (or, quite simply, by mass unemployment is rendering the previous controls inoperative). The problem is to keep "in their place," from generation to generation, those who have no fixed place; and for this, it is necessary that they have a genealogy. And also to unify in the imagination the contradictory imperatives of nomadism and social heredity, the domestication of generations, and the disqualification of resistances.

If these remarks are well founded, then they may throw some light on what are themselves the contradictory aspects of what I shall not hesitate to call the self-racialization of the working class. There is here a whole spectrum of social experiences and ideological forms we might mention: from the organization of collectivities of workers around symbols of ethnic or national origin to the way in which a certain workerism, centered on criteria of class origins (and, consequently, on the institution of the working-class family, on the bond which only the family establishes between the "individual" and "his class") and the over-valorization of work (and, consequently, the virility which it alone confers), reproduces, within the ambit of "class consciousness," some part of the set of representations of the "race of workers."[17] Admittedly, the radical forms of workerism, at least in France, were produced more by intellectuals and political apparatuses aiming to "represent" the working class (from Proudhon down to the Communist Party) than by the workers themselves. The fact remains that they correspond to a tendency on the part of the working class to form itself into a closed body, to preserve gains that have been made and traditions of struggle, and to turn back against bourgeois society the signifiers of class racism. It is from this reactive origin that the ambivalence characterizing workerism derives: the desire to escape from the condition of exploitation and the rejection of the contempt to which it is subject. Absolutely nowhere is this ambivalence more evident than in its relation to nationalism and to xenophobia. To the extent that in practice they reject official nationalism (when they do reject it), the workers produce in outline a political alternative to the perversion of class struggles. To the extent, however, that they project onto foreigners their fears and resentment, despair and defiance, it is not only that they are *fighting competition*; in addition, and much more profoundly, they are trying to escape their own exploitation. It is a hatred of *themselves*, as proletarians—insofar as they are in danger of being drawn back into the mill of proletarianization—that they are showing.

To sum up, just as there is a constant relation of reciprocal determination between nationalism and racism, there is a relation of reciprocal determination between "class racism" and "ethnic racism," and *these two determinations are not independent*. Each produces its effects, to some extent, in the field of the other and under constraints imposed by the other. Have we, in retracing this overdetermination in its broad outline (and in trying to show how it illuminates the concrete manifestations of racism and the constitution of its theoretical discourse), answered the questions we posed at the beginning of this chapter? It would be more accurate to say that we have reformulated them. What has elsewhere been called the excess which, by comparison with nationalism, is constitutive of racism turns out at the same time to be a shortfall as far as the class struggle is concerned. But, though that excess is linked to the fact that nationalism is formed in opposition to the class struggle (even though it utilizes its dynamic), and that shortfall is linked to the fact that the class struggle finds itself repressed by nationalism, *the two do not compensate one another*; there effects tend, rather, to be combined. The important thing is not to decide whether nationalism is first and foremost a means of imagining and pursuing the unity of state and society, which then runs up against the contradictions of the class struggle, or whether it is primarily a reaction to the obstacles which the class struggle puts in the way of national unity. By contrast, it is crucially important to note that, in the historical field, where *both* an unbridgeable gap between state and nation and endlessly re-emerging class antagonisms are to be found, nationalism necessarily takes the form of racism, at times in competition with other forms (linguistic nationalism, for example) and at times in combination with them, and that it thus becomes engaged in a perpetual headlong flight forward. Even when racism remains latent, or present only in a minority of individual consciousnesses, it is already that internal excess of nationalism which betrays, in both senses of the word, its artic-ulation to the class struggle. Hence the ever recurring paradox of nationalism: the regressive imagining of a nation-state where the individuals would by their nature be "at home," because they would be "among their own" (their own kind), and the rendering of that state uninhabitable; the endeavor to produce a unified com-munity in the face of "external" enemies and the endless rediscovery that the enemy is "within," identifiable by signs which are merely the phantasmatic elab-oration of its divisions. Such a society is, in a real sense, a politically alienated society. But are not all contemporary societies, to some degree, grappling with their own political alienation?

NOTES

1. Pierre Ayçoberry, *The Nazi Question: An Essay on the Interpretation of National Socialism* (1992–73), trans. R. Hurley (London: Rout ledge & Kegan Paul, 1981).
2. See the theorizations of Karl Popper, *The Open Society and Its Enemies* (2 vols.), 5th ed. (revised) (London: Routledge & Kegan Paul, 1966); and, more recently, of Louis Dumont, *Essays on Individualism: Modern Ideology in Anthropological Perspective* (Chicago: University of Chicago Press, 1986).
3. The personification of capital, a social relation, begins with the very figure of the *capitalist*. But this is never sufficient in itself for arousing an emotional reaction. This is why, following the logic of "excess," other real-imaginary traits accumulate: lifestyle, lineage (the "200 families"*), for-eign origins, secret strategies, racial plots (the Jewish plan for "world domination"), etc. The fact that, specificalty in the case of the Jews, this personification is worked up in combination with a process of fetishization of money is clearly not accidental.
4. Matters are further complicated by the fact that the lost unity of "Christian" Europe, a mythic figuration of the "origins of its civilization," is thus represented in the register of race at the point when that same Europe is embarking upon its mission of "civilizing the world," i.e., submitting the world to its domination, by way of fierce competition between nations.
5. Cf. Benedict Anderson, *Imagined Communities* (London: Verso, 1983), pp. 92–93.
6. L. Poliakov, *The History of Anti-Semitism* (4 vols.), trans. R. Howard (London: Routledge &

*The idea that 200 families held most of the wealth of France and used it to exert political power was current in France in the 1930s, being quoted by Daladier at the Radical Congress of 1934. It seems probable that the figure 200 derived from the number of shareholders allowed to attend the annual meeting of the Bank of France.

Kegan Paul, 1974); M. Duchet & M. Rebérioux, "Préhistoire et histoire du racisme," in P. de Commarond and C. Duchet, eds., *Racisme et société* (Paris: Maspero, 1969); C. Guillaumin, *L'idéologie raciste. Genèse et langage actuel* (Paris-The Hague: Mouton, 1972); "Caractères spécifiques de l'idéologie raciste," *Cahiers internationaux de sociologie* LIII (1972); "Les ambiguïtes de la catégorie taxinomique "race" in L. Poliakov ed., *Hommes et bêtes: Entretiens sur la racisme (I)* (Paris-The Hague: Mouton, 1975); Eric Williams, *Capitalism and Slavery* (Chapel Hill: University of North Carolina Press, 1944).

7. And one which substitutes itself, in the French case, for the "ideology of the three orders," a basically theological and juridical ideology, which is, by contrast, expressive of the organic place occupied by the nobility in the building of the state (feudalism properly so-called).

8. L. Poliakov, *History of Anti-Semitism*, Vol. 2, pp. 222–32.

9. Louis Chevalier, *Labouring Classes and Dangerous Classes in Paris during the First Half of the Nineteenth Century*, trans. F. Jellinek (London; Routledge & Kegan Paul, 1973).

10. Cf. G. Netchine, "L'individuel et le cottectif dans les representations psychologiques de la diversité des êtres humains au XIXe siecle," in L. Poliakov, ed., *Ni juif ni grec: Entretiens sur le racisme (II)* (Paris-The Hague: Mouton. 1978); L. Murard and P. Zylberman, *Le Petit Travailleur infatigable ou le prolétaire régénéré. Villesu-sines, habitat et intimités au XIX siecle* (Fontenay-sous-Bois: Editions Recherches,1976).

11. Cf. H. Arendt, "Antisemitism," Part One of *The Origins of Totalitarianism* (London: André Deutsch, 1986), pp. 68–79; L. Poliakov, *History of Anti-Semitism*, Vol. 3, pp. 328–37; Karl Polanyi, "Appendix 11: Disraeli's 'Two Nations' and the Problem of Colored Races," *The Great Transformation* (Boston: Beacon Press, 1957), pp. 290–94.

12. Frederick Winslow Taylor, *Principles of Scientific Management*, 1911. See the commentaries by Robert Linhart, *Lénine, les paysans, Taylor* (Paris: Seuil, 1976); and Benjamin Coriat, *L'Atelier et le chronomètre* (Paris: Christian Bourgeois, 1979). See also my study, "Sur le concept de la division du travail manuel et intellectuel" in Jean Belkhir *et al.*, *L'Intellectuel, l'intelligentsia et les manuels* (Paris: Anthropos, 1983).

13. Clearly, the "bestiality" of the slave has been a continual problem, from Aristotle and his contemporaries down to the modern slave trade (the hypersexualization to which it is subject is a sufficient indication of this); but the industrial revolution brought about a new paradox: the bestial body of the worker is decreasingly *animal* and increasingly technicized and therefore humanized. It is the panic fear of a *super-humanization* of man (in his body and his intelligence which is "objectivized" by cognitive sciences and the corresponding techniques of selection and training), rather than his *sub-humanization*—or, in any case, the reversibility of these two—which discharges itself in phantasies of animality and these are projected for preference onto the worker, whose status as an "outsider" [*étranger*] confers upon him at the same time the attributes of an "other mate," a rival.

14. See Etienne Balibar, Immanuel Wallerstein, *Race, Nation, and Class* (London: Verso Press, 1991), Chaps. 1 and 3.

15. Not only in the sense of individual filiation, but in the sense of a "population" tending toward the practice of endogamy; not only in the sense of a transmission of skills (mediated by schooling, apprenticeship and industrial discipline) but in the sense of a "collective ethic," constructed in institutions and through subjective identification. Alongside the works already cited, see J. P. de Gaudemar, *La Mobilisation générale* (Paris: Editions du Champ Urbain, 1979).

16. Daniel Bertaux, *Destins personnels et structure de classe* (Paris: PUF, 1977).

17. C. G. Noiriel, *Longwy: Immigrés et prolétaires, 1880–1980* (Paris: PUF, 1985); J. Frémontier, *La Vie en bleu: Voyage en culture ouvrière* (Paris: Fayard, 1980); Françoise Duroux, "La Famille des ouvriers: mythe ou politique?" unpublished thesis, Université de Paris VII, 1982.

Part II.
Constructive Realism

9. The Contribution of Race to Culture
Alain L. Locke

THE PROPOSITION THAT RACE is an essential factor in the growth and development of culture, and expresses culturally that phenomenon of variation and progressive differentiation so apparently vital on the plane of the development of
organic nature, faces a pacifist and an internationalist with a terrific dilemma,
and a consequently difficult choice. Even so, granted that race has been such a
factor in human history, would you today deliberately help perpetuate its idioms
at the cost of so much more inevitable sectarianism, chauvinistic prejudice,
schism, and strife? It amounts to this, then, can we have the advantages of cultural differences without their obvious historical disadvantages? For we must
remember that national and racial prejudices have been all through history con-
current with such traditional differences, and have grown up from the roots of
the engendered feelings of proprietorship and pride.

History has made this question a grave dilemma. Or rather the chauvinistic
interpretation of history—which is orthodox. Theoretically the question can be
straddled; but practically it is time to front-face the sharp paradoxes of the situation, even at the risk of being impaled. The issue is particularly unavoidable in
our day, when we have side by side with our conscious and growing internationalism a resurgence everywhere of the spirit of nationalism and the principle of
the autonomy and self-determination of national and racial groups. We have
carried the principle into the inner boundaries of many nations, and have
aroused expectant and clamorous minorities, where before there were repressed
and almost suffocated minor groups.

Alain L. Locke, "The Contribution of Race to Culture," *The Student World* 23 (1930): 349–53;
reprinted by permission of Moorland-Spingarn Research Center, Howard University.

215

Personally I belong to such a minority, and have had some part in the revival of its suppressed hopes; but if I thought it irreconcilable with the future development of internationalism and the approach toward universalism to foster the racial sense, stimulate the racial consciousness, and help revive the lapsing racial tradition, I would count myself a dangerous reactionary, and be ashamed of what I still think is a worthy and constructive cause.

The answer to this dilemma, in my opinion, lies behind one very elemental historical fact, long ignored and oft-forgotten. There is and always has been an almost limitless natural reciprocity between cultures. Civilization, for all its claims of distinctiveness, is a vast amalgam of cultures. The difficulties of our social creeds and practices have arisen in great measure from our refusal to recognize this fact. In other words, it has been the sense and practice of the vested ownership of culture goods which has been responsible for the tragedies of history and for the paradoxes of scholarship in this matter. It is not the facts of the existence of race which are wrong, but our attitudes toward those facts. The various creeds of race have been falsely predicated. The political crimes of nations are perpetuated and justified in the name of race; whereas, in many instances, the cultural virtues of race are falsely appropriated by nationalities. So that in the resultant confusion, if we argue for raciality as a desirable thing, we seem to argue for the present practice of nations and to sanction the pride and prejudice of past history. Whereas, if we condemn these things, we seem close to a rejection of race as something useful in human life and desirable to perpetuate.

But do away with the idea of proprietorship and vested interest—and face the natural fact of the limitless interchangeableness of culture goods, and the more significant historical facts of their more or less constant exchange, and we have, I think, a solution reconciling nationalism with internationalism, racialism with universalism. But it is not an easy solution—for it means the abandonment of the use of the idea of race as a political instrument, perhaps the second most potent ideal sanction in the creed of the Western nations—the "Will of God" and the "good of humanity" being the first. But we are in a new era of social and cultural relationships once we root up this fiction and abandon the vicious practice of vested proprietary interests in various forms of culture, attempting thus, in the face of the natural reciprocity and our own huge indebtedness, one to the other, to trade unequally in proprietary and aggressive ways. There are and always will be specialized group superiorities; it is the attempt to capitalize these by a politics of civilization into theoretical and practical group supremacies which has brought the old historical difficulties.

Freed from this great spiritual curse, the cult of race is free to blossom almost indefinitely to the enrichment and stimulation of human culture. On the grand scale, as between East and West—European, Asiatic, African; and on the small scale as well, within the borders of our political units, as the self-expression and spiritual solidarity of minorities. I have often thought that the greatest obstacle that has prevented the world from realizing unity has been a false conception of what unity itself meant in this case. It is a notion, especially characteristic of the West, that to be one effectively, we must all be alike and that to be at peace, we must all have the same interests. On the contrary, apart from the practical impossibility of such uniformity, and its stagnant undesirability, we have, in the very attempt to impose it, the greatest disruptive force active in the modern world today.

That way, with its implications of "superior" and "inferior," "dominant" and "backward," "legitimate" and "mongrel," is the path of reactionism and defeat. If this all too prevalent psychology is to survive, then it is a modern crime to encourage minorities and preserve races, either in the physical or the cultural sense; for one is only multiplying the factors of strife and discord. But the modern world is doing just these things, hoping meanwhile for internationalism, peace, and world cooperation. It is easier and more consistent to change our false psychology than to stem the rising tide of resurgent minorities, which have every right and reason for self-expression which the older established majorities ever had; and in addition the moral claims of compensation. The new nations of Europe, Zionism, Chinese and Indian nationalism, the awakened American Negro and the awakening Africa have progressed too much to be pushed back or snuffed out. The revision of thought which we are speaking about now as an ideal possibility, tomorrow will be a practical necessity, unless history is tragically to repeat itself in terms of other huge struggles for dominance and supremacy. The best chance for a new world lies in a radical revision of this root idea of culture, which never was soundly in accordance with the facts, but which has become so inveterate that it will require a mental revolution to change it.

For a moment let us look at some of its anomalies. Missionarism, so dear to our Western hearts, is one of them, and one of the gravest. The very irony of self-asserted superiority and supremacy of an adopted Oriental religion turned against the Oriental world as an instrument of political and cultural aggression ought to chasten the spirit of a rational Christianity. Or, to rake another instance, the Aryan myth has no validity if political expediency demands a rationalization of the domination of an Asiatic branch of Aryans by a European branch of Aryans. America, for example, appropriates as characteristically "American" the cultural products of their Negroes, while denying them civic and cultural equality. A North Teutonic tribe, with a genius for organization, appropriates a Palatinate culture-history and what was largely a South German culture, and sets out to dominate the world under its aegis. These are typical anomalies. And they are not cited in a spirit of accusation. They could be matched for almost every nation or race or creed, and are cited, to prove by the force of their mutual self-contradiction, their common underlying fallacy. Shall the new nations, the insurgent minorities, the awakening races adopt the same psychology, advance in the name of their race or nation the same claims, avow the same antiquated sanctions? Inevitably—unless there is rapid and general repudiation of the basic idea, and a gradual but sincere abandonment of the old politic of cultural aggression and proprietary culture interests. We began by talking about the cult of race—but this is not beside the point. For the cult of race is dangerous and reactionary if the implications of the creeds of race are not disposed of or revised. There can be two sorts of modern self-determination— one with the old politic of revenge and aggressive self-assertion, another with a new politic of creative individuality and cultural reciprocity.

With this new ideology lies the only hope for combining the development of a greater solidarity of civilization successfully with a period of greater intensification and fresh creativeness in our individual cultures. Divorced from the political factors, this is possible. It is not an accident that Switzerland is the foster home of internationalism. By good historical fortune it has arrived at culturally neutral nationhood, and so is a prototype of the reconstructed nationality of the future. We may just as naturally have several nations sharing a single culture as, on the other hand, have several cultures within a single nation. But we must revert to the natural units of culture, large or small, rather than try to outrival one another, like Aesop's ox-emulating frogs, in these artificially inflated, politically motivated cultures. Let us notice that the same motive is responsible for two sorts of cultural violence, not always associated in the common mind— external aggression for building up artificial combinations for the sake of power and size, arbitrary internal repressions for the sake of dominance and uniformity.

To summarize, the progress of the modern world demands what may be styled "free-trade in culture" and a complete recognition of the principle of cultural reciprocity. Culture-goods, once evolved, are no longer the exclusive property of the race or people that originated them. They belong to all who can use them; and belong most to those who can use them best. But for all the limitless exchange and transplanting of culture, it cannot be artificially manufactured; it grows. And, so far as I can understand history, it is always a folk-product, with the form and flavor of a particular people and place, that is to say, for all its subsequent universality, culture has root and grows in that social soil which, for want of a better term, we call "race."

10. Race and Nature: The System of Marks

Colette Guillaumin

THE IDEA OF RACE AND OF A "NATURAL" GROUP

The Idea of Race

THE IDEA OF RACE. What is this self-evident notion, this "fact of nature"? It is an ordinary historical fact—a social fact. I deliberately say *idea* of race: the belief that this category is a material phenomenon. For it is a heterogeneous intellectual formulation, with one foot in the natural sciences and one foot in the social sciences. On the one hand, it is an aggregate of somatic and physiological characteristics—in short, race as conceived by the physical anthropologists and the biologists. On the other hand, it is an aggregate of social characteristics that express a group—but a social group of a special type, a group *perceived as natural,* a group of people considered as materially specific in their bodies. This naturalness may be regarded by some people as fundamental (a natural group whose nature is expressed in social characteristics). Or it may be regarded by others as a secondary fact (a social group that "furthermore" is natural). In any case, in the current state of opinion, this naturalness is always present in the approach which the social sciences take, and which the social system has crystallized and expressed under the name of "race."

Colette Guillaumin, "Race and Nature: The System of Marks, the Idea of a Natural Group and Social Relations," trans. Mary Jo Lakeland. *Feminist Issues* (Fall 1988), pp. 25–43, reprinted with the permission of *Transaction*.

So apparently it's all very simple. A purely "material" approach to observed characteristics, on the one hand; and on the other hand, a mixed approach, more interested in sociosymbolic traits than in somatic traits, all the while keeping the latter present in the mind, in the background in some way or another. But with no profound clash between the two approaches; it's indeed a matter of the same thing in both cases. And equilibrium seems assured with the natural sciences referring to physical forms and the classical social sciences referring to social forms. Nevertheless, one might expect from the latter that their classifications and commentaries, even if they render discreet homage to the natural sciences, would still declare their specificity, first by defining with precision their concerns and then by questioning the meaning in social terms of the fact that certain social categories are reputed to be natural. In fact, the social sciences are fascinated by the natural sciences, in which they hope to find a methodological model (which at the very least is debatable), but in which also (and this is the most serious matter) they believe they find an ultimate justification.[1] This attitude is not unrelated to the social reasons which lead to the usage of the idea of nature in the classification of social groups.

But, to proceed, let us accept for the moment that the division is effective and that equilibrium is realized between the disciplines, and let us take for established fact a separation between diem, at least in their explicit concerns. So we have, on the one hand, a *supposedly natural* taxonomy, that of physical anthropology, population genetics, etc., declaring the existence of "natural" groups of humans, finite and specific (whites, blacks, brachycephalics, dolichocephalics, etc.); and on the other hand, a *social* taxonomy, that of history and sociology, taking into account the relational and historical characteristics of groups (slaves, the nobility, the bourgeoisie, etc.). The two types of classification can overlap or not, can have common areas or have no meeting point.[2] An example of *nonoverlap*: the blacks of the American social (read racial) system obviously have nothing (or very little) to do with the blacks and whites of physical anthropology in the anthropological meaning of the term. An example of *overlap*: the whites and blacks of the apartheid system are indeed what anthropology designates them as. But let us note that this is only at the price of another category, which is, if you wish, nonexistent or out of consideration—the "coloreds"—bringing together both an aggregate of socioeconomic criteria (an aggregate without which and outside of which this group would literally not be *seen*) and an ideological *denial*—the denial of the nonexistence of naturally finite groups. The denial is constructed as follows:

First step: The fantasizing initial position postulates that an unbreachable barrier separates human groups, that races are radically dissimilar from each other.

Second step: The reality nevertheless is that this barrier does not exist, since the continuity between groups is proven in action by individuals who, belonging to two (or several) "races," show that there is only one.

Third step: Then comes the denial: "I do not want to know that there is no barrier, because I assert that there is one, and I consider null and void any con-tradiction of that barrier. I don't see it, it doesn't exist." In other words, the con-stitution of a "colored" group says that *it is not true that there is no* unbreachable barrier between "blacks" and "whites." By the creation of this "nongroup" no evidence exists of the continuity between groups, for the evidence of it is turned into a particular and independent entity. That class formed by people belonging in fact to one *and* the other group is declared to belong to neither the one nor the other, but to itself.³ And thus the system proclaims that human groups are natural, and that in one's natural materiality one can belong to one or the other of these groups (or to some other *group*) but in no case to both one *and* the other. But the reality meanwhile is that people do belong to one *and* the other (or to some other groups).

A first questioning can already begin: the two preceding statements—that certain (social) blacks are whites (in the United States) and that a group belongs to both one *and* the other group (in South Africa)—are exactly the opposite of what is implied by the idea of race itself, which is supposed to be a *natural closed category*, and which thereby certifies the status of a group that is first of all fixed and secondly hereditary. In the impassioned proclamations of the social system, there is the fantastic and *legalized* affirmation (we will return to this) that the boundaries between the groups are beyond the reach of, and anterior to, human beings—thus immutable. And in addition, these boundaries are considered as obvious, as the very avowal of common sense ("You are not going to tell me that there are no races, no!" and "That is plain to see!").⁴ And on the other hand, one cannot but charge such affirmations with lack of reality when one looks at what actually goes on and when one tries to apply the most ordinary rules of logic to it. For what goes on is the opposite of the impossibility that they affirm to us—no barrier nor separation, but a close association, a deep social and mate-rial imbrication which far outstrips the simple somatic continuity between the groups so violently denied.

The Idea of a "Natural" Group

Material "imbrication"? Social "imbrication"? Yes, for supposedly "natural" groups only exist by virtue of the fact that they are so interrelated that effec-tively each of the groups is a function of the other. In short, it's a matter of social relations within the same social formation. One doesn't care to assert natural-ness when there is economic, spatial, and other independence among groups. Only certain specific relations (of dependence, exploitation) lead to the postu-lation of the existence of "natural heterogeneous entities." Colonization by the appropriation of people (traffic in slaves, later in laborers) and of territories (that of the last two centuries) and the appropriation of the bodies of women (and not solely of their labor power) have led to the proclamation of the specific nature of the groups that endured or still endure these relations.

In fact, the groups concerned are *one and the same natural group* if one accepts this classification in terms of nature. The social idea of natural group rests on the ideological postulation that there is a closed unit, endo-determined [determined from within], hereditary, and dissimilar to other social units. This unit, always empirically social, is supposed to reproduce itself and within itself. All this rests on the clever finding that whites bear whites and blacks bear blacks, that the former are the masters and the latter the slaves, that the masters bear masters and the slaves slaves, and so on, and that nothing can happen, and that nothing does happen, to trouble this impeccable logic. The children of slaves are slaves, as we know, while the children of slaves can also be—and often are—the children of the master. What "natural" group do they belong to? That of their mother? That of their father? That of their slave mother or that of their master father? In the United States in the eighteenth century, the person who was on either side (the mother or the father), the child of a slave was a slave. The child of a slave man and a free woman was a slave (in Maryland as far back as the seventeenth century); the child of a slave woman and a free man was also a slave (in all the slave states). What "natural" group did they belong to? It was said (this line of argument developed in the United States) that the child of a slave woman was a slave "because it is difficult to dissociate a child from its mother," but what becomes of this argument when the slave child is the child of a free woman? If it is "difficult to dissociate a child from its mother, shouldn't it be free? In Maryland a free woman who married a slave saw her children born slaves.

We can move one step further if we take into consideration the social relationships of sex in this matter. They clarify the relationships of "race" (theoretically involved in slavery) better than considerations about "maternity." The child and the wife are the property of the husband-father, which is forgotten. A woman slave is the property of the master as a slave; her child is therefore the property of the master, a free woman is the property of her husband as a wife and—her husband being the property of the master as a slave—her children are the property of the master, thus slaves. She herself, moreover, was obliged to serve the master as long as her husband was living.

In addition, the sexed division of humanity is regarded as leading to and constituting two heterogeneous groups. The fantasy implies that men make men and women make women. In the case of the sexes, emphasis is more and more placed on intragroup homogeneity: men with men, women with women, in their quasi-speciation. This can be seen in the scientized expressions used in discussing parthenogenesis and in the half-reproving, half-condescending attitude which surrounds fathers who father "only" girls. But, for the time being, men are the children of women (a fact which is well known, perhaps too well known).

What is less known seems to be that women are the children of men. To what "natural" group do they belong? Being a man or being a woman, being white or being black means to belong to a social group regarded as natural, but certainly not to a "natural" group.

And moreover, the American system—first a slave system, later transformed into a racial system in the nineteenth century with the abolition of slavery—has well and truly defined belonging to a "race" according to class criteria, since the whites who had (or might have had) a supposed slave ancestor were (and still are) "blacks." Thus, a greatgrandparent—that is, one out of eight direct genitors (since we have eight grandparents)—or even one grandparent out of sixteen makes you belong to a determined social group, under the mask of naturalness— the most adulterated naturalness in this case. For logically, if one takes the suggestions of natural realism literally (and not figuratively), having seven white grandparents certainly means being white. But it is not so! You are not white, you are "black," for it is the social system that decides. The social situation is that you are black because that is the way the (social) definitions have decided it. Why then speak of presocial, outside-of-society, "scientific" classification—in a word, of "natural" classification? It is this which makes us ask ourselves about this "natural" that claims to be natural while being something else than what it claims to be, a Natural that defines a class by something other than that which is effectively at work in constituting a class. In short, beneath this single notion there stretches a network of relationships covered with a justifying mask—that of Nature, of our Mother Nature.

The denial of reality in the apartheid system illustrates this extraordinary operation of masking. This system claims—having found another, more subtle means of defining membership in a group—that there is no material mixing between groups. There are supposed to be two races, one white, the other black, each exhibiting its own characteristics and its own nature, and another race, completely different, without any relation to the preceding ones, a pure product in and of itself. Institutionally separate, the "coloreds" constitute the "other" race, the third element that renders any questioning of the system irrelevant.[5]

These two examples of naturalist false consciousness have been taken from Western industrial society and refer to two historical extreme points: the sequels of the period of capital accumulation (plantation slavery) and the contemporary technological society of South Africa. This is not by chance, for the development of the idea of race is coextensive with that spatial and temporal zone. But it is more than doubtful that this idea still has spatial limits today.

THE SYSTEMS OF "MARKS"

The Conventional Mark

During the two preceding centuries, the geographical localization of productive forces has been the determining factor in the *form* taken by the imputation of naturalness to social groups. The European labor force, in Europe itself, produced a certain number of products (metal ingots, cloth, weapons, etc.) which served as the means of exchange in Africa, especially in the Gulf of Guinea, for a labor force directly transported to the Americas (the South, the Caribbean, and the North) to cultivate the land by "industrial" (or intensive) exploitation. This agriculture, which at first had been extensive and devoted to luxury products (tobacco, indigo, etc.), rapidly became intensive, with the growing first of sugarcane and then of cotton to be exported to Europe. This triangular traffic, as it is called, maintained the European labor force in Europe for mining and manufacturing and exported the African labor force to America for the industrial-agricultural production of tropical products. But the recruitment of the labor force was not immediately so neatly divided. During the seventeenth century, the American agricultural slavery system recruited in both Europe and Africa; the indentured slaves of that period came from the two old continents.[6] It is then as a byproduct of, and in a manner dependent on, geographical origin that skin color acquired a role, insofar as the occasion presented by the search for a labor force and the extension of the triangular traffic offered the possibility for "marking." For, if the idea of naturalness is modern, written into the industrial-scientific society, it is not the same, on the other hand, for the sociosymbolic system of marks put on social groups. This latter system concerns a large number of historical and contemporary societies. It is not linked, as the race system will be, to the position of the dominated as such. It comes into play at all levels of the relationship, dominating and dominated, although the mark has specific characteristics according to the level, as we shall see.

Distinct from the idea of nature,[7] and even in a sense contrary to it, since it bears witness to the conventional and artificial inscription of social practices, the system of marks has been present for a very long time as the accompaniment of social cleavages. It still exists, although it is not always noticed, and in its most constant form it is too familiar to be seen. The fact that men and women dress differently, with clothes that are not cut in the same way (draping persists to some extent in women's clothes, while it has disappeared from men's) is an example of marking that continues to be generally unrecognized.

Nevertheless, people recognized the dress differentiation between the bourgeoisie and the nobility during the feudal period of the eighteenth century, which gave the nobility the right to furs, jewels, bright colors, and metallic cloth, and gave the bourgeoisie almost a monopoly on the wearing of black.[8] This distinction disappeared when the noble class melted into the bourgeoisie during the nineteenth century, after the bourgeois revolutions. These latter, by abolishing clothing prohibitions, are the source of so-called peasant "regional" costumes, in which color, lace, and embroidery express a newly acquired right. It is well known that during the Middle Ages the members of nondominant religions wore a clothing mark such as the yellow pointed hat or the yarmulke (varying according to regions and period) of the Jews, the yellow cross for the Cathars, and so forth. The nobles marked their various family groups (groups that, from the fifteenth to the eighteenth century, were called "races") with "coats of arms" on movable objects such as harnesses, shields, armor, vehicles, paintings, servants (objects like the others), or on their buildings, on the porticos, gates, and the like. In the sixteenth and seventeenth centuries, the galley slaves, the deported prostitutes, and then the slaves, until the nineteenth century, were marked by an *immovable* sign, directly inscribed on the body (physical marking of slaves was abolished in 1833 for France), as, in the twentieth century, deportees were marked by the Nazi state; this same state imposed a cloth badge on Jews before it started to exterminate them. We know that today military personnel and street cleaners (among others) wear a uniform, but we have forgotten that only a short while ago (in the nineteenth century) a man's shaving his beard was a sign of being in domestic service; the tonsure of Catholic priests, ringlets of very orthodox Jews, and long hair for women and short for men were (or still are) some of the many signs and marks, either external or inscribed on the body, that expressed (and imprinted) the fact of belonging to a definite social group. And there is a very long list of such signs and marks.

The characteristics of the mark vary, and its indelibility, as well as its more or less close proximity to/association with the body, is a function of: (1) the assumed permanence of the position that it is a sign of and (2) the degree of subjection that it symbolizes. The convict under the *ancien regime*, the contemporary concentration camp victim, and the American slave bore the mark on their body (tattooed number or brand), a sign of the *permanence* of the power relationship. The dominating group imposes its fixed inscription on those who are materially subject to them. The mark of status is inscribed in a reversible fashion when it signifies *contractual* subordination: transitory bodily adaptations, such as shaving the beard or not (domestic service), the wearing of a wig (marriage), the tonsure (religious vows), the length of hair. Marking by clothing, much more subject to change in one sense, is without doubt the zero expression of belonging to a *social station*[9] or, if you prefer, the expression of place in social relations. It is only in the division between the sexes that the clothing mark persists in a permanent fashion today. For, although a person puts on a uniform (professional, military, or other) for work—that is, for a specified time and in a limited area—a person is, on the contrary, at every moment when dressed, and in all circumstances, in the uniform of sex. In short, the idea of visually making known the groups in a society is neither recent nor exceptional.

Naturalization of the System of Marking and Development of the Idea of a Natural Group

However, the idea of classifying *according* to somatic/morphological criteria is recent and its date can be fixed: the eighteenth century. From a circumstantial association between economic relations and physical traits was born a new type of mark ("color"), which had great success. Later developments turned it from the traditional status of *a symbol* to that of a *sign of a specific nature* of social actors. Then began the fabrication of taxonomies that were to be progressively qualified as "natural." This naturalness was not obvious at the beginning, when the concern for form unquestionably overshadowed it.[10] The taxonomies were transformed into classification systems based on a morphological mark, in which the latter is *presumed to precede* the classification, while social relationships created the group on which the mark—because of the social relationship—is going to be "seen" and attached. The taxonomies thus served as anchoring for the development of the idea of race, but the idea of endo-determinism spread little by little onto the schema of marking, which was completely classical at its beginning.

However that may be, the morphological "mark" doesn't precede the social relationship, any more than branding or the tattooing of a number do. I alluded above to the triangular traffic and to the role played by the spatial/temporal extension of this process. At the end of the seventeenth century and at the beginning of the eighteenth, the capture of a labor force for the Americas from just one region of the world—the Gulf of Guinea and East Africa—to the exclusion of Europe, played the role of catalyst in the formation of the idea of race, which was done through the means of the classic "mark." The accidents of economic history furnished in this case *a ready-made* form. But in fact the process of the appropriation of slaves had *already* been going on for around a century, when the first taxonomies that included somatic characteristics appeared: the mark *followed* slavery and in no way preceded the slave grouping. The slave system was *already* constituted when the inventing of the races was thought up.

This system developed from something completely different than the somatic appearance of its actors. It is heartrending to hear so many well-intentioned people (then as now) question themselves about the reasons that could exist for "reducing the blacks to slavery" (contempt, they think; visibility; who knows what else?). But no "blacks" per se were reduced to slavery; slaves were made—which is very different. All these strange reasons are sought and advanced as if "being black" existed in itself, outside of any social reason to construct such a form, as if the symbolic fact asserted itself and could be a cause. But the idea of "reducing 'the blacks' to slavery" is a modern idea which only came about at a specific historical juncture, when the recruitment of slaves (who at the beginning were blacks *and* whites) was focalized. People were enslaved wherever they could be and as need dictated. Then, at a certain historical moment, from the end of the seventeenth century on, slaves ceased to be recruited in Europe because their labor power from then on was needed there, with the development of industrialization. Consequently they were taken only from a specific and relatively limited region of the world, constituting one of the poles of the triangular traffic. During the period of European/African recruitment, there was not (not yet) a system of marking other than that used for this purpose (branding). So, a fortiori, neither was there any reflection about the somatic/physiological "nature" of slaves. This reflection, moreover, only appeared after the marking by the somatic sign itself. The taxonomies preceded the racist theories.

THE "NATURE" OF THE EXPLOITED

During the nineteenth and twentieth centuries there have been (and moreover still are) many scholars looking for a "naturalness" in classes and exploited groups. For example, the presumption and affirmation of a genetic and biological particularity of the working class, expressed in the form of a lesser intelligence, was—and still remains—one of the strongpoints of the naturalist discourse. It must also be said that this approach is strongly opposed; it may even be censured. Nevertheless, the censure only occurs when it is a matter of the white, male, urban part of the exploited class. All censure or hesitation disappears at the moment that it is a question of the female part, or the immigrant part, or the neo-colonized part in the relations of exploitation. Nature is nature, isn't it?

The obsession with the natural mark (proclaimed as the "origin" of social relationships) operates today with great effectiveness. It doesn't do so with the same facility in all circumstances. But whatever the twists and turns of the line of argument, the natural mark is presumed to be the intrinsic *cause* of the place that a group occupies in social relationships. As such this "natural" mark differs from the dress mark or the mark inscribed on the body known by premodern societies. For the old mark was recognized as imposed by social relationships, known as one of their consequences, while the natural mark is not presumed to be a mark but the very *origin of* these relationships. It is supposed to be the internal (therefore natural) "capacities" that determine social facts. This is a throwback to the idea of endogenous determinism in human relationships, an idea characteristic of mechanistic scientific thought.

In short, the modern idea of a natural group is the fluid synthesis of two systems: (1) the traditional system of the mark, purely *functional*, in which there is no endogenous implication and which is no different than the marking of livestock and (2) the archaeo-scientific deterministic system which sees in any object whatever a substance which secretes its own causes, which is *in itself its own cause*. What interests us here is the social group, and its practices are supposed to be the product of its specific nature.

For example: "It is the nature of women to clean up the shit," a statement that (practically throughout the world) means: "Women are women; it's a natural fact; women clean up the shit; it's their nature that makes them do it; and besides, since this is a specialization of genetic origin, it doesn't disgust them, which is itself proof that for them it's natural." In the same way (in the United States), "It's the nature of blacks not to work" means: "It's a natural fact; blacks are unemployed; that's the way their nature makes them: and moreover they are lazy and don't want to do a stroke of work, which shows very well that for them it's natural to be out of work." Notwithstanding that women don't "like" shit more than men do (which is to say, not at all) and that blacks don't "like" to do less work than whites do (which is to say, not any more), what we have here is an intentionally purely subjective critique of their states of mind. On the other hand, that which refers to the effective experiences of the groups of "women" and "blacks" (cleaning up, unemployment), that which refers to the facts is correct: women do clean up the shit, and being black condemns one to unemployment—but *the relationship between the facts is false*.

The spontaneous idea of nature[11] introduces an erroneous relationship between the facts; it changes the very character of these facts. And it does this in a particular way: nature proclaims the permanence of the effects of certain social relations on dominated groups. Not the perpetuation of these relations themselves (on which no one cares to fix their eyes, and that is understandable; they are like the sun, they burn), but the permanence of their effects—the permanence of shit and of unemployment. The crux of the question really is: a *social relationship*, here a relationship of domination, of power, of exploitation, which secretes the idea of nature, is regarded as the product of traits internal to the object which endures the relationship, traits which are expressed and revealed in specific practices. To speak of a specificity of races or of sexes, to speak of a natural specificity of social groups is to say in a sophistical way that a particular "nature" is *directly productive* of a social practice, and to bypass the *social relationship* that this practice brings into being. In short, it is a pseudo-materialism.

The idea of the nature of the groups concerned precludes recognition of the real relationship by concentrating attention first (with the explanation to follow) on isolated, fragmented traits, presumed to be intrinsic and permanent, which are supposed to be the direct causes of a practice which is itself purely mechanical. It is thus that slavery becomes an attribute of skin color, that non-payment for domestic work becomes an attribute of the shape of sexual organs. Or more exactly, *each* of the numerous obligations imposed by the precise relationships of race and sex are supposed to be a natural trait, with the multiplicity of these natural traits becoming merged to indicate the specific nature of the social group that suffers the relationship of domination. At this precise point the idea of a natural group is invented—of "race," of "sex"—which inverts the reasoning.

CURRENT FORM OF THE IDEA OF NATURE IN SOCIAL RELATIONSHIPS

Some ideas of race and sex can be said to be imaginary formulations, legally sanctioned and materially effective. Let us look at these three points one after the other.

Natural Groups: Imaginary Formulations

It is certainty not an accident that the classic arguments about the nonpertinence of the idea of race (I would say, moreover, more aptly, of the idea of a natural group) have been made about natural categories that are not very "distinguishable," and have been made in the case of those where the quality of the mark is rather ambiguous and even wholly evanescent. Both Jean-Paul Sartre, in the past, in his *Réflexions sur la question juive*, and Jacques Ruffié today, in his *De La biologie à la culture*, use the same subject to support, in an immediately convincing fashion, the fact that races don't exist. Although their perspectives are different, both of them refer to a group, the Jews, who, whatever the time and place, are not physically distinguished from the dominant group.[12] Showing that belief in the natural characteristics of sociality is illusory, that this belief has been built up by a coercive history, is certainly much easier in the case where no fallacious distraction in terms of physical evidence or visibility is possible. The absence of visual criteria, which might support a counterattack by supporters of the natural inscription of social characteristics, helps considerably in arguing a case that is in itself extremely difficult.

But, all things considered, is it such a good tactic? I don't believe that one can overcome preconceived ideas and commonplace beliefs—which go hand in hand with a unanimous and naive belief in "races" and other natural groups— by a rational argument, making appeal to the suspension of judgment and to waiting for an examination of the facts. It seems to me that, on the contrary, it would be more logical to treat the problem by what is most "evident" about it to the eyes of the believers in naturalness, and not by what seems at first view to support the argument of the ideological character of naturalness. What is "least visible" is a trap in this field. For one is not operating within a classical framework of discussion, where the terms of the debate are common and the definitions approximately shared. One is well and truly in a situation of conflict. The idea of the endo-determined nature of groups is precisely *the* form taken by the antagonism between the very social groups which are concerned. First let us try to start from scratch and take another approach, which calls into question, at their level of highest visibility, the ideas of visual evidence themselves.

No, it is not a matter of fact that the idea of race, since its historical appearance, is found both in common sense and in the sciences.[13] Although physical traits, elsewhere and in the past, have certainly drawn attention, this was done without making distinctions and with a non-classifying attitude that has become difficult for us to understand. In short, such traits were noticed little more than baldness, eye color, or size are today—interesting certainty, but not the basis for discrimination.[14] Today we are confronted with fierce realities, for which it is not enough to say they don't exist. We see them, we draw conclusions—(1) classifying conclusions and (2) conclusions about *nature*—stages which are historically and analytically distinct, as we have seen by following the passage from the conventional mark to the natural mark, but which today are mingled, almost syncretically. Moreover, these classifying conclusions are not false, since people do belong to a group, a social group which is defined by its practices within one relationship (among many).[15] It is not by virtue of its (constructed) membership that the group is defined, despite the perception imposed on us by a naturalist apprehension that places the somatic nature of social actors as the origin of classifications and practices.

So there is both truth and falsehood in these classifications—truth (a group), falsehood (the "somatic nature" of the group)—and the falsehood lives on the truth. Appearance (color, sex) furnishes very good information about work (and even about the jobs within a line of work), about pay (or non-pay), and even, if there is one, about the wage level. In 1977 (and still today) in France, for example, if one encounters a woman, one surely encounters someone who does domestic work gratis and probably someone also who, without pay or sometimes for pay, physically cleans the youngest and oldest people in a family or in public or private establishments. And there is a very good chance one will encounter one of those workers at the minimum wage or below who are women. This is not nature; it is a social relationship. In France, if one encounters a Mediterranean man—and it is by design that I don't use a word indicating nationality, because nationality has nothing to do with it, while the region of the world is the determining factor—there is a very good chance that one will encounter one of those workers with a specific type of contract or even one who risks having none at all, and maybe not even a residence permit, someone who works longer hours than other workers, and does this in a construction trade, the mines, or heavy industry. In short, he is one piece of the very structural "labor cushion," which also includes the 46 percent of women who have access to a paid job. If one encounters in France a Caribbean or West Indian man or woman, it is very likely that one encounters someone employed in the service sector—in hospitals, transportation, communications—and precisely someone employed in the public sector. In France, if one encounters a Mediterranean woman, one will very likely encounter someone who also works in the service industries, but not in the public sector; she will be working in the private sector, for an individual employer or a collective employer (a company)—a cleaning woman, a *concierge*, a kitchen employee. One will encounter someone who, for less than the minimum wage (as a woman), does domestic work (as a Mediterranean person), and who does family domestic work (as a woman) gratis.

So here we have these obvious "natural" groups, whose activities, presumed to be "natural" like those who do them, are only the actualization of a very social relationship. It is important to find out how these groups are reputed to be "natural," and natural *first and foremost*: to find out how that is the "logical consequence" of that nature to some people, who consider that one is born with a precise place and task in life, or how it is an "abominable injustice" to others, who think it is cruel and unjustifiable to confine to the "lower strata" or quasi-castes the members of these groups, who, poor things, can do nothing about where they naturally belong. Although the conception of what is wished for varies, the perception of reality is the same—there are natural groups. It is indisputable that nature, which serves us today as portable household god, is the ideological form of a certain type of social relationship. But, stratum or caste ("nature," no less!), it is also true that attention is focused on the subject in order to refuse to see the relationship that constituted it.

The idea of the somatic-physiological internal specificity of the social groups concerned is an imaginary formulation (in the sense that naturalness exists in the mind) associated to a social relationship. This relationship is identifiable through the criteria we have noted, which are completely material, historical, technological, and economic. These traits are connected to a naturalist affirmation whose contradictions, logical silences, and affirmations (all the more confident because based on unclarified implications) demonstrate ambiguity and dubiousness. And the imaginary character of a term of the connection is invisible—thanks to nature.

Imaginary Formulation, Legally Sanctioned

Legally, and not, as has been claimed for a century, scientifically sanctioned. And the two terms—*legal* and *scientific*—form a pair in the social system. In the case of the natural, the legal plays the role of guarantee theoretically ascribed to scientific fact.

The *institutionalization*, the transformation of the idea of a natural group into a category sanctioned at the level of the state, was not done by the scientific community, despite all its efforts in that direction, but was in fact done by the legal system. Race became an effective legal category *as a category of nature* (that is, a category of non-divine, non-sociohuman origin) at the end of the nineteenth century in the United States (the Jim Crow laws), in 1935 in Nazi Germany (the Nuremberg laws), and in 1948 in South Africa (the apartheid laws). These discriminatory, interdictory, segregating laws, which touch practically all areas of life (marriage, work, domicile, moving about, education, etc.), stipulate the interdictions as a function of racial criteria *by name*. It is not the fact of their being interdictions that is new—interdictions were not created yesterday—but the fact that they write into the law the "natural" membership of citizens in a group. The failure to devise logical naturalist categories by scientific means was only a superficial episode in a process that could do without them. The law came to furnish the sociogovernmental, institutional sanction which had not been produced by the channel from which it had at first been expected, even though the scientific field itself had not given up pursuing it.

The gigantic and grotesque enterprise of physical anthropology that Nazism launched in order to enunciate "scientifically" its racial-legal "truth" was not an enigmatic dysfunction, but the result of a logic of previous social relationships. This scientific justification, unceasingly proclaimed and actively researched in all possible directions, proved to be as elusive as it was foreseeable. And particularly elusive, since, aiming at a *functionality* of the idea of race, they tried, looking for a legitimation of a natural order, to create indicators that could coincide with a previous definition of "Aryans" and "Jews" according to the Nazi system. Frenzy by the dominant group about the racial or sexual "nature" of the groups concerned bursts out in periods of open conflict or explicit antagonism. Witness the works on the various human "races" in the post-slavery United States,[16] or the Jews in Nazi Germany, on the particularities of sexual chromosomes in the whole industrial world since the 1960s, and on the chemophysiological or genetic nature of deviance in the contemporary USSR. Whether it be in the United States, in colonizing France, in Nazi Germany, or in the transnational patriarchal system, it remains impossible to claim—despite the efforts in which considerable means and great energy were (and are) invested—that human heterogeneity is demonstrated or demonstrable.

So then, it is a legal category and a *natural* category of the law. For it is not at all true that when one leaves the domain of the natural sciences in order to enter the realm of the law, one renounces the idea of nature. Quite the contrary. What is involved is the same nature and a guarantee directed at the *same* objective. The law, more than science, came to serve as witness of and assurance for the strong, usable belief in the endo-determined character of groups in a given society. This transference shows that race is a category peculiar to social rela-

tionships, springing from them and in turn orienting them. The actual relationships come to he expressed in one of the two possible superstructural forms: legal
institutions or science.

Imaginary Formulation, Legally Sanctioned, Materially Effective

The social sciences themselves have a strangely ambiguous relationship, both
reluctant and submissive, with the idea of a natural group. They are reluctant in
that they don't accept the thesis that races are, insofar as they are a natural category, an effective, nonmediated cause of social relationships (the proponents of
the naturalist thesis are found mostly among physicists, physical anthropologists,
or psychologists). They are submissive in that they nevertheless accept the idea
of a natural category, but as something dissociated from social relationships and
somehow able to have a pure existence. This results in an untenable position. A
total abstention from the idea of naturalness would be an easier position to
maintain. But the ideological implications of the idea of nature and of natural
groups *cannot be passed over*, and therefore it occupies—even if one is loath to
see it—a central place in almost all social relations. Ideologically hidden (if the
ideology is hidden beneath the "obviousness" of it, as I think), the "natural"
form, whether it be common knowledge or already institutionalized, is at the
center of the *technical means* used by the relationships of domination and power
to impose themselves on dominated groups and to go on using them.

As a technical/legal category, the proclamation of the existence of natural
groups enters the order of material facts. The law is the expression of the ideo-
logical/*practical* techniques of the system of *domination*. One finds there the privileged guarantee of what is ideologically supposed to not need guarantee in social
rules, since it is a fact of nature. Who can go against nature, the law of the world,
the writing down of which can only be a nullity or a tautology? In affirming the
specificity of groups, nature passes through legal inscription; it is affirmed as a
social fact at the same time that it claims to be the origin of and the reason for
human society. It is a sinister game of "one is supposed to act as if . . ." and then,
in fact, one does "act as if."

In fact, a natural characteristic (race, sex), being a legal category, intervenes
in social relationships as a constraining and impelling trait. It inscribes the
system of domination on the body of the individual, assigning to the individual
his/her place as a dominated person; but it does not assign any place to the dom-
inator.[17] Membership in the dominant group, on the contrary, is legally marked
by a convenient lack of interdiction, by unlimited possibilities. Let me explain.
Legally nothing prevents a member of the dominant group (which, moreover, is
only a "natural" group by negation; it is "neither" this, "nor" that) from taking

up the activities of the dominated categories. Such a person can become a migrant farm worker, do home sewing, do the laundry gratis for a whole domestic group, be paid to do typing, not be paid to care for, wash, and feed children. Outside of a low wage or none at all, this person wouldn't encounter anything but sarcasm, contempt, or indifference. In any case, there would be no barrier to doing it, but this person wouldn't do it—it's just a theoretical possibility. For (1) while no one would prevent someone from doing it, (2) no one would require it. The two propositions are only meaningful in combination; *each* is important in itself *and when taken together.*

However, everything keeps the members of the dominated groups from (1) getting paid for jobs that are socially defined as being jobs performed without pay and (2) becoming part of certain state or religious establishments. They are forbidden to them. And I am not even speaking here of the usual barriers, so effective in barring access to high salaries, to personal independence, to freedom of movement. The dominated persons are in the symmetrical and inverse situation of the dominators, for (1) everything prohibits certain activities to them and (2), on the contrary, everything requires them to do domestic work gratis, to be laborers, to work at (or below) the minimum wage level. And this is done with an array of resources, including legal resources.

CONCLUSION

The invention of the idea of nature cannot be separated from domination and the appropriation of human beings. It unfolded within this precise type of relationship. But appropriation which treats human beings as things, and from that draws diverse ideological variations, is not enough in itself to lead to the modern idea of natural groups. Aristotle, after all, talked about the nature of slaves, but it was not with the meaning that we give today to this word. The word *nature*, applied to any object, fixed its purpose in the world order, an order which at that time was regulated by theology. In order for the modern meaning of the word to come into being there had to be another element, a factor internal to the object. Endogenous determinism, which ushers in scientific development, will come, by attaching itself to the "purpose," to form this new idea of the "natural group." For, beginning with the eighteenth century, rather than appealing to God to explain material phenomena, people turned to analyzing mechanical causes in the study of phenomena, first physical phenomena and then living phenomena. The stake, moreover, was the conception of Man, and the first materialism was to be mechanistic during this same century (see *L'Homme machine* by Julien Offray de La Mettrie).

If what is expressed by the term *natural* is the pure materiality of the implicated objects, then there is nothing less natural than the groups in question, which are constituted *by* a precise type of relationship: the relationship of power, a relationship which makes them into things (both destined to be things and mechanically oriented to be such), but which *makes* them, since they *only* exist as things within this relationship. This is the social relation in which they are involved (slavery, marriage, migrant labor), and which makes them such at every moment. Outside of these relations they don't exist; *they cannot even be imagined.* They are not givens of nature but naturalized givens of social relationships.

Translated by Mary Jo Lakeland

Notes

1. For a critical presentation of this position, see the collective work, *Discourse biologique et ordre social*, ed. Pierre Achard *et al*. (Paris: Seuil, 1977), which endeavors to demonstrate this fascination and constant reference at work.

2. In fact, the same problem arises in classical physical anthropology, for the "natural" position is practically untenable. But it is with the social sciences that the present discussion is concerned.

3. At the time that the present article was written, an evening newspaper, in a review of recent books, in French on South Africa, used the term *métis* (half-breed) to refer to the "colored" group. Correct in the logical sense, this is false in the social sense, the South African particularly. The word *colored* exists precisely in order to censor the word *half-breed*. Everybody knows that half-breed is what is referred to—that is not the question—but *nobody wants to know it.*

4. But it would be pointless to keep resorting (as is the case) to reaffirmations of morphosomatic evidence if—as is often said (even among social scientists)—the somatic traits were "striking" and "obvious" and were, because of that, the cause of racial prejudice, conflicts, and power relations between groups.

5. *Colored* and not *uncolored*, an appellation that would logically be just as pertinent. This shows what the referent of the system is.

6. On the process that separated the two strands of the recruitment of forced labor, the European and the African, see Eric Williams, *Capitalism and Slavery* (Chapel Hill: University of North Carolina Press, 1944).

7. I mean here the idea of "nature" in the present scientific sense. The theological societies gave to this word the meaning of "internal order," a meaning always present within the contemporary idea, but until the nineteenth century it *did not include* an endogenous determinism, which is a fundamental characteristic today.

8. An allusion to this practice can be found in Tallement des Réaux (a leading member of a bourgeois banking family) in the seventeenth century: "She called him over to a comer of the room to ask him if he didn't find that black suited me well. At that time young people didn't wear black so early in the day as one does now."

9. I distinguish here between dependence and belonging. Belonging—"being" in a social station, in a religion—is supposed to be both permanent *and* subject to change. One could be ennobled or change one's religion in certain circumstances. Dependence implies a direct relationship, either contractual or coercive: The "indentured" servant, the cleric bound by his vows, and the appropri-

ated slave were considered to be in an irreversible situation for a specific term of time (which could be limited but which also could be for an entire lifetime).

10. Carl von Linné, the first great taxonomist of the human species, had, as in his vegetable classifications (which it may be noted in passing were, all the same, his essential preoccupation), a conception of method that did not place him at all within an empiricist perspective. His system is a set of statements of principle. He would probably have been very surprised if one had connected him to some endo-determinism, which today necessarily accompanies the idea of nature.

11. "Spontaneous idea": that is, an idea which is tightly associated with—or indissociable from—a specific historical relationship, and which is always present at the heart of this relationship.

12. Even supposing that one accepts this kind of argument, one can also point out that the "obvious distinction" between a Tunisian and a Dutch person is completely invisible to someone who is neither North African nor European, as I have been able to note on numerous occasions. In any case these distinctions are less than those that distinguish between social classes or the sexes, where weight, height, etc. are differentiated.

13. I take the liberty of referring to some of my own previous works: Colette Guillaumin, L'idéologie raciste. Genèse et langage actuel (Paris: Mouton, 1972); "Les caractères specifiques de l'idélolgie raciste," Cahiers Internationaux de Sociologie 53 (1972); and "The Idea of Race and Its Elevation to Autonomous, Scientific and Legal Status," in Sociological Theories: Race and Colonialism (Paris: UNESCO, 1980).

14. One can only ask oneself why it is so frequently argued (and by important scholars) that the somatic—so-called racial—mark (in fact, skin color) is supposed to be so much more relevant than eye color or hair color and that it is supposed to have so much more value as a discriminating factor than the latter, which "can differ from parent to child." It is forgotten curiously quickly that, as a matter of fact, racial characteristics such as skin color can be different between parents and children (in the United States and the West Indies a white parent can have a black child). And this difference is more important than the shade of eye color or hair color not because it is more visible, but because it is socially proclaimed to be racial and assumes the characteristic of constraining violence. Here we have again an example of the lack of reality in the propositions that are presented as evidence of simple common sense.

15. For—let me repeat it—if there was not a social group, the physical trait (whatever it might be) would not be discriminating.

16. See, for example: John S. Haller, Outcasts from Evolution, Scientific Attitudes of Racial Inferiority 1859–1900 (Urbana: University of Illinois Press, 1971); and Marvin Harris, The Rise of Anthropological Theory (New York: Crowell, 1968).

17. And it is at this precise point where we find the break with the traditional system of marks, which conventionally applied to all opposing groups. The groups of slaves, of deported prostitutes, of condemned criminals are in an intermediate classification, between those based on the conventional mark and the natural mark, in which the mark on the body was imposed only on the dominated persons.

11. Biology and the New Racism

Martin Barker

ALTHOUGH IT IS NECESSARY to spend time establishing the link between the new Tory racism and David Hume, it is not the most obvious link to make. Nor is it the most obviously powerful, compared with the link with biology. It is the use of the concept of instincts that gives the new racism the appearance of scientific validity. It is in the context of particular aspects of biology, ethology, and sociobiology that we must took at it.

Tory ideology claims that it is biologically fixed that humans form exclusive groups, and that these groups succeed internally insofar as they close up against outsiders. Or as someone else put it:

> The biological nation . . . is a social group containing at least two mature males which holds as an exclusive possession a continuous area of space, which isolates itself from others of its kind through outward antagonism, and which through its defence of its social territory achieves leadership, cooperation and a capacity for concerted action.[1]

The writer of this, Robert Ardrey, is a popularizer of the scientific claims of human ethology, a version of neo-Darwinism that has come to conclusions demonstrably like those of the Tory party.

In recent years, however, the claims of the human ethologists have been the subject of hot controversy. Their prime adversaries have presented yet another neo-Darwinist account: sociobiology. And yet that theory also arrives at the same conclusions about "race." So could it be that Tory policies are, in fact,

Martin Barker, "Biology and the New Racism," *The New Racism*. New York: Greenwood Publishing Group, 1981, pp. 12–29, reprinted with the permission of Greenwood Publishing Group, Inc.

merely following the dictates of biology as has been claimed? Or is it rather that these supposedly scientific theories are themselves suspicious, and in fact scientific ideologies? Just what is the relation of science and politics in a case like this? Before these questions can be answered, we need to know something more about the theories. We must see just what conclusions are offered by ethology and sociobiology, and how they are arrived at.

What are the two schools, and who are their protagonists? Human ethology derives from the work of a large number of writers, many of them European; notable among them are Konrad Lorenz, Niko Tinbergen, Desmond Morris, and their public relations man Robert Ardrey.[2] Both schools have a taste for popularization, with Morris leading the way in Britain with serializations of his books in the tabloid newspapers. There are strong lines of continuity, both personal and doctrinal, between the ethologists and the prewar eugenicists. Lorenz, in particular, had a somewhat dubious role in the German race-biology climate. Allen Chase cites one of the worst expressions of this:

> There is a close analogy between a human body invaded by a cancer and a nation inflicted with subpopulations whose inborn defects cause them to become social liabilities. Just as in cancer the best treatment is to eradicate the parasitic growth as quickly as possible, the eugenic defence against the dysgenic social effects of afflicted subpopulations is of necessity limited to equally drastic measures. (Lorenz, quoted in Chase, p. 349)[3]

Lorenz, postwar, was somewhat milder, albeit he still held to such an organicist view of society.

But from the late 1960s, a major challenge developed to some key ideas of the ethologists, deriving this time from America. In 1976, the bulk of these criticisms, and an alternative neo-Darwinism, were brought together in Edward Wilson's *Sociobiology—the New Synthesis*.[4] A number of authors have rehearsed the history of this controversy. Michael Ruse gives a useful summary of the sociobiologists' side.[5] The argument centered on the mechanism by which Darwinian selection was supposed to take place.

The Darwinian revolution, effectively begun in 1859 with the publication of *On the Origin of Species*, was built around the idea of natural selection. Natural selection was a summary term for the processes whereby, within a species, organisms selectively survived. Those with characteristics slightly better adapted to the particular environments and general circumstances in which the species lived would, on average, survive better and longer—and would, therefore, have greater chances to pass on the genes for those adapted characteristics to offspring. By the slow accumulation of these differences, species change and develop.

All this is fine, beautifully simple, and has all the advantages of a naturalistic account. But it is in applying it that the problems arise. For among the key variables of any environment in which organisms have to survive are others of its own kind. This is problem enough in relation to plants. But when we come to a vast number of species of animals—insects, birds, fish, mammals—there is the additional factor of *society*. Under the heading of society would come sexual relations, the rearing of offspring and forms of cooperative behavior, as well as competition for resources. What is the role of social life in natural selection?

Although it is not normally formulated quite in this way by the ethologists and sociobiologists, it seems a fair characterization of the debate to say that this is what it is all about. According to the ethologists, selection takes place at the level of the group: hence the term "group selectionist." What this means is best seen through an example. Among flocking birds, it is common that when a hawk approaches, the first bird to sight it gives an alarm call, which has the effect of warning the whole flock. Why does this happen? Common sense would say, to warn the others. But evidence suggests that the birds that do this put themselves at greater risk by standing out from the rest of the flock. How does such a piece of behavior evolve if it is harmful to the individual? Is it a piece of altruistic behavior?

The group selectionists said yes. It is a piece of behavior that has evolved because of its use to the species as a whole. You can apply this idea in many tempting ways: to the runt in the litter of pigs that gives up trying to live "for the benefit of the others"; to the ritual element in the fighting among wolves that prevents the victor killing the loser. Characteristics tend to survive, it was argued, for the good of the species—or better, for the social population. A social population is any relatively separate subgroup of a species within which mating, rearing, and other social activities take place.

The ethologists were in the main zoologists, animal watchers; their problem was to interpret behavior that they saw. Their critics, on the other hand, contained a fair sprinkling of geneticists and biologists. They fired a Darwinian objection; it didn't seem to be possible that group selection could actually work.

Take the bird alarm. At some point this bit of behavior must have been added to the flocks' repertoire. But if giving the alarm tended to attract predators to the bird who made it, then on average it would have been less likely to survive than those birds who gave no alarm, but who still benefited from any warnings given. The genetic predisposition to behave this way would have canceled itself out. So the idea of group selection, however attractive, would not work in evolutionary terms.

This is what the individual selectionists argued, and, out of their increasingly self-conscious applications of this idea came sociobiology. Its main proponents, apart from Wilson, have been W. Hamilton, R. Trivers, John Maynard Smith (all represented in Clutton-Brock and Harvey), and Richard Dawkins.[6] But the sociobiologists have found supporters in other disciplines, including the social sciences. I shall have occasion to refer to these as well.

For all their differences, on a large number of occasions the two schools find themselves very largely arguing the same case. For this reason I have called them together the "new instinctivists." But it is of some importance to see how each arrives at the racist conclusions that are the subject of this book.

THE ETHOLOGISTS AND RITUAL AGGRESSION

Why do we need to do this? A common term shared by this book [7] and by those it criticizes is the Darwinian theory of evolution. I am totally committed to an evolutionary account of the origins and nature of human beings, as of all other species, in terms of natural selection and adaptation. However, I want to dispute what this means in practice. If it turned out that the findings of either the ethologists or of the sociobiologists were necessitated or directly warranted by the very nature of Darwinian theory, I believe we would have no option but to accept them—however unpalatable. In reality, I want to demonstrate that no such straight line of derivation is either achieved or achievable. To see this, it is necessary to know exactly how the ethologists derive their ideas.

I shall begin with Ardrey and Morris, who set out the conclusions that the ethologists draw, and then trace their route of emergence. I am not attempting a full account or critique of their views, only of how they typically move from premises to, in this case, a racist conclusion. Morris has a (for him) very careful discussion of racialism. He notes that there is a strong tendency for people to look at differences between nations and to argue that these (perhaps temperamental) differences must be biologically based: thus the Germans are laborious, the Italians excitable, Americans expansive, the British stiffupper-lipish, and so on. He scorns this idea: "Even as superficial assessments of acquired national character these generalizations are gross oversimplifications."[8] But, he claims, the real fault and danger comes from reading these traits as innate.

Clearly Morris is not being racist in a traditional sense.[9] But the new racism shows in his next step. Why do people believe this illogical idea that national characters are innate, asks Morris? It is "nothing more than the illogical wishful thinking of the *in-grouping tendency*." What is this?

> The whole human species has a wide range of basic behaviour patterns in common. The fundamental similarities between any one man and any other man are enormous. One of these, paradoxically, is the tendency to form distinct groups and to feel that you are somehow different, really deep-down different, from members of other groups. (*Naked Ape*, p. 128)

This is an innate tendency; and it is the same as what Lorenz calls "pseudospeciation" and Ardrey "nation-forming." And it makes inevitable a pessimistic political conclusion:

> I am not arguing that there can be a worldwide brotherhood of man. That is a
> naive utopian dream. Man is a tribal animal and the great super-tribes will
> always be in competition with one another. (Ibid., p. 126)

Morris has argued that although the "badge" of color of your skin does not indicate any necessary difference under the skin, it is inevitably treated as though it
did. And a condition of the success of "in-groups" is, in large part, the attitude
taken toward outsiders:

> There is, unhappily, an inverse relationship between external wars and internal
> strife. The implication is clear enough: namely that it is the same kind of frus-
> trated aggressive energy that is finding an outlet in both cases. Only a brilliantly
> designed supertribal structure can avoid both at the same time. (Ibid., p. 116)

This last qualification is very odd since we are never given any guide as to what
will be a brilliant design, who a brilliant designer, and how you go about reorga-
nizing instinctual responses as suggested. By contrast, Ardrey does not worry too
much about qualifications of this sort. His support of apartheid in South Africa
witnesses the direction of his ideas. Ardrey has always been treated with reserve
by the professional ethologists, who are a bit embarrassed by him. But for all his
exaggerated statements, he is committed to the same central concepts as they,
and shares a lot of their "evidence"—coming to conclusions, in a way, much
more logically than the others.

His main conclusion is a stronger restatement of Morris, that there is an
inverse relation between the internal strength of a nation and the external hostility in which it is involved:

> Nothing in animal example or primate precedent offers any but the conclusion
> that territory is conservative, that it is invariably defensive, that the biological
> nation is the supreme natural mechanism for the security of a social group.[10]

Well-defined borders and a relation of defensiveness therefore are the essential
requirements of a strong social order.

Even supposing that there were not a hundred other questions and objections to put up against this way of thinking, how is this supposed to have come
about? How do Morris, Ardrey, and Lorenz know that this is how it works, and
that it is innate? For an innate disposition is nor. the sort of thing that appears
immediately in experience. It is a hypothetical explanation of data.

The ethologists, almost without exception, began from the problem of "aggression." Normally, this term refers loosely to a grouping of forms of behavior,
including the actions of nations toward each other, the actions of children
sorting out the rules of a game, a certain style of playing football, strategies in
chess, and even aspects of foreplay in sex. But the ethologists have taken this

confused hotchpotch and have offered to re-present it as a sharp concept by confronting it with the requirements of evolutionary theory. They have a paradigm type-case of aggression—intraspecific killing—accounting for which will explain all the others.

Their strategy has been to ask a question that seems at first sight problematic: How is uncontrolled aggression between members of the same species compatible with the Darwinian selection and survival of a species? "If a species is to survive, it simply cannot afford to go round slaughtering its own kind. Intraspecific aggression has to be inhibited and controlled."[11] But aggression cannot just be got rid of. It has powerful evolutionary functions. Lorenz listed the key ones: distribution of the species within its environment, so that food stocks are available to those able to make best use of them; sexual selection, so that the "strongest" genes get passed on; brood defense against predators; and the creation of social ranking orders that are regarded as necessary for coordinated action. The problem, then, is this: By what process is it ensured that these essential functions are fulfilled without, unfortunately, wiping out the species in the process? Ethology's answer is *ritualization*.

If we consider again those functions of aggression listed by Lorenz, clearly, unlike the taking of prey, they are not necessarily best served by killing your opponent, if only for the reasons that killing may take much time and energy, and may result in you yourself being injured. If there were a way in which an instinctual rule could be built in such that you fight only insofar as it is needed, and winner be declared without any damage done, the species would be well served. This is what Lorenz and others claim to have discovered. For example, when the mate cichlid fish gets very excited about the possibility of mating, he behaves in a very peculiar way; he

> assumes an attitude of broadside display, discharges some tailbeats, then rushes at his mate, and for fractions of a second it looks as if he will ram her—and then the thing happens which prompted me to write this book; the mate does not waste time replying to the threatening of the female; he is far too excited for that, he actually launches a furious attack which, however, is *not directed at his mate* but, *passing her by narrowly, finds its goal in another member of his species.* Under natural conditions this is regularly the territorial neighbour.[12]

Lorenz's analysis of this and similar cases is the core of the ethological theory, including its application to human beings. Indeed, he went on to say that his special case "is very significant for our theme, because analogous processes play a decisive role in the family and social life of a great many higher animals and man."[13]

Lorenz is a good Darwinian. This account of ritualization will only work if it can be shown how it could have become part of what he calls our "inherited inventory." He has shown why we have to behave like this for survival's sake; in

King Solomon's Ring[14] he has shown why socially organized predators, in particular, need effective ritualization of aggression. Think of wolves: their success depends both on their powerful cooperation and their powerful jaws. Out-of-control aggression among them would result in much less cooperation among them, and many fewer wolves. The fighting behavior of wolf against wolf is a paradigm of ritualization; the loser bares its throat, its most vulnerable part, to the victor, who instantly stops attacking.

But to show that something needs to be present is not to show how it could have developed. Aggression cannot be got rid of. But maybe it can be released in a safer direction. And so ritualization is said to involve *redirected aggression*.

Redirection of aggression means that potentially damaging behavior that is stimulated by one conspecific is directed away toward another. Thus, the male cichlid was aroused by his mate, but attacked a neighbor. Without this, says Lorenz, there could be no society to speak of. Indeed, the very strength of society is in inverse proportion to the strength of the deflected aggression. If we love our partners, relatives, and countrymen a lot, that can only be because we have adequately displaced our aggression. And all this has to be instinctual: "The phylogenetic process of ritualization creates a new autonomous instinct which interferes as an independent force in the great constitution of all other instinctive motivations."[15] And its primary function is to induce "mutual understanding between members of a species." This is a claim to which Lorenz repeatedly returns.

But how is this to be maintained? One of the sociobiologists' challenges runs as follows: suppose there is such a group-beneficial trait as ritualization. What is to prevent a genetic cheat from arising? Imagine one wolf that does not restrain itself when faced with a bare throat. Think how it would benefit in a society of ritualizers. It would pass on more of its cheating genes. So, even supposing that a tendency to act for the group's benefit could emerge, it would soon cancel itself out.

This is always presented as though no answer was possible. In fact, there was one all along:

> There are certain social behaviour patterns useful to the community but against the interests of the individual. . . . The social system arising in this way remains by its very nature unstable. If, for example, in the jackdaw, *Coleus mondedula* L., a defence reaction has evolved in which every individual bravely defends a fellow against a predator, it is easy to see that a group with this behaviour pattern has better chances of survival than one without it, but what prevents the occurrence within the group of individuals lacking this comrade-defence reaction?[16]

The answer Lorenz gives is important. For it reveals the continuities with prewar instinctivist accounts of society; and it will be a key to unlocking the objections of the sociobiologists. His answer is: we don't know (yet) for certain, but the mechanism must be something like a social antibody mechanism. Just as the body has defense mechanisms against mutant cells (and outside invaders), so the "social organism" must have a way of policing troublemakers. This will have to have been genetically coupled with the original group-formation mechanism, and the two must mutually entail each other. Otherwise society could not persist. And as evidence that such mechanisms do work, Lorenz quotes cases where animals have displayed feelings of remorse or guilt, presumably showing that the individuals can also discipline themselves.

We thus get, from the application of Darwinian requirements to the facts of species' aggression, the following results: to the extent that a species requires social organization, it must ritualize and redirect its aggression. This produces populations that are internally socially structured and militant against outsiders. This is "pseudospeciation,"[17] and it is genetically rooted. And human culture is to be understood in this way, not as man-made, but as built by selection:

> Without traditional rites and customs representing a common property valued and defended by all members of the group, human beings would be quite unable to form social units exceeding in size that of the primal family group. [18]

At the family level, simple unitary instincts such as brood protection are strong enough. But for the higher levels of social organization, a "true autonomous instinct" is required, called "militant enthusiasm" (*In Aggression*, p. 234).

A combination of this, and a reconstruction of human prehistory[19] explains the horrible human propensity to go to war:

> In human evolution, no inhibitory mechanisms preventing sudden manslaughter were necessary, because quick killing was impossible anyhow; the potential victim had plenty of opportunity to elicit the pity of the aggressor by submissive gestures and appeasing attitudes. No selection pressures arose in the prehistory of mankind to breed inhibitory mechanisms preventing the killing of conspecifics until, all of a sudden, the invention of artificial weapons upset the equilibrium of killing-potential and social inhibitions.[20]

We are not, of course, told how and why humans had this propensity to develop weapons. The only explanation given is that humans had a generalized exploratory attitude that led to science and technology. This provided Morris with a justification for a contemptuous dismissal of any evidence about human tendencies derived from traditional societies; they had not developed, so they could not properly be called human. For it is part of our fundamental nature to explore, and thus to develop.[21]

What worries Lorenz and Morris about this human condition is that certain things can set off militant enthusiasm and then unrestrained aggression will tend to follow. One general cause they all stress is overpopulation.[22] This is a potential cause because over-population interferes with the things that bind a society together: organization of property and personal distance; social hierarchies; customs and traditions. Part of the problem can be put down to the creation of cities. When John Doe took up urban life, "he had become a citizen, or super-tribesman, and the key difference was that in a super-tribe *he no longer knew personally each member of his community.*"²³ But that was precisely why the cultural symbols of unity became uniquely important, and why anything that interfered with them would be deadly: "The balanced interaction between all the single norms of social behaviour characteristic of a culture accounts for the fact that it is usually highly dangerous to mix cultures."²⁴ Although his examples are all of traditional societies, Lorenz insists that this is true of any culture.

Lorenz in many places discusses the effects of the weakening of social controls; in particular, he has constructed an explanation of "boredom" in youth, "hatred" between generations, and lawless anarchy in youth subcultures, based on the decline in clear hierarchies and strong traditions.²⁵ But the root of these effects is what interests us here. It is still the inevitable creation of in-groups and out-groups, based on the innate principles of redirection of aggression, which is the ethologists' solution to the Darwinian problem of society.

THE ASSUMPTIONS OF ETHOLOGY

It would be possible to spend hours and days showing the individual flaws, howlers, contradictions, and false "evidences" that make up human ethology. Many have done so. But it would not serve my purpose of showing that the project of arguing in their way is in principle wrong; that, therefore, their explanations" of war, rape, aggression, hierarchy, racialism are not just questionable and indeed wrong, but also ideologically laden. To show this, we need to took again at the structure of the account I have just reviewed. For it shows several assumptions that are not subjected to analysis, without which the ethological argument could not even begin.

All these assumptions are connected with what Chase rightly referred to as the continued *preformationism* of instinctivism. Preformationism has taken many forms; at one time, it was believed that male sperm contained a tiny homunculus that simply grew when implanted in the woman. The doctrine now takes the somewhat more subtle form of believing that for each bit of behavior of an organism, there is an appropriate bit of genetic material (or gene difference for each difference in behavior).²⁶ First is the assumption that all animal behavior and human behavior must be understood by looking at its contribution to the survival of the organism. According to Lorenz, there really is no other sort of genuine explanation.²⁷ Natural selection operates through selective survival of organisms; therefore behaviors that have survived must be there because of their capacity to add to the survival chances of the organism. QED.

The naive attractiveness of this notion should not blind us to its uses and implications. For this is the reality that underlies Morris's comment that "biologically speaking, man has the inborn task of defending three things: himself, his family, and his tribe."[28] They are tasks because they are essential, says Morris, to the survival of the gene pool of that species or population. Now, if it could be proved that human behavior is not guided by such tasks," the whole ethological program would collapse.

The second assumption is perhaps best seen by asking what it is, according to the ethologists, that causes the modern problem of war. I have already hinted at the assumption here, when commenting on Morris's talk of the development of weaponry. Essentially, the ethologists' case is that something has been put biologically out of balance. Morris's talk of the supernormal stimuli of moder n advertising is mirrored in one of Lorenz's more cautious, "scientific" works:

> In many omnivorous animals, for example, a mechanism exists that causes them to prefer food with a minimum content of fibre and a maximum of sugar, fat and starch. In the "normal" conditions of wild life, this phylogenetically adapted releasing mechanism is of obvious survival value, but in civilised man it gives rise to a search for supernormal objects, the addiction to which actually amounts to a vice detrimental to health (e.g. white bread, chocolate etc., which cause constipation and obesity in millions).[29]

Again, in one of his most recent works, he explains that humans have it in their natures only to work when it is necessary, an innate laziness that was not harmful when conditions enforced work. But now "modern civilisation" has flattened that enforcement; the absence of serious challenges is seen as dangerous to the species.[30] This same pattern of argument, then, is used to explain problems of war, overeating, laziness, conflict between generations. In this pattern there is an opposition between normal, natural environments and a supposedly artificial environment in which modern persons live.

The ethologists are notoriously unclear about what is the naughty factor in modern society that is supposed to have corrupted us. It is variously called civilization, technology, cities, overpopulation (though, contra Chase, this is usually seen as a result, not a cause). The imprecision is in itself revealing, but not as significant as the sheer use of the opposition. For we are being shown an implicit assumption: that neo-Darwinism requires species to be "victims" of their environment. Natural selection equals the ability of environments to select out, weed out the unfit for those environments. If a species evolves characteristics that enable it to escape natural selection, that is unhealthy. Ironically, given their frequent misplaced attacks on "environmentalism," it turns out to be an odd form of environmental determinism. For example, Morris describes as follows the condition of prehominid beings when the forests receded: "Only if the environment gave them a rude shove into greater open spaces would they be likely to move."[31] And being shoved into a different environment gave minimal choices about lifestyle or social structure: either man would compete with the carnivores or with the herbivores. The idea of humans becoming, in effect, innate changers of environments is inconceivable to the ethologists, because of this assumption of theirs. For it would be to deny that "environment" always signifies an independent variable, controlling natural selection. Any breach of this rule is, by definition, "artificial" or an "unbiological environment."[32]

The third assumption, which interlaces with the others, is that human behaviors are unitary: this is a point of tremendous significance. Consider the term "aggression" again. What reason is there, merely from examining its behavioral elements, to suppose that there is one common determining factor to war, murder, rape, sport, and chess playing? It is an assumption of the ethologists (and all other instinctivists) that there are common unitary bases to widely different behaviors. To explain, therefore, is to find a common motivation pattern.

This shows in Lorenz's discussion of the Great Parliament of the Instincts. He explains how big functions of the organism (like mating) are built up out of "relatively independent elements." There can be interaction between these elements, of course; but even interactions presuppose something else, that what interacts is preformed. Therefore, the nature of the interactions is predetermined: "In reality, all imaginable interactions can take place between two *impulses which are variable independently of each other*."[33] Thus aggression + sex drive was turned into group adhesion and militant enthusiasm against outsiders. And, because the elements of the combination are preformed and remain relatively independent of each other, no new level of behavior beyond the limits of the elements is possible. But their continued independence is a preformationist assumption.

None of these assumptions is warranted by a Darwinian account, as we shall see. Indeed, it can be shown to be inconsistent with them. This point will become the major substance of my last chapter. But for now it is enough to see that the ethologists cannot stick to these assumptions themselves. They need to contradict them in order to have what I could call a "natural history of evil," that is, a picture of what it is in human behavior that has allowed so much to go wrong, and what could put it right.

Thus Lorenz, despite his assertion that everything ought to be explained as a function of its contribution to evolutionary survival, argues that there are "so-called luxury forms, i.e., structures whose form is not caused by the selection pressure of a system-preserving function, not even by one that was active in the past.[34] And it is supposed to be this additional baggage that expresses the forces of artificial civilization and all the deviations from Darwinian logic.

But we have been given no guide for assigning behaviors, rites, and customs, institutions to one side or the other. All we have is a bald dualism; when one side can't account, the other must do. Let me show how this works by exploring in detail one example from Morris.

He invites us to see our hierarchical social behavior through Darwinian eyes, by a comparison with baboons. It is true, he admits, that the evolutionary connection is very distant, but that is not the point. For baboons were organized to face an environment similar to that which we faced when the prehominids left the lush forests for the open plain (this is Assumption 2 at work):

> The value of the baboon/human comparison lies in the way it reveals the very basic nature of human dominance patterns. The striking parallels that exist enable us to view the human power game with a fresh eye, and see it for what it is: a fundamental piece of animal behaviour.[35]

Thus is Assumption I now brought into play; for what is "animal behaviour" but behavior innately programmed for its survival benefit? So, how do we use this comparison? A typical way would be to look at the roles of the dominant males in each case: "It is always the dominant male baboon that is in the forefront of the defence against an attack from an external enemy. He plays the major role as protector of the group."[36] But, I hear you cry, that doesn't happen in humans. Precisely, says Morris, and that just goes to show how "civilization," the "artificial" life of modern man, has corrupted an inherent mechanism: "If only today's leaders were forced to serve in the front lines, how much more cautious and 'humane' they would be when taking their decisions."[37] But why? It can only be because, with the artificial conditions removed, the impulse to ritualize would reassert itself and all would be well again—that is Assumption 3. For ritualization is now separated out as a unitary process, with definite ends and natural tendencies that must be pursued.

In this example from Morris we have a perfect illustration of the arbitrary way in which Darwinian premises are used in order to permit a shift between explanation and condemnation. Where the analogy fails it becomes a mode of condemnation; and a random extra factor, inexplicable in terms of this version of Darwinism, called "artificial civilisation," has to do the job of explaining why the analogy broke down. All three preformationist assumptions are needed in order to continue the myths.

What emerges, though, is that ethology contains assumptions that are not only unquestioned, but unquestionable by the "science" of ethology. For any human behavior that appears to challenge the basic theory is classified as "artificial" and therefore deviant. But the distinction between natural and artificial lives and environments is not a scientific one; it is a moral and political distinction. On all these grounds, we have a case for regarding ethology as *ideological science*. I prefer this wording to calling it simply "ideology," since it is a very important part of the force of ethology that it presents itself as science, that it uses a structure of interconnecting concepts and elaborate methods, and that it appears to be above politics. The ideology is in the very science.

SOCIOBIOLOGY AND THE SELFISH GENE

It is with these remarks as a basis that we must examine the nature of the dispute between the ethologists and the sociobiologists. For without doubt, it arose within biology as a dispute between scientists. And the sociobiologists are keen to point out the implications of this fact. In July 1979, I was present at a conference at which Richard Dawkins asked that certain faults be forgiven, because the sociobiologists had been directing their attention specifically at the group selectionists. And indeed, the debate between these two groups has been particularly sharp since the publication, in 1962, of Wynne-Edwards's group selectionist study of animal behavior.[38]

What makes the debate so sharp? Ostensibly, it is purely a debate about genetics, about the mechanism whereby Darwinian selection takes place. This debate has been rumbling on since the original formulation of evolutionary theory, beginning as a dispute between Darwin and Alfred Wallace, the codiscoverers of natural selection. But there is much more involved in the question of mechanism than a purely genetic argument.

If we review for a moment what the ethologists were doing, we can see that they were trying to solve some very particular problems. They were worried about the evolutionary functions of aggression: How could fighting members of one's own species be good for that species and incorporated in its behavioral repertoire? And how could aggression, genetically rooted, be genetically restrained, so that its functions could be benignly fulfilled? All this boils down to explaining the genetic possibility of society, of certain forms of "altruism." For unrestrained aggression would be the death of society, if not of the species. The ethologist's solution was *ritualization*.

For a time, the ethologists had the edge over the individual selectionists for popularity. Among geneticists, that was probably not so. But Lorenz and company had never been shy of popularizing, and in forms that would appeal; and many of their ideas soaked into popular opinion (or became part of the rationale given for common opinion). The recent counterblast from the sociobiologists, who have also had a strange penchant for popularization, has probably now made them the more popular. What they have attacked is the idea of selection at the level of the group. I have already briefly illustrated this at the beginning of the chapter; now I want to consider its significance.

The ethologists' solution to their problems had been premised on the central need for society. There had to be society for sexual, protective, and distributive purposes. Ritualization, as a possible genetic mechanism, had the beautiful advantage of simultaneously providing society's need for altruism and restraining aggression. I put it like this, for if we do not see the ethologists as first and foremost solving the problem of society, we will not be able to understand why, for the sociobiologists, aggression is not the central problem.

Not that aggression disappears for the sociobiologists: it is simply given a different place in the picture. The ethological claim is specifically rejected:

> The ethological claims as to the facts of animal aggression are therefore challenged. As might be expected, Lorenz's group selection hypotheses are also questioned. In particular, the sociobiologists want to work from, and only from, individual selection. Now, in a sense, they can do this easily: perhaps even more easily than someone like Lorenz. The sociobiologists make no *a priori* assumptions about the good of the species, and hence have no need of special explanations as to why one organism might attack a fellow. Thus, all other things being equal, in the eyes of the sociobiologists the parasitic wasp larva is indifferent as to whether it is attacking a fellow or a member of a different species.[39]

Every member of a species, according to sociobiology, potentially treats every other as a resource for food and as a competitor for mating, territory, and so forth. Aggression is therefore just the natural relation of members of the same species. And the challenge to the ethological view of animal aggression was made by referring to the many known cases where animals *have* killed conspecifics.

We must be careful here about the status of this evidence. Lorenz and his cothinkers had long known that, especially in some species (and, important for them, that included human beings), ritualization was not as strongly developed as in others (see, for example, Lorenz, *On Aggression*, Chapter 10, on rats). And in addition, they were fond of quoting studies that showed that under certain sorts of pressure, rape, murder, and cannibalism could develop in animal species. So this evidence was not new, and it was accounted for by reference to a natural thinness of the barriers preventing "murderous" aggression, or as "deviance" resulting from abnormal pressures of such things as overcrowding or food shortages.

Wilson has argued, and Ruse has quoted him, that the ethologists in a sense just missed the necessary information: "I have been impressed by how often such behaviour becomes apparent only when the observation times devoted to a species passes the thousand hour mark."[40] This is not a good argument. The ethologists had in fact pioneered the systematic observation of animals' behavior. They knew many of these "facts"; they just had a different strategy for coping with them. The sociobiologists do not disagree with ethologists primarily on matters of empirical evidence, but on the ways of handling data. They have a different conceptualization of the evidence, in which the idea of "deviant" aggression is largely removed. Instead, it is accounted for by an a priori position, that individual genes—and as their bearers, individual organisms[41]—necessarily and always seek to maximize their own chances of survival. And that means, *ab initio*, that all other members of your species are your natural competitors.

But that does not get rid of the problem of society. On the contrary, it makes it necessary to consider it in a new form. This is the reason why Wilson, speaking for them all, wrote about "the central theoretical problem of sociobiology: how can altruism which by definition reduces personal fitness, possibly evolve by natural selection?"[42] By definition, indeed. Genes and their organisms (nicely named "gene machines" by Dawkins) behave in such a way as to maximize their own fitness. No malice is imputed. Simply, genes and organisms that did not do this will not have had much of a future. For an organism is only to be called altruistic if it behaves "in such a way as to increase another such entity's welfare at the expense of its own."[43] This odd definition of altruism has all the signs of making a dangerous circular argument.

The sociobiologists' confidence in these definitions flows straight from their picture of fundamental evolutionary theory. But it lands them with the problem of accounting for all forms of social behavior: If evolution by definition favors the selfish, how could there ever be altruism? Their answer is, only if it is a special form of selfishness: "There are special circumstances in which a gene can achieve its own selfish goals best by fostering a limited form of altruism at the level of individual animals.[44]

Much energy and inventiveness have gone into inventing many various forms of altruism. But the prime form is *kin altruism*. The mechanism of its possibility is straightforward: genes are defined as selfish because unselfish ones would not reproduce so successfully, and would gradually disappear from any population. But suppose that an organism is programmed to look after only related organisms, ones with shared genes. The chances are, then, that even if this costs the life of the protector, the gene for protection will have been saved.[45]

Kin altruism is thus consistent with sociobiological premises. But how does all this relate to racism? We can see this if we take note of an important criticism of sociobiology and how it is responded to. This account of kin altruism had been met with some very powerful arguments from, for example, Marshall Sahlins.[46] Kin altruism seems to expect organisms to undertake some amazing calculations of genetic relatedness; for clearly, the degree to which it is evolutionarily beneficial depends upon the likelihood that the organism being helped shares the particular genes. And that is mathematically calculable; a parent-child or a sibling relation will be 50 percent; grandparents and aunts and uncles 25 percent; cousins $12\frac{1}{2}$ percent; and so on.[47] Sahlins has rightly been scornful of the idea that such detailed calculations can take place.

But the sociobiologists do have a reply, which has two parts. First, it is commonly emphasized that organisms don't actually do the calculating. They behave as if they had calculated:

> I have made the simplifying assumption that the individual animal works out what is best for his genes. What really happens is that the gene pool becomes

filled with genes which influence bodies in such a way that they behave *as if* they had made such calculations.[48]

But how? Gene inheritance is only marginally written in one's face. In some species there might be very specific identifiers (for example, the smell-chemicals, pheromones, that carry precise information in insect species); in others, it might rather be a learned discrimination, via the social rearing pattern.

It was this second possibility that gave rise to what can be called a "pseudo-biological" process. Tiger and Shepher, in their study of the Israeli kibbutzim, give an example of this. Noting that there seemed never to be sexual relations among children reared together in kibbutzim, they claimed that this must be because of a misfiring incest-avoidance trait that was genetically implanted.[49] A BBC Horizon program on their work called this "fooling the genes"; for the children apparently were avoiding incestuous relations because they had been brought up as though they were brothers and sisters. Thus a genetic "requirement" was mediated via a social pattern.

It is really the combination of these two strands that makes sociobiology's addition to the justification of racism. Listen to David Barash:

> If we admit to the possibility that human behaviour has been selected to maximise inclusive fitness, then our preoccupation with genetic relatedness and our responses to it are certainly no surprise. In fact anything else would require some explanation.
>
> Genetic relatedness often declines dramatically beyond the boundaries of a social group . . . and, significantly, aggressiveness increases in turn. Hostility towards outsiders is characteristic of both human and non-human animals. Physical similarity is also a function of genetic relatedness, and human racial prejudice, directed against individuals who look *different*, could well have its roots in this tendency to distinguish in-group from out-group.[50]

Exactly the same line of argument is offered by Pierre van den Berghe, former liberal sociologist of race relations, in an unpleasant article.[51] In it, he argues that all racial dislike has a genetically based component. He goes through an account of the derivation of racism, ethnocentrism, and nationalism, all from the same source: kin altruism. A breeding population over a long span of time develops sufficient genetic closeness and closedness for such "powerful sentiments" to develop, whose "blind ferocity" and imperviousness to rational arguments are "but a few indications of their continued vitality and their primordiality"[52]: "As hominids became increasingly formidable competitors and predators to their own and closely related species, there was a strong selection pressure for the formation of larger and more powerful groups." Thus the creation of "super families" or nations "necessarily meant organising *against* other competing groups, and therefore maintaining ethnic boundaries" (p. 405).

Thus is racism rooted in the genes, in the specific style of sociobiology. Limited altruism within a genetic community has its counterpart in open selfishness, hostility, and aggression toward competitive outsiders. Of course, if they had kept their distance. . . . But I took care to say that this was the particular contribution of sociobiologists. In fact, while denying the ethologists' framework of explanation, they have kept many of their particular conclusions; and that has included the use both of territorialism and of ritualization of aggression. Thus sociobiology can offer a series of reasons why racism should be regarded as genetically programmed in us.

It must be pretty obvious that there is a close convergence between the style of racism that I described earlier, and the "explanations" of ethnocentrism and racial prejudice just outlined. In both, it is possible to deny any assertion of superiority. It is simply that it is natural to isolate oneself behind cultural and genetic barriers: what the two schools of instinctivism offer is a gloss on the word "natural." In this chapter, I have only tried to show the process of derivation of this conclusion. I have made a few preliminary remarks on the ethologists, but I do not want much to return to them. The sociobiologists have become the senior partners now, and I shall direct my main fire against them. Much that I say, however, would apply without change to the ethologists.

The sociobiologists declare themselves deeply upset at any charge of being racist. Barash, for example:

Concern has been expressed that human sociobiology represents racism in disguise: This is simply not true. Sociobiology deals with biological universals that may underlie human social behaviour, universals that are presumed to hold cross-culturally and therefore cross-racially as well. What better *antidote* for racism than such emphasis on the behavioural commonality of our single species.[53]

He is even prepared to concede that the early pseudobiology of "races" and of *laissez faire* capitalism was a misuse of Darwinism. But that could not be true this time?

Exactly the same case is put forward by Michael Ruse (pp. 76–79), who also cannot see that a racist theory could be anything other than asserting that Jews are degenerate or blacks inferior. But the new Tory racists are saying something much simpler, and Wilson for one apparently agrees: "Nationalism and racism, to take two examples, are the culturally nurtured outgrowths of simple tribalism."[54] And they all agree that "simple tribalism" (whatever that may be) is just kin altruism in action. It is simply the extension of loving one's family—at least, if all the preceding theory is correct.

NOTES

1. Robert Ardrey, *The Territorial Imperative* (London: Collins, 1967), p. 191.

2. See Konrad Lorenz, *Evolution and Modification of Behavior* (Chicago: University of Chicago Press, 1965), *On Aggression* (London: Methuen, 1967), *Civilised Man's Eight Deadly Sins* (London: Methuen, 1973), and "The Enmity between Generations and Its Probable Causes," in A. Tiselius and S. Nilsson (eds.), *The Place of Values in the World of Fact* (Stockholm: Almqvist & Wiksell, 1970); Nikolas Tinbergen, *The Study of Instinct* (Oxford: Oxford University Press, 1951), and "On War and Peace in Man and Animal," in H. Friedrich (ed.), *Man and Animal* (London: Paladin, 1972); Desmond Morris, *The Naked Ape* (London: Corgi, 1968), *The Human Zoo* (London: Corgi, 1971), *Intimate Behavior* (London: Cape, 1971), and *Manwatching* (London: Cape, 1977); and Robert Ardrey, *The Territorial Imperative, The Social Contract* (London: Collins, 1970), and *African Genesis* (London: Collins, 1961).

3. Allan Chase, *The Legacy of Malthus* (New York: Knopf, 1977). Lorenz's biographer, Alec Nesbitt, rather disputes the significance of this period of Lorenz's writings; to my mind inconclusively, since he is only concerned to disprove personal Nazism. I am much more worried by the simple continuity of basic concepts and what they warrant. Nesbitt, *Konrad Lorenz* (London: Dent, 1976), Chap. 7.

4. Wilson, *Sociobiology—the New Synthesis* (Cambridge, MA: Harvard University Press, 1976); see also Wilson, *On Human Nature* (Cambridge, MA: Harvard University Press, 1978).

5. Michael Ruse, *Sociobiology—Sense or Nonsense?* (Dordrecht: Reidel, 1979), Chap. 2.

6. T. H. Clutton-Brock and Paul Harvey (eds.), *Readings in Sociobiology* (New York: Freeman, 1978); Richard Dawkins, *The Selfish Gene* (Oxford: Oxford University Press, 1976), and "Sex and the Immoral Gene," *Vogue* (1977).

7. [The author refers here to the volume from which this essay was excerpted: *The New Racism* (London: Junction Books, 1981)—Ed.]

8. Morris, *The Human Zoo*, p. 127.

9. Morris in fact is very ambivalent on the question of innate differences. In *The Human Zoo* (p. 189), he claims that it has never been proved that there are innate differences between populations (he dislikes the word "race" advisedly). On the other hand, he is prepared to repeat the age-old myth (p. 134) that contraception restricted to the "educated classes" will lead to an overall genetic deterioration, as there is probably a genetic component to differences in intelligence; and the poor, unintelligent won't understand how to use some forms of contraception. What this shows, I think, is moder n ethology's whole ambiguous relationship to prewar eugenicism.

10. Ardrey, *The Territorial Imperative*, p. 253.

11. Morris, *The Naked Ape*, p. 139.

12. Lorenz, *On Aggression*, pp. 144–45.

13. Ibid., p. 145.

14. Lorenz, *King Solomon's Ring* (London: Methuen, 1961).

15. Lorenz, *On Aggression*, p. 72.

16. Lorenz, *Civilised Man's Eight Deadly Sins*, p. 32.

17. Ibid., p. 49.

18. Lorenz, *On Aggression*, p. 226.

19. Something of which the ethologists are very fond. But see the complete demolition of their, and related, accounts in Leakey and Lewin's marvellous book, *Origins* (London: MacDonald & Jane, 1977). Leakey has since disappointed many admirers by his concessions to sociobiological views in the later *People of the Lake* (London: MacDonald & Jane, 1979).

20. Lorenz, *On Aggression*, p. 207.

21. Morris, *The Naked Ape*, p. 10.

22. See Chase, *The Legacy of Malthus*, Chaps. 6 and 7.

23. Morris, *The Human Zoo*, p. 21.

24. Lorenz, *On Aggression*, p. 225.

25. See Lorenz, "Enmity between Generations."

26. The fallacy in this, and the alternative, are set out in Chaps. 7–9 [of *The New Racism*—Ed.].

27. Lorenz, *On Aggression*, p. 1.

28. Morris, *The Human Zoo*, p. 111.

29. Lorenz, *Evolution and Modification of Behavior*, pp. 26—27.

30. Lorenz, *Civilised Man's Eight Deadly Sins*, p. 25.

31. Morris, *The Naked Ape*, p. 17.

32. See, e.g., Morris, *The Human Zoo*, pp. 27, 115.

33. Lorenz, *On Aggression*, p. 75; my emphasis.

34. Lorenz, *Civilised Man's Eight Deadly Sins*, pp. 46—47.

35. Morris, *The Human Zoo*, p. 51.

36. Ibid., p. 50.

37. Ibid., p. 113.

38. V. C. Wynne-Edwards, *Animal Dispersion in Relation to Social Behavior* (Edinburgh: Oliver & Boyd, 1962).

39. Ruse, *Sociobiology*, p. 25.

40. Ibid.

41. Though that step is highly problematic.

42. Wilson, *Sociobiology—the New Synthesis*, p. 3.

43. Dawkins, *The Selfish Gene*, p. 4.

44. Ibid., p. 2.

45. We can see from this why kin altruism is the paradigm of altruism, compared with, say, reciprocal altruism, another commonly quoted sort. For this latter consists, in one organism agreeing with another, as it were, on a "you scratch my back, I'll scratch yours" principle—usually aiding each other in competition with a third. This ability may be mutually beneficial, but it has nothing to do with the specific gene differences between individuals that form the core of the sociobiologist's account, since the cooperating individuals can be totally unrelated genetically.

46. Marshall Sahlins, *The Use and Abuse of Biology* (London: Tavistock, 1977).

47. In fact, of course, the mathematical calculation is vastly more complicated than this, for many reasons. There are dominant genes that are more likely to reappear in any combination; in a small population of animals, there are likely to be generally shared genes in different proportions throughout the population, because of inbreeding. But the sociobiologists will play their games, so who are we to interfere?

48. Dawkins, *The Selfish Gene*, p. 108.

49. Lionel Tiger and Joseph Shepher, *Women in the Kibbutz* (Harmondsworth: Penguin, 1977).

50. David Barash, *Sociobiology and Behavior* (London: Heinemann, 1978), pp. 310–11. In order to guard against charges of selective quotation, let us see how Barash continues: "Clearly, this suggestion of a possible evolutionary basis for human racial prejudice is not intended to legitimise it, just to indicate why it may occur. Behaviour patterns that may have been adaptive under biological conditions are inappropriate and even dangerous under the cultural innovations of today" (p. 311). Why this is no defense, and is indeed worse than no defense, will become apparent in Chap. 8 [of *The New Racism*—Ed.]. Note only for now the continuity with the dualism of the ethologists, between "natural" biology and "artificial" culture.

51. Pierre van den Berghe, "Race and Ethnicity: A Sociobiological Perspective," *Ethnic and Racial Studies* 1 (1978). And see also Wilson's use of a distinction between hardcore (kin only) and softcore (ethnic community) altruism in his *On Human Nature* (pp. 155–63); also Dawkins: "Con-

ceivably, racial prejudice could be interpreted as an irrational generalisation of a kinselected tendency to identify with individuals physically resembling oneself and to be nasty to individuals different in appearance" (*The Selfish Gene*, p. 108).

52. Dawkins, *The Selfish Gene*, p. 104.
53. Barash, *Sociobiology and Behavior*, p. 278.
54. Wilson, *On Human Nature*, p. 92.

12. On Race, Racism, and Ethnicity
Claudia Card

THESE REFLECTIONS EXPLORE STRANDS of thought suggested primarily in essays by three thinkers whose work has been helpful to me for thinking about race, racism, ethnicity, and ethnocentrism.[1] I do not develop a thesis so much as raise questions and explore some interrelated themes and considerations surrounding these concepts.

The thinkers to whom I refer are W. E. B. Du Bois, Marilyn Frye, and María Lugones.[2] W. E. B. Du Bois, in his 1897 essay "The Conservation of Races," offers a positive outlook on race from an internal point of view, that is, from the point of view of those who have been racialized.[3] He offers a positive view of the potentialities of identifying as members of a race, however negatively the concept of race may have originated in the unfriendly projects of others. In doing so he seems to suggest the possibility of non-racist uses of the concept of race, other than simply to acknowledge or address its racist uses by others. In contrast, in her essays on being white and being gendered, Marilyn Frye offers a negative picture of race, treating the concept as external, as imposed upon a people by outsiders whose interests were to mark them for domination, to set them apart as inferior, to prohibit intermarriage, and so on.[4] María Lugones suggests yet another dimension, that of interaction, in her essays "Pedagogy and Racism," "Hablando cara a cara/Speaking Face to Face: An Exploration of Ethnocentric Racism," and other essays that address issues arising from cultural confrontations and interpenetrations.[5] She stresses the interactive nature of racism, which sug-

Claudia Card, "On Race, Racism, and Ethnicity," in Linda A. Bell and David Blumenfeld, eds., *Overcoming Racism and Sexism.* Lanham, Md.: Rowman & Littlefield, 1995, pp. 141–52, reprinted with permission from Rowman & Littlefield.

gests the possibility that the concept of race may also develop interactively, regardless of how it originated. These views are not necessarily alternatives. Each of these thinkers has had his or her purposes for stressing different aspects of race. Yet they might fit together as complementary elements of a more comprehensive view.

If "race" may have internal, external, and interactive aspects, "racism" suggests first and foremost a negative external view, that is, a negative view held toward members of another group. Like "sexism," "racism" refers to oppressive behaviors, policies, and attitudes ranging from institutionalized murder to unwitting support of insensitive practices by the well-intentioned.[6] In analyses of racism, the very concept of race is often problematized in ways analogous to the problematizing of gender in analyses of sexism. Worlds seem imaginable in which neither concept structures social relations. Neither races nor genders appear to be natural kinds.[7] In 1945, Ashley Montagu argued that there are no races, on the ground that behaviors cannot be meaningfully correlated with biological ancestry.[8] However, social construction does not make races unreal, even if it makes them arbitrary and unnatural. I say "if" because Du Bois's essay raises the possibility that races need not continue to be totally arbitrarily delineated, even if they are cultural constructions and were initially arbitrary.

"Racism" appears to be a contraction of the earlier "racialism," suggesting the verb "to racialize" which, in turn, suggests social construction and for that reason may be a preferable term.[9] Being race-conscious, however, is not necessarily racializing: it is one thing to *make* something a matter of race and another to *acknowledge* that this has been done. After five centuries of Euro-American racializing of Africans, Asians, and Native Americans, it would seem as irresponsible for white people suddenly to act as though races did not matter as it would be for men suddenly to act as though gender did not matter. For Du Bois, however, race consciousness was not only about oppression. He took issue with the integrationists regarding possible sources of pride and what might be of value in the preservation of races for African Americans and for humanity in general. He was not thinking first of all of holding whites accountable for black oppression. He was concerned here with the development of black talent and genius.

The *American Heritage Dictionary* speculates that the word "race" may come from the Latin, *ratio*, meaning "a reckoning, account." What "accounts"? What "reckonings"? Rendered by whom to whom? One answer is that the "reckonings" or "accounts" of the conquered were produced by the conquerors, thus embedding their own biases in the concept of race. This interpretation supports the view of race as a construction externally imposed, as in Marilyn Frye's understanding of the concept, that is, applied first to others. Another possible answer, however, is that the "reckoning" or "account" refers to one's own record of one's ancestors, handed on to one's descendants, documenting their heritage. This interpretation suggests an internal view of race, that is, a conception applied first of all to oneself. The latter interpretation is also compatible with a negative view, however, insofar as it may be combined with insider chauvinism and hostility regarding outsiders.

"Race," as sometimes used in the late nineteenth century by Charlotte Perkins Gilman in *Women and Economics*, refers to a people who share a lineage (a biological ancestry) and a social history.[10] This might be an interesting idea conceived as applying to oneself if individual races were not defined too broadly—if they were not, say, reduced to four or five in the world. Neither she nor Du Bois does so. They usually identify races not by color but by nationality or geographic origin. When races are defined so broadly that one can list them on the fingers of one hand, intraracial differences become more significant than interracial differences, and it is difficult to claim that racial groups so conceived share a social history.

Among social critics, *ethnicity* is often embraced as something positive, while *race* more often arouses suspicion and skepticism. Yet the differences are not always clear or obvious.[11] Both suggest birthplaces and birthrights. Both races and ethnicities may become dispersed through the homelands of others. Like "national," "ethnic" may suggest geographic origins.[12] Like "race," it suggests heritage. However, "race," unlike "ethnicity," suggests the biological as well as the sociopolitical. Thus, Pierre L. van den Berghe defines "race" as "a group that is *socially* defined but on the basis of *physical* criteria" and ethnic groups as "socially defined but on the basis of *cultural* criteria."[13] Because the social heritage of race is commonly one of oppression or privilege, it is plausible that races are products of conquest, a way of maintaining social hierarchy and of preventing intermarriages that would entail property dispersals and consequent power dispersals.

"Race" suggests color more readily than does "ethnicity." "Ethnic" can be used as a euphemism for "racial" where it is thought impolite (or impolitic) to refer to color (as "erotic" in "erotic art" can be a euphemism for "pornographic" where it is thought impolite or impolitic to refer directly to sex). Today in the United States, "ethnic" is popularly used (misused) to refer to anything that isn't white Anglo-Saxon Protestant (WASP), as in the "ethnic" section of the library, "ethnic" restaurants, and the like, as though WASP were not itself an ethnic concept. If one accepts van den Berghe's distinction between race and ethnicity, WASP appears to be a hybrid of race (white) and ethnicity, with ethnicity identified in two ways: by linguistic origin (Anglo) and by religious connection (Protestant). When "ethnic" is used to refer to groups other than WASP, it can refer both to nonwhite races and to non-Anglo ethnicities. Thus, Thomas Sowell's *Ethnic America* offers chapters on Germans, Jews, Italians, Chinese, Japanese, Puerto Ricans, Mexicans, and blacks, identifying only blacks by color.[14]

"Ethnicity," as distinct from "race," suggests culture, especially folk culture, produced by people who share a history that is usually tied to a geographical territory. In the case of Jewish ethnicity, the shared history is tied to a religion or, at least, a body of texts. Either way leaves it open whether co-ethnics share *biological* ancestry. Ethnic groups sometimes fall within racial groups and in other cases cut across them. Ethnicity seems to cut across race in the case of Jewish blacks and whites and to fall under it in the case of whites who may be Italian or German. W. E. B. Du Bois treats Slavic as a race within which there are Russian and Hungarian ethnicities. But is Slavic a racial identification? Or an ethnic one? Like "Anglo" and "Semitic," "Slavic" names a language group, which suggests ethnicity. Yet, according to Amoja Three Rivers, the term "slave" comes from "Slavic."[15] If slavery is a racializing practice, perhaps the Slavs were thereby racialized at a certain time in history.

There appears a certain asymmetry between race and ethnicity. No noun "ethnicism" corresponds to "racism." Instead, there is "ethnocentrism," referring to one's attitude regarding one's *own* ethnicity and only by implication, if at all, to one's attitudes toward others. "Racism" (or "racialism"), on the other hand, refers first to one's (usually hostile) attitudes toward *other* races, only by implication suggesting arrogance regarding one's own. Their structures thus seem opposite. There are, of course, terms such as "ethnic prejudice" (and more specific terms, such as "anti-Semitism") and "race supremacist" for attitudes running the other direction in each case.

María Lugones once argued that ethnocentrism need not be racist, meaning that it need not involve a negative attitude toward others. In her early essay "Pedagogy and Racism," she used the analogy of a mother saying that her child is "the most beautiful in the world," meaning simply that the child is the center of the mother's attention but not intending objectively the comparative value judgment that the words seem to imply. If ethnocentrism could be the analogue of this, it suggests a healthy pride and joy. However, in "Hablando cara a cara/Speaking Face to Face" María Lugones presents a revised conception of ethnocentrism as basically arrogant, arguing that an *absorption in one's own culture* (like a mother's absorption in her child) is *not necessarily enthnocentric*. Yet she retains the idea that ethnocentrism—although arrogant—is not necessarily racist. Ethnocentrism becomes racist, she argues, when it involves the idea of the racial state.[16] Racist ethnocentrism combines the orientations of racism and ethnocentrism.

Because histories and ancestries crisscross and their boundaries are arbitrary and vague, race identifications are bound to be arbitrary, regardless of their motivations. They may be *more* arbitrary than ethnic ones if one's ethnicity—enculturation—is less liable to multiplicity than one's genealogy. It may seem as though one's ethnicity is liable to serious multiplicity, in that biculturalism is common, especially among the oppressed in ethnocentrically racist societies. However, biculturatism need not involve *identifying with or identifying oneself as a member* of both cultures. It may simply be a matter of facility in negotiating one's way in another culture. One who is bicultural might think of oneself as a

" 'world'-traveler," in María Lugones's sense of that term, without necessarily identifying oneself as *belonging* to "worlds" in which one travels well.[17]

Neither one's race nor one's ethnicity seems reducible to one's loyalties. An interesting question, however, is what significance, if any, one's self-identification has for one's racial or ethnic identity, perhaps especially if one's ancestry or one's cultural heritage is evidently mixed.[18] Identifying someone as a member of a certain race may suggest either that they *do* identify with a certain ancestry and history or that the speaker thinks they *should* identify with it, perhaps for political reasons. From a political point of view, the latter sort of view need not be arbitrary, even if the relevant biological ancestry were evidently mixed. Further, whether one chooses to identify with a race may not be decisive for how others identify one, and how others identify one may come to have implications for what the racial category means. There is also such a thing as refusing to face up to one's identity; there is such a thing as "passing." Yet, there is also such a thing as justifiably disowning a heritage, although the resulting implications for one's identity may be unclear. If I disown my Protestant heritage, I may have changed my identity *somewhat*, but I do not cease thereby to be WASP.

I have been told that I hail from a line of Scots. Should I identify with that? I do not voluntarily identify with Scottish ethnicity. I love music but have a low tolerance for bagpipes. I like plaids but do not wear skirts, not even kilts. And I seem not to have inherited proverbial Scottish attitudes toward money. Yet such things may not be decisive for who I am. My sensibilities and dispositions may be inherited from Gaelic ancestors with whom I have no particular higher-order desire to identify. Even my attitudes and values may be influenced by a more palpable Presbyterianism which I do not willingly embrace. Such characteristics may have enabled me throughout my life to hook into advantageous social networks and to develop what assets I have that others value in me (and that I value in myself). If such influences are transmitted through the parenting process, and if they construct me ethnically, my ethnicity may have tittle to do with my choices or voluntary identifications. Being an ethnic Scot may be part of my moral luck, something to be taken into account if I am to appreciate the political meanings of my relationships and interactions with others and avoid the arrogance that María Lugones identifies as ethnocentric. To regard as *simply human* the attitudes, values, sensibilities, and dispositions that define *one's ethnicity* is a form of arrogance that might justifiably be regarded as ethnocentric, however unwittingly it is done.

Just as combating ethnocentrism may require developing a consciousness that many of one's values, attitudes, and so forth have roots in one's ethnic heritage, anti-racism may require—as it has, in my case—developing a higher-order race consciousness: becoming conscious, for instance, of how one has learned to process perceptions of racial difference (in order to deny them, for example). Such consciousness goes against the grain of my upbringing. Terms like "color conscious," in my corner of Anglo culture, conjure up such thoughts as that if people are classified by readily visible physical characteristics such as color, these characteristics will not be treated as value-neutral and then masses of people will be instantly targetable by each other for friendship (as in elitist cliques) or hostility (as in people of color being tracked by white security guards in predominantly white department stores), independently of who they are as individuals."[19] "Racial" thinking blocks getting to know people. Hasty generalization is not the worst danger. Generalizing at all in terms of race about highly undesirable or highly desirable characteristics (such as intelligence) is readily enlisted in the service of oppression. Yet among those who are in fact targets of racism, instant recognition of potential friends or potential enemies can be necessary for survival. Instant recognition of contexts in which racism is a potential danger can be necessary for effective resistance by anyone. In the context of what María Lugones calls "the racial state," color consciousness facilitates positive contacts among the oppressed as well as oppressive contacts of dominant with subordinate. It facilitates political separatism of the oppressed as well as segregation and oppressive avoidance by the dominant.[20] The segregationist potentialities are terrifying: capture, concentration of peoples, imprisonment, enslavement. Yet they are hardly a reason to reject color consciousness in a society that is *already* racist—rather the opposite: such dangers can hardly be combatted without it. This creates a challenge for white people in a society such as the United States: how to be race or color conscious without being racist or in other ways oppressive. As Pat Parker put it in her poem "For the white person who wants to know how to be my friend":

> The first thing you do is to forget that i'm Black.
> Second, you must never forget that i'm Black.[21]

One may ask, must color consciousness, or race consciousness, be at best only a necessary evil? Can good purposes, other than resistance to oppression, be served by race consciousness? Good for whom? I want to say good for those on both sides, or at least on the oppressed or subordinated side, of a given racial distinction. W. E. B. Du Bois was interested in the good of affirming racial identity for African Americans. But he also spoke of its value to humanity. His idea was that different cultural developments distinguish racial groups and that it takes many generations to produce these cultural developments. He feared that if races were not conserved—if, for example and in particular, African Americans assimilated to European Americans—valuable cultural developments would be lost. The focus on culture by Du Bois may suggest a concern more with ethnicity than with race. And yet, how separable are they, if he is also right that significant cultural developments require many generations? Du Bois, in his essay on conserving races, seems to think of race as having internal aspects, which he identifies as cultural potentialities that may require generations to realize, as well as whatever external aspects may be defined by practices of others. Neither seems originally the object of individual choice, although individuals can affirm or deny them.

In my liberal Anglo upbringing, race was supposed to be morally irrelevant at least partly because individuals have no *control* over their racial identity, and individuals were supposed to have control over who they *really are*. One can adopt or reject many aspects of an ethnicity—as I do with the Scots. Perhaps for this reason, Anglo liberals have not worried historically about the importance of ethnicity as they have about that of race. Race has been thought totally involuntary—except for the choice whether to procreate (which can, of course, affect the race of one's offspring although it does not affect one's own racial identity).

Marilyn Frye's essay, "On Being White," challenges the assumption that one has no control with respect to one's race by arguing that one can at least choose where to place one's loyalties. This approach preserves the idea that the individual, morally speaking, is basically revealed by her choices. At any rate, it does not challenge that idea. I have come to question, however, such historically liberal reasons for regarding race as morally irrelevant. Although who I am is importantly affected—and revealed—by my choices, I do not choose everything that is important to my identity, nor even all of it that matters morally. I am a relational being, and my choices alone are not decisive for all my relations. A heritage that has given me privileges or liabilities from birth, whether I affirm it or reject it, is important to who I am and who I can become. Even whether I have a heritage to which to be loyal or disloyal is not the product of my choices.

"Heritage" is a slippery term. If one thinks of it as whatever led up to one's existence, it seems that everyone has a heritage. But what makes a past *one's own* is not just causal precedence. When a heritage is a cultural legacy, one can be disinherited or alienated from it. One can be robbed of one's culture. Cultures of one's ancestors may have been annihilated. They may have been appropriated by others and assimilated into their cultures.[22] Thus, not all have the privilege of being able to claim a heritage. Nor do all want to claim as their heritage some of the pasts that produced them (rape and slavery, for example). Amoja Three Rivers writes: "One of the most effective and insidious aspects of racism is cultural genocide. Not only have African Americans been cut off from our African tribal roots, but . . . we have been cut off from our Native American roots as well. Consequently most African Native Americans no longer . . . even know for certain what people they are from."[23] If "race" in its internal aspect refers to certain aspects of cultural heritage—as is suggested in Du Bois's usage in "The Conservation of Race"—an insidious aspect of racism seems to be the *destruction* of races. (This is compatible, of course, with its also constructing races). Laurence Thomas points out in his discussions of the evils of American slavery that it takes only seven generations to complete cultural genocide, to erase the memories. For some whose Native American ancestors succumbed to European diseases, it may have been faster.[24]

Perhaps race and ethnicity come together, to some extent, in the notion of a heritage. Cultural genocide may be less complete than it appears if what is primarily destroyed are the means of *identifying* cultural developments but not necessarily those developments themselves. Further, in pondering the question of what significance if any, one's *biological* heritage has for one's social identity, I want to ask: What counts as "biological"? Marilyn Frye once wrote, in thinking about gender: "Enculturation and socialization are misunderstood . . . if one pictures them as processes which apply layers of cultural gloss over a biological substratum. It is with that picture in mind that one asks whether this or that aspect of behavior is due to 'nature' or 'nurture.' "[25] She went on to develop a very bodily picture of gender, concluding that if that makes it "biological," then "biological" means only "of the animal." Likewise, much of what is "biological" in race may not be genetic and what is "cultural" in ethnicity may not be chosen. Thus, it may be more significant for self-understanding to know one's earliest unchosen caretakers and the often also unchosen social contexts of their lives, and *their* early caretakers and the social contexts of *their* lives (and so on), than to know the sources of one's genes. This distinction is obscured when childrearing is done by biological kin. Yet either sort of history might be considered a "genealogy." I conclude with three examples of genealogies where what is of interest are the histories of parenting:

1. An issue of *Lilith*, a few years ago, contained an article on Indian Catholic Jews of New Mexico, descendants of sixteenth-century "conversos" (Jews forced to convert to Christianity) who fled the Inquisition in Mexico.[26] These descendants are reported to be practicing Catholics who still also practice Jewish customs privately at home without knowing what they mean or even that the customs are Jewish.[27] Some, having accidentally discovered the Jewish meanings, are now, apparently, talking about *discovering their Jewish heritage*. And what customs do they likewise practice without knowing their Native American meanings?

2. Enslaved Africans in the Americas were often separated from biological kin at early ages and raised by others who were enslaved from totally different regions of Africa. Such foster parents may have borne little resemblance to the children's biological kin and may not even have spoken a related language. If a common African American heritage has been developing in this country, undocumentable generations of such parenting under conditions of slavery may be a more significant factor in its unification than the genetic impositions of white rapists who claimed to own African slaves and their descendants.

3. And what is the heritage of white people in the United States who were raised by black servants or slaves? Or, for that matter, of white people generally in the United States today? The culture of white people in the United States is at least as mixed in its genealogy as the genealogy of the Indian Catholic *conversos* of New Mexico, as a result of generations of enforced interracial caretaking and forms of cultural appropriation.[28]

NOTES

1. The May 1991 conference "Racism and Sexism: Differences and Connections, sponsored by the Georgia State University Department of Philosophy, was a major stimulus to these reflections, which I first set down in response to a call for essays on race and racism by the Midwest Society of Women in Philosophy later that same year. For comments on that early draft I am grateful to Jeffner Allen, Howard McGary, and Joann Pritchett.

2. These three thinkers were represented on the program of the Georgia State conference: W. E. B. Du Bois in the presentation by Lucius Outlaw, Marilyn Frye in her presentation reflecting on her own earlier essays on the topic, and María Lugones in her presentation on anger.

3. *W. E. B. Du Bois Speaks: Speeches and Addresses 1890–1919*, ed. Philip S. Foner (New York: Pathfinder, 1970), 73–85. This essay was the subject of Lucius Outlaw's presentation at the 1991 Georgia State conference.

4. Marilyn Frye, *The Politics of Reality: Essays in Feminist Theory* (Trumansburg, N.Y.: The Crossing Press, 1983) and *Willful Virgin: Essays in Feminism 1976–1992* (Freedom, Calif.: The Crossing Press, 1992).

5. "Pedagogy and Racism" was presented in Minneapolis at a conference of the Midwest Society of Women in Philosophy in 1984 and printed in Carleton College's *Breaking Ground* 6 (Spring 1984): 38–43. It was later revised and expanded as "Hablando cara a cara/Speaking Face to Face: An Exploration of Ethnocentric Racism," in Gloria Anzaldúa, ed., *Making Face, Making Soul: Haciendo Caras* (San Francisco: Aunt Lute, 1990), pp. 46–54. See also María Lugones, "Playfulness, 'World'-Travelling, and Loving Perception," *Hypatia* 2, no. 2 (Summer 1987): 3–10, and "Hispaneando y lesbiando: On Sarah Hoagland's Lesbian Ethics," *Hypatia* 5, no. 3 (Fall 1990): 138–146.

6. See, for examples of the latter, Amoja Three Rivers, *Cultural Etiquette: A Guide for the Well-Intentioned*, 1990 (distributed by Market Wimmin, Box 28, Indian Valley, VA 24105).

7. Although sexual differentiation into *female* and *male* is natural for human beings (however ambiguous it may turn out in particular instances), it does not follow, as a matter of logic, *that femininity* and *masculinity* are also natural, where these concepts are understood to refer not to gross anatomical structure or chromosomal composition but to psychological dispositions or traits and social expectations.

8. Ashley Montagu, "'Ethnic Group' and 'Race,'" *Psychiatry* 8 (1945): 27–33, reprinted in Montagu, *Race, Science and Humanity* (New York: Van Nostrand, 1963). See also Ashley Montagu, *Man's Most Dangerous Myth: The Fallacy of Race* (Cleveland: Meridian, 1964).

9. An essay by Marcus G. Singer first called my attention to this history, "Some Thoughts on Race and Racism," *Philosophia* (Philosophical Quarterly of Israel), 8, nos. 2–3 (Nov. 1978): 153–83.

10. Charlotte Perkins Gilman, *Women and Economics* (New York: Harper Torchbooks, 1966). This work was first published in 1898. Sometimes the author used "race" in referring to the human species, and at other times to refer to more specific human groups.

11. In *Racist Culture: Philosophy and the Politics of Meaning* (Cambridge, MA: Blackwell, 1993), 74–78, David Theo Goldberg presents "ethnorace" as one of the masks of race.

12. See also Goldberg, *Racist Culture*, 78–80, on "race as nation."

13. Pierre L. van den Berghe, *Race and Racism: A Comparative Perspective*, 2d ed. (New York: Wiley, 1967, 1978), 9–10.

14. Thomas Sowell, *Ethnic America* (New York: Basic Books, 1981).

15. Three Rivers, *Cultural Etiquette*, p. 9.

16. On the idea of the racial state, see Michael Omi and Howard Winant, *Racial Formation in the United States from the 1960s to the 1980s* (New York: Routledge, 1986), pp. 57–69.

17. In "Playfulness, 'World'-Travelling, and Loving Perception," María Lugones introduced a

conception of "world"-travel as the willful exercise of an acquired flexibility, developed sponta-neously out of necessity by members of a minority in an oppressive society, in shifting from a con-struction of life in which one is at home although others are outsiders, to other constructions of life in which some of these former outsiders are at home, or more nearly at home and in which one may figure oneself as an outsider. To illustrate, she elaborated on what it meant for her to travel to the "world" of her mother, explaining that she was unable to love her mother well until she could do this. Such "world"-travel has the potentiality to develop new aspects of oneself, even new "selves." It seems not, however, to create new ethnic *identities*, perhaps because one's ethnicity has a histor-ical element that remains unchanged by "world"-travel.

18. For a critique of the concept of race based on problems presented by mixed race, see Naomi Zack, *Race and Mixed Race* (Philadelphia: Temple University Press, 1993).

19. For another example of invidious tracking, see Cornet West's account of what occurred when he tried to hail a taxi on the corner of 60th Street and Park Avenue in Manhattan, in *Race Matters* (Boston: Beacon, 1993), p. x.

20. I here follow Malcolm X and Marilyn Frye in using "separatism" to refer to the voluntary separation from an oppressor by the oppressed, in the interests of the oppressed, and "segregation" to refer to separations from the oppressed imposed by an oppressor, in the interests of the oppressor. See *The Autobiography of Malcolm X*, with the assistance of Alex Haley (New York: Grove, 1964), p. 246, and Frye, *Politics of Reality*, p. 96

21. Pat Parker, *Movement in Black* (Oakland, Calif.: Diana Press, 1978), p. 68.

22. Regarding cultural death and cultural appropriation, see Laurence Mordekhai Thomas, *Vessels of Evil: American Slavery and the Holocaust* (Philadelphia: Temple University Press, 1993), on the "natal alienation" of descendants in the Americas of enslaved Africans.

23. Three Rivers, *Cultural Etiquette*, p. 8.

24. This is not to deny the survival of any Native American cultures but only to acknowledge that some have undoubtedly been killed.

25. Frye, *Politics of Reality*, p. 35.

26. They have also been called "marranos," which means "pigs" in Spanish.

27. Maria Steiglitz, "New Mexico's Secret Jews," *Lilith* (Winter 1991), 8–12. Cf. La Escondida, "Journal Toward Wholeness: Reflections of a Lesbian Rabbi" (also on contemporary descendants of conversos in New Mexico) in *Twice Blessed; On Being Lesbian, Gay, and Jewish*, ed. Christie Balka and Andy Rose (Boston: Beacon Press, 1989).

28. For an example of cultural appropriation, see Alice Walker's story of Joel Chandler Harris, who wrote down and published the Uncle Remus tales, in *Living by the Word* (New York: Harcourt, Brace, Jovanovich, 1988), pp. 25–32.

13. Why There Are No Races
K. Anthony Appiah

THERE ARE TODAY TWO very different and competing philosophical notions of what it is to give an adequate account of the meaning of a word or expression.[1]

One—I'll call it the "ideational" view of meaning—which goes back at least to the seventeenth century and the Logic of Port Royal, associates the meaning of a term, like "race," with what the Port Royal Logicians called an "idea."

The other picture of meaning—the "referential" view—suggests that what it is to explain what the word "race" means is, in effect, to identify the things to which it applies, the things we refer to when we speak of "races."

The simplest ideational theory of meaning is that what we learn when we learn a word like "race" is a set of rules for applying the term. Everybody who knows what the word "race" means learns the same rules: so that, while people have different beliefs about races, they share some special beliefs—I'll call them the criteria beliefs—that define the concept.

For various reasons semanticists have given up on theories of that sort. They are more likely to suggest that what is required, to know what "race" means, is that you should believe most of the criteria beliefs, but not that you should believe any particular ones. The explicit definition that fixes the common notion of those who understand the word "race" will then be given like this: A race is something that satisfies a good number of the criteria beliefs. I'll call this the "vague criteria theory."

The theory has important consequences. First, it doesn't draw a sharp line

Anthony Appiah, "Why There Are No Races," excerpts from *Color Conscious*, ed., Anthony Appiah, Amy Gutmann. New Jersey: Princeton University Press, 1996, reprinted with the permission of Princeton University Press.

between not knowing what the word "race" means and having unconventional views about races. That boundary is vague, because the expression "a good number" is vague.

Second, it allows that among the criteria beliefs, there can be some that are not held by everybody who uses the word "race." For example: *Most sub-Saharan Africans are of the Negro race. There are only a few races.* There are clearly people who count as understanding the term "race" who don't believe these things. Physical anthropologists, for example, who felt the only useful notion of race classified people into scores of kinds.

This theory makes it hard to argue against the existence of races. But it suggests a way to understanding the race concept: explore the sorts of things people believe about what they call "races" and see what races would have to be like for these things to be true of them. We can then inquire as to whether current science suggests that there is anything in the world at all like that.

Now, suppose there just isn't one such thing in the world; then, on this view, there are no races. It will still be important to understand the criteria, because these will help us to understand what people who believe in races are thinking; and that will be important, even if there are no races, because people act on their beliefs, whether or not they are true. To use an analogy I have often used before, we may need to understand talk of "witchcraft" to understand how people respond cognitively and how they act in a culture that has a concept of witchcraft, whether or not we think there are, in fact, any witches.

The ideational view leads to exploring contemporary thought and talk about races. But I think this is likely to produce a confusing picture because current ways of talking about race are the residue of earlier ways of thinking about race; so it turns out to be easiest to understand contemporary talk about "race" as the pale reflection of a more full-blooded race discourse that flourished in the last century.

What route to understanding the race-concept is suggested by the referential account of meaning?

Consider an example: looked at from the point of view of current theory, early nineteenth-century chemists apparently classified some things—acids and bases, say—by and large correctly, even if a lot of what they said about those things was pretty badly wrong. From the point of view of current theory, you might argue, an acid is, roughly a proton donor.[2] And we are inclined to say that when Sir Humphrey Davey—who, not having any idea of the proton, could hardly be expected to have understood the notion of a proton donor—used the word "acid," he was nevertheless talking about what we call acids.

In explaining why it seems proper to think that he was referring to the things we call proton donors, even though much of what he believed about acids is not true of proton donors, we can borrow the "causal theory of reference": if you want to know what object a word refers to, they say, find the thing in the world that gives the best causal explanation of the central features of uses of that word. If you want to know what the name "New York" refers to, find the object in the world that is at the root of most of the causal chains that lead to remarks containing the expression "New York."

So, in the case of acids, we believe the stuffs "out there" in the world that really accounted for the central features of Davey's "acid" talk really were acids, and that that is what accounts for our sense that Davey was not simply talking about something else.

How can we use these ideas to develop a referential account of the concept of race? Well, we need to explore the sorts of things people have said about what they call "races" and see whether there is something in the world that gives a good causal explanation of their talk. If there is one thing in the world that best explains that talk, then that will be what the word "race" refers to; and that can be true, even if it would surprise most people to know that that was what they were really talking about—just as Sir Humphrey Davey would have been surprised to discover that, when he said "acids" he was talking about—referring to—proton donors.

On the causal theory, what it is for something to be the best candidate for the job of the referent of the word "race" in the speech of a community, is for it to be the thing that best causally explains their talk about "races." So what we need to do, on this view, is to explore the history of the way the word "race" has been used and see if we can identify through that history some objective phenomenon that people were responding to when they said what they said about "races."

Semantical considerations thus steer us toward historical enquiry. Parenthetical observation: the history I am going to explore is the history of the ideas of the intellectual and political elites of the United States and the United Kingdom. You might ask why I don't look at the words of more ordinary people: race is statistically most important in ordinary lives. A good question, I say. (This is what you say when you think you have a good answer.) The reason is itself embedded in the history: as we shall see, throughout the nineteenth century the term "race" came increasingly to be regarded, even in ordinary usage, as a scientific term. Treating it as a scientific term meant not that it was only for use by scientists, but that scientists and scholars were thought to be the experts on how the term worked. That is, with the increasing prestige of science, people became used to using words whose exact meanings they did not need to know, because their exact meanings were left to the relevant scientific experts.

In short, there developed a practice of *semantic deference*: people used words like "electricity" outside the context of natural philosophy or physical science, assuming that the physicists could say more precisely than they could what it meant. The same goes for "race" and the science of biology.

End of parenthesis.

In Thomas Jefferson's *Autobiography*—begun on January 6, 1822—the third

President of the United States reproduces his original draft of the Declaration of Independence, with the passages deleted by the Congress "distinguished by a black line drawn under them."[3] There are only two paragraphs entirely underlined in black; and the second, and by far the longer of them, gives, as grounds for complaint against "the present king of Great Britain,"[4] the fact that he encouraged slavery and its attendant wrongs. So far, I think, we can feel that Thomas Jefferson was not simply ahead of his times but that, allowing for changes in rhetorical taste, he is our moral contemporary.

But soon enough Jefferson makes an observation that disrupts this happy illusion: "Nor is it less certain," the former President writes, "that the two races, equally free, cannot live in the same government."[5] For Jefferson, who offers here no defense of his view, this is a piece of common sense. Here is a point at which we see something important about Jefferson's way of thinking about race: *it is a concept that is invoked to explain cultural and social phenomena,* in this case, the supposed political impossibility of a citizenship shared on terms of equality between white and black races.

If we want to know the sources of Jefferson's stern conviction, we can turn to Query XIV of the *Notes on the State of Virginia,* published four decades earlier. Emancipation is inevitable, Jefferson has argued, and it is right. But blacks, once emancipated, will have to be sent elsewhere. Jefferson anticipates that we may wonder why, especially given "the expense of supplying, by importation of white settlers, the vacancies they will leave."

> Deep rooted prejudices entertained by the whites; ten thousand recollections, by the blacks, of the injuries they have sustained; new provocations; the real distinctions which nature has made; and many other circumstances, will divide us into parties, and produce convulsions which will probably never end but in the extermination of the one or the other race.—To these objections, which are political, may be added others, which are physical and moral. The first difference which strikes us is that of colour. . . . is this difference of no importance? Is it not the foundation of a greater or less share of beauty in the two races? . . . Add to these, flowing hair, a more elegant symmetry of form, their own judgment in favour of the whites, declared by their preference for them, as uniformly as is the preference of the Oranootan for the black woman over those of his own species. The circumstance of superior beauty, is thought worthy attention in the propagation of our horses, dogs, and other domestic animals; why not in that of man?[6]

Apart from this difference of color with its attendant aesthetic consequences, Jefferson observes that there are other relevant differences:

> Comparing them by their faculties of memory, reason, and imagination, it appears to me, that in memory they are equal to the whites; in reason much

inferior. . . . The Indians . . . will often carve figures on their pipes not destitute of design and merit. . . . They astonish you with strokes of the most sublime oratory; such as prove their reason and sentiment strong, their imagination glowing and elevated. . . . Misery is often the parent of the most affecting touches in poetry.—Among the blacks is misery enough, God knows, but no poetry. . . .[7]

Here is his concluding negative judgment:

I advance it as a suspicion only, that the blacks . . . are inferior to the whites in the endowments both of body and mind. . . . Will not a lover of natural history then, one who views gradations in all the races of animals with the eye of philosophy, excuse an effort to keep those in the department of man as distinct as nature has formed them. This unfortunate difference of colour, and perhaps of faculty, is a powerful obstacle to the emancipation of these people.[8]

For Jefferson the political significance of race begins and ends with color.

Jefferson's discussion is representative of late eighteenth-century discussions of race because it brings together considerations that we are likely to think should be kept distinct. Jefferson answers the question—can blacks and whites live equally together—with appeals to what we would call differences in physiology and moral and cognitive psychology, distinctions which, if they are real, we too are likely to regard as "distinctions which nature has made."

Not only, then, is race, for Jefferson, a concept that is invoked to explain cultural and social phenomena, it is also grounded in the physical and the psychological natures of the different races; it is, in other words, what we would call a *biological concept*.

I say that it was what we would call a biological concept, because the science of biology did not exist when Jefferson was writing the *Notes*. What did exist was Natural History; and Jefferson, as we see, was a "lover of natural history," who saw race as a natural historical notion, as much as was the idea of species that Linnaeus had developed.[9] To think of race as a biological concept is to pull out of the natural history of humans a focus on the body—its structure and function—and to separate it both from mental life—the province of psychology—and from the broader world of behavior and of social and moral life. Jefferson's discussion, with its movement from questions of the morphology of the skin, to discussions of sexual desire, to music and poetry, strikes us as a hodge-podge, because we live now with a new configuration of the sciences; and, more especially, with the differentiation from the broad field of natural history, of anatomy, physiology, psychology, philology (i.e., historical linguistics), sociology, anthropology, and a whole host of even more specialized fields that gradually divided between them the task of describing and understanding human nature.

But, while Jefferson conceives of racial difference as both physical and moral, he was not committed to the view that race explained all the rest of the moral and social and political matter that is drawn into his portrait of the Negro. He leaves open the possibility "that nature has given to our black brethren, talents equal to those of the other colors of men"; and throughout the *Notes* Jefferson writes, as here, with real affection and respect about Indians. For him, the differences between whites and Indians hardly constitute a difference of essential natures.

If we move on another fifty of so years from Jefferson's *Autobiography*, we enter a new intellectual landscape: in which there is no longer any doubt as to the connection between race and what Jefferson calls "talent."

In 1867 Matthew Arnold published his lectures *On the Study of Celtic Literature*, in which he argues for the view that the ancient literature of the Celts—of Ireland and Wales, in particular—is part of the literary heritage of Britain; even of those Britons in England who by then conceived of themselves as heirs to a Saxon heritage and were inclined, by and large, to hold the Irish Celts, in particular, with contempt.

Here is how Arnold makes his case:

> Here in our country, in historic times, long after the Celtic embryo had crystallised into the Celt proper, long after the Germanic embryo had crystallised into the German proper, there was an important contact between the two peoples; the Saxons invaded the Britons and settled themselves in the Britons' country. Well, then, here was a contact which one might expect would leave its traces; if the Saxons got the upper hand, as we all know they did, and made our country be England and us be English, there must yet, one would think, be some trace of the Saxon having met the Briton; there must be some Celtic vein or other running through us.
>
> [T]hough, as I have said, even as a matter of science, the Celt has a claim to be known, and we have an interest in knowing him, yet this interest is wonderfully enhanced if we find him to have actually a part in us. The question is to be tried by external and internal evidence; the language and physical type of our race afford certain data for trying it, and other data are afforded by our literature, genius, and spiritual production generally. Data of this second kind belong to the province of the literary critic; data of this first kind to the province of the philologist and the physiologist.[10]

What Arnold lays out in these passages is the essence of what I call racialism. He believed—and in this he was typical of educated people in the English-speaking world of his day—that we could divide human beings into a small number of groups, called "races," in such a way that the members of these groups shared certain fundamental, heritable, moral, intellectual, and cultural characteristics with each other that they did not share with members of any other race.

The discussion of Celtic literature makes it plain that Arnold believes the racial essence accounts for more than the obvious visible characteristics of individuals and of groups—skin color, hair, shape of face—on the basis of which we decide whether people are, say, Asian or African-Americans. For a racialist, then, to say someone is a Celt or a Negro is to say more than that they have inherited a distinctive skin or hair: it is to invoke other important inherited characteristics—including moral and literary endowments.

Arnold makes the same sort of appeal to race—this time at a greater level of generality, discussing the contrast between Indo-European and Semitic races—in *Culture and Anarchy*, a work that is much more widely known. In these essays, based on articles that first appeared in *Cornhill Magazine* in 1867 and 1868, and then in book form in 1869, Arnold wrote:

> Science has now made visible to everybody the great and pregnant elements of difference which lie in race, and in how signal a manner they make the genius and history of an Indo-European people vary from those of a Semitic people. Hellenism is of Indo-European growth, Hebraism of Semitic growth; and we English, a nation of Indo-European stock, seem to belong naturally to the movement of Hellenism. But nothing more strongly marks the essential unity of man than the affinities we can perceive, in this point or that, between members of one family of peoples and members of another.[11]

Hebraism is Arnold's name for the tendencies in Western culture that are owed to its Judaeo-Christian religious heritage. He is not, then, an enemy of Hebraism: every race, he insists here as much as in *On the Study of Celtic Literature*, has emblematic excellences as well as distinctive defects. The ideal for Britain, Arnold argues, is to construct a judicious mixture of Hebraism and Hellenism: the British, lacking Semitic blood, are not, by nature, Hebraists.[12]

These passages from the two sources, taken together, reveal a great deal of the structure of racialist thinking. Arnold displays both the flexibility of the view and some of its characteristic obscurities. Part of the flexibility flows from the fact that racial classification proceeds, as we see, at different levels: the Saxons and the Celts are both Indo-European. Differences between them are differences within the broader Indo-European race. In the United States, the differences between the Irish and the Anglo-Saxons could be used to account for the cultural and moral deficiencies—real or imaginary—of Irish immigrants; but their whiteness could be used to distinguish them from the Negro.

But there is also something of a muddle here: if the Celtic and the Saxon essences are so opposite, what is an individual like who inherits both of them? What would a man be like who was steady and sentimental; or who suffered from commonness and humdrummery and ineffectualness and self-will?

Arnold has no theory of how the character of a race survives through the generations, transmitted in the bodies of its members; no account of the laws that govern the interactions of racial essences. Without these, racialism makes no particular predictions about racial hybrids: a fact that is of the greatest importance since, if we are considering races at the taxonomic level of Celt and Saxon, there were very few peoples known to Arnold and his contemporaries who could plausibly have been thought to be un-mixed.

Also lacking is an answer to the question how we balance the effects of race and the effects of environment. *Culture and Anarchy* is in large measure about why the British are not Hellenic enough. If the British inherit naturally the tendencies of Hellenism with their Indo-European blood and language, why is British culture not too suffused with Hellenism (as the theory should predict) but too dominated by Hebraism?

There is no doubt that these questions could have been answered, but without answers to questions such as these, what is masquerading as an empirical, even a scientific theory, is remarkably insensitive to evidence. These deficiencies in Arnold are found in other race thinkers of the period—and, they are by no means limited to those who addressed the less physical, that is, the moral or cultural, traits of races.

Arnold represents, then, a theory couched in terms of the new vocabulary of "race," whose authority derives, in part, from its association with the increasing prestige of the natural sciences. (You will have noticed that in the excerpts from the Celtic literature lectures, Arnold uses the word "data" several times.) And the most important theoretical development in the growth of a biological conception of race had already occurred by the time Arnold published *Culture and Anarchy* in 1869. For on November 24, 1859, Charles Darwin had published a work whose full title reads: *The Origin of Species by Means of Natural Selection or the Preservation of Favoured Races in the Struggle for Life.*

The word "race" had been used in this way to refer to kinds of animals and plants, as well as to kinds of people, for some time; but there is no doubt that even for a mid-nineteenth-century ear this title promises something of relevance to the study of human difference.

Darwin suggested, with characteristic caution, in *The Origin of Species*, that his theory might throw light on "the origin of man and his history"; the implication being that human beings developed, like other modern organisms, out of earlier forms. Taken to its "logical conclusion," this view suggested the oneness not only of all human beings—related by common descent—but, at least potentially, the common ancestry, and thus unity, of all life.

Darwin thought of species as essentially classificatory conveniences[13]; he was interested in how populations changed their character and separated from each other, not in drawing boundaries between them. But his theory allowed that the accumulation of differences by selection could gradually produce kinds—varieties or species—that were measurably different; and thus suggested a mode of classification in which kinds that were more closely related by evolution should be classified together.

Thus, the increasing acceptance of Darwin's theory of natural selection gave scientific support to the idea that human kinds—races—like animal and plant species could be both evolutionarily related and biologically distinct. Furthermore, even though human races were not mutually infertile, the theory of evolution suggested a way of thinking of varieties as being in the process of speciation: races might not be species, but they were, so to speak, moving in that direction.

Once we have the modern genetic picture we can see that each person is the product of enormous numbers of genetic characteristics, interacting with each other and an environment, and that there is nothing in the theory of evolution to guarantee that a group that shares one characteristic will share all or even most others. Characteristics on different chromosomes are, as Mendel said, independently assorted. Indeed, it turns out that in humans, however you define the major races, the biological variability within them is almost as great as the biological variation within the species as a whole.

Even limiting oneself to the range of criteria available to nineteenth-century comparative anatomists, it is hard to classify people objectively into a small set of populations; and whichever way you do it, it will turn out that, for biological purposes, your classification will contain about as much human genetic variation as there is in the whole species.

"Race, then, as a biological concept picks out, at best, among humans, classes of people who share certain easily observable physical characteristics, most notably skin color and a few visible features of the face and head.

We have followed enough of the history of the race concept and said enough about current biological conceptions to answer, on both ideational and referential view, the question whether there are any races.

On the ideational view, the answer is easy. From Jefferson to Arnold, the idea of race has been used, in its application to humans, in such a way as to require that there be significant correlations between the biological and the moral, literary, or psychological characters of human beings; and that these be explained by the intrinsic nature (the "talents" and "faculties" in Jefferson; the "genius," in Arnold) of the members of the race.[14]

That has turned out not to be true.

Once you have the modern theory of inheritance, you can see why there is less correlation than everyone expected between skin color and things we care about: people are the product nor of essences but of genes interacting with each other and with environments, And there is little systematic correlation between the genes that fix color and the like and the genes that shape courage or literary genius. So, to repeat, on the ideational view we can say that nothing in the world meets the criteria for being a Jeffersonian or an Arnoldian race.

The biological notion of race was meant to account only for a narrower range of characteristics, namely, the biological ones, by which I mean the ones important for biological theory. There are certainly many ways of classifying people for biological purposes, but there is no single way of doing so that is important for most biological purposes that corresponds, for example, to the majority populations, by skin color, of each continent or subcontinent. It follows that, on an ideational view, there are no biological races either: not, in this case because nothing fits the loose criteria, but because too many things do.

On the referential view, we are required to find something in the world that best explains the history of usage of the term. Two candidates suggest themselves for the biological uses of "race": one is the concept of a population that I have been using for a while now. It can be defined as "the community of potentially interbreeding individuals at a given locality."[15] There are interesting discussions in the literature in population genetics as to how one should think about where to draw the boundaries of such communities: sometimes there is geographic isolation, which makes interbreeding in the normal course of things much less likely. But the population concept is generally used in such a way that we speak sometimes of a population defined by one geographical region and also, at other times, of a wider population, defined by a wider range, of which the first population is a part; and at yet other times of populations that are overlapping.

I have no problem with people who want to use the word "race" in population genetics.[16] Many plants and animals do in fact have local populations that are isolated from each other, different in clustered and biologically interesting ways, and still capable of interbreeding if brought artificially together; and biologists both before and after Darwin could have called these "races." It's just that this doesn't happen in human beings. In this sense, there are biological races in some creatures, but not in us.

A second candidate for the biological referent would simply be groups defined by skin color, hair, and gross morphology, corresponding to the dominant pattern for these characteristics in the major subcontinental regions: Europe, Africa, East and South Asia, Australasia, the Americas, and perhaps the Pacific Islands. This grouping would encompass many human beings quite adequately and some not at all; but it would not provide us with a concept that was central to biological thinking about human beings. And, once more, if we used this biological notion, it would have very little established correlation with any characteristics thought to be important for moral or social life.

The bottom line is this: you can't get much of a race concept, ideationally speaking, from any of these traditions; you can get various possible candidates from the referential notion of meaning, but none of them will be much good for explaining social or psychological life, and none of them corresponds to the social groups we call "races" in America.

NOTES

1. This essay excerpts a much fuller discussion to be found in K. Anthony Appiah and Amy Gutmann, *Color Conscious: The Political Morality of Race* (Princeton: Princeton University Press, 1996).

2. This is the so-called Bronsted theory of the Danish physical chemist Johannes Nicolaus Bronsted.

3. *Thomas Jefferson: Complete Writings*, Thomas Jefferson (New York: Library of America, 1984), p. 18.

4. Ibid., p. 21.

5. Ibid.

6. Jefferson, *Notes of the State of Virginia* (1781–82), in *Writings*, p. 264.

7. Jefferson, *Notes*, p. 206.

8. Jefferson, *Notes*, p. 270.

9. Carolus Linnaeus, *Systema Naturae*, in which people are classified as *Homo sapiens*, appears in 1735.

10. Matthew Arnold, *On the Study of Celtic Literature*, in *On the Study of Celtic Literature and on Translating Homer* (New York: MacMillan and Co., 1883), pp. 66–67.

11. Matthew Arnold, *Culture and Anarchy*, ed. Samuel Lipman (New Haven: Yale University Press, 1994), p. 95.

12. Arnold's fairly benign mobilization of the idea of a Celtic race here contrasts favorably with contemporary and later uses of it in discussions of the Irish character both in England and the United States. In late nineteenth-century America, the place of the Irish "race" within the broader European races was distinctly below that of the Anglo-Saxon and Nordic "races" and, in some contexts, closer to that of Negro.

13. See George W Stocking, *Race, Culture and Evolution* (New York: Free Press, 1968): "Darwin's own position on the question of human races was equally congenial to polygenist thinking. Although he thought it a matter of indifference whether human races were called species or subspecies, he granted that a naturalist confronted for the first time with specimens of Negro and European man would doubtless call them 'good and true species' " (p. 46).

14. That is, *not* produced by the fact that people who have certain physical appearances are treated in ways that produce differences.

15. Ernst Mayr, *Populations, Species and Evolution* (Cambridge: Harvard University Press, 1970), p. 82.

16. I think, however, that this usage carries two risks: first, it gives an ill-deserved legitimacy to ideas that are mistaken, because those who listen in to these conversations may not be aware of the fact that the usage here does not correspond at all to the groups that have mostly been called races in Europe and America; second, because speaking this way, you can actually find yourself relying, illicitly, on those other modes of classification. Still, if you can avoid these two dangers, there's no problem.

Constructivist Explanations of Racism

14. The Construction, Deconstruction, and Reconstruction of Difference

Paula Rothenberg

THE CONSTRUCTION OF DIFFERENCE is central to racism, sexism, and other forms of oppressive ideologies. Few theorists have better understood the importance of constructing difference and the centrality of that construction to racism (and by extension, other forms of oppression) than Albert Memmi (1971, pp. 186–195). At a time when liberal theoreticians still grounded their political philosophy on a metaphysic that accepted "natural" differences between women and men, and then set out to win certain rights for women by arguing over which differences provided a legitimate basis for limiting women's rights and which did not, Memmi had already recognized that difference was created not discovered. "Making use of the difference is an essential step in the racist process," he wrote, "but it is not the difference which always entails racism; it is racism which makes use of the difference" (1971, p. 187). This insight prompted Memmi to define racism as

> the generalized and final assigning of value to real or imaginary difference, to the accusers benefit and at his victim's expense, in order to justify the former's privileges or aggression. (1971, p. 185)

Note that it is the process of assigning value to difference, not whether the difference is real or imagined, that is the key to the process by which "the racist aims to intensify or cause the *exclusion*, the *separation* by which the victim is placed outside the community or even outside humanity" (Memmi, 1971, p.

Paula Rothenberg, "The Construction, Deconstruction, and Reconstruction of Difference," *Hypatia* 5:1 (Spring 1990): 42–57, reprinted with the permission of *Hypatia* and the author.

187). Placing the victim outside humanity is of course essential if one is to justify the inhumanity of slavery and colonialism. Placing the victim outside the
community (of equals, or adults, or decent women) is essential if one is to rationalize the violence and the denial of personhood that lies at the heart of sexism.

What Memmi failed to notice, however, is the two-sided or dialectical
nature of the process wherein difference is defined. For it is not only the racist
or sexist who constructs difference but the victim of each or both who seeks to
create difference as well. At times the "victim" has done so in response to the
racism and/or sexism of the society in order to survive, but at other times movements made up of those "victims" have sought to redefine difference as part of a
struggle for power and personhood.[1] At least in part this is because the particular
paradigm for expressing race or gender difference that holds sway in society at
any given moment carries with it both implicit and explicit prescriptions for
social policy. At certain moments in history, oppressed people have been able to
exert control over the process of defining difference with a view to reconstructing difference in what they perceive to be their own interest. Social, political, and intellectual disagreements or struggles over both the appropriate social
construction of race and gender and disagreements about the appropriateness of
particular paradigms of race and gender can best be understood as disputes over
the nature of difference that the society is prepared to establish and, by implication, the nature of the social policies it is prepared to entertain.

THE CONSTRUCTION OF DIFFERENCE

If we undertake a historical survey of the construction of difference in the
United States, we find that difference claims have been expressed in the vocabulary of numerous different ideologies. In spite of the historical specificity which
determines the form and content of each particular claim, we can distinguish
three fundamental categories according to which race and gender difference has
been alleged: difference in nature, difference in moral sensibilities, and difference in culture and/or values (Whitbeck, 1975). Claims about difference in
nature have been the most numerous and have assumed the most diverse forms.
At times they have been attributed to biology, to physiognomy, to genetic
makeup, and so forth. Difference in moral sensibilities has alternately been
treated as either innate or acquired, and the cultural/value differences have
received similar treatment. It is not uncommon for one or more of these categories of difference to be used in combination.

Claims about difference are often difficult to deal with precisely because
they are offered under the guise of value-free descriptions yet smuggle in normative considerations that carry with them the stigma of inferiority. Where

white, male, middle-class, European heterosexuality provides the standard of and the criteria for rationality and morality, difference is always perceived as deviant and deficient.[2] In addition, though difference claims are usually couched in the language of the academy, most often bearing the trappings of the natural or social sciences, difference claims are essentially metaphysical. Even though they often point to or allege some readily observable difference, such as skull size, brain weight, or family structure, a reasoned refutation of the empirical claim rarely results in a change in attitude on the part of those who allege difference. They merely seek some other vocabulary or conceptual framework in which to reformulate their charge. This has led some thinkers to suggest that racism (and, by extension, sexism) have the belief status of delusions, which by definition are impervious to contrary evidence (Pierce, 1974, p. 513).

THE NATURE/BIOLOGY PARADIGM

Underlying all racism and sexism is the notion of a natural or biological difference alleged to separate the groups in question in a fundamental, inevitable, and irreversible way. This natural difference is then called upon to explain any and all observable differences in opportunity or achievement between white people and people of color or men and all women. Science, medicine, religion, and the law have all made important contributions to the force and longevity of this theory, providing "evidence" to ground this basic claim of natural inferiority. The strength of the paradigm lies in its ability to translate readily observable physical differences in appearance into qualitative and even "moral" differences.

While the idea of natural difference is central to both racism and sexism, it functions somewhat differently in each. In the case of race, the nature/biology paradigm is used to portray a difference in nature between whites and blacks so fundamental and so enormous as to exclude black people from the human community and thus make it possible for otherwise kind and decent people to carry out the unspeakable acts of inhumanity and violation that constitute the history of slavery and its aftermath.

Sexism works differently. Since men have mothers and often have wives, daughters, and sisters as well, the nature/biology paradigm expresses a weaker form of difference with respect to gender. Women are not portrayed as excluded from humanity but as separated from the relevant community, be it the community of men or adults. While racist ideology has entertained the question as to whether or not black people were part of the human species and has, at times, answered in the negative; sexist ideology has simply sought to exclude women by virtue of their nurture from membership in the community that enjoyed or had a proper claim to certain privileges or rights.

The weak version of this same paradigm, which evolves after the Civil War and is bound up with the Industrial Revolution, offers white women a "separate sphere." Here difference is seen as endowing white women with certain noble or positive attributes which fit them for certain important roles that men are unable to fulfill. This complementary paradigm of gender difference replaces natural inferiority with "different and better if not equal." In doing so, it manages to preserve the sense of difference which excludes all women from certain areas and functions (and rights and privileges), but sugarcoats this exclusion with the assurance that that sphere isn't worthy of women anyway.

No comparable weak version of the paradigm exists for race nor does the weak version itself apply to black women. Beginning with slavery, black women are excluded from the community of women who need and deserve "special protection" and who inhabit a "separate sphere." Historically, white people have denied the existence of gender difference within the black community at the very same time that "separate sphere" sex roles functioned as part of male identity and privilege in the white world. This denial of gender difference became part of the construction of difference that is racism. To put it another way, the difference in appropriate social roles for women and men that was the mark of "civilized" society was denied to the black community, whose members, not coincidentally, were consistently portrayed as having a bestial or animal nature. This difference in the social construction of gender within each race must be understood as part of the construction of difference that is central to racism.

In the case of both race and gender, the way difference is defined by the nature/biology paradigm performs certain critical functions. First, it implicitly and explicitly defines or establishes hierarchy as natural, that is, present in the natural order of things. Second, it absolves those in power from any responsibility for the condition of the inferior group and thus blames the victim for its victimization. Third, it undercuts all efforts to alter relations between the races or the sexes since it portrays the difference as one of kind, not degree. Social policy and practice must be predicated on difference and ought not seek to mitigate suffering caused by it.

While the nature/biology paradigm is often portrayed (and even dismissed) as crude and unsophisticated, it has never been entirely replaced or supplanted. In fact, additional paradigms have been generated at different historical moments to meet the changing economic, social and political conditions and their attendant needs, but these new paradigms always function within the context of the nature/biology paradigm; they never replace it. The relation between old and new paradigms is very much like that among the contents of "Grandmother's trunk" in the children's memory game, where though new items are added with each turn the old items persist and remain an integral part of each recitation.

CHALLENGES TO THE NATURE/BIOLOGY PARADIGM

Challenges to the nature/biology paradigm take many forms but all have in common the desire to portray difference as a matter of degree, not kind. While they need not be committed to the idea that there are no differences between people, and even entertain the idea that there can be differences of race and/or gender, they emphasize the social nature of the categories "race" and "gender" and try to move from a normative to a descriptive use of the concept of difference.

The "separate but equal" approach to race relations and the "different but equal" or liberal model for gender roles are early examples of attempts to modify the nature/biology model by beginning to incorporate the idea of difference as degree while still retaining a strong hold on the difference in kind paradigm. For example, the Justices in *Plessy v. Ferguson* (1896), which effectively establishes "separate but equal" as the nation's policy of race relations for almost sixty years, go to great pains to maintain that separating the races in public education, transportation, and other areas is simply a way of recognizing difference but involves no normative judgment. In fact, they specifically assert that such segregation does not "necessarily imply the inferiority of either race to the other. . . ." Portraying the other as "equal" though different paves the way for future accommodation. After all, negotiations or accommodations are only possible between equals.

THE ETHNICITY PARADIGM

During the latter portion of the nineteenth century and the first half of the twentieth, the biologistic/Social Darwinist paradigm of race still predominates but the legal doctrine of separate but equal helps undermine its force, and gradually race difference comes to be redefined using the ethnicity paradigm. This paradigm functions both descriptively and prescriptively, bringing with it its celebration of cultural pluralism (Wolff, 1965). Now race difference is no longer irrevocably "other" and no longer places people of color, in Memmi's words, "outside of humanity." The ethnicity paradigm goes beyond "separate but equal" to offer a picture of society where race is simply one more difference on the all-American continuum of ethnic diversity.[3]

The implications and consequences of this portrayal of difference are enormous. Because the adoption of ethnicity as the dominant paradigm for race transforms race from a biological to a social category, it presents a progressive alternative to the crude and unyielding nature/biology paradigm it attempts to replace or supplement. At the same time, by denying both the centrality and uniqueness of race as a principle of socioeconomic organization, it redefines difference in a way that denies the history of racism in the United States and thus denies white responsibility for the present and past oppression and exploitation of people of color. Further, while one version of the paradigm celebrates diversity in the form of cultural pluralism, another version regards difference as a problem and offers as its solution "assimilation." The emergence of black nationalism during the 1960s, as well as Garvey's Pan Africanism of the 1920s, can be understood as a direct response to the inadequacies of this paradigm and an attempt on the part of black Americans to redefine difference in what they perceived to be their interests.

By focusing on the dynamics of colonialism, the nation-based paradigm for race reasserts the unique history of people of color in the United States and points to the inadequacy of the ethnicity paradigm. The popular movement to replace "Negro" and "colored" with "black" and "Afro-American" represented a dramatic attempt on the part of black Americans to reassert race as the primary social-political-economic category and principle of social organization and to reject outright all solutions to "the negro problem" that proselytized assimilation.[4] The cultural nationalism of the period, which was perhaps most visible to white Americans in the form of *dashikis* and *afros*, was part of the group's attempt to assert its own power to define and create difference. Looked at in this way, the nation-based paradigm and its attendant linguistic and lifestyle recommendations represented an attempt of black Americans to assert their right to define difference specifically by rearticulating the meaning of "separate but equal."

EMBRACING GENDER DIFFERENCE

During the latter portion of the nineteenth century, the "separate sphere" gender paradigm is modified and ultimately replaced by a picture of gender which portrays women as "different but equal."[5] Predicated on the notion of difference, the liberal paradigm for gender raises the possibility that at least some gender difference may be social rather than natural or biological. Part of the justification, offered by Mill and others, for introducing a principle of "perfect equality" between the sexes is that such a principle will not suppress whatever natural differences exist. The "different but equal" model for gender relations prevails for a considerable period of time. Its essential ambiguity about the nature and origins of difference between the sexes guarantees that the "nature/ biology" paradigm it seeks to replace will continue to exert considerable control at both the psychological and social level. In a context where wealthy, white males set the standard, race, and gender paradigms that assert either "separate" or "different" but "equal" will always perform the dual function of implicitly evaluating as "inferior" what they purport to be describing as "different."

During the sixties and seventies we find attempts by significant sectors of the white women's movement to redefine difference in ways which parallel struggles carried out by the black community. Just as the nation-based paradigm challenges ethnicity by heightening race difference instead of trying to deny or de-emphasize it, the radical feminism typified and precipitated by Shulamith Firestone's *The Dialectics of Sex* (1971) and the more recent feminist essentialism which portrays feminine nature as different than and preferable to "maleness" represent attempts by women to identify and embrace sex difference rather than apologize for it. At certain points, Firestone's argument bears remarkable similarity to Mill's, insofar as both argue that traditional ways of formulating social policy about gender convert a physical fact to a legal right, subsuming the history of gender relations under the principle of "might makes right." Early radical feminism quite dramatically embraces the nature/biology paradigm for gender, only to stand it on its head. The thrust of the paradigm as it expresses and perpetuates male domination is that nature/biology can't be changed; it is immutable. Firestone and others (following Rousseau of *The Social Contract* and John Stuart Mill) suggest that the proper way to deal with natural inequality is to overcome it, not institutionalize it. What we have here is an attempt on the part of the women's movement to assert its right to redefine difference.

Other segments of the women's movement entered the political struggle over definition by offering androgyny as the proper paradigm for gender.[6] The androgyny paradigm, now very much out of favor, shares many similarities with the ethnicity paradigm for race. Now gender difference is clearly portrayed as a matter of degree, not kind. In place of a model which assumes two sexes, the androgyny paradigm portrays gender difference as points on the continuum of gender. Difference now reflects not two separate and different sexes, but a whole range of human possibilities.

The androgyny paradigm has been criticized in much the same way as the ethnicity/cultural pluralism model for race. Both have been charged with building in an essentially conservative picture of the (static) components (i.e., "qualities" and "groups") that constitute the reality they seek to describe. Further, by prematurely seeking to replace male and female with "human," the androgyny paradigm is guilty of rendering both race and gender difference invisible at a time when differences based on gender, as they impact on people's lives, need to be uncovered and dismantled, not covered over. This parallels the charge that the ethnicity paradigm denies race its unique history of slavery and colonization, rendering the very factors that create its virulence invisible.

Finally, at those times when racial oppression has been regarded as the most serious kind of injustice in the society, white women have attempted to employ race as the paradigm for gender in order to appeal to those male social reformers who failed to acknowledge the extent and severity of women's oppression as women. During the 1850s and 1860s, feminists drew parallels between the situation of white women and the situation of blacks, arguing that in the eyes of custom and the law, white women's status was equivalent to that of *Negro* slaves. In her famous speech before the New York State Legislature in 1854, Elizabeth Cady Stanton spends considerable time drawing this parallel. And again, more than a hundred years later, during the 1960s and 1970s, feminists once again attempted to draw this analogy as part of their effort to redefine gender difference in a way that would capture the attention of white, male activists who considered racism a serious evil but tended to trivialize charges of sexism.[7] Such attempts have often rightfully angered black Americans, who have argued that they improperly equated the situation of middle-class white women with the brutalization suffered by black people under slavery. It must also be noted that the very same white women who drew this analogy participated in fostering the invisibility of black women, both by drawing the analogy in the first place and by failing to speak out about the double burden of black women's exploitation in the second.

CONTEMPORARY PARADIGMS AND THEIR CRITICS

In the contemporary period we find considerable confusion over what explicit paradigms are to be adopted for race and gender. Literature in philosophy as well as the social sciences reflects a concern on the part of some to identify "the new racism," alternately referred to as "symbolic racism," "modern racism," or even (with a touch of irony) "civilized racism."[8] While analysts disagree over some of the specific features and implications of these "new" racisms, all are concerned with distinguishing their more subtle contemporary manifestation from so-called old-fashioned racism, which is seen as crude and explicit. The new racism expresses itself by using "code words" in place of explicitly racist language and arguments.

In *Racial Formations in the US*, Omi and Winant define code words as "phrases and symbols which refer indirectly to racial themes but do not directly challenge popular democratic or egalitarian ideals . . ." (1986, p. 120). As an example of this approach, they point to the way in which the earlier, explicit attack on school integration has been replaced by an attack on busing, which is rejected on the grounds that it interferes with "the family's" or "the parent's" right to decide where their children will attend school or with "the community's" right to decide upon appropriate housing patterns and school districts. Having made similar observations, Donald Kinder, who has written extensively on "symbolic racism," sets out to explain why so many white Americans express a commitment to "equality of opportunity" while opposing concrete efforts to bring about racial equality (Kinder & Sears, 1981; Kinder, 1986). Rejecting both the earlier prejudice model and the later self-interest account, Kinder formulates the concept of symbolic racism to account for the new phenomenon he observes. He points to

> a blend of anti-black affect and the kind of traditional American values embodied in the Protestant Ethic. Symbolic racism represents a form of resistance to change in the racial status quo based on moral feelings that blacks violate such traditional American Values as individualism and self reliance, the work ethic and discipline. (Kinder & Sears, 1981, p. 416)

Kinder and others who offer this account of the new racism have been taken to task by others who argue that it underestimates the continued virulence of old-fashioned racism with its explicit assumption of black inferiority and its straightforward commitment to segregationist sentiments (Weigel & Howes, 1985; Sniderman & Tetlock, 1986). And Kinder himself has recently responded to his critics by acknowledging that he and others "claimed too much when we declared that white America had become, even in principle, racially egalitarian and that traditional forms of racial prejudice had been replaced by symbolic racism. Old fashioned racism remains alive and all too well" (1986, p. 161).

What are we to make of the current debate about the nature and extent of racism in contemporary American society? Returning to the perspective of this paper, we can understand competing theories as reflecting a struggle over how difference is to be constructed in the present period and over who is to have the power to define difference.

Politicians and intellectuals have joined forces, intentionally or unintentionally, to make race invisible. It is this invisibility which is both highlighted and reinforced by accounts of the New Racism, accounts which, on the one hand, seem appealing to many of us because they capture something of what we sense to be the flavor of "a new racism," and disturbing, on the other, because we fear they contribute to the mythology that "*real* racism" is a thing of the past.

Understanding contemporary racist ideology requires that we recognize that the "old fashioned" notion of racial difference as natural and fundamental persists alongside contemporary formulations of that doctrine which now point to difference as moral deficiency. By correlating physical and moral deficiencies with observable differences in physical appearance, the nature/biology paradigm obtains a virtual stranglehold on thought processes that continues to this day, making it very difficult to persuade the uninitiated that this paradigm is really already part of the social construction of race and gender and nor a reflection of natural difference at all. The nature/biology paradigm has not been replaced, it has simply been supplemented by additional and more sophisticated expressions of racism and sexism that have the effect of continuing to reinforce the so-called crude paradigm, while at the same time allowing people to avoid confronting that crude model or taking responsibility for it.

According to the new racism, the problem with people of color in general and blacks in particular is that they are not willing to work hard and defer gratification.[9] Their failure to attain economic self-sufficiency and social recognition lies in an essential difference in their nature. This difference legitimately excludes them from the community of citizens who deserve either or both support and sympathy from the government or "the American People." Note here that people of color, according to this ideology, are already excluded from the community that is intended by the phrase "the American People," which is then understood to be circumscribed by a certain set of values "we" (as opposed to "they") all share.[10]

What we are witnessing in the contemporary period is the resurrection of the nature/biology paradigm, now in a more dangerous and more ideologically loaded form.[11] The political ideology of the day is Conservative with a capital "C," and Conservatism always relies upon some theory of natural and fundamental difference to explain and justify the inequality of opportunity and conditions which it fails to find problematic. In its older, crude version, the nature/biology paradigm is quite straightforward about the fundamental difference between the races that separates them irrevocably. In its new, sophisticated version, the blatant racism is muted and its assertion of fundamental difference between the races appears to be its unavoidable (perhaps even regrettable) conclusion, nor its premise.

According to the new ideology, we are enjoined from ever seeing race difference. The differences we notice are differences in moral character. Since race has been obliterated as a category, the only way to explain differences in achievement is by pointing to individual difference. If blacks as a group fail to achieve, the implication is that there is something in their nature that prevents them from achieving. To say that they lack a commitment to the Protestant work ethic and a willingness to delay gratification is simply a polite way of restating the old litany that "blacks are shiftless and lazy," but in this more sophisticated form we are left with pointing out a moral deficiency or a deficiency of character which can claim to be colorblind.[12]

The work of two contemporary black social scientists, Thomas Sowell (1981) and William J. Wilson (1978), have helped to gain credibility for the neo-conservative approach by de-emphasizing the significance of race as a factor in contemporary American society. In particular, Sowell's discussion of the relative economic success or lack of success enjoyed by members of various ethnic and racial groups in the country can easily be interpreted as supporting the implicit ascription of moral deficiency.

The current refusal to acknowledge the existence of race difference leads to a redefinition of race as once again a biological or natural category, and actually brings us much closer to a return to the biologistic/Social Darwinist paradigm. Now there are no races, just human beings. Some of those human beings are morally deficient (or grow up in deviant families, which amounts to shorthand for the same claim) and hence don't/won't/can't achieve. Many of these morally deficient human beings are blacks, so there must be something in the nature of black people that explains this failure. Success proves that you have worked hard and delayed gratification and deserve to succeed. "Failure" simply indicates that you were deficient in those moral qualities or character attributes that guarantee success. At the heart of the "new racism" is a reconstruction of difference which returns to a paradigm which both explains and justifies why certain individuals are excluded from the community of those whose efforts government is there to support. Government is to create and enforce conditions which guarantee equality of opportunity so that all those who work hard can succeed. Addicts and criminals (and, by implicit equation, "lazy blacks") have excluded themselves from that community. Their failure to achieve is simply proof that they were never members of it and didn't deserve to be. We return to the earliest formulation of classical liberal ideology, with its emphasis on individualism, and its insistence that hierarchy is part of nature, now fused with a revitalized Social Darwinism.

The only alternative paradigm that has been proposed for race in the most recent period comes from Jesse Jackson's Rainbow Coalition. Jackson's rainbow is of course awash with the color that was left out of the ethnicity paradigm, color that is totally absent from the New Right's return to a modified Social Darwinism, but it is an analogy that thus far has had limited usefulness for formulating social policy. The thing about rainbows is that as soon as you begin to get close to them, they fade and ultimately disappear, an account that some would argue provides a disturbingly accurate account of the Rainbow Coalition's role in both the 1988 Democratic campaign and its aftermath. While Omi and Winant and others like the rainbow analogy because it moves beyond a purely racially based agenda (1986, pp. 142–143), in the current climate it's not clear whether this will prove to be a viable political strategy for coalition building or a (perhaps unavoidable) move in the direction of a paradigm that plays right into the contemporary preoccupation with denying the existence of race. Viewed in this light, Jackson's announcement in December of 1988 that henceforth black Americans were to be called "African Americans" suggests an attempt on his part to revitalize the ethnicity paradigm as a way to reassert the existence of black Americans as a group. If we are, in fact, experiencing a resurrection of the biology/nature paradigm combined with emphasis on a rabid individualism, redefining difference by adopting the term "African American" may be the best chance black people have to reassert their common history at a time when the New Right seeks to focus on individual opportunity and merit.

If we turn our attention to the construction of gender during the contemporary period we find a similar return to a nostalgic past where gender difference and female biology or sexuality lies at the heart of social organization. Far from wishing to obliterate gender as it has done with race, the New Right sees gender difference everywhere and is prepared to use it to justify differences in opportunity or achievement where appropriate. Where the ideal woman of the late 1970s was portrayed as a kind of superwoman who could and *should* be able to combine successfully her multiple roles of corporate attorney, girl scout leader, femme fatale, super mom, loving wife, PTA volunteer, gourmet cook, little league coach, bonsai gardener, and fashion model, the ideal woman a decade or so later is encouraged to self-define as a wife and mother with an emphasis on the latter. Unable to actually turn back the clock on some of the concrete gains that white, middle-class women have made in the labor force, the new right is prepared to close its eyes to that participation as long as women with careers embrace the ideology that defines their primary role as wife and mother. The media is filled with stories about highpowered professional women who put their careers on hold or find a way to convert full-time careers to part-time, home-based work, in order to stay home and raise their kids. Politicians and media portrayals made it clear that these women are allowed to build a work life into their homelife as long as they assure us that their primary source of satisfaction and fulfillment lies in motherhood not work (sic). Highly visible women in society, from Supreme Court Justices to law school deans to best-selling authors, are presented to us as women who stayed home and took their motherhood role seriously, thus earning the right to pursue their careers later.

While social pressure to return to the home during childrearing years has increased on middle- and upper-class white women, cuts in food stamps and Medicaid along with a new emphasis on "workfare" seem determined to insure that poor women and women of color are out of the home and in the labor force filling the jobs that no one else wants at wages no one else will accept. This continues the phenomenon we noticed earlier of using the construction of gender difference between women of different races as another way of constructing race (and, one might add, class) difference.

Where early stages in the contemporary women's movement focused on analyzing "sex-role socialization," the later stages have been concerned with understanding the construction of gender. This move reflects a new and more profound understanding of the way the constitution of difference lies at the heart of sexism, an understanding which parallels Memmi's insights about racism. In the mid-seventies Gail Rubin (1975) wondered about the claim that men and women are polar opposites, different as night and day. Stepping back to reflect on what many took to be obvious, Rubin pointed out a very different reality

> In fact, from the standpoint of nature, men and women are closer to each other than either is to anything else—forests, mountains, kangaroos or coconut palms. The idea that men and women are more different from one another than either is from anything else must come from somewhere other than nature.... The idea that men and women are two mutually exclusive categories must arise out of something other than a non-existent "natural" opposition. (1975, p. 179)

More recently, Catherine MacKinnon has argued that "gender is not difference, gender is hierarchy . . . the idea of gender difference helps keep male dominance in place" (1987, p. 3). Writing from a similar perspective, Zillah Eisenstein has suggested that "equality of opportunity is simply a form of male privilege" (1984, p. 67), and Carol Gilligan has urged us to listen to a different voice" (1982).

In both its theory and its practice, the contemporary women's movement has demonstrated a determination to deconstruct gender combined with a strong commitment to redefining difference. In an important essay Audre Lorde has asked us to recognize that "it is not our differences which separate women, but our reluctance to recognize those differences and to deal effectively with the distortions which have resulted from ignoring and misnaming those differences" (1984, p. 115). She concludes, "Now we must recognize differences among women who are equals, neither inferior nor superior, and devise ways to use each others' difference to enrich our visions and our joint struggles" (p. 122).

Responding to Lorde's challenge, the women's movement has begun to search for a metaphor that will facilitate the project Lorde envisions. A popular poster celebrating international women's solidarity adopts the slogan "One Ocean, Many Waves," while the 1987 National Women's Studies Association Conference used the theme of "Weaving Women's Colors," and the 1989 New Jersey Research Conference on Women, Celebration of Our Work at Douglass College, bears the title "Mosaics of Inclusion." Each of these represents an attempt to find a metaphor for difference that reflects both diversity and unity. Each is an attempt to move beyond a portrayal of women which is narrowly white, professional, and Western in nature to one which recognizes and celebrates difference.

THE CHALLENGE OF THE 1990s

The challenge that faces progressive movements as we move into the 1990s is enormous. In the face of a return to an implicit dependence on the nature/biology paradigm for expressing both race and gender difference, how can we reinstate the "deconstruction" projects of the seventies and create the basis for forging broad-based political coalitions that can transform the political-social-economic agenda and priorities of the nation? While attempts to recognize and analyze the social construction of gender and race were important intellectual projects a decade or two ago, this relatively sophisticated conceptual project has been made even more difficult by the conservative ideological bias that permeates much of popular culture and communication during the current period. At a "common-sense" level, the natural difference paradigm is reinforced constantly in the most casual interaction between people: dark skin is not light skin; women's bodies are not male bodies. In the presence of such obvious physical differences, most people find it difficult even to entertain the notion of race and gender as social and political categories. What can it mean to claim that difference is created by racism and sexism, not simply and (appropriately) reflected by them?

Those of us committed to social change must look for the answer by focusing on the essential contradictions that lie at the heart of the new conservatism—conservatism that is committed simultaneously to asserting fundamental natural differences between races while seeking to make race invisible—a conservatism that, in addition, is committed to asserting fundamental natural differences based upon gender, yet is unable to institutionalize this difference as the basis for social policy with the force and comprehensiveness it once could. Once again, our project is to turn the natural difference paradigm on its head. We must simultaneously deconstruct the social construction of difference that constitutes racism and sexism while we reconstruct difference as unlimited human and humane possibilities. This means that we must use every opportunity to show the way in which race and gender difference has been constructed in order to justify racism and sexism, at the same time that we teach ourselves and others to name and value the differences that help to define each of us but which are the very strengths of the community we seek to create. We must do this at every opportunity by focusing on the contradictions between conservative rhetoric and the reality of the lives of women and men who live and work in a multiracial, multicultural, class society. Local, regional, and national organizing around issues that expose the contradictions inherent in the prevailing paradigms provide the best longterm hope for redirecting economic and social policy toward human interests.

NOTES

1. The former occurs when oppressed people participate in the creation of difference in order to protect themselves from violating or seeming to violate the norms of behavior established by those in power.

2. Audre Lorde has described what she calls this "mythical norm" as "white, thin, young, heterosexual, christian and financially secure" (1984, p. 116).

3. My discussion of the ethnicity paradigm and challenges to it is based upon the analysis offered by Michael Omi and Howard Winant in their important book *Racial Formations in the United States* (1986). Even at those points where I disagree with their analysis, I am indebted to it.

4. Commenting on the impetus for replacing "colored" and "Negro" with "black," Robert Baker writes: "All of these movements and their partisans wished to stress that Afro-Americans were different from other Americans and could not be merged with them because the difference between the two was as great as that between black and white" (1981, p. 163).

5. In their fascinating account of a hundred and fifty years of the experts' advice to women, *For Her Own Good*, Barbara Ehrenreich and Deirdre English refer to these views respectively as "sexual romanticism" and "sexual rationalism" (1979, p. 21).

6. For some accounts of the androgyny paradigm and its critics, see, for example, Caroline Bird (1968), Ann Ferguson's "Androgyny As an Ideal for Human Development" (1977), and Betty Roszak's "The Human Continuum" (1971, pp. 297ff), as well as Mary Daly's (1975) "The Qualitative Leap beyond Patriarchal Religion" and Janice Raymond's "The Illusion of Androgyny" (1975).

7. See Gail Rubins "Woman as Nigger" (1971, pp. 230ff).

8. Omi and Winant quote political scientist Merle Blacks as pointing out that "Reagan's kind of civilized the racial issue" (1986, p. 135).

9. This stereotypical portrayal is not applied to Asian Americans or to Cuban Americans at the present time.

10. This trick of exclusion has a long history. Portraying civil rights for blacks and women as a special interest, for example, sets things up so that extending civil rights to these groups appears to take something away from everybody else instead of enhancing democracy for all.

11. This in contrast to Omi and Winant, who argue that "we are witnessing the resurrection of the ethnicity paradigm in a new form" (1986, p. 141).

12. See, for example, Jeffrey Prager's discussion of Ronald Reagan's portrayal of black Americans during his 1985 State of the Union Address. Prager points out that Reagan subtly attempted to divide black Americans into two groups, those who were "virtuous black workers" and those who were "menacing addicts, criminals, etc." (1987, p. 70).

REFERENCES

Baker, Robert. 1981. " 'Pricks' and 'Chicks': and A Plea for 'Persons.' " In *Sexist Language*. M. Vetterling-Bragin, ed. Totowa, N.J.: Littlefield Adams.

Bird, Caroline. 1968. *Born Female: The High Cost of Keeping Women Down*. New York: McKay.

Daly, Mary. 1975. "The Qualitative Leap beyond Patriarchal Religion." *Feminist Quarterly* 1 (4): 29ff.

Ehrenreich, Barbara, and Deirdre English. 1979. *For Her Own Good: 150 Years of the Experts' Advice to Women*. Garden City, N.Y.: Anchor Press/Doubleday.

Eisenstein, Zillah R. 1984. *Feminism and Sexual Equality*. New York: Monthly Review Press.

Ferguson, Ann. 1977. "Androgyny as an Ideal for Human Development." In *Feminism and Philosophy*. See Vetterling-Braggin (1977).

Firestone, Shulamith. 1971. *The Dialectic of Sex*. New York: Bantam Books.

Gilligan, Carol. 1982. *In a Different Voice*. Cambridge, MA: Harvard University Press.

Kinder, Donald R. 1986. "The Continuing American Dilemma: White Resistance to Racial Change 40 Years after Myrdal." *Journal of Social Issues* 42 (2): 151–71.

Kinder, Donald, R. and D. O. Sears. 1981. "Prejudice and Politics: Symbolic Racism versus Racial Threats to the Good Life." *Journal of Personality and Social Psychology* 40: 414–43.

Lorde, Audre. 1984. "Age, Race, Class, and Sex: Women Redefining Difference." In *Sister Outsider*. Trumansburg, N.Y.: The Crossing Press.

MacKinnon, Catherine A. 1987. *Feminism Unmodified*. Cambridge, MA: Harvard University Press.

Memmi, Albert. 1971. *Dominated Man*. Boston: Beacon Press.

Omi, Michael and Howard Winant. 1986. *Racial Formation in the United States*. New York: Routledge and Kegan Paul.

Pierce, Chester M. 1974. "Psychiatric Problems of the Black Minority." In *American Handbook of Psychiatry*. New York: Basic Books.

Prager, Jeffrey. 1987. "American Political Culture and the Shifting Meaning of Race." *Ethnic and Racial Studies* 10 (1): 62–81.

Raymond, Janice. 1975. "The Illusion of Androgyny." *Quest* 2 (1).

Roszak, Betty. 1971. "The Human Continuum." In *Masculine/Feminine*. See Roszak, Betty and T. Roszak (1971).

Roszak, Betty, and T. Roszak, eds. 1971. *Masculine/Feminine*. New York: Harper Colophon Books.

Rubin, Gail. 1971. "Women as Nigger." In *Mascline/Feminine*. See Roszak 1971.

———. 1975. "The Traffic in Women: Notes on the 'Political Economy' of Sex." In *Toward an Anthropology of Women*. Rayna R. Reiter, ed. New York: Monthly Review Press.

Sniderman, Paul M., and Philip E. Tetlock. 1986. "Symbolic Racism: Problems of Motive Attribution in Political Analysis." *Journal of Social Issues* 42: 129–50.

Sowell, Thomas. 1981. *Ethnic America*. New York: Basic Books.

Vetterling-Braggin, Mary, and Frederick A. Elliston, *et al.* 1977. *Feminism and Philosophy*. Totowa, N.J.: Littlefield Adams.

Weigel, Russell H., and Paul W. Howes. 1985. "Conceptions of Racial Prejudice: Symbolic Racism Reconsidered." *Journal of Social Issues* 41 (3): 117–38.

Whitbeck, Caroline. 1975. "Theories of Sex Difference." *The Philosophical Forum* 5 (1–2): 54–80.

Wilson, William Julius. 1978. *The Declining Significance of Race*. 2d ed. Chicago: University of Chicago Press.

Wolff, Robert Paul. 1965. "Beyond Tolerance." In *A Critique of Pure Tolerance*. Boston: Beacon Press.

15. National Identity Framed in the Logics of Racialization: Aspects, Figures, and Problems of Differentialist Racism

Pierre-André Taguieff

IN THIS ESSAY, I set out to address two interwoven ideological phenomena, which seem complementary and have been noticeable in France of late: the complacent and trivial reference to "identity crisis" (or the crisis of identities) as well as the collective overemphasis on nationalism, racism, and "integrity-ism." Individual identity, which had replaced collective identity, is in disarray. Consequently, and predictably, this situation has entailed a host of compensations and dislocations, as well as self-identifying and whitewashing. The present paper does not pretend to break any new ground because the identity theme has been studied before, and its widespread usage and diverse meanings have been isolated in scientific or learned discourse, in "spontaneous" social talk or in elaborate political speeches.

In 1974, as he was starting the now-celebrated interdisciplinary course on "identity," Claude Lévi-Strauss stated: "The theme of identity finds itself not only at a crossroads, but at several crossroads. Every academic discipline, including ethnology and, particularly, anthropology, finds an interest in it" (Lévi-Strauss, 1977, p. 91). My basic thesis assumes that the notion of identity, which apparently lacks a clear, distinct, and effective definition, has been readily embraced by modern political myths. The illusion of a unified, homogeneous, unique (i.e., outstanding, original), substantial individual and/or collective identity is thriving despite the emergence of a critical discourse. This is a minor ideological illusion which is easy to conceptualize, but it also is one which critical reasoning has yet to curb.

Pierre-André Taguieff, "National Identity Framed in the Logic of Racialization," *Mots/Les langages du politique* 12 (1986): 91–128. Trans. Bernard Pony. Reprinted with the permission of Presses de Sciences Po.

Writing on the non-holistic characteristics of identity, Lévi-Strauss stressed, rightly, that, "Despite being spatially removed and despite being highly heterogeneous, when one considers their cultural content, none of the societies randomly sampled seem to have a substantial identity of their own. Within these societies identity has been broken up into many elements. As a result, finding a synthesis within each of them has, in varying degrees, been problematic." Thence, one can "assume that identity has its relations of uncertainty, too." (Lévi-Strauss, 1977, p. 11).

But an ethnologist can be likened to Sirius shining down on earth, for the former runs the risk of not enlightening us on the theme discussed here. An ethnologist will approach, or decypher, the theme of identity from the top down; he/she is informed yet detached. While the above approach is necessary for our understanding, we must realize that political mythologies have overemphasized, unified, and substantialized collective identities; they have also made them the essence of strong beliefs and the repository for certainty. These collective identities have been, so to speak, frozen, and, to paraphrase Proudhon, they have been elevated into absolutes and idols. What follows is an attempt to challenge these ideological and political absolutes—a colossal task, indeed.

ASSESSING IDENTITY AND DIFFERENCE

Identity: An Essential and Abstruse Term

It has generally been challenging to theoretically assess identity, which is a clear/abstruse notion. According to Willard V. O. Quine, this challenge has its roots in a logical and epistemological paradox:

> Identity, though a simple and basic idea, has been difficult to effectively explain beyond synonyms. To argue that x and y are identical, is to argue that they are one and the same; every one thing being identical only to itself. Yet, for all its simplicity, the term "identity" has raised more questions than it has provided answers for. One may be tempted to ask, what use is the notion of identity if to identify an object to itself is trivial, and if to identify an object to another is in itself a false proposition. (Quine, 1973, p. 236)

In yet another attempt to comprehend the terms "difference" and "identity," we must repeat what Valéry wrote on "liberty" in 1938:

> Liberty is of those words that are overly used but are meaningless; it is a musically-sounding word that actually says little, that asks more questions than it

can answer. In our mind, the notion of liberty has been engrained and shaped by theology, metaphysics, moral values and politics. It is a word that is relished in controversy, dialectic and eloquence; a word ever-present in fallacious analyses and in high-flown sentences, as well. (Valéry, *Fluctuations sur la liberté*)

At the risk of equivocating, I should suggest that the issue here is not whether thinking on the term "community," being the various modes in which humans live together, can actually be formed by looking beyond "identity," "difference," and the individual. By adopting such an approach, I will scrutinize these enigmatic entities known as "collective identities," which may refer to a nation, an ethnic group, a region, a minority or majority group, a people, or even a race. In this essay, I have had to rely on my "tribe's" imperfect language, a language where common words can be extremely polemical and equivocal—which may explain why lexical eugenism and other attempts to reform our language have failed miserably.

However, I agree with Quine, when he writes that identity is not about how sentences are constructed in relation to one another. Instead, it is about enunciating relations between objects. "Only objects are self-identical, not words," Quine further remarked Quine, 1973, p. 237). Therefore, a valid statement about identity must take into consideration our actual knowledge of the world around us. Put succinctly, semantic knowledge has to be complemented by a broader based, encyclopedic knowledge.[1]

Assessing the use of the notion of identity along a "trivial-false" paradigm, we can conclude that a statement on identity is neither trivial nor false, if both terms used provide some information and achieve the same objective (e.g., "la France est la patrie des droits de l'homme" /France is the land of human rights). The words or groups of words "France" and "la patrie des droits de l'homme" are not identical, but the encyclopedic entities they refer to are. Here ties the usefulness of the notion "identity": to give world-based meaning that is one and "real" to different terms or nouns in a statement, whether in everyday parlance, as in this tautology, "La France est la France" (France is France).[2]

Statements about identity are essential in order to represent for ourselves what is real—a functional capacity not found in human languages. Quine agreed with the foregoing point in these terms:

> If our language represented subject-matter perfectly, to the point that there was a single name for each thing, statements about identity would certainly be useless. But ours is not such a language. [So] . . . to do away with redundancy and such complex nouns as "the twenty-fifth president of the United States" and "the first president of the United States," would be to strike at the root of the problem. The usefulness of a language lies, in part, in its inability to copy reality in such a way that one thing is called by one name only. The notion of identity is, therefore, essential because it fills a vacuum for it minimizes the shortcomings of a language. (Quine, 1973, p. 236)

THE MAKING OF COMMON AUTHORITARIANISM AND DIFFERENTIALIST RACISM

A basic requirement for any natural language is its ability to allow for the formulation of statements on the presumed identity of X, a collective entity which is assumed to be different from Y, the latter a known and "defined" collective identity, with X being also different from any other collective identities (whether they are, or can be, known). However, if everyday discourse and the equivocal terms it contains must not be challenged, an attempt can at least be made to clarify, explain, and disentangle some of the ideological knots they have been made into. Nationalism, xenophobia, racism, or anti-Semitism, which are doctrines and political attitudes that have exalted identity as they have repudiated difference, are among the easiest to define. Still, to systematically study the large corpus associated with such problematic ideology can be an awe-inspiring undertaking. In light of this, the present study has been narrowed to focus only on the state of that ideology in France in the last decade.

Beginning in 1981, antisocialist discourse in "liberal" and "national" Right circles has increasingly been woven around narrowly defined, modern myths of a French identity, but against "foreign" collective differences perceived as being dangerous. I find striking the movement that advocates a return to a closed, inward-looking nationalism, whether this is expressed as sentiment or as a doctrine (of nationalism as public opinion or as doctrine, see Girardet, 1970, p. 9). I find it striking because it has intertwined two ideological, almost simultaneous, processes. On the one hand, a sizeable segment within the "liberal" conservative and neo-Gaullist Right has rallied behind the ideas of the new, metapolitical Right (e.g., GRECE and Club de l'horloge), and are espousing themes synonymous with the kind of nationalism heretofore confined outside the walls of Parliament.

These themes—values and norms (national identity, security, authority, morals)—have permeated the so-called far-Right discourse. A case in point: L. Pauwels and Alain Griotteray, the latter a hybrid liberal Gaullist, wrote in *Le Figaro-Magazine* an article which could be entitled "Reagano-Papism," where these authors longed for an authoritarian, xenophobic neonationalism and, in the same breath, total economic liberalism and traditionalist moralism. Another article, by Jean-Yves Le Gallou and the Club de l'horloge (Le Club has fast become a standard-bearer for xenophobic neonationalism in France), makes a variety of ideological points and provides "scientific" modes of legitimation. Rather than being an extreme statement by the moderate Right—or a softening of the rhetoric of the far Right—it is an attempt by Right-wingers to become mainstream. Their rhetoric has focused on these ideological points: the threat to national identity, lack of security (delinquency by the lower classes and laxity by leaders), unemployment, social-racial "parasitism," the immigration invasion, and the providence-state conflict.

It should also be noted that the ideas or themes put forth by the Right have been, in a great measure, influenced by Left-wing discourses. Known as "retortion," this strategy can be defined as expropriation, self-legitimation, and dis-legitimation of the enemy. It is a culturally based, discursive, and ideological technique meant to combat the Left on its own turf, by using in attack the adversary's [the Left's] themes: "the right to difference" is one such theme. It was a slogan used in the 1960s and 1970s within regional and "nationalitarist-minoritarist" circles on the left. Today, however, "the right to difference" rests on a Manichean-type division, such as *Us vs. Foreigners*. As such, the "right to difference" has clearly become synonymous with "neo-racism." We have thus gone from "the right for self-determination" to "a duty for citizens to remain within their own country, by themselves, and to be themselves." This nationalist thought, propelled by fertile imagination, is woven around a self-serving fragmentation of mankind where *I/Us* stands opposite *non-I*.

This view advocates a stratification of French society in which nationals/citizens have political, legal, social, and economic benefits, but the same view holds that foreigners, and more particularly the most foreign of all (non-Europeans), must be denied every such right. Thus, the nationalist ideology places a premium on the racial background of individuals within the nation-state. To be inducted into the "nationals" category, one will have to become naturalized (the naturalization process has been construed as being a rejection of one's cultural background, which amounts to cultural self-denial). Still, a careful look shows that the nationalist discourse is caught up in a "double bind," because it has also been argued that the cultural background of a naturalized "national" will not be entirely wiped out.

The Right has been revitalized, and its fine-sounding sloganeering, including "the right to difference," has given a political meaning to (genetic) science ("biopolitics"), and such slogans appear to be both "biologist" and "culturalist." The more subtle "culturalist" position has been used in order to maneuver around openly racist language and thinking, such as the zoology-inspired typology that has attempted to divide mankind into distinct races, where all members within each race must fit a common theoretical profile (a holotype). But the realization that a race is generically diverse, and that the polymorphous nature of every race around the globe renders quixotic any genetics-based legitimation of racism, makes impossible a race-based scientific study of mankind. As recently as 1979, the careful ideology watcher was unable to detect the rise of this populist nationalism, its themes and arguments, because it lacked media exposure at the time.

THE CONCEPT OF DIFFERENTIALIST RACISM AND ITS RHETORIC FOUNDATION

The differentialist discourse can be characterized as follows:

1. There is a semantic focus on difference and/or identity
2. There is a rejection of a race-based vocabulary; instead, the use of euphemistic and lexical substitutions has sought to replace obvious, or "classical," racism with differentialism (which, to the critic, is neoracism nevertheless). This relationship comes to mind: race→ethnic group→civilization→culture→mentality→tradition→roots→identity/difference.
3. There is heavy reliance on quotes and themes that are borrowed from political adversaries—a discursive heterogeneity that focuses on the other (foreigner, adversary, enemy).
4. Differentialism evolves in a polemic milieu with political forces, ideological orientations—a milieu where interacting interests are furthered. Its strategy, "retortion," as it has been called, rests on borrowed points and ideas from other, opposing ideological and political quarters, and it seeks to change their discourse around so as to defeat its initial purpose.
5. The lack of reference to a specific corpus in the differentialist discourse makes it difficult to clearly pinpoint coherent, well-defined ideological and political camps: there are themes dear to neo-feminists or groups advocating regional identity that are at once found alongside "pagan," far-Right intellectuals and far-Leftists who have rejected the universalist approach to social problems.

Discursive polemology, the science we are grappling with here, deals with the definition of the essence of politics. Essentially, there is talk of politics because social actors clash over who will wield power and, consequently, because a friend-enemy relation emerges, whether one's enemy has to be over-powered (*hostis, polemios*), or whether defeating an enemy does not necessitate their being exterminated (*inimicus, ekhthros*). Political discourse involves a symbolic cultural and ideological war in which your enemy must be eliminated or your adversary disqualified. Therefore, political rhetoric should rest on paradigms involving logic that is known to all and that has been mutually agreed to.

THE ANTINOMY OF THE CLOSE COMMUNITY AND DETACHED INDIVIDUAL

National-Racist Ideologizing: The "Right to Difference" and Ethnocidal Liberalism

Hypothetically speaking, the core of the current ideological controversy deals with the many and often "perverted" effects associated with regarding the "right to difference" as a supreme right. We have called these effects "perverted" because, on the one hand, the phrase "right to difference" has been accepted by the methodological individualism school. The differentialist norm, which has been adopted by regionalist and nationalist movements, has had unintentional, unwanted, or contrary effects, and has caused these movements to accept a "separate development" position, a position traditionally associated with racists. On the other hand, the "perverted" effects are the product of a calculated, strategic, ideological and political rhetoric promoting cultural warfare. Thus, nationalism has inched toward racism by stressing the "right to difference."

But what is the underlying racist vision and what are the hidden political motives behind the making of the "right to difference" into an absolute? Our task here is to challenge differentialist racism, a nonclassical racism, and to champion minority cultures. It is to also protect the "rights of peoples."[3] The principle of difference presupposes that the principle of universality must assume a secondary and a lower station. As the turning of "difference" into an absolute is in stark opposition to the positive appreciation of "difference," so is differentialist racism vis-à-vis the positive acceptance (tolerance) ethos.

The Antinomy of Communitarism and Individualism

Intercultural differences and hegemonic struggles pointing to a cultural division along the lines "dominant" cultures/"dominated" cultures, as well as the scientific findings of a limitless, inter-individual genetic variation, have led to conflicting interpretations. The ideological and political advocacy of difference has to be considered on two levels—one inter-individual, the other inter-cultural (or inter-ethnic). Between these two symbolic bridges, analogies and metaphors continue to be built, removed, and then rebuilt. This situation has spawned a mix of differentialist, para-ethnologic and para-genetic speeches. A philosophical or political appraisal of those facets of differentialism has yet to be undertaken.

The analysis of the discourse of specialists and that of the professional ideologies seems to command our attention at a time when it is important that we reflect on genetic and cultural diversity, in an effort to challenge reductionism (e.g., sociobiology, which has reduced culture to biology) as well as disciplinarian protectionism, which, quite casually, bases the idea of cleavage on the distinction nature-culture. Together, ideologizing and professionalizing have begotten an antinomy as they have wandered about the political field, being communitarist at one time, individualist at another. In other words, they have embraced both Right-wing differentialist racism and Left-wing anti-racism and apolitical universalism. On the one hand, the Right has made communitarism, or ethnopluralism, into a self-serving double absolutization: difference between communities (ethnic groups, races, peoples, etc.) and belonging to one's own community. Here, cultural difference becomes an insuperable boundary, and membership in a given community is limited to who meets certain cultural characteristics. Such logic stands in opposition to the three pillars of modern ideology: individualism, universalism, and egalitarianism. The communitarist ideology stresses the primacy of the group at the expense of the individual, and perceives this relationship as the making of destiny. But in the mind of the Right, this involves a closed, inward-looking community. Thus, neo-racist schools of thought have viewed the communitarist ideology in genetic and racially based terms, while the "ethist" (ethos?) schools or such neo-racist entities as GRECE have approached it in cultural terms.

This integrity-ism stresses original-community membership and rests on an absolute/anti-individualist doctrine. This doctrine implies a de-realization (making not-real) of the individual, the roots of which can be traced to either Hegel, Bonald, Comte, Vacher de Lapouge, or Robert Jaulin. Actually, the goal of this ideology is to preserve the identity of one's group. Social links are then based solely upon bloodline (racist schools), or mutual destiny is based upon a common past (culturalist or neo-traditionalist schools). The first position can be seen as a holistic reaction to a social environment with strong individualistic values and norms, with a took being cast to the past (race purity) or to the future (romantic post-individual society). There is a "regressive" mode of thinking (pre-individualist utopia) and a "progressive" one, which is a meliorative, post- individual is tic vision of society (eugenism, socialism, selectionism).

On the other hand, there is an unrestrained shift toward radical and exclusivist individualism (absolutization of individual or individuo-universalism), as is the case with scientists and geneticians in particular, who have crossed swords with racism. (see A. Jacquard, 1982 or F. Jacob). This position regards the individual as absolute, self-contained, and it extols the individual as being the bearer of universal traits and having a bright future. In this theoretical framework, one goes freely from the individual to the universal, and vice versa. According to this approach, the closed community is no more, having been replaced by an "outside-the-world individual."[4]

THE INDIVIDUALISTIC FOUNDATIONS OF HUMANITARIAN ANTI-RACISM

As Albert Jacquard wrote in 1978, in *Eloge de la différence. La génétique et les hommes*, we must "love the differences that exist between humans," because "the first lesson genetics has taught us is that individuals are different to be put in classes, to be evaluated or be assigned a certain order" (p. 207). If "our differences are our wealth, our greatest need, therefore, is to be unique in order to actually 'be,' our obsession is to be acknowledged as being original and irreplaceable. The greatest gift we can receive from 'the other' is that, by merely being different from us, they enhance our own uniqueness and originality" (pp. 206–207).

If difference is our wealth which we must protect, then this *true* wealth takes on qualitative, exceptional, and incomparable value, far beyond the quantitative models that have been based on money and capital—symbols par excellence of bogus wealth. In a later publication dealing with "human rights," Albert Jacquard examined the individualist ideology by asking an insightful question: "Is society in the service of the individual, or is the individual in the service of society?" (Jacquard, 1982, p. 186). An answer to this question will certainly improve our understanding of human rights, but "no scientific reasoning can effectively address it." Again, Jacquard's views on both the individualistic and differentialist responses to human rights: "The task at hand is to allow for unfettered individual growth; it is to value difference (i.e., non-equality) without imposing any value judgement" (p. 187).

Can such balance be achieved, in actuality? Individualism, being the ideology that favors individual development free from social constraints, can in part be traced to the seminal and doctrinal thoughts of Rousseau. Neo-Rousseauites have repudiated Durkheim's sociologism, but have advocated "natural education" and sheathing or protecting the individual from society. As they argue that the individual is an autonomous, exclusive, and supreme being, they have explained the dual model—embryonic and "personalist"—associated with the individualist ideal in terms penned by Ellen Key at the turn of the century: "Education should center around the fact that nature works at its own pace, under no constraints, with man's only role being to insure that the environment can allow such a process."[5] The individualist ethos allows for and values differences, as it rejects both money and society when they are not "in the service" of the individual.

However, this approach shirks the thorny question of interpersonal relationships by arguing that individual behavior is not controlled by negative passions (envy, jealousy, resentment), and that man is not naturally evil (note Rousseau's influence). The individualist/humanitarian argument is dominated by two views: (scientific or) genetic polymorphism and the Universal Declaration of Human Rights created by the United Nations. On the one hand, there is "scientific" individualism, while on the other ethnic personalism (the latter being associated with Kant, Levin, or humanitarianism, which is the best known of the three). Here are Vilfredo Pareto's comments on what he termed "the humanitarianism of our time":

> What a pity it is to blame others for our own shortcomings. It is a tendency for unhappy individuals to blame their environment for their unhappiness and to sympathize with everyone who is suffering. [Humanitarianism] offers no sound and logical reasoning; rather, it is one sensation after the other, with such arguments as: "I am unhappy, society is to blame. If another individual is unhappy, then, society must (also) be to blame. I and that individual are in the same bind. I must sympathize with that companion of mine, the same way I do me." (Pareto, 1932, Vol. 1, pp. 602–603)

Thus, humanitarianism rationalizes a feeling, veils a desire for revenge, while at the same time providing a means for one's ego to share in the pain of others. According to this approach, "Society is at fault when some people live in poor economic conditions. In the same vein, this approach holds society responsible for thieves and assassins, who are considered to be our unfortunate brothers worthy of our kindness and sympathy" (Pareto, 1932, p. 603).

Somewhere between the position favoring asocial individualism and that favoring abstract universalism, we can locate the "liberal"/"anti-totalitarian" idea of the 1980s, which in essence sought to wrest the individual from the "yoke of communitarianism." It must be noted that since 1979–80, some French proponents of liberal individualism have been trying to adapt the American myth of exclusive individual interest. This type of economics-based (economist) individualism is fundamentally without ethical values and norms, and borrows from a founding myth of the United States: man is but "a small particle of ego-centrism."[6] This liberal individualism, supported by competition and egotistical rivalry, faces a central and insuperable contradiction. On the one hand, it offers a theoretical paradigm of free and harmonious individual development, but, on the other, it presents a paradigm of struggle and rivalry, where individuals seek to safeguard or further their own interests.

ANALOGOUS ANTINOMIES

Theoretically, the main effect of absolute individualism, whether it is found on the Left (humanitarianism) or on the Right (competition liberalism), is to obliterate any social linkages by closing off the individual into strict hedonism or stoicism. This can be explained in two ways: (1) "Be happy and enjoy yourself to the fullest, here and now!" (2) "Work and you will deserve happiness!" (in grander ways, to paraphrase Kant). A close scrutiny of absolute individualism shows it in an impasse, for it fails to produce any answers to the following questions: Why are there communities and not (only) individuals? And why are there contracts and irreducible gatherings as opposed to interindividual alliances!

The antinomy involves totalism and individualism, doctrines that, respectively, extol closed communities and celebrate the individual without any linkages except for those that directly connect him/her with universal figures. In a strictly metapolitical sense, this antinomy can be constructed from diverse angles by opposing the following: romantic spirit vs. classical spirit; "Catholic"-traditionalist (and community) model vs. "Protestant" (individual-universalist) model; man of culture (differentiation and organicity) vs. man of civilization (universalist humanism, globalism); traditional world (suprahuman values) vs. modern world (man-centered values).

Individualism, where the individual is viewed as supreme being and lives according to self, and belongs to only oneself (this being the lowest expression of the autonomy ideal), is poor materialism peculiar to demagogues anxious to dictate ideology. It is low-level revolutionarist rhetoric (centered around calls for pay raises, hatred of the upper classes); it also is liberal as it deals with "initiative and self-love" (A. Laurent, *De l'individualisme*), which has, unabashed, turned itself into the "normal" man's theory. Jean Starobinski has recently said that Rousseau experienced an identity crisis, when he "longed for self-identity over a considerable length of time" (Starobinski, 1984, p. 759).

NATIONALISM AND RACISM: BASIC ARGUMENTS

The Nationalist Problematic: An Assessment of Its Rhetoric and Ideology

This segment addresses the dominant exclusionary modes, legitimated as "nationalist" or "republican," in 1980 France—a culturally heterogeneous society. Without specifically researching the established links that have pulled "nationalism" and "racism" together, it strikes me that nationalist ideology and discourses bear strong similarity to the so-called racist discourse. In light of this observation, it has become necessary to address the relationship between these two ideologies: Can nationalism be without racism?

Although nationalism has been expressed without resorting to the doctrinal form of racism, modern racist ideology has taken place within an ideological and political framework supplied by nationalism. Also, if nationalism can be expressed without appearing to endorse the doctrine promoting race purity or race superiority, it is because Republican ideology, out of universalist considerations, has tamed or even eliminated such discourse. It can be argued that nationalism, when not restrained by Republican universalism, is a poison. However, the ideology behind nationalism and Republicanism rejects both the thought of an infra-national community, replete with minority or regionalist cultures, and the prospect of a supra-national community (European federation).

The hypothesis that racism and nationalism are intrinsically linked cannot be corroborated by political and intellectual history, because several anthropologists have theorized that the existence of races cannot scientifically support the emergence of political nationalism (or the principle of nationality). This theory has also challenged the view that the idea of nation can be traced to race. As far as doctrinal and obvious nineteenth-century racism is concerned, there is an ambivalence vis-à-vis the nationalist idea that is being examined here. Doctrinal racism is as much an ideological legitimation of nationalism (e.g., Hitler's *Mein Kampf*) as it is a means of challenging the scientific ideals of nationalism and uncovering its inconsistencies (thus verifying anthropological findings).

For its part, anti-nationalist racism assumes many forms: it is either a raciological legitimation or a traditionalist legitimation of nationalism (Barrès). Le Bon and Lapouge have not yet assumed a firm position in regards to the relations between zoological races, "ethnic groups," "historical races," and peoples. Also, those anthropologists with national-socialist inclinations have found it hard to reconcile the science of race with such nationalisms as pan-Germanism.

Addressing an international congress in Moscow in 1892, Paul Topinard suggested a clear-cut distinction be made between the various aspects of race (the domain of physical anthropology) and nationality (being a complex set of historical legacies that are coupled with a feeling of membership, and are coated with faith and dogma, all of which cannot be studied as a science), before concluding:

> Nationality has no link to anthropology, nor does it to race. It is the product of history, and, as such, is linked to government (of any form). Every nationality grows from modest beginnings to a higher station, owing to wisdom, a spirit of continuity, as well as all kinds of successes—on the battlefield, in diplomacy, in science, and in the letters. A people's genius, its spirit of unity, its flag held high and erect—all of these are a nationality's characteristics. Nationality is a fact you cannot demonstrate or argue. It is a faith that creates heroes and martyrs, brings friends, admirers, as well as enemies and the envious. It is a dogma! (Topinard, 1892, p. 170)

Thus, national identity—the mode of collective identity associated with the belonging to a nation—appears nondescript; it is a thing the existence of which the individual is cognizant, yet a concept he/she is unable to define. Although national identity is no objective scientific reality, it can nonetheless be identified as a historical fact that lies beyond debate.

When one considers patriotism and nationalism—modern "myths" and "expression of will," to use Georges Sorel's term's (Sorel, 1972, p. 38)—one gets a sense of the limited impact of critical discourse on this specific reality that takes on the form of collective passions. A reason why critics have been unsuccessful at comprehending and eradicating the myths that are patriotism and nationalism is because "a myth cannot be refuted, for it can be likened to the deeply-held convictions of a group, for it is the expression, in language and movement, of these very convictions" (Sorel, 1972, p. 38). A recent survey of France-bound migration from North Africa shows that, "Because of the very nature of peoples, we can foresee a time when these Beurs [North African emigrés], the latest immigrants to be integrated into French society, will perceive later-in-time arrivals as invaders threatening the mythical identity of France. At that time, the Beurs will have become 'beaufs,' for having migrated to France earlier. And someday, when telling their story, we will say, 'here is how one becomes French' " (Françoise Gaspard & Claude Servan-Schreiber, 1985, p. 216).

USING THE INEQUALITY CRITERION WRONGLY OR ANTI-RACISM'S TRUNCATED APPRAISAL OF RACISM

Most observers of the nationalist populist phenomenon have looked for specific texts and pamphlets by the National Front that would allow them to pin down the "racism" gripping this party, its leader Jean-Marie Le Pen, or his top aides. When such an investigation fails to identify the racist overtones used, and therefore falls short of its anticipated results, these observers are loathe to identify the National Front as a racist organization. But "racism" has dominated the discourse held by the nationalist-populists, where it has become ingenuously disguised from the 1970s on. There is a constant reference to race, a call for the exploitation, or eradication, of the "inferior" races, which unearths thoughts of racial colonialism (sanctioning exploitation and domination) and phobia-motivated racism (which is reminiscent of Hitlerian racism and the extermination of the Jew, then viewed as being demonic and soiled).

A rhetorical question posed by xenophobic nationalism deals with identifying those who are excluded ("foreigners"/"the undesirable"/"the invaders"/ "the aggressors"); it also deals with finding a way to legitimize their exclusion. A mode through which exclusion has taken place is the categorization of Maghrebins (North Africans) in a fixed category on the basis of their facial or physical appearance. "Le Maghrébin" has become a metaphorical stigmatization of the

North African émigré used both by the Right and Left. Such a technique enables those ideologues to maneuver around—to use Le Pen's terms—"taboo topics," by not using more obvious names such as "Arabs" or "Jews" in public addresses, in an attempt to avoid offending members of these groups.

MIXOPHOBIA AND THE LOGICS OF EXCLUSION

At the heart of mixophobia (racism fused with nationalism) lies a fear of race mixing, a situation that would obliterate those cultural and biological boundaries which ensure a normal existence. Xenophobia is fundamentally mixophobic because it opposes race mixing, which is said to cause the disappearance of what is pure (the extinction of purity). Jean-Marie Le Pen, president of the National Front, an organization that has become the standardbearer for mixophobia, once observed:

> There is a multiplicity of races and cultures around the world, but there is a kind of utopic movement that advocates "globalism" and seeks to level all cultures in order to create an admixture that will obliterate the differences between people and, more particularly, between the races. This is an utterly contemptible venture because these diverse races were created by God and, because of this, must live on. . . . Those equalitarian theories have not shown the slightest regard for the desire by each race of men (and breed of dogs) to remain different. What this movement has actually done is to show how artificial and unnatural it really is. (Le Pen quoted in Jean Marcilly, 1984, p. 192)

The foregoing quote is characteristic of the nationalist discourse, a discourse woven around three logics of exclusion: differential ism, inegalitarianism, and preferentialism. But what best defines this type of discourse is the centrality which the theme of racial difference has assumed. This theme is used in order to discard attempts to level or make uniform the human races (indifferentiation). The nationalist discourse adheres to the idea of absolute racial inequality without verbally or explicitly admitting to it.

The three logics of exclusion are channels for racist ideology. They have been used together in statements or separately to express a variety of racist ideals. The nationalist view presupposes that inter-ethnic differences are value-laden (which is a normative view of an empirical fact: the division of mankind into races essentially based on skin color). Additionally, it presupposes an affirmation of inter-individual inequality and, indirectly, the inequality between races and ethnic groups. Finally, it presupposes the expression of preference in the following logical or axiomatic order: "I prefer my daughters over my nieces, my nieces over my neighbors. . . . I prefer my fellow countrymen, France and the

French, as well as Europeans and nationals from NATO countries."[7] This state-ment moves from the obvious (racial difference) to the subjective, which is a self-serving and self-centered hierarchy of feeling and preference.

Consonant with this position, the next quotation (pp. 167–168) opens by acknowledging difference but soon goes on to enunciate the author's preferences:

> I pay tribute to the diversity and variety that is found in our world where dif-ferent races, ethnic entities and cultures coexist, but I readily establish a dis-tinction between people and between peoples/nations. I cannot argue that Switzerland is as large a country as the United States, nor can I argue that the Bantu have the same ethnological abilities as Californians, because an argu-ment to the contrary would fly in the face of reality. Citizens are equal by law, yet people are not naturally equal. Additionally, if it is accurate that all people deserve the same amount of respect, it is also accurate that hierarchies, prefer-ences and affinities are self-evident. I am French . . . I prefer the French. I am connected to the world in a series of self-centered, hierarchical arrangements, which link me to my family, my *commune*, my workplace, and to my provincial or national community.

The nationalist discourse assumes that the inegalitarian ideology and the racist overtones in differentialist and preferentialist statements, as is the case above, will be easy to infer or uncover. Such an approach provides a (rhetorical) way around direct and obvious reference to race-based inequality. An analogy is used in order to maneuver from inter-individual relations (which is an ideological level where the inegalitarian thesis is acceptable) to interracial relations (a level where the inegalitarian thesis is repudiated). For instance, in response to the sensitive question, "Do you believe in the existence of superior human beings and unequal races?" Le Pen said, "I will reply, without hesitation, in the affir-mative to the first part of your question; yes, there are superior minds and human beings. [But] egalitarianism is a myth and a stupid idea, because there exists undeniable differences between the races" (Le Pen, 1985, p. 8).

The analogy that is established between the "individual" and the "racial" allows for a subtle expression of the inegalitarian thesis. In so doing, nationalists have assumed what may appear to be a neutral stance on the issue of difference. The view held by Le Pen that, "As individuals are unequal (as everybody knows), so are the races," but it is better to use "different" in lieu of "unequal." "Such wording finds its roots as far back as 1945. Since then anti-defamatory rules have prevented the French populace from speaking its mind."

In what follows, Le Pen resorts to differentialism but stops short of overtly endorsing the inegalitarian thesis:

> A tribe out of Africa may boast top-caliber athletes who are yet to be bested by whites; and, in music, African Americans may have given the world the unri-

valed polyphonies of the Negro spirituals. However, in the scientific and technological areas, these groups, have not performed as well as whites. Still, no
people can summarily be categorized as being superior nor as being inferior;
peoples are different and, as a result, their physical and cultural differences must
be respected. (Le Pen, 1985, p. 8)

By using analogy and differentialism, and by substituting race with such nouns
as races, ethnic groups, peoples, tribes, blacks/whites, Americans and Africans,
Le Pen can afford to discard any "summary" statements associated with the
world view which he (actually) represents and champions. A close reading of his
statement shows that although he claims to reject such adjectives as "superior"
and "inferior," the well-known nationalist leader points to a universal hierarchy
of differential racial abilities: that black people are superior in track and field,
and that they have some musical ability cannot be denied; that white people are
superior in science and technology is obvious (physical ability vs. intelligence
and competence).

In sum, the nationalist discourse conveys and legitimizes its xenophobic
views (directed at foreigners) and racist stance (which involves a biologizing
hierarchy of rejected groups) by resting on three, often interconnected, logics:

1. The logics of difference per se: since races and/or peoples have God-
   given, differential characteristics, they do not have to be compared to
   one another or be evaluated in relation to one another.
2. The self-centered logics of preference: according to this mode, the evaluation of (human) groups is only based on "distance," a criterion devised
   by the evaluator. Such evaluation is a concentric (self-centered) arrangement with "me" at the center: me/my family/my friends/my neighbors/my
   village/my commune/my region/my country (nation)/my continent/our
   allies. This evaluation paradigm, which is in essence self-centered, is built
   around four antinomies: near/distant; alike/unlike; homogeneous/hetero-
   geneous; friend/enemy. The preferentialist view sounds like an absolute
   political egocentrism, a view that appears in an ideological context that
   is fundamentally different from nationalism, and which may even be in
   utter opposition to it (e.g., the federalist perspective that expressly rejects
   imperial unitarianism as it is advocated by the nation-state).
3. The logics of eminence or inequality: The schematic superior/inferior
   arrangement is transferred from the inter-individual level to the inter-
   ethnic level. The relativity of innate abilities and talents, as well as their
   uneven allotment among individuals, becomes elaborated into incomplete and relative hierarchies between races and peoples—"blacks are
   better at using their feet, whites their head" (it takes all sorts to make the
   world go round!).

In each of these logics, the analogy of the "individual" and the "racial" is central. To be a racist, these days, is to be able to move spontaneously or tactically (strategically?) from one of these logics to the next, and to take advantage of different systems of images, symbols, and metaphors.

The cross-roads term "identity," both essential and abstruse, gives place to some paradoxes in the field of ideologico-political discourse. The antinomy between individuo-universalism (absolutization of individual) and communitarism (absolutization of an exclusive type of group belonging) mainly underlies most of the conflicts taking the form of the opposition nationalismracism/humanirarism-anti-racism. Three operations characterize the last fifteen years of French racist speeches: the "racialization" of vocabularies of culture, religion, traditions and mentalities; the rhetorical shifting from the inegalitarian argument to the differentialist argument—(Mixophobia is the term suggested for designating the presently dominant form of racism integrated in nationalism, the bible of which being propagated by the national-populist discourse (Le Pen) and legitimated by the differentialism of the New Right)—; the systematic use of a strategy of "retortion," defined as an operation of reusing-appropriation, self-legitimation and dislegitimation of the enemy. When interweaving nationalism and racism, the racist arguments can both justify and contest nationalist doctrines in the name of bioanthropological sciences. An analysis of J. M. Le Pen's recent texts cause to distinguish three logics of racisation: differentialist, preferentialist, and inequalitist.

Key-words: identity/difference, racism, nationalism, communatarism, retortion, differentialist/preferentialist/unegalitarian logics.

Translated by Bernard Pony

NOTES

1. For a study of semantic knowledge and encyclopedic knowledge, see Dan Sperber, *Le Symbolisme en général* (Paris: Hermann, 1974), p. 103.

2. Jean Touchard, *Le Gaullisme, 1940–1969* (Paris: Le Seuil, 1978), p. 57; on tautology, see Chaim Perelman and L. Otbrechts-Tyteca, *Traité de l'argumentation* (Paris: P.U.F. 1958), vol. 1, p. 290: or more definitional statements such as "La France est le pays de la qualité" (France is the land of quality) (Louis Rougier, *La France en marbre blanc* [Génève: Constant Bourquin, 1947]), p. 47.

3. See Alain de Benoist, *La Cause des peuples*, 1982, pp. 55–56.

4. See L. Dumont, *Homo Hierarchicus* (Paris: Gallimard, 1978), p. 235.

5. Ellen Key, *Le siècle de l'enfant* (1900), quoted in J. P. Schmid, *Le maître-camarade et la pédagogie libertaire*, 1936 (Paris: Maspero, 1971), p. 113.

6. Richard Hofstadter, *The American Political Tradition* (New York: A. A. Knopf, 1948), trans. D. Wandby, *Bâtisseurs d'une tradition* (Paris; Seghers, 1966), p. 14.

7. Jean-Marie Le Pen, *Les Français d'abord* (*The French First and Foremost*) (Paris: Carrère/Lafon, 1984), pp. 170–239.

16. Racism and Anti-Racism in Brazil: A Postmodern Perspective

Antonio Sérgio Alfredo Guimarães

ANY STUDY OF RACISM in Brazil must begin by reflecting on the very fact that racism is a taboo subject in Brazil. Brazilians imagine themselves as inhabiting an anti-racist nation, a "racial democracy." This is one of the sources of their pride and, at the same time, conclusive proof of their status as a civilized nation.

This anti-racist claim has deep roots in both factual and literary history. Since the abolition of slavery in 1888, Brazil has not experienced legal segregation or overt racial conflicts. In literature, since the pioneering studies of Freyre in the early 1930s and Pierson in the 1940s, and as late as the 1970s, the professional research of sociologists and anthropologists has reassured both Brazilians and the rest of the world that the Brazilian pattern of race relations is relatively harmonious. In the latest edition of Cashmore's *Dictionary of Race and Ethnic Relations* (1994), the summarization of the entry on Brazil reads:

> In short, Brazil may be described as a society where class distinctions are marked and profound, where class and color overlap but do not coincide, where class often takes precedence over color, and where "race" is a matter of individual description and personal attractiveness rather than of group membership. (p. 9)

AUTHOR'S NOTE: This chapter benefited from a scholarship research fund granted by CAPES/ Fulbright for 1993–94, during which time I worked with the Afro-American Studies Program at Brown University. I am grateful for the comments and suggestions of Michel Agier, Benjamin Bowser, Nadya Castro, Anani Dzidzieyno, and Lucia Lippi.

Antonio S. A. Guimarães, "Racism and Anti-Racism in Brazil," in Benjamin Bowser, ed., *Racism and Anti-Racism in World Perspective*. Thousand Oaks, Calif: Sage Publications, Inc., 208–226, reprinted with the permission of Sage Publications, Inc.

In this chapter, I argue that this interpretation of race and racism in Brazil is due to a certain political and social Western *problématique*, largely supplanted from the 1970s onward, but still present in Brazil. This *problématique* includes the meaning of race and racism. My main concerns are twofold: first, I argue that the language of color and class has always been used in Brazil in a racialized way. Color variations "naturalized" harsh categorical racial inequalities that could disrupt the self-image of a racial democracy. Second, I show the historical, native, and political issue of racism and anti-racism in Brazil. Although my primary sources are social-scientific literary discourses, I refer to the popular, grassroots usage of these discourses as well. Before these issues are addressed, I must briefly reconstitute the idea of "race as a floating signifier" and the changing agenda of anti-racism in the West.

THE CHANGING AGENDA OF WESTERN ANTI-RACISM

The field of scientific inquiry broadly known as "race relations" is of North American inspiration. Social scientists frequently took the U.S. pattern of race relations as a standard for comparison and contrast in their understanding of race in other societies, especially Brazil. Elevated as an archetype, the U.S. pattern molded the formation of race relations studies in Brazil. The U.S. type exhibited a segregationist, conflictive, violent pattern of relations commonly known as *Jim Crow*, which had precise rules of group affiliation based on biological reasoning that defined race. The Brazilian type, in contrast, paraded a sophisticated etiquette of distancing, sharp status, economic differentiation, egalitarian laws, and an ambiguous but very complex system of identification based mainly upon color nuances.

Why were these two systems put in sharp contrast? Why were their functional similarities unnoticed during the dominance of structural-functionalism in sociology? Three main reasons account for this dualism. First, the political agenda of anti-racism itself stressed the legal and formal status of citizenship instead of its actual organization in Brazilian society. This agenda reflected mainly the liberal interests prevailing in the United States, South Africa, and the European colonies. In Brazil, this agenda was advanced by white, middle-class intellectuals who overlooked the popular, black anti-racism of their time, which clashed against the barriers raised by color prejudice. By differentiating prejudice from discrimination and putting the former into the realm of individual privacy, erudite anti-racism operated, functionally, as an ideological effort to obscure real, existing racism.

Second, the definition of *race* as a biological concept concealed both the actual character of color distinctions and its constructed, social, cultural

dynamic in Brazilian society. If race was about concrete biological differences, so
went the reasoning, then color was not a race-related notion, but a subjective
and preferential notion.

Third, the search for objective realism in the social sciences that looked for
definite essences and causal explanations neglected the web of slippery discursive images that concealed racism under class or status metaphors. The symmetry of the language of race and class in Brazil, although noticed, was largely
misinterpreted as a proof of the insignificance of race.

The focus on formal structure and the search for Objectivity were world
trends. In fact, during the aftermath of World War II, anti-racism was too simple
and clear-cut in its aims: to show the unscientific, mythological character of
races and the barbaric, inhuman consequences of racism. Both goals operated in
a field of obvious realism and vivid experience in Europe: the Holocaust and the
demise of *race* as a scientific concept.

The postwar agenda of intellectual anti-racism had two obvious targets: segregation in the United States and apartheid in South Africa, the two remaining
systems of formal state racism. This agenda could be measured concretely by
objective change in formal social organization—the dismantling of formal legal
segregation. This was a convenient logic for white Brazilians that obscured the
historical, assimilationist racism of Brazil.

But Anglo-American elite anti-racism was a no less active participant in
the mystification and idealization of Brazil as a racial paradise. In a recent book
edited by Hellwig (1992), one cannot find a single observation of racial discrimination in Brazil by African American travelers or social scientists from
1910 to 1940, and from 1940 to 1960, the registered evidence is usually
explained by class reasoning.

Perceptions began to change only when civil rights laws were enacted in the
United States. Only then could unequal racial opportunities be seen clearly
operating and reproducing themselves through social mechanisms—schooling,
unemployment, historic poverty, and urban de facto segregation. The changing
perceptions of racial discrimination in the United States influenced both the
Anglo-American perception of Brazil and the agenda of Western anti-racism.
Thereafter, the identification of structural racial inequalities disguised in class or
status terms became an important issue. Brazilian and North American racism
had become much more alike.

North American black nationalism and the feminist revolution of the 1970s
shed another light on the structuring of anti-racist perceptions; the universalist
and assimilationist view of postwar intellectual anti-racists was called racist
because it favored the cultural annihilation of African origins and did not see
the relation between cultural genocide and black subordinate status. The
women's movement stressed the way sexual differences had been historically
"racialized" to naturalize and justify social and cultural hierarchies.

The historical framework of changing perceptions was completed more recently by the massive immigration of Third World people (East Indians, Caribbeans, Latin Americans, Africans, Chinese, Koreans) toward European and North American democracies. Now these immigrants are viewed as "unassimilables": colored strangers presenting sharp religious (Islam), linguistic (Arabic or Spanish speakers), or cultural (Rastafarian) threats to the native white populations. These were the ingredients for awareness of a "new racism" and a new look at race in Brazil. What is now obvious is that when it comes to race,

> culture is conceived along ethnically absolute lines, not as something intrinsically fluid, changing, unstable and dynamic, but as a fixed property of social groups rather than a relational field in which they encounter one another and live out social, historical relationships. When culture is brought in contact with race it is transformed into a pseudo-biological property of communal life. (Gilroy, 1993, p. 24)

THEORIZING RACISM

The changing anti-racist agenda reverberated in the social thinking about racism. In the 1970s, from the point of view of its structures, functions, and mechanisms, race was defined as "a group of people who in a given society are socially defined as different from other groups by virtue of certain real or putative physical differences" (van den Berghe, 1970, p. 10). With this definition, race could no longer be distinguished from gender, ethnicity, or class.

In fact, if one examines any list of characteristics said to define and specify race, one sees that the structural and functional characteristics presented are shared by many other social hierarchies. The theorists of the 1970s, however, could not live with this ambiguity. Most of the time, even when defining race and race relations in a flexible manner, they were not conscious that their definitions encompassed other forms of hierarchy. One exception to this pattern was van den Berghe (1970), who, reflecting on this ambiguity, wrote:

> It became increasingly clear to me over the years that the subject had no claim to a special place in a general theory of society. In other words, race and ethnic relations are not sufficiently different from other types of social relations—nor, conversely, do various types of race and ethnic relations have enough that is exclusively common—to justify special theoretical treatment. (p. 9)

In the 1980s, the ride of poststructuralism that came from France brought self-consciousness to the ambiguous definition of *race*. Deconstructionism in the social sciences favored the widespread use of *race* as a metaphor. The analysis of the discursive field of racism, both old (biological images) and new (cultural differentialism), was based on the same underlying reality disguised as different empirical phenomena.

Again, social scientists remained unable to distinguish racism from discriminations arising from other social hierarchies (gender, class, ethnicity, sexuality). To call racism any kind of discrimination based on "essentialist" or objective constructions transforms racism into a political metaphor.

Delacampagne (1990) provides a good example of this broad reconceptualization of racism and its metaphorical use:

> Racism, in the modern sense of the term, does not necessarily begin as soon as one speaks of the physiological superiority, or cultural superiority, of one race or another; it begins when one makes (alleged) cultural superiority directly and mechanically dependent on (alleged) physiological superiority, that is, when one group *derives* the cultural characteristics of a given group from its biological characteristics. Racism is the reduction of the cultural to the biological, the attempt to make the first dependent on the second. Racism exists wherever it is claimed that a given social status is explained by a given natural characteristic. (pp. 85–86)

The definition is imprecise partially because it reduces the idea of "nature" to a biological notion. But there are many ways to connect social hierarchies to biological differences. In the general sense, "natural" signifies an ahistoric or transhistoric order, devoid of related and particular interests, thus representing only one general attribute of the human species or the divinities. This presumed natural order may rest upon different bases: a theological justification (divine origin), a scientific justification (endodetermined), or a cultural justification (historical necessity).

Consequently, all social hierarchies appeal to natural order, yet they may be justified and rationalized in different ways. The economic order can be justified as a product of individual virtue (the poor are poor because they lack noble sentiments, virtues, and values); by the same token, women are said to occupy subordinate positions due to the characteristics of the female gender, and Africans or African descendants were enslaved or kept in an inferior position because their race was thought to be intellectually and morally incapable of civilization. In each case, when a natural order limits social formations, systems of rigid and inescapable hierarchies emerge. But note that in the three cases outlined, a "scientific" theory of nature (biology and genetics) was used only in the latter two cases.

This process of naturalization seems to be a necessary trait of all social hierarchies. As Guillaumin (1992) observes,

> the ideological implication of the idea of nature (and natural groups) cannot be abolished from social relations in which they occupy a central place. Ideologically hidden (since ideology lurks under "evidence"), the "natural" form,

whether it is common sense or institutionalized practice, is one of the main technical means used by the dominant groups in their relations with subordinate groups. (p. 192)

Certainly, one can use racism as a metaphor for any type of naturalization resulting from systematic discriminatory practices. This, however, is a loose usage of the term, because race could be empirically absent but lending its figurative meaning to the discriminatory discourse. My presumption is that if one speaks of some discriminatory practices as sexism, class discrimination, or ethnism, that is because race is subsumed under other differences or is only a trope of irreducible differences. With this new thinking about race, the more complicated and subtle imbedding of race in class and cultural differences in Brazil comes under new attention. To use Gates's (1985) words:

Race has become a trope of ultimate, irreducible difference between cultures, linguistic groups, or adherents of specific belief systems which—more often than not—also have fundamentally opposed economic interests. Race is the ultimate trope of difference because it is so very arbitrary in its application. (p. 5)

RACE AND COLOR

In the literature relating to race relations in Brazil, as Wade (1993) points out, "the distinction between appearance and ancestry is often left unclarified and made to parallel a distinction between the insignificance and the significance of 'race' " (p. 28). In contrast to the United States, races in Brazil are not defined by the rule that there is no clear rule of biological descendance for belonging to a racial group, but rather, classifications of physical appearance and an "interplay between a variety of achieved and ascribed statuses" (Harris, 1974). This would mean that there are no racial groups in Brazil, only "groups of color" (Degler, 1991, p. 103).

Sociologists widely accepted the idea that, in Brazil and in Latin America in general, there was no racial prejudice, just "color prejudice." Azevedo (1955) writes, "Since color and somatic traits function, to a great degree, as symbols of status, resistance to inter-marriage suggests both class and race prejudice, or better, color prejudice" (p. 90). Wright (1990) is even more explicit in his discussion of Venezuela: "But Venezuelans consider only those individuals with black skin as black. Color rather than race—appearance rather than origin—play far more important roles in influencing the Venezuelans' perceptions of individuals" (p. 3).

As Fernandes (1965) points out, the idea of color prejudice is better used as a native's notion, first conceptualized by the Frente Negra Brasileira (Black Brazilian Front) in 1940. The group referred to the peculiar type of racial discrimination that oppresses Brazilian blacks, one wherein color-viewed as a spontaneous, natural fact—and not race—viewed as an artificial, abstract, scientific concept—is decisive.

The conception of color as natural phenomenon rests on the pretense that physical appearance and phenotypical traits are neutral, objective, biological facts. But that is just the way in which in Brazil, color is a figure for race. When scholars incorporate in their discourse color as the criterion for constituting "objective" groups, they refuse to perceive Brazilian racism. Their conclusion is superficial and formalistic. Without history and clear rules of descendance, there would be no races, just spontaneous groups of color.

But there is nothing spontaneously natural about phenotypical traits or color. Gates (1986) says,

> It takes little reflection, however, to recognize that these pseudoscientific categories are themselves figures. Who has seen a black or red person, a white, yellow or brown [person]? These terms are arbitrary constructs, not reports of reality. But language is not only the medium of this often insidious tendency; it is the sign. Current language use signifies the difference between cultures and their possession of power, spelling out the distance between subordinate and superordinate, between bondsman and lord in terms of their "race." (p. 6)

This position is strengthened by the argument that nothing in skin color, hair type, width of nose, or thickness of lips is more naturally visible or discriminating than other traits, such as foot size, height, eye color, or any other physical trait. Such traits have meaning merely within a preexisting ideology (an ideology that creates the facts it organizes), and only because of this do they function as meaningful classifications or criteria.

In sum, a person can only have a color and be classified in a color group if an ideology exists in which the color of people has meaning. That is, people do not have any color except within racial ideologies, *stricto sensu*.

RACISM IN A SOUTH AMERICAN WAY

What is the ideology that particularizes racism in Brazil? The distinctiveness of Brazilian racism, or Latin American racism in general, comes from the fact that the Brazilian nationhood was not formed, or "imagined" to use Anderson's (1992) metaphor, as a community of ethnic, dissimilar individuals coming from all parts of Europe, as was the United States. Brazil is an amalgam of Creoles from different ethnic and racial backgrounds whose race and ethnicity were lost to gain Brazilian nationhood. Brazil generously offered a comfortable penumbra to hang over everyone's ancestry. Color remained the only trace of race, or better, became its coded name. Colonial racism, founded upon the idea of the ethnic purity of white settlers or conquerors, gave way after independence to the idea of mixed-blooded, mestizo nations (Skidmore, 1979; Wade, 1993; Wright, 1990), or to a *nação morena* in the Brazilian case, whose citizenship was granted by place of birth, not by ancestry.

Of course the United States or South Africa, for example, presents a similar place-of-birth citizenship; however, they have developed an image of themselves more as a European transplantation (the ethnic melting pot) than a multirace mixture. Their extreme sense of racial community has corresponded with nationality based upon "mixophobia"—the aversion toward racial mixture, to use Taguieff's (1987) term. To understand it further, one must comprehend how whiteness is defined in Brazil.

The other main characteristic of race relations in Latin America is the existence of an oligarchical order in which race (color), status, and class are intimately linked. Oboter (1995) writes:

> As a result of extensive miscegenation throughout the colonies, racial classifications, social status, and honor evolved into a hierarchical arrangement that Lipschütz has called a "pigmentocracy." As Ramón Gutiérrez has described, this was a racial system whereby whiter skin was directly related to higher social status and honor whereas darker skin was associated both with "the physical labor of slaves and tributary indians" and, visually, with "the infamy of the conquered." The Spanish notion of *pureza de sangre*, or purity of blood, was thus imbedded in the New World aristocracy's understanding of the inter-related concepts of race, social status, and honor. (p. 28)

In Brazil, this system of hierarchy is layered with gradations of prestige, where social class (occupation and income), family origin, color, and formal education are buttressed by a dichotomy expressed as highborn/rabble and elite/masses. But the hierarchy and the dichotomies are founded on the racial dichotomy of white/black, which has sustained the slavocratic order for three centuries.

Da Costa (1988) recognizes this origin of color prejudice in Brazil when she writes about the Second Empire: "Racial prejudice served to maintain and legitimize the distance between a world of privileges and rights and one of deprivation and duties" (p. 137). The nineteenth-century liberal doctrine that held that the poor were poor because they were inferior found legitimacy in Brazil in the cultural destruction of Africans by European social customs and the conditions of poverty and cultural unpreparedness of free blacks and mestiços. The servile condition of slaves, like the poverty and misery of free blacks and mestiços, was taken as a sign of racial inferiority.

As Da Costa (1988), Fernandes (1965), and others have so well demonstrated, the entire Brazilian elite (including the Abolitionists) was prisoner to this logic, which justified social inequalities. For liberals, slavery was only an obstacle to their ideas. They did not have a critical reflection on race relations and did not care about the condition of blacks after Abolition. The admission of universal human equality was placed on the level of theory (dogma), beyond any contact with, or commitment to, the interests of real people. As today, this theory coexisted with a great social distance and a sense of superiority in relation to blacks, mulattos, and the general populace.

In fact, the idea of color, despite being affected by class hierarchies (thus, "money whitens," as does education), is founded upon a peculiar notion of race. This notion revolves around the dichotomy of whiteness/blackness just as in the Anglo-Saxon world. This working definition is peculiar in terms of its definition of "whiteness," that is, the rule that defines group belonging. In Brazil, whiteness was not formed through the exclusive ethnic melting pot of European people, as in the United States (Lewis, in press; Oboler, 1995; Omi and Winant, 1986); on the contrary, "whiteness" absorbed mixed-race, tight mulattos who could exhibit the dominant symbols of Europeans: a Christian upbringing and Portuguese literacy. By extension, the rules of belonging minimized the black pole of this dichotomy, thereby separating mestiços from blacks. The meaning of the word *black*, therefore, crystallized the absolutely different, the non-European. By this meaning, a real black could not be a complete Christian (should exhibit some syncretic animist beliefs) or a cultivated man (black women were not even considered in the identification reasoning). Therefore, in Brazil, only those with very dark skin suffer the same degree of prejudice and discrimination as black Africans. Those with varying degrees of mestiçagem may enjoy, according to their degree of whiteness (both chromatic and cultural, as white is a feature of Europeanness), some of the privileges reserved for whites.

Dzidzienyo (1979) was perhaps the first to note this peculiarity of race relations in Brazil. Defining the "hallmark of the much-vaunted Brazilian 'racial democracy' " was

> the bias that white is best and black is worst and therefore the nearer one is to white, the better. The hold which this view has on Brazilian society is all pervasive and embraces a whole range of stereotypes, role-playing, job opportunities, life-styles, and, what is even more important, it serves as the corner-stone of the closely-observed "etiquette" of race relations in Brazil. (p. 3)

Corroborating Dzidzienyo's thesis, Cleveland Donald Jr., a black American journalist visiting Brazil in 1972, noted, "In fact, it does not matter that the Brazilian mulatto is not a 'Negro'; far more important is the fact that he is never White" (cited in Hettwig, 1992, p. 212).

CHANGING PATTERNS OF RACISM IN BRAZIL

Any analysis of Brazilian racism Must consider at least three major historical processes: the process of nation formation; the intermingling of race in the discursive, ideological field with the other major social hierarchies of class, status, and gender; and the transformations of the socioeconomic order and its regional effects.

A discussion of nationhood is of foremost importance because in Brazil, as suggested before, the rules of nation-belonging were intended to subsume and suppress ethnic, racial, and community feelings. The Brazilian nation was first thought of as culturally uniform in terms of religion, race, ethnicity, and language. In this idea of nation, Brazilian racism could only be characterized by a fear of others, making it necessary to negate others' differences, however they may be defined (Taguieff, 1987, p. 29).

But negation of differences does not mean that universal, enlightened racism is necessarily a hidden racism, one that is ashamed to say its name. On the contrary, in the beginning of the twentieth century, Brazilian fear of others was still explicit. The fundamental grounding of Brazilian racialism at this time rested upon a peculiar adaptation of scientific racism. If every racism has a particular history, whitening is what specifies Brazil's. According to Skidmore (1993), this doctrine was based

> on the assumption of white superiority—sometimes muted by leaving open the question of how "innate" inferiority might be, and using the euphemisms "more advanced" and "less advanced" races. But to this assumption were added two more. First, the black population was becoming progressively less numerous than the white for reasons which included a supposedly lower birth rate, higher incidence of disease, and social disorganization. Second, miscegenation was "naturally" producing a lighter population, in part because whiter genes were stronger and in part because people chose partners lighter than themselves. (pp. 64–65)

In summary, the particularity of Brazilian racialism resided in the importation of racist theories from Europe, excluding two important conceptions—"the innateness of racial differences and the degeneracy of mixed bloods—in order to formulate their own solution to the 'Negro problem' " (Skidmore, 1993, p. 77). White blood was thought to purify, dilute, and exterminate black blood, thus opening the possibility for mestiços to elevate themselves to a civilized state. Whitening was the response of a wounded national pride assaulted by doubts and qualms about its industrial and economic genius. It was a way to rationalize the feelings of racial and cultural inferiority suggested by scientific racism and the geographical determinism of the nineteenth century.

Freyre, Pierson, and the whole project of social anthropology represented a blow against this shameless racism. Although I do not intend to discuss the academic merits or pitfalls of these works, I do examine some of their ideas in the perspective of a changing nationhood.

When Pierson (1942), Azevedo (1955), and others conducted their research, the second Brazilian-born generations of Italian, Spanish, German, and Japanese immigrants were climbing the social and economic ladder of the southern states. São Paulo would become the major industrial city in Latin America. The old stock of Brazilians, mainly from the sertão, were emigrating in large numbers to São Paulo and entering subordinate positions in the labor market. The traditionally imagined Brazilian nationality was, as a result, under profound stress. This stress came from the fact that the "new Creoles" (the native-born children of recent immigrants) did not present the same cultural uniformities as the older ones and maintained some sense of community and ethnic belonging. This novelty was far more important because these new Brazilians were situated in the consolidated, dynamic, industrial and agricultural areas of southern and southeastern Brazil, toward which the cultural national axis of the country was turning—toward Rio de Janeiro, São Paulo, and Rio Grande do Sul.

The historic cultural areas of Bahia, Pernambuco, and Minas Gerais remained almost untouched in their racial composition by the new wave of immigration (Merrick and Graham, 1979; Skidmore, 1993). Freyre's work and the social anthropology of the 1940s and 1950s were done in Pernambuco and Bahia, as part of the reaction of established Brazilianhood to the cultural challenge represented by the new economic axis of São Paulo. In this sense, racial democracy as reinterpreted by the cultural anthropology of Freyre (1938) can be said to be a founding myth of a rapidly transformed nation.

It would be an error, however, to think that the culturalist thought of the mid-twentieth century—after Freyre and Pierson—changed the racist assumptions of whitening. Actually, the whitening thesis was adapted to the basic tenets of social anthropology and came to signify the mobility of mestiços within the social hierarchy. On the one side, whitening was an empirical statement of fact, an upward mobility track followed by blacks; on the other side, it presupposed a racist view of blackness to which the theory remained silent and acritical.

The Eurocentric perspective of the culturalist version of whitening can be found in Freyre (1938), Pierson (1942), Azevedo (1955), and all the most prominent and progressive Brazilian anthropologists of the 1950s:

> Through mixing and other socio-biological factors, the darker group, of black phenotype, is slowly being absorbed in the ethnic caldron; the white group is growing faster and the mestiços increase in numbers, registered in statistics as *pardos* (brown), to be ultimately submerged, through mixing, by the group predominantly of European heritage. (Azevedo, 1955, p. 51)

Whitening hereafter signified the capacity of Brazil (defined either as an extension of Europe or as a country wherein a new race was born) to absorb and integrate mestiços and blacks. This capacity implicitly requires a willingness of people of color to repudiate their African or indigenous ancestry. Thus, whitening and racial democracy are, in fact, concepts of a new racialist discourse. The racist substance to these concepts resides in the idea, at times implicit, that there are three founding races of Brazilian nationality that have made different contributions and have qualitatively different cultural potential. The color of people, like their customs, is an index of the positive or negative value of these races. At the core of this thought is the supposition that the mark of color is indelible not only because it signals inferior ancestry, but also because it symbolizes the presumed inferiority of this race.

It also means, implicitly, a very definitive notion of Brazilianness. Writing about the colored elites in Bahia, a city where 80 percent of the population has a census-declared African ancestry, Azevedo (1955) successively says:

> Because of its architecture and its urban style, its antiquity, and its moderate rhythm of life, Bahia is considered today Brazil's most European city. (p. 25)

> Bahia considers itself one of the most Brazilian communities in the whole country by virtue of its reduced number of foreigners and by virtue of being constituted by the original elements who settled in Brazil. (p. 38)

> No other Brazilian state which has a large black population shows such a high degree of racial mixture (mestiçagem) as Bahia. This demonstrates that Bahia is probably the most important Euro-African ethnic melting pot in Brazil. (p. 48)

In these passages, the discursive slippage between Europeanness, Brazilianness, and mestiçagem clearly reveals the "European" character of this imagined nationhood, operating through the Creolization of Europeanness by the whitening of mestiçagem.

These same passages, which uncover a racialized nationhood—typical of the northeastern elites of Brazil—also unravel the strains to this nationhood brought by the European immigrant wave of 1890 to 1920, when thousands of Italians, Spaniards, Portuguese, Germans, and Japanese settlers entered the southern states in a partially official policy of whitening.

The whiteness produced by the southern melting pot is very different from the consolidated, colonial melting pot Azevedo (1955) refers to. The main difference lies in the fact that those whites did in truth mix in the Brazilian middle class and, to a much lesser degree, the working classes. The *paulista* (from São Paulo) working class was racially transformed through the absorption of northeastern immigrants, mainly blacks and mestiços (Andrews, 1991). Indeed, the rapid upward mobility of European immigrants is testimony to the relative lenience of Brazilian society toward Europeans, in contrast to the subordinate assimilation of Africans.

Japanese descendants offer, in this respect, an extremely interesting case. Although placed outside the imagery of Brazilianness (they are still called *nisei*), they were not assimilated into the white-black status gradient inherited from slavery but entered directly into the class gradient of the competitive order. As a result, they found enough leeway and arranged sufficient cultural and economic capital to make a better journey through the Brazilian society than those of African descent.

The new ethnic communities of immigrant descendants who, at first, saw and were seen by Brazilians (the traditional) as foreigners were absorbed into the Brazilian mainstream. They were also incorporated into the southern Brazilian elites and ended up redefining the racialized others, mainly working-class or underclass "traditional Brazilians," as *baianos* (Bahians) and *nordestinos* (northeasterners). Baianos and nordestinos are black or mixedrace Brazilians from the working class; they have become the special targets of Brazil's new racism.

THEORIZING ABOUT RACISM AND ANTI-RACISM IN BRAZIL

There is something very special in this racism that comes also from the peculiar way Brazilianness is imagined. As Anderson (1992) argues, the nation in Latin America was mainly defined by "substantial landowners, allied with somewhat smaller number of merchants, and various types of professionals (lawyers, military men, local and provincial functionnaires)" (p. 48). Despite the fact that all Brazilians did not gain economically, the potential for conflict was averted by elite actions. This was done by incorporating mixed-race blacks and Native Americans more "as potential recruits to mixedness" (Wade, 1993, p. 3) than as full citizens. In fact, mixed-race blacks and Native Americans were excluded from the beginning through the very process of their emancipation, as an underclass.

Brazilian racism has a pre-republican origin. Reis (1993) shows how Africans in the mid-nineteenth century, manumitted or not, were discriminated against in Bahia and forced back to rural areas or to Africa. Africans were the first "other," the absolute different, and when there were no Africans left but Creoles, black became a figure for Africanness.

This holds true for the upper classes and the lower classes alike. In the popular usages of Brazilianness, mainly in the soccer subculture, Creoles who do not fit the ideal mixed-race pattern of *morenidade* are called *negão* if black or *alenão* (German) or *galego* (Galician) if white. This apparent chromatic symmetry of black and white applied by and for poor people is reversed in the chromatotogy of status, whereby they distinguish between a *branco fino* (those of pure European lineage) and a *branco da terra*, the mixed-Creole white (Azevedo, 1955; Pierson, 1942), thereby stressing the importance of being European.

To mark the origins of this racism, Fernandes (1965) calls it the "slave metamorphosis," to mean how black, the skin color, was used from Abolition onward as a signifier for subordinate, underclass Brazilians.

Actually, racism in Brazil has been played mainly through the contradictory game of a broadly defined citizenship, guaranteed by formal juridical rights, on the one side, but largely ignored, not enforced, and structurally limited by poverty and everyday state violence, on the other side. Racism is perpetrated through the curtailment of citizenship and the social distance created by huge economic, cultural, and social inequalities separating blacks from whites, poor from well-to-do, north from south.

Elites in Brazil, encompassing landowners, capitalists, intellectuals, and middle classes, represent a factual, broad compromise between wild exploitation and *bonne conscience*. On one side, elites can boast a radical, modern legislation; on the other side, they can be sure the sophisticated laws are highly inoperative. Universal franchise, for example, until recently (1988) was limited to literate people, which represented disenfranchisement for the black illiterate mass. Still another example: racism was first considered a misdemeanor by a Congressional Act of 1951 (Lei Afonso Arinos, no. 1390); in 1988, as a result of lobbying by the black movement, the new democratic constitution made racism a felony. To this date, however, nobody has been sentenced on a racist charge. On the contrary, victims' attorneys opt for charges that stand a better chance for winning the case (Guimarães, 1994). This is the current Brazilian pattern of racism, which does not show its face and hides behind enlightened universalism, masking itself as anti-racism and denying the full presence of the other, the African Brazilian or the Native Brazilian.

How does anti-racism unmask a racism that does not recognize itself as racism, that naturalizes the other through chromatic metaphors, regionalism, and class etiquette?

Marxist thought, which strongly influenced the doctrines and actions of the emerging Brazilian middle class in the 1960s, 1970s, and 1980s, did nothing to reverse this status quo. On the contrary, Marxist insistence that races are nonexistent and color is an epiphenomenon merely gave racial democracy a socialist bent. Or rather, transformed it into an ideal to be achieved only through class struggle. Marxist thought adapted very well to the idea of capitalism (here a trope for Europeanness) as a civilizing force, to which the people of the entire world would naturally have to submit before reaching the socialist stage. Even when the inherent racism of these cultural theories and refined color classifications (which substitute bipolar classification) is recognized, the counter-argument remains that in Brazil racism is "milder." Its mildness is suggested by the relative conformity of the black population and the absence of legal mechanisms to thwart inequality and discrimination.

In a certain sense, the ideal of racial democracy is really a founding myth of Brazilian nationality and can only be denounced as myth, as broken promises. In fact, the studies by Andrews (1992), Castro and Guimarães (1993), Hasenbalg (1979), Lovell (1989), N. Silva (1980), P. C. Silva (1993), Telles (1992), and others unmask the mildness of Brazilian racial democracy. They show the profound inequalities that separate blacks from other groups. They reveal a de facto job, residential, and educational segregation between white and non-white.

A critical challenge for those who struggle against racism in Brazil is to show not only inequalities, but their daily reproduction by institutions of production (public and private enterprises), institutions of public order (the police, the judicial and correctional systems), and educational and health care institutions. This is an important way through which one can hope to displace the centenarian, invisible veil that wraps the dichotomies of elite/masses and white/black in Brazilian society.

For the African Brazilian population, those who call themselves *negroes* (blacks), anti-racism must mean first the admission of race; that is, a perception of themselves—the racialized others—as the racialized "we." It means the reconstruction of the self, drawing upon African heritage—the Afro-Brazilian culture of *candomblé, capoieira*, and *afoxés*, but also upon the cultural and political reservoir of the "Black Atlantic" legacy—the civil rights movement in the United States, the Caribbean cultural renaissance, and the fight against apartheid in South Africa.

The new cultural forms of the black movement in Latin America and Brazil (Agier, 1993; Agier and Carvalho, 1992; Wade, 1993) have stressed the process of black reidentification in ethnic terms. It seems that only a racialized discourse can sustain a sense of pride, dignity, and self-reliance, largely destroyed by a century of invisible, universalist, enlightened racism. This ethnic resurgence is constructed upon a land to be retrieved, such as the former Maroon territories, or the transformation, largely symbolic, of poor urban areas into black neighborhoods or new Maroons—*quilombos*. Second, there is need for the culture to redeem and repurify, in contact with an imaginary Africa, the Africa brought and maintained as memory.

This concrete, popular agenda of anti-racism is still fiercely combatted by Brazilian nationalists, all over the political spectrum, who believe in the official, mythological anti-racism of Brazil. They are very susceptible to what they call the reverse racism of black organizations, or the importation of foreign categories and feelings. In truth, nothing harms the Brazilian ideal of assimilation more than the cultivation of differences. Even within the black movement, one can hear dissident views, dissenting against a narrow definition of blackness or the essentialism involved in any ethnic formation.

Trapped at the crossroads of different types of racism, Latin American intellectuals, mainly those who view themselves through European lenses, must begin to realize that racism does not exist outside a particular history. There is no absolute, metahistorical concept of race or racism. By exploring the linkages between racism and anti-racism in the Brazilian context and situating them in the broader world system, one can hope to contribute to rescuing Brazilian race relations from its myths. That is the only way Latin American anti-racists can fight not others' but their own racism.

REFERENCES

Agier, M. (1993). "Ilê Aiyê: A invenção do mundo negro." Unpublished manuscript.

Agier, M., and M. R. Carvalho. (1992, November 12–13). "Nation, race, culture: La trajectoire des mouvements noir et indigène dans la societé brésilienne." Presented at the meeting "Nation, État, Ethnicité," Association des Chercheurs de Politique Africaine, Centre d'Études d' Afrique Noire, Bordeaux, France.

Anderson, B. (1992). *Imagined communities*. London: Verso.

Andrews, G. (1991). *Blacks and Whites in São Paulo, Brazil, 1899–1988*. Madison: University of Wisconsin Press.

Andres, G. R. (1992). "Desigualdade racial no Brasil e nos Estados Unidos: Uma comparção estatística." *Estudos Afro-Asiáticos* 22: 47–84.

Azevedo, T. (1955). *As elites de cor, um estudo de ascenso social*. São Paulo: Cia Editora Nacional.

Cashmore, E. (1994). *Dictionary of Race and Ethnic Relations*. 3rd ed. London: Routledge.

Castro, N. G., and J. A. Guimarães. (1993). "Desigualdades raciais no mercado e nos locais de trabalho." *Estudos Afro-Asiáticos* 24: 23–60.

Da Costa, E. V. (1988). *The Brazilian Empire: Myths and Histories*. Belmont, Calif.: Wadsworth.

Degler, C. N. (1991). *Neither Black Nor White*. Madison: University of Wisconisn.

Delacampagne. (1990). "Racism and the West: From Praxis to Logos." In D. T. Goldberg (Ed.), *Anatomy of Racism* (pp. 85–86). Minneapolis: University Minnesota Press.

Dzidzienyo, A. (1979). *The position of Blacks in Brazilian society*. London: Minority Rights Group.

Fernandes, R. (1965). *A inegração do negro na sociedade de classes*. 2 vols. São Paulo: Cia Editora Nacional.

Freyre, G. (1938). *Casa grande & senzala: Formação da família brasileira sob o regime da economia patriarcal*. Rio de Janeiro: Schmidt.

Gates, H. L., Jr. (1985). "Editor's introduction: Writing 'Race' and the Difference It Makes." In H. L. Gates Jr., ed., *Race, Writing, and Difference* (pp. 1–20). Chicago: University of Chicago Press.

Gilroy, P. (1993). *Small Acts: Thoughts on the Politics of Black Cultures*. London: Serpent's Tail.

Guillaumin, C. (1992). *"Race et nature," sexe, race et pratique du pouvoir: L'idée de nature*. Paris: Côté-Femmes Éditions.

Guimarães, J. A. (1994). *Racial Conflicts in Brazilian Law*. Providence, R.I.: Brown University, Afro-American Studies Program.

Harris, M. (1974). *Patterns of races in the Americas*. New York: Norton.

Hasenbalg, C. (1979). *Discriminação e desigualdades raciais no Brasil*. Rio de Janeiro: Gral.

Hellwig, D. J. (ed.). (1992). *African American Reflections on Brazil's Racial Paradise*. Philadelphia: Temple University.

Lewis, E. (in press). "Race, the State and Social Construction: The Multiple Meanings of Race in the Twentieth-Century." In S. I. Kutler (ed.), *The Encyclopedia of the United States in the Twentieth Century*. New York: Scribner.

Lovell, P. (1989). "Income and Racial Inequality in Brazil." Unpublished doctoral dissertation, University of Florida.

Merrick, T., and D. Graham. (1979). *Population and Economic Development in Brazil*. Baltimore: Johns Hopkins University Press.

Oboler, S. (1995). *Ethnic Labels, Latino Lives: Identity and the Politics of Re-presentation*. Minneapolis: University of Minnesota Press.

Omi, M., and H. Winant. (1986). *Racial Formation in the United States, from the 1960's to the 1980's*. London: Routledge.

Pierson, D. (1942). *Negroes in Brazil: A Study of Race Contact in Bahia*. Chicago: University of Chicago Press.

Reis, J. I. (1993). "A greve negra de 1857 na Bahia." *Revista USP* 18: 8–29.

Silva, N. (1980). "O preço da cor: Diferenciais raciais na distribuiçao de renda no Brasil." *Pesquisa e Planejamento Econômico* 10, no. 1: 21–44.

Silva, P. C. (1993). "Negros à luz dos fornos: Representações do trabalho e da cor entre metalugicos da moderna indústria baiana." Master's thesis, Universidade Federal da Bahia, Salvador.

Skidmore, T. (1993). *White into Black*. Durham, NC: Duke University Press.

Taguieff, P. A. (1987). *La force du préjugé: Essai sur le racisme et ses doubles*. Paris: Gallimard.

Telles, E. (1992). "Residential Segregation by Skin Color in Brazil." *American Sociological Review* 57: 186–97.

Van den Berghe, P. (1970). *Race and Ethnicity*. New York: Basic Books.

Wade, P. (1993). *Blackness and Race Mixture: The Dynamics of Racial Identity in Colombia*. Baltimore: Johns Hopkins University Press.

———. (1994). "Race, Nature and Culture." *Man (N.S.)* 281: 17–34.

Wright, W. R. (1990). *Café con Leche: Race, Class, and National Image in Venezuela*. Austin: University of Texas Press.

17. Reflections on the Comparative History and Sociology of Racism

George M. Fredrickson

HISTORIANS WHO DEAL WITH black-white relations in the United States often refer to "racism" but rarely do they define the term precisely or develop a theoretical understanding of what it refers to that deeply affects their treatment of such matters as slavery, segregation, or black urbanization. Some use the word only when referring to a very specific set of doctrines that arose in the nineteenth century and were discredited in the mid-twentieth, while others apply it casually and loosely to everything that is said and done when one group of people devalues and mistreats another that it believes to be genetically different from itself. For some purposes, perhaps, nothing much is lost by inattention or lack of analytical rigor. But the historian of comparative race relations needs sharper tools and stronger conceptualizations; otherwise he or she is likely to find a vague and undifferentiated attitudinal racism almost everywhere or a pure doctrinal racism in very few places for limited periods. It is high time that historians devoted the same intense effort to understanding race as a transnational social and historical phenomenon that they have sometimes applied to class, gender, and nationalism. In my view, the term racism refers to something real, significant, and devilishly complex that needs to be conceptualized and analyzed if we are to comprehend some central aspects of American and world history.

When sociologists and historians first wrote about racism in the period between World War II and the 1960s, they generally meant an explicit ideology

George M. Fredrickson, "Reflections on the Comparative History and Sociology of Racism," in *American Studies in Southern Africa: Symposium Proceedings*, unpublished. This is a condensed version of "Understanding Racism: Reflections of a Comparative History," in *The Comparative Imagination* (Berkeley and Los Angeles: University of California Press, 1998), pp. 77–87.

331

based on the belief that population groups that could be distinguished from each other by physical appearance or ethnic descent were different and unequal in genetically determined mental and behavioral capabilities. As recently as 1967, for example, the British sociologist Michael Banton defined racism as "the doctrine that a man's behavior is determined by stable inherited characteristics deriving from separate racial stocks having distinctive attributes and usually considered to stand to one another in relations of superiority and inferiority."[1]

Such a doctrine or ideology could serve to justify or rationalize a range of policies, depending on the circumstances and aims of the racializing group. The principal possibilities were the subordination and unequal segregation of the "others," their exclusion or expulsion from a community or nation, or, in the most extreme case, their physical annihilation. Hitler's view of the Jews and what should be done with them, the southern white supremacist's conception of the African American's place in nature and society, and the notions that underlay the "White Australia" policy were obvious and unambiguous examples of racism in this strict sense.

Since the 1960s, however, there has been a tendency to apply the term to attitudes and practices viewed as objectively harmful to the interests and aspirations of people previously designated as racially inferior, even though an explicit doctrine of innate racial differences is no longer being invoked as a rationale. Where groups defined as racially distinct remain unequal in rights or opportunities, members of underprivileged groups and their champions thus have a tendency to describe the attitudes and practices that sustain this inequality as "racist," even though claims of genetic superiority and inferiority are no longer being made. This view implies that a covert and implicit racism continues to operate after the intellectual foundations of a racist view of the world have been discredited. For the historian, there is the additional problem of trying to deal with patterns of discrimination that emerged *before* doctrinal or ideological racism was articulated by Western ethnological thinkers. In an early effort to grapple with this problem, I made a distinction between ideological and "societal" racism, with the latter referring to practices that treated a subaltern group as if it were inherently inferior to the socially dominant group, even though an explicit doctrine of innate racial differences had not yet been promulgated and widely accepted.[2]

What we need for comparative historical analysis is a theoretical understanding of racism that is broad enough to take account of contemporary usage and also covers past discriminatory practices that were not motivated or justified by classic racist doctrine. But in seeking such breadth we must be careful to avoid giving credence to view that racism is an essential or the primordial human response to diversity, something that inevitably takes place when groups that *we* would define as racially different come into contact. It must be remembered that we are doing the defining and that the historical record shows that the designations or categories we are using did not always exist and were in fact constructed or invented by our ancestors. I agree with historian Barbara Fields that "race" and all the ideas and attitudes associated with it are the product of social contexts that change over time and not the reflection of some "transhistorical" impulse that is rooted in objective human differences. But Fields and other historians who argue that "class" is real and "race" is not are captives of a theory of social relationships that arbitrarily privileges one form of social inequality over others. If class is defined very loosely as "the inequality of human beings from the standpoint of social power," there is no disagreement, although it is hard to make analytical use of such an all-encompassing concept. Problems emerge when Fields invokes "the more rigorous Marxian definition involving social relations of production." Is it really true, as she claims, that class in this sense "can assert itself independently of people's consciousness" while race cannot?³ People certainly do differ in economic power and position, but such differences have literally no meaning until they enter people's consciousness and are interpreted in some fashion. The specifically Marxist conception of two essential and perpetually antagonistic classes is not a necessary or purely logical deduction from the realization of economic inequality in a capitalist society. There could be more than two essential classes, and classes do not have to be viewed as inevitably at war. Class is as much a historical and social construct as race, which also builds on differences that clearly exist but are not meaningful until interpreted in some way.

Besides differing in their relation to the means of production or to the market, people really do differ in physical characteristics, immediate or remote ancestry, and inherited cultural traits. Race emerges from the interpretation or construction of such non-economic differences to create a sense of group solidarity or peoplehood that can provide the basis for a claim of dominance or privilege over those considered outside of the group. If class refers to the universal fact that all societies have economies, race arises from the equally pervasive fact that all human beings have a sense of family or kinship. The construction of race is fundamentally different from the making of class only if one accepts a particular philosophy or metaphysic of history that cannot be empirically verified and fails to account for much of the history of human inequality. Although race and class are both historical inventions—creative interpretations of alternative types of human differences—it would be a mistake to infer that, once invented, they do not become durable and enormously influential ways of perceiving the world. The construction of class may lead to class conflict, revolution, and socialist societies. The construction of race may lead to secession in defense of racial slavery, the creation of social orders based on racial caste, or to gas ovens for stigmatized peoples.

A good point of departure for understanding the relationship of race and class is Max Weber's writings on social hierarchy as a general phenomenon and stratification based on ethnicity or race as a special case. For Weber, "status," or the unequal assignment of honor and prestige to individuals or groups, may vary independently from "class," which he defines precisely as the economic advantage or disadvantage that comes from objective relationships to a capitalistic market. Status may be based on aristocratic de.scent or the ability to maintain a prestigious lifestyle, but in multiethnic societies it can also be derived simply from membership in an ethnic or racial group that has a history of being dominant over other groups.[4]

Using Weber's concept of "ethnic status" to get at the nature of racism allows us to sidestep the debate on the difference between race and ethnicity. As Donald L. Horowitz has argued persuasively, in a broad-ranging comparative study of "ethnic conflict," the designation of people by skin color and the mistreatment of them on that basis has no special features that would distinguish it in any definitive theoretical way from group domination based on religion, culture, or the simple belief that some people have defective ancestry. It is only because Western culture has developed the peculiar notion that people can change religion or culture and be assimilated into a group other than the one in which they were born that the distinction has arisen. But even in the West, the ascription of ethnic status has often been derived from something other than skin color or reputed non-white ancestry. Northern Ireland has most, if not all, of the characteristics of what British sociologist John Rex calls a "race relations situation." A Catholic could certainly convert to Protestantism, but it is not only extremely unlikely that he would do so, but also doubtful whether he could thereby win full acceptance into the Protestant community. The key element in ethnicity is descent, and ethnic status emerges when a group of people with a real or fictive common ancestry assert their dominance over those who are believed to be of a different and inferior ancestry. The Burakhumin of Japan are descendents of a caste that once engaged in occupations that other Japanese considered unclean or impure. They do not differ in any apparent way in phenotype or culture from other Japanese; but the discrimination against them, on grounds of descent alone, closely resembles the color discrimination of Western societies. One might conclude, therefore, that racism, or something so much like it as to be virtually indistinguishable, has no essential relation to skin color or other obvious physical characteristics and need not even be based on significant cultural differences. The essential element is the belief, however justified or rationalized, in the critical importance of differing lines of descent and the use of that belief to establish or validate social inequality.[5]

Ethnic status—the sense of being top dog because of one's ancestry—may come from the conquest or earlier enslavement of other ethnic groups or simply from being the original inhabitants of an immigrant-receiving society. To a degree that Weber did not anticipate, such a sense of social superiority could also develop in societies that considered themselves ethnically homogeneous, placed great value on this lack of diversity, and were therefore unwilling to receive ethnic strangers into their national community—one thinks of the history of Australia and Japan, for example. Lest we fall into essentialism, however, we have to bear in mind that the operative group definitions and boundaries are not fixed but are in fact constructed or reconstructed in response to changing historical circumstances. At the same time, we must also avoid overestimating how easily they change or how directly responsive they are to short-term historical developments. Constructed racial categorizations may endure for very long periods, as the career of the patently illogical "one-drop rule" for defining African American ethnicity clearly exemplifies.[6]

Racism, then, can be defined as an ethnic group's assertion or maintenance of a privileged and protected status vis-à-vis members of another group or groups who are thought, because of defective ancestry, to possess a set of socially relevant characteristics that disqualify them from full membership in a community or citizenship in a nation-state. A racist society functions like a private club, in which the membership conceives of itself in a certain way and excludes those who do not fit in. (This analogy is especially apt, because under the "black hall" system all members do not have to be strongly prejudiced against an applicant for membership; they merely have to defer to the prejudices of others.) Such a sense of ascribed identity and entitlement naturally inclines its beneficiaries to defend their group position if they believe it to be threatened. Many years ago the Weberian sociologist Herbert Blunter caught the essence of racism when he described race prejudice as an anxious sense of "group position."[7]

In contrast to the traditional definitions of racism, this one puts less emphasis on precisely how the alleged deficiencies of the "other" are described and explained and more on how a group defines itself and its prerogatives. The essence of racism is caught by such old American expressions as "give him a white man's chance" or "she's free, white, and twenty-one." The complaint that Euro-Americans are discriminated against because special efforts are being made to increase the number of blacks or other people of color in educational institutions or occupational fields in which they have been historically underrepresented would not be racist if it were based on an accurate perception of Euro-American disadvantage, but it would be if, as often seems to be the case, it exaggerated or imagined that disadvantage and assumed, consciously or subconsciously, that it is right and natural for whites to predominate in positions of prestige and authority. Racism as a general phenomenon is not tied to any specific set of beliefs about what makes a given minority undeserving of equal treatment. We know from the history of anti-Semitism and anti-Japanese discrimination in the United States that racism of a virulent sort can be directed at groups believed to be *superior*, at least in their competitive efficiency, to an in-group seeking to protect its position. Using this definition, we would have no problem in considering the South African regime of the late 1980s to be racist even though it was edging toward a willingness to "share" power with Africans and refrained from invoking doctrines of innate racial inferiority to justify its presumption that whites must retain de facto social and economic dominance in a reformed, "multi-racial" South Africa. Similarly, those opponents of antidiscrimination or affirmative action programs in the United States who, implicitly or explicitly, base their resistance on fears of losing something to which they feel entitled by ethnicity or ancestry are clearly racist despite the fact that they talk about acquired culture or competence rather than genetics. Even in Brazil, that allegedly most non-racist of color-differentiated societies, an element of racial-status consciousness is clearly evident when a person of dark complexion finds that he or she must have more money or education than a white to attain a comparable social position.[8]

If Weber's concept of ethnic status helps us to understand racism in a general and theoretical way, it is not sufficient in itself to make sense of the history of racism in different societies. As the examples of black-white relations in the United States, Brazil, and South Africa suggest, racism varies greatly in intensity and in the role in plays in specific social structures, economies, and cultures. What accounts for differences in the nature and effects of racism in various color-coded societies? How do we explain the growth and decline of racist attitudes and policies within a single nation's history? Anyone who has lived in the United States during the last three or four decades should realize that racism— or status consciousness based on race—changes over time in its strength and capacity to shape a social order. Blacks are far from equal in American society, but their status has obviously improved in significant ways, and white racism, while still very much alive, has declined in power and intensity. How do we account for such changes?

Variability and change in ethnic status and consciousness depend to a considerable extent on variations or changes in the power relationship among ethnic groups. To the degree that an oppressed and stigmatized group can somehow gain in physical resources, political power, and cultural recognition or prestige, it can induce or force a dominant group to share its rights and privileges. This in turn can gradually erode the material and even the psychological foundations for a *Herrenvolk's* sense of itself as a group with clearly defined borders and a collective sense of entitlement. Unfortunately, the process is reversible; loss in power, for whatever reason, normally entails a loss of status or prestige. Emancipation from slavery or other forms of directly coerced labor does not by itself empower a group to challenge its subordinate status and the stigma that continues to be associated with servile ancestry, but it does unsettle the power equation by opening new possibilities for action to challenge the racial order as well as new dangers of marginalization, expulsion, or even extermination.

Many historical examples could be offered from the history of countries like the United States, Brazil, and South Africa to show how political or economic power affects consciousness of ethnic status. One of the most important reasons why free people of color in Brazil had greater opportunities for upward mobility than their American counterparts in the era of slavery, and were thus in a position to win a greater degree of social acceptance, was the vital role that they played in the plantation economy as growers of foodstuffs, herders of livestock, and catchers of escaped slaves. The "free Negroes" of the Old South could not play such a role because there was a large population of non-slaveholding whites to service the plantation economy.[9] But the acquisition of political power by southern African Americans during the Reconstruction era gave them, during the relatively brief period when they could exercise their right to suffrage, an influence over public policy greater than that enjoyed by freedpeople in Brazil after *their* emancipation, which was completed in 1889. Laborers' lien laws, giving the worker priority over the merchant in the division of the planter's crop after the harvest, were a tangible result of this temporary gain in political leverage."

But nothing is more dangerous for a racialized minority fighting for equality than a partial and precarious accession of power. Majority backlash is the normal response; if not resisted by a national government acting for its own purposes, popular resistance to minority rights can readily erase most of the gains made under an earlier dispensation of national power. This in a nutshell is the story of the decline and fall of Radical Reconstruction in the southern states. The subsequent disfranchisement of southern blacks after white supremacists regained control was congruent with efforts to place them at the mercy of employers or landlords and restrict their opportunities to acquire wealth and property or to follow occupations other than sharecropper, laborer, or servant. The partial success of this effort made it possible for whites to stereotype turn-of-the-century blacks as radically and irremediably inferior. Only when blacks migrated in great numbers to the relatively freer atmosphere of the North after 1914 did they again have a chance to acquire the resources and political clout to challenge the Jim Crow system and begin to elevate their ethnic status in ways that eventually impelled whites to abandon their claims to a racial hierarchy sustained by law.

Recent developments in South Africa also reflect changes in the racial power equation, despite the fact that Africans are still denied the right to vote and hold office. The government's decision to attempt some form of conciliation that points to the enfranchisement of the black majority is due in large part to the leverage that black protesters have gained over the South African economy—internationally, through the ability of the anti-apartheid movement to promote sanctions and disinvestment, and domestically, through their growing influence as organized workers or consumers and their ability to resist white rule in ways that could make the country ungovernable and thus undermine the security and prosperity of the white minority.[11]

Such examples suggest that racism is not a constant and unalterable fact of life in ethnically divided societies. For Weber, status was only one of three analytically distinguishable but overlapping and interacting sources of social inequality. Others were "class," as determined by objective relationships to the market, and "party," meaning ability to influence public decisions through political organization and access to suffrage and officeholding.[12] As Weberian sociologists have often pointed out, inequalities of class, status, and party do not always coincide.[13] A main historical dynamic is the interaction of one form of inequality with the others—how stratification of one kind conflicts with the others or reinforces them, as the case may be. Under a system of racial slavery, there is of course little or no contradiction; the three Weberian categories coincide almost perfectly. Blacks in the Old South had almost no access to social prestige, government, or the marketplace. After emancipation, however, the three types of inequality could vary independently. At the height of the Jim Crow era at the turn of the century, an approximation to the early pattern of total subordination was almost achieved—but not quite. Because there was now an emerging black middle class, albeit one that was restricted to a segregated economy, there was no longer such a close fit between class and racial caste as during the stave era. Furthermore, as we have seen, the exclusion of southern blacks from American politics was mitigated to some extent by accelerating migration to the North, where the right to vote and hold office persisted. But the ethnic status of blacks in the nation as a whole, as reflected in the generally unfavorable or derogatory stereotypes projected by the dominant culture and in the pervasiveness of social segregation and discrimination, may have been at a low point in the period between 1910 and the Great Depression. One recalls here the segregation of the federal civil service in 1913, the popularity of the blatantly racist film *Birth of a Nation*, the official U.S. admonition to French authorities in 1917 to discourage fraternization between French civilians—especially women—and black soldiers out of deference to the belief of most white Americans in black inferiority and social unacceptability, and the bloody race riots and resurgence of the Ku Klux Klan in the immediate postwar years. But this was also the period when the NAACP won its first court victories and came close to getting anti-lynching legislation through Congress. In addition to limited political leverage, black migration to the North brought access to industrial jobs and better educational facilities.[14]

The persistence of a sharply defined ethnic-status hierarchy in the United States between World War I and the 1940s—a time when blacks were making some economic and political advances—does not prove that ethnic status is unaffected by changes in political and economic empowerment. In the long term, as developments in the 1950s and 1960s demonstrated, substantial and durable gains in one respect can be translated into gains in the others. Racism gains much of its strength and legitimacy from ingrained cultural attitudes, which of course change more slowly than the social and economic structures with which they were once associated in a direct and transparent way. But change they do, and it would be difficult to maintain indefinitely a culturally sanctioned sense of status in the face of substantial changes in the class and power position of a subordinate group. Racism does have a life of its own, but not in the sense that it can persist without changing its character and gradually losing some of its force in the face of dramatic and durable improvements in the material and power position of a disadvantaged ethnic group. Some might argue that this is getting the cart before the horse, that you cannot gain economic and political empowerment for an oppressed minority without changing the status attitudes of a dominant group. But what I am in fact advancing is a kind of inter-reactionist or feedback model of change. Increases in power affect attitudes, and changing attitudes open access to power.

How, one might ask, does such a process get started? Studies of the history of race relations in several societies suggest that something extraneous to the racial order has to occur, normally some larger economic or political develop-ment that calls for adjustment by the society as a whole in ways that have acci-dental or unintended advantages for subordinated status groups, before such a dialectic can be set in motion.

Major wars or intense international competition among nations can have such a catalytic effect on race relations. The Paraguayan war of 1865–70 speeded Brazil on the path to slave emancipation because it became necessary to use thousands of slaves as soldiers and to reward them for their participation by freeing them.[15] Black Americans were of course freed from bondage as the result of a Civil War that was fought primarily for the preservation of the federal union and not for their liberation. As a result of the necessities and opportunities of war, emancipation and the use of black troops became a means to the end of national integrity. The victories of the civil rights movement a century later were aided, perhaps decisively, by the belief of influential and powerful whites that Jim Crow was a serious liability in America's competition with the Soviet Union for the "hearts and minds" of Africa and Asia.[16] If white South Africa has become serious about the dismantling of apartheid and negotiating with African nationalists, it is because black resistance and the threat of international sanc-tions have raised fears that, unless something is done to accommodate blacks within a capitalistic framework, a future South Africa will have no place at all for an affluent and acquisitive white minority. What all these examples suggest is that, in times of national peril or catastrophe, inclusive forms of nationalism, sometimes encouraged by a belief that survival on any terms available requires a redefinition of citizenship, may prove stronger than ethnic-status consciousness and open the way to lowering or even eliminating barriers to the participation and empowerment of oppressed racial groups.

A more fundamental and less contingent force that undermines traditional racial hierarchies and the status claims they engender are long-term trends in the structure and value systems of modern societies away from "ascription" and toward "achievement" as a basis for status and power. We need not adopt the naive view that these trends are irresistible or that industrial capitalism is a direct and automatic solvent of ethnic stratification—the long career of apartheid in South Africa and of group conflict in Northern Ireland show that this is not the case—to recognize that ethnic hierarchies become more problematic and vulnerable when they are the only form of ascribed status that persists in an open and publicly sanctioned way. The role of explicit racist ideology, when it was in its heyday in the period between the mid-nineteenth century and the Second World War, was to rationalize the conspicuous exceptions to the prevailing model of a liberal, open-class society that could be found in places like South Africa, the American South, and various colonies of European nations.

But the period since World War II has seen an international revulsion against racism, inspired in large part by the increasing role in international affairs and organizations played by the emerging nations of Asia and Africa.[17] Another important impetus for change is the internationalization of capitalist enterprise, a development that has made racial prejudice a liability for those who would seek to compete with the Japanese and other Asians for world markets. Vast international inequalities that correlate roughly with color persist, but the current tendency to talk of the resulting conflict as pitting rich nations against poor ones may reflect the nature of this struggle better than the language of race, which would have been more appropriate in the age of conquest and colonization.

The trend toward a worldwide struggle based on "class" in the Weberian sense, or between those who have a favored access to markets and scarce resources and those who do not, is to some extent paralleled within industrialized nations with strong traditions of racial or ethnic inequality. It is clear to most observers of contemporary Brazil that the central issue is the vast differential between a rich minority and an impoverished majority. The fact that people of darker skin are disproportionately represented among the poor is evidence of a long history of slavery and racial prejudice but is not the central fact about the current situation. Emancipating the poor as such would seem to be the main challenge, despite the exposure of subtle but persistent forms of discrimination that has recently compelled Brazilians to recognize that they do not in fact have a "racial democracy."[18]

Even in South Africa, as has already been suggested, an analysis based in part on an assessment of the prospects for class conflict or accommodation may give a better sense of the forces currently at work than one that sees the struggle exclusively in racial or ethnic terms. Racism is of course the historical force that gave this version of capitalist industrialization its peculiarly segmented quality. But two theoretically color-blind ideologies, freemarket capitalism and Marxian socialism, have gained in strength at the expense of a statist and corporatist doctrine of white supremacy, on the one hand, and a racially defined black nationalism, on the other; workers and employers alike seem increasingly ready to view the struggle in class terms.[19] Contrary to what one might expect from Marxist-Leninist theory, such a redefinition or reconstruction of the situation may actually increase the prospects for a peaceful transition of power; for history shows that class adjustments and compromises are easier to bring off than the reconciliation of groups that view their differences as primarily ethnic or racial. But South Africa still has a way to go before it achieves a viable combination of majority rule and minority rights. Significant differences remain over how much power the majority should have and how it should be exercised. The government and the white electorate may still cling to the hope that they can keep the substance of white power and privilege by giving up the trappings and allowing a middle-class black minority to share their advantages. Only by coming to terms with black workers and peasants can they keep South Africa from blowing up or degenerating into chaos.

What of current black-white relations in the United States? Historically speaking, racism—in Weberian terms, Euro-American status consciousness—has tended to predominate over any consciousness of class that transcends racial categories. The inability of the southern Populist movement of the late nineteenth century to build an interracial political coalition in the face of its opponents' appeals to racial solidarity is a well-known example of this tendency. Another is the notorious difficulty of uniting white and black workers in a collective struggle for class interests, as reflected in the long history of anti-black discrimination by organized labor and the failure of socialist movements to attract substantial black support. During the height of the Great Depression, when it appeared to many that there were unprecedented opportunities for class action across racial lines, W. E. B. Du Bois was driven, despite his sympathy for Marxism, to espouse the economic self-segregation of blacks, because he despaired of the capacity of white workers to overcome their cultural racism.[20] Three decades later, after the civil rights movement had freed southern blacks from de jure segregation and de facto disfranchisement, advocates of black power and black nationalism came to a similarly pessimistic assessment of the ability of American society to overcome racial segmentation. The Kerner Report's 1968 description of the nation as "moving toward two societies, one black and one white—separate and unequal"—was evidence of a general sense in the late 1960s that the United States was still a society stratified by race or ethnic status and not merely by economic or class differences.[21]

Ten years later, however, a leading black sociologist, William Julius Wilson, argued that race was declining in significance and that the situation of blacks in American society could now best be approached in terms of class.[22] Wilson, who has refined and elaborated his argument in a more recent work on the black "underclass,"[23] based his case primarily on the growth of a substantial black middle class that he believed was being successfully integrated into the larger American middle class. This was in sharp contrast to the earlier situation of black elites, who had been condemned by racism to seek higher status exclusively within the segregated African-American community. But the price of this desegregation of elites was that blacks who could not qualify for middle class opportunities, because of lack of skills, education, and employment possibilities, were stranded in the ghettos without middle-class leadership or behavioral examples. Consequently, their condition had worsened, and the nation faced the major social problem summed up in the phrase "black underclass." Underclass disabilities, Wilson concluded, were primarily 'a matter of class rather than race and needed to be addressed as such, mainly through social-democratic or New Deal–type policies.

Wilson's theories are controversial and have been sharply criticized by those black sociologists and historians who believe that racism is not only alive and well but perhaps even stronger than ever.[24] I find much of value in Wilson's analysis and believe that the social democratic policies he recommends would alleviate inner-city poverty and demoralization. But he has somewhat overstated his case and has not always made it sufficiently clear that he has identified an uneven and reversible trend rather than an accomplished reality. It is certainly true that the black middle class suffers substantially less than in the past from specifically racial discrimination, but the affirmative action policies that made such advancement possible are now endangered by decisions of the Rehnquist Supreme Court and the civil rights policies of Republican administrations. Recent campus incidents suggest that black achievers and aspirants for middle-class status are not immune from harassment by white middle-class kids, who resent what they view as special privileges or unfair advantages for African Americans, and subtle but effective forms of discrimination persist in white collar employment, corporate bureaucracies, and the professions. Middle-class assimilation, in other words, is not as complete or as certain as Wilson sometimes implies. Furthermore, it would be hard to deny that the black underclass is feared and despised by many whites, not merely for its poverty and statistical propensity to commit crimes or use drugs but also for reasons of race. Clearly the Willie Horton stereotype, as employed by the Bush presidential campaign in 1988, is racially charged and not merely the product of class anxieties. What has changed is that education and wealth can, to some extent, often to a considerable extent, compensate for the stigma of African appearance and ancestry. (Although it might be hard to convince a middleclass African American trying to hail a taxicab in a big city of this fact.) But to be both poor and black is to be doubly disadvantaged. Until this changes, it cannot truly be said that race is no longer significant and that the United States can confront its inequalities exclusively in terms of class.

But Wilson's problematic interpretation of current race relations may have some value as prophecy. The deepening economic deprivation and insecurity that relatively large numbers of blacks share with somewhat smaller proportions of other racial and ethnic groups makes it conceivable that a sense of class division could eventually eclipse race consciousness as the main source of public conflict in American society. Status based on race and the politics of status protection stubbornly persist and may even increase in hard times—as the rise of David Duke graphically shows—but they lack ideological legitimacy and no longer, as in the past, sustain a functional segmentation of labor based on race. Opportunities for the construction of class and the deconstruction of race may now exist to an unprecedented degree, because blacks are no longer consistently and categorically relegated to lowercaste status, a development that changes basic social alignments and makes class-based responses to the growth of social and economic inequality more likely. Although the opposite extreme of a home-grown fascism based on a heightened Euro-American ethnicity is also a possible outcome of the struggle over a shrinking economic pie, the preponderance of evidence suggests to me that a decisive and lasting reversion to racial scape-goating is somewhat less likely than an uneven advance toward racial democracy. My comparative historical perspective permits the hope, if not the confident expectation, that a plausible combination of circumstances and initiatives could lead to the end of racism as a principal determinant of inequality in the United States. To paraphrase Martin Luther King Jr.—Will it matter so much what kind of ship our ancestors came over in, when we realize that we are all in the same boat now?

NOTES

1. Michael Banton, Race Relations (New York: Basic Books, 1967), p. 8. Realizing the narrowness and limited applicability of this definition, Banton used the term "racialism" to cover the attitudinal and institutional aspects of racial domination. In my own work, I have reserved the term racialism for thinking that assumes significant innate racial differences but refrains from interpreting these differences in an overtly hierarchical fashion. See *The Black Image in the White Mind: The Debate on Afro-American Character and Destiny, 1817–1914* (New York, 1971; Middletown, Conn., 1987), Chap. 4. In another book published in 1967, the American sociologist Pierre van den Berghe also defined racism as a specific form of ideology that necessarily involves the belief that "organic, genetically transmitted differences (real or imagined) between human groups are intrinsically associated with the presence or absence of certain socially relevant abilities or characteristics," and made the point that "Western racism is a fairly well-defined historical phenomenon; it came of age in the third or fourth decade of the nineteenth century, achieved its golden age approximately between 1880 and 1920, and has since entered its period of decline." See *Race and Racism: A Comparative Perspective* (New York, 1967), pp. 11, 15.

2. See George M. Fredrickson, *The Arrogance of Race: Historical Perspectives on Slavery, Racism, and Social Inequality* (Middletown, Conn., 1988).

3. Barbara J. Fields, "Ideology and Race in American History," in J. Morgan Kousser and James M. McPherson, eds., *Region, Race, and Reconstruction: Essays in Honor of C. Vann Woodward* (New York, 1982), pp. 150–51 and passim.

4. Max Weber, *Economy and Society: An Outline of Interpretive Sociology*, Guenther Roth and Claus Wittich, eds. (Berkeley, 1978), 385–98, 926–39.

5. Donald L. Horowitz, *Ethnic Groups in Conflict* (Berkeley. 1985), pp. 41–54. See also John Rex, "The Concept of Race in Sociological Theory," in Sam Zubaida, ed., *Race and Racialism* (London, 1970), pp. 35–55.

6. See F. James Davis, *Who Is Black? One Nation's Definition* (University Park, Pa., 1991).

7. Fredrickson, *The Arrogance of Race*, pp. 210–11; Herbert Blumer, "Race Prejudice as a Sense of Group Position," *Pacific Sociological Review*, 1 (1958): 3–7.

8. On Brazil see especially Carl N. Degler, *Neither Black Nor White: Slavery and Race Relations in Brazil and the United States* (New York, 1971); I. K. Sundiattal "Late Twentieth Century Patterns of Race Relations in Brazil and the United States," *Phylon* 47 (1987): 62–76; and George Reid Andrews, Blacks and Whites in Sao Paulo, Brazil (Madison, Wisc., 1991).

9. Degler, *Neither Black Nor White*, pp. 44–46; Marvin Harris, *Patterns of Race in the Americas* (New York, 1964), pp. 84–89.

10. See Eric Foner, *Reconstruction: America's Unfinished Revolution* (New York, 1988).

11. See George M. Fredrickson, "Can South Africa Change?" *The New York Review of Books*, October 26, 1989, pp. 48–55, and "The Making of Mandela," ibid., September 27, 1990, 20–28.

12. Weber, *Economy and Society*, pp. 926–939.

13. See, for example, Ira Katznelson, *Black Men, White Cities: Race, Politics, and Migration in the United States, 1900–1930 and Britain, 1948–1968* (London, 1973), pp. 18–2 1.

14. On the black migration and some of its consequences see James R. Grossman, *Land of Hope: Chicago, Black Southerners, and Great Migration* (Chicago, 1989).

15. Degler, *Neither Black Nor White*, p. 77.

16. Fredrickson. *Arrogance of Race*, p. 267; Harvard Sitkoff, *The Struggle for Black Equality, 1964–1980* (New York, 1981), pp. 16–17.

17. A good account of the international campaign against racism can be found in Paul Gordon Lauren, *Power and Prejudice: The Politics and Diplomacy of Racial Discrimination* (Boulder, Colo., 1988).

18. Sundiatta, "Patterns of Race Relations," pp. 74–75. The extent and persistence of racial inequality in Brazil, as well as the belated rise in the 1970s and 1980s of an anti-racist movement in that country, are discussed in Andrews, *Blacks and Whites in São Paolo.*

19. On these ideological developments, see Stanley Greenberg, *Legitimating the Illegitimate: State, Markets, and Resistance in South Africa* (Berkeley, 1987), and Julie Frederikse, *The Unbreakable Thread: Non-Racialism in South Africa* (Bloomington, Ind., 1990).

20. W. E. B. Du Bois, *Dusk of Dawn: An Essay Toward the Autobiography of a Race Concept* (New York, 1940), Chap. 7.

21. *Report of the National Advisory Commission on Civil Disorders* (New York, 1968), p. 1.

22. William Julius Wilson, *The Declining Significance of Race: Blacks and Changing American Institutions* (Chicago, 1978).

23. William Julius Wilson, *The Truly Disadvantaged: The Inner City, the Underclass, and Public Policy* (Chicago, 1987).

24. See, for example, Alphonso Pinkney, *The Myth of Black Progress* (Cambridge, England, 1984), and Clayborne Carson, "Why the Poor Stay Poor," *Tikkun* (July/August 1988): pp. 67–70.

Part III.

Reason, Race, and Morality

18. Antiblack Racism and Ontology

Lewis R. Gordon

WE HAVE NOW COVERED sufficient ground to state the importance of an ontological description of antiblack racism. Sartrean ontology poses the question of
the significance of a contingent relationship between the self and the Other. As
we have seen, this is a relationship of conflict in the sense that relationships
aren't established simply by the basic situation of two freedoms attempting to
face each other, but also by the effort of the chosen, ongoing project of making
those relationships. On this score, Fanon identifies three limitations of Sartre's
ontology—one dealing with his treatment of the Other and the other two
dealing with the role of ontology in the study of the black situation. In regard to
the first, Fanon writes:

> Though Sartre's speculations on the existence of The Other may be correct (to
> the extent, we must remember, to which *Being and Nothingness* describes an
> alienated consciousness), their application to a black consciousness proves fal-
> lacious. That is because the white man is not only The Other but also the
> master, whether real or imaginary. (1967, p. 138 n24)

The second limitation is located in Fanon's assessment of the relationship
between the historical situation of colonialism and antiblack racism:

> In the *Weltanschauung* of a colonized people there is an impurity, a flaw that
> outlaws any ontological explanation. . . . Ontology—once it is finally admitted

Lewis R. Gordon, "Antiblack Racism and Ontology," *Bad Faith and Antiblack Racism*. New Jersey:
Humanities Press International, Inc., 1995, pp. 130–137, reprinted with the permission of Humanities Press International, Inc.

as leaving existence by the wayside—does not permit us to understand the being of the black man. For not only must the black man be black; he must be black in relation to the white man. . . . The black man has no ontological resistance in the eyes of the white man. (pp. 109–110)

In criticizing Alioune Diop's assessment of the Reverend Placide Tempels's effort to state a Bantu ontology,[1] Fanon formulates the third limitation:

Be careful! It is not a matter of finding being in Bantu thought, when Bantu existence subsists on the level of thought, when Bantu existence subsists on the level of nonbeing, of the imponderable. It is quite true that Bantu philosophy is not going to open itself to understanding through a revolutionary will: But it is precisely in that degree in which Bantu society, being a closed society, does not contain that substitution of the exploiter for the ontological relations of Forces. Now we know that Bantu society no longer exists. And there is nothing ontological about segregation. Enough of this rubbish. (pp. 185–186)

We will begin with the first.

Fanon reminds us that the social world—the world of Absence confronted by the presence of Others—is rich with meanings that articulate the confrontation of freedoms. How can the black be a freedom if his confrontation with the white is never, at least institutionally, that of master over the Other in a situation? Does this mean that the black can never be master in and over his situation? Or more abstractly, does this mean that the black can never be a subject? This is how things appear when Fanon writes, "The Martinican does not compare himself with the white man qua father, leader, God, he compares himself with his fellow against the pattern of the white man" (p. 215).

Insofar as the black can only achieve equality among blacks in an antiblack world, we agree with Fanon. The ruling principle of such a world is "separate but equal"—equality among, like kinds. This conclusion is obvious from our analysis of blackness as a mode of being beneath the scheme of whiteness in an antiblack world. Yet a conclusion of a Sartrean analysis is that antiblack racism is a contingent (though not accidental) feature of our world. There could very well have been an interpretation of blackness as fullness and whiteness as the emptiness that threatens it. For example, the expression "colored" suggests an alternative group who exists without color. But even this example is susceptible to an obvious problem: would not the "white" in this case really be the black? Fanon refers to a *black* consciousness. Isn't such a notion a form of bad faith, the spirit of seriousness, on its face?

It is—to the extent that there is no, at the basic ontological level of consciousness of transphenomenal Being, black nor white consciousness. But "what" kind of consciousness is there? We face a qualitative and quantitative concern.

Qualitative: Since there are reflective white and black consciousnesses—that is, knowledge of each consciousness' situation in a given society—is there a qualitative distinction between white and black pre-reflective consciousnesses? Does it make sense to speak of such consciousnesses?

Quantitative: Does it make sense to speak of more than one pre-reflective consciousness?[2]

Perhaps we should work backward. Pre-reflective consciousness is "empty." It seems to function at first glance, I venture to say, like Schopenhauer's notion of Will. Being ontological, there is no principle of individuation located in its domain. "It is true we see the individual come into being and pass away," says Schopenhauer, "but the individual is only phenomenal, exists only for the knowledge which is bound to the principle of sufficient reason, to the *principium individuationis*. Certainly, for this kind of knowledge, the individual receives his life as a gift, rises out of nothing, then suffers the loss of this gift through death, and returns again to nothing.[3] There are deterministic elements in Schopenhauer that differentiate him from Sartre and provide a rich response to Sartre's notion of the situation. For example,

> We find that although the will may, in itself and apart from the phenomenon, be called free and even omnipotent, yet in its particular phenomena enlightened by knowledge, as in men and brutes, it is determined by motives to which the special character regularly and necessarily responds, and always in the same way. We see that because of the possession on his part of abstract rational knowledge, man, as distinguished from the brutes, has a choice, which only makes him the scene of the conflict of his motives, without withdrawing him from their control. This choice is therefore certainly the condition of the possibility of the individual character, but is by no means to be regarded as freedom of the particular volition, i.e., independence of the law of causality, the necessity of which extends to man as to every other phenomenon. (Schopenhauer, 1883, p. 388)

But in the main, the basic units of their thought are pre-reflective and ontological. Like, albeit not identical with, the for-itself, "The will, which, considered purely in itself, is without knowledge, and is merely a blind incessant impulse, as we see it appear in unorganized and vegetable part of our own life, receives through the addition of the world as idea, which is developed in subjection to it, the knowledge of its own willing and of what it is that it wills. And this is nothing else than the world as idea, life, precisely as it exists" (p. 354). Pre-reflective consciousness functions like an empty set in formal logic; all derivations can flow from it. This consequence poses no special problem, given our articulation of human reality as contradictory, paradoxical, And ironic; its emptiness is a precondition of its freedom. Qualitatively, then, no human being distinct beyond the fact of his perspective on the world.

One may hasten to impute a form of universalism here, but this would be an error since, being empty, such universality is meaningless. For meaning, we have to step outside of the pre-reflective level by-itself, for such an in itself formulation would be in bad faith in the first place, and consider what we have interpreted Sartre to be arguing for in his description of the body as a pre-reflective *perspective*; an appreciation of the context of choice, what we have called the residue of mediation, or the inter-play between pre-reflection and reflection, awareness and knowledge, seeing and being seen. Put differently, we face the question of what is imposed upon a situation. Every individual faces a situation not only as a freedom, but also as a freedom facing a collectivity of freedoms, a freedom with a perspective (the body) facing a collectivity of perspectives. The Other, in this case, is more than a concrete individual Other. The Other is ALL. The Other is tantamount to the Freudian notion of the super ego. Although it may be problematic to speak of a plurality of pre-reflective consciousness, it certainly makes sense to speak of a plurality of perspectives. The question is whether pre-reflective consciousness calls for a perspective other than the plurality of perspectives to constitute the *I*. Phyllis Sutton Morris has argued that the body fulfills all the conditions of the *I* qua perspective of consciousness.[4] Morris seems to be correct, insofar as her point pertains to the first ontological description of the body (the body as consciousness). I cannot see as an object my body as I live it, just as *I* am not identical with *me*. In the presence of the Other as the Other who, as the Third, looks back at us, there is a minimum of three perspectives: *his* and ours.

Our analysis of antiblack racism rests upon the notion of the Third's being The Antiblack Racist—a figure treated as a fundamental perspective of the antiblack world. The consequence of such an institutional or cultural imposition is the reality, as pointed out by Fanon, of our various social roles in an antiblack world. The type of being we meet the Other as is already situated for most of us. We must choose, but what we must choose *as* is already set for us. Try as I may, whenever I choose, no matter what I choose to choose *as*—what I choose to "be"—the fact of the matter is that it always turns out to be a black man who chooses.[5]

So it would seem that we agree with Fanon. Let us see.

Ontology can be regarded not only as a study of what "is" the case, but also a study of *what is treated as being the case* and *what is realized as the contradiction of being the case*. By following the path of articulating what is treated as being the case, by appealing to interpretations of reality in the given social situations that serve as matrices of choice, and by emphasizing the importance of negativity, of Absence, in critical ontology we have been able to raise the question of whether all ontologies are ultimately "distorted" ontologies. This is the case because, by way of their commitment to identity relations between meanings and being, human being and essence, ontologies often ascribe necessity instead of contingency to being. In short, all ontologies asserted as ONTOLOGY may carry residues of the spirit of seriousness; they may fall into the error of treating ontology as solely the study of Presence, and they may regard Absence on the level of an in-itself, abstract universalism. We have seen many instances of the perils of committing ourselves to what *must be the case* as far as existence is concerned. We lose sight of the contingency of being when we fail to appreciate that what is the case doesn't always have to be the case. No black has to be black. No white has to be white. But we must also stand back and add—provided we remember that the wider situation upon which these interpretations are based is itself contingent, although not necessarily "accidental." For example, the feminist effort to establish a policy of nonsexist language "has derived some strength and, I suppose, plausibility, in the eyes of philosophical practitioners because of one simple fact: until quite recently, those engaged in philosophical reflection in the western academy *have been* white men. This fact is as much a result of the presumption as it is a determinant of it. We can say of this fact, however contingent, that 'it is no accident.' Though it could not be 'rationalized' by all the philosophy in the world, it is of a piece with the entire history of the United States, and for what is still called 'western civilization'" (Pittman, 1992–93, p. 5). Blacks *are* black and whites *are* white *in an antiblack world*.

So we return to Fanon's view that whites cannot be the Other to blacks. Is a black in bad faith when he says, "I *am* the Other if the Other means inferior object in the presence of a white," in an antiblack world?

Well, first, such a black isn't a figure in bad faith primarily because he is recognizing his *situation*, if he means by the expression that the Other means he who is Absence. This does not mean that he is not recognizing his freedom. Knowing his situation makes his options, however poverty stricken, clear, which in turn brings him face to face with his role in the matter—the anguish of his choice. To exist himself—to live—in an antiblack world as though he were not seen as black, an Other, would be sheer self-denial.

But, we ask, how meaningful is any of his actions in changing his situation?

Our formal goal is an ontological one. Since we reject the notion of a pure," unmediated ontology in itself as opposed to a mediated or interpreted ontology,[6] our discussion of existence should not stand as a discussion of what "is" without presenting interpretations of the positive dimensions of what it means "to be." We suggest that "to be" is to be-as-at-least-one-situation-or-another. This is not identical with being-at-least-one-situation-or-another. Yet description of an antiblack ontology as a distorted ontology—an ontology *in* bad faith instead of one perpetually threatened by bad faith—suggests an ontological perspective that is not distorted. Such an ontological perspective stands true without mediation. This suggestion, interestingly, brings us back to the liberation question, for this undistorted ontology seems to depend on a rejection of the "must be" attitude. It calls for a recognition of contingency "in-itself." To liberate ourselves from an ontological perspective of pure presence (and the attitudes that accompany it), we need to admit, at bottom, that our situation doesn't have to be as it is. We need to embrace the negative aspects of existence in the form of existential or radical conversions hinted at in *Being and Nothingness*. Thus, although the bad-faith situation of institutional bad faith puts the black in conflict with the white subject as his Other, it doesn't follow that part of that conflict cannot mean the black's effort to transform that relationship. The whole point of the black's being able to recognize there being something wrong with the relationship of his objectification rests on his awareness of the possibility of an alternative situation-that he has a perspective on the world, that he is a human being. It is this awareness that makes the type of revenge situations described earlier possible. In his treatment of the situation of slaves and masters in the slave colony of San Domingo, C. L. R. James provides support for our view of human awareness:

> The difficulty was that though one could trap them like animals, transport them in pens, work them alongside an ass or a horse and beat both with the same stick, stable them and starve them, they remained, despite their black skins and curly hair, quite invincibly human beings; with the intelligence and resentments of human beings. To cow them into the necessary docility and acceptance necessitated a régime of calculated brutality and terrorism, and it is this that explains the unusual spectacle of property-owners apparently careless of preserving their property: they had first to ensure their own safety.[7] (James, 1989, pp. 11–12)

The fundamental problem with Fanon's rejection of a possible ontological description of that situation is that it fails to appreciate the *existential* dimensions of the black situation. This is probably the reason for Fanon's proviso, "once [such an ontology] is admitted as leaving existence by the wayside." The ontology he is criticizing is the form that demands ontology to look at the black from the "outside." Yet his own experience of being the black man seen as being seen—"Look, Negro!"—can only be understood as a realization of perspectivity, as an existential situation. His analysis calls for, and in fact is, an appreciation of the body as an ontological figure constantly confronted by the possibility of a bad-faith reduction of itself, a reduction into pure Presence or pure Absence. That the black body is interpreted as a black body by way of the two dimensions of being-seen and seen-as-being-seen calls for an assessment of such interpretations. This assessment we have already made: that such assessments call for an analysis from the critical standpoint of bad faith. Sartrean ontology is such a critical ontology.

To an extent, then, we have already described antiblack racism in a way that reveals its critical ontological or, better, existential dimensions. What is existential about racism is that it is a form of bad faith, which is a phenomeno-logical ontological or existential phenomenological concept. The ethnophilo-sophical aims of Tempels, against which Fanon was arguing, are different from ours.[8] It is in recognition of the limitations of the ontological scope of ethnic categories that we have from the outset rejected the prefix "African" as in African-American, as the focus of our study. When Fanon writes, "What use are reflections on Bantu ontology when one reads elsewhere [of Apartheid in South Africa]?" we respond that ontology, understood from the standpoint of bad faith, offers basic reasons for the failure of *Bantu* ontology. Such an ontology isn't basic; it attempts to formulate human reality not only in terms of a specific form of human reality—specifically Baluba society (see Mbiti, 1970, p. 14)—but also in terms of a metaphysics of *presence*, that is, forms of being-in-itself. Ontology, properly understood, reveals that human being can only be positively universal-ized in bad faith, precisely because human being also *lives* as a negative, nihi-lating being. Apartheid, for example, was an effort to ossify man.

Antiblack racism is a form of bad faith because it is an effort to evade facing human beings in their ambiguity or, as we prefer, in the flesh. This means that antiblack racism is ontologically significant since bad faith is an ontological cat-egory. That antiblack racism is politically significant is already conceded by Sartre and Ration. The relationship between bad faith and antiblack racism results in the following remarkable conclusion: not only does it challenge Fanon's death sentence on ontological studies of race, but it also challenges the view that existential ontology, as developed in *Being and Nothingness*, is without political distinction.

These considerations bring us to a matter in which the relationship between bad faith and antiblack racism is of great importance: the problem of legitimacy in the human sciences. How can there be a science of human beings, the chal-lenge goes, if there is no ontological dimension of human beings? Similarly, how can one study antiblack racism and black people when there are already prob-lems involved in studying people? A clue rests in what is at bottom required of the interpreter of human phenomena. Husserl's discussion of the body is helpful here. He writes, "If we stick to our de facto experience of someone else as it comes to pass at any time, we find that actually the *sensuously seen body* is expe-rienced forthwith as *the body of someone else* and not as merely an indication of someone else" (Husserl, 1960, sec. 55, p. 121). The demand then becomes an admission of what we see: "What I actually see is not a sign and not a mere ana-logue, a depiction see: in any natural sense of the word; on the contrary, it is someone else" (p. 124). To *see* human beings requires an admission of the onto-logical challenge of human encounter. The critical ontological role of the con-cept of bad faith in the study of human phenomena is that of a hermeneutical scheme in which to understand human *beings* in the face of the rejection of human *nature* and a reductive view of history. Fanon's "sociogenic" approach, which employs the methodological tools available to the situation under concern, is an effort toward such an analysis. This method is demonstrated in the entire Fanon corpus as a form of critical existential phenomenological description of the relationship between social-scientific "data" and the human effort to be made evident, to be seen as human, amid the data. That is why Fanon's "subjects" always at some point "speak," come through, in his work. Human beings, he suggests, require case-study analyses to be understood. This is not to disregard physiological and macro data. It is instead to offer considerations from which the data can contribute to descriptions of actual human beings.

What existential phenomenology has to offer anyone concerned with the study of race, then, are explanations of three aspects of antiblack racism. The first is that the concept of bad faith hits the core of the existential situation of blacks by providing an account of why black men and women feel responsible for their condition. They are oppressed by a sadist's realization of both his anonymity and their freedom. At the end of *Black Skin, White Masks*, Fanon prays, "O my body, make of me always a man who questions!" But he knows that as a black man he *lives* the question—Why? Why *us*? Why *me*? Some years later, this questioning led to a realization similar to our own:

> I shall be found to use terms like "metaphysical guilt," or "obsession with purity." I shall ask the reader not to be surprised: these will be accurate to the extent to which it is understood that since what is important cannot be attained, or more precisely, since what is important is not really sought after, one falls back on what is contingent. This is one of the laws of recrimination and of bad faith. The urgent thing is to rediscover what is important beneath what is contingent. (1967, p. 18)

The second insight is the self-reflective dimension of examining the world from the standpoint of bad faith. The only privilege the inquirer into antiblack racist phenomena has is his situation as a human being, a situation that leaves him constantly in the face of a possible slide into bad faith. His inquiry, like all "good" inquiry, must be a critical inquiry.

The third insight is that, just as in the wake of God's devastation man is born, so too in man's devastation racism is born. In Fanon's own words, "The disaster and the inhumanity of the white man lie in the fact that somewhere he has killed man" (1967, p. 231). One fights against racism to liberate human beings. It is with this assessment of the implications of antiblack racism that we now begin an exploration of "God" in an antiblack world.

NOTES

1. Placide Tempels, *Bantu Philosophy*, translated by Colin King, with a foreword by Margaret Read (Paris: Présence Africaine, 1959). The revised French version, translated by A. Rubbens, of which Fanon is probably referring when he considers Diops introduction, was published by Présence Africaine in 1949 and was based on a version, by the same translator, that first appeared in 1945 in Etizabethville, Belgian Congo (now Lubumbashi), published by Editions Lovania, 1945. This edition is no longer in print. See "Note by the English Translator" in the 1959 version.

2. Similar questions are raised by Maurice Natanson in his "Problem of Others in *Being and Nothingness*," in Schilpp, The Philosophy of Jean-Paul Sartre [(LaSalle, Ill.: Open Court, 1981), p. 332 i.e., of *Bad Faith and Antiblack Racism*]. Natanson raises these questions in the context of the relation between Sartre's description of others and mundane experience, p. 333. Since we have argued in our Part II that racism has to be understood in its mundane dimensions as well, it was inevitable that we find ourselves facing variations of Naranson's questions, since the realm of the mundane, the everyday, the natural attitude, is the social world of others. See also Natanson's *Journeying Self: A Study in Philosophy and Social Role* (Reading, Mass.: Addison-Wesley, 1970) for the various challenges to Sartrean philosophy posed by the perspective of sociality, especially in terms of Alfred Schutz's arguments in *The Phenomenology of the Social World*.

3. Arthur Schopenhauer, *The World as Will and Idea*, vol. 1. trans. R. B. Haldane and J. Kemp (London: Kegan Paul, Trench, Trubner, 1883), 354.

4. See her *Sartre's Concept of a Person: An Analytic Approach* (Amherst: University of Massachusetts Press, 1976).

5. See also Taylor 1992, 71, for a similar conclusion.

6. See particularly our discussion of the image and indistinct consciousness in Chapter 10, above of *Bad Faith and Antiblack Faith*.

7. *The Black Jacobins: Toussaint L'Ouverture and the San Domingo Revolution*, 2d ed., rev. (New York: Vintage Books, 1989), 11–12.

8. For a more developed, critical discussion of Tempels's work, see Hountondji (34–46). Note also John Mbiti's *African Religions and Philosophy* (Garden City, N.Y.: Anchor Books, 1970), esp. pp. 13–14.

REFERENCES

Fanon, Frantz. 1967. *Black Skin, White Masks*. Translated by Charles Lamm Markmann. New York: Grove Press.

Hountondji, Paulin. 1983. *African Philosophy: Myth and Reality*. Translated by Henri Evans, with the collaboration of Jonathan Rée. Introduction by Abiola Irele. London: Hutchinson University Library for Africa.

Husserl, Edmund. 1960. *Cartesian Meditations: An Introduction to Phenomenology*. Translated by Dorion Cairns. Dordrecht: Martinus Nijhoff Publishers.

James, C. L. R. 1989. *The Black Jacobins: Toussaint L'Ouverture and the San Domingo Revolution*. 2d ed., rev. New York: Vintage Books.

Pittman, John, ed. Fall—Spring 1992–93. "Introduction: African-American Perspectives and Philosophical Traditions." *Philosophical Forum: A Quarterly* 24, no. 103: 1–296.

Taylor, Charles. 1992. *Multiculturalism and "the Politics of Recognition": An Essay by Charles Taylor*. Commentary by Amy Gutmann, ed., Steven Rockefeller, Michael Walzer, and Susan Wolf. Princeton, N.J.: Princeton University Press.

19. Critical Race Theory: The Decline of the Universalist Ideal and the Hope of Plural Justice— Some Observations and Questions of an Emerging Phenomenon
Gerald Torres

[C]onsider what effects, which might conceivably have practical bearings, we conceive the object of our conception to have. Then, our conception of these effects is the whole of our conception of the object.

—C. S. Peirce[1]

No particular results then, so far, but only an attitude of orientation, is what the pragmatic method means. The attitude of looking away from first things, principles, "categories," supposed necessities; and of look going towards last things, fruits, consequences, fact. . . . [The] pragmatist talks about truths in the plural. . . .

—W. James[2]

My single mistake has been to seek an identity with any one person or nation or with any part of history. . . . What I see now, on this rainy day in January, 1968, what is clear to me after this sojourn is that I am neither a Mexican nor an American. I am neither a Catholic nor a Protestant. I am a Chicano by ancestry and a Brown Buffalo by choice.

—O. Z. Acosta[3]

THINK ABOUT JUSTICE. WHEN I say the word "justice," how do you understand it? Do you conceive of it as representing a single thing? How is your conception of justice formed? What stands behind your conception of justice? What background highlights the features of your conception of justice? I think it important

Gerald Torres, "Critical Race Theory: The Decline of the Universalist Ideal and the Hope of Plural Justice—Some Observations and Questions of an Emerging Phenomenon." *Minnesota Law Review* 75, no. 993 (1991): 993–1007, reprint with the permission of University of Minnesota Law School.

to start by questioning our conceptions of justice because doing so highlights both the difficulty and importance of my task. That task is to demonstrate that at least two of the goals of the civil rights movement may be incompatible, at least as they are commonly understood.

The claim for justice at the heart of the civil rights movement had moral force because it was the demand for a single thing: that differently situated people be treated fairly and equally.[4] But our allegiance to pluralism, a concept implicit in the mapping of our political universe, may equally be loyalty to a single thing. Justice, as it has taken concrete form in our civil rights jurisprudence, may require a weak form of pluralism, or a strong form of pluralism may require many kinds of justice.

Pluralism is the concept that has come to define culture and ethnicity within our legal system. Pluralism is not a "thing," however, but an approach to politics and, through politics, law. According to at least one version of our political story, the evolution of our law reflects the continued moral progress of our society.[5] To the extent that the law also reflects at least one version of the social consensus on justice, the moral progress also reflects an evolution toward a more just society. Because our society not only projects our culture but also expresses and creates it, we would expect evolving notions of cultural pluralism to be reproduced in politics and in law. Particularity may be celebrated but, in keeping with James and Peirce, the question remains just what is being celebrated. My premise is that "community,"[6] characterized as "democratic pluralism," has become the conceptual link between competing particularities and the existence (or hoped for existence) of a universal social, political, economic, and "ethnic" American culture. The deployment of "community" as a substitute for "cultural pluralism" within the structure of existing political discourse has the effect of denying cultural differences by defining pluralism as a purely political category.

An initial question, then, is what is the difference between cultural pluralism and political pluralism? In the context of contemporary political discourse, cultural pluralism does not exist outside the realm of a cultural difference that is expressed in terms of interest groups or as a marginalized, non-threatening other. Virginia Governor Douglas Wilder and the Reverend Jesse Jackson have demonstrated that culturally subordinated people can only have their interests heard by collapsing the broader goals of "cultural liberation," as haltingly expressed in the civil rights movement, into the structure of major-party interest-group coalition building. The recent re-election campaign of North Carolina Senator Jesse Helms demonstrated that, to secure a polity free from the voice of the dispossessed, all that is needed is to raise the specter of an alien, threatening other.[7] Thus, political pluralism, as currently understood, has no room for the full expression of the culturally distinct needs of subordinate groups. Those groups only have expression to the extent that they translate their needs into the language of "interests." By restricting the claims of subordinate groups to "interests," political discussion on the construction of "the good" is severely limited. "The good," as the term is commonly used, refers to the construction of the context within which rights (and thus first order interests) may be asserted and contested. By constraining a reconstruction of "the good," "interests" will continue to be defined in terms congenial to the continued domination by those who control the distribution of social goods.[8] The technique is formal neutrality as to "interests." Thus, according to this understanding, both procedural and normative barriers exist in contemporary political discourse to the inclusion of those who would seriously destabilize the current distribution of political power.

The "cultural nationalism" that emerged toward the end of the resurgent mass civil rights movement was an attempt to construct an antagonistic cultural foundation that would facilitate the assertion of claims by those whose "interests" were first given voice within the context of "civil rights." Stokely Carmichael (now known as Kwame Toure), one of the original proponents of Black Power, put it this way:

> "Integration" as a goal today speaks to the problem of blackness not only in an unrealistic way but also in a despicable way. . . . [It] reinforces, among both black and white, the idea that "white" is automatically superior and "black" is by definition inferior. . . .
> "Integration" also means that black people must give tip their identity, deny their heritage. . . . The fact is that integration, as traditionally articulated, would abolish the black community. The fact is that what must be abolished is not the black community but the dependent colonial status that has been inflicted upon it.[9]

Cultural nationalism thus opposed civil rights as a definition of the political program that subordinate groups should follow. Those within conventional political discourse perceived as deeply threatening the idea that groups want to participate in the social life of the "nation," yet stand aloof from the demands that differentiating characteristics be discarded. We saw the response to the threat in the state-sanctioned violence that was meted out against black people and native people, and we continue to see it today in the "English only" movement. The inchoate cultural nationalism of that age might be understood as a response of members of a group who were the objects rather than the subjects of social change.

By declaring that a cultural foundation was necessary for the political changes that were proposed during the struggle against Jim Crow, elements within the civil rights movement attempted to articulate the notion that recognition and preservation of group membership is important to community building and to the creation of justice. "Justice is neither a term of explanation nor of classification, but of experience."[10] The experience of justice is not just a residue, however, but the sense that we have participated in the system that both defines and creates it.

This construction raises the critical question of how these concepts of cultural and political pluralism differ from mere interest-group pluralism? Is group integrity essential to the process of the creation and definition of a just society?[11] As Frank Michelman,[12] among others,[13] has demonstrated in his recent work, both the republican ideal (as reconstituted in the "new civic republicanism") and the strongly liberal-pluralist strains in American political consciousness start from an unstated but common assumption: that the definition of citizenship presupposes a general, as opposed to particular, will and that this generality requires that the law be blind to group interests, at least where the group is smaller than the nation and where recognizing the "subgroup's" legitimacy risks undermining the solidarity of the state. I do not mean to understate the tension between republicanism of either the new or old variety and liberal-pluralism with this characterization.

This common assumption has two very broad implications for politics and law. First, our identity (and thus our interests) is rooted in some broad culture defined by the political contours of our present nation-state. Second, to the extent that there are contests over that identity and shares of goods that are distributed socially, we define ourselves in terms of shifting interest groups. These interest groups are largely affiliational. We choose to commit to them or not. Mostly, however, we do not.[14] Even groups based on filiation are either redefined to fit the affiliational model or marginalized.[15]

The interest-group model of politics is based upon an essentially privatized contractual model of social life within the context of a dominant political ethos. The ethos might be defined as the general commitment to public fair play. Each undifferentiated citizen must be treated like every other, and we all have the opportunity to affiliate in order to exercise state power to our advantage within constitutionally defined boundaries. Within the procedurally defined boundaries of "fair play," however, affiliated citizens struggle through the representation of their interest to achieve the maximum benefit regardless of the social cost. The theory obviously encompasses cost shifting as a major strategy. Since the cipher-citizen can shift from alliance to alliance as opportunity and need present themselves, costs will only weigh most heavily on those who are unpersuasive and choose to remain in a losing arrangement. The pressures both of the republican model and of the liberal-pluralist interest group model aim to strip unimportant features like race or ethnicity or gender from the definition of citizen participant.

Interest group pluralism begins from these premises. Under this view, as Iris Young puts it, "Friends of the Whales, the National Association for the Advancement of Colored People, the National Rifle Association, and the National Freeze Campaign all have the same status, and each influences decision making to the degree that their resources and ingenuity can win out in the competition for policymakers' ears."[16] The main effort of the opponents of the civil rights movement is to characterize the movement for "equal rights" as just another special interest group. This restructuring of the debate both debases the nature of the claims that have evolved in the civil rights struggle and disguises the efforts of "racial management" that characterizes current state policy toward minority groups.[17]

My view of cultural/political pluralism starts from a different premise. Turn again to Iris Young for a preliminary statement, but remember her definition here is still one of political rather than cultural pluralism:

> By an interest group I mean any aggregate or association of persons who seek a particular goal, or desire the same policy, or are similarly situated with respect to some social effect—for example, they are all recipients of acid rain caused by Ohio smokestacks. Social groups usually share some interests, but shared interests are not sufficient to constitute a social group. A social group is a collective of people who have affinity with one another because of a set of practices or way of life; they differentiate themselves from or are differentiated by it least one other group according to these cultural forms.[18]

The basic idea is that cultural groupings, as I have defined them elsewhere,[19] may have distinct interests in common, but it is not those interests that define them. To reduce those groupings to the political expression of their interests in the sense Young uses is to debase the culture that supports and identifies the group. Thus, to say that a cultural subgrouping is merely an interest group is to assume from the outset that the political expression of the group's cultural life captures the essence of the collectivity and defines any particular member of the group. Such a move, of course, protects the dominant cultural grouping from confronting a destabilizing "other," and forces the subordinate group to adopt the dominant group's definition of themselves if they wish to share in the distribution of social goods. This process, while structurally concealing the translation at work, formally provides "groups" with a model of participation in the discourse of the polity. Under this model, however, it is a discourse of exclusion.

To the extent that the above description captures in a schematic fashion the complexity of the social relations that have produced the specific historical forms that "pluralism" has taken, specific attention must be paid to the ideological structures that mask systemic domination and subordination. Any theorizing about structures of domination and subordination must recognize that no system is a seamless web. Every system is a living system composed of actors engaged in the construction of "everyday life." Any analysis of "cultural pluralism" as a potentially viable form of political pluralism must recognize the oppositional content of everyday resistance. Much of this resistance will he partial and found in the marginal spaces of the dominant culture and society. Mere marginality must not be valorized as such, however, since the margins may be where resistance occurs, but marginality is not resistance in itself.

> For the benefits of marginality to be reaped, marginality must in some sense be chosen. Even if, in one's own individual history, one experiences one's patterns of desire as given and not chosen, one may deny, resist, tolerate or embrace them. One can choose a way of life which is devoted to changing them, disguising oneself or escaping the consequences of difference, or a way of life which takes on one's difference as integral to one's stance and location in the world. If one takes the route of denial and avoidance, one cannot take difference as a resource. One cannot see what is to be seen from one's particular vantage point or know what can be known to a body so located if one is preoccupied with wishing one were not there, denying the peculiarity of one's position, disowning oneself.[20]

To remain critical, however, theorizing about pluralism or marginality must remain rooted in a historically specific practice and must reject the notion of the representative intellectual.[21] No theory can be applied without modification to the field of study for which it was constructed, since the objects of that study are constantly creating ways of knowing and patterns of being. A critical theory will accept the notion that various autonomous and competing groups will have to cooperate in ways that support the integrity of the various groups within the polity, without using the concept of polity to collapse real differences. These competing groups will be both cultural, in a broad sense, and political, in a narrow sense. Recreating a theory of pluralism will entail escaping the decentering and deculturizing nature of conventional contemporary pluralism. Theorizing must reject the idea of a trans-historical subject of politics.

The struggle is against domination and for autonomy, and thus a theory must specify each without privileging a specific version by reference to a transhistorical subject. Resistance at the margin is never "for itself," because the specific actors are never "for themselves" as historical individuals, but are linked with others, and the others define the individual. Non-identity is presumed in identity, the subject and the object are always one. Difference within the subject is never overcome or suspended. Difference is merely repressed through social and discursive power. Looking at the idea of equality illustrates this point.

Equality has been interpreted in our law as sameness: those who are similarly situated should be treated similarly; the same things should be treated the same.[22] This construction, while formally attractive, submerges much that is both interesting and important about the question of equality. It transforms similarity into sameness. Equality, as the post-modernists[23] have shown us, has at least two important meanings for the law. First, there is the idea of identity: these things (or people, or situations) are the same; therefore, they should be treated the same.

(This construction is contained within the ideal of universal citizenship.) Second is the idea of equivalence: in some important respects—that is, from an intersubjective perspective—these two things or these two people are sufficiently similar to require equivalent treatment. Equivalence does not require identical treatment, but requires that treatment take into specific account the subject's particularity.[24]

The term "postmodernism" has been used to express dismay over the collapse of modernism, as well as to express hope over the decline of totalizing modes of description and explanation. The postmodern critique begins with the admonition to guard against attempts to ground value in any foundationalist or basic normative conception like humanity, nature, or reason. Postmodern theorists insist on the local contingency of value. One way out of the problem of contingency is to adopt a position that grounds value in "interpretive communities."[25] Maintaining the integrity of local communities of meaning grounds the intellectual within the social needs of the community.[26]

Jean-François Lyotard, a central figure in the current debate over postmodernism, contrasts the "grand narratives" that attempt to unify all of human history within the story of emancipation (the promise of the Enlightenment and the French and American Revolutions) with the language games that control the interpretive integrity of local communities.[27] Lyotard, in exploring the "differend,"[28] looks to those situations where power and language intersect. As he puts it: "[Every] phrase, even the most ordinary one, is constituted according to a set of rules (its regimen). . . . Phrases from heterogeneous regimens cannot be translated from one into the other."[29] Pretending that they can be translated with no damage to the structure of meaning underlying the disputes is to presume the legitimacy of one perspective and the illegitimacy of the other. More than that, however, where cultural differences are at stake, the definition of the local community is central. An attempt to universalize the narrative by universalizing cultural discourse suspends the capacity of the subordinate group even to argue for their exclusion.[30] He notes that "[a] case of differend between two parties takes place when the 'regulation' of the conflict that opposes them is done in the idiom of one of the parties while the wrong suffered by the other is not signified in that idiom."[31] Lyotard distrusts the "integrity of interpretive communities" as much as the "tendency toward totalizing explanation."[32]

By constituting themselves as separate "language games,"[33] the various and competing spheres of cultural knowledge seek to maintain their autonomy and explanatory power. The function of these language games is to keep cultural values from infecting the separate realms of politics and economics and to disguise the pervasive role of power in the various realms of cultural discourse.[34] An attempt to de-culturalize a discourse is an attempt to understand the conceptions within that discourse as "pure." This purity is a resurrection of the claim to a universalizing (or totalizing) explanatory power within a distinct, or at least relatively autonomous, realm.[35] To struggle against the power displaced in language games that disguise the differend is to struggle against what Gramsci called the hegemony of everyday life through which social and economic relations are enforced, amplified, and contested.[36] Lyotard recognizes that this process is part of the practice of politics. We live our lives in a series of separate realities, and in each one of those spaces a specific kind of politics is possible. The many possibilities for action across different discursive realms is a direct refutation of the notion that there is a single sense of politics or single strategic political idea.

Constituting the postmodern in opposition to the modern or to the metaphysical is a counter-hegemonic act.[37] It is an oppositional practice. The ensemble of social and linguistic relations that constituted the "modern" acted to mask social difference. Yet, if theorizing the postmodern is to constitute a counter-hegemonic activity, then it must be done with a clear understanding of the historical specificity of our own cultural practices and with the aim of bringing the practices of our discipline in line with oppositional forces in society that are struggling against the various forms of cultural domination. How do we transform our practices and what will postmodern legal theorizing look like? Lyotard would suggest that the answers to those questions cannot be predetermined. However, until critics of the dominant discourse position themselves within the structures they hope to transform, they cannot hope even to identify the differend or to respond to the totalizing impulses of every specific language game. Thus, current "theory" is necessarily inadequate to the task, especially if it locates itself within a universalizing story of emancipation. For example, Marxism is inadequate not just because it has failed materially in Eastern Europe, but because it partook of the oppressive ideal of a single historical subject. No single ruling discourse of social life or autonomy is possible or even desirable.

To argue that pluralism requires multiplicity of voices for liberation to remain relatively autonomous seems to invite chaos. But to reject that conception in favor of some version of homogeneity is a nostalgic and totalizing vision. Multiplicity implies a decentralized ideology and economy and, ultimately, a non-hierarchical culture. Yet, this postmodern vision is not one that suggests either the pure determinism of culture nor the pure autonomy of voluntary association. Postmodernism requires building from the micro-politics of opposition to an opposition that can challenge the extant distribution of power, but not to establish an alternative hegemonic structure. A postmodern discourse of justice rejects that as a goal. Theory does not precede ideology, and thus the eclecticism of theory mirrors the historical specificity of the project of building a postmodern politics. This is one of the problems that Lyotard confronted as 'a form of both "narrative solidarity" and "essentialism."

Marilyn Frye, in *The Politics of Reality*, reports enjoining men to think about how to stop being men, and when thinking about her whiteness she enjoins herself to stop being white.[38] Yet how does one stop being "white" or how does a man stop being a "man"? Frye's remonstration highlights the problem in any theory of pluralism: filiation versus affiliation both for being and for action. Her injunction also throws into relief Lyotard's notion of the determinative power of narrative structures. There are groups to which we belong or, perhaps more descriptively, into which we are thrown. A mere act of will cannot disaffiliate us from these groups. Even our attempt to hold ourselves apart merely reconfirms our membership.[39]

To take Frye's categories as examples, a man is both male biologically described, and male socially described. Every man is a member of both groups. Feminists like Frye and Professor Catharine MacKinnon[40] distinguish between the two categories and argue that the socially constructed category "male" describes a fully articulated view of the world and the subject's place in it. Short of a sex-change operation, the biological determinant remains unchangeable, but it does not determine the social content of maleness. Biologically *and* culturally, men are thrown into the category "male." To "stop being a man," in the sense that Frye intends, means critically to evaluate the privileges and political views and positions that are attendant to the role. Yet it also means to understand politics *as a man*. From this perspective a "male" can choose to act in ways that reinforce structures of privilege and domination or he can oppose them, but he cannot escape his grouping with other men. Similarly, when Frye struggles with racism from the perspective of her whiteness she can reject the impulse to act in ways that reinforce the privilege of "whiteness," but she must do so from the perspective that her situation entails.[41] The quotation from Acosta at the beginning of this essay states in very personal terms the conflict and promise in recognizing how we can convert filiation into affiliational terms; it also illustrates the problem of the differend.[42]

The determinative power of narrative structures arises when either one or the other definition of group structure and membership is given priority. Among the practical problems facing Critical Race Theory or Critical Pluralist Theory is how to regulate the conflicting idioms in a way that does not depend upon a universalizing norm or vision of the good.[43] These theorists need to reform conceptions of democratic representation in a way that supports the underlying legitimizing justifications of democracy without systematically repressing the capacity for minority self-determination. There must be strong democratic support for group difference and, from those differences, complex equalities. The interest group model of representation described fails in this task. A pure majoritarian model would also fail where it does not weight to culturally specific definitions of the good.

I began by asking whether justice could be conceived of in the plural. In this essay, I have tried to suggest why, by and large, the answer has been no. The answer has been "no" because of the assumption that all cultural differences that matter are either outside the idiom of politics or else are convertible into the form of interest group discourse that represses differences that matter. The dilemma is tragic and old.

> The tragic consists of a legal double bind. Antigone, Creon, Oedipus, Agamemnon, Eteocles—all owe allegiance to both the edicts of their city and to the customs of their family lineage. Living under this tragic double bind is unbearable, which is why each of them chose *his* or *her* univocal law. . . . Their denial of the conflicting law proves however hubristic.[44]

NOTES

1. Peirce, "How to Make Our Ideas Clear," in *Values in a Universe of Chance* (1958) p. 124.

2. James, "What Pragmatism Means," in *Pragmatism: The Classic Writings*, (H. Thayer, ed. 1970) pp. 209, 214, 220. Compare this formulation with that suggested by E. P. Thompson:

> But outside the university precincts another kind of knowledge production is going on all the time. I will agree that it is not always rigorous. I am not careless of intellectual values, nor unaware of the difficulty of their attainment. But I must remind a Marxist philosopher that knowledges have been and still are formed outside the academic procedures. Nor have these been, in the test of practice, negligible. They have assisted men and women to till the fields, to construct houses, to support elaborate social organizations, and even, on occasion, to challenge effectively the conclusions of academic thought.

3. O. Z. Acosta, *The Autobiography of a Brown Buffalo* (1972), p. 199. Compare Acosta's vision with that of Richard Rodriguez in *The Hunger of Memory: The Education of Richard Rodriguez* (1982) pp. 28–40, 58–73.

4. I recognize that this characterization is unfair to the complexity of the civil rights movement, but it does capture the essence of the initial claim for "equal rights" as citizens. I realize many in the civil rights movements articulated "justice" as more than the call for equality of opportunity; it was also the call for a more transformative elimination of all the socially constructed barriers to equal results. See, e.g., Pellet, "Race Consciousness," 1990, *Duke Law Journal* (1990): 758.

5. See, e.g., A. Bickel, *The Supreme Court and the Idea of Progress*, p. 19 (1978); G. Gilmore, *The Ages of American Law*, pp. 4, 101–104.

6. Community refers here to the idealized polity within which differences are regulated by reference to a common understanding of the general good. Community as a virtue shows up in the current literature surrounding "civic republicanism" and in the dialogic left. See Delgado, "Zero-Based Racial Politics: An Evaluation of Three Best-Case Arguments on Behalf of the Non-White Underclass," *Georgetown Law Journal*, 78 (1990: 1929, 1937–39); *infra* notes 12–13.

7. Newspaper accounts of Senator Helms's stump speeches, alleging that his opponent Harvey Gantt was fundraising in the bars of San Francisco, combined with his television advertisement suggesting that quotas would deny deserving white men of their jobs, created an electoral climate of "us versus them," with very little question about who the "them" was. The television advertisement was captured well in this report:

> In the TV spot, the camera focused in on the hands of a white man wearing a wedding ring crumpling up what is apparently a job rejection letter.

As dramatic music played in the background a voice said: "You needed that job. And you were the best qualified. But they had to give it to a minority because of a racial quota. Is that really fair? Harvey Gantt says it is. Gantt supports Ted Kennedy's racial quota law that makes the color of your skin more important than your qualifications."

Mandel, "Quotas: A Potent but Perilous Political Issue," Investor's Daily, November 23, 1990, p. 32, col. 1. Gantt opposed job quotas.

A Washington Post editorial noted:

In the closing days of his campaign, Helms appealed not only to racism but to homophobia as well. He accused his opponent, Harvey Gantt, of accepting money from gay groups—funds raised, Helms said, in gay bars. "Why are homosexuals buying this election for Harvey Gantt!" a Helms newspaper ad asked. . . .

Cohen, "Helms the Hater," Washington Post, November 8, 1990, p. A31, col. 1.

8. "[T]he right to decide what is true is not independent of the right to decide what is just." J. Lyotard, The Postmodern Condition: A Report on Knowledge, (1984), p. 8.

9. S. Carmichael and C. Hamilton, Black Power: The Politics of Liberation in America, 54–55 (1967).

10. Torres and Brewster, "Judges and Juries: Separate Moments in the Same Phenomenon," Law & Inequality 4 (1986): 171, 187.

11. See Kymlicka, "Liberalism, Individualism, and Minority Rights," in Law and the Community: The End of Individualism? (1989), p. 181; Torres and Mitun, "Translating Yonnondio by Precedent and Evidence: The Mashpee Indian Case," Duke Law Journal (1990): 625, 654–59.

12. See Michelman, "Conceptions of Democracy in American Constitutional Argument: Voting Rights," Florida Law Review 41 (1989): 443, 445–47.

13. See, e.g., Sunstein, "Beyond the Republican Revival," Yale Law Journal, (1988); Sullivan, "Rainbow Republicanism," Yale Law Journal 97 (1988): 1713, 1714, 1716.

14. Take, for example, the pejorative content in conventional political discourse of the phrase "special interests."

15. Useful examples are the Sons of Italy or the Black Panthers. Discussions with Kendall Thomas have been very helpful on this point.

16. Young, "Polity and Group Difference: A Critique of the Ideal of Universal Citizenship," Ethics 99 (1989): 250, 266.

17. See Torres, "Local Knowledge, Local Color: Critical Legal Studies and the Law of Race Relations," San Diego Law Review, 25 (1988): 1043, 1062–68.

18. I. M. Young, Justice and the Politics of Difference, 186 (1990).

19. See Torres, Local Knowledge, pp. 1061–66, n. 17.

20. M. Frye, The Politics of Reality: Essays in Feminist Theory, (1983), pp. 149–50.

21. Questions about the role of the intellectual in social movements has a history dating at least back to Marx. Italian Marxist Antonio Gramsci developed the idea of "organic intellectuals," who viewed themselves not as members of a separate, detached, reflective community, but who were instead intimately linked to the social class from which they came. This connection informed their intellectual work. For a version of this analysis in the legal context, see Matsuda, "When the First Quail Calls: Multiple Consciousness as Jurisprudential Method," Women's Rights Law Report, 11 (1989): 7, 7–10, and Matsuda, "Looking to The Bottom: Critical Legal Studies and Reparations," Harvard C. R.–C. L. L. Rev., 22 (1987): 323, 324–26, 362–63.

22. See, e.g., Western, "The Empty Idea of Equality," Harvard Law Review, 95 (1982): 537, 539–40.

23. For an interesting discussion and critique of postmodernism, see D. Harvey, *The Condition of Postmodernity* (1989).

24. See, e.g., C. MacKinnon, *Feminism Unmodified* 37 (1987):

I will also concede that there are many differences between women and men. I mean, can you imagine elevating one half of a population and denigrating the other half and producing a population in which everyone is the same? What the sameness standard fails to notice is that men's differences from women are equal to women's differences from men. There is an *equality* there. Yet the sexes are not socially equal. The difference approach misses the fact that hierarchy of power produces real as well as fantasied differences, differences that are also inequalities. What is missing in the difference approach is what Aristotle missed in his empiricist notion that equality means treating likes alike and unlikes unlike, and nobody has questioned it since. Why should you have to be the same as a man to get what a man gets simply because he is [a man]? Why does maleness provide an original entitlement, not questioned on the basis of its gender, so that it is women—women who want to make a case of unequal treatment in a world men have made in their image (this is really the part Aristotle missed)—who have to show in effect that they are men in every relevant respect, unfortunately mistaken for women on the basis of an accident of birth!

25. S. Fish, *Is There a Text in This Class?* (1980) pp. 303–21.

26. See, e.g., R. Rorty, *Contingency, Irony and Solidarity* (1989). For a critical review of Rorty's project, see West, "The Politics of American Neo-Pragmatism," in *Post-Analytic Philosophy* 259 (1985).

27. J. Lyotard, *Postmodern Condition*, pp. 23–27, n. 8.

28. Lyotard defines "the differend" as "a case of conflict, between (at least) two parties, that cannot be equitably resolved for lack of a rule of judgment applicable to both arguments." J. Lyotard, *The Differend*, (1988) p. xi.

29. Ibid., xii. "Phrase" is defined this way:

Phrase: . . . the English cognate has been used throughout rather than the semantically more correct *sentence* for a number of reasons. The term, as Lyotard develops it here, is not a grammatical—or even a linguistic—entity (it is not the expression of one complete thought nor the minimal unit of signification), but a *pragmatic* one, the concern being with the possibility (or impossibility) of what can (or cannot) be "phrased," of what can (or cannot) be "put into phrases." . . . A phrase is defined by—as it, in fact, defines—the situating of its instances (addressor, addressee, referent, sense) with regard to one another. Rather than defining a grammatical or semantic unit, a *phrase* designates a particular constellation of instances, which is as contextual as it is textual—if it is not indeed precisely what renders the "opposition" between text and context impertinent. (194)

30. Ibid., p. 157.

31. Ibid., p. 9.

32. See J. Lyotard, *Postmodern Condition*, pp. 11–41, n. 8 (discussing the strengths and weaknesses inherent in each model of knowledge).

33. Ibid., p. 62.

34. Ibid., p. 64.

35. Ibid., p. 62.

36. Gamsci's notion of hegemony is discussed in Lears, "The Concept of Cultural Hegemony: Problems and Possibilities," *American Historical Review* 90 (1985): 567, 568–71.

37. Hegemony is a term with a complicated lineage and it is often used in contradictory ways. In the sense that I mean it here, hegemony might usefully be compared to Lyotard's idea of terror. Lyotard argues that:

> Within the framework of the power criterion, a request (that is a form of prescription) gains nothing in legitimacy by virtue of being based on the hardship of an unmet need. Rights do not flow from hardship, but from the fact the alleviation of hardship improves the systems performance. The needs of the most underprivileged should not be used as a system regulator as a matter of principle: since the means of satisfying them is already known, their actual satisfaction will not improve the systems performance, but only increase its expenditures. The only counterindication is that not satisfying them can destabilize the whole. It is against the nature of force to be ruled by weakness. . . .

> Such behavior is terrorist. . . . By terror I mean the efficiency gained by eliminating, or threatening to eliminate, a player from the language game one shares with him. He is silenced or consents, not because he has been refuted, but because his ability to participate has been threatened (there are many ways to prevent someone from playing). The decision makers' arrogance, which in principle has no equivalent in the sciences, consists in the exercise of terror. It says: "Adapt your aspirations to our ends—or else." (J. Lyotard, *Postmodern Condition*, pp. 62–64, n. 8 footnotes omitted).

A counter-hegemonic act resides in the destabilization of the system that excludes the "unmet need."

38. M. Frye, *Politics of Reality*, p. 127, n. 20.

39. See, e.g., S. Steele, *The Content of Our Character*, (1990), pp. 70–75, 93–109 (discussing the conflict between racial and individual aspects of identity and tension between raceless class values and patterns of racial identity); Carter, "The Best Black," *Reconstruction* 1 (1990): 6, 7 (discussing the "Best Black" syndrome that sets some blacks apart from the rest of their culture, yet reinforces their membership).

40. C. MacKinnon, *Feminism Unmodified*, pp. 54–55, n. 24.

41. See, e.g., Pellet, *Race Consciousness*, pp. 839–40, n. 4 (discussing psychological forces driving white progressives and liberals to advocate integration).

42. See note 31.

43. Linda Hirschman, in an interesting article, "The Virtue of Liberality in American Communal Life," *Michigan Law, Review* 88 (1990): 983, struggles with the "pre-modern" foundations for defining the good (998–1002). In doing so, she attempted to construct redistributist claims within the context of existing American culture (1011–22). Her explication of the good life remains resolutely flexible within the redistributist ideal.

44. Shurmann, "A Brutal Awakening to the Tragic Condition of Being: On Heideggers *Beitrage zur Philosophie*," in *Art, Politics, and Technology: Martin Heidegger 1889–1989, an International Colloquium at Yale* (K. Harries, ed., 1992).

20. Racism and Rationality: The Need for a New Critique

David Theo Goldberg

IT IS WIDELY CONSIDERED that racism is inherently irrational. This common belief has substantial support from the social sciences and careful philosophical analysis. Kurt Baier (1978), for example, considers racists irrational because their beliefs are "hypothetical or deluded" (p. 126); and Marcus Singer (1978) insists that "the theory of racism. . . is self-contradictory as well as confused" (p. 176). From the moral point of view, no more need be said: racism is immoral because it is by nature irrational.

The general policy implication commonly drawn from this is that racism can be eradicated for the most part by education. Proponents point to the strides made since 1964 in the United States. Yet two sorts of critical consideration suggest some skepticism about this claim. First, though much ground has been covered in attacking racist beliefs, the many effects of racist practices remain very much in evidence. To cite but one telling statistic, twenty years after the Kerner Commission, black family wealth in the United States remains one-tenth of that for white families. This, of course, raises the central issue of racism's relation to power. Second, it is a fairly common assumption of studies supporting the thesis of racism's inherent irrationality that it is a social psychosis and that racists are socially sick. This assumption undermines moral condemnation of racism, at least in part, for the mentally ill cannot be held responsible for acts caused by their disease; nor for such maladies do we usually think moral education the appropriate response. I will return to these questions of racism, power, and education later in the article.

David T. Goldberg, "Racism and Rationality: The Need for a New Critique," *Philosophy of the Social Sciences* 20, no. 3 (1990): 317–348, reprinted with the permission of *Philosophy of the Social Sciences*.

I argue that the prevailing presumption about racism's irrationality is flawed. I will follow Jarvie and Agassi (1970) in distinguishing between a weak and a strong sense of rationality, between rationality in action and rational belief. An action will be rational if there is a desired end or goal toward which it is properly directed; a belief is rational if it is consistent with some accepted criterion of rationality, for example, if it meets sufficient evidence, avoids reasonable doubt, or is open to criticism and revision. As Jarvie and Agassi pointed out, a rational person accordingly may be one who acts or believes rationally, or both (pp. 172–73). A theory will be rational if it consists in a set of rational beliefs. I will argue negatively that the set of irrational racist beliefs and practices is considerably smaller than commonly believed and that racism certainly is not inherently irrational; and positively that some forms of racism will turn out rational in both the weak and strong senses.

Lest my motives be misunderstood, I should emphasize that it is not in any way my aim to provide a rationalization for racism. Rather, if it turns out that some racist beliefs and actions are capable of meeting otherwise acceptable standards of rationality, then they cannot be dismissed on narrow grounds of irrationality. A different sort of social condemnation will have to be offered. The same point can be made also about other forms of aversive social discrimination.

Many *define* racism as irrational, but this precludes even posing the problem whether racism can be rational under any interpretation. The question of racism's rationality, at least intuitively, is not an ill-conceived one. The question therefore presupposes a definition of racism that is neutral in respect of its rational status.

I characterize racism in terms of a model for picking out racists on the basis of the kinds of beliefs they hold. This presupposes depicting the general content of racist beliefs. Racists are those who explicitly or implicitly ascribe racial characteristics of others which purportedly differ from their own and others like them; these characteristics may be biological or social. Yet the ascriptions must not merely propose racial differences. They must assign racial preferences, or explain racial differences as natural, inevitable, and therefore unchangeable, or express desired, intended, or actual inclusions or exclusions, entitlements, or restrictions.[1] Racist acts based on such beliefs fall under the general principle of "discriminatory or exclusionary behavior against others in virtue of their being deemed members of different racial groups." In some instances, nevertheless, expressions may be racist merely on grounds of their effects. The mark of racism in these cases will be whether the discriminatory expression reflects a persistent pattern or could reasonably have been avoided. Racist institutions, by extension, are those whose formative principles incorporate and whose social functions serve to institute and perpetuate the beliefs and acts in question.

A dominant element in this characterization of racist expression is *exclusion* on the basis of (purported) racial membership, whether the exclusion is merely intended, actual, or (implicitly) rationalized. This captures in the most conceptually minimal form the sense of social power—again whether desired, actual, or rationalized—that is a central mark of racist beliefs, practices, and institutions. Conceived in this way, racism need not be about exploitation in the strong sense of forcing, coercing, or manipulating racial others to maximize surplus value for the ruling racial class, though, of course, racism has often served this end (on the conceptual relation between race and class, cf. Boxill, 1983; Goldberg, 1989b; Harris, 1983). Nor need racism involve any appeal to superiority and inferiority as justification for the exclusion(s). For racism may simply be about domination in the weaker sense of being in a position to exclude others from (primary) social goods, including rights, to prevent their access, or participation, or expression, or simply to demean or diminish the other's self-respect. And as recent examples attest, the justificatory appeal may be merely to racially based cultural differences, to concerns to preserve the indigenous culture rather than to supposed inferiorities (cf. Baker, 1981; Gilroy, 1987; Goldberg, 1989c). Again, I will return later to this relation between racism and power.

I should add that I am not committed by this definition to maintaining that racists must appeal to a (coherent) conception of race. While some racists may, there are those for whom racial characteristics may be only loosely and perhaps unthinkingly ascribed of others. At the very least, it is of *conceptual* necessity that racists are (often only implicitly) committed to some notion of race. A child's expression, or a childlike one, will be characterized as racist on this view in part because of the (implicit) racial ascription involved, which it is the task of conceptual reconstruction to lay bare.

Thus whether racism can be rational in any circumstance turns on the rationality of the racist beliefs, ascriptions, and acts at issue. Generally, two classes of arguments are offered to support the contention that racism is by nature irrational. For the sake of convenience, I refer to these as logical arguments and moral arguments, respectively. Each class consists of two subclasses. The logical arguments divide between accusations concerning stereotyping and those concerning inconsistencies. The former divide in turn between those stressing the centrality to racist thinking of category mistakes, on one hand, and empirical errors from overgeneralizations, on the other. Accusations of inconsistency divide into claims of inconsistencies between attitude and behavior in the first instance, and contradictions in racist beliefs in the second. The arguments from morality claim that racism is always imprudent, failing as means to well-defined ends, on one hand, and that racist acts achieve ends other than moral ones, on the other.

THE LOGIC OF RACISM

It is generally agreed that racism is commonly expressed in terms of stereotypes. In addressing this question of the logic of racism, then, we need to develop an account of stereotypes and their relation to categories.

Social psychologists and philosophers commonly hold that placing sensory data under categories is central to human experience. Application of categories enables human cognition by ordering data we would otherwise find chaotic. The data organized are so large that they would be impossible to assimilate if considered monadically. Categorizing simplifies the complexity of the surrounding world: it condenses potentially overwhelming data to manageable proportions, it enables identification, and it serves ultimately as a guide to action. On this view, scientific classifications are simply natural extensions of our ordinary cognitive facility.

Basically, the same cognitive functions pertain for social cognition, for the same general purposes (categorizing and identification) and reasons (simplicity), and to the same general ends (a guide to action). In perceiving and thinking about others with whom we have social contact, the economy of thought demanded to navigate the complexity of social experience is promoted and reinforced by characterizing individuals in terms of groupsclasses, ethnics, races, religions, and so on. The less familiar we are with the individuating characteristics of the persons in question, the more likely we are to treat them in terms of their ascribed group membership.[2]

It is necessary to find some criterion for differentiating acceptable forms of categorizing from the unacceptable, the rational from the irrational. A general proposal is to conceive stereotypes as transgressions of the rational limits of category use, that is, as irrational categories. This is just another version of the usual presumption that stereotyping is inherently irrational and still requires that criteria of rational categorizing be offered. Social scientists generally consider stereotyping to be a species of social categorizing, for it involves fundamentally the same kinds of purposes, reasons, and ends as were identified earlier for categories in general (cf. Miller, 1982, p. 31).

However, stereotyping is thought to involve an "economy and efficiency of thought only at the expense of accuracy" (Newcomb and Charters 1950, p. 214). Yet stereotypical categories differ from those of ordinary functional thought in respect only of their *tendency* to rigidify, to harden our attitudes toward others, not in any necessity that they do. "Rigidity" consists in the agent's refusal to admit of alteration in the light of countervailing evidence, or in the denial that any such evidence in fact exists. While many cling resolutely to their stereotypes, thereby establishing their apparent stability over time, it cannot be assumed that this rigidity is an essential feature of stereotypes. For the little research that has been undertaken fails to exclude the distinct possibility that the rigidity more properly characterizes individual agents than the stereotype as such (Fishman, 1956, pp. 35ff; Tajfel, 1973, p. 84).

So rational and irrational stereotypes can be differentiated only on the basis of whether they commit errors—conceptual, logical, or factual—when ascribed in respect of the database at hand. It is commonly considered that racist stereotyping and thinking invariably commit such errors, and hence that they must be irrational. A representative text claims simply that "anti-semitism . . . consists of faulty habits of thought characterized by simplism, overgeneralization and errors of logic" (Wuthnow, 1982, pp. 181–182). I will examine each of these errors in relation to racist thinking,

BASIC ERRORS

Conceptual Errors and Category Mistakes

Racism appeals *ex hypothesi* to the concept of *race* as the basis for discriminations. Many find here the grounds for their objection to racism. A racist tends to explain the behavior of others by attributing it causally to racially transmitted dispositional traits of the agents in question rather than to the effects of environmental conditions in which agents find themselves at the time. But *race*, it is argued, is a spurious taxonomic unit of the human species. This "fundamental attribution error" functions by replacing the proper set of conceptual factors in the causal explanation of the behavior with a set only apparently more appropriate (Allport, 1954, p. 109). To attribute human social differences causally to racial membership, as racists must, is to commit a category mistake: it is to confuse social kinds with natural kinds. Actual differences are "explained" in terms of some ghostly group biology, and so racism must be irrational.

This criticism ignores the fact that no one seriously objects to discrimination *between* members of different races, only *against* them. We speak of "black business" and "black self-respect" or "Jewish political interests" without thereby demeaning members of the group to whom we refer. A casting director for a film on Martin Luther King rightly differentiates between black and nonblack applicants for the main role. She does not discriminate against a nonblack applicant by failing to consider him. Requirements of the role determine not that she exclude the white actor, simply that she consider only blacks for the role. Thus any nonblack candidate would fail to qualify for consideration on the same grounds as the white. However, if the casting director refused to consider a white (or a black) model because of racial membership, though that be irrelevant to the film role or the product advertised, this would amount to a case of racial discrimination against the person(s) in question.[3]

Interpreted as statistical generalizations across phenotypes, "race" may be viably employed as a taxonomic unit, though with limited scope. Actual racial classification of, say, black and white may differ according to the phenotypical markers employed or stressed. Racist implications follow only if the putative racial memberships are supposed to include or exclude agents from some favorable or unfavorable social arrangement or as signs of some inherent qualities or abilities. The notion of "passing for white" reflects such a racist social arrangement: historically, it has been deemed preferable to be considered white. Similarly, racial membership determined by near ancestry is part of a historical arrangement that was clearly racist. The Texas Statute Book of 1911, for example, defined as "black" any person with but "a drop of black blood." Nevertheless, determination of racial membership by ancestry is not necessarily racist in conception. An evenhanded application of the criterion carrying no socially biased implications need not discriminate against anyone qua racial member. Such an application would be strictly neutral between placing a person with one white and one black parent in the racial group "black," "white," or some third category. An agent need not be racist then merely by use of some version of the concept "race." So it cannot be the mere use of race which is objectionable.

The accusation of category mistake must rest on the assumption that racists inevitably impute biological determination to individual behavior. Racists need not make the causal claims central to the "fundamental attribution error." This error is characterized as a "tendency" of racist reasoning. Though cited as a "logical fallacy," social psychologists offer only *examples* of the error in place of objective criteria of acceptable causal reasoning. On the other hand, racists may resort to racial categories as simply signifying descriptive differences. These differences are taken in turn not as biological attributions but as the social basis for signs of certain modes of exclusion. Though it may be accused of introducing many demons, racism cannot be so readily condemned as irrational for encouraging conceptual ghosts.

Overgeneralizations and the Facts of the Matter

In the standard view, racist thinking always functions by way of stereotyping. It is assumed that individuals are squeezed into hard and fast categories by the rigid application to them of racial stereotypes. Racial stereotyping is taken to overgeneralize by its nature from a narrow database of empirically perceived racial characteristics to their assumed status as core traits of the alien racial stock. The characteristics in question are then supposed to harden into a stereotype of the other race, its ideal features, which any individual identified as a member is thereby thought a priori to possess. Thus racial stereotypes are defined as over-generalizations of agents' experiences of members of another race. Individual members of a race are ascribed racial characteristics which they may, in fact, fail to reflect. Treatment of all racial members is enjoined on the basis of possessing these characteristics, and so those members who lack the relevant traits will be treated—perhaps adversely—on grounds inapplicable to them (Allport, 1954, pp. 103–104).

Two related claims are embedded in this argument. The first is that unavoidable factual errors arise in ascribing the putative racial traits to individuals, especially where the ascribed traits are aversive. The second is that every form of racial stereotyping suffers the fallacy of universalizing from particular characteristics or from individual members. Problems of scope afflict both claims.

The argument underlying the first claim is that racists fail to notice the extent of individual differences in respect of a given property (e.g., ability, intelligence, or culture) within the group under observation (Tajfel, 1973, pp. 8085); or the degree of overlap in respect of such traits between members of the observed group and those of the racist's own (Campbell, 1967, pp. 823–835). This supposedly leads racists to be too readily convinced of the accuracy of their racial attributions (Allport, 1954, pp. 166, 167). Where available evidence conflicts with their stereotypes, racists may be led to distort the evidence—via selection, accentuation, and interpretation— thereby corroborating the applicability of the given stereotype (Stephan and Rosenfield, 1982, p. 119).

Racists often fail to recognize individual intragroup differences and intergroup similarities. Yet nothing in the standard view of racist thinking establishes the much stronger assertion that it fails *necessarily* to recognize these differences and similarities. Nor is it established that stereotypes inevitably involve factual errors. In some cases (for example, "Oriental eyes"), a bare stereotype may capture the facts rather accurately. Moreover, it is not necessary to racist thinking that racial stereotypes be substituted for observation. I noted earlier that the racist may use the stereotype simply to assist in observations of others' characteristics, to order data otherwise potentially overwhelming. Where relevant information is unavailable and decisions immediately pressing, there are cases in which the agent may rationally appeal to the stereotype at hand. Bertrand Russell's statistically based claim that more people of genius tend to be Jewish may prompt a granting body to award a Jewish scientist rather than a non-Jewish applicant, other things being equal and no further information being available. It is not clear either that racial stereotypes necessitate in those holding them a dogmatic conviction of accuracy and validity in their racial attributions or that they inexorably distort counter-evidence. Again, the dogmatic convictions and tendencies to distort may prove in many cases to be a function of agents' personalities.

Racial stereotypes may lead to factual errors and in those cases, may be dismissed for the most part as irrational. It's not essential to their nature that they involve such errors, and there may be instances where they cannot reasonably be expected to know better.[4] R. A. Jones (1982) argued that the factual errors often committed in stereotyping are not indicative of deficient categorizing or processing functions. They follow largely from shortcuts that for the most part operate ably in ordinary information processing and which render our categorizing easier. It follows that the basic operations of stereotyping are no different from those of categorizing (p. 41). So the fundamental issue in establishing agent irrationality on the basis of factual errors in racial stereotyping concerns the determination—in cases of lack or falsity of information about races—of the agent's culpability: Ought the agent properly to have known more about the racial group or individual in question? Like other questions of culpability, the verdict here can only be established contextually. In this respect, racist thinking appears to be no different than other forms of social thought.

There are similar problems with the scope of the overgeneralization claim. Particular races may be characterized in terms of probabilistic or statistical generalization of trait possession by their members. It is accordingly open to the racist to discriminate on the same basis against a race and its members. Stereotypes are probability estimates of differential group trait characteristics. They are constructed as abbreviated measures of the believed degree of trait incidence among members of given groups compared with the agent's comparable beliefs about the population at large. Agents may believe, for example, that "Jews are stingy" or that "blacks are lazy" to varying degrees: that all or 60 percent or merely 30 percent of the racial group are characterized as such. This degree of belief or estimate is furnished by plugging the agent's many relevant judgments into a Bayesian statistical formula. Given the availability of objective statistical data (e.g., contributions by Jews to secular charities, productivity levels of blacks and whites at the same level of employment, and so on), the degree of accuracy of agents' stereotypes may be computed. There is potentially available, then, an objective measure against which to assess the validity of agents' social judgments.

This formulation solves problems confronting any analysis of racial stereotyping. Agents are not committed to extending the stereotyped beliefs about a group to all its members; they can allow exceptions to the generalization. In this way, an agent may hold a stereotypical belief about a group, treat the relevant proportion of the group accordingly, and yet consistently insist that though some of one's best friends are group members, they lack the characteristics in question. An agent may believe, for example, that one's Jewish friends are generous while adhering to the stereotype "stingy Jews" (to the degree, say, of 0.6). This suggests that stereotypes have only partial extension, altering and corroding, the more familiar that agents become with group members. Clearly, this model represents much more closely the way in which we respond to others—as individuals and as group members—within the complexity of our social relations.

A measure for the degree of rationality of an agent's social stereotypes can be constructed in light of the relevant group information objectively available and taken into consideration. by the agent. Familiar with members of a race whom he is capable of identifying "macrodiacritically"[5]—for example, blacks— a racist may construct an aversive stereotype on the basis of his fairly extensive experience of group members in relation to his experience of the population at large: For example, "40 percent of blacks encountered in a given city have criminal records compared with 20 percent of whites." The racist may construct from this a predictive estimation of his future experiences and probable behavior responses. He may even be open to careful modification of his behavior as a result of failed predictions and new experiences. Thus he would seem to meet Jarvie and Agassi's (1970) strictest demands on rational agency.[6]

It follows that racist thinking is not simply a matter of overgeneralization grounded in conceptual mistakes and generating factual errors. It is not simply the impaired psychological functioning of an authoritarian personality as opposed to a tolerant one. Racist thinking is capable, in some cases, of avoiding both primary features of stereotyping: that is, the tendency *to rigidify* our conceptions of individuals *by ignoring* their differences in the face of some idealized group conception. This conclusion that racist beliefs do not necessarily transgress criteria of rationality will be corroborated by a careful examination of the second subclass of logical arguments cited to support the contention that racism is inherently irrational.

LOGICAL ERRORS

The prevailing presumption that the logic of racism is commonly characterized by inconsistency and contradiction assumes two forms: first, that there are undeniable inconsistencies between the relevant attitudes of agents and their behavior; and second, that racist stereotyping and thought consist in contradictory beliefs about members of the race in question. There are shortcomings with both formulations of this "racist logic."

Attitude-Behavior Inconsistency

Social psychologists generally hold that there is an inconsistency between the relevant attitudes of agents and their behavior. Though racists may express overtly benign attitudes toward members of another race, it is claimed that their behavior will be inconsistent with these expressed attitudes. By contrast, logical theory reveals that only propositions (or their bearers, such as statements or sentences) may be inconsistent, not disparate entities like attitude and behavior. More directly, social psychologists have treasured this claim of "attitude-behavior inconsistency" as a scientific thesis generating research programs. Yet subsequent research in social psychology has failed to furnish any clearly defined results in support of the hypothesis (cf. Liska, 1975, p. 19).[7]

The common assumption underlying these inconsistency claims, at least in the social psychological literature, is that the beliefs constituting the attitudes in question are alone capable of causing behavior directly and uniquely. However, attitudes (qua beliefs) are incapable in themselves of causing behavior directly. More than the bald beliefs, attitudes may express intentions, dispositions, or desires—generally motives—to act. There is nothing about the nature of racists that necessitates inconsistencies between their racist motives to act, truly admitted, and their acts. Indeed, it is doubtful that the claim of such inconsistency is coherent. Without the relevant disposition, intention, or desire to impel action in accord with or to aim at the consequences projected by the belief, the attitude alone can have no direct determinative (causal) effect on the agent's behavior. Attitudes in the narrow sense of beliefs can only affect actions indirectly—by fashioning desire or expressing a motive in the relevant sense (cf. Hare, 1980).

It follows from the conjunction of these logical and conceptual truths that agents can harbor only inconsistent beliefs. The beliefs in question are either reflected in particular premises (for example, descriptive claims about the member of a race, or the race as such, against which the agent bears a grudge) or in moral or prudential universals (believing, for instance, that members of a race ought both to be treated with respect and to be used merely to the agent's own ends). The universal claims can only be inapplicable, strictly speaking, to particular premises; agents' desires or motives can only conflict with each other (where an agent has two mutually exclusive motives to act). Consider an agent who reveals truthfully that he or she has a nondiscriminatory attitude toward a race or member at Time 1. If, then, at Time 2 the agent is seen to act toward that race or member in a manner that conflicts with this attitude, the general reasons must be these: either the agent has altered his or her attitude, or a competing attitude has come to exert greater influence, or the introduction of some desire or changed motive has now taken hold.[8] In other words, racist action will generally (though not exhaustively) turn out rational in the weak sense of aiming at a desired end.

These conceptual confusions underlie the failure of the psychological research to establish the claimed "attitude-behavior inconsistency." Liska (1975) concluded that recent research reveals "a significant relationship between attitudes and behavior" (p. 15). He admitted, however, that it is completely unclear from the research whether the relationship is such that behavior affects attitude or attitude affects behavior. The supposed inconsistency is not "an anomaly" nor is it "an insignificant datum" (pp. 245–259). It is simply no inconsistency at all.

Contradictions in Beliefs

The dominant view of racist logic is that it consists in straightforwardly contradictory and hence irrational beliefs. This "contradictory belief thesis" is not merely a hypothesis about the psychological state of individual racists. It represents the logic of racist beliefs and must be assessed as such. Gordon Allport is the clearest and most influential representative of this widespread view, and so I will concentrate on his presentation.

Relying on results reported in *The Authoritarian Personality* (Adorno et al., 1950, pp. 605–653), Allport (1954) cited the following set as a paradigmatic instance of contradictory beliefs:

J_1. Jews tend to keep apart, excluding gentiles from Jewish social life, remaining a foreign element in American society.

and

J_2. Jews pry too much into Christian activities, seeking too much recognition and prestige from Christians, going too far in hiding their Jewishness.

Allport admits that "there is somewhat less self-contradiction" in respect of "Negro" stereotypes, yet insists that "contradiction is by no means absent" as witnessed by:

B_1. Negroes are lazy and inert.

and

B_2. The Negro is aggressive and pushing.

Alternatively, the following set is deemed inconsistent:

B_3. The Negro knows his place.

and

B_4. Force is needed to keep the Negro in his place.

Items of the kind J_1, B_1, and B_3 constitute a "subscale of seclusiveness"; those of kind J_2, B_3, and B_4 constitute a "subscale of intrusiveness." Since Adorno et al. (1950) had found that the two subscales converged to the degree of 0.74, Allport (1954) concluded that the same racist agents who believed that Jews or blacks are seclusive tended also to believe that Jews or blacks are intrusive (Allport, 1954, pp. 194–98).

Nevertheless, contradictions are subject to far more stringent logical prerequisites than Allport acknowledged. First, in strict terms, contradictions assume the form "a and –a." Second, the agent must hold both constituent beliefs of the contradictory set in respect of the same people or well-defined group, not some vaguely constituted and shifting population. Third, the beliefs must be held within the same delimited time span. Allport's conception of contradiction clearly violates each of these strict criteria. At best, the "subscale of seclusiveness" could only indirectly contradict the "subscale of intrusiveness," that is, where the properties constituting one subscale, given the appropriate context, controverted those making up the other. Now the measure of 0.74 suggests that the same agents tended to believe that the given racial group was marked by the apparently contradictory characteristics. But the study eliciting this correlation failed to establish whether the racists tested held these beliefs about all members of the race in question, and, if only about some, whether the contradictory beliefs were predicated of the same group members. Further, the study failed to confirm that the apparently contradictory beliefs were held simultaneously or at least within a narrowly defined time span. Each agent surveyed marked off the properties considered characteristic of Jews or "Negroes" in the abstract, without reference to specific individuals. That a racist may believe "a" and that given some other background setting, may believe "–a" does not entail that the racist believes "a and –a." There need be nothing irrational in believing that Jews, in general, are stingy while admitting that one's close Jewish friends are generous.[9]

In particular, the properties which Allport offered as examples do not exhibit the proper logical form: Jews, it is believed, only *tend* to keep apart, remaining foreign to *American* society (J_1) while seeking too much from *Christians* (J_2). Tendential judgments in terms of differing predicates cannot contradict each other. To use Allport's "Negro" examples, it may be that under some interpretations, the terms "laziness" and "inertia" (B_1) contradict "aggression" and "pushiness" (B_2), or that "knowing one's place" (B_3) contradicts "needing force to keep one in one's place" (B_4). But it is not obviously so. The study failed to establish that racists predicate these claims of the *same* "Negroes" or in respect of the same kind of behavior of the racial group. A racist may believe that "a Negro" is lazy and inert when it comes to work, but aggressive and pushy about rights.

The logic of racist thought is characterized less by contradictions and internal inconsistencies than commonly assumed. This is corroborated by the fact that group (racial) stereotypes do not arise randomly. They are determined by the relative probabilities of trait possession by members of a given (racial) group, the nature of historical contacts between agents and members of the stereotyped group, by the dynamics of group identification and membership identity, as well as by sociopolitical, economic, and cultural conditions. Deeply influenced by this intricate web of specific factors which ·serve to define any social actor, the (potential) racist may construct what amounts to an implicit yet coherent theory of character for members of the group in question. It is in light of this picture that group members' behavioral expectations and the agent's responses are projected. The point to be emphasized here is that "the implicit theory generally is *internally consistent* and is unlikely to contain any sharply contradictory traits" (Stephan and Rosenfield, 1982, p. 96; my emphasis).

So racism is not inherently irrational on logical grounds. It need involve no inconsistency between attitudes and acts, for such inconsistency is ill-conceived. Nor must a racist hold contradictory beliefs, for clearly a racist need not. This highlights prior conclusions. On one hand, a racist act may conflict with an affirmative attitude expressed at an earlier time by the racist. Here, however, the act may be affected by a changed attitude in relation to the specific desire or motive at issue, or the act may conflict with a currently held belief. In the latter case, an aversive desire or motive on the agent's part is most likely at odds with the belief in question. The agent would be considered irrational in this but not in the former instance where the attitude has changed in the relevant way. On the other hand, where a racist holds contradictory beliefs about a race or (some of) its members, he or she is in this respect clearly irrational. But where both beliefs are conscious, it is unlikely that they would be held simultaneously. Finally, racism need not function by way of stereotyping in the narrow sense of employing the techniques of dismissal, rigidity, and plain ignorance. It is not simply that the "logic" commonly ascribed to such stereotyping is inapplicable to the general operations of racism, but rather that the "logic" is inadequately formulated in and of itself.

We have failed to establish that racism is necessarily irrational on strict logical grounds. Accordingly, we must now turn to inquire whether the claim to racism's irrationality can be established on the wider basis of prudential or moral reasoning.

RACISM, PRUDENCE, AND MORALITY

An agent is rational, on the standard account, if the ends, aims, and purposes proposed and pursued are mutually coherent and the means used to attain them are conducive to fulfilling these pursuits. These two conditions of agent rationality—the prudential considerations of means—ends consistency and the coherence of ends—are interdependent. Nevertheless, in determining whether the various forms of racism are capable of meeting these conditions, clarity requires that they be addressed seriatim.

The Imprudence of Racism

The prudential condition obviously rests on the way in which ends are circumscribed. The clearest attack on the rationality of racism on grounds of imprudence has been economic in nature, and so I will cast my discussion here in terms of the economic end of profit. Determination of the means appropriate to maximizing profit will include defining investment possibilities, predicting probable outcomes for each, and specifying the optimum conditions (for example, labor hiring and wage policies, working conditions, and so on) under which each of these policies may be instituted. What has to be decided are the institutional forms and behavior conducive to the highest possible returns on investment, given prevailing market conditions. The objection that racism is economically irrational translates into the claims that racist expression—the "taste to discriminate"—ultimately proves unprofitable (cf. Becker, 1957, p. 6; cf. Prager 1972, pp. 118–119, 121); that given certain social factors, the neutral calculus of economic profit never discriminates on racial grounds; and that where discrimination occurs, it is always extra-economic or "exogenously determined" (Becker, 1957, p. 109; cf. Prager, 1972, p. 125; and Godelier, 1972, pp. 30–35). Thomas Sowell (1975) stated the argument thus:

> In short, empirical evidence confirms what economic analysis would predict: that regulated industries have more discrimination than unregulated industries when this depends only on economic considerations. (p. 167)

Nevertheless, it is now a well-established historical fact that racially discriminatory laws and practices have enabled the profit ratio to be maintained or increased both on the micro- and macrolevels, and, indeed, have been intentionally introduced at times with this end in view. While we must view his hypothetical calculations with considerable caution, Lester Thurow (1969) estimated that white economic gains or "Negro" losses from discrimination in the United States amount to approximately $15 billion annually (p. 135; Prager, 1972, p. 143); and the massive and continuing gains to South African whites from apartheid are inestimable (Greenberg, 1987, pp. 123–176; Innes, 1984; Wolpe, 1972; Goldberg, 1986a; Cell, 1982). A closer look at the prevailing claims from "economic reason" will reveal the terms under which racism may prove to be prudentially rational, that is, rational in the weak sense identified earlier. I am concerned here only with specifying the conditions of racism's economic rationality and should not be thought thus to imply that racism has no extra-economic determinants.

In a review of two provocative books by Thomas Sowell, Christopher Jencks (1983) distinguished among four kinds of economic discrimination: myopic, malicious, statistical, and consumer-directed (pp. 37–38; cf. Banton,

1983). *Myopic discrimination* is the refusal to employ any properly qualified member of a specified racial group because of a misjudgment about the job performance of some group members. It is economically irrational, for it causes the discriminating employer to hire less-qualified workers without decreasing the wage bill. *Malicious discrimination*, against the group as a whole but not directly against any individual member, is considered economically irrational on the same grounds. In support of this claim, Jencks suggested the example of an individual employer who refuses to hire a more qualified black for fear that extending some economic power to blacks will undermine white social supremacy in general. Similarly, middle-income whites who support economic discrimination against blacks as a whole are deemed irrational, for it can be shown that the former experience loss of income as well (Reich, 1981, p. 110; cf. Prager, 1972, p. 126). Yet it is not clear that malicious discriminators need be irrational, for white social and political supremacy may be both a cherished and a tested means of maintaining the profit ratio or social benefits above the level otherwise attainable. Third, it has been demonstrated already that what Jencks called *statistical discrimination* may meet ordinary standards of rationality. Jencks admitted that the employer who refuses to hire members of a racial group on the basis of statistical evidence that its members are generally less productive or more likely to fall afoul of the law is acting rationally in the economic sense.

Fourth, *consumer-directed discrimination* is that form of discrimination motivated not by antipathies of the discriminating employer or supplier but by consumers of the product or by those wishing to maintain the good's value. For example, a real estate agent serving a prestigious neighborhood acts in their own long-term economic interest, and perhaps in the best economic interests of the clientele, by refusing to sell property of one client to members of a particular race, where it is clear that this would result immediately and inevitably in lower property values for the neighborhood in general. Implicit here is the realistic assumption that only a small percentage of the restricted racial group could afford housing in such a neighborhood. Of course, the agent may thereby delimit the highest price for that client and so act contrary to the latter's economic interest (unless the client owned other property in the area). Yet this objection cannot be generalized from *any* particular client to a denial of maximized profit for *all* clients. The temporal consideration necessary for the generalization to be effective transgresses the condition that property values fall more or less immediately. For a clearer instance, consider the case of a Jewish employer who, while personally not antagonistic toward Arabs, refuses to hire Arab personnel because all businesses in the community have been threatened by boycott should they employ Arabs. This employer is hardly proceeding contrary to good economic reason by acting accordingly (cf. P. Singer, 1978, pp. 188–91).

So, some forms of racist discrimination facilitate the general end of profit or utility maximization. These forms will be considered economically rational. This conclusion will be supported by analyzing the rationality of white workers who defend the maintenance of job color barriers to guarantee their own jobs and preserve higher wage levels by eliminating competition (cf. Boggs, 1970, p. 155; Prager, 1972, pp. 137–38; Boston, 1988; Wolpe, 1972). This conclusion may be generalized: where ends, aims, and purposes are predetermined and rationality is weakly defined in purely instrumental terms, racist expressions which engender the ends in question must be rational (provided the ends themselves meet prudential requirements).

This suggests that the microlevel analyses of racism's rationality thus far addressed may be subsumed under a macrolevel account. It may be claimed that the psychological, social, and cultural rationales for racist expression are explained in the last analysis only in terms of their functionality for the capitalist mode of production, as "rational ideological response(s) to the realities" of capitalism. On this view, racism has both systemic and ideological implications, for it structures, strengthens, stabilizes, and legitimizes relations of class privilege and racial exclusion (Prager, 1972, pp. 130, 133, 137; cf. Prager, 1987a, 1987b, and Banton, 1987; Gabriel and Ben-Tovim, 1977).[10] In short, racism is rational only insofar as it serves the interests of capital and white privilege.

Viewed in this way, racism is treated as "false consciousness," a "system of beliefs and attitudes that distort reality" (Miller, 1984, pp. 45–46; cf. Prager, 1972, p. 138). Thus, though racism may prove rational at the level of individual psychology, or personality formation (Miller, 1987, p. 97), or accumulation of wealth, it involves intellectual defects by distorting and undermining real social and human interests (cf. Miles, 1989, p. 42; Reich, 1981). Despite the recognition that racist ideas are distasteful, blacks, for example, continue to remain structurally subordinate both intra- and internationally. At the wider level, then, racism generates contradictions, in general, between its functionality and its disfunctionality. Racism may serve to maintain profit, power, and privilege, but does so at the cost of longterm resentment, reaction, and instability. So, at the macrolevel, racism seems irrational (cf. Miller, 1987, pp. 97–98; Prager, 1987a, 1987b).

There is much that is compelling about this picture of racism. Many have demonstrated that the rise of racism is coterminous with the development of capitalism and colonialism, and that changes in the forms that racism has assumed can largely be related to transformations in the capitalist mode of production and its class relations (cf. Miles, 1989; Gilroy, 1987; Goldberg, 1987; Jordan, 1968; Cox, 1948). But while these determinants for the most part account for the genesis of racism, they fail to exhaust the range of its possibilities and transformations. At some point, offspring assume autonomy from progenitors. There are cases where exclusion takes place *in virtue of* and not merely rationalized by racist discourse (Goldberg, 1989a; cf. Prager, 1987a, 1987b, and Banton, 1987). This is reflected in the fact that racist discrimination may occur intraclass, as it may interclass, and that racism could conceivably afflict classless societies. It is possible then that racism could persist despite eradicating classes or capitalism, just as racism could be eliminated without eradicating (capitalist) class differentiation (cf. Goldberg, 1989b; Gates, 1989). Moreover, the maintenance of profit, power, and privilege may not be inconsistent with resentment, reaction and instability. The greater the risk, the higher the rare of return: the latter may turn out to be the conditions under which maintenance of the former are truly put to the test. Thus while racism is highly likely to exacerbate social inequities and tension, it is not clear that it need promote (dialectical) contradiction.

A general account of racism must integrate its determinants and effects at the levels of the economic and the psychological, the social and the individual, the political and the moral. I will address this in conclusion. But first I turn to the claim that racism's inherent irrationality consists in the incoherence of its ends.

The Immorality of Racist Ends

In a nonobjectivist view of values, individual ends considered in isolation are arbitrary and subjective. The only way to determine whether an agent's end is rational is on the basis of its cohering with a given system of ends. The question here is whether racist discriminations considered as ends-in-themselves—as racist beliefs held and practices undertaken for their own sakes—are capable of cohering with our other ends. To hold racist beliefs or undertake racist practices as ends-in-themselves and not merely, say, for their profitability is literally to adhere to and act for the sake of the racist principles. It is to believe or act thus not only because of any advantages that these expressions may afford but in the face of conceivable or actual disadvantages. Where social ends are racist, social institutions are fashioned in their light, and this, of course, enables realization of these ends. Social structure in South Africa attests to this. Now, there is no inherent inability of racist principles to cohere with other ends like social affluence, retention of state power, domination, and the like. It follows that the view of racism's inherent irrationality is left to depend on the argument that racist ends or principles are inconsistent with moral ones.

This argument must hold generally that moral ends conjoin in a body of universal principles—honesty, truth, justice, liberty, and so forth—determined by perfectly rational legislating beings subject only to common, objective—that is, rational—laws. No principles other than these or those consistent with them are moral, for no other principles are socially rational. Racist principles would not be chosen, for they are inconsistent with principles of liberty and justice. Hence racism must be irrational.

On this argument, an end is a proper member of the empire of ends by virtue of being rationally chosen by an ideal legislator. To determine whether a racist principle would be morally acceptable, it must first be established whether it is rational. We cannot, on pain of circularity, simply claim its immorality a priori and infer its irrationality from this. Nor may we presume so readily that any racist principle per se will be inconsistent with principles of liberty and justice. It is at least conceivable that a policy of separate development meets rational standards of freedom and equality. Though the policy separates social, political, and cultural institutions on racial grounds, it could guarantee distributively equal levels of resources to the separate institutions.[11] Of course, this "egalitarian apartheid" is merely a conceptual possibility; yet it cannot be objected here that experience has proved otherwise for two reasons. First, though separatism historically has mainly been proposed by and in the interests of dominant groups, it has received some support among those dominated (e.g., blacks and Palestinians). And second, the general form of the argument at hand is an a priori one; so rational possibility is a sufficiently strong counter.

The benevolent utilitarian has a more appealing formulation of the argument. Concerned with maximizing benevolent treatment for all, the utilitarian can extend equal liberty and justice to each as a means of maximizing utility, average or aggregate. Maintenance of liberty and justice would be guaranteed for all, and, by implication, so would moral indictment of institutional racism.

The assumption of equal liberty and justice for all as a means to utilitarian ends must realistically presuppose an economy of scarce resources. From positions of equal liberty, participants compete for the same goods. It is then open for some to argue in justification either of their claims to the goods or of their successful domination of the competition that they deserve the disproportionate distribution on *empirical* grounds. These grounds might include racially based considerations. The utilitarian could appeal, for instance, to needs based on putatively racial characteristics. More fundamentally, the claim could be rationalized paternalistically as follows: despite equal rights to liberty and justice abstractly considered, the "less civilized" level of development of some races renders them incapable of the best administration of their resources from the perspective of maximizing their own utility.[12] So, there is no necessity in terms of this utilitarian principle to condemn racially discriminatory practices. One possible response open to the benevolent utilitarian here is to insist that liberty and justice have intrinsic utility. But this is no longer a factual claim, and the utilitarian retreats thereby to deontological high ground.

The standard view of deontological deliberation determines a unique moral obligation for each act context by reasoning from a premise to which all rational agents would assent, via intermediate steps (description of context and so on) which anyone would be capable of comprehending, to a conclusion with which all would agree and hence are compelled to accept. To fail to accept the conclusion signifies either incompetence or irrationality. However, formulated in this way, moral reason is even more stringent than the concept of rationality basic to the strictest sciences. Rationality in science consists in suggesting hypotheses and undertaking to revise them by checking them against the facts

(Jarvie and Agassi, 1970, p. 178). In any case, the nature of morality itself seems to belie such rigor: in keeping with scientific reason, one of the marks of the moral is that disputes be open to rational disagreement, that moral claims are revisable (Cavell, 1976, pp. 254ff).

It might be argued that racist contentions are not something on which there can be *rational* disagreement. They transgress the revisability condition and so must be irrational. On this view, racist beliefs are intrinsically indisputable, and those who espouse and act on them are not open to being persuaded otherwise. Yet there is nothing in the nature of racist beliefs that render them inherently indisputable: some have claimed that even apartheid can be reformed (for the dispute at issue here, cf. Goldberg, 1986a). So, the argument seems to reduce to a question about the dogmatic nature of racists. A racist may respond, not insincerely, that one is open to being persuaded otherwise; one simply has not been offered reasons compelling enough to overthrow one's racist beliefs. For example, after long and vehement commitment to apartheid, the Nederduits Gereformeerde Kerk (Dutch Reformed Church) recently declared it inimical to the spirit of God. Similarly, Peter Urbach (1974) once argued that the hereditarian research program concerning intelligence is progressive in the sense of anticipating novel facts, while the environmentalist program could only account for these facts on an ad hoc basis (pp. 115–125). The anticipated facts that Urbach had in mind included the degree of family resemblances in IQ, IQ-related social mobility, and most notably a ten- to fifteen-point differential in sibling regression for American "Negroes" and whites (pp. 133–135). Urbach's arguments presupposed the prevailing data at the time furnished by Burt, Shuey, and Jensen. The data have since been discounted as fraudulent and biased (cf Kamin, 1974; Gould, 1981; Lewontin, Rose, and Kamin, 1984, Chap. 5). Presumably, Urbach would be concerned to revise his thesis, if not to renounce it, as a result of these later considerations. These examples suggest that there are also cases where racist beliefs turn out rational in the strong sense.

The revisability objection to the possibility of racism's rationality can be interpreted in strictly moral terms. Here, the objection is not equivalent to the logical one that racism refuses revision nor to the criticism that racism conflates natural and social kinds, that appeals to "race" as biological grounds for differential social treatment always involve unjustified values as the motive for such differences. Nor is it just the point of empirical sociologists that racists are found never to alter their views. Rather, the objection consists in the moral claim that "race" never commands categorically: it is incapable of grounding a moral imperative. "Race" is, by definition, a "morally irrelevant category," and discriminations on the basis of "race" are thus irrational (Rawls, 1971, pp. 149–150; Cohen, 1979; Wasserstrom, 1979, pp. 84ff; M. Jones, 1985, p. 223).

The Rawlsian formulation of the objection is the strongest, and I will restrict my remarks to it. Rawls is surely right that any appeal to racial considerations is to be excluded from the *ideal* principles of justice rationally chosen in the original position. Yet appeals to racial considerations turn out irrational, and hence immoral, because the impossibility of their coming out rational is assumed to be a structural feature of the hypothetical choice situation itself. Rawls assumes away contingent differences between people that in actual contexts could conceivably make a moral difference. "Race" turns out to be a "morally irrelevant category" because it is presumed to be.

The difficulties facing the strict moral rationalist here are highlighted in those cases where agents find self-interested prudential considerations competing with rational choices made behind the veil of ignorance. Like Kant, Rawls's moral argument assumes the overriding compulsion of moral claims in conflict with prudential ones. Nevertheless, as Philippa Foot (1978) argued, the claim that moral considerations are overriding from the moral point of view is tautologous and uninteresting. Common cases can be cited where an agent may be deemed rational for acting on prudential considerations in the face of competing moral ones (see pp. 181–188). Moreover, the moral rationalist who holds ideally to the irrelevance of "race" is hard put to distinguish between the moral unacceptability of "discriminating against" and the oftentimes permissible "differentiating between" members of a race. This makes it more difficult, at least prima facie, to justify preferential treatment on the basis of race. Nevertheless, such programs are not, on the face of it, irrational nor are they morally irrelevant.

I do not mean to imply by this set of arguments that rationality plays no part in establishing the immorality of racism. There are clearly cases where racist beliefs and the practices to which they give rise may be dismissed as unacceptable because they are irrational. Nevertheless, irrationality can serve only as a sufficient condition for racism's immorality. The immorality of racism for the most part turns on something more substantive than the rational status of the beliefs and practices in question. We usually condemn racism as immoral not because it fails to satisfy formal requirements of rationality, like consistency, nor because race is an irrelevant moral criterion, but rather because it picks out persons so as to exclude them from rights or entitlements which we think should be available to all or to subject them to behavior that we think no one should have to suffer. Indeed, even in those cases where racist beliefs and acts are dismissed as irrational, this seems to signal a deeper disapprobation. Mostly, we find racism wrong because it is somehow unfair or unjust. In short, we dismiss it on grounds of deeply cherished values.

One way of trying to sharpen the distinction at issue is to deem racism wrong for the *unreasonable* claims and behavior that it encourages or causes. The distinction between rationality and reasonableness is embedded in our contemporary moral tradition: it is explicit, for example, very early in Rawls's work (195 1, p. 179; cf. Scanlon, 1984, pp. 110ff), and many moral theorists intend the latter when using the former. "Rationality" is largely formal in extension, setting the standards for "explaining, arguing, proving and deliberating" (Baier, 1984, p.

194). Reasonableness also involves the formal criteria of rational consistency, coherence, conceptual clarity, generalizability, and so forth. But it signifies more than this, including substantive conceptions of fairness, moderation, genuine autonomy, support by grounded reasons, emphasis on non-fatalistic ideas, and respect for persons and counterclaims. A reasonable person is one open to being persuaded otherwise by the best available arguments. In short, a rational person might not be reasonable, though a reasonable person cannot help but be rational. Thus while racism need not be irrational, it is inherently unreasonable and, as such, unacceptable.

Now it might turn out that this hypothesis is faced by difficulties similar to those I have shown afflicting the view that racism is inherently irrational. It is beyond my scope to pursue these issues here. Yet, should this turn out to be so, it suggests a deeper point about the nature of racism. "Racism" has come to designate a very wide range of phenomena. So, while we may be able to say roughly what in general we find wrong with racism, there may be no single moral condemnation strictly appropriate to all types. This would commit us to developing multiple strategies for revealing that racism is wrong. A given racist token would turn out immoral by reflecting a type that has been shown for some reason to be wrong; it may differ from the reason why another racist token of a different type turns out unacceptable. Clearly, the existential hurt suffered by the victim of racist discrimination and its characteristic wrongfulness may differ for different kinds of cases. Certainly, they will not just have to do with the ascription of morally irrelevant characteristics. In some cases, the hurt and wrong will be functions of being made the object of categories from which there is no escape. If one is called stupid, there may at least be ways of showing why the characterization is wrong—in this or other cases. By contrast, if one is deemed incompetent for racist reasons, the most one can often hope to show the racist is that the designation is unfitting in spite of one's race. But here one can think of at least two different sources for the hurt and wrong. On one hand, they may be a function of having the culture, history, and products of the group to which one is committed being demeaned, dismissed, or disregarded; on the other, they may be a function of being placed in a group to which one chooses to show no allegiance. The first is a straightforward case of disrespect; the second is a case of denying autonomy.[13] Again, these may differ from cases where the cause of hurt is tied to the historical weight of being called a "nigger" or a "kike," deemed a sly Arab, considered incapable of more than athleticism or entertainment, or slighted as usurious moneylender. Of course, circumstances must establish whether the accompanying wrongs here are instances of disrespect or lack of autonomy, or simply rationalized instances of the denial of a right to equal treatment. The blanket notion of irrationality at best serves to hide these distinctions and at worst draws attention away from the wrongfulness of rational racism, leaving uncontested and so seemingly legitimate any racist expressions not clearly irrational.

CONCLUSION

Thus the conceptual, logical, prudential, and moral arguments supporting the thesis that racism is inherently irrational fail under scrutiny to exhaust the entire range of racist propositions, beliefs, and acts. There are clearly many examples where racist actions turn out rational in the weak instrumental sense of effecting ends or goals. A fuller account of social rationality involving a more complete specification of human psychology and the structures of social life will bear this out. For here, beliefs will turn out rational in terms of their ability to comfort and protect against anxiety, to organize vague feelings, to provide a sense of identity, to facilitate participation in a cause, and so forth (Abelson, 1976). The view that many racist acts turn out weakly rational assumes greater plausibility in this light. Yet I have suggested that some racist beliefs will be strongly rational, for they satisfy widely accepted formal criteria of rationality. To illustrate the sophistication of contemporary cases of rational racism in both the weak and the strong senses, I offer the following examples.

The first example concerns immigration restrictions. Maintenance and promotion of cultural tradition are widely considered morally acceptable ends. A general policy to foster these ends preserves prima facie regard for members of the various cultures in question. Some societies claim to find as a necessary means for realizing these ends the enforcement of immigration restrictions on members of "alien" cultures. Quotas of this kind need not be overtly racist in formulation: consider the ruling that "only persons with families domiciled in Britain in 1850 will be granted British citizenship." It is possible to universalize the policy without contradiction, for Tory parliamentarians have readily acknowledged that "alien" cultures may want to protect their own heritage, that they ought to do so, and that this would necessitate similar immigration restrictions on their behalf (Baker, 1981, pp. 16–20; Dummett and Dummett, 1982, pp. 58–92; Cohen, 1988).

Consider also the case of a white female district attorney in the United States who uses the majority of her peremptory challenges to exclude blacks from the jury in the case of trials involving black defendants. She correctly believes from long experience and statistical studies that the more black jury members there are, the less likely she is to obtain a jury decision in such cases (cf. *Batson v. Kentucky*, 1986).

It might be argued that neither case is racist. There is no attribution of biologically determined characteristics to the excluded group that purports to render its members inferior or inept. Yet this restricts racism to its older forms.[14] Though neither case need be overtly racist in formulation, both meet my definition of racism given earlier. The first is racist in intending to exclude racial others, the second, in effect. The prosecutor's professional aim is to secure prosecution. Should social statistics about black jury members alter, the prosecutor would be willing to change her strategy accordingly. So she is clearly aware of the effects. Both cases pointedly involve exclusion of members of a given racial group and, as policy, both would affect the excluded group adversely. Group members are (to be) excluded because of racial membership from entitlements available to others in a different racial group. In neither case is the policy self-defeating. Each is consistent and coheres with interests central to the society in question. So, clearly, both are rational in the weak sense.

Yet these cases surely involve morally invidious undertakings. The former aims to, and the latter does, exclude on the basis of racial membership. The first case is tied to a pattern of historical exclusion, exploitation, and invidious treatment. The second case, if generalized as a policy, would go far in perpetuating blacks' exclusion from access to and active participation in the institutions of justice. The rights to equal protection under the law and trial by fair cross section of the community would be violated. Such a policy would increase the probability of procedural unfairness. In general, black defendants would be open to penalties in ways that whites would not. Trial outcomes might be skewed by undermining the likelihood of jury divergence, for example, in interpreting the facts.

A different case will reveal that racist beliefs or theory could be rational in the strong sense. I have already suggested that Urbach's (1974) hereditarianism structured in terms of Lakatosian methodological considerations is an example of this sort. Pierre van de Berghe's (1981) commitment to a sociobiological explanation of racism provides a more recent example. The sociobiological paradigm holds that, like other animals, members of the various human races have reached the point via selection of kin preference. Reproductive partiality to kin is supposed to maximize the inclusive fitness of the intrabreeding kin. Human organisms are simply frameworks for the natural selection of reproductively successful genes, and genes favoring intrakin relations have purportedly exhibited selective advantage. Racism emphasizes genetically heritable phenotypes in selection of sexual partners, and all other fraternal relationships are for the sake of this reproductive end. Racial phenotypes are accordingly considered the most reliable markers of kinship or genetic relatedness. Racism turns out to be genetically functional (pp. xii, 29–35; Wilson, 1975, pp. 562ff). The sociobiological implication is that racial exclusion is understandably universal in both the temporal and spatial senses. As with Urbach's hereditarianism, sociobiology makes of racism a natural phenomenon. Explanation of its occurrence becomes rationalization of its inevitability. Theoretical commitment to sociobiology under this interpretation implies rational commitment to racist beliefs.

That forms of racist expression may sometimes turn out rational in both the strong and weak senses has implications for how racism is both conceived and resisted. I have suggested that racist beliefs, and the acts and institutions they license, cover a wide range. This has to do with the fact that "race" is chameleonic and parasitic in character, insinuating itself into more legitimate forms of social and scientific expression. Racist discourse is able to modify its mode of articulation and thus assumes renewed significance in terms of prevailing scientific and social theories as well as cultural and political values at given times. It becomes less surprising, then, that forms of racist discourse may be accommodated by any conception of rationality that does not discount it a priori. The consequent resemblance of racism's categorical functions to more acceptable forms of social and scientific thinking suggests one reason why racist discourse in some form or another continues to enjoy social effect, if not always open endorsement. This similarity renders racist discourse seemingly more acceptable, consciously or unconsciously, more *normal* than its extreme forms sometimes suggest (cf. Foucault, 1977, pp. 63–108).

The relative conceptual autonomy of racist discourse from other discourses, while articulated in terms of them, suggests that racism not only serves and fuels relations of power but may sometimes define them. On one hand, given relations of power obviously may be articulated and so reified in racist terms. Yet it should not be thought that the relations of power always are or need be those between capitalist and working class. It is conceivable that racism articulated the relations between slave and slaveholder, serf and feudal lord, though whether this was historically the case is an empirical question. And examples abound of racially articulated power relations between individuals within or that have nothing to do with class membership. On the other hand, relations of power may be constituted in virtue of racist discourse. Here, the very definition of power owes its raison d'être to pregiven racial formations (cf. Foucault, 1978, pp. 149–150; Goldberg, 1989a).

Thus there is no single unified phenomenon of racism, only a range of racisms. This lack of any more than a general identity to instances of racist discourse has implications for resistance. Just as a plurality of strategies may be required for moral condemnation, so no single mode of resistance to racism will succeed exhaustively. Racism's adaptive resilience entails that we have to respond with sets of pragmatic oppositions appropriate to each form that racism assumes. Institutionally, overcoming apartheid (Goldberg, 1987) must take on forms different from opposition to racist jury practices or discriminatory employment and housing practices in the United States (Goldberg, 1990); ideologically, the appropriate kinds of response to claims of racial superiority or inferiority will differ from those to racially interpreted cultural differences (Goldberg, 1989a); and scientifically, critical attack on racist metaphors and concepts insinuated into standard theoretical articulation (Stepan, 1989) will differ from the responses appropriate to scientific theories supporting racist hypotheses (Stepan, 1982; Stepan and Gilman, 1988). In general, the ways in which we are to resist rational articulations of racism will diverge from critical opposition to irrational racisms, as, indeed, also will the appropriate responses to rational racisms in the weak and strong senses.

Thus we should not be too optimistic about the effectivity of moral education. Given this account, moral education may be an appropriate way to respond to some forms of racism, but its scope and effects are likely to be very limited. First, as Prager (1987b) pointed out, there is no necessary relation between the growth of knowledge and its effect on the dominant representation of others, and probably even less on more subtle discriminatory articulations (p. 471). The limits of moral education in combating racism will likely be magnified in those cases where racism is more deeply embedded in the social structure and its accompanying discourse of articulation. Here, nothing short of structural transformation and discursive displacement will help. Second, moral education aims to encourage agents to give up racist behavior by altering racist feelings and thoughts. This line of attack seems inverted: One can never be sure that, or when, the moral education has been effective; and there are all sorts of ways to restrict discriminatory expressions directly without having first to alter thinking (cf. Dummett, 1986, p. 14; M. Jones, 1985, p. 226). Third, moral education is always undertaken in, and so is likely to reflect, a given social context. In a racist social setting, there is an increased tendency for racial constructs to insinuate themselves into the presuppositions, language, and thinking of public morals (cf. Brandt and Muir, 1986, p. 64; Goldberg, 1986b).

While these concluding remarks require elaboration elsewhere, I can only suggest here that, in the final analysis, moral resistance to racism must necessarily assume political, legal, economic, and cultural forms. And yet, any such form of resistance to racism must likewise be underwritten by moral commitment.

NOTES

Work on this topic was partially funded by a grant from Drexel University, Philadelphia. I take this opportunity to thank Bernard Baumrin, Peter Caws, Arthur Collins, Peter Lupu, and Howard McGary for their incisive comments on earlier versions or particular parts of this article. I thank also Alan Goldman for his interesting comments on a version I read at the American Philosophical Association Eastern Division meeting in Washington, D.C., December 1985. Of course, any mistakes remain entirely my responsibility.

1. In this characterization, as elsewhere in the article, disjuncts are intended inclusively.

2. It may be objected that this characterization captures only ethnocentric ascriptions, not racist ones. For while ethnocentric stereotypes may weaken with familiarity, the very point of racist ideology in terms of which racial stereotypes get their force is to maintain exclusions—either by stiffening or altering their form—at the very points at which the exclusions threaten to evaporate. While this is no doubt true in some instances of racial stereotyping, it is inadequate as a general characterization of the differences on two counts. First, some forms of ethnocentric stereotyping may

function in just the same ways—for example, fundamentalist stereotyping of more liberal religious practices. Second, not all racism is rigid in this way—for example, in becoming more familiar with blacks, some white South Africans now concede that "we would not mind black neighbors as long as they can afford it" (Coetzee, 1986).

3. For similar examples, see P. Singer (1978, p. 188) and M. Jones (1985, p. 223).

4. There may be cases of Aristotle's acting *by reason of* rather than *from* ignorance, where the agent cannot be expected to know better and so where responsibility for the act is mitigated (Aristotle, 1946. III.1: 1110b15ff).

5. A "pandiacritic race" is one for which every member is easily identifiable; a "macrodiacritic race" is signified by an identification rate of over 80 percent; a "mesodiacritic race" has between 30 percent and 80 percent identifiability; and a "microdiacritic race" is that for which members are less than 30 percent recognizable (cf. Keith, 1928; Allport, 1954, pp. 132–133).

6. An example of this is unfortunately not difficult to find: see Putnam (1961, pp. 6–7). We should also remember that the history of science (and not just the history of racial science) would be distorted if we restrict rationality only to true beliefs (Jarvie and Agassi, 1970, p. 188). Here, rationality requires simply that the evidence be the best available.

7. Whether there is evidence of something like this inconsistency concerning other issues in fields like anthropology is a question beyond my present scope.

8. The object of my criticism is much more modest than the widely held belief-desire theory of action as such. Rather, it is the unsophisticated application of this model in social psychology to corroborate the presumption of racism's irrationality.

9. Kelman (1981) suggested that it even may not be inconsistent for an agent to exhibit some personal racial prejudice while supporting anti-discrimination legislation: different ends and considerations are at issue. This point bears also on the "attitude behavior inconsistency" discussed earlier.

10. Banton (1987) assumed that individuals are basically rational in calculating the effects of alternative courses of action for achieving their subjective goals, and that values of differences in skin color enter the utility function as one among other variables. Macrolevel determinations for Banton are simply accumulations of individual, microlevel ones. By contrast, for Prager (1987b), irrational assumptions about racial difference are basic to macrolevel collective representations about the other. These irrational racist assumptions then serve to determine microlevel choices of individuals (p. 469). While I am sympathetic to Prager's suggestions concerning the irreducibility of racial determinations, I will argue that the racial assumptions need to be irrational.

11. This may include separate institutions for the group forming as a result of mixed marriages. The son of H. F. Verwoerd, architect of apartheid, continues to insist that this egalitarian separateness represents the proper spirit of apartheid. Such a conception of a racist social structure can be attacked not by appealing to principles of liberty and equality but on grounds of the overriding value of genuine mutual integration, whether consequential or inherent.

12. Examples include Mill's (1859) argument about "nations in their nonage" and Carleton Putnam's (1961) comments about blacks in America. Of course, beliefs, of this kind will turn out largely to be false. But to rule out the argument at hand, utilitarianism would have to establish that such beliefs are *inherently* false.

13. I am aware that Kant took respect and autonomy to be, in some sense, morally (and perhaps conceptually) equivalent. Yet one can still argue that the autonomy or respect denied in the one case at hand differs from that in the other case. The constraints on autonomy that are the product of the attack on self-respect seem to me to differ, at least in degree if not kind, from the lack of autonomy in denying one the capacity to determine self-identity.

14. Some refer to explanatory beliefs of this kind as *racialism*, to contrast them with those beliefs prompting *racist* practices. At any rate, nothing seems to hang on this distinction (see Appiah, 1989).

REFERENCES

Abelson, R. P. 1976. "Social Psychology's Rational Man." In *Rationality and the Social Sciences*. edited by S. I. Benn and G. Mortimore. London: Routledge & Kegan Paul.

Adorno, T. W., E. Frenkel-Breunswik, D. Levinson, and R. Sanford. 1950. *The Authoritarian Personality*. New York: Harper & Row.

Allport, G. 1954. *The Nature of Prejudice*. Boston: Beacon.

Appiah, A. 1989. "Racisms." In *Anatomy of Racism*, edited by D. T. Goldberg. Minneapolis: University of Minnesota Press.

Aristotle. 1946. *Collected Works of Aristotle*, edited by R. P. McKeon, New York: Random House.

Baier, K. 1978. "Merit and race." *Philosophia* 8:121–51.

———. 1984. "Rationality, Reason and the Good." In *Morality, Reason and Truth*, edited by D. Copp and D. Zimmerman. Totowa, NJ: Rowman & Alanheld.

Banton, M. 1983. "Categorical and Statistical Discrimination." *Ethnic and Racial Studies* 6:269–83.

———. 1987. "United States Racial Ideology as Collective Representation." *Ethnic and Racial Studies* 10:466–68.

Barker, M. 1981. *The New Racism*. London: Junction Books.

Becker, G. 1957. *The Economics of Discrimination*. Chicago: University of Chicago Press.

Boggs, J. 1970. *Racism and the Class Struggle*. New York: Monthly Review Press.

Boston, T. 1988. *Race, Class and Conservativism*. Boston: Allen & Unwin.

Boxill, B. 1984. *Blacks and Social Justice*. Totowa, NJ: Rowman & Alanheld.

Brandt, G., and D. Muir. 1986. "Schooling, Morality and Race." *Journal of Moral Education* 15:58–67.

Campbell, D. 1967. "Stereotypes and the Perception of Group Differences." *American Psychology* 22:823–35.

Cavell, S. 1976. *The Claim of Reason*. Oxford: Oxford University Press.

Cell, J. 1982. *The Highest Stage of White Supremacy*. Cambridge: Cambridge University Press.

Coetzee, J. M. 1986. "Tales of Afrikaners." *Sunday Times Magazine*, 9 March.

Cohen, C. 1979. "Why Racial Preference Is Illegal and Immoral." *Commentary* 67 (June): 40–51.

Cohen, S. 1988. *A Hard Act to Follow: The Immigration Act of 1988*. Warwick: Centre for Research in Ethnic Relations.

Cox, O. C. 1948. *Caste, Class and Race*. New York: Modern Reader.

Dummett, A. 1986. "Race, Culture and Moral Education." *Journal of Moral Education* 15:10–15.

Dummett, A., and M. Dummett. 1982. "The Role of Government in Britain's Racial Crisis." In *Race in Britain*, edited by C. Husband. London: Open University Press.

Fishman, J. 1956. "Examination of the Process and Functions of Social Stereotyping." *Journal of Social Psychology* 43:27–64.

Foot, P. 1978. "Are Moral Considerations Overriding?" In *Virtues and Vices*. Los Angeles: University of California Press.

Foucault, M. 1977. "Two Lectures." In *Power/Knowledge*, edited by Colin Gordon. New York: Pantheon.

———. 1978. *The History of Sexuality, Volume I*. New York: Random House.

Gabriel, J., and G. Ben-Tovim. 1977. "Marxism and the Concept of Racism." *Economy and Society* 7:118–42.

Cates, H. L., Jr. 1989. "Critical Remarks." In *Anatomy of Racism*, edited by D. T. Goldberg. Minneapolis: University of Minnesota Press.

Gilroy, P. 1987. *There Ain't No Black in the Union Jack*. London: Hutchinson.

Godelier, M. 1972. *Rationality and Irrationality in Economics*. New York: Monthly Review Press.

Goldberg, D. T. 1986a. "Reading the Signs: the Force of Language." *Philosophical Forum*, Double Issue on Apartheid 18:71–93.

Goldberg, D. T. 1986b. "A Grim Dilemma about Racist Referring Expressions." *Metaphilosophy* 17:224–29.

———. 1987. "Raking the Field of the Discourse of Racism." *Journal of Black Studies* 18:58–71.

———. 1989a. "The Social Formation of Racist Discourse." In *Anatomy of Racism*, edited by D. T. Goldberg. Minneapolis: University of Minnesota Press.

———. 1989b. "Racist Discourse and the Language of Class." In *Race and Class as Patterns of Twentieth-Century Exploitation*, edited by A. Zegeye, J. Maxted, and L. Harris. London: Hans Zell (Butterworth).

———. 1990. "Polluting the Body Politic: Racist Discourse and Urban Location." In *Racism and the Postmodern City*, edited by M. Keith and M. Cross. London: Unwin & Hyman.

———, ed. 1989c. *Anatomy of Racism*. Minneapolis: University of Minnesota Press.

Gould, S. J. 1981. *The Mismeasure of Man*. New York: Norton.

Greenberg, S. 1987. *Legitimating the Illegitimate*. Berkeley: University of California Press.

Hare, R. M. 1980. "Prediction and Moral Appraisal." In *Midwest Studies in Philosophy III*, edited by P. French, T. Uehling, and H. Wettstein. Minneapolis: University of Minnesota Press.

Harris, L., ed. 1983. *Philosophy Born of Struggle*. Dubuque, IA: Kendall/ Hunt.

Innes, D. 1984. *Anglo American and the Rise of Modern South Africa*. New York: Monthly Review Press.

Jarvie, I. C., and J. Agassi. 1970. "The Problem of the Rationality of Magic." In *Rationality*, edited by Bryan Wilson. Oxford: Blackwell.

Jencks, C. 1983. "Thomas Sowell vs. Special Treatment for Blacks." *New York Review of Books* 30, no. 4, March.

Jones, M. 1985. "Education and Racism." *Journal of Philosophy of Education* 19:223–34.

Jones, R. A. 1982. "Perceiving the Other." In *In the Eye of the Beholder*, edited by A. G. Miller. New York: Praeger.

Jordan, W. 1968. *White over Black*. Chapel Hill: University of North Carolina Press.

Kamin, L. 1974. *The Science and Politics of IQ*. Potomac, MD: Erlbaum.

Keith, A. 1928. "The Evolution of the Human Species." *Journal of the Royal Anthropological Society* 58:305–21.

Kelman, S. 1981. "Cost-Benefit Analysis: An Ethical Critique." *Regulation*, January–February.

Lewontin, R., L. Kamin, and S. Rose. 1984. *Not in Our Genes*. New York: Pantheon.

Liska, A., ed. 1975. *The Consistency Controversy*. New York: Wiley.

Miles, R. 1989. *Racism*. London: Routledge.

Mill, J. S. 1859. *On Liberty*. Various editions.

Miller, A. G. 1982, *In the Eye of the Beholder*. New York: Praeger.

Miller, R. 1984. *Analyzing Marx*. Princeton, NJ: Princeton University Press.

———. 1987. *Fact and Method*. Princeton, NJ: Princeton University Press.

Newcomb, T., and W. Charters. 1950. *Social Psychology*. New York. Dryden.

Prager, J. 1972. "White Racial Privilege and Social Change: An Examination of Theories of Racism." *Berkeley Journal of Sociology* 17:117–50.

———. 1987a. "American Political Culture and the Shifting Meaning of Race." *Ethnic and Racial Studies* 10:62–81.

———. 1987b. "The Meaning of Difference: A Response to Michael Banton." *Ethnic and Racial Studies* 10:469–72.

Putnam, C. 1961. "*Race and Reason*." Washington, DC: Public Affairs Press.

Rawls, J. 1951. "Outline of a Decision Procedure for Ethics." *Philosophical Review* 60:171–92.

———. 1971. *A Theory of Justice*. Cambridge, MA: Harvard University Press.

Reich, M. 1971. "The Economics of Racism." In *Problems in Political Economy*, edited by D. Gordon. 2d ed. Lexington, MA: D. C. Heath.

———. 1981. *Racial Inequality*. Princeton, NJ: Princeton University Press.

Scanlon, T. M. 1984. "Contractualism and Utilitarianism." In *Utilitarianism and Beyond*, edited by A. Sen and B. Williams. Cambridge: Cambridge University Press.

Singer, M. 1978. "Some Thoughts on Race and Racism." *Philosophia* 8:163–85.

Singer, P. 1978. "Is Racial Discrimination Arbitrary?" *Philosophia* 8:187–203.

Sowell, T. 1975. *Race and Economics*. New York: McKay.

Stepan, N. I. 1982. *The Idea of Race in Science*. London: Macmillan.

———. 1989. "Race and Gender: The Role of Analogy in Science." In *Anatomy of Racism*, edited by D. T. Goldberg, Minneapolis: University of Minnesota Press.

Stepan, N. L., and S. Gilman. 1988. "Appropriating the Idioms of Science: Strategies of Resistance to Biological Determinism." Unpublished manuscript.

Stephan, W., and D. Rosenfield. 1982. "Racial and Ethnic Stereotypes." In *In the Eye of the Beholder*, edited by A. G. Miller. New York: Praeger.

Tajfel, H. 1973. "The Roots of Prejudice: Cognitive Aspects." In *Psychology and Race*, edited by P. Watson. Chicago: Aldine.

Thurow, L. 1969. *Poverty and Discrimination*. Washington, D.C.: Brookings Institute.

Urbach, P. 1974. "Progress and Degeneration in the IQ Debate (1)." *British Journal for the Philosophy of Science* 25: 99–135.

van den Berghe, P. 1981. *The Ethnic Phenomenon*. New York: Elsevier.

Wasserstrom, R. 1979. "On Racism and Sexism." In *Today's Moral Problems*. New York: Macmillan.

Wilson, E. O. 1975. *Sociobiology*. Cambridge: Belknap.

Wolpe, H. 1972. "Capitalism and Cheap Labor Power in South Africa: From Segregation to Apartheid." *Economy and Society* 1: 425–56.

Wuthnow, R. 1982. "Anti-Semitism and Stereotyping." In *In the Eye of the Beholder*, edited by A. G. Miller. New York: Praeger.

21. The Heart of Racism
Jorge L. A. Garcia

THE PHENOMENON OF RACISM having plagued us for many centuries now, it is somewhat surprising to learn that the concept is so young. The second edition of *The Oxford English Dictionary* (1989) dates the earliest appearances of the term "racism" only to the 1930s.[1] During that decade, as the shadow of Nazism lengthened across Europe, social thinkers coined the term to describe the ideas and theories of racial biology and anthropology to which the Nazi movement's intellectual defenders appealed in justifying its political program. Thus, Ruth Benedict, in a book published in 1940, called racism "the dogma that one ethnic group is condemned by nature to congenital inferiority and another group is destined to congenital superiority"[2] (Benedict, 1940).

These origins are reflected in the definition that the *Oxford English Dictionary* still offers: "The theory that distinctive human characteristics and abilities are determined by race."[3] Textbook definitions also echo this origin: "Racism— a doctrine that one race is superior" (Schaefer, 1990, p. 27). Recently, however, some have argued that these definitions no longer capture what people mean when they talk of racism in the moral and political discourse that has become the term's primary context. Some on the political Left argue that definitions reducing racism to people's beliefs do not do justice to racism as a sociopolitical reality. Robert Miles records the transition in the thought of Ambalvaner Sivanandan, director of Britain's Institute Of Race Relations, who abandoned his earlier account of racism (1973) as "an explicit and systematic ideology of racial superiority," because later (1983) he came to think that "racism is about

Jorge L. A. Garcia, "The Heart of Racism," in the *Journal of Social Philosophy* (forthcoming), reprinted with permission of the *Journal of Social Philosophy* and the author.

power not prejudice." Eventually, he saw racism as "structures and institutions with power to discriminate" (quoted at Miles, 1989, p. 54).[4] From the Right, the philosopher Antony Flew has suggested that, to identify racism with "negative beliefs" about "actual or alleged matters of fact" is a "sinister and potentially dangerous thing"—it "is to demand, irrespective of any evidence which might be turned up to the contrary, that everyone must renounce certain disapproved propositions."[5] Flew worries that this poses a serious threat to intellectual freedom, and proposes a behavioral understanding of "racism" as "meaning the advantaging or disadvantaging of individuals for no better reason than that they happen to be members of this racial group rather than that."

I agree with these critics that, in contemporary moral and political discourse and thought, what we have in mind when we talk of racism is no longer simply a matter of beliefs.[6] However, I think their proposed reconceptions are themselves inadequate. In this paper, I present an account of racism that, I think, better reflects contemporary usage of the term, especially its primary employment as both descriptive and evaluative, and I sketch some of this view's implications for the morality of race-sensitive discrimination in private and public life. I will also briefly point out some of this account's advantages over various other ways of thinking about racism that we have already mentioned—racism as a doctrine, as a socioeconomic system of oppression, or as a form of action. One notable feature of my argument is that it begins to bring to bear on this topic in social philosophy points made in recent criticisms of modernist moral theory offered by those who call for increased emphasis on the virtues. (This voice has hitherto largely been silent in controversies within practical social philosophy.)

I. A VOLITIONAL CONCEPTION OF RACISM

Kwame Anthony Appiah rightly complains that, although people frequently voice their abhorrence of racism, "rarely does anyone stop to say what it is, or what is wrong with it" (Appiah, 1990, p. 3). This way of stating the program of inquiry we need is promising, because, although racism is not essentially "a moral doctrine," *pace* Appiah, it is always a moral evil[7] (Appiah, 1990, p. 13). No account of what racism is can be adequate unless it at the same time makes clear what is wrong with it. How should we conceive racism, then, if we follow Appiah's advice "to take our ordinary ways of thinking about race and racism and point tip some of their presuppositions" (Appiah, 1990, p. 4)? My proposal is that we conceive of racism as fundamentally a vicious kind of racially based disregard for the welfare of certain people. In its central and most vicious form, it. is a hatred, ill-will, directed against a person or persons on account of their assigned race. In a derivative form, one is a racist when one either does not care at all or does not care enough (i.e., as much as morality requires) or does not care in the right ways about people assigned to a certain racial group, where this regard is based on racial classification. Racism, then, is something that essentially involves not our beliefs and their rationality or irrationality, but our wants, intentions, likes, and dislikes and their distance from the moral virtues.[8] Such a view helps explain racism's conceptual ties to various forms of *hatred* and contempt. (Note that "contempt" derives from "to contemn"—not to care [about someone's needs and rights].)

It might be objected that there can be no such thing as racism because, as many now affirm, "there are no races." This objection fails. First, that "race" is partially a social construction does not entail that there are no races. One might even maintain, though I would not, that race terms, like such terms as "person," "preference," "choice," "welfare," and, more controversially, such terms as "reason for action," "immoral," "morally obligatory," may be terms that, while neither included within, nor translatable into, the language of physics, nevertheless arise in such a way and at such a fundamental level of social or anthropological discourse that they should be counted as real, at least for purposes of political and ethical theory.[9] Second, as many racial anti-realists concede, even if it were true that race is unreal, what we call racism could still be real (Appiah, 1992, p. 45). What my account of racism requires is not that there be races, but that people make distinctions in their hearts, whether consciously or not, on the basis of their (or others') racial classifications. That implies nothing about the truth of those classifications.[10]

Lawrence Blum raises a puzzling question about this. We can properly classify a person S as a racist even if *we* do not believe in races. But what if S herself does not believe in them? Suppose S is a white person who hates black people, but picks them out by African origin, attachment to African cultures, residence or rearing in certain U.S. neighborhoods, and so on. Should we call S racist, if she does not hate black people *as such* (i.e., on the basis of her assigning them to a black race), but hates all people she thinks have been corrupted by their internalizing undesirable cultural elements from Harlem or Watts, or from Nairobi or the Bunyoro? I think the case underdescribed. Surely, a person can disapprove of a culture or a family of cultures without being racist. However, cultural criticism can be a mask for a deeper (even unconscious) dislike that is defined by racial classifications. If the person transfers her disapproval of the group's culture to contempt or disregard for those designated as the group's members, then she is already doing something morally vicious. When she assigns all the groups disliked to the same racial classification, then we are entitled to suspect racism, because we have good grounds to suspect that her disavowals of underlying racial classifications are false. If S hates the cultures of various black groups for having a certain feature, but does not extend that disapproval to other cultures with similar features, then that strongly indicates racism.

Even if she is more consistent, there may still be racism, but of a different sort. Adrian Piper suggests that, in the phenomenon she calls "higher order discrimination," a person may claim to dislike members of a group because she thinks they have a certain feature, but really disapprove of the feature because she associates it with the despised group. This "higher order discrimination" would, of course, still count as racist in my account, because the subject's distaste for the cultural element derives from and is morally infected by race-based disregard.

We should also consider an additional possibility. A person may falsely attribute an undesirable feature to people she assigns to a racial group because of her disregard for those in the group. This will often take the forms of exaggeration, seeing another in the worst light, and withholding from someone the benefit of the doubt. So, an anti-Semite may interpret a Jew's reasonable frugality as greed; a white racist may see indolence in a black person's legitimate resistance to unfair expectations of her, and so on.

Thinking of racism as thus rooted in the heart fits common sense and ordinary usage in a number of ways. It is instructive that contemptuous white racists have sometimes called certain of their enemies "nigger-lovers." When we seek to uncover the implied contrast-term for this epithet, it surely suggests that enemies of those who "love" black people, as manifested in their efforts to combat segregation, and so on, are those who hate black people or who have little or no human feelings toward us at all. This is surely borne out by the behavior and rhetoric of paradigmatic white racists.

This account makes racism similar to other familiar forms of intergroup animosity. Activists in favor of Israel and of what they perceive as Jewish interests sometimes call anti-Semites "Jew-haters." Wistrich, for example, says that "'anti-Semitism,' which never really meant hatred of [all] Semites, but rather hatred of Jews, has come to be accepted in general usage as denoting all forms of hostility toward Jews and Judaism throughout history" (Wistrich, 1992, p. xv). He opposes this expansion of meaning, especially extending the term to cover opposition to the religion of Judaism. According to him, those who coined the term for their own doctrines were "not opposed to Jews on religious grounds, but claimed to be motivated by social, economic, political, or 'racial' considerations."[11] What is important for us is to note that *hostility* toward Jews is the heart of anti-Semitism.

It is also worth noting that, immediately prior to the coining of the term "racism," even some of the early anti-Nazi polemicists referred to their subject as "race hatred."[12] This suggests such thinkers may have realized that the true problem was not so much the doctrines of the scientists of race biology and race anthropology, but the antipathy these doctrines rationalized and encouraged.

Racism also seems, intuitively, to be structurally similar to xenophobia and the anti-homosexual malice sometimes called homophobia. However, xenophobia is commonly understood not primarily as consisting in holding certain irrational beliefs about foreigners, but in *hatred* or disregard of them. This suggests that racism should, as I here claim, be considered a form of disaffection.[13] The gay activists Kirk and Madsen urge that we reclassify some so-called homophobes as "homohaters." They cite studies indicating that many people who detest homosexuals betray none of the telltale physiological signs of phobia, and remind us that what is at stake is primarily a hostility toward homosexual persons on account of their homosexuality.[14] Again, by analogy, racism should be deemed a form of disregard.

On my account, racism retains its strong ties to intolerance. This tie is uncontroversial. Marable, for example, writes of "racism, and other types of intolerance, such as anti-Semitism . . . [and] homophobia" (Marable, 1992, pp. 3, 10). Intolerant behavior is to be expected if racism is hatred.[15] How, after all, can one tolerate those whom one wants to injure, and why ought one to trouble oneself to tolerate those whom one disregards?

Such an account of racism as I propose can both retain and explain the link between the two "senses of" racism found in some dictionaries: (i) belief in superiority of R1s to R2s, and (ii) interracial "antagonism."[16] I suggest that we think of these as two elements within most common forms of racism. In real racists, I think, (ii) is normally a ground of (i) (though sometimes the reverse is true), and (i) is usually a rationalization of (ii). What is more important is that (i) may not be logically *necessary* for racism. (In some people, it may nonetheless be a psychological necessity.) However, even when (ii) is a result of (i), it is (ii) and not (i), that makes a person a racist. (Logically, not causally.)

My view helps explain why racism is always immoral. As Stephen Nathanson says, "Racism, as we ordinarily speak of it. . . . implies . . . a special disregard for other groups. Hence, there is a sense in which racism is necessarily immoral" (Nathanson, 1992, p. 9).[17] Its immorality stems from its being opposed to the virtues of benevolence and justice. Racism is a form of morally insufficient (i.e., vicious) concern or respect for some others. It infects actions in which one (a) tries to injure people assigned to a racial group because of their racial identity or (b) objectionably fails to take care *not* to injure them (where the agent accepts harm to R1s because she disregards the interests and needs of R1s because they are R1s). We can also allow that an action is racist in a derivative and weaker sense when it is less directly connected to racist disregard; for example, when someone (c) does something that (regardless of its intended, probable, or actual effects) stems in significant part from a belief or apprehension about other people, that one has (in significant part) because of one's disaffection toward them because of (what one thinks to be their) race. Racism, thus, will often offend against justice, not just against benevolence, because one sort of injury to another is withholding from her the respect she is owed and the deference and trust that properly express that respect. Certain forms of paternalism, while benevolent in some of their goals, may be vicious in the means employed. The paternalist may deliberately choose to deprive another of some goods, such as those of (licit) freedom and (limited) self-determination in order to obtain other goods for her. Here as elsewhere, the good end need not justify the unjust means. Extreme paternalism constitutes an instrumentally malevolent benevolence: one harms A to help her. I return to this below in my discussion of "Kiplingesque" racism.

If, as I maintain, racism is essentially a form of racially focused ill-will or disregard (including disrespect), then that explains why "'Racism' is inescapably a morally loaded term. To call a person a racist is to impugn his character by suggesting deliberate, malign discrimination . . . " (Lichtenberg, 1992, p. 5).

My account of racism suggests a new understanding of racist behavior and of its immorality. This view allows for the existence of both individual racism and institutional racism. Moreover, it makes clear the connection between the two, and enables us better to understand racism's nature and limits. Miles challenges those who insist on talking only of "racisms" in the plural to "specify what the many different racisms have in common" (Miles, 1989, p. 65). This may go too far. Some philosophers have offered respected accounts of common terms that seem not to require that, every time A is an F and B is an F, then A and B must have some feature in common (other than that of being-an-F, if that is a feature). Nominalism and Wittgenstein's "family resemblance" view are two examples. However, if we are not dealing with two unrelated concepts the English terms for which merely happen to have the same spelling and pronunciation (like the bank of a river and the bank that offers loans), then we should be able to explain how the one notion develops out of the other.

Some think that institutions and the like are racist when they are structures of racial domination, and that individual beliefs are racist when they express, support, or justify racial superiority. Both, of course, involve denying or violating the equal dignity and worth of all human beings independent of race. This sort of approach contains some insight. However, it leaves unclear how the two levels or types of racism are related, if they are related at all. Thus, such views leave us rather in the dark about what it is in virtue of which each is a form of racism. Some say that institutional racism is what is of central importance; individual racism, then, matters only inasmuch as it perpetuates institutional racism. I think that claim reverses the order of moral importance, and I shall maintain that the individual level has more explanatory importance.

At the individual level, it is in desires, wishes, intentions, and so on that racism fundamentally lies, not in actions or beliefs. Actions and beliefs are racist in virtue of their *coming from* racism in the desires, wishes, and intentions of individuals, not in virtue of their *leading to* these or other undesirable effects. Racism is, for this reason, an interesting case study in what we might call "infection" (or " input-centered" or backwards-looking) models of wrongdoing, in contrast to the more familiar consequentia list and other result-driven approaches. Infection models of wrongdoing—according to which an action is wrong because of the moral disvalue of what goes into it rather than the non-moral value of what comes out of it—seem the best approach within virtues-based ethics. In such ethical systems, actions are immoral insofar as they are greedy, arrogant, uncaring, lustful, contemptuous, or otherwise corrupted in their motivational sources.[18] Finally, desires, wishes, and intentions are racist when they either *are*, or in certain ways reflect, attitudes that withhold from people, on the basis of their being assigned to a particular race, levels or forms of good will, caring, or wellwishing that moral virtue demands.[19] At its core, then, racism consists in vicious attitudes toward people based on their assigned race. From there, it extends to corrupt the people, individual actions, institutional behavior, and systemic operations it infects. Some, however, seem not to think of racism in this way, as something that, like cruelty or stupidity, can escalate from its primary occurrence in individual people to infect collective thought and decision making of organizations, and, from there, to contaminate the behavior of institutions as well. So to think of it is to see the term as not merely descriptive and evaluative, but also as having some explanatory force.

How is institutional racism connected to racism within the individual? Let us contrast two pictures. On the first, institutional racism is of prime moral and explanatory importance. Individual racism, then, matters (and perhaps occurs) only insofar as it contributes to the institutional racism which subjugates a racial group. On the second, opposed view, racism within individual persons is of prime moral and explanatory import, and institutional racism occurs and matters because racist attitudes (desires, aims, hopes, fears, plans) infect the reasoning, decision making, and action of individuals not only in their private behavior, bur also when they make and execute the policies of those institutions in which they operate. I take the second view. Institutional racism, in the central sense of the term, occurs when institutional behavior stems from (a) or (b) above or, in an extended sense, when it stems from (c). Obvious examples would be the infamous Jim Crow laws that originated in the former Confederacy after Reconstruction. Personal racism exists when and insofar as a person is racist in her desires, plans, aims, most notably when this racism informs her conduct. In the same way, institutional racism exists when and insofar as an institution is racist in the aims, plans, and the like that people give it, especially when their racism informs its behavior. Institutional racism begins when racism extends from the hearts of individual people to become institutionalized. What matters is that racist attitudes contaminate the *operation* of the institution; it is irrelevant what its original point may have been, what its designers meant it to do. If it does not operate from those motives (at time T1), then it does not embody institutional racism (at T1). On this view, some phenomena sometimes described as institutionally racist will turn out not to be properly so describable, but others not normally considered to be institutionally racist will fit the description. (I return to this below.)

Not only is individual racism of greater explanatory import, I think it also more important morally. Those of us who see morality primarily as a matter of suitability responding to other people and to the opportunities they present for us to pursue value will understand racism as an offense against the virtues of benevolence and justice, in that it is an undue restriction on the respect and goodwill owed people. (Ourselves as well as others; racism, we must remember, can take the form of self-hate.) Indeed, as follows from what I have elsewhere argued, it is hard to render coherent the view that racist hate is bad mainly for its bad effects. The sense in which an action's effects are bad is that they are undesirable. But that it is to say that these effects are evil things to want and thus things the desire for which is evil, vicious. Thus, any claim that racial disadvantage is a bad thing presupposes a more basic claim that race hatred is vicious. What is more basic morally is also morally more important in at least one sense of that term.[20] Of course, we should bear in mind that morality is not the same as politics. What is morally most important may not be the problem whose rectification is of greatest political urgency.

II. IMPLICATIONS AND ADVANTAGES

There are some noteworthy implications and advantages of the proposed way of conceiving of racism.

First, it suggests that prejudice, in its strict sense of "pre-judgment," is not essential to racism, and that some racial prejudice may not be racist, strictly speaking. Racism is not, on this view, primarily a cognitive matter, and so it is not in its essence a matter of how or when one makes one's judgments. Of course, we can still properly call prejudice-based beliefs racist in that they *characteristically* either are rooted in prior racial disregard, which they rationalize, or they foster such disregard.[21] Whether having such a belief is immoral in a given case will depend in large part on whether it is a rationalization for racial disaffection. It may depend on *why* the individual is so quick to think the worst of people assigned to the other racial group. Of course, even when the order is reversed and the prejudice does not whitewash a prior and independent racial disaffection, but causes a subsequent one, the person will still be racist because of that disaffection, even if she is not racist in holding that belief, that is, even if she does not hold it for what we might call "racist reasons." My guess is that, in most people who have been racists for some expanse of rime, the belief and the disregard will reinforce each other.

A person may hold prejudices about people assigned to a race without herself being racist and without it being racist of her to hold those prejudices.[22] The beliefs themselves can be called racist in an extended sense because they are characteristically racist. However, just as one may make a wise move without acting wisely (as when one makes a sound investment for stupid reasons), so one may hold a racist belief without holding it for racist reasons. One holds such a belief for racist reasons when it is duly connected to racial disregard: when it is held in order to rationalize that disaffection or when contempt inclines one to attribute undesirable features to people assigned to a racial group. One whose racist beliefs have no such connection to any racial disregard in her heart does not hold them in a racist way, and if she has no such disregard, she is not herself a racist, irrespective of her prejudices.

Second, when racism is so conceived, the person with racist feelings, desires, hopes, fears, and dispositions is racist even if she never acts on these attitudes in such a way as to harm people designated as members of the hated race. (This is not true when racism is conceived as consisting in a system of social oppression.) It is important to know that racism can exist in (and even pervade) societies in which there is no systematic oppression, if only because the attempts to oppress fail. Even those who think racism important primarily because of its effects should find this possibility of inactive racism worrisome, for, so long as this latent racism persists, there is constant threat of oppressive behavior.

Third, on this view, race-based preference (favoritism) need not be racist. *Preferential* treatment in affirmative action, while race-based, is not normally based on any racial disregard. This is a crucial difference between James Meredith's complaint against the University of Mississippi and Allan Bakke's complaint against the University of California at Davis Medical School (see Appiah, 1990, p. 15). Appiah says that what he calls "extrinsic racism has usually been the basis [1] for treating people worse than we otherwise might, [2] for giving them less than their humanity entitles them to" (Appiah, 1992, p. 18). What is important. to note here is that (1) and (2) are not at all morally equivalent. Giving someone less than her humanity entitles her to is morally wrong. To give someone less than we could give her, and even to give her less than we would if she (or we, or things) were different is to treat her "worse [in the sense of "less well"] than we otherwise might." However, the latter is not normally morally objectionable. Of course, we may not deny people even gratuitous favors out of hatred or contempt, whether or not race-based, but that does not entail that we may not licitly choose to bestow favors instead on those to whom we feel more warmly. That I feel closer to A than I do to B does not mean that I feel hatred or callousness toward B. I may give A more than A has a claim to get from me and more than I give B, while nevertheless giving B everything to which she is entitled (and even more). Thus, race-based favoritism does not have to involve (2) and need not violate morality.

Appiah recognizes this fact, saying that "intrinsic racism," because of its ties to solidarity, fraternity, and even "family feeling," is often merely "the basis for acts of supererogation, the treatment of others better than we otherwise might, better than moral duty demands of us" (Appiah, 1990, p. 11). However, he warns ominously, "This is a contingent fact. There is no logical impossibility in the idea of racialists whose moral beliefs lead them to feelings of hatred for other races while leaving them no room for love for members of their own" (Appiah, 1990, p. 12). But why should the fact that this remains a logical possibility incline us to condemn racial preference? When the possibility is actualized, and someone feels not special regard for those who share assignment to her own racial group (along with adequate affection for people assigned to other groups), but hatred for those allocated to other groups (whether or not there is affection for people allocated to her own), then we have illicit antipathy not licit favoritism. When this ugly possibility is not actualized, however, then we need some independent argument against favoritism.[23] Appiah invokes Kant for this purpose (Appiah, 1992, p. 18; 1990, pp. 14, 15). However, the invocation is insufficient. There is no obvious inconsistency in willing that a moderate form of race preference, like other moderate forms of kinship preference, should be a universal law of nature, as Kant's own principal test of universalization requires.[24]

Discrimination *on the basis of* race, then, need not be immoral. It is discrimination *against* people because of their racial assignment that cannot but be immoral. Christopher Jencks says "we need formal discrimination in favor of blacks to offset the effects of persistent informal discrimination against them."[25] Suppose Jencks's claim about our need for discrimination is true. Can racial favoritism ever be justified? It will help to remind ourselves that discriminating *in favor of* R1s need not entail discriminating *against* R2s.[26] The latter consists in acting either (i) with intention of harming R2s or (ii) with hardhearted racist indifference to the action's foreseeable ill effects on R2s,[27] or (iii) from racist beliefs held because of racist disaffection. Similarly, racial self-segregation need not be immoral. It may be especially suspect when white people do it, because we have good historical reason to be suspicious that what is presented as merely greater than morally required concern for fellow white people really involves less than morally required concern for black people. It may also be ill advised even when it is black people who do it. However, in neither case must it be immoral.[28] In neither case must it be racist.

According to this conception of racism, de jure racial segregation violates political morality primarily because (and, therefore, when) it expresses a majority's (or minority's) racial indifference, contempt or ill-will. It is therein vicious, offending against the virtues of both benevolence and justice. However, it need not have such origin, a fact illustrated by recent suggestions to establish separate academies to deal with the educational challenges confronting young black males, and by efforts to control the racial demography of public housing projects in order to avoid problems that have sometimes arisen when such projects became virtually all-black or virtually all-white. Whatever the social merit of such proposals, in cases like these, even if the segregation in the end *proves* immoral, this is not *intrinsic*. There must be some special additional factor present that makes it immoral. De facto racial segregation (mere separation or disproportional representation) need not be morally problematic at all when it happens to result from decently and responsibly motivated individual or social actions.[29] However, it will be immoral if its bad effects on, say, R1s are accepted out of racist hardheartedness, that is, out of racist indifference to the harm done R1s. This will sometimes, but not always, be the case when harms are disproportionally distributed across the various racial groupings to which people are assigned.

Fourth, on this view of racism, racist discrimination need not always be conscious. The real reason why person P1 does not rent person P2 a room may be that P1 views P2 as a member of a racial group R2, to whose members P1 has an aversion. That may be what it is about P2 that turns P1 off, even if P1 convinces herself it was for some other reason that she did not rent. As racist discrimination need nor always be conscious, so it need not always be intended to harm. Some of what is called environmental racism, especially, the location of waste dumps so as disproportionally to burden black people, is normally not intended to harm anyone at all. Nevertheless, it is racist if, for example, the dumpers regard it as less important if it is "only," say, black people who suffer. However, it will usually be the case that intentional discrimination based on racist attitudes will be more objectionable morally, and harder to justify, than is unintentional, unconscious racist discrimination. Rac*ial* discrimination is not always rac*ist* discrimination. The latter is always immoral, because racism is inherently vicious and it corrupts any differentiation that it infects. The former—racial discrimination—is not inherently immoral. Its moral status will depend on the usual factors—intent, knowledge, motive, and so on—to which we turn to determine what is vicious.

This understanding of racism also offers a new perspective on the controversy over efforts to restrict racist "hate speech." Unlike racially *offensive* speech, which is defined by its (actual or probable) effects, racist *hate* speech is defined by its origins, that is, by whether it expresses (and is thus an act of) racially directed hate. So we cannot classify a remark as racist hate speech simply on the basis of *what* was said, we need to look to *why* the speaker said it. Speech laden with racial slurs and epithets is presumptively hateful, of course, but merely voicing an opinion that members of R1 are inferior (in some germane way) will count as racist (in any of the term's chief senses, at least) only if, for example, it expresses an opinion held from the operation of some predisposition to believe bad things about R1s, which predisposition itself stems in part from racial disregard.[30] This understanding of racist hate speech should allay the fears of those who think that racial over-sensitivity and the fear of offending the over-sensitive will stifle the discussion of delicate and important matters beneath a blanket of what is called political correctness. Racist hate speech is defined by its motive forces, and, given a fair presumption of innocence, it will be difficult to give convincing evidence of ugly motive behind controversial opinions whose statement is free of racial insults.

III. SOME DIFFICULTIES

It may seem that my view fails to meet the test of accommodating clear cases of racism from history. Consider some members of the Southern white aristocracy in the antebellum or Jim Crow periods of American history—people who would never permit racial epithets to escape their lips, and who were solicitous and even protective of those they considered "their Negroes" (especially black servants and their kin), but who not only acquiesced in but actively and strongly supported the social system of racial separatism, hierarchy, and oppression. These people strongly opposed black equality in the social, economic, and political realms, but they appear to have been free of any vehement racial hatred. It appears that we should call such people racists. The question is: Does the account offered here allow them to be so classified?[31]

This presents a nice difficulty, I think, and one it will be illuminating to grapple with. There is, plainly, a kind of hatred that consists in opposition to a person's (or group's) welfare. Hatred is the opposite of love, and, as to love someone is to wish her well (i.e., to want and will that she enjoy life and its benefits), so one kind of hatred for her is to wish her ill (i.e., to want and will that she not enjoy them).[32] It is important to remember, however, that not all hatred is wishing another ill for its own sake. When I take revenge, for example, I act from hate, but I also want to do my enemy ill *for a purpose* (to get even). So, too, when I act from envy. (I want to deprive the other of goods in order to keep her from being better off than I, or from being better off than I wish her to be.) I have sometimes talked here about racial "antipathy" ("animosity," "aversion," "hostility," etc.), but I do not mean that the attitude in question has to be especially negative or passionate. Nor need it be notably ill-mannered or crude in its expression. What is essential is that it consists in either opposition to the well-being of people classified as members of the targeted racial group or in a racially based callousness to the needs and interests of such people.

This, I think, gives us what we need in order to see part of what makes our patricians racists, for all their wellbred dispassion and good manners. They stand against the advancement of black people (as a group, even if they make an exception for "their Negroes"). They are averse to it as such, not merely doing things that have the *side* effect of setting back the interests of black people. Rather, they *mean* to retard those interests, to keep black people "in their place" relative to white people. They may adopt this stance of active, conscious, and deliberate hostility to black welfare either simply to benefit themselves at the expense of black people or out of the contemptuous belief that, because they are black, they merit no better. In any event, these aristocrats and their behavior can property be classified as racist.

Recall, too, that even if the central case of racism is racial hatred (malevolence), the racial disaffection that constitutes racism also extends to racial callousness, heartlessness, coldness, or uncaring. (We might group these as the vice of non-benevolence). These too are racism, for it is surely vicious morally to be so disposed toward people classified as belonging to a certain racial group that one does not care whether they prosper or suffer, and is thus indifferent to the way in which the side effects of one's action disadvantage them.[33] Indeed, I think that, as described, our genteel, oppressive members of the gentry go beyond this to manifest a kind of practical hostility: they consciously and actively act to suppress black people. However, even those who do not go that far are still racist. (Dr. King famously reminded us that to the extent that the good are silent in the face of evil, they are not [being] good.) Morally, much will depend on what these agents mean to do. Do they seek to deprive black people of various positions and opportunities precisely because they wish black people not to have these things because the things are good? If so, this is a still deeper type of race malice.[34]

It may not be clear how the understanding of racism offered here accommodates the commonsense view that the attitudes, rhetoric, behavior, and representatives of the mindset we might characterize as the "white man's burden"-view count as racist.[35] One who holds such a Kiplingesque view (let's call her K) thinks non-whites ignorant, backwards, undisciplined, and generally in need of a tough dose of European "civilizing" in important aspects of their lives. This training in civilization may sometimes be harsh, but it is supposed to be for the good of the "primitive" people. Moreover, it is important, for our purposes, to remember that K may think that, for all their ignorance, lack of discipline, and other intellectual and moral failings, individuals within the purportedly primitive people may in certain respects, and even on the whole, be moral superiors to certain of their European "civilizers." Thus, Kipling's notorious coda to "Gunga Din."[36]

The matter is complex, of course, but I think that, at least in extreme instances, such an approach can be seen to fit the model of racism whose adoption I have urged. What is needed is to attend to and apply our earlier remarks about breaches of respect and the vice of injustice. An important part of respect is recognizing the other as a human like oneself, including treating her like one. There can be extremes of condescension so inordinate they constitute degradation. In such cases, a subject goes beyond more familiar forms of paternalism to demean the other, treating her as utterly irresponsible. Plainly, those who take it upon themselves to conscript mature, responsible, healthy, socialized (and innocent) adults into a regimen of education designed to strip them of all authority over their own lives and make them into "civilized" folk condescend in just this way.[37] This abusive paternalism borders on contempt, and it can vio-

late the rights of the subjugated people by denying them the respect and deference to which their status entitles them. By willfully depriving the oppressed
people of the goods of freedom, even as part of an ultimately well-meant project
of "improving" them, the colonizers act with the kind of instrumentally malevolent benevolence we discussed above. The colonizers stunt and maim in order
to help, and therein plainly will certain evils to the victims they think of as beneficiaries. Thus, their conduct counts as a kind of malevolence insofar as we take
the term literally to mean willing evils.[38]

Of course, the Kiplingesque agent will not think of herself as depriving
responsible, socialized people of their rights over their lives; she does not see
them that way and thinks them too immature to have such rights. However, we
need to ask why she regards Third World peoples as she does. Here, I suspect,
the answer is likely to be that her view of them is influenced, quite possibly
without her being conscious of it, by her interest in maintaining the social and
economic advantages of having her group wield control over its subjects. If so,
her beliefs are relevantly motivated and affected by (instrumental) ill-will, her
desire to gain by harming others. When this is if so, then her beliefs are racist
not just in the weak sense that their content is the sort that characteristically is
tied to racial disaffection, but in the stronger and morally more important sense
that her own acceptance of these beliefs is partially motivated by racial disaffection. She is *being* racist in thinking as she does. I conclude that the account of
racism offered here can allow that, and can help explain why many people who
hold the white-man's-burden-mentality are racist; indeed, why they may be
racist in several different (but connected) ways.

Having said all this about some who are what I have called Kiplingesque
racists and about some "well-meaning" Southern aristocrats, I must admit that
my account suggests that some people in these situations, some involved in
racially oppressive social systems, will not themselves be racist in their attitudes,
their behavior, or even in their beliefs (at least, in the stronger sense of being
racist in holding her beliefs). I do not shrink from this result, and think it should
temper our reliance on the concept of collective responsibility. There are real
cases where people share in both wrongdoing and blameworthiness, but collective responsibility for racism is philosophically problematic (in ways I cannot
here pursue) and, I think, it is neither so common nor so important morally as
some maintain (see May, 1992).

IV. SOME CASES

John Cottingham asks us to imagine that "walking down the street, I come
across two beggars, both equally in need of assistance, and I have only a single

banknote, so that I cannot assist both." If, moreover, "one of the mendicants is white and the other black, may not a black passer-by legitimately choose to give his banknote to the latter for no other reason than 'he's one of my race'?" (Cottingham, 1986, pp. 359, 362). He also asks us to imagine ourselves in a position heroically to rescue only one of two people trapped in a burning building. If they are of different races, may I legitimately direct my supererogatory efforts to saving the one who is of my own race?[39]

The view of racism suggested here can help us see how to think about such cases. It indicates, at least, that its being done from non-malicious racial partiality need not tend to render an action wrong. For a black person or a white one, to give to the black mendicant out of racial preference seems to me unobjectionable, so long as the gift is not likely to mean the difference between life and death. Giving preferentially to the white mendicant is more suspicious, but there is no more vicious ("wrong-making," as some say) tendency *inherent* in this preference than there is in the other. (I see little or none in the other.) However, if "Because he's black [like me or like the ones I prefer]" states a morally acceptable answer to the question why someone gave to the black beggar, when she acts from the pro-black preference, then do we not have to say that "Because he's black" (or "Because he isn't white [as I am and as are the ones I prefer]") is a legitimate answer to the question why one did not give to the black beg at when she acts from a different preference? And mustn't we avoid being committed to this, and admit that the latter answer is clearly racist and illegitimate? Well, no; we do not have to admit that. To explain a failure to help someone by saying "Because he's black" sounds ugly, because, given the history of antiblack attitudes and behavior in this society, it sounds as if the agent were acting in order to deprive black people of certain goods. This is likely racist. In our case, however, this answer is merely a misleading way of saying that this person lost out, not on his rights, but on special favors, and not because of ill-will toward black people but because of extra good will toward some other group. Once the explanation "Because he's black" is itself explained, I think, some of our initial suspicion of racism evaporates. (Of course, we might still deem the conduct undesirable and insensitive.)

What of the rescues from the burning building? Even here, I suspect, appeals to race are not as such immoral. They may, however, be inappropriate to the gravity of what is at stake. Surely, it would be objectionable to make the two trapped people play a game, or pick a number, to decide who gets saved. For similar reasons, it would be improper to subject them to a questionnaire and then save the one whose answers were "correct" in matching one's own trivial preferences. No one should lose her life even in part because her favorite color, or football team, or musical performer is different from mine. That is not because there is anything wrong with my having such preferences or, normally, with acting from them. It is because it mocks the seriousness of what is at stake and demeans the persons involved to bring such frivolous matters into these deliberations. By the same token, it may be that strictly racial preference, though innocent in itself, remains too trifling a basis for choice to be made the crux in so weighty a matter. Exactly what seems objectionable about these procedures is hard to specify, but surely it centers on the contrast between the comparative insignificance of the decisive factor (race) and the gravity of what is to be decided (life and death). It makes it more difficult to attend to the importance and solemnity of the end, when we must deal with means that we have trained ourselves to take none too seriously.[40] Race, of course, is a more serious matter in our society than are sports or color preferences, primarily because of its historical overemphasis in programs of oppression and their rationalization. In itself, and more properly, it forms no deep part of one's identity, I think; but, like rooting for the sports teams of one's neighborhood or hometown or school, it may be associated psychologically with interpersonal connections of a more serious nature.

Nonetheless, while perhaps racial classification as such cannot bear the moral weight of life and death choices, the notions of race and of shared race may be masking work done by more serious features and affinities: for example, heightened compassion for those with a history of shared or comparable suffering, a sense of kinship, shared community (not of race but) of social/political connection, and so on. In any case, within a properly virtues-based ethical theory, the important question is not (i) what has B done that legitimizes A's abandoning her? but (ii) in what way is A vicious toward B (cruel? unjust? callous?) if A prefers to help C even when that precludes her also helping B? It is not at all clear that or how attending to affinities connected with the admittedly crude notion of race must always suffice to render A's choice vicious.

Consider the related problem of disfavoritism.[41] Suppose persons D and E both have more regard for people assigned to every race than morality requires of them. D plays favorites, however, loving (people she considers to be) members of R1 more than she loves those of any other racial group. E plays disfavorites (as we might say), specialty reserving (people she considers to be) members of R1 for less concern than she has for others. Is what E does/feels racism? Is it morally permissible?

It seems to me that what E does is not racism, because her so-called disfavoritism is only a special case of favoritism. She picks out all (people she considers to be) *non*-members of R1 for preferential good treatment (that is, better than that she accords R1s). This is likely to be more dangerous socially than are standard cases of favoritism, because it threatens more easily to degenerate into insufficient regard for R1s (or even into antipathy toward them). It is thus a dangerous business, but it lacks the moral ugliness of true racism.

Perhaps it would be a better world without any such racial favoritism. The more important human interconnections, after all, are those founded on joint projects, shared understandings, and common commitments. In short, they are ones that help more fully to humanize us, that bind us one to another in binding us to what is greater than ourselves. All that is a separate matter, however, and one that has no direct bearing on our question of whether acting from such favoritism is permissible.[42]

What should we say of some different cases, discussed by Andrew Hacker and Gertrude Ezorsky, among others, in which a person who herself harbors no racial disregard or disrespect nonetheless accedes to others' racism by refusing to hire, promote, or serve those assigned to a targeted racial group? Here the agent's action is infected, poisoned by racial hatred. It has such hate in its motivational structure, and that is the usual hallmark of racist behavior. I think what crucially distinguishes this agent's behavior is that it is not *the agent's own* hatred. I suggest that in addition to the two forms of racist disaffection we have already identified—the core concept of racial malevolence and the derivative concept of a race-based insufficiency of good, will—we can allow that an action may be called racist in an extended sense of the term when it is poisoned by racism, even where the racial disaffection that corrupts it does not lie in the agent's own heart but in those to whom the agent accedes. Thus, the agent in our example, while not herself racist, performs an action that is in an important way infected by other people's racism. I doubt we should simply say, without qualification, that her own action is racist, but it is surely morally objectionable.[43] Her action *reflects* the racial disaffection that constitutes racism, although it may not *express* or manifest any racist motivation in the agent. (It may, as I note below, but also it may not.) Actions of this sort are morally objectionable, but the moral objection to them will not normally be so severe as is that to actions in which the agent's own racial antipathy motivates her to try to harm members of the targeted group. They may reflect an insufficiency of goodwill, but they may also fall short of actual malevolence.[44] We should, however, note different and more vicious cases. Consider a person who denies service, or promotion, or admission, or employment to people assigned to group G1 in order to appease people with a racial disaffection directed against them. Now, suppose further that she herself cooperates in the latter's malevolence by *trying* to harm those classified as G1s in order to placate their enemies. (This would be a form of what moral theologians have called "formal cooperation.") When the agent goes that far, she has internalized racist malice into her own intentions, and has thus corrupted her actions in a more grievous way than has the person who merely goes along with neighboring racists in her external actions. This is so whether or not her *feelings* toward people assigned to G1 are hostile.

What should we say of a case Judith Lichtenberg raises, in which, acting from racial fear, a white person crosses the street to avoid black pedestrians she perceives as possible dangers?[45] Lichtenberg thinks it acceptable for the fearful (and prejudiced?) white person to cross the street in order to avoid proximity with the black teenagers who approach her at night (p. 4). She sensibly suggests that this is not racist if the person would respond in the same way with white teenagers. "She might well do the same if the teenagers were white. In that case her behavior does not constitute racial discrimination." (Of course, her behavior now raises a question of age discrimination, but, like Lichtenberg, I will not pursue that topic.) Helpfully, Lichtenberg cites several factors she thinks relevant to deciding when it is unjust to take race into account. How much harm does the victim suffer? How much does the agent stand to suffer if she does not discriminate? Is the person who discriminates acting in a public or official capacity?

Lichtenberg maintains that the black teenagers suffer "a minimal slight—if it's even noticed." She even suggests that the white person might spare their feelings "by a display of ulterior motivation, like [pretending to] inspect the rosebushes on the other side" of the street in order to make it look as if it were her admiration for the flowers, and not her fear of black people, that motivated her to cross the street. The latter pretense is, in my judgment, insulting and unlikely to succeed. More important, this appears to be a guilty response, as if the person is trying to cover up something she knows is wrong. I think that fact should cause Lichtenberg and her imagined agent to reconsider the claim that the action is unobjectionable. It is also quite wrongheaded to think that the harm of insult is entirely a matter of whether a person has hurt feelings. Does it make a difference that the victims suffer little direct and tangible harm? Some, but not much. After all, by that criterion, egregiously racist behavior such as engaging in caricatures or telling jokes that mock black people would be justified if done in an all-white setting.

According to Lichtenberg, it is acceptable for the white woman to try to avoid the black teenager on the street, but much harder to justify her racially discriminating when he applies for a job. It will be difficult to maintain this position, however. How is this woman—so terrified of contact with young black males that she will not walk on the same side of the street with them—simply to turn off this uneasiness when the time comes for her to decide whether to offer a job to the black Male? Suppose that the job is to help out in her family's grocery store, and that this is likely to mean that the woman and the teenager will be alone in the store some evenings? Lichtenberg's advice, that the woman indulge her prejudice in her private life but rigorously exclude it from her official conduct, seems unstable. Indeed, Lichtenberg seems to assume that the woman can take refuge in bureaucracy, that she will be the personnel officer who does the hiring, while it is other people who will actually have to work in proximity with the new employee. It is the worst of liberal bad faith, however, for this woman to practice her tolerance in official decision making, but only on the condition that it is other people who will have to bear the burden of adjusting to the pluralistic environment those decisions create and of making that environment work. (Compare the liberal politician who boldly integrates the public schools while taking care to "protect" her own children in all-white private schools.)

Lichtenberg assumes that private discrimination is less serious morally, but this is doubtful. The heart is where racism, like all immorality, begins and dwells. Even if some moral *virtue*-traits were differentially distributed along racial lines (and even if that were for generic rather than historical reasons), each individual would still retain the right to be given the benefit of the probability that she is *not* herself specialty inclined toward vice. Of course, this sort of racial discrimination need not be racist, since it can be entirely unconnected to any racial disaffection, just as it may not be irrational if it is a response to a genuine statistical disparity in risk. (Similarly, there need be nothing immoral in age-based discrimination should the woman seek to avoid being on dark streets alone with teenagers but not with the elderly.) Nevertheless, such conduct runs substantial risk of reinforcing some of the ugly racial stereotypes that are used to rationalize racial antipathy, and there is reason to avoid relying upon it.

Our view of institutional racism is both narrower and wider than some others that have been offered. To see how it is narrower, that is, less inclusive, let us consider the practice of word-of-mouth job-recruitment, in which people assigned to a privileged racial group, who tend to socialize only with one another, distribute special access to employment benefits to social acquaintances similarly assigned. Some deem this institutional racism, because of its adverse impact on those considered members of the disadvantaged group (see, for example, Ezorsky, 1991). Miles protests against those who expansively identify institutional racism with, as he puts it, "all actions or processes (whatever their origin or motivation) which result in one group being placed or retained in a subordinate position by another." In his eyes, the practice of world-of-mouth recruitment is not racist because, although it has an admittedly disproportionally adverse impact on people assigned to the disadvantaged racial group (e.g., African Americans), it has similar impact on members of other groups—ethnic, gender, economic—that are underrepresented among the elite (Miles, 1989, pp. 52, 61).

One can, however, respond that this fact does not show the practice is not an instance of institutional racism. It may be an instance of institutional racism and, at the same time, an instance of institutional sexism, of institutional classism, and so forth.[46] Miles's critics have a point. I think, however, what this shows is that we go wrong when we try to identify institutional racism merely by examining the effects of institutional practices. On the view taken here, the practice, while possibly undesirable and perhaps even unjust, is not racist unless it stems from racist antipathy or lack of empathy or from negative beliefs born of such disaffection, in the hearts of the people who carry out the practice .[47]

Consider, similarly, the so-called old-boy network.[48] Person F, upon hearing of an opening at his place of employment, tells the people he thinks of (who are all white males like himself) about the job and recommends one of them (Person G) to the boss, who hires him. Ignoring the exaggeration is calling anything so informal an "institution," let us explore whether this institution of the old-boy network is racist. Is F (or F's behavior) racist? Is G (or G's behavior) racist? Some are ready to offer affirmative answers. What should we say? First, G cannot be racist just for receiving the job; that's not sufficiently active. What about G's act of *accepting* the job? That can be racist. I think, however, that it *is* racist only in the exceptional circumstance where the institutions are so corrupt that G should have nothing to do with them. Second, F may be racist insofar as his mental process skips over some possible candidates simply because the stereotypes he uses (perhaps to mask his racial disaffection from himself and others) keep him from thinking of them as possible job candidates. Third, one needs some further reason not yet given to label racist the practice of the old-boy network. It may work "systematically" to the detriment of black people. That, however, merely shows that, in our society, with our history of racism, black people can be disadvantaged by many things other than race-based factors. (Glenn Loury offers several other examples of this, interestingly including the custom of endogamy among both white and black people.[49]) What is important to note is that it is misleading to call all these things racist, because that terminology fails to differentiate the very different ways in which and reasons for which they disadvantage people. This classification and broad use of the term, then, fails adequately to inform us, and, of more practical importance, it fails to direct our attention (and efforts) to the source of the difficulty. It doesn't identify for us *how* things are going wrong and thus *what* needs to be changed.

Some accounts of institutional racism threaten to be excessively broad in other ways. Some implicitly restrict institutional racism to operations *within* a society—they see it as one group maintaining its social control over the other.[50] This is too narrow, since it would exclude, for example, what seem to be some clear cases of institutional racism, such as discrimination in immigration and in foreign assistance policies. However, if this restriction to intragroup behavior is simply removed from these accounts, then they will have to count as instances of institutional racism some actions which do not properly fall within the class. Suppose, for example, the government of a hostile planet, free of any bigotry toward any earthling racial group, but unenamored of all earthlings, launches a missile to destroy the earth. Suppose it lands in Africa. This institutional (governmental) action has a disproportionally adverse impact on black people, but it is silly to describe it as racist. (It remains silly even if the aliens decide to target *all* their attacks on the same continent—say, because its size or subterranean mineral deposits make it easier for their tracking systems to locate—and the effect thus becomes "systematic.") Talk of racism here is inane because the action, its motivation, and its agents are entirely untainted by any racial disaffection or prejudice. By the same token, however, although the agents of many earthly institutions *are* tainted by racism (e.g., in the U.S. government), that fact cannot suffice, even in combination with adverse impacts, to make its actions institutionally racist. The racism has first to *get into* the institutional conduct somehow by informing, the conduct of individual agents. In contrast, proponents of expansive accounts of institutional racism, by focusing on the action's effects, end tip in the untenable position of claiming that racism somehow *comes out of* institutional behavior, while simultaneously denying that it must ever even get *into the* action at the action's source in the aims, beliefs, desires, hopes, fears and so on of the agents who execute institutional policy.[51]

We can also profitably turn our account to an interesting case Skillen offers. He writes:

> Suppose Dr Smythe-Browne's surgery has been ticking over happily for years until it is realized that few of the many local Asians visit him. It turns out that they travel some distance to Dr Patti's surgery. Dr Smythe-Browne and his staff are upset. Then they realize that, stupidly, he has never taken the trouble to make himself understood by or to understand the Asians in his area. His surgery practices have had the effect of excluding or at least discouraging Asians. Newly aware, he sets out to fix the situation.
>
> By the same token as his practices have been "consequentially," not "constitutively" discriminatory, they have been "blind," lacking in awareness.
>
> The example shows the possibility of a certain sort of "racism" that, if we must attribute blame, is a function of a lack of thought (energy, resources, etc.). If that lack of thought is itself to be described as "discriminatory" it would need to be shown Dr Smythe-Browne showed no such lack of attention when one of the local streets became gentrified. . . . In such cases, it is not racial sets as such that are the focus of attention, but race as culturally "inscribed." In other words, one is concerned with people in respect of how they identify themselves and are identified by others (for example, intimidating institutions or outright racists). (Skillen, 1993, p. 81)

Despite what Skillen implies, that an institution intimidates some racial groups ("sets") does not make it racist. Flew is right about the insufficiency (even the irrelevance) of mere effects to establish racism, as he is right about the sufficiency of racism to establish immorality.[52] Otherwise, the interplanetary attacks in our earlier example would count as instances of institutional racism. Moreover, that Smythe-Browne was thoughtless about what might be needed to attract Asians in no way shows his conduct was racist, not even if he was more sensitive and interested in how to attract "yuppies" brought close by local gentrification. Insensitivity to certain race-related differences is not racist, even if one is sensitive to class-related differences or to differences associated with other racial differences. Smythe-Browne does not so much "discourage" Asians as fail to encourage them. Psychologically and ontologically, that is a very different matter, and those differences are likely to correlate with moral differences as well. (Failure to encourage is likely merely to be, at worst, an offense of *non*-benevolence rather of *male*volence.) *Perhaps* the Asians were "invisible" to

Smythe-Browne in ways that he is culpable for. To show this, however, more would need to be said about why he did not notice them, their absence, and their special interests. Is it that he cares so little about Asians and their well-being? If there is nothing like this involved, then there is no racism in Smythe-Browne's professional behavior, I say. And if there is something like this involved, then Smythe-Browne's conduct is not purely "'consequentially'. . . discriminatory." It is corrupted by its motivation in racial disaffection.

When it comes to defending racial preferences against Flew's strictures, however, Skillen shows more insight. He adds further detail to his case, asking us to suppose that Dr. Smythe-Browne decides that the only way to cope with the situation is to get an Asian doctor, preferably female, onto the staff. He advertises the job, and finding a good person of the sort he needs, she joins the practice, whereas a number of, in other respects at least, equally good applicants (white, male for the most part) do not. Is this "racism"? Skillen thinks not, and I think he argues his point well. Is it not, in Flew's terms, a case of "discriminating in favor of a racially defined subset out of a total set"? Well, not necessarily. Dr Smythe-Browne's criteria remain medical. His selection is legitimate insofar as we accept that medicine is a human and communicative "art" in respect of which socially significant variables are relevant. In that sense, it is simply not the case that bypassed candidates with better degree results were necessarily "better candidates" (Skillen, 1993, p. 82).

With this understanding and assessment, I agree wholeheartedly. Dr. Smythe-Browne's hiring preference here seems to me to exemplify the sort of race-based distinction that is in its nature and its morality quite different from racist discrimination.[53]

As I mentioned, this account of institutional racism is also more inclusive than some. Flew's account, for example, is too narrow in ways I shall point out below. Usually, people apply the term institutional racism only to practices that reinforce existing intergroup power relations. However, a company of people, all of whom are assigned to an oppressed racial group, may harbor reactive racist attitudes toward all those designated as members of the dominant group, and may institutionalize their racism in such institutions as they control: excluding people considered members of the resented group from access to certain schools, scholarships, employment positions, or memberships not out of fraternal/sororal solidarity with others similarly oppressed, nor out of a concern to realize more just distribution of benefits, but simply from resentful racial antipathy. That is racism in the operations of a social organization, institutionalized racism, and should therefore count as institutional racism. This bears out an observation of Randall Kennedy's.

> Some argue that, at least with respect to whites, African Americans cannot be racist because, as a group, they lack the power to subordinate whites. Among

other failings, this theory ignores nitty-gritty realities. Regardless of the relative strength of African-American and Jewish communities, the African Americans who beat Jews in Crown Heights for racially motivated reasons were, at the moment, sufficiently powerful to subordinate their victims. This theory, moreover, ignores the plain fact African Americans—as judges, teachers, mayors, police officers, members of Congress and army officers—increasingly occupy positions of power and influence from which they could, if so minded, tremendously damage clients, co-workers, dependents, and beyond, the society as a whole. (Kennedy, 1994, 34)

The approach taken here opens the door to the sort of research H. L. Gates has recently called for. He writes, "[W]e have finessed the gap between rhetoric and reality by forging new and subtler definitions of the word 'racism.' Hence a new model of institutional racism is one that can operate in the absence of actual racists. By redefining our terms we can always say of the economic gap between black and white America: the problem is still racism . . . and by stipulation it would be true. But the grip of this vocabulary has tended to foreclose the more sophisticated models of political economy we so desperately need" (Gates, 1993, 48).

V. OTHER VIEWS

This way of understanding the nature of racism contrasts with certain other views from the literature. Elizabeth Young-Bruehl and Cornel West have recently articulated the common view that white male sexual insecurity is at the heart of white racism. "White fear of black sexuality is a basic ingredient of white racism. . . . Social scientists have long acknowledged that interracial sex and marriage is the most *perceived* source of white fear of black people—just as the repeated castrations of lynched black men cries out for serious psychocultural explanation" (West, 1992, pp. 86-87. Also see Young-Bruehl, 1992).

Suppose that West and Young-Bruehl are right to think that most of the white racists around today (or in history) were driven to their racism through fear of black male sexuality. Even if this claim about the psychological causes of racism is true, it leaves unaffected our claim about what racism consists in. It is implausible to think such insecurity essential to (a necessary condition for) racism, even for white racism, because if we came across someone who hated black people, thought us inherently inferior, worked to maintain structures of white domination over us, and so on, but came to all this for reasons other than sexual insecurity, we would and should still classify her attitude as racism. Nor is this hypothesis a near-impossibility; we may come across such people quite often, especially, when we consider other forms of racism—hostility against Asians, for example. "Psychocultural explanation" is unlikely to reveal (logically) necessary truths about the nature of racism.

Finally, let us examine the views offered by Anthony Flew and Anthony Skillen in the recent exchange to which we have already several times attended (Skillen, 1993; Flew, 1990). Skillen writes[54]:

> According to Antony Flew, when people, beliefs or practices are spoken of as "racist," one of three sorts of thing is usually being said. These express three concepts of "racism." But only one of the them, the first, is valid.
>
> (1) "Racism as unjust discrimination." In this first of Flew's senses, to be racist" is to discriminate *in favor of* [emphasis added] or against people for no other or better reason than that they belong to one particular racial set and not another. Since the "defining characteristics" of a race are "skin pigmentation, shape of skull, etc." and since such attributes are strictly superficial and properly irrelevant to (almost) all questions of social status and employment," racism in this sense is as grotesquely unfair as to disqualify competing candidates because they are bald, or blond, or red-headed. So this is a valid use of the term "racist," which both picks out a recognisable practice, colour discrimination, and indicates why it is abominable.
>
> (2) "Racism as heretical belief." In this second sense, to be racist is to *believe* that there are substantial inherited differences among racial sets in attributes relevant to important practical questions. Such differences in accompanying characteristics might be differences in intelligence . . . in aggressiveness, etc. . . . But, Flew contends, the person accused of racism in this sense (provided they are not simply aiming to throw up a smoke-screen for true racism—racism 1), is accused wrongly (p. 73).
>
> (3) "Institutionalized racism" [emphasis added]. In this third sense, "institutions" (schools, firms, government courts) are said to be racist when their routine practices, however "legitimated" have the *effect* [Skillen's emphasis] of and typically, It is alleged, the unadmitted purpose, of excluding or disadvantaging racial sets. Against this Flew argues, again a priori, that institutions cannot have intentions and hence cannot be the target of moral blame (p. 74).
>
> In Flew's terms, then, "racism 3" (pervasive "disadvantage") is falsely represented as a function of "racism 1" by representing the claims of inherited inferiorities ("racism 2") as a legitimating smoke-screen. Thus armed, "anti-racism" becomes the ideology of a genuine and abhorrent racism with blacks getting preference simply on the basis of the color of their skin. . . . [According to Flew's p. 66: "Discriminating in favor of a racially defined subset out of the total set of all those worse off than the majority . . . is paradigmatically racist" (quoted at Skillen, p. 74).]

Skillen rejects Flew's narrow view of what properly counts as racism in favor of his own more expansive conception. "On the contrary, I [Skillen] see racism, which is by no means peculiar to Europeans, as being like misogyny, bigotry, and chauvinism in its *straddling the theory practice (beliefaction) dichotomy* essential to Flew's scheme of things. *Racism, in my view, is a belief validated or 'ideological' disposition or attitude.* As such, *racism is not just a feature of this or that individual but a largely cultural matter*" (emphases added, except Skillen emphasizes "cultural") (Skillen, 1993, p. 75). "[R]acism is a complex of ideological attitudes and practices, more or less bound up with institutionalised barriers. . . . In all cases there is an exercise, through ideology, of power" (Skillen, p. 87).

The volitional account of racism, advocated here, captures what is valuable in the views of Flew and Skillen, while helping to identify and correct their difficulties. As regards Flew, it is not clear what counts as "discrimination" for him. Does a mere differentiation I make in my head count? (For example, thinking all Xs are stupid, corrupt, lazy, greedy, conniving? Thinking they tend disproportionally to be stupid, etc.?) Or must I go on to *do* things to some Xs? If the latter, then what kinds of things? Must it involve withholding real benefits? (How about just keeping away from them?) What if I do things, but don't really do much of anything *to* Xs? (Suppose I malign the intelligence or character of Xs when I speak to my fellow Ys.) What counts as "discriminating" for Flew? I suspect his criterion is too behavioral and insufficiently centered in the racists' desires and goals. Further, Flew's rejection as racist of discrimination in favor even of those socially assigned to an oppressed racial group merely misses the distinction made above between *racist* discrimination and modes of discriminating that are merely race-based. In addition, one wonders about Flew's concession that someone accused of racism for holding so-called heretical beliefs will not escape the charge if, in offering factual claims to defend her position, she is "simply aiming to throw up a smoke-screen for [unjust discrimination]." What if she throws out a smoke-screen without aiming to, or without consciously aiming to?

Contra Skillen's position, it is not clear that a "belief-validated disposition or attitude" does straddle the beliefaction divide. If the "attitude" is the doxastic attitude of belief, then racism doesn't straddle, it's just a belief. Nor need it straddle if the "disposition" is a disposition to perform certain (which?) actions. Much depends on how one understands dispositions (and beliefs), but, assuming that a belief is not just a disposition to act, then that would place racism on the action/practice side. (The disposition would count as racist, however, only if it stood in the right relationship to certain beliefs.)

Skillen nicely counters Flew by pointing out that expressing a negative view of the capabilities of blacks "is paradigmatic of racism. [However] Flew excludes it from racism proper. . . . [Such] utterances . . . can't, on Flew's view, be racist at all, because racism by proper definition is morally abominable, whereas [Flew thinks that] morally to condemn a belief is to be categorically mistaken" (Skillen, 1993, p. 77). So, "not only can beliefs be racist but racism typically entails a belief 'system.' Hence Flew's dissection of 'racism in the second sense' [i.e., as belief] involves considerable misdirection" (p. 79). Skillen adds that "the person who sees the world in terms of the sort of essentialising divisions [drawn by those who think races like species or natural kinds] is at least suffering from a shortfall of vision. If his racism is sincere, he ought not to be 'condemned' and vilified . . . though he may need to be argued with, contested and, if he is in position of power, fought" (p. 79). For me, typically holding such beliefs is racist because one holds them in part to justify racial antipathy, ill-will, or disregard. So, some people can be condemned for holding these beliefs, *pace* both Flew and Skillen. In any case, someone with such beliefs is likely to have racist desires and volitions whether they cause, or are caused by, the beliefs. It is important to observe, *pace* Skillen, first, that racism need entail no "system" of beliefs and, second, while various institutions and other elements of the cultural environment may nurture racism and derived racist beliefs, racism nevertheless lies fundamentally in individuals.

Racism has, according to Skillen, an "institutional character." "If it is the case that individuals, not institutions, have intentions or goals, we need to say that institutions operate through individuals, that our intentions are structured by institutions (going home, teaching, keeping the country or the club white and so on). . . . Racism, like sexism or confessional discrimination, can be an implicit thing, taken for granted, a traditional part of the way we've always done things" (Skillen, 1993, p. 80).

> [A]s Flew's . . . objection charging the opponent of "institutionalised racism" with definition in terms of "consequences" bears out, his main concern is not with institutions whose racism is more or less constitutive of their identity [as in a club or school founded to give whites refuge from integration]. . . . [but] with regulative practices: tests, entry requirements, employment practices, which, *as it turns out*, result in poor outcomes for members of certain racial sets. (p. 81, original emphasis)

This is wrongheaded for reasons that should by now be clear. No institutional practices can be racist—nor malicious, dishonest, or in any other way morally vicious—merely because "as it turns out" they have undesirable effects. Flew is right that an institution can be racist in the way it is constituted, and Skillen is right that institutions can also be racist in their operations, even when innocently founded. However, Skillen goes too far when he claims that its effects alone can suffice to make an institution racist. Institutional racism exists, as we said, when the racism in individuals becomes institutionalized. To become institutionalized, racism must infect the institution's operations by informing the ends it adopts, or the means it employs, or the grounds on which it accepts undesirable side effects (as is normally the case in "environmental racism"), or the assumptions on which it works. Failing any such basis, Skillen is unable to explain how racism gets into the institution to corrupt its behavior. Any suggestion that it gets into the institution and its behavior after the fact, from the behavior's effects, is incoherent. Skillen's error is to confuse output-driven concepts, such as being dangerous or harmful or lethal, with a moral concept such as racism. Output-driven concepts can be useful for moral judgment, because they help us to ask the right questions about why the agent (here the institution) acted as it did and why it did not abandon its plans in favor of some less harmful course of action. Answers to these questions can help us to decide whether the action is negligent or malicious or otherwise vicious. However, output-driven concepts cannot suffice to ground assigning any moral status, because vice and virtue are by nature tied to the action's motivation. Effects can only be (defeasible) evidence of motivation.[55]

Finally, Skillen is correct to observe that institutions often shape individual intentions and actions. Institutional racism will often exist in reciprocal relation to individual racism. The racism of some individual (or individuals) first infects the institution, and the institution's resultant racism then reinforces racism in that individual or breeds it in others. Once individual racism exists, institutional racism can he a powerful instrument of its perpetuation. This reciprocity of causal influence, however, should not blind us to the question of origins. Individual racism can come into the world without depending on some prior institutionalization. (It could come to be, say, as a result of some twist in one person's temperament.) The converse is not true. Institutional racism can reinforce and perpetuate individual racism. Unless an institution is corrupted (in its ends, means, priorities, or assumptions) by a prior and independent racism in some individual's heart, however, institutional racism can never come to exist.

Nevertheless, we should take care not to overstate the dependence of institutional racism upon the individual. Institutional racism appears to be capable of continuing after individual racism has largely died out. Think of a case where, for example, officials continue, uncomprehendingly, to implement policies originally designed, and still functioning to disadvantage those assigned to a certain racial group. Indeed, I strongly doubt that the qualifier "and still functioning" is necessary. Institutional racism can exist without actually functioning to harm anyone. Suppose, a few generations back, some R1s designed a certain institutional procedure P specifically to harm R2s, an oppressed racial group, though the designers were never explicit about this aim. Later, anti-R2 feeling among R1s faded away, and in time real social equality was achieved. The R1s, however, are a traditionalist lot, and they continue faithfully to execute P out of deference to custom and their ancestors. P no longer specially harms R2s. (Perhaps it excludes those who come from some specific, traditionally poor R2 neighborhoods from various privileges, and R2s are no longer disproportionally represented in those neighborhoods [which, perhaps, are also no longer disproportionally poor].)

In that case, it appears that the racism of the earlier generation persists in the institutional procedure P, even though P no longer specially harms R2s. This indicates that institutional racism, no less than individual racism, can be either effective or ineffective, either harmful or innocuous. Institutional racism, then, is a bad thing; but it is a bad thing not simply because of its actual effects, but sometimes merely because of its aims. The study of people's aims directs the social theorist's attention into their hearts, to what they care about, to what they have set themselves on having, or being, or making, or doing. Such is the stuff of the moral virtues, of course. Neither the social theorist nor the moral theorist can continue to neglect them if she wishes to understand the world. Or to change it.

VI. CONCLUSION

These reflections suggest that an improved understanding of racism and its immorality call for a comprehensive rethinking of racial discrimination, of the preferential treatment programs sometimes disparaged as "reverse discrimination," and of institutional conduct as well. They also indicate the direction such a rethinking should take, and its dependence on the virtues and other concepts from moral psychology. That may require a significant change in the way social philosophers have recently treated these and related topics.

NOTES

I am grateful to many people who discussed these matters with me. Henry Richardson, Martha Minow, David Wilkins, David Wong, Anthony Appiah, Susan Wolf, Dennis Thompson, Glenn Loury, and Judith Lichtenberg offered thoughtful comments on earlier drafts of some of this material. Discussions with Russell Hittinger, Ken Taylor, and others also profited me greatly. I am especially indebted to Lawrence Blum for repeated acts of encouragement and assistance, including reading and discussing my manuscripts and letting me read from his unpublished work, and I thank him and an audience at Rutgers University's 1994 conference on philosophy and race, for making suggestions and raising forceful objections.

My work was made possible by generous sabbatical support from Georgetown University, by research assistance from Rutgers University, and by grants from the National Endowment for the Humanities and from Harvard's Program in Ethics and the Professions. This paper would not have been written without the stimulation and the opportunity for reflection afforded me at the annual Ford Foundation Fellows conferences. To all these institutions I am indebted.

1. The same dictionary dates the cognate, "racist," as both adjective and noun, to the same period, but places the first appearances of "racialism" and "racialist" three decades earlier.

2. Miles begins a summary of his review of the first uses of the term in the effort of certain intellectuals to attack the pseudo-scientific defenses of the Nazi movement by saying that "the concept of racism was forged largely in the course of a conscious attempt to withdraw the sanction of

science from a particular meaning of the idea of 'race'"; and he chides these early critics on the grounds that their interpretation of racism, "by focusing on the product of nineteenth century scientific theorizing, tended to presume that racism was always, and therefore was only, a structured and relatively coherent set of assertions. . . . Such a definition [is problematic insofar as it] excludes less formally structured assertions, stereotypical ascriptions and symbolic representations. . . ." (Miles, 1986, pp. 47, 48).

3. Merriam-Webster's *Ninth New Collegiate Dictionary* offers a secondary definition: "racial prejudice or discrimination."

4. For a negative appraisal of Sivanandan's thought, see David Dale, "Racial Mischief: The Case of Dr. Sivanandan," in Palmer, 1986, pp. 82–94.

5. Discussing an account of racism offered by Britain's Commission for Racial Equality, Flew writes: [A] sinister and potentially dangerous thing here is the reference to actual or alleged matters of fact—to 'negative beliefs'. . . . For this is to demand, irrespective of any evidence which might be turned up to the contrary, that everyone must renounce certain disapproved propositions about average or universal differences and similarities as between races and racial groups: difference and similarities, that is, either in respect of biology or in respect of culture. To concede such a demand to the often Marxist militants of race relations is to open the door to purges: not only of libraries and of textbooks and of curricula; but also of people. It is not ten years since many a campus in the U.S.A. was ringing with calls to 'Sack' and even to 'Kill Jensen'—Jensen being a psychologist who dared to publish evidence suggesting that there may be genetically determined average differences between different races and racial groups in respect of other than their racial defining characteristics" (Flew, 1986, p. 22). I critically examine Flew's view of racism at the end of this essay.

6. Banton suggests that we should restrict our usage of the term, withholding its application from many people we nowadays call racists. In his view, these people are not racists because they use arguments of cultural superiority in preference to the doctrines of biologically based superiority the term was coined to pick out (Banton, 1970). This proposal is unrealistic, and serves to illustrate what makes unacceptable the excessively conservative approach to word meaning of those who still insist that racism consists solely in certain beliefs, ideology, doctrines, and theories.

7. That is not to say that its definition must include a moral evaluation. The acutilitarian must hold that non-optimific behavior is always wrong simply in virtue of what it is and what morality is, but she need not think the term "non-optimific" includes a moral evaluation in its definition. Similarly, a divine-command theorist may judge every act against God's will to be immoral *eo ipso*, without thinking this wrongness analytically derivable from the meaning of "against God's will."

8. According to Miles, the term "racism" originally denoted certain pseudo-scientific doctrines. I think the term changed its meaning, and speculate that this change occurred as race became important less for the discredited beliefs than for attitudes and resultant social practices (see Miles, 1989, Chaps. 2, 3). On the linguistic history, also see the *Oxford English Dictionary*, 2nd edition.

9. Compare David Wiggins and John McDowell on Kantian moral realism (see Wiggins, "Truth, Invention, and the Meaning of Life," in Wiggins, 1987; and McDowell, 1986).

Although in conversation Appiah has denied any such dependence, there is reason to worry that his position may covertly rely on a form of scientism, the supposition that no serious use of a once pseudo-scientific term is permissible if it plays no role within legitimate science. In any case, he seems to allow that neither the fact that the concept of race is inexact in its criteria and extension, nor the fact that it was the subject of a discredited science, nor the fact that it was used to justify unjust social practices is by itself sufficient to show that the notion must be banished from speech. (Perhaps he thinks they are jointly sufficient, but that remains to be shown.) Moreover, he is willing to talk informally of this person being black and that one white, so he and I are not so far apart. I do not see why this informal, but acceptable, way of speaking cannot be extended to allow us call such talk acceptable (albeit informal) racial classifications. Of course, informal talk of races cannot be accepted if racial terms must really be scientific. That, however, returns us to our question why anyone should think that.

Appiah's criticism of talk of races on the grounds that there are no "racial essences" suggests that he may presuppose a metaphysical essentialism that does not count against using racial terms on the looser bases of Wittgensteinian "family resemblances": perhaps a combination of surface and ancestral features, ordered in no one way, underlies the legitimate application of race terms to many but not all persons.

10. Miles objects to some early accounts of the nature of racism on the grounds that they "tended to remain inextricably entangled with, and consequently to legitimate, the idea of 'race'" (Miles, 1989, p. 48).

11. After an Arab dismissed a charge of anti-Semitism by the late Meir Kahane, on the grounds that Arabs are themselves a Semitic people, I once heard Kahane sensibly (if not necessarily accurately) respond by amending his charge to that of "Jew-hater." Of course, Kahane himself was often described, with some justification, as an Arab-hater. The connection between racism and anti-Semitism may be more than analogical. It is sometimes said that anti-Semitism is itself a type of racism. Thus, Miles writes of "that form of racism which others label anti-Semitism" (Miles, 1989, p. 68). It is worth remarking that, whereas Wistrich thinks anti-Semitism "the longest hatred," Castoriadis claims that the Hebrew Bible is, because of its exaltation of the Jews, the oldest extant racist document (Castoriadis, 1992, p. 3). I think that Castoriadis's view serves as a *reductio* of understanding racism as a matter of beliefs. Whether or not one thinks God selected the Jews for a special role in human salvation, this election hardly constitutes the sort of contemptuous or aversive dismissal of others that properly counts as racist.

12. "Critics of scientific theories of race prior to this decade [the 1930s] did not use a concept of racism to identify their ideological object. For example, in a wide-ranging critique published in the late 1920s, Friedrich Hertz referred to 'race hatred'" (Miles, 1989, p. 42).

13. As I said at the outset, the term "xenophobia" also suggests that this aversion to others is accompanied or caused by fear of them, but I do not think this association carries over to "racism."

14. They write, "'Homophobia' is a comforting word, isn't it? It suggests that . . . all who oppose, threaten, and persecute us [that is, homosexuals] are actually scared of us! [However, f]ear need have nothing to do with it. A well-designed study . . . demonstrat[ed] that although some 'homonegative' males respond to homosexual stimuli with the 'tell-tale racing heart' of phobia, plenty of others don't." Kirk and Madsen condemn "the specious 'diagnosis'" of homophobia as a "medically exculpatory euphemism," and offer a proposal: "Let's reserve the term 'homophobia' for the psychiatric cases to which it really applies, and find a more honest label for the attitudes, words, and acts of hatred that are, after all, the real problem." As for their own linguistic procedure, "when we really do mean 'fear of homosexuals,' [them] 'homophobia' it will be; when we're talking about hatred of homosexuals, we'll speak (without the hyphen) of 'homohatred,' 'homohating,' and 'homohaters.' We urge the reader to follow suit" (see Kirk and Madsen, 1989, pp. xxii–xxiii). This is sensible advice, though some caveats are in order. First, we should bear in mind that not every fear is a phobia. Second, even the quasi-scientific term "homonegative" tends to lump together such very different matters as (i) a person's personal aversion to her own engaging in homosexual activities, (ii) her concern over perceived social effects of other peoples' homosexual conduct, and (iii) her holding the belief that such conduct is morally impermissible. Hatred of homosexual persons is immoral (although, as Kirk and Madsen point out, to see it simply as a medical condition tends to exculpate). Moral disapproval of homosexual practices, whether on medical, moral, or religious grounds, is a different matter, however, and it may often be an unrelated one. Third, to use the prefix "homo" to mean "homosexual" is objectionable for obvious reasons, so it seems preferable to speak of "homosexual-haters" and "homosexual-hatred," retaining the hyphen. This would also make it clear, as "homophobia" does not, that what is to be condemned is an attitude of ill-will or contempt toward certain people, and not a moral judgment on certain practices.

15. The Freudian theorist Elizabeth Young-Bruehl, in an unpublished paper, argues that anti-Semitism differs from racism in that anti-Semitism, which she thinks rooted in a combination of assumed male Gentile sexual superiority and economic and intellectual inferiority, aims to exterminate its targets, while racism, which she thinks rooted in assumed white male sexual inferiority, seeks to keep its victims around for humiliation (Young-Bruehl, 1992). I suspect all this is wrongheaded for reasons I sketch at the end of this essay. For our purposes, what is important is that no such causality is essential to racism or anti-Semitism, because we should label haters of Jews or black people anti-Semites and racists even if we knew their hatred had different causes.

16. I shall use such terms as R1 and R2 to refer to racial groups, and such expressions as R1s and R2s to refer to people assigned to such groups. This usage holds potential for some confusion, since the plural term R1s is not the plural of the singular term R1, but I think the context will always disambiguate each instance of this usage.

17. Two caveats. First, since our interest is in the central sense(s) of the term "racism," I see little reason to add Cottingham's qualifier, "there is a sense in which," to our claim that racism must be illicit. Any sense of the term in which racism is not illicit must be decidedly peripheral. Second, Cottingham seems to think of this "disregard" as primarily a matter of negative evaluative beliefs, while I reject any such doxastic account and construe "disregard" as disaffection or malice.

18. See Slore, 1994, and Garcia, 1986.

19. I will not try to identify minimal levels of goodwill such that having less is against the virtue of benevolence, nor minimal levels of respect such that less offends against justice. I doubt these levels can be identified in abstraction, and it will be difficult or impossible for us to determine them even in minutely described particular situations. Throughout, I generally restrict my talk of disrespect and other forms of disregard to cases where the levels are morally vicious, offending against the moral virtues of benevolence, and justice, respectively.

20. See Garcia, 1986, 1987.

21. In a way similar to my non-doxastic account of racism, John Dewey seems to have offered an account of race prejudice that is non-doxastic. Recent scholarship reminds us that, for Dewey, prejudice was not primarily a matter of hasty judgment, but of a fear of, and aversion to, what is unfamiliar. Gregory Pappas expounded Dewey's view in his paper, "Dewey's Philosophical Interpretation of Racial Prejudice," presented at a session of the 1992 Ford Fellows Conference in Irvine, California.

22. See Appiah, 1992.

23. Iris Young offers the interesting suggestion that modernist moral theory's aversion to partiality, like its aversion to appeals to feelings, and its insistence on the irrelevance of gender, ethnicity, and other aspects of personal or group experience, history, and situatedness, originate as parts of an endeavor to eliminate from the viewpoint of the moral judge those factors that are deemed inessential to her as a rational agent and that serve to differentiate her from others. This effort is perhaps most evident in Kant's famous insistence that an agent's moral requirements be rooted in her (universal) reason, and not be contingent upon her desires (unlike "hypothetical imperatives"), test the requirements vary across persons and times, as he thought all substantive desires did. Young also thinks the impartialist unfairly presents impartiality as the only alternative to egoism (see Young, 1990, Chap. 4). If that is right, then the impartialist position rests upon several dubious assumptions, most notably, assumptions about the constituents of the moral agent's identity (or "essence"), about the irreducible variability of desires and feelings, and about the supposed gap between human passions and desires, on the one hand, and abstract reason, on the other. All these assumptions are currently undergoing philosophical reconsideration (see especially Blum, 1994).

24. Note that action from maxims that pass Kant's universalizability test is therein permissible, not necessarily obligatory.

25. Quoted in Hacker, "The New Civil War," p. 30.

26. Arguing against some writers who use the slogan "Preference is not prejudice" to support

their view that moderate racial preference is permissible, Miles complains, "[T]o prefer is to rank and to choose to value something or person or group, and therefore necessarily to preclude some other thing, person or group (Miles, 1989, p. 8). What Miles says is true, but it does nothing to prove the controverted point that excluding person S1 in the course of expressing greater than morally required regard for S2 is the moral equivalent of excluding S1 out of less than morally required concern for S1. That said, I do certainly not wish to associate myself with the further doctrines of the thinkers Miles is criticizing, who use the inflammatory example of preferring to marry within one race as an example of supposedly innocent preference. In a society such as ours, any such "preference" is likely to be informed by and to result in part from an aversion to interracial marriage as "race treachery" or "miscegenation." Such a preference is not at all innocent, in my view, having roots in deep-seated racial antipathy.

In personal correspondence, Glenn Loury has expressed misgivings about my view, reminding me that "what ends in personal viciousness towards the 'other' finds its beginning in the more benign celebration of the virtues of one's 'own kind.'" I wonder whether, in fact, racial antipathy does always begin in such a benign attitude. However, even if it does, the danger that it may lead to racial antipathy is a reason to be cautious of racial favoritism. It is not a reason to condemn this partiality as malign nor, more to the point, as racist. Even the framers of a recent California measure proposing to outlaw racial preferences observe a distinction between discriminating against A and according B a preference. "The anti-affirmative action measure is essentially a simple declaration: 'Neither the State of California nor any of its political subdivisions shall use race, sex, color, ethnicity, or national origin as a criterion for either discriminating against or granting preferential treatment to, any individual or group in the operation of the state's system of public employment, public education, or public contracting'" (Schrag, 1995, p. 18). The drafters may, however, make the distinction merely to close a possible linguistic loophole, and not deem it a distinction that marks any genuine and morally significant difference. With that, of course, I disagree.

27. I say "foreseeable" effects rather than "foreseen" because S's racist contempt may be the reason she does not bother to find out, and thus does not foresee, some of the bad effects of her behavior.

28. I think this undermines an argument recently offered by Gomberg. He argues against what has been called "moderate patriotism," which "includ[es limited] preference for fellow nationals," on the grounds that any argument in defense of it will also legitimize what he calls "moderate racism," which allows someone to "discriminate against black or Hispanic people or against immigrants" so long as one is careful not to "violate their fundamental rights" (p. 147). Assuming that such "moderate racism" is unjustifiable, then so too is moderate patriotism or any form of preference. The problem is that it is hard to see why Gomberg's "moderate racism" need be unjustifiable, or even why it is racism. His analogy with patriotism suggests that what Gomberg has in mind is merely a mild form of preference for people of one's own racial group. This will sometimes be suspicious morally, especially when the one discriminating on the basis of race belongs to a group that has enforced and benefited from forms of discrimination that are racist, that is, that are driven by racial disaffection. However, it is unclear that there is anything morally troubling in same-race favoritism by those on the bottom, or by those who live in a situation, unlike ours, where favoritism has been historically divorced from race hatred. Similarly, there seems to be nothing morally troubling in other-race favoritism, at least, there is nothing morally troubling where this favoritism is likely to be divorced from hatred of one's own racial group, as is the case with other-race favoritism by those from historically oppressing groups.

Indeed, while same-race favoritism, by people considered members of the oppressing group, and other-race favoritism, by those allocated to the oppressed group, are disturbing morally, I think that, to the extent this discomfort is legitimate, it will be rooted in our suspicion that it is really race hatred masking as mere favoritism, or in our worry that such a practice, should it become widespread, will have the bad effect of exacerbating the comparatively disadvantaged position of those assigned to the historically oppressed group. The latter worry may be serious, but it is a concern about the general effects of a social (or personal) policy, not a concern that individuals may be treated unjustly. As such, it is much less significant morally.

(Since writing this, I have seen a similar point made in Stephen Nathanson's response to Gomberg. Nathanson sensibly writes that "a racial preference might not be inherently wrong or evil. American Blacks have been an oppressed group that has needed special attention. Whites are not similarly oppressed as a group. Thus, a person with a special affection and concern for whites might not be equally justified in promoting their interests. . . ." Actions done from such favoritism will even "be wrong if they require neglect of the much more pressing need of others" [Nathanson, 1992, pp. 10, 11].)

In this connection, it is worth noting that Appiah rejects what he calls "intrinsic speciesism," adherents of which think it would be morally permissible "to kill cattle for beef, even if cattle exercised all the complex cultural skills of human beings" (Appiah, 1992, p. 19). Such a position is to be condemned, of course, but we can condemn it without necessarily rejecting the view ("moderate speciesism"?) that even in the world of Appiah's cosmopolitan cattle, we may, and perhaps even should, show greater concern for members of our own species simply because of their relation to us. The impermissibility of such favoritism does not follow from the recognition that there are moral limits on the ways in which we may treat the various others outside the favored group. I can think morality allows and even demands that I care specially for my family without thereby committing myself to thinking that we may slaughter, butcher, and eat the folks next door.

29. See Carter, 1991.

30. For a helpful discussion of the controversy surrounding efforts to identify and regulate hate speech, and of the different grounds offered for these restrictions, see Simon, 1991.

31. Lichtenberg reminds us that such figures are often seen as paradigms of racism, though, unfortunately, she ties this to her claim that black people and white people tend to have fundamentally different understandings of the nature of racism. "The white picture of the racist is the old-time Southern white supremacist" (p. 3). Surely, it is not merely what is sometimes disparaged as "thinking white" to see such people as paradigmatic instances of racism.

32. "When you love a man you want him to live and when you hate him you want him to die" (Confucius, Analects, Bk. 12, sec. 10).

33. This sort of disregard, consisting in a lack of concern for whether one's actions harm black people, may lie behind some manifestations of the phenomenon called "environmental racism," in which hazardous wastes, it has been alleged, tend to be dumped disproportionally in areas with largely black populations. Sociologist Robert Bullard and former NAACP executive director Benjamin Hooks have done much to focus attention on this problem.

34. Contrast a religious school that (like the Westminster Academy, in the newspapers a few years back) refuses to hire non-Christians. This policy deprives those who would otherwise have been hired of prestige and salary. However, this deprivation is incidental to the policy's purpose, benign or benighted as it may be, of securing a certain sort of instruction by hiring only instructors with certain relevant convictions.

35. Philip Kircher directed my attention to this topic.

36. "Though I've belted you and flayed you, By the livin' Gawd that made you, You're a better man than I am, Gunga Din." Rudyard Kipling, "Gunga Din," in Kipling: a Selection of his Stories and Poems (Garden City: Doubleday, n.d.).

37. It is in the form of Kiplingesque, "white man's burden"-racism that racism most nearly approaches the structure of sexism. Sexism is, of course, a form of social bias to which many assume racism is structurally similar, and those who introduced the notion of sexism as a concept of social explanation explicitly modeled it on (their understanding of) racism: In general, however, I think the similarity is not great. Sexism appears normally to be a form of condescension, wherein males deprive women of authority and power in order to protect them from the consequences of their supposed immaturity and weakness. This sort of disrespect can violate the virtue of justice in just the

ways I have been describing. However, noticing that racism in certain peripheral forms can resemble what sexism seems to be in its essence (or, at least, in its most central forms) helps reveal the fundamental dissimilarity between these two social vices more than it supports the widespread assumption that sexism is just the same sort of thing as racism, victimizing women instead of black people and with gender replacing race as the grounds of victimization. (For a sophisticated comparative account of racism and sexism, see Thomas, 1980.)

38. See Garcia, 1987.

39. I follow him in assuming that the prospective agent stands in no special personal relationship to either of the trapped people (e.g., son), and occupies no role that specially calls for impartiality (e.g., paid village firefighter).

40. I think this problem also besets various schemes of randomization, such as flipping a coin and throwing dice, though this drawback is seldom noticed by philosophers, so blinded by their attachment to the goat of impartiality that they cannot see the grotesquerie of the means sometimes suggested for achieving it. (Hursthouse makes a similar point in Hursthouse, 1990.)

41. Robert Audi raised this problem with me in conversation.

42. A world without partiality to family members, in contrast, would surely be a worse one, less rich in virtues and in other goods.

43. I am inclined to think we should say a racist act in the strict sense is one that is done from racist attitudes (in the agent, whether settled dispositions or a passing episode of nasty whimsy), rather than merely being one done in acquiescence to other's racist attitudes. A's act is not cowardly merely because it is one in which A accedes to B's cowardice. (Consider the remark: "OK, we'll take the longer way to school if it will calm you down, but I still say there's no real danger we would be attacked by dogs if we took the shortcut." Here the speaker accedes to the listener's cowardice, but does not therein act from her own cowardice.) Likewise with racism.

44. This action of hers reflects an insufficiency of goodwill, whether or not she does something or feels something else (e.g., regret, sympathy) that manifests some measure of fellow-feeling. It just is not enough. (I am, of course, aware that at this point I am relying merely on intuition; I offer here no suggestion of how much goodwill morality requires, let alone any theoretical justification for drawing this line at one place rather than another.)

45. Reflecting on this case should help inform our Answers to related questions: What should we say of those, white or black, who lock car doors when driving through black neighborhoods but not white ones? Or of store owners (again, white or black) who will not admit black teenagers to their premises?

46. Larry Blum pointed out to me the availability of this line of response to Miles.

47. It is also doubtful whether such an informal practice, not tied to any organizational structure in particular, and part of no determined policy, properly counts as institutional behavior at all. However, I will not pursue that classificatory matter here. Philosophers and other social thinkers nowadays use the term "institution" in quite a broad and vague way, and this is not the place to try to correct that practice. (That "institution"? For a step toward a more discriminating use, see the brief discussion of "institutions" and "practices" in MacIntyre, 1984, Chap. 14.)

48. This phenomenon is closely related to that of word-of-mouth job recruiting. There are, however, some distinctions. The old-boy network is defined by an educational elite of private schools (which often embeds a still more restricted elite who are members of secret societies, dining halls, and special clubs). This educationally elite network may also extend its privileging beyond recruitment to include admission to restricted social occasions and establishments where business is conducted, and where participants may advance employment, get informal help and advice, influence to gain preference in academic admissions and fellowships, award contracts and consultantships, gain immunity from having to pay for misconduct, and secure other social and economic privileges.

49. Loury, 1992.

50. For instance, "[T]he essential feature of racism is . . . the *defense* of a system from which advantage is derived on the basis of race" (D. Wellman, quoted at Miles, 1989, p. 52. Emphasis added).

51. This reflection illuminates a further example. Young-Bruehl says, "A current law [in the United States] which has as its known consequence that women using federally funded family planning clinics—a majority of whom are women of color—will be deprived of information to make informed reproductive choices is, simply, racist" (Young-Bruehl, 1992, p. 10). The law she seems to have had in mind was an executive order, which, because of court action, was never enforced. Young-Bruehl's classification of it as racist is highly implausible. Presumably, the requirement was part of a general policy of getting the government out of the provision and support of abortion—a policy which also militates against funding overseas abortion-"providers" through foreign aid, against federal facilities performing abortions on government property (such as military bases) or in U.S. protectorates or the federal district, against using federal payments to employees' insurance funds to pay for abortions, and against using federal insurance payments to provide abortions. Some of these restrictions will wind up having a statistically disproportionate impact on minority women and children; some will not. (Some will interpret this impact as specialty burdening minority women, others as specialty protecting minority children.)

It does not appear, however, that any beliefs or feelings or desires about race enter into these policies in their design or execution. Thus, those who agree with Young-Bruehl, if they mean to rise above nasty rhetoric to serious argument, need to reveal to us where, when, and how the racism gets *into* this institutional practice, if they are going to back up their claim that this law is a manifestation or instance of institutional racism. Of course, they might instead claim that the law is racist because of the racist conduct of those who execute it. This will probably be true of some administrators. In just the same way, however, it is true of some of the law's opponents that they are motivated by a racist desire to reduce the numbers of black people, especially the poor female ones who are most likely to be lost should the government make abortion cheap and easy while it leaves the having and rearing of children a disproportionally heavy financial burden. Advocacy of facilitated abortion access, no less than opposition to it, *can* be marked by both racism and sexism. That fact does nothing to support Young-Bruehl's one-sided criticism.

52. It is not clear what Skillen thinks about the latter point. I agree that some people with racist beliefs should not be condemned morally, but that is because I think that racist beliefs, don't make one a real racist and that the beliefs are racist only in a derivative sense. Does Skillen agree?

53. One must, however, take care not to proceed too far down this path. One must assure that the white candidates are not victims of reverse racism. For it would normally be wrong to keep out black candidate, even if the white patients related better to white physicians. One may not bow to primary racism by becoming illicitly collaborative in its workings. Consider a retailer who won't hire a black salesperson because she correctly believes the clientele will be put off. That is secondary racism—intending to exclude (even if not to hurt), in compliance with others' wishes to hurt by excluding. Even if A's exclusion of B is not itself racist—i.e., not derived from A's ill-will toward B's group—nevertheless, it may be illicit as impermissible collaboration in C's racism toward B's group. Insofar as A excludes B in mere deference to C's disregard for B's rights and needs, then A acts wrongly by cooperating in C's unjust treatment of B. Even C may be partly to blame for A's misconduct, insofar as C has influenced or pressured A so to behave. (This influence might consist merely in a pervasive climate of fear; it need be neither explicit nor specifically addressed to B in particular.)

54. Throughout this discussion, I have had to rely on Skillen for a presentation of Flew's views. Flew's paper is difficult to locate and the periodical in which it appeared is no longer published. Fortunately, Skillen is aware of the difficulty and takes extra care to present Flew's views at length, separating summary from interpretation or critique. I follow his practice in presenting sometimes extensive verbatim passages quoted from Flew.

55. I am aware that the charge I here level against Skillen would also militate against all forms

of direct, optimizing consequentialism, and against other result-driven accounts of wrongdoing, such as the satisficing consequentialism Slote discussed. (For more on this, see Sloth, 1985; Garcia, 1990, 1993.)

REFERENCES

Adams, Robert. 'The Virtue of Faith." In Adams, *The Virtue of Faith*, pp. 9–24. Oxford: Oxford University Press, 1987.

Appiah, Anthony. "Racisms." In *Anatomy of Racism*, pp. 3–17. Edited by D. T. Goldberg. Minneapolis: University of Minnesota Press, 1990.

———. *In My Father's House: Africa in the Philosophy of Culture*. Oxford: Oxford University Press, 1992.

Banton, Michael. "The Concept of Racism." In *Race and Racialism*, pp. 17–34. Edited by Sami Zubaida. New York: Barnes & Noble, 1970.

Banton, Michael, and Robert Miles. "Racism." In *Dictionary of Race and Ethnic Relations*. 2d ed. Edited by E. Ellis Cashmore. London: Routledge, 1988.

Blum, Lawrence. "Antiracism, Multiculturalism, and Interracial Community: Three Educational Values for a Multicultural Society." Office of Graduate Studies and Research, University of Massachusetts at Boston, 1991.

———. *Moral Perception and Particularity*. Cambridge: Cambridge University Press, 1994.

———. "Individual and Institutional Racism." Unpublished paper read at Smith College, February, 1993.

Carter, Stephen. *Reflections of an Affirmative Action Baby*. New York: Basic Books, 1991.

Castoriadis, Cornelius. "Reflections on Racism." *Thesis Eleven Number* 32 (1992): 1–12.

Cohen, Marshall, et al. Editors. *Marx, Justice, and History*. Princeton: Princeton University Press, 1980.

Cottingham, John. "Partiality, Favouritism and Morality," *Philosophical Quarterly* 36 (1986): 357–73.

Ezorsky, Gertrude. *Racism and Justice*. Ithaca: Cornell University Press, 1991.

Flew, Antony. "Clarifying the Concepts." In *Anti-Racism—An Assault on Education and Value*, pp. 15–31. Edited by Frank Palmer. London: Sherwood, 1986.

———. "Three Concepts of Racism." *Encounter* 73 (September 1990).

Garcia, J. L. A. "Virtue Ethics." In *Cambridge Dictionary of Philosophy*. Edited by Robert Audi. Cambridge: Cambridge University Press, forthcoming.

———. "Current Conceptions of Racism." Unpublished.

———. "African-American Perspectives, Cultural Relativism, and Normative Issues." In *African-American Perspectives on Biomedical Issues: Philosophical Issues*, pp. 11–66. Edited by Edmund Pellegrino and Harley Flack. Washington: Georgetown University Press, 1992.

———. "The New Critique of Anti-Consequentialist Moral Theory." *Philosophical Studies* 71 (1993): 1–32.

———. "The Primacy of the Virtuous," *Philosophia* 20 (1990): 69–91.

Gates, Henry Louis, Jr. "Let Them Talk: A Review of 'Words that Wound: Critical Race Theory, Assaultive Speech and the First Amendment,' " by Mari J. Matsuda, Charles R. Lawrence III, Richard Delgado, and Kimberle, Williams Crenshaw. *New Republic*, September 20 & 27, 1993 (double issue), pp. 37–49.

Gilligan, Carol. *In a Different Voice*. Cambridge: Harvard University Press, 1982.

Goldberg, David Theo. "Racist Exclusions." *Philosophical Forum* 26 (1994): 21–32.

———. "The Semantics of Race." *Ethnic and Racial Studies* 15 (1992): 543–69.

———. "The Social Formation of Racist Discourse." In *Anatomy of Racism*, pp. 295–318. Edited by D. T. Goldberg. Minneapolis: University of Minnesota Press, 1990.

Gomberg, Paul. "Patriotism Is Like Racism." *Ethics* 101 (1990): 144–50.

Green, Judith. "King's Historical Location of Political Concepts." *APA Newsletter on Philosophy and the Black Experience* 91 (1992): 12–14.

Hacker, Andrew. *Two Nations: Black and White, Separate, Hostile, Unequal.* New York: Scribner's, 1992.

———. "The New Civil War." *New York Review of Books*, April 23, 1992, pp. 30–33.

Hursthouse, Rosalind. "Virtue Theory and Abortion." *Philosophy and Public Affairs* 20 (1993): 223–46.

Kamm, F. M. "Non-Consequentialism, the Person as an End-in-Itself, and the Significance of Status." *Philosophy and Public Affairs* 21 (1992): 354–89.

Kennedy, Randall. "Some Good May Yet Come of This." *Time*, February 28, 1994, p. 34.

Kirk, Marshall and Hunter Madsen. *After the Ball: How America Will Conquer Its Fear and Hatred of Gays in the '90s.* New York: Doubleday, 1989.

Larrabee, Mary Jane, ed. *An Ethic of Care.* New York: Routledge, 1993.

Lichtenberg, Judith. "Racism in the Head, Racism in the World." *Philosophy and Public Policy* (Newsletter of the Institute for Philosophy and Public Policy, University of Maryland) 12 (1992).

Loury, Glenn. "Why Should We Care About Group Inequality?" *Social Philosophy and Policy* 5 (1987–1988): 249–71.

———. "The Economics of Discrimination." *Harvard Journal of African-American Public Policy* 1 (1992): 91–110.

———. "The New Liberal Racism: A Review of Andrew Hacker's Two Nations." *First Things* (January 1993): 39–42.

Lukes, Stephen. *Marxism and Morality.* Oxford: Oxford University Press, 1987.

Lyas, Colin, ed. *Philosophy and Linguistics.* New York: St. Martin's, 1969.

MacIntyre, Alasdair. *After Virtue.* 2d ed. Notre Dame: University of Notre Dame Press, 1984.

Marable, Manning. *Black America: Multicultural Democracy in the Age of Clarence Thomas and David Duke.* Open Magazine Pamphlet Series, #16. Westfield, N.J., 1992.

May, Larry, ed. *Collective Responsibility.* Lanham, Md.: Rowman and Littlefield, 1992.

McDowell, John. "Values and Secondary Qualities." In *Morality and Objectivity*, pp. 110–29. Edited by Ted Honderich. London: Humanities, 1985.

Miles, Robert. *Racism.* London: Routledge, 1989.

Murphy, Jeffrie, and Jean Hampton. *Forgiveness and Mercy.* New York: Cambridge University Press, 1988.

Nathanson, Stephen. "Is Patriotism Like Racism?" *APA Newsletter on Philosophy and the Black Experience* 91 (1992): 9–11.

Noddings, Nell. *Caring.* Berkeley: University of California Press, 1986.

Okin, Susan Miller. *Justice, Gender and the Family.* New York: Basic Books, 1989.

Piper, Adrian M. "Higher Order Discrimination." In *Identity, Character, & Morality*, pp. 285–309. Edited by Owen Flanagan and Amelie Rorty. Cambridge: MIT Press, 1990.

Rothenberg, Paula. *Racism and Sexism: an Integrated Study.* New York: St. Martin's Press, 1988.

Schaefer, Richard. *Racial and Ethnic Groups.* 4th ed. Glenview: Scott, Foresman, 1990.

Schrag, Peter. "Son of 187." *New Republic*, January 30, 1995, pp. 16–19.

Part IV.
Postscript

22. What, Then, Is Racism?
Leonard Harris

WHAT, THEN, IS RACISM? Racism is a polymorphous agent of death, premature births, shortened lives, starving children, debilitating theft, abusive larceny, degrading insults, and insulting stereotypes forcibly imposed.[1] The ability of a population to accumulate wealth and transfer assets to their progeny is stunted by racism. As the bane of honor, respect, and a sense of self-worth, racism surreptitiously stereotypes. It stereotypes its victims as persons inherently bereft of virtues and incapable of growth. Racism is the agent that creates and sustains a virulent pessimism in its victims. The subtle nuances that encourage granting unmerited and undue status to a racial social kind are the tropes of racism. Racism creates criminals, cruel punishments, and crippling confinement, while the representatives of virtue profit from sustaining the conditions that ferment crime. Systemic denial of a populations humanity is the hallmark of racism.

Integral to race-based denials of humanity are unspeakable terrors, holocausts, vicious rapes, cruel beatings, tortures, and maiming rituals. It is never enough, in racist societies, to exploit and degrade. Humiliation and symbolic subjugation of even the dead of the suppressed population are required to sustain a sense of superiority, honor, healthiness, purity, and control in the dominant population. And too often, self-effacement, inferiority complexes, insecurity, and hopelessness are features developed by segregated and stereotyped persons. Thus, for example, in 1904 Vicksburg, Mississippi,

> when the two Negroes were captured, they were tied to trees and while the funeral pyres were being prepared they were forced to suffer the most fiendish tortures. The blacks were forced to hold out their hands while one finger at a time was chopped off. The fingers were distributed as souvenirs. The ears of the mur-

derers were cut off. Holbert was beaten severely, his skull was fractured, and one of his eyes, knocked out with a stick, hung by a shred from the socket. . . . The most excruciating form of punishment consisted in the use of a large corkscrew in the hands of some of the mob. This instrument was bored into the flesh of the man and woman, in the arms, legs and body, and then pulled out, the spirals tearing out big pieces of raw, quivering flesh every time it was withdrawn.

The Holbert family was accused of defending their home against white intruders—the actual criminals. Since they were perceived as inherent criminals, and bereft of the entitlements accorded persons considered members of the moral community, no trial was needed. Quivering flesh, taken by avid corkscrewers, was thrown to the crowd for souvenirs. The bodies were burned, and after cooling, pieces of charred flesh were taken from the ashes by men, women, and children for souvenirs. Shopkeepers and women of class occasionally used severed hands as ornamentation. This ritual of violence was not isolated to Mississippi. Corkscrewing flesh, bodily souvenirs, and public burning were reserved rituals for blacks. With the invention of cameras, photographs of the crowd gloating over the bodies became a common feature of the ritual.

Whether the madness occurs in Cambodia, Rwanda, Germany, Croatia, Guatemala, or America, when persons are described, ascribed, stereotyped, and symbolized as racially abject, the fact of one's phenotype—imagined or apparent—is used to warrant degrading representatives of the subjugated population. Each individual is either treated, or subject to be treated, in every social and business environment as a representative of a kind—a kind, the embodiment of which is always subject to humiliation—from conception to beyond death. Under British colonial domination, Welsh children were seen as born dirty, mired in eternal filth, and beyond concern except as workers; Japanese leather workers, Burakumin, are incapable, from the standpoint of "pure" Japanese, from parenting worthy children, they are condemned from conception; Australian adoptive mothers and fathers separated light-and dark-skinned Aborigine siblings, showered foster parental love on light-skinned children, and abandoned dark-skinned children in accordance with public policy intended to systemically destroy the darker population. Racism is a mother demanding that her servants kill her child, immediately upon its issue from her womb, because "it" is of the wrong race; or when a country's president, such as Thomas Jefferson, keeps his interracial children as slaves; or a Cherokee chief trades his half-castes for horses. Racism is the degradation and humiliation of a population as a totally abject collective, beyond redemption.

When "real" means social realities that are historically inevitable, natural, or invariably a feature of every society, then races are not real. Universal and trans-historical human traits, such as agnate love or the ability to think in past and future tenses, do not necessarily cause the existence of racial identity or any particular racial identity. Races, as biological kinds matching social kinds, do not exist. That is, there are no necessary correlations between racial biologies and cultures. The science of ethnology is not one that describes character traits according to racial biologies. Rather, ethnology is a science that can describe the relationship of character traits to values, heritage, and practices. Racial groups, as social kinds, are constructions.

Groups are real in the sense that they are historically inevitable, natural, and invariably a feature of every society. Trans-historical groups, such as women, men, families, or workers are always biological kinds closely matching social kinds.[2] There are universal character traits associated with such formations. There are, in effect, gender, age, capacities, and patterns associated with trans-historical kinds. And none of these kinds are racial kinds.

If there were only one person on the planet, that person would not have a biological race. That is, they would not have a non-adaptive, genetically determined character trait caused by a stable population of common descent.[3] If that person believed that they had a biological race, they would be mistaken. If their biology or genetic makeup was affected by this mistaken belief, they nonetheless remain malleable. That is, they remain capable of having different beliefs and behaviors.

If the only person on the planer believed that acquired cultural characteristics are transmitted in a racially significant way, they would be wrong. If that one person could use an artificial incubator and the resources of a sperm/egg bank, the next generation need not manifest cultural or character traits identical to their forbears outside of the same social situation.

Constructions, socially and individually created, influence our lives. Some constructions are morally odious. Racial identities, especially when such identities are treated as inherent to every member, transhistorical, natural, and inevitable, are odious. Such racial identities are inextricably tied to, and invariably indebted to, degrading, demeaning, and misguided stereotypes. There simply are no virtues nor any sense of self-worth that could not be better achieved than through the pernicious idea of race.

There are compelling reasons for persons terrorized by race to band together, define themselves, and work on behalf of themselves. There are, for example, compelling reasons for such persons to marry within networks of the same social kind because such networks provide support and sustenance. The idea that Africans, for example, should unite to end destructive national identities and unnecessary borders that divide geographically, politically, and culturally similar peoples is warranted. Moreover, Africans should defeat the continuing remnants of foreign elitism. Alexander Crummel, Edward Wilmot Blyden, and Kwame Nkrumah were right: Pan-African unity is a positive good. Seeking Pan-African unity for the reason of Negro uplift, however, has gone the way of seeking Wolof, Welsh, and Tasmanian uplift through Wolof, Welsh, and Tasmanian national unity—impossible accomplishments. The background reality within which language groups as racial kinds, such as Wolof, Welsh, and Tasmania, could become nation-states no longer exists. Analogously, a world in which relatively isolated groups can be reasonably counted as races, or as having the possibility of race-based nations, no longer exists. Moreover, native speakers are entrapped in a limited world of opportunity unless they also know a world dominant language. It is the terror of history, and the malleability of humanity, that destroys the security of closed raciated networks and makes the realization of racial ideals, such as an all-white Europe, all-yellow Japan, or all-black Africa, superfluous.

It is misguided to believe that English-speaking Jamaicans, Arabic-speaking Turks, and French-speaking Polynesians are unauthentic, free only if they could return to the time before colonialism or move into a time when the colonial culture is completely shed; or a time when alien religions, languages, or racial kinds are purged from an imagined pure cultural background.

Alain L. Locke's argument that victims of racism need a racial identity as a source of unity and as a resource to defend themselves has strong appeal, as long as the source of their victimization is racial and its destruction is aided by racial union among victims. That is, so long as the oppression is arguably caused by, or is strongly correlated to, the sort of racism in which the racial identity of the oppressor is a substantive variable determining the misery of the oppressed. Background realities change. Neither mulattos, mestizos, nor mixed Asians are trans-historical. What they are, as groups, is far too unstable, transitory, continually redefined, and always disappearing to warrant commitment in the way that commitment to trans-historical realities can gain such warrant. Racial preservationists, that is, those who believe that existing groups are a sort of natural community and their members entitled to sustain whatever identity they currently foster, are analogous to environmentalists who believe "nature" is the static, unchanging, and unaffected physical surrounding they immediately inhabit. That is, they are analogous to persons who support completely untenable pictures of themselves and others.

The death of racial identity is no bellwether that racism is dead. Yet, liberation of any social race from oppression by racism requires ending the racial identity of the oppressor and the oppressed. For a racist, the goal of imagined superior races is always to dominate or destroy all others. For an anti-racist, the goal should include the negation of all institutions, interests, and benefits that sustain oppression by race. In addition, for an anti-racist, it should also include the negation of race as such—the negation of social constructions which link biology and culture, biology and character, biology and potential, and biology and rights.

Antiblack, anti-Welsh, or anti-colored racism necessarily has as its ultimate interest and object ending the need for "anti," leaving nothing in its wake. The primary interest of any social race, if its members are to be liberated from debilitating stereotypes, is the negation of all identity by race and empowerment through control of assets.

In a nonracist world, social races would not exist. No one would be obligated for non-moral reasons, such as fear of ostracism or the need for self-protection from prejudice, to marry within a predetermined racial group; no one would be born into a race; no one would have a non-moral duty to be the representative of a race. Even if racialism continued in a non-racist world, through default (for example, because socially like constructed kinds preferred their own), that would not warrant a description of such a society as racist. If 70 percent of every existing raciated population married internally, that would tell us the obvious—these people like themselves and those they know the most about. It would also hide what we know—racial groups come and go out of existence, and the definition of membership in such groups is continually redefined. In a racist world, however, the oppressed have obligations to one another. Without some form of internal unity, Gypsies, Jews, Kurds, black South Africans or numerous other groups would be unable to protect themselves from unspeakable horrors and holocausts.

History's terror, its seemingly careless concern for the wishes of the vanquished, makes hopes for stable racial kinds the erotica of necrophilia. History's intentional and unintentional terrors—its mutations, destructions, genocides, assimilations—often leave languages, cultures, and races as museum relics.

Racial constructions divide the world. The divisions often rest on perceptions of cultures as representing different races. Locke frequently criticized the conflation of race and culture—treating cultures as if they were the sole creation of a race; treating nations as if their justification should be based on promotion of a racial ideal. Cultural kinds can gain regard and cultural exchanges and transitions can occur without seeing peoples as the elixir of a race. The pathology of self-hatred, for example, associated with the high rate of Asian-American women who marry white American men, is not solved by romanticizing an ideal, pure Asian race and promoting Asian-only marriage. If the pursuit of status is one strong motivating force in deciding on one's mate, it is predictable that pathologies of self-hatred would accompany the degrading reality of white American racism. Ending "white" as a status marker may have far greater impact on ending race-based pathologies than achieving a numerical arrangement of same-racial-kind marriages. Ending the perception of Asians as a pure racial kind, and thereby contributing to the negation of the idea of people as representing the elixir of a race or culture, may generate far more regard for Asian culture as a living reality—assimilable, malleable, and complex.

Racism is one of humanity's egregious and unnecessary forms of terrorizing. Social reality always changes. Various practices used to generate status—such as scarification, ownership of eunuchs, displaying enemy skulls, and various institutions such as slavery, serfdom, male suffrage, and caste-based rights—have slowly, grudgingly declined. Racism, contrary to a pessimist view of future possibilities, is not a permanent feature of future societies.

The answer to "What, then, is racism?" is disconnected in a complex way from the answer to "Why, then, does race or racism exist?" If the concept of race exists because people frequently mistake phenotypes for natures, that does not tell us why the concept of race persists, especially when phenotypes are a minor feature of racial differentiations. If racism exists because of kin nepotism, the current cause of racism is in no way answered. The current cause of racism, for example, may be the consequence of class struggle. Racism might exist because humans are irrational egotists, because kin nepotism is ubiquitous, or because racial mythology is a convenient trope in the service of nation state formations to unite trading partners. The current cause of racism may have nothing to do with its origin. Moreover, answers to "what" questions require depictions of what exists—pictures of individuals and groups—and what subtle, salient, coercive, compelling, and enigmatic variables contribute to how the "what" functions now and how it is likely to function in the future.

Our beliefs about what will happen in the future often condition, if not determine, what beliefs we have now and what we do now. Our attitude toward reality differs, for example, depending on whether we believe racism is permanent or whether it is a defeatable social condition. Explanations, whether they use a notion of mechanical causation or teleological causation; whether pragmatist, historical materialist, structuralist or otherwise, invariably help us imagine what we believe will happen in the future. The explanation form we prefer influences how we understand change, for example, whether we believe that change occurs for purposeful reasons or whether we believe that the world is dysteleological; whether change proceeds through random chaos, dialectically, or rationally; whether change is fundamentally the result of intentional action and explained by accounts of intentionality, and so on. Moreover, the ontological elements we believe exist, for example, races, classes, nations, civilizations, or peoples, influence what we believe can happen.

The explanation we prefer, and its ontological elements, should be based on strongly warranted belief, if not certain truth. We should not risk our lives, as police, soldiers, or nurses, nor place the lives of our loved one's at risk without a genuine belief that our actions are at least strongly warranted. We should not risk the lives of current persons nor future generations on the basis of weak accounts or for instrumental reasons that are not based on reasoned beliefs about what will happen.

I argue for a moderate form of objectivism, one that takes seriously explanations that consider groups real ontological entities. An objectivist believes at least that there are facts about the human world independent of contingent cultural or social ideas. Groups, for an objectivist, can exist independently as objective causal agents. That is, the cause or influential force of group phenomenon is engined by variables that are nor strictly contingent for their power on fleeting ideas. Evolutionists or historical materialists are examples of philosophic orientations that are objectivist in orientation. Our biologies or material interests, in substantive and salient ways, drive group events. Races do not exist as trans-historical objective entities, and insofar as that is the case, I consider constructivist views of race to be valuable contributions to our understanding of reality.

Constructivists believe that facts about the human world are absolutely dependent on contingent cultural or social ideas. Groups do not exist for the constructivist independent of cultural or social ideas. The causal agency for groups is dependent on constructed ideations, that is, groups are in some substantive way a feature of individual or social ideas. Phenomenologists, existentialists, and vitalists are examples of constructivist-oriented philosophies. Even if social entities are considered real by philosophers with these orientations, they are not real in any substantive way independent from uncaused choices, phenon, or some form of unexplainable indeterminancies rooted in consciousness or ideology. Intentions are thus crucial salient and coercive variables.

Objectivists have, in my opinion, an interesting theoretical advantage over constructivists: given their respective theories of explanation such as functionalist or structuralist, they proffer what the future holds. The future can be presaged, if not predicted, because material reality shapes, in a substantive way, events independent of unpredictable modes of consciousness. Who lives and dies, how long they live, what diseases they are subject to suffer from without adequate health care, who owns and profits from businesses, and thus whose children have bright futures are all shaped by the egregious fiscal realities in racist societies. Victims of racism, for example, live more often than not near toxic waste sites, they drink industrially polluted water, and suffer preventable ill health. People are born into these disadvantages and struggle, heroically, to overcome daily humiliation and the expropriation of their wealth. Evolutionists, for example, believe that fitness, adaptation, mutation, and survival are the sorts of conceptions needed to explain what groups have survived in the past and which sort will likely succeed in the future—usually without telling us which group will invariably succeed. Definite methods for shaping future societies can be plausibly inferred from such explanations. Neither individual existential moments of choice nor phenomenological forms of sense experience drives social change on evolutionary accounts. Biologies, geographies, and a host of variables inclusive of sense experience drive what evolutionists see as possible human futures. Marxists, as another example, often believe that risking their lives on behalf of the working-class struggle to overthrow the bourgeoisie means risking their lives in ways that will benefit the enhancement and thriving of all future persons. Thinking in terms of how objective, real groups or forces will shape the future is characteristic of objectivist approaches.

Philosophies that cannot proffer what traits and what sort of groups shape the future are at best parasitic on philosophies that purport to tell us what will happen. Where, for example, hospitals should be located or what the criteria should be for college admission are influenced by explanations of group behavior. Where to place a hospital is not given by philosophies that offer no substantive guidance to believe that our selection will have short and long-term desired effects. Such philosophies can react to where the socialist, communist, capitalist, Muslims, Christians, or Buddhists place a hospital, but they cannot offer strong guidance concerning where to place one's loyalties for the purpose of creating a definitive future.

Objectivists can argue that a given recommended community is preferred across fleeting, contextual, and constructed identities and will come into existence. It is parasitic to simply condemn the realities created or predicted by others while remaining agnostic about the efficacy of such predictions. Every society is already compelled to react to, and be affected by, universally influential social entities—religious communities, multinational corporations, class interests, regionally united nations—that define their teleology and community in objectivist terms. Given that social entities are often egregiously treated as metaphysical absolutes and undifferentiated wholes, there are nonetheless no viable explanations that reasonably offer projections that do not use some array of social entities as an explanadum.

Anti-racists are always in the position of reacting to a world of dominant powers in hopes of creating an alternative world. Anti-racists who can affect the variables with the greatest impact on the future arguably can have a substantive impact. It is not, then, immaterial to know as best as we can what variables will affect what happens in the world and what social entities will have the greatest impact on abating conditions of misery.

A good deal of what happens in the world and what affects us, unfortunately, has nothing to do with our social constructions—including constructed racial social kinds. This is one reason why, I have suggested, the death of racial identities is no bellwether for the death of racism. How we construct racial kinds is not sufficient to explain substantively what happens to such groups. That is, ideation of racial kinds may have little or nothing to do with what happens to those kinds or what affects those kinds have. Intentions, desires, purposes, choices, and heuristic categories may be relatively benign. Perceiving persons as freely choosing agents, independent selves, unencumbered by antecedent ties or obligations, may not be of much value for explanatory efficacy.

As a way of seeing why racial social kinds may be relatively weak causal variables as well as relatively weak agents in pursuit of teleological interests, imagine that Alain L. Locke, a constructivist, was right in believing that races, as biological kinds, are not real. Further, assume that social races—the beliefs, habits, customs, and informal institutional regulations defining racial groups— are significant causal variables. In addition, assume that races can have teleologies (for example, a race can be said to contribute to a multicultural society if it is also the bearer of an enriching culture). Assume also that Locke was right in believing that civilizations and peoples (i.e., ethnic groups, nations, tribes, linguistic groups), when they can sustain themselves, shape history. It is then arguable that civilizations and peoples, and the traits that define their success, will help us in substantively deciding what traits to support when faced with hard decisions over scarce resources.

Civilizations and peoples are not, however, coterminous with races. If civilizations and peoples cause historical change, race is a trope within those historical forces. As social constructions, it is not just that social racemembership criteria radically change over relatively short periods of time, but that as causal variables they are subordinate to much more compelling and salient forces, for example, a civilization's march to standardize production, a people's effort to sustain territories identified as owned by that people, a material class interest, or the pursuit of status by ownership and control of revered symbols or sources of wealth. If particular civilizations or peoples shape history, they can be said to do so if they are contiguous, continuous, and ontologically trans-historical. As Locke recognized, however, races do not have such historical coherency. The analysis of race in France, for example, tells us nothing about race in China or postcolonial Algeria if we accept a constructivist picture of reality. Constructivists see reality in nonsequential fashion, that is, historical epochs, social races, and forms of identity are unique. The multitude of races that have come and gone out of existence has not left any social race as a viable historical entity. The convergence of incipient variables, independent of race markets, perpetuates forms of racism; that is, rules, regulations, practices, codes, and modes of transferring wealth often function to sustain lower-class statuses, poor health services, and greater exposure to dangerous waste products for a social race, while the same variables favor another race. It is not race that is the cause of the misery. The vicious force of white supremacy, for example—given that St. Clair Drake and Martin Bernal are right in believing that white supremacist ideology has continued unabated for over a thousand years—is not a "race" with inherent causal traits but a polymorphic arrangement of incipient variables that conjoin to make possible the completely inhumane force of white supremacist ideology and behavior.[4] The disjunctions between race, civilization, and peoples renders race not as a salient variable, but at best a contributor. Possibly, this is why explanations and predictions that rely on stable and assumed trans-historical races—stable entities—have been notoriously wrong.

Populations oppressed, terrorized, exploited, and degraded by race are not invested with world historical missions any more than the populations engaged in demonic racial oppression.[5] Locke's view, if interpreted to mean that races contribute to social growth by manifesting a racial historical mission, is misguided. The teleology of race, even if a racial identity can be said to have contributed to a culture, is the negation of racial identity. One way to see this is the following: if there are historical agents such as the working class, moral consciousness, or civilizations, then such agents seek to create a reality and thereby satisfy their teleologies. That is, historical agents have, as an abiding interest or mission, the creation of a certain situation that embodies their goals. The historical mission of the working class, on Marx's account, for example, is the creation of a world in which the working classes' interest is realized universally. The working class would then, in effect, cease to exist as a class since there would be no other classes. Analogously the interest of the oppressed by race is the ending of race-based oppression. Minimally, this includes ending the conditions that create racial disparity and what it is to be stereotyped—inclusive of the negation of race. Consequently, if, as Locke believed, races can make contributions in some way distinguishable from cultural ones, such contributions or missions make sense solely within a limited, short-term historical context. The sense of self-worth racial unity offers and its use as a bulwark against egregious racism has at best temporary pragmatic merit—no virtues are inculcated, no one can actualize their natures, no one gains union with good faith, no liberated consciousness is gained, and no tragedy is avoided. Racial identity is, as Locke notes, a temporary surcease.

There are no arguments that could justify making hard decisions about allocating scarce resources for the long term on preferential treatment of specific races. If our explanation of social races as causal variables is cogent, we cannot make the sort of inference about how to allocate scarce resources the way that we can use ideas about civilizations or peoples as causal variables to help inform decisions. Civilizations and peoples do not carry the sort of odious identification with degrading prejudice that is integral to race.

Racism is explained by objectivist criteria in a more convincing fashion than constructivist criteria, and it can offer long-term suggestions for creating community. Yet, without constructivist insights into how visceral race is, objectivist explanations can mistake anabsolutes for more Substantive social objects, discount the influence of social constructions, and mistake contingent communities for natural communities.

Constructivist accounts are analogous to cautionary tales. Cautionary tales foreshadow terrible consequences if we fail to weigh appropriately competing motivations. If, as in the ancient Egyptian *Instruction of Ani*, motivation springs from our hearts, the seat of intuitive wisdom, then it is opposed to the certainty of tradition. The intuitions of each generation are not likely the same across generations. Khonshotep, the son, is committed to applauding instructions of his heart, and his father, the certain truth of tradition. Analogously, constructivists advise of the deeply important role our hearts play in shaping reality. If, as in Goethe's *Faust*, intuited religious faith and the search for certain knowledge are in conflict, the warning is that a probable decline of the soul will occur because the desire for certain knowledge is itself misguided. The warning of the constructivist, in a similar way, is that absolute access to an unmediated social reality is itself misguided. Statuses, for example, may be accorded through legal institutions in one society but through family lineage in another, making the nature of honor or racist insult contingent on the context—an important constructivist insight. Constructivist accounts help picture the web of significations and marks of exclusion and inferiority with attention to the personal, the daily, and concrete specificity.

It is objectivist criteria of what exists, across contexts, that I suggest we use to decide when situations count as racist. It is not just humiliations, stereotypes, and false forms of categorizing persons that define racism, it is the racial slavery of children, the hunger of the starving and the charred remains of racial populations designated for extermination. If, for example, we define racism in historical materialist terms, there is a way to define racism whether the society uses institutional rules or family lineage to accord status. A historical materialist will consider the material sources that influence behavior. In addition, in the absence of adequate information about whether a situation is racist—and it is arguable that we rarely have adequate information—appeal to stable definitions has advantages that subjective definitions lack. Stable definitions offer, for example, criteria we can use to evaluate changes, such as whether the conditions creating racial misery are increasing or decreasing.

The ineffable character, and incongruous nature, of multiple identities that normally inhabit human consciousness is never stable and always subject to change. Constructivist explanations picture the vicissitudes of constantly shifting identities and efforts to avoid, or cop out of, forms of identity. "As a culture, we call ourselves Spanish when referring to ourselves as a linguistic group and when copping out. It is then that we forget our predominant Indian genes. ... We call ourselves Hispanic or Spanish-American or Latin American or Latin when linking ourselves to other Spanish-speaking peoples of the Western Hemisphere and when copping out. We call ourselves Mexican-American to signify we are neither Mexican nor American, but more the noun 'American' than the adjective 'Mexican' (and when copping out)."[6] *Mestizo* may affirm both Indian and Spanish heritage, *raza* may refer to a Chicano's racial identity; *tejanos* may be Chicanos from Texas. *Metis* or *metissage* is the racial base of Euro-Asians, but Euro-Asians as mixed, in some form, with Europeans by definition. Simultaneously, Europeans, misconceived as paradigmatically white, are seen as white on a foreground of Bosnian, Slavic, Belarussian and numerous other ethnic identities. That fact that racial realities are contingent on subjective or social ideation is compatible with a constructivist picture of what exists. However, all forms of identity involve copping out. Some forms are pathological, for example, forms that engender self-hatred. The reality of copping out is not a tragic or inherently debilitating feature of social reality. There are no authentic racial kinds hiding beneath our skins and no static social reality that requires a romantic racial solution.

What, then, is oppression? Or rather, what is non-contextual oppression?

Objectivists can answer both questions with something other than claims about contextual identities, feelings, local descriptions, and fleeting ascriptions. An objectivist can contend that class, nation, and gender identities are more likely to be identities rooted in, caused by, or closely associated with invariant human features. That is, an objectivist can contend that such entities are features not strongly contingent on constructions, such as ascriptions, descriptions, and depictions of group membership, but exist and function in certain ways regardless of constructions. Racist practices might be understood as completely unnecessary, never a feature of a truly liberated consciousness, and always dysfunctional.

Quaint platitudes about the importance of democracy, dialogue, critical thinking, and communal discourse, as well as romantic appeals to the obligations of the wealthy, are grossly inadequate solutions to the sinister motives of racists and the egregious joys and power secured by the monetary profit from situations of racism—the wages usurped from death and shattering lives. In a world that has increasingly destroyed substantive distinctions between peoples, while simultaneously maintaining contrived divisions of race, it is relatively easy to ignore the suffering of persons stigmatized as abject and beyond redemption while applauding cultural pluralism. The existing arrangement of assets—who owns factories, who controls health care, who gains from disposing of toxic waste in poor neighborhoods and underdeveloped countries, who profits from the sale of policing supplies—already structures differential life chances along lines of racial constructions. Directly changing these arrangements requires far more than the paternalism associated with maintaining racially and culturally segregated enclaves. Quaint platitudes, hoped-for changes in corrupt intentions, and shifts of intuited ideology are extremely weak causal variables as sources for change—changed ownership, control, participation, and access to material reality will have far greater impact on creating a deraciated and socially viable world.

Racial oppression allows us to ignore the suffering of the oppressed by race, because the immiserated are tucked away in prisons, rural hovels, illegal drug dens, and communities that offer their members little to no real opportunity for gainful employment, let alone ownership or control. The death of racist oppression, regardless of the context or transient form of identity construction, requires creating fiscally empowered oppressed populations, new realities, and the actualization or blossoming of the deepseated, warranted traits that unite humanity.

The Holberts, lynched but not forgotten, burned and dismembered, but not bereft of honor, should have defended their homes—the killing of vicious aggressors and the enmity of an amoral community not withstanding. No person should be encouraged to develop traits of submissiveness, especially those faced with living their lives in a world that marks them as abject, wretched, and inherently inferior. There is no reason to be self-effacing or complacent, whether one is a pacifist or not.[7] Anti-racists should be confident, demanding, uncompromising, and aggressive. Destroying racism will require more revolutions. They may be violent revolutions or they may be nonviolent, direct-action movements, based on philosophies of pacifism and the power of conscience. In either case, power concedes nothing without demand, compulsion, expropriation, and radical redistribution of control over the resources that make life possible.

There are competing views of racism that would not approach explanations in the above way. However, I do not believe that other explanatory approaches should depict the miseries any less vividly or recommend any milder actions to destroy the terror of race and racism.

Race is a trope undergirding North and South American, African, Asian, and European identities. Without communal unity between and among populations of these regions, a unity that subordinates and negates supremacist racial realities, the creation of universal human liberation is stunted.

Racism is one of history's unnecessary, fickle terrors. The forces that unite humanity—such as common dominators of class interest, inclinations to pursue status, disdain for injustice to members of one's perceived community—can be marshalled to aid the destruction of sinister, unintentional, and structural racial formations of oppression. If attacked vigilantly and without compromise, racism will also be one of history's irretrievable terrors.

NOTES

1. I mean by death the actual destruction of life and thereby futures, exemplified in Joseph C. Miller's *Way of Death* (Wisconsin: University of Wisconsin Press, 1988). The social import of death, I believe, is well explored in Orlando Patterson's *Slavery and Social Death* (Cambridge, MA: Harvard University Press, 1982).

2. See, for example, Donal E. Brown, *Human Universals* (Philadelphia: Temple University Press, 1991). Also see Alain Locke, "Values and Imperatives," Leonard Harris, ed., *Philosophy of Alain Locke* (Philadelphia: Temple University Press, 1989, pp. 34–50). I am indebted to Frank Kirkland, Hunter College, for his 1992 critical comments on my views of ontology, "Race and the Nature of Social Entities: Or Trying to Make It [Race] Real Compared to What," unpublished. Also see Richard J. Bernstein, *Beyond Objectivism and Relativism* (Philadelphia: University of Pennsylvania Press, 1983).

3. See, for example, Richard C. Lewontin, *Not in Our Genes* (New York: Pantheon Books, 1984).

4. See St. Clair Drake, *Black Folks Here and There* (Los Angeles: Center for Afro-American Studies, 1987); Martin Bernal, *Black Athena* (New Brunswick, N.J.: Rutgers University Press, 1987).

5. See my arguments against racial teleologies in "Agency and the Concept of the Underclass," ed., Bill E. Lawson, *Philosophy and the Underclass* (Philadelphia: Temple University Press, 1992), pp. 33–56. "Historical Subjects and Interests: Race, Class, and Conflict," ed., Michael Sprinkler *et. al.*, *The Year Left* (New York: Verso, 1986), pp. 91–106. Also see my argument against color-blind romanticism in "Postmodernism and Racism: An Unholy Alliance," eds., Fred L. Hord, J. S. Lee, *I Am Because We Are: Readings in Black Philosophy* (Amherst: University of Massachusetts Press, 1995), pp. 367–382.

6. Anzaldua, G., *Borderlands/La Frontera* (San Francisco: Spinsters/Aunt Lute, 1987), p. 63.

7. An excellent example of the stalwart character of pacifists with deep moral commitments to human uplift is explored in Greg Moses, *Revolution of Conscience* (New York: The Guillford Press, 1997).

Selected Bibliography

Abelson, R. P. "Social Psychology's Rational Man." In *Rationality and the Social Sciences*, S. I. Benn and G. Mortimore, eds. London: Routledge & Kegan Paul, 1976.

Acosta, Oscar Zeta. *The Autobiography of a Brown Buffalo*. San Francisco: Straight Arrow Books, 1972.

Adler, Elkan Nathan. *London*. Philadelphia: Jewish Publication Society of America, 1930.

Adorno, Theodore, *et al. The Authoritarian Personality*. New York: Harper and Row, 1950.

Agier, M. "Ilê Aiyê: A invenção do mundo negro." Unpublished manuscript, 1993.

Agier, M., and M. R. Carvalho. "Nation, race, culture: La trajectoire des mouvments noir et indigène dans la société bresilienne." Presented at the meeting "Nation, État, Ethnicité," Association des Chercheurs de Politique Africaine, Centre d'Études d'Afrique Noire, Bodeaux, France, November 12–13, 1992.

Ahern, Wilbert H. "Assimilationist Racism: The Case of the 'Friends of the Indian,'" *Journal of Ethnic Studies* 4:2 (1976): 23–32.

Aldrich, Mark. "Progressive Economists and Scientific Racism: Walter Willcox and Black American 1895–1910," *Phylon* 40:1 (1979): 1–14.

Alex, La Gama. *Apartheid*. New York: International Publishers, 1971.

Allen, Robert. *Black Awakening in Capitalist America*. New York: Doubleday, 1969.

Allen, Theodore W. *The Invention of the White Race*. London: Verso, 1994.

Allport, Gordon W. *The Nature of Prejudice*. Redding, MA: Addison-Wesley Publishing Company, 1954.

Alvarez, Julia. *How the Garcia Girls Lost Their Accents*. Chapel Hilt, NC: Algonquin Books, 1991.

Anderson, Benedict. *Imagined Communities*. London: Verso Books, 1983.

Andersen, Margaret, and Patricia Hill Collins, eds. *Race, Class and Gender*. Belmont, CA: Wadsworth Press, 1991.

Andradoe, Antonio Aberto banha de. *O anti-racismo da accao civilizadora dos portuguesses*. Lisbon: Bertrand, 1953.

Andrews, George. *Blacks and Whites in São Paulo, Brazil, 1899–1988*. Madison, WI: University of Wisconsin Press, 1991.

Andrews, G. R. "Desigualde racial no Brasil e nos Estados Unidos: Uma comparção estatística." *Estudos Afro-Asiaticos* 22 (1992): 47–84.

451

Anson, Robert S. *Best Intentions: The Education and Killing of Edmund Perry*. New York: Vintage Books, 1987.

Anthias, Floyd, and Nita Yuval-Davis. *Racialized Boundaries: Race, Nation, Gender, Color and the Anti-racist Struggle*. New York: Routledge, 1992.

Apostle, Richard A., C. Y. Glock, T. Piazza, and M. Suelzle. *The Anatomy of Racial Attitudes*. Berkeley, CA: University of California Press, 1983.

Appel, Stephen W. "'Outstanding Individuals Do Nor Arise from Ancestrally Poor Stock': Racial Science and the Education of Black South Africans," *Journal of Negro Education* 58:4 (Fall 1989): 544–57.

Appiah, Anthony, K. *Assertions and Conditionals*. Cambridge: Cambridge University Press, 1985.

———. *In My Father's House: Africa in the Philosophy of Culture*. New York: Oxford University Press, 1992.

———. "Racisms." *Anatomy of Racism*. Minneapolis: University of Minnesota Press, 1990.

———. "Racism and Moral Pollution," *Philosophy Forum* 18 (Winter-Spring 1987): 185–202.

Appiah, Anthony K., and Amy Gutman. *Color Consciousness: The Political Morality of Race*. Princeton, NJ: Princeton University Press, 1996.

Aristotle. *Collected Works of Aristotle*, ed. R. P. McKeon. New York: Random House, 1946.

Arnold, A. James. *Modernism and Negritude—The Poetry of Poetics of Aime Cesaire*. Cambridge, MA: Harvard University Press, 1981.

Aronson, Elliot. *The Social Animal*. San Francisco: W. H. Freeman, 1972.

Ashtor, Eliyahu. *The Jews and the Mediterranean Economy, 10th–15th Centuries*. London: Variorum Reprints, 1983.

Azevedo, Thales. *As elites de cor, um estudo de ascenso social*. São Paulo: Cia Editora Nacional, 1955.

Baier, Kurt. "Merit and Race," *Philosophia* 8 (November 1978): 121–51.

———. "Rationality, Reason and the Good," *Morality, Reason and Truth*. Totowa, NJ: Rowman & Alanheld, 1984.

Bailey, Frederick G. *Civility of Indifference: On Domesticating Ethnicity*. New York: Cornell University Press, 1996.

Bailyn, Bernard. *Voyagers to the West*. New York: Vintage, 1988.

Baird, Robert M., and Stuart M. Rosenbaum, eds. *Bigotry, Prejudice and Hatred: Definitions, Causes and Solutions*. Amherst, NY: Prometheus Books, 1992.

Baker, Paul T. "The Biological Race Concept as a Research Tool," *American Journal of Physical Anthropology* 27:573 (1967): 21–27.

Baker, Robert. "'Pricks' and 'Chicks': A Plea for Persons." In *Sexist Language*, ed. Mary Vetterling-Bragin. Totowa, NJ: Littlefield Adams, 1981.

Baksh, I. J. "Stereotypes of Negroes and East Indians in Trinidad: Re-examination," *Caribbean Quarterly* 25:1–2 (1979): 52–71.

Balibar, Etienne. *Cinq études du materialisme listorique*. Paris, France: F. Maspero, 1974.

———. *On the Dictatorship of the Proletariat*. Atlantic Highlands, NJ: Humanities Press, 1976.

Balibar, Etienne and Imanuel Wallerstein. *Race, Nation, Classe: les identités ambiques*. Paris, France: Editions la Decouverte, 1988.

Balla, Ignatius. *The Romance of the Rothschilds*. London: Eveleigh Nash, 1913.

Banton, Michael. "The Concept of Racism," *Race and Racialism*. New York: Barnes & Noble, 1970.

———. *The Ideal of Race*. London: Tavistock, 1977.

———. *The Race Concept*. Canada: Douglas David and Charles Limited, 1975.

———. *Race Relations*. New York: Basic Books, 1967.

———. *Racial and Ethnic Competition*. Cambridge: Cambridge University Press, 1983.

———. *Racial Theories*. Cambridge: Cambridge University Press, 1987.

Barash, David P. *Sociobiology and Behavior*. New York: Elsevier, 1982.

Barbot, Marie-Jose. *Racie sans race: Japanese Shiritagaranai Nihonjin*. Tokyo: Kashiwa Shob, 1983.

Barken, Elazar. *The Retreat of Scientific Racism*. Cambridge: Cambridge University Press, 1992.

Barker, Anthony J. *The African Link: British Attitudes to the Negro in the Era of the Atlantic Slave Trade, 1550–1807*. London: Frank Cass, 1978.

Barker, Martin. *The New Racism*. Maryland: Altheia Books, 1981.

Barker, Martin, and Annelogy Beezer. *Readings into Cultural Studies*. New York: Routledge, 1992.

Barton, N. H., and G. M. Hewitt. "Analysis of Hybrid Zones," *Annual Review of Ecology and Systematics*, vol. 16 (1985): 113–48.

Barrett, Stanley. "Racism, Ethics and the Subversive Nature of Anthropological Inquiry," *Philosophy of Social Science*. 14 (March 1984): 1–26.

Bar-Tal, Daniel. "Causes and Consequences of Delegitimization: Models of Conflict and Ethnocentrism," *Journal of Social Issues* 46:1 (Spring 1990): 65–81.

Barzun, Jacques. *Race: A Study in Modern Superstition*. London: Methuen, 1938.

Bateson, Patrick, ed. *Mate Choice*. New York: Cambridge University Press, 1983.

Battersby, James L. *Paradigms Regained: Pluralism and the Practice of Criticism*. Philadelphia: University of Pennsylvania Press, 1991.

Baxter, Paul, and Basil Sansom, eds. *Race and Race Difference*. New York: Penguin Books, 1972.

Becker, Gary S. *The Economics of Discrimination*. Chicago: University of Chicago Press, 1957.

Bell, Derrick A., Jr. *And We Are Not Saved: The Elusive Quest For Racial Justice*. New York: Basic Books, 1987.

———. *Confronting Authority: Reflections of an Ardent Protester*. Boston: Beacon Press, 1994.

———. *Faces at the Bottom of the Well: The Permanence of Racism*. New York: Basic Books, 1992.

———. *Race, Racism and American Law*. Boston: Little, Brown and Company, 1980.

Bell, Linda A., and David Blumenfeld. *Overcoming Racism and Sexism*. Boston: Rowman and Littlefield Publishers, Inc., 1995.

Belliotti, Raymond A. *Seeking Identity*. Lawrence, KS: Kansas University Press of Kansas, 1995.

Belok, Michael. "Ethnicity and Social Control," *Review Journal of Philosophy and Social Science* 2 (Summer, 1977): 118–28.

Benedict, Ruth. *Patterns of Culture*. Boston: Houghton Mifflin, 1934.

———. *Race and Racism*. London: Routledge Publishing Co., 1942.

———. *Race, Science, and Politics*. New York: Modern Age Books, 1940.

Berghe, Pierre L. van den. *Ethnic Phenomenon*. New York: Elsevier, 1981.

———. *The Ethnic Phenomenon*. Westport, CT: Greenwood Publishing, 1987.

———. *Human Family Systems*. New York: Elsevier, 1979.

———. *Race and Ethnicity: Essays in Comparative Sociology*. New York: Basic Books, 1970.

———. *Race and Racism*. New York: Wiley, 1967.

———. *Race and Racism: A Comparative Perspective*. New York: Wiley, 1978.

Bernal, Martin. *Black Athena*. New Brunswick, NJ: Rutgers University Press, 1987.

Berry, Brewton. *Race and Ethnic Relations*. Boston: Houghton Mifflin, 1958.

Berry, Mary F. *Black Resistance/White Law: A History of Constitutional Racism in America*. New York: Appteton-Century-Crofts, 1971.

Berthoff, Rowland. "Conventional Mentality: Free Blacks, Women, and Business Corporations as Unequal Persons," *Journal of American History* 76:3 (December, 1989): 753–84.

Bickel, Alexander M. *The Supreme Court and the Idea of Progress*. New Haven: Yale University Press, 1978.

Biddiss, Michael D. *Father of Racist Ideology—The Social and Political Thought of Count Gobineau*. New York: Weybright & Talley, 1970.

Billig, Michael. "Patterns of Racism: Interviews with National Front Members," *Race and Class* (Autumn 1978): 161–79.

Bird, Caroline. *Born Female: The High Cost of Keeping Women Down*. New York: McKay, 1968.

Birt, Robert E. "A Returning to the Source: The Philosophy of Alain Locke," *Quest* (December 1990): 103–13.

Blauner, Bob. *Black Lives, White Lives.* Berkeley, CA: University of California Press, 1989.

Blauner, Robert. *Racial Oppression in America.* New York: Harper & Row, 1972.

Block, N. J., and Gerald Dworkin, eds. *The IQ Controversy: Critical Readings.* New York: Pantheon Books, 1976.

Blum, Lawrence. *Moral Perception and Particularity.* Cambridge: Cambridge University Press, 1994.

Boas, Franz. *Race, Language and Culture.* New York: MacMillan Company, 1940.

Bobo, L. "White Opposition to Busing: Symbolic Racism or Realistic Group Conflict?" *Journal of Personality and Social Psychology* 45 (1983): 1196–1210.

Boggs, James. *Racism and the Class Struggle.* New York: Monthly Review Press, 1970.

Bolt, Christine. *Victorian Attitudes to Races.* London: Routledge and Kegan Pauli, 1971.

Bose, Nemai Sadhan. *Racism, Struggle for Equality and Indian Nationalism.* Firma: KLM, 1981.

Boston, Thomas D. *Race, A Different Vision.* 2 vols. New York: Routledge, 1996.

———. *Class & Conservatism.* Boston: Unwin Hyman, 1988.

Bourdieu, Pierre. "What Makes a Social Class? On the Theoretical and Practical Existence of Groups," *Berkeley Journal of Sociology* 32 (1987): 1–6.

Bourne, Jenny. "Towards an Anti-Racist Feminism," *Race and Class* 25:1 (Summer).

Bowers, C. A. *Elements of a Post-Liberal Theory of Education.* New York: Teachers College Press, 1987.

Bowser, Benjamin P. "Race Relations in the U.S.," *Journal of Black Studies* 15:3 (March 1985): 307–24.

———. *Racism and Anti-Racism in World Perspective.* Thousand Oaks, CA: Sage Publications, 1995.

Bowser, Benjamin P., R. Alvarez, et al., eds. *Discrimination in Organizing Using Social Indicators to Manage Social Change.* San Francisco, CA: Jossey-Bass, 1979.

Boxer, C. R. *Race Relations in the Portuguese Colonial Empire: 1415–1825.* Oxford, England: Clarendon Press, 1963.

Boxill, Bernard. *Blacks and Social Justice.* Totowa, NJ: Rowman & Alanheld, 1984.

———. "How Injustice Pays," *Philosophy and Public Affairs* 9:4 (Summer 1980): 359–71.

Boyer, Pascal. *Tradition as Truth and Communication.* Cambridge, MA: MIT Press, 1985.

Boyer, Robert, and P. Richardson. *Culture and the Evolutionary Process.* Chicago: University of Chicago Press, 1985.

Bracken, Harry M. "Philosophy and Racism," *Philosophia* 8:2–3 (1978): 241–60.

Braithwaite, F. S. "Race and Class Differentials in Career (Value) Orientation," *Plural Societies* 7:2 (1991): 17–31.

Brandt, George, and D. Muir. "Schooling, Morality, and Race," *Journal of Moral Education* 15, 1986, 58–67.

Braxton, Joanne M., and Andree N. McLaughlin, eds. *Wild Women in the Whirlwind.* New Brunswick, NJ: Rutgers University Press, 1990.

Brereton, B. "The Foundations of Prejudice: Indians and Africans in the 19th Century," *Caribbean Issues* 1:1 (1974): 15–28.

Brierly, John K. *A Natural History of Man.* Madison, NJ: Fairleigh Dickinson University Press, 1970.

Brittan Arthur. *Sexism, Racism, and Oppression.* Oxford: Blackwell, 1984.

Brooks, D. H. M. "Why Discrimination Is Especially Wrong," *Journal of Value Inquiry.* 17 (1983): 305–12.

Brown. Michael E. "The Viability of Racism: South Africa and the United States," *Philosophy Forum* 18 (Winter-Spring 1987): 254–69.

Bruening, William. "Racism: A Philosophical Analysis of a Concept," *Journal of Black Studies* 5:1 (1974): 3–18.

Burgest, David R. "Sexual Games in Black Male/Female Relations," *Journal of Black Studies* 21:1 (1990): 103–116.

Burkey, Richard. *Racial Discrimination and Public Policy in the United States.* Lexington, MA: Health Lexington, 1971.

Burnham, Dorothy. "Science and Racism," *Freedomways* 15:2 (1975): 89–95.

Butler, John Sibley. *Entrepreneurship and Self-Help among Black Americans: A Reconsideration of Race and Economics.* Albany, NY: SUNY University Press, 1991.

Butter, Judith. *Gender Trouble: Feminism and the Subversion of Identity.* New York and London: Routledge, 1990.

Byron, Raymond. *Affirmative Action at Work: Law, Politics and Ethics.* Pittsburgh, PA: Pittsburgh University Press, 1991.

Camejo, Peter. *Racism, Revolution and Reaction, 1861–1877: The Rise and Fall of Radical Reconstruction.* New York: Monad Press, 1976.

Campbell, D. "Stereotypes and the Perception of Group Differences." *American Psychology.* 22 (1967): 823–35.

Card, Claudia. "Race, Racism, and Ethnicity," in Linda Bell and David Blumenfeld, eds. *Overcoming Sexism and Racism.* Lanham, MD: Rowman and Littlefield, 1994.

Carmichael, Stokley, and Charles Hamilton. *Black Power: The Politics of Liberation in America.* New York: Vintage Press, 1967.

———. *Black Power-The Politics of Liberation in America.* London: Cape, 1968.

Cashmore, Ernest. *Dictionary of Race and Ethnic Relations.* London: Routledge and Kegan Paul, 1994.

———. *The Logic of Racism.* London: Allen & Unwin, 1987.

Cassirer, Ernest. *The Myth of the State.* New Haven, CT: Yale University Press, 1946.

Castles, S., H. Booth, and T. Wallace. *Here for Good: Western Europe's New Ethnic Minorities.* London: Pluto Press, 1984.

Castoriadis, Cornelius. "Reflections on Racism," *Thesis Eleven* 32 (1992): 1–12.

Carter, Stephen. *Reflections of an Affirmative Action Baby.* New York: Basic Books, 1991.

Castro, Nei G., and J. A. Guimarães. "Desigualclades racials no mercado e nos locais de trablho." *Estudos Afro-Asiáticos.* 24 (1993): 23–60.

Cavalli-Sforza, Luieji L. "Genetic Drift in an Italian Population," *Readings from Scientific American: Biological Anthropology.* New York: Freeman, 1969.

———. *The History and Geography of Human Genes.* Princeton, NJ: Princeton University Press, 1994.

Cavalli-Sforza, L. L., and M. Feldman. *Cultural Transmissions: A Quantitative Approach.* Princeton, NJ: Princeton University Press, 1982.

Cavell, S. *The Claim of Reason.* Oxford: Oxford University Press, 1976.

Cell, John. *The Highest Stage of White Supremacy.* Cambridge: Cambridge University Press, 1982.

Centre for Contemporary Cultural Studies. *The Empire Strikes Back.* London: Hutchinson, 1982.

Champigny, Robert. *Humanism and Human Racism: A Critical Study of Essays by Satre and Camus.* The Hague: Mouton, 1972.

Chase, Allan. *The Legacy of Malthus: The Social Costs of the New Scientific Racism.* New York: Knopf, 1977.

Chase, Stuart. *The Tyranny of Words.* London: Methuen, 1938.

Chavez, Linda. *Out of the Barrio: Toward a New Politics of Hispanic Assimilation.* New York: Basic Books, 1991.

Churchill, Ward. *Fantasies of the Master Race: Literature, Cinema and the Colonization of the American Indians.* Monroe, ME: Common Courage Press, 1992.

Clauser, Edwin G., and Jack Bermingham. *Pluralism, Racism and Public Policy.* Massachusets: Bun G. K. Hall , 1981.

Clegg, Jenny. *Fu Manchu and the "Yellow Peril": The Making of a Racist Myth.* New York: Trentham Books, 1994.

Coetzee, J. M. "Tales of Afrikaners." *Sunday Times Magazine*, March 9, 1986.

————. *White Writing: On the Culture of Letters in South Africa*. New Haven, CT: Yale University Press, 1989.

Cohen C. "Why Racial Preference Is Illegal and Immoral," *Commentary* 67 (June 1979): 40–51.

Cohen, Robin, *The New Healots*. Brookfield, VA: Gower, 1987.

Cohen, S. Allen. *Hard Act to Follow: The Immigration Act of 1988*. Warwick, England: Centre for Research in Ethnic Relations, 1988.

Coles, Robert, and Jane Hollowell Coles. *Women of Crisis*. New York: Detacorte Press/Seymour Lawrence, 1978.

Colleyn, Jean-Paul. "The Color of Words," *Revue de l'Institut de Sociologie* 3:4 (1983): 467–79.

Collins, Patricia Hill. *Black Feminist Thought*. London: Harper Collins Academic, 1990.

Colman, A. M. "Scientific Racism and Evidence on Race and Intelligence," *Race* 14:2 (1972): 137–53.

Cottingham, John. "Partiality, Favouritism and Morality," *Philosophical Quarterly* 36 (1986): 357–73.

————. "Race and Individual Merit," *Philosophy* 55 (October 1980): 525–31.

Couper, Kristin. "Racism and Anti-Racism in the United Kingdom," *MediterraneanPeoples* 51 (April-June 1990): 83–93.

Cox, Oliver C. *Caste, Class and Race*. New York: Doubleday, 1948.

Crilds, John Brown. "Afro-American Intellectuals and the People's Culture," *Theory and Society* 13:1 (1984): 69–90.

Cross, William E. *Shades of Black: Diversity in African-American Identity*. Philadelphia, PA: Temple University Press, 1991.

Crummelt, Alexander. *Destiny and Race*. Amherst, MA: University of Massachusetts Press, 1992.

Curtin, Phillip D. *Cross-Cultural Trade in World History*. Cambridge, England: Cambridge University Press, 1984.

————. *The Image of Africa: British Ideas and Action, 1780–1850*. London: Macmillan, 1965.

Curtis, Lewis P. *Anglo-Saxons and Celts*. Bridgeport, CT: University of Bridgeport Press, 1968.

Da Costa, Emília. V. *The Brazilian Empire: Myths and Histories*. Belmont, CA: Wadsworth, 1988.

Daly, Mary. "The Qualitative Leap beyond Patriarchal Religion." *Feminist Quarterly* 1, no. 4 (1975): 29 ff.

Darrough, Masako N., and Robert H. Blank, eds. *Biological Differences and Social Equality Implications for Social Policy*. Westport, CT: Greenwood Press, 1978.

Das Gupta, Tania. *Racism and Paid Work*. Toronto: Garamond Press, 1996.

Davis, Angela Y. *Women, Race & Class*. New York: Vintage Books, 1983.

Davis, James. *Who Is Black?: One Nation's Definition*. University Park, PA: Penn State University Press, 1991.

Davis, Michael. "Race as Merit," *Mind* 92 (July 1983): 347–67.

Davis, Richard. *The English Rothschilds*. Glasgow: Collins Publishers, 1983.

Dawkins, Richard. *Extended Phenotype*. Oxford: Oxshire, 1982.

————. *The Selfish Gene*. New York: Oxford University Press, 1976.

Day, Beth. *Sexual Life between Blacks and Whites: The Roots of Racism*. New York: World Publishing, Times Mirror, 1972.

Degler, Carl N. *Neither Black nor White: Slavery and Race Relations in Brazil and the United States*. New York: The Macmillan Company, 1991.

de Kiewiet, Cornelius. *A History of South Africa–Social and Economic*. London: Oxford University Press, 1948.

Delacampagne, Christian. *L'invention de Racisme: Antiquité et moyen age*. Paris: Fayard, 1983.

————. "Racism and the West: From Praxis to Logos," *Anatomy of Racism*. Minneapolis, MN: University of Minnesota Press, 1990, 85–86.

De Lepervanche, Marie, and Gillian Bottomley eds. *The Cultural Construction of Race*. Sydney: Sydney Association for Studies in Society and Culture, 1988.

————. *Intersexions: Gender, Class, Culture, Ethnicity*. Australia: Allen and Unwin, 1991.

Delgado, Richard, ed. *Critical Race Theory: The Cutting Edge*. Philadelphia, PA: Temple University Press, 1995.

————. "Critical Race Theory," *Sage* 19:2 (May 1992): 3–29.

Demarco, Joseph P. "The Concept of Race in the Social Thought of W. E. B. Du Bois" *The Philosophical Forum* 3:2 (1972): 227–242.

De Silva, Kingsley M., et. al. *Ethnic Conflict in Buddhist Societies*. Boulder, CO: Westview Press, 1988.

De Vos, George D., et. al. *Japan's Invisible Race*. Berkeley, CA: University of California Press, 1966.

Dikotter, Frank. *The Discourse of Race in Modern China*. Stanford, CA: Stanford University Press, 1992.

Dobzhansky, Theodosius. *Genetics of the Evolutionary Process*. New York: Columbia University Press, 1970.

————. *Mankind Evolving*. New York: Bantam Press, 1981.

Dollard, John. *Caste and Class in a Southern Town*. New York: Doubleday, 1957.

Dollard, John, et al. *Frustration and Aggression*. New Haven, CT: Yale University Press, 1939.

Domínguez, Virginia. *White by Definition: Social Classification in Creole Louisiana*. New Brunswick, NJ: Rutgers University Press, 1986.

Dower, John W. *War Without Mercy: Race and Power in the Pacific War*. New York: Pantheon, 1986.

Dovidio, John F., and Samuel L. Gaetner. *Prejudice, Discrimination, and Racism*. Plympton, MA: Academy Publishing, 1986.

Drake, St. Clair. *Black Folks Here and There*. Los Angeles, CA: Center for Afro-American Studies, 1987.

Drescher, Seymour. "The Ending of the Slave Trade and the Evolution of European Scientific Racism," *Social Science History* 14:3 (Fall 1990): 415–450.

D'Souza, Dinesh. *The End of Racism: Principles for a Multiracial Society*. New York: The Free Press, 1995.

Du Bois, W. E. B. "The Conservation of Races," Howard Brotz, *Negro Social and Political Thought, 1850–1920*, New York: Basic Books, 1966, pp. 203–331.

————. *The Crisis* (December 1947).

————. *Dusk of Dawn*. New York: Harcourt Brace, 1940.

————. *The Souls of Black Folk*. New York: Penguin Books, 1903/1989.

DuBois, Ruiz. *Unequal Sisters*. New York: Routledge, 1994.

Dubow, S. "Afrikaner Nationalism, Apartheid and the Conceptualization of Race," *Journal of African History* 33:2 (1992): 209–37.

Dummett, Ann. *A Portrait of British Racism*. New York: Penguin Books, 1973, Hammondsworth.

————. *A Portrait of English Racism*. New York: Penguin Books, 1973.

————. "Race, Culture and Moral Education," *Journal of Moral Education* 15 (January 1986): 10–15.

Dummett, Ann, and M. Dummett. *Race in Britain*. London: Open University Press, 1982.

Dumont, Louis. *Homo Hierarchicus*. Paris: Gallimard, 1978.

Durkheim, Emile. *The Rules of Sociological Method*. New York: The Free Press, 1938.

Dzidzienyo, A. *The Position of Blacks in Brazillian Society*. London: Minority Rights Group, 1979.

Eastland, Terry, and William Bennett. *Counting by Race*. New York: Basic Books, 1979.

Ehrenreich, Barbara, and Deidre English. *For Her Own Good: 150 Years of the Experts' Advice to Women*. Garden City, NY: Anchor Press Doubleday, 1979.

Ehrlich, Howard J. *The Social Psychology of Prejudice*. New York: Wiley, 1973.

Einstein, Zillah R. *Feminism and Sexual Equality*. New York: Monthly Review Press, 1984.

Elizondo, Virgule. *The Future Is Mestizo: Life Where Cultures Meet*. Crossroad Bloomington Publishing Company, 1988.

Essed, Philomena. *Everyday Racism*. Claremont, CA: Hunter House, 1990.

Ezorsky, Gertrude. *Racism and Justice*. Ithaca, NY: Cornell University Press, 1991.

Faith, Berry. "Black Poets, White Patrons: The Harlem Renaissance Years of Langston Hughes," *Crisis* 88:6s, (1981): 278–83, 306.

Fanon, Franz. *Black Skin, White Masks:* New York: Grove Press, 1967.

Fei, Hsiano-tung. *Chung-hua min tsu tu. yuan ti ke chu.* Peiching: Chung yang min tsu hsueh yuan chu pan she, 1989.

Feinslaver, Rabbi Alexander. *The Talmud for Today.* New York: St. Martin's Press, 1980.

Feis, Herbert. *Europe: The World's Banker, 1870–1914.* Clifton, NY: Kelley, 1974.

Ferguson, Ann. "Androgyny as an Ideal for Human Development." in Mary Vetterling-Bragin and F. A. Elliston *et. al.*, *Feminism and Philosophy.* Totowa, NJ: Littlefield adams, 1977.

Fernandes, Florestan. A. *Integração do Negro na Sociedade de Classes*, 2 vols. São Paulo: Cia Editora Nacional, 1965.

Field, Geoffrey. "Nordic Racism," *Journal of the History of Ideas* 38 (July-September 1977): 523–40.

Finley, Moses I. *Ancient Slavery and Modern Ideology.* New York: Pelican, 1983.

Firestone, Shulamith. *The Dialectic of Sex.* New York: Bantam Books, 1971.

Fish, Stanley. *Is There a Text in This Class?* Cambridge, MA: Harvard University Press, 1980.

Fishman, J. "Examination of the Process and Functions of Social Stereotyping," in *Journal of Social Psychology* 43 (1956): 27–64.

Fitzpatrick, Peter. "Racism and the Innocence of Law," *Journal of Law and Society* 14:1 (Spring 1987): 119–32.

Flecha, Ramon, and Jesus Gomez. *Racismo: no, gracias, ni moderno, ni postmoderno.* Barcelona: Roure, 1995.

Flew, Antony. "Clarifying the Concepts," *Anti-Racism—An Assault on Education and Value.* London: Sherwood, 1986, pp. 15–31.

———. "Education against Racism: Three Comments," *Journal of Philosophy Education* 21 (Summer 1987): 131–37.

———. "Three Concepts of Racism," *Encounter* 75 (July/August 1990): 63–66.

Fontaine, Pierre-Michel, ed. *Race, Class and Power in Brazil.* Los Angeles: Center for Afro-American Studies, 1985.

Foot, Philippa. *Virtues and Vices.* Los Angeles: University of California Press, 1978.

Forbes, Jack D. *Black Africans and Native Americans: Color, Race and Caste in the Evolution of Red-Black Peoples.* London: Blackwell, 1988.

Fortney, Nancy D. "The Anthropological Concept of Race," *Journal of Black Studies* 8:1 (1977): 35–54.

Foucault, Michael. *Power/Knowledge.* New York: Pantheon, 1977.

Fox-Genovese, Elizabeth. *Within the Plantation Household: Black and White Women of the Old South.* Chapel Hill, NC: University of North Carolina Press, 1988.

Franbenburg, R. *White Women, Race Matters: The Social Construction of Whiteness.* Minneapolis, MN: University of Minnesota Press, 1983.

Franklin, John H. *Color and Race.* Boston: Beacon Press, 1968.

Fredrickson, George M. *Arrogance of Race.* Middletown, CT: Wesleyan University Press, 1988.

———. *The Black Image in the White Mind: The Debate on AfroAmerican Character and Destiny, 1817–1914.* New York: Harper and Row, 1971.

———. *Inner Civil War.* New York: Harper-Row, 1965.

———. *White Supremacy.* New York: Oxford University Press, 1981.

Freye, Gilberto. *The Masters and the Slaves (Casa-grande & senzala): A Study in the Development of Brazilian Civilization*, trans. Samuel Putman. New York: Putnam, 1946.

———. *Sobrados e mucambos: decadencia do patriarchado rural no Brasil.* Sao Paulo: Companhia editora nacional, 1936. Serie 5a, vol. 64, of *Biblioteca pedagogica brasileira.*

Fried, Morton, H. *The Notion of Tribe.* Menlo Park, CA: Cummings Publishing, 1975.

Friedman, Lawrence. *The White Savage: Racial Fantasies in the Postbellum South*. Old Tappan, NJ: Prentice Hall, Inc., 1970.

Froman, Judy. *An Examination of the United Nations General Assembly Resolution 3379 (xxx), 10 November 1975*. New York: United Nations, 1991.

Fromm, Eric. *The Fear of Freedom*. London: Routledge and Kegan Paul, 1942.

Frye, Marilyn. *The Politics of Reality*. Trumansburg, NY: Crossing Press, 1983.

Gabel, Joseph. "Racism and Alienation," *Praxis International* 2:4 (January 1983): 421–37.

Gabriel J., and G. Ben-Tovim. "Marxism and the Concept of Racism," *Economy and Society* 7 (1977): 118–42.

Gadamer, Hans Georg. *Reason in the Age of Science*, trans. Frederick G. Lawrence. Cambridge, MA: MIT Press, 1982.

Garcia, Jorge L. A. "African-American Perspectives, Cultural Relativism, and Normative Issues," *African-American Perspectives on Biomedical Issues: Philosophical Issues*. Washington, DC: Georgetown University Press, 1992, p. 1166.

———. "Goods and Evils," *Philosophy and Phenomenological Research* 47 (1987): 385–412.

———. "Tunsollen, The Seinsollen, and the Soleinsollen," *American Philosophical Quarterly* 23 (1986): 267–276.

———. "Virtue Ethics," in the *Cambridge Dictionary of Philosophy*, ed. Robert Audi. Cambridge: Cambridge University Press, 1995, pp. 840–42.

Gaspard, Françoise, and Claude Servan-Schreiber. *La fin des immigrés*. Paris, Le Seuil. 1985.

Gates, Henry L. "Let Them Talk: A Review of 'Words that Wound': Critical Race Theory, Assaultive Speech and the First Amendment," *New Republic* (September 20 & 27, 1993): 37–49.

———. "Race," *Writing and Difference*. Chicago: University of Chicago Press, 1986.

———. *The Signifying Monkey*. New York: Oxford University Press, 1988.

Gates, Henry L., and Cornet West. *Future of the Race*. New York: A. A. Knopf, 1996.

Gates, Henry Louis, et. al. *Speaking of Race, Speaking of Sex: Hate Speech, Civil Rights, and Civil Liberties*. New York: New York University Press, 1994.

Giddens, Anthony, and David Held. *Classes, Power, and Conflict: Classical and Contemporary Debates*. Berkeley, CA: University of California Press, 1982.

Giddings, Paula. *When and Where I Enter: The Impact of Black Women on Race and Sex in America*. New York: Bantam, 1984.

Gilbert, Martin. *The Jewish History Atlas*. 3ed. Jerusalem: Steinatzky Press, 1975.

Gilligan, Carol. *In a Different Voice*. Cambridge, MA: Harvard University Press, 1982.

Gilman, Sander L. "Anti-Semitism and the Body of Psychoanalysis," *Social Research* 57:4 (Winter 1990): 993–1017.

Gilroy, Paul. *Ain't No Black in the Union Jack*. London: Hutchinson, 1987.

———. *The Black Atlantic: Modernity and Double Consciousness*. Cambridge, MA: Harvard University Press, 1993.

———. *Small Acts: Thoughts on the Politics of Black Cultures*. London: Serpent's Tail, 1993.

Girardet, Raoul. *Le Nationalime Français, 1871–1914*. Paris, 1970.

Gitlin, Todd. *The Twilight of Common Dreams: Why America Is Wracked by Culture Wars*. New York: Metropolitan Books, Henry Holt and Company, 1995.

Glass, Marvin. "Anti-Racism and Unlimited Freedom of Speech: An Untenable Dualism," *Canadian Journal of Philosophy* 8 (September 1978): 559–75.

Glausser, Wayne. "Three Approaches to Locke and the Slave Trade," *Journal of the History of Ideas* 51:2 (April-June 1990): 199–216.

Glazer, Nathan. "Blacks and Ethnic Groups: The Difference and the Political Difference it Makes," *Journal of Social Problems* 18 (Spring): 444–61.

Godelier, Maurice. *Rationality and Irrationality in Economics*. New York: Monthly Review Press, 1972.

Goldberg, David Theo. *Anatomy of Racism.* Minneapolis, MN: University of Minnesota Press, 1990.
———. "A Grim Dilemma about Racist Referring Expressions," *Metaphilosophy* 17 (October 1986): 224–29.
———. "Polluting the Body Politic: Racist Discourse and Urban Location." *Racism and the Postmodern City.* London: Unwin & Hyman, 1990.
———. "Racism and Rationality: The Need for a New Critique," *Philosophy Social Science* 20:3 (Summer 1990): 317–50.
———. *Racist Culture: Philosophy and the Politics of Meaning.* Cambridge: Blackwell Publishers, 1993.
———. "Racist Discourse and the Language of Class," *Race and Class as Patterns of Twentieth Century Exploitation,* 1989b.
———. "Raking the Field of the Discourse of Racism," *Journal of Black Studies* 18 (1987): 58–71.
Goldberg, David, and Michael Krausz, eds. *Jewish Identity.* Philadelphia: Temple University Press, 1993.
Goldin, Ian. *Making Race.* New York: Longman, 1987.
Gomberg, Paul. "Patriotism is Like Racism," *Ethics* 101 (1990): 144–150.
Gonzalez, Lelia, and Carlos Hasenbalg. *Lugar de negro.* Rio de Janeiro: Editora Marco Zero, 1982.
Gordon, Allport. *The Nature of Prejudice.* Boston: Beacon Press, 1954.
Gordon, Lewis R., ed. *Bad Faith and Antiblack Racism.* Atlantic Highlands, NJ: Humanities Press International, Inc., 1995.
———. *Existence in Black: An Anthology of Existentialist Black Philosophy.* New York: Routledge, 1997
———. *Fanon.* Cambridge, MA: Blackwell Publishers, 1996.
Gossett, Thomas. *Race: The History of an Idea in America.* New York: Schoken, 1965.
Gould, Stephen Jay. *The Mismeasure of Man.* New York: W. W. Norton, 1983.
Graham, Richard, ed. *The Idea of Race in Latin America, 1870–1940.* Austin, TX: University of Texas Press, 1990.
Grant, Michael. *From Alexander to Cleopatra: The Hellenistic World.* New York: Scribner, 1982.
———. *The Jews in the Roman World.* New York: Scribners, 1973.
Greene, John C. *The Death of Adam: Evolution and Its Impact on Western Thought.* Ames, Iowa: Iowa State University Press, 1959.
———. "Some Early Speculations on the Origin of Human Races," *American Anthropologist* 56:1 (1954): 31–41.
Green, Judith. "King's Historical Location of Political Concepts," APA *Newsletter on Philosophy and the Black Experience* 91 (1992): 12–14.
Green, Rayna. *Women in American Indian Society.* New York: Chelsea House Publishers, 1992.
Greenbaum, Susan. "What's in a Label? Identity Problems of Southern Indian Tribes," *Journal of Ethnic Studies* 19:2 (Summer 1991): 107–26.
Greenberg, S. *Legitimating the Illegitimate.* Berkeley, CA: University of California Press, 1987.
Gregory, Steven, and Roger Sanjek, eds. *Race.* New Brunswick, NJ: Rutgers University Press, 1994.
Gregory, Ian. "The American Debate on the Negro's Place in Nature, 1780–1815." *Journal of the History of Ideas* 15:3 (1954): 384–96.
———. "T. W. Moore on the Ethics of Discrimination," *Journal of the Philosophy of Education* 17 (1983): 127–30.
Griaule, Marcel. *Conversations with Ogotommelii.* Oxford, England: Oxford University Press, 1965.
Gross, Barry R. *Reverse Discrimination.* Amherst, NY: Prometheus Books, 1977.
Grove, David J. *The Race vs. Ethnic Debate.* Denver, CO: Center on International Race Relations, University of Denver, 1974.
Guillaumin, Colette. *L'Idéologie raciste.* Paris: Mouton, 1972.
———. "The Practice of Power and Belief in Nature, Part II. The Naturalist Discourse" *Feminist Issues* 1 (1981).

———. "Race et nature: Système des marques, idée de groupe naturel et rapports sociaux," *Pluriel-Débats* (1977).

———. *Racism, Sexism, Power, and Ideology.* New York: Routledge, 1995.

———. *Sexe, race et pratique du pouvoir. L'idée de Nature.* Paris: Côte-femmes, 1992.

Guimarães, Antonio S. A. *Classes Trabalho E Differenciacao Social a Brasil.* Bahia: Centro de Recursos Humanos, Universidade Federal da Bahia, 1990.

———. *Repensando uma Decada a Construcao, Actualidades brasileiras.* Bahia: Universidade Federal da Bahia, Centro Editorial e Didatico, 1994.

Guimarães, Antonio Michel Agier, and Nadya A. Castro. *Imagens e Identidades Do Trabalho.* São Paulo: Editora Hvcitec; Brasilia, DF: Institut Français de Recherche Scientifique pour la Development Cooperation, 1995.

Gyekye, Kwame. *An Essay on African Philosophical Thought—The Akan Conceptual Scheme.* Cambridge: Cambridge University Press, 1987.

HMSO. *Race Relations Act 1976,* Chapter 74, 1976.

HMSO. *Policy for the Inner Cities,* Cmd 6845, 1977.

Hacker, Andrew. *Two Nations.* New York: Ballantine, 1992.

Hall, Stuart. *New Times: The Changing Face of Politics in the 1990's.* New York: Verso, 1990.

———. *Questions of Cultural Identity.* London: Sage Publishing, 1996.

———. "Race, Articulation and Societies Structured in Dominance," *Sociological Theories: Race and Colonialism.* Paris: UNESCO, 1980.

Hallen, Barry, and Jhon O. Sodipo. *Knowledge, Belief, and Witchcraft.* London: Ethnographica Press, 1986.

Halter, John S. *Outcasts from Evolution. Scientific Attitudes of Racial Inferiority 1859–1900.* Urbana. IL: University of Illinois Press, 1971.

Hanke, Lewis. *Aristotle and the American Indians—A Study in Race Prejudice in the Modern World.* New York: Hollis and Carter, 1959.

Hare, Richard, M. *Midwest Studies in Philosophy III.* Minneapolis, MN: University of Minnesota Press, 1980.

Harmon, Charles L., ed. *Darwin's Legacy.* San Francisco: Harper & Row, 1983.

Harris, Leonard. "Historical Subjects and Interests: Race, Class, and Conflict," Michael Sprinkler, et al., eds., *The Year Left.* New York: Verso, 1986, 91–106.

———. "Postmodernism and Racism: An Unholy Alliance," ed. Fred L. Hord, J. S. Lee, *I Am Because We Are.* Amherst, MA: University of Massachusetts Press, 1995, 367–82.

———. "Prolegomenon to Race and Economics," ed., Thomas D. Boston, *A Different Vision.* New York: Routledge, 1996, pp. 136–54.

Harris, Leonard, ed. *Philosophy Born of Struggle.* Dubuque, IA: Kendall Hunt Pub. Co., 1984.

———. *Philosophy of Alain Locke.* Philadelphia, PA: Temple University Press, 1989.

Harris, Leonard, Abebe Zegeye, and Julia Maxted. *Exploitation and Exclusion: Race and Class in Contemporary US Society.* London: Hans Zell Pub., Co., 1991.

Harris, Marvin. *The Rise of Anthropological Theory.* New York: Crowell, 1968.

Harris, Trudier. *Exorcising Blackness.* Bloomington, IN: Indiana University Press, 1984.

Hartsock, Nancy. "Rethinking Modernism," *Cultural Critique* 0882–4371 (Fall 1987): 187–206.

Harvey, David. *The Condition of Postmodernity.* Oxford: Blackwell, 1989.

Hauserman, Nancy R., Masako N. Darrough, and Robert H. Blank, eds., *Biological Differences and Social Equality.* Westport, CT: Greenwood Press, 1983.

Hay, Denys. *Europe: Emergence of an Idea.* Edinburgh: Edinburgh University Press, 1968.

Heilke, Thomas W. *Voegelin on the Idea of Race: An Analysis of Modern European Racism.* Baton Rouge, LA: Louisiana State University Press, 1990.

Helbling, Mark. "African Art: Albert C. Barnes and Alain Locke," *Phylon* 43:1 (1982): 57–67.

———. "Alain Locke: Ambivalance and Hope," *Phylon* 40:3 (1979): 291–300.

Hellwig, David. J., ed. *African American Reflections on Brazil's Racial Paradise*. Philadelphia: Temple University Press, 1992.

Herm, Gerhard. *The Phoenicians: the Purple Empire of the Ancient World.* trans. Caroline Hiller. New York: William Morrow, 1975.

Herrnstein, Richard, and Charles Murray. *The Bell Curve*. New York: The Free Press, 1994.

Hersch, Jeanne. "The Concept of Race," *Diogenes* 59 (Fall 1967): 114–33.

Hertzberg, Arthur, ed. *The Zionist Idea*. New York: Doubleday, 1959.

Hirschfeld, M. *Racism*. London: Gollancz, 1938.

Hobsbawm, Eric, and Terence Ranger, eds. *The Invention of Tradition*. Cambridge: Cambridge University Press, 1983.

Hofstadter, Richard. *The American Political Tradition*. New York: A. A. Knopf, 1948.

Hollinger, Robert. "Can a Scientific Theory Be Legitimately Criticized, Rejected, Condemned, or Suppressed on Ethical or Political Grounds," *Journal Value Inquiry* 9 (Winter 1975): 303–6.

Holmes, Eugene C. "Alain Locke–Philosopher, Critic, Spokesman," *Journal of Philosophy* 54 (February 1957): 113–18.

Hook, Sidney. "Discrimination, Color Blindness, and the Quota System," *Reverse Discrimination*, ed. Barry R. Gross. New York: Prometheus Books, 1977: 88–96.

hooks, bell. *Yearning: Race, Gender and Cultural Politics*. Boston: South End Press, 1990.

Hord, Fred. *I Am Because We Are*. Amherst, MA: University of Massachusetts Press, 1995.

Horne, Gerald. *Reversing Discrimination*. New York: International Publishers Co., Inc., 1992.

Horowitz, Maryanne C. *Race, Class, and Rank*. New York: University of Rochester Press, 1992.

Horsman, Reginald. *Race and Manifest Destiny: The Origins of American Racial Anglo-Saxonism*. Cambridge, MA: Harvard University Press, 1981.

———. "Scientific Racism and the American Indian in the Mid-Nineteenth Century," *American Quarterly* 27 (1975): 2152–2168.

Houston, Lawrence N. *Psychological Principles and the Black Experience*. Boston, MA: University Press of America, 1990.

Howe, Irvin. *World of Our Fathers*. New York: Harcourt Brace Jovanovich, 1976.

Hughes, C. Alvin. "We Demand Our Rights: The Southern Negro Youth Congress, 1937–1949," *Phylon* 48:1 (1987): 38–50.

Husserl, Edmund. *Cartesian Meditations: An Introduction to Phenomenology*. Dordrecht: Martinus Nijhoff Publishers, 1960.

Ignatiev, Noel. *How the Irish Became White: Irish-Americans and African-Americans in 19th-Century Philadelphia*. New York: Verso, 1995.

Ignatiev, Noel, and John Garvey, eds. *Race Traitor*. New York: Routledge, 1996.

Ikonne, Chidi. "Rene Maran and the New Negro," *Colby Library Quarterly* 15:4 (1979): 224–39.

Innes, Duncan. *Anglo American and the Rise of Modern South Africa*. New York: Monthly Review Press, 1984.

Ireland, Thomas. "Discussion: The Relevance of Race Research," *Ethics* 84 (January 1974): 140–45.

Irele, Abiola. "The African Imagination," *Research African Literatures* (special issue on Critical Theory and African Literature) 21, no. 11 (Spring 1990): 49–67.

Israel, Jonathan I. *European Jewry in the Age of Mercantilism*, 2d ed. New York: Oxford University Press, 1989.

Jacquard, Albert. *Au peril de la science*. Paris: Le Seuil, 1982.

———. *Eloge de La Différence. La Génétique et les hommes*. Paris: Le Seuil, 1978.

James, Cyril. L. R. *The Black Jacobins: Toussant L'Ouverture and the San Domingo Revolution*, 2d ed., rev. (New York: Vintage Books, 1989).

James, William. *Pragmatism*. New York: Longman, Green, and Co., 1907.

Jarvie, Ian C., and J. Agassi. *Rationality*. Oxford: Blackwell, 1970.

Jay, Martin. *The Dialectical Imagination—A History of the Frankfurt School and the Institute of Social Research*. London: Heinemann, 1973.

Jencks, Christopher. "Discrimination and Thomas Sowell," *New York Review of Books* (March 3, 1983): 33–38.

Jennings, James, ed. *Race, Politics, and Economic Development*. London: Verso, 1992.

Johnson, Charles. *Being and Race*. Bloomington, IN: Indiana University Press, 1988.

Jones, Malcolm. "Education and Racism," *Journal of Philosophy of Education* 19 (December 1985): 223–34.

Jones, R. A. "Perceiving the Other." *In the Eye of the Beholder*. New York: Praeger, 1982.

Jordan, Winthrop D. *White over Black: American Attitudes toward the Negro, 1550–1812*. Chapel Hill, NC: University of North Carolina Press, 1968.

Juteau-Lee, Danielle. "La Production de l'ethnicite ou la part réelle de l'idéal," *Sociologie et sociétés* 1983.

Kahneman, Daniel, Paul Slovic, and Amost Tversky. *Judgement Under Uncertainty*. Cambridge: Cambridge University Press, 1982.

Kallen, Horace M. "Alain Locke and Cultural Pluralism," *Journal of Philosophy* 54 (February 1957): 119–26.

Kamin, Leon. *The Science and Politics of IQ*. Potomac, MD: Erlbaum, 1974.

Karcher, C. L. "Melvilles Gees–Forgotten Satire on Scientific Racism," *American Quarterly* 27:4 (1975): 152–68.

Kastein, Josef. *History and Destiny of the Jew*, trans. Huntley Paterson. New York: Viking Press, 1933.

Katz, Judy. *White Awareness Handbook for Anti-Racist Training*. Norman, OK: University of Oklahoma, 1978.

Katz, D., and J. Braly. "Verbal Stereotypes and Racial Prejudice." *Journal of Abnormal and Social Psychology* 30 (1933): 175–93.

Katz, Phyllis, and Dalmes A. Taylor. *Eliminating Racism*. New York: Plenum Press, 1988.

Kaufmann, Walter. *Nietzsche: Philosopher, Psychologist, Anti-Christ*. New York: Vintage, 1958.

Kayyali, Abd Al Wahhab. *Zionism, Imperialism, and Racism*. London: Vroom Helm, 1979.

Keith, A. "The Evolution of the Human Species," *Journal of the Royal Anthroplological Society* 58 (1928): 305–21.

Kelman, S. "Cost-Benefit Analysis: An Ethical Critique," *Regulation* January–February 1981.

Kelsey, George. "The Racist Search for the Self," *Journal of Religious Ethics* 6:2 (Fall 1978): 240–356.

Ketchum, Sara Ann. "Implicit Racism," *Analysis* 36 (January, 1996): 91–95.

Kimlica, Will, "Liberalism, Individualism, and Minority Rights," in Allan C. Hutchinson and Leslie J. M. Green, *Law and the Community: The End of Individualism?* Toronto: Carswell, 1989, p 297.

Kimlica, Will, ed. *The Rights of Minority Cultures*. Oxford: Oxford University Press, 1995.

Kinder, David R., and David O. Sears. "Prejudice and Politics: Symbolic Racism versus Racial Threats to the Good Life," *Journal of Personality and Social Psychology* 40:3 (1981): 414–43.

King, Joyce E. "Dysconscious Racism: Ideology, Identity, and the Miseducation of Teachers," *Journal of Negro Education* 60:2 (Spring 1991): 133–46.

King, Martin L. *Stride toward Freedom*. New York: Harper & Row, 1958.

Kitcher, Philip. *Abusing Science*. Cambridge, MA: MIT Press, 1982.

———. *Advancement of Science*. New York: Oxford University Press, 1993.

———. *Lives to Come*. New York: Simon & Schuster, 1996.

———. *Vaulting Ambition*. Cambridge, MA: MIT Press, 1985.

———. "Species," *Philosophy of Science*. 51 (1984): 308–33.

Knowles, Louis, and Kenneth Prewitt, eds. *Institutional Racism in America*. Old Tappan, NJ: Prentice Hall, 1969.

Koel, Joel. *White Racism*. New York: Columbia University Press, 1984.

Korman, Abraham. *The Outsiders: Jews and Corporate America*. Lexington, MA: Lexington Books, 1988.

Kornblith, Hilary. *Naturalizing Epistemology*. Cambridge, MA: MIT Press. 1985.

Kotkin, Joel. *Tribes*. New York: Random House, 1993.

Kotkin, Joel, and Yoriko Kishomoto. *The Third Century*, New York: Crown, 1988.

Kovel, Joel. *White Racism: A Psychohistory*. London: Free Association, 1988.

Kranzler, David. *Japanese, Jews and Missionaries*. New York: Yeshiva University Press, 1976.

Kumar, Dharma. *The Cambridge Economic History of India, Vol. II: 1757–1970*. New Delhi: Cambridge University Press, 1982.

Kuper, Leo, ed. *Race, Science and Society*. New York: Columbia University Press, 1975.

LaCapra, Dominick, ed. *The Bounds of Race*. Ithaca, NY: Cornell University Press, 1991.

Laclau, Ernesto. "The Impossibility of Society," *Canadian Journal of Political and Social Theory* 7:12 (1983): 21–24.

Leicester, Mal. "Racism, Responsibility and Education," *Journal of Philosophy Education* 22 (Winter 1988): 201–6.

Lelyveld, Joseph. *Move Your Shadow: South African, Black and White*. New York: Times Books, 1985.

Leone, Bruno. *Racism*. Minnesota: Greenhaven Press, Inc. 1986.

Le Pen, Jean-Marie. *Les Français d'abord*. Paris: Carrère/Lafon, 1984.

———. *National Hebdo*. Paris, 1985.

Leslie, Charles, P. J. M. McEwan, O. D. Wilson, C. O. Lovejoy, and J. P. Rushton. "Scientific Racism: Reflections on Peer Review, Science and Ideology," *Social Science and Medicine* 31:8 (1990): 891–905.

Leventhal, Dennis A. *The Jewish Community of Hong Kong*, rev. ed. Jewish Publication Society of Hong Kong, 1988.

Lévi-Strauss, Claude. *L'identité*. Paris: Grasset, 1977.

Levin, Jack, and William Levin. *The Function of Discrimination and Prejudice*. New York: Harper & Row, 1982.

Levitas, Ruth, ed. *The Ideology of the New Right*. London: Polity Press, 1986.

Lewis, Arthur. *Racial Conflict and Economic Development*. Cambridge, MA: Harvard University Press, 1985.

Lewontin, Richard. C. *The Analysis of Variance and the Analysis of Causes Reprinted in the IQ Controversy*. New York: Pantheon (1974).

———. *Human Diversity*. San Francisco: Freeman, 1982.

Lewontin, Richard C., Steven Rose, and Leon J. Kamen. *Not in Our Genes: Biology, Ideology, and Human Nature*. New York: Pantheon Books, 1984.

Lichtenberg, Judith. "Racism in the Head, Racism in the World," *Philosophy and Public Policy* (newsletter of the Institute for Philosophy and Public Policy, University of Maryland) 12, no. 1 (Spring–Summer 1992): 3–5.

Lieberman, Leonard. "The Debate Over Race: A Study in Sociology of Knowledge," *Phylon* 29 (1968): 127–41.

Ling, Amy. *Between Worlds: Women Writers of Chinese Ancestry*. New York: Pergamon Press, 1990.

Liska, Allen. *The Consistency Controversy*. New York: Wiley, 1975.

Livingstone, F. B. "On the Nonexistence of Human Races," in A. Montagu, ed., *The Concept of Race*. New York: Free Press of Glencoe, 1964, pp. 46–60.

Locke, Alain L. *Race Contacts and Interracial Relations*. Washington D.C.: Howard University Press, 1992.

———, ed. *The New Negro*. New York: Albert and Charles Boni, Inc., 1925.

Locke, Alain, and Bernhard J. Stern, eds. *When Peoples Meet*. New York: Committee on Workshops, Progressive Education Association, 1942.

Lorenz, Konrad. *On Aggression*, trans. Marjorie K. Wilson. San Diego, CA: Harcourt Jovanovich, 1974.

Lorde, Audre. "Age, Race, Class and Sex: Women Redefining Difference," in *Sister Outsider*. Trumansburg, NY: The Crossing Press, 1984.

Lorimer, Douglas A. *Colour, Class and the Victorians*. Leicester: Leicester University Press, 1978.

Lovett, Peter. *Income and Racial Inequality in Brazil*. Doctoral dissertation, University of Florida Press, 1978.

Lundberg, George. *Foundations of Sociology*. New York: MacMillan, 1939.

Lyotard, Jean-François. *The Postmodern Condition: A Report on Knowledge*, trans. Geoff Bennington and Brian Massumi. Minneapolis: University of Minnesota Press, 1984.

MacCoby, Hyam. *Revolution in Judea*. New York: Taplinger, 1980.

MacIntyre, Alasdair. *After Virtue*. Notre Dame, Ind: University of Notre Dame Press, 1981.

MacKinnon, Catherine A. *Feminism Unmodified: Discourses on Life and Law*. Cambridge, MA: Harvard University Press, 1987.

Madhavan, M. C. "Indian Emigrants: Numbers, Characteristics and Economic Impact" *Population and Development Review* 113 (September 1985): 460.

Maiz-Suarez, Ramon. "Celtic Race and Myth in the Origins of Galician Nationalism: Manuel M. Murguia," *Revista Espanola de Investigaciones Sociologicas* 25 (January-March 1984): 137–80.

Malvaeaux, Julienne. "The Economic Interests of Black and White Women: Are They Similar?" *The Review of Black Political Economy* 14:1 (Summer 1985): 5–28.

Marable, Manning. *Beyond Black and White*. London: Verso, 1995.

———. *Blackwater: Historical Studies in Race, Class Consciousness, and Revolution*. Ohio: Black Praxis Press, 1981.

———. *The Crisis of Color and Democracy*. Monroe, ME: Common Courage Press, 1992.

———. *Race, Reform and Rebellion*. Jackson, MS: University of Mississippi Press, 1984.

Marcilly, Jean. *Le pen sans Bandeau*. Paris, 1984.

Marquez, Benjamin. "The Politics of Race and Assimilation: The League of United Latin American Citizens, 1929–40," *Western Political Quarterly* 42:2 (June 1989): 355–75.

Mason, Ernest D. "Alain Locke on Race and Race Relations," *Phylon* 40:4 (1979): 342–50.

Matustik, Martin. *Postnational Identity*. New York: Guilford Press, 1993.

Marxs, Karl, and Friedrich Engels. "The Communist Manifesto" in *Karl Marx and Frederick Engels Selected Works*, vol. 1, Moscow: Foreign Languages Publishing House, 1962.

May, Larry. *The Morality of Groups*. Notre Dame, IN: University of Notre Dame Press, 1987.

Mayr, Ernst. *Animal Species and Evolution*. Cambridge, MA: Harvard University Press, 1963.

———. *Populations, Species, and Evolution*. Cambridge, MA: Harvard University Press, 1970.

———. *Systematics and the Origin of Species*. New York: Columbia University Press, 1942.

McCalman, Ian D. "Africa and Negro-American Nationalism: From Negritude to Black Revolution," *Australian National University History Journal* 7 (1970): 42–59.

McClendon, McKee J. "Racism, Rational Choice, and White Opposition to Racial Change: A Case Study of Busing," *Public Opinion Quarterly* 49:2 (1985): 214, 233.

McConahay, John, and Joseph Hough, Jr. "Symbolic Racism," *Journal of Social Issues* 32:3 (1976): 23–45.

McCord, David, and William Cleveland. *Black and Red: The Historical Meeting of Africans and Native Americans*. Atlanta, GA: Dreamkeeper Press, Inc., 1990.

McGary, Howard, and Bill Lawson. *Between Slavery and Freedom*. Bloomington, IN: Indiana University Press, 1992.

McKay, Nellie. "Black Theater and Drama in the 1920's: Years of Growing Pains, *Massachusetts Review* 28:4 (May 1, 1987): 615–26.

Mbiti, John. *African Religions and Philosophy*. Garden City, NY: Anchor Books, 1970.

Memmi, Albert. *Dominated Man*. Boston: Beacon Press, 1971.

———. *Portrait du colonisé*. Paris: Buchet/Chastel, 1957.

Menkitti, I. A. "The Resentment of Injustice: Some Consequences of Institutional Racism," *Philosophical Forum* 9 (Winter-Spring 1977–78): 227–49.

Merrick, Thomas, and D. Graham. *Population and Economic Development in Brazil.* Baltimore, MD: Johns Hopkins University Press, 1979.

Michaels, Walter Benn. *Our America: Nativism, Modernism, and Pluralism.* Durham, NC: Duke University Press, 1995.

Miles, Robert. *Capitalism and Unfree Labour: Anomaly or Necessity?* London: Tavistock, 1987.

———. "Racism," in *Dictionary of Race and Ethnic Relations,* 2d ed., ed. E Ellis Cahsmore. London: Routledge, 1988, pp. 276–79.

———. *Racism.* London and New York: Routledge, 1989.

———. *Racism after "Race Relations."* London and New York: Routledge, 1994.

———. *Racism and Migrant Labour: A Critical Text.* London: Routledge and Kegan Paul, 1982.

———. "Recent Marxist Theories of Nationalism and the Issue of Racism," *British Journal of Sociology* 38:1 (1987): 24–43.

Mill, J. S. *On Liberty* (1859) Indiana: Hackett Publishing Co., 1978.

Miller, Arthur G. *In the Eye of the Beholder.* New York: Praeger, 1982.

Miller, Joseph C. *Way of Death.* Madison, WI: The University Of Wisconsin Press, 1988.

Miller, Richard. *Analyzing Marx.* Princeton, NJ: Princeton University Press, 1987.

———. *Fact and Method.* Princeton, NJ: Princeton University Press, 1987.

Mills, Charles. *The Racial Contract.* Ithaca, NY: Cornell University Press, 1997.

Montagu, Ashley. *The Concept of Race.* New York: Free Press of Glencoe, 1964.

———. "The Concept of Race," *American Anthropologist* LXIV (1962): 919–28.

———. *The Idea of Race.* Lincoln, NE: University of Nebraska Press, 1965.

———. *Man's Most Dangerous Myth: The Fallacy of Race.* Cleveland, OH: World, 1964.

———. *Race, Science, and Humanity.* New York: Van Nostrand Reinhold, 1963.

———. *Sociobiology Reexamined.* New Jersey: Oxford University Press, 1980.

Moore, Robert. *Racism and Black Resistance in Britain.* London: Pluto Press, 1975.

Moraga, Cherrie, and Gloria Anzaldua, eds. *This Bridge Called My Back: Writings by Radical Women of Color.* New York: Kitchen Table: Women of Color Press, 1983.

Moreland, Lois B. *White Racism and the Law.* Columbus, OH: Charles E. Merrill Publishing Company, 1970.

Morner, Magnus. *Race Mixture in the History of Latin America.* Boston: Little, Brown & Company, 1967.

Morrison, Toni. 1992. *Playing in the Dark: Whiteness and the Literary Imagination.* Cambridge, MA: Harvard University Press.

Morton, Frederick. *The Rothschilds: A Family Portrait.* New York: Atheneum, 1962.

Morton, Patricia. *The Historical Assault on Afro-American Women.* Westport, CT: Greenwood Press, 1991.

Moses, Greg. *Revolution of Conscience.* New York: Guilford Press, 1997.

Mosley, Albert G., and Nicholas Capaldi. *Affirmative Action.* Lanham, MD: Rowman & Littlefield, 1996.

Mosse, George L. *Toward the Final Solution: A History of European Racism.* London: Dent and Sons, 1978.

Motoyoshi, Michelle E. "The Experience of Mixed-Race People: Some Thoughts and Theories," *Journal of Ethnic Studies* 18:2 (Summer 1990): 77–94.

Mowlana, Hamid. *Global Information and World Communication? New Frontiers.* New York: Longmans, 1986.

Mudimbe, V. Y. *The Invention of Africa.* Bloomington, IN: Indiana University Press, 1988.

Muga, David A. "The Marxist Problematic as a Model Interdisciplinary Approach to Ethnic Studies," *Journal of Ethnic Studies* 17:4 (Winter 1990): 53–80.

Muhlstein, Anka. *Baron James: Rise of the French Rothschilds.* New York: Vendome Press, 1982.

Mumford, Lewis. *Ethnics and Civilization.* New York: Harcourt Brace, 1934.

Munford, Clarence. "Ideology and Racist Mystification in America," *Revolutionary World* 17:18 (1976): 57–85.

Murphy, Jeffrie G. *Evolution, Mortality, and the Meaning of Life.* Latham, MD: Rowman and Allenheld, 1982.

Murphy, Rhoads. *The Outsiders: The Western Experience in India and China.* Ann Arbor, MI: University of Michigan Press, 1977.

Myrdal, Gunnar. *An American Dilemma.* New York: Harper Bros., 1944.

Nairn, Tom. *Break-up of Britain.* London: Verso, 1981.

Nam Tae y. *Racism, Nationalism, and Nation-Building in Malaysia and Singapore.* Meertu: Sadhna Prakashan, 1973.

Nasr, Marilin. *Surat-al-Arab wa-al-Islam fi al-madrasiyah al-Faransiyah.* Bayrut: Markaz Dirasat al-wadah al-Arabuyah, 1995.

Nathanson, Stephen. "Is Patriotism Like Racism?" *APA Newsletter on Philosophy and the Black Experience* 91 (1992): 9–11.

National Council of the Churches of Christ. *Indicators of Institutional Racism, Sexism and Classism, Some Suggested Responses.* New York: National Council of Churches, 1992.

Newcomb, Theodore, and W. Charters. *Social Psychology.* New York: Dryden, 1950.

Neugebauer, Christian. "Hegel and Kant—A Refutation of Their Racism," *Quest* (June 1991): 50–73.

Nickel, J. W. "Discrimination and Morally Relevant Characteristics," *Analysis* 32:4 (1972): 113–14.

Nietzsche, Friedrich. *The Birth of Tragedy and the Genealogy of Morals,* trans. Francis Golffing. Garden City, NY: Doubleday Anchor edition, 1956.

Nikolinakos, M. "Notes on an Economic Theory of Racism," *Race: A Journal of Race and Group Relations* 14 (April 1985): 365–81.

Nisbert, Richard, and Led Ross. *Human Inference.* Old Tappan, NJ: Prentice Hall, Inc., 1980.

Noel, Donald L. *The Origins of American Slavery and Racism.* Ohio: Charles E. Merrill, 1972.

Ochillo, Yvonne. "The Race-Consciousness of Alain Locke," *Phylon* 47:3 (1986): 173–81.

Omi, Michael, and Howard Winant. *Racial Formation in the United States: From the 1960s to the 1980s.* New York: Routledge & Kegan Paul, 1986.

———. "Racial Theory in the Post War United States: A Review and Critique," *Sage* 12:2 (May 1987): 3–45.

Oruka, H. Odera. *Sage Philosophy.* New York: E. J. Brill, 1990. "Philosophical Sagacity in African Philosophy." *The International Philosophical Quarterly* 23 no. 4 (December 1983): 383–93.

O'Shaughnessy, Martin. "Modern Languages and Anti-Racism," *British Journal of Language Teaching* 26:2 (Fall 1988): 71–73.

Outlaw, Lucius. *On Race and Philosophy.* New York. NY: Routledge, 1996.

Paliaro, Harold E. *Racism in the Eighteenth Century.* Cleveland, OH: The Press of Case Western Reserve University, 1973.

Palmer, Frank, ed. *Anti-Racism—An Assault on Education and Value.* London: Sherwood Press, 1986.

Pareto, Vilfredo. *The Mind and Society—A Treatise on Sociology,* 4 Vols., Dover Books, 1963.

———. *Traité de sociologie générale.* Paris, 1932.

Park, Robert Ezra. *Race and Culture.* New York: The Free Press, 1950.

Parsons, Talcott. *The Social System.* Illinois, IN: Free Press, 1951.

Parsons, Talcott, and Edward Shils. *Towards a General Theory of Action.* New York: Harper and Row, 1962.

Patterson, Orlando. *Ethnic Chauvinism: The Reactionary Impulse.* New York: Stein and Day, 1977.

———. *Slavery and Social Death.* Cambridge, MA: Harvard University Press, 1982.

Peterson, William, Michael Novak, and Phillip Gleason. *Concepts of Ethnicity*. Cambridge, MA: Harvard University Press, 1982.

Pettigrew, Thomas F., ed. *Prejudice*. Cambridge, MA: Harvard University Press, 1982.

———. *Racial Discrimination in the United States*. New York: Harper & Row, 1975.

Phillips, Jenny. *Symbol, Myth and Rhetoric: The Politics of Culture in an Armenian-American Population*. New York: AMS Press, 1989.

Phizacklea, Annie, ed. *One-Way Ticket: Migration and Female Labour*. London: Routledge & Kegan Paul, 1983.

Pierce, Charles S. "How to Make Or Ideas Clear." *Values in a Universe of Chance*. Garden City, NY: Doubleday, 1958.

———. *Values in a Universe of Chance*. Stanford: Stanford University Press, 1958.

Pierce, Chester M. "Psychiatric Problems of the Black Minority," in *American Handbook of Psychiatry*. New York: Basic Books, 1974.

Pierson, Donald. *Negroes in Brazil: A Study of Race Contact in Bahia*. Chicago: University of Chicago Press, 1942.

Piper, Adrian M. "Higher Order Discrimination," *Identity, Character, & Morality*. Cambridge, MA: MIT Press, 1990, pp. 285–309.

———. "Two Kinds of Discrimination," *Yale Journal of Criticism* 6 (1993): 25–74.

Pittman, John P., ed. "Introduction: African-American Perspectives and Philosophical Traditions," *Philosophical Forum*. 24: 103 (Fall-Spring 1992–93): 1–296.

Poliakov, Leon. *The Aryan Myth: A History of Racist and Nationalist Ideas in Europe*. London: Heinemann, 1974.

Popkin, Richard. "Hume's Racism," *Philosophical Forum* 9 (Winter/Spring, 1977–78): 211–26.

———. "The Philosophical Bases of Modern Racism," *Journal of Operational Psychology* 5:2 (Spring/Summer, 1974): 24–36.

Porterfield, Ernst. *Black and White Mixed Marriages*. Chicago, IL: Nelson-Hall, 1984.

Portocarrero Maisch, Gonzalo. *Racismo y mestizaje*. Lima: Stir Casa de Estudio del Socialismo, 1993.

Powell, Thomas. *The Persistence of Racism in America*. Lanham, MD: Littlefield Adams Quality Paperbacks, 1993.

Prager, Jeffrey. "American Political Culture and the Shifting Meaning of Race," *Ethnic and Racial Studies* 10:1 (1987): 62–81.

———. "The Meaning of Difference: A Response to Michael Banton," *Ethnic and Racial Studies* 10 (1987b): 469–72.

———. "White Racial Privilege and Social Change: An Examination of Theories of Racism," *Berkeley Journal of Sociology* 17 (1972–73): 117–50.

Pulman, C. *Race and Reason*. Washington, DC: Public Affairs Press, 1961.

Puzzo, Dante. "Racism and the Western Tradition," *Journal of the History of Ideas* 25 (October, 1964): 579–86.

Quine, Willard. *Méthodes de logique*, trans. M. Clavelin. Paris, 1973.

Radin, Paul. *The Racial Myth*. New York: Whittlesey House, 1934.

Rattray, Robert S. *Ashanti Law and Constitution*. London: Oxford University Press, 1929.

Rawls, John. "Outline of a Decision Procedure for Ethnics," *Philosophical Review* 60 (1971): 171–92.

———. *A Theory of Justice*. Cambridge. MA; Harvard University Press, 1971.

Raymond, Janice. "The Illusion of Androgyny," *Quest* 2 (1) 1975.

Recinos, Harold J. *Hear the Cry: A Latino Pastor Challenges the Church*. Westminster: John Knox Press, 1989.

Reed, John, and Clive Wake, eds. *Senghor Prose & Poetry*. New York: Oxford University Press, 1965.

Reich, M. *Racial Inequality*. Princeton, NJ: Princeton University Press, 1981.

Reiman, Jeffrey H. *Justice and Modern Moral Philosophy*. New Haven, CT: Yale University Press, 1990.

———. *Police and Society*. Lexington, MA: Lexington Books, 1975.

———. *The Rich Get Richer and the Poor Get Prison: Ideology, Class, and Criminal Justice*. New York: John Wiley & Sons, 1979.

Reis, Roberto, and David W. Foster, eds. *Bodies and Biases: Sexualities in Hispanic Cultures and Literature*. Minneapolis: University of Minnesota Press, 1996.

Rex, John. *Race and Ethnicity*. Milton Keynes: Open University Press, 1986.

———. *Race Relations in Sociological Theory*. London: Weidenfeld & Nicolson, 1970.

Rex, John, and D. Mason. *Theories of Race and Ethnic Relations*. Cambridge: Cambridge University Press, 1986.

Rex, John, and Sally Tomlinson. *Colonial Immigrants in a British City*. London: Routledge and Kegan Paul, 1979.

Richards, Janet Radcliff. "Discrimination," *Aristotelian Society Supplemental*, vol. 59 (1985): 53–82.

Riesman, Frank, and Harry Boyte. *The New Populism*. Philadelphia, PA: Temple University Press, 1986.

Robinson, Cedric, J. *Black Marxism*. London: Zed Press, 1983.

Roediger, David R. *The Wages of Whiteness: Race and the Making of the American Working Class*. London: Verso, 1992.

Root, Maria P. P., ed. *The Multiracial Experience: Racial Borders as the New Frontier*. Thousand Oaks, CA: Sage Publications, 1996.

Rorty, Richard. *Contingency, Irony, and Solidarity*. Cambridge: Cambridge University Press, 1989.

Rose, Arnold M. *Race, Prejudice and Discrimination*. New York: Knopf, 1951.

Rose, S., J. L. Forsythe, and A. Chase. "Legacy of Malthus–Social Costs of the New Scientific Racism," *Race & Class* 20:4 (1979): 115–20.

Ross, Howard. "Oppression, Racism, and the Status of Blacks in American Society", *Cogito* 3 (Summer 1985): 39–55.

Ross, Robert. *Racism and Colonialism*. The Hague: Martinus Nijhoff Publishers, 1982.

Rosazk, Betty, and T. Roszak, eds. "The Human Condition," in Betty Roszak and T. Roszak, eds. *Masculine/Feminine*. New York: Harper Colophon Books, 1971.

Roth, Byron M. "Social Psychology's 'Racism,'" *Public Interest* 98 (Winter 1990): 26–36.

Rothenberg, Paula, *Racism and Sexism*. New York: St. Martin's Press, 1988.

———. ed., *Feminist Frameworks*. New York: McGraw-Hill, 1978.

———. ed., *Race, Class, and Gender in the United States*. New York: St. Martin's Press, 1995.

Ruben, David-Hillel. "The Existence of Social Entities." *Philosophical Quarterly* 34:129 (October 1982): 295–310.

Rubin, Gail. "The Traffic in Women: Notes on the 'Political Economy' of Sex," in Rayna R. Reiter, ed. *Toward an Anthology of Women*. New York: Monthly Review Press, 1975.

———. "Women as Nigger," Betty Roszak and T. Roszak, eds. *Masculine/Feminine*. New York: Harper Colophon Books, 1971.

Rushton, Alan R. *Genetics and Medicine in the United States, 1800–1922*. Baltimore: The Johns Hopkins University Press, 1994.

Rushton, J. Phillipe. *Race, Evolution, and Behavior*. New Brunswick, NJ: Transaction Press, 1995.

Russell, Kathy, Midge Wilson, and Ronald Hall. *The Color Complex: The Politics of Skin Color Among African Americans*. New York: Harcourt Brace Jovanovich, Publishers, 1992.

Said, Edward W. *Orientalism*. New York: Pantheon Books, 1978.

Saintoul, Catherine. *Racie et l'ethnocentrisme dans la litterature indigeniste de la zona andine*. Buenos Aires: Ediciones del sot, 1988.

San Juan, Epifanio, Jr. "Problems in the Marxist Project of Theorizing Race," *Rethinking Marxism* 2:2 (Summer 1989): 58–82.

———. *Racial Formations/Critical Transformation: Articulation of Power in Ethnic and Racial Studies in the United States*. Atlantic Highlands, NJ: Humanities Press International, Inc., 1992.

Sartre, Jean-Paul. *Anti-Semite and Jew*. New York: Schocken Books, 1948.

———. *Being and Nothingness: A Phenomenological Essay on Ontology.* New York: Washington Square Press, 1956.

Scanlon, T. M. "Contractualism and Utilitarianism," *Utilitarianism and Beyond.* Cambridge, MA: Cambridge University Press, 1984.

Schillp, Paul A., ed. The Philosophy of Jean-Paul Sarte. LaSalle, IL: Open Court, 1981.

Schmid, J. P. *Le maître-camarade et la pédagogie libertaire.* Paris, 1936.

Schniappa, E. "Sophistic Rhetoric: Oasis or Mirage?" *Rhetoric Review* 10:1 (1978): 5–18.

Schopenhauer, Arthur. *The World as Will and Idea.* London: Kegan and Paul, Trench, Trubner, 1883.

Schutte, Ofelia. *Cultural Identity and Social Liberation in Latin American Thought.* Albany, NY: State University of New York Press, 1993.

Schutz, Alfred. *The Phenomenology of the Social World.* Evanston, IL: Northwestern University Press, 1967.

Schwartz, Barry, and Robert Disch, eds. *White Racism: Its History, Pathology and Practice.* New York: Dell Publishing Co., Inc., 1970.

Schwartz, L., and M. Schwartz. "The Legacy of Malthus—The Social Cost of the New Scientific Racism," *Contemporary Sociology* 1:15 (1982): 501–504.

Seliger, M. "Race Thinking during the Restoration," *Journal of the History of Ideas* 19 (April 1958): 273–82.

Senghor, Leopold. "On Negritude: The Psychology of the African Negro," *Diogené* 37 (1962).

Sheehan, Thomas. "A Normal Nazi," *New York Review of Books* (January 14, 1992).

Sher, George. "Groups and Justice," *Ethics* 87:2 (January 1977): 174–81.

Shulman, Steven. "Racial Inequality and White Employment: An Interpretation and Test of the Bargaining Power Hypothesis," *Review of Black Political Economy* 18:3 (Winter 1990): 5–20.

Singer, Milston. *When a Great Tradition Modernizes.* New York: Praeger, 1972.

Singer, Marcus G. "Is Racial Discrimination Arbitrary?" *Philosophia* 8 (November, 1978): 185–203.

———. "Some Thoughts on Race and Racism," *Philosophia* 8:2–3 (1978): 241–60.

Sivanandan, Ambalavaner. *A Different Hunger: Writings on Black Resistance.* London: Pluto Press, 1982.

———. *Black America.* London: Institute of Race Relations, 1993.

———. *Race and Resistance.* London: Race Today Publications, 1983.

Sizemore, Barbara. "The Politics of Curriculum, Race, and Class," *Journal of Negro Education* 59 (Winter 1990): 77–85.

Skidmore, Thomas. *White into Black.* Durham, NC: Duke University Press, 1993.

Skidmore, Thomas E., and Bradford E. Burns. *Elites, Masses, and Modernization in Latin America, 1850–1930.* Austin: University of Texas Press, 1979.

Skillen, Anthony. "Racism: Flew's Three Concepts of Racism," *Journal of Applied Philosophy* 10 (1993): 73–89.

Slote, Michael. "Agent-Based Virtue Ethics." A paper presented as a University of Santa Clara conference on virtue ethics, March, 1994.

———. *Common-Sense Morality and Consequentialism.* London: Routledge & Kegan Paul, 1985.

Smedley, Audrey. *Race in North America.* Boulder, CO: Western Press, 1993.

Smith, Anthony. *The Human Pedigree.* London: George Allen & Unwin, 1975.

Smith, Tony. *The Patterns of Imperialism: The United States, Great Britain, and the Late-Industrializing World Since 1815.* Cambridge, England: Cambridge University Press, 1981.

Sniderman, Paul, Thomas Piazza, Philip E. Terlock, and Ann Kindrick. "The New Racism," *American Journal of Political Science* 35:2 (1991): 423–47.

Sniderman, Paul, Philip E. Terlock, and Donald R. Kinder. "Symbolic Racism: Problems of Motive Attribution in Political Analysis," *Journal of Social Issues* 42:2 (1986): 129–50.

Snyder, Louis L. *Macronationalisms: A History of Panmovements.* Westport CT: Greenwood Press, 1984.

Sodipo, John O. "Some Philosophical Aspects of the African Historical Experience." In *African Philosophy*, edited by Claude Sumner. Adis Ababa: Chamber Printing House, 1980.

Sollors, Werner, ed. *Beyond Ethnicity*. Oxford: Oxford University Press. 1986.

———. *The Invention of Ethnicity*. New York: Oxford University Press, 1989.

Sorel, George. *Réflexions sur la violence*. Paris: M. Rivière, 1972.

South, Scott J., and Richard B. Felson. "The Racial Patterning of Rape," *Social Forces* 69:1 (September 1990): 71–93.

Sowell, Thomas. *The Economics and Politics of Race*. New York: Quilt, 1983.

———. *Ethic America*. New York: Basic Books, 1981.

———. *Preferential Policies: An International Perspective*. New York: William Morrow, 1990.

———. *Race and Cult: A World View*. New York: Basic Books,, 1994.

———. *Race and Economics*. New York: McKay, 1975.

Spear, Percival. *India: A Modern History*. Ann Arbor, MI: University of Michigan, 1961.

Spengler, Oswald. *The Decline of the West*. New York: Knopf, 1928.

Sperber, Dan. *Le Symbolisme en Général*. Paris, 1974.

Sprinkler, Michael, et al., eds. *The Year Left*. New York: Verso, 1986.

Squadrito, Kathleen. "Racism and Empiricism," *Behaviorism* 7 (Spring 1979): 105–15.

Stamp, Kenneth. *The Peculiar Institution*. New York: Knopf, 1956.

Starobinski, Jean. "Rousseau et Voltaire," *Critique*. 449 (October 1984).

Steele, Shelby. *The Content of Our Character*. New York: St. Martin Press, 1990.

Stein, Edward. *Forms of Desire*. New York: Routledge, 1992.

Steinberg, Stephen. *Turning Back: The Retreat From Racial Justice in American Thought and Policy*. Boston, MA: Beacon Press, 1955.

———. *The Ethnic Myth: Race, Ethnicity, Class in America*. Boston: Beacon Press, 1981.

Stepan, Nancy Leys. *The Idea of Race in Science: Great Britain, 1800–1950*. London: Archon Books, 1982.

Stepan, Nancy Leys, and S. Gilman. "Appropriating the Idioms of Science: Strategies of Resistance to Biological Determinism." Unpublished manuscript. 1988.

Stephan, W., and D. Rosenfield. "Racial and Ethnic Stereotypes," *In the Eye of the Beholder*. New York: Praeger, 1982.

Stevens, Frank S. *Racism: The Australian Experience*. New York: Taplinger Pub. Co., 1972.

Stolcke, Verena. *Racismo y sexualidad en la Cuba colonial*. Madrid: Alianza Editorial, 1992.

Synder, Louis. *The Idea of Racialism*. Princeton, NJ: Princeton University Press, 1962.

Tabe, Noboru. *Indian Entrepreneurs at the Crossroads*. Tokyo: Institute of Developing Economies, 1970.

Taguieff, Pierre-André. *Face au racisme*. 2 vols. Paris: Editions La Découverte, 1991.

———. *La force du préjugé: essai sur le racisme et ses doubles*. Paris: Gallimard, 1987.

———. *Les Fins de l'antiracisme*. Paris: Editions Michalon, 1995.

———. "National Identity Framed in the Logic of Racialization," *Mots/Les langages du politique* 12 (1986): 91–128.

Taguieff, Pierre-André, and Gil Delannoier. *Théories du nationalisme*. Paris: Editions Kime, 1991.

Taguieff, Pierre-André, and Philippe Petits. *Fins de République Menacée*. Paris: Textuel, 1996.

Tajfel, Henri. "Cognitive Aspects of Prejudice," *Journal of Social Issues* 25:4 (1960): 79–97.

———. "The Roots of Prejudice: Cognitive Aspects," in P. Watson, *Psychology and Race*. Chicago: Aldine, 1973.

Takaki, Ronald. *Strangers from Different Shores: A History of Asian Americans*. New York: Penguin Books, 1990.

Tamir, Vicki. *Bulgaria and Her Jews: The History of a Dubious Symbiosis*. New York: Yeshiva University Press, 1979.

Tatum, B. D. "Talking about Race, Learning about Racism—The Application of Racial Identity Development Theory in the Classroom," *Harvard Educational Review* 62:1 (1992): 1–24.

Taylor, C. M. "Dubois, W. E. B. Challenge to Scientific Racism," *Journal of Black Studies* 11:4 (1981): 449–60.

Taylor, Charles. *Multiculturalsim and the Politics of Recognition.* Princeton, NJ: Princeton University Press, 1992.

Tawney, Robert H. *Equality.* New York: Harcourt, Brace, 1952.

Teague, Bob. *The Flip Side of Soul: Letters to My Son.* New York: Quilt, 1990.

Telles, E. "Residential Segregation by Skin Color in Brazil," in *American Sociological Review* 57 (1992): 186–97.

Tempels, Placide. *Bantu Philosophy.* Paris: Presence Africaine, 1959.

Tenebaum, Joseph. *Race and Reich.* New York: Twayne, 1957.

Terris, Martin. "An Ancient Basis for African Philosophy." *Second Order* 5 (July 1976): 27–36.

Thalberg, Irving. "The Justification of Institutional Racism," *Philosophical Forum* 3 (Winter, 1972): 243–264.

———. "Reverse Discrimination and the Future," *Philosophical Forum* 5 (Fall–Winter 1973): 294–308.

Thomas, Brinley. *International Migration and Economic Development.* Paris: UNESCO, 1961.

Thomas, Laurence. "Racism and Sexism: Some Conceptual Differences," *Ethics* 90 (1980): 239–50.

———. *Vessels of Evil.* Philadelphia: Temple University Press, 1993.

Thornton, Russell. *American Indian Holocaust Survival: A Population History Since 1492.* Norman, OK: University of Oklahoma Press, 1987.

Ture, Kwame, and Charles Hamilton. *Black Power.* New York: Vintage, 1992. (Reissue, with new afterword of 1967 edition.)

Thurow, Lester C. *Poverty and Discrimination.* Washington, DC: Brookings Institute, 1969.

Tocqueville, Alexis de. *The European Revolution and Correspondence with Gobineau,* John Likas, ed. New York: Anchor Books, 1959.

Todd, Gitlin. *The Twilight of Common Dreams: Why America is Wracked by Culture Wars.* New York: Metropolitan Books, Henry Holt and Company, 1995.

Todorov, Tzvetan. *The Conquest of America.* New York: Harper and Row, 1984.

Toll, William. *The Resurgence of Race.* Philadelphia, PA: Temple University Press, 1979.

Topinard, Paul. *De la race en anthropologie.* Paris: G. Masson, 1892.

Torres, Gerald and Donald P. Brewster. "Judges and Juries: Separate Moments in the Same Phenomenon," *Law & Inequality.* 4 (1986) 171–188.

Touchard, Jean. *Le Gaullisme, 1940–1969.* Paris: Le Seuil, 1978.

Trivers, Robert. *Social Evolution.* Redwood City, CA: Benjamin Cummings, 1985.

Trorre Espinosa, Carlos de la. *El racismo en ecuador.* Ecentro andino de accion Popular-CAAP, 1996.

Tuckman, Barbara. *Bible and Sword.* New York: Ballantine, 1984.

Turner, Jonathan H., and Royce Singleton, Jr. "A Theory of Ethnic Oppression: Toward A Reintegration of Cultural and Structural Concepts in Ethnic Relations Theory," *Social Forces* 56:4 (1978): 1001–1018.

Uebel, Thomas E. "Scientific Racism in the Philosophy of Science: Some Historical Examples," *Philosophical Forum* (Fall 1990): 1–18.

UNESCO. *The Race Question in Modern Science.* Paris: UNESCO, 1956.

———. *Sociological Theories: Race and Colonialism.* Paris: UNESCO, 1980.

Unsuriyah wa-al Sahyuniyah. *Al-unsuriyah wa-al-Sayuniyah.* al-Qahairah: Ittihad al-Muhamin al-Arab, 1990.

U.S. Bureau of the Census. *Census of Population: General Population Characteristics–United States* (Vol. CP-1-1), Washington, DC: Government Printing Office, 1990.

Urback, P. "Progress and Degeneration in the IQ Debate," *British Journal for the Philosophy of Science* 25 (1974): 99–135.

Van Dyke, Vernon. *Equality and Public Policy.* Chicago, IL: Nelson-Hall, 1990.

Vetterling, Braggin Mary, ed. *Sexist Language.* Totowa, NJ: Littlefield Adams, 1981.

Vetterling, Braggin Mary, and F. A. Elliston, et. al. *Feminism and Philosophy.* Totowa: Littlefield Adams, 1971.

Varet, Gilbert. *Racisme et philosophie.* Paris: Denoel, 1973.

Wacker, R. Fred. *Ethnicity, Pluralism, and Race.* New York: Greenwood Press, 1983.

Wade, Peter. *Blackness and Race Mixture: The Dynamics of Racial Identity in Columbia.* Baltimore, MD: Johns Hopkins University Press, 1993.

Wagley, Charles. "On the Concept of Social Race in the Americas." *Contemporary Cultures and Societies of Latin America.* New York: Random House, 1965, pp. 531–45.

Wagner, Roy. *The Invention of Culture.* Chicago, IL: University of Chicago Press, 1975.

Wandby, D. *Bâtisseurs d'une tradition.* Paris: Selghers, 1966.

Washbrook, David A. *The Emergence of Provincial Politics.* Cambridge, 1976.

———. "Law, Sate and Agrarian Society in Colonial India," *Modern Asian Studies.* 15:3 (1981): 649–721.

Washbrook, David A, and C. J. Baker. *South India: Political Institutions and Political Change.* Delhi: Macmillan Co. of India, 1975.

Wasserstrom, Richard A. "On Racism and Sexism." *Today's Moral Problems.* New York: MacMillan, 1979.

———. *Philosophy and Social Issues.* Notre Dame: University of Notre Dame Press, 1980.

Waters, H. "Anti-Racist Science Teaching," *Race & Class* 30:1 (1988): 104–6.

Weber, Max. *General Economic History.* New York: The Free Press, 1950.

Weigel, Russell H., and Paul W. Howes. "Conceptions of Racial Prejudice: Symbolic Racism Reconsidered," *Journal of Social Issues* 41:3 (1985): 117–38.

Weiner, Michael. *Japan's Minorities.* New York: Routledge, 1997.

Weinroth, Jay. "Nation and Race: Two Destructive Concepts," *Philosophical Forum* 15 (June 1979): 67–86.

Wellman, David T. "Prejudiced People Are Not the Only Racists in America," *Portraits of White Racism.* New York: Cambridge University Press, 1977.

West, Cornel. "A Genealogy of Racism: On the Underside of Modern Discourse," *The Journal* 1:1 (Winter/Spring 1984): 42–60.

———. *Keeping Faith: Philosophy and Race in America.* New York: Routledge, 1993.

———. *Prophesy Deliverance: An Afro-American Revolutional Christianity.* Philadelphia: Westminster, 1982.

———. *Race Matters.* Boston: Beacon Press, 1993.

Wetherell, Margaret, and J. Potter. *Mapping the Language of Racism.* New York: Columbia University Press, 1992.

Whitbeck, Caroline. "Theories of Sex Difference," *Philosophical Forum.* 5: 1–2 (1975): 54–80.

Wieviorka, Michel. "Racism and Modernity in Present-Day Europe," *Thesis Eleven* 35 (1993): 51–61.

Wiggins, David. *Needs, Value, Truth.* New York: Blackwell, 1987.

Williams, Eric. *Capitalism and Slavery.* Chapel Hill, NC: University of North Carolina Press, 1994.

Williams, Patricia J. *The Alchemy of Race and Rights.* Cambridge: Harvard University Press, 1991.

———. "On Being the Object of Property," *Signs* 14:1 (1988): 5–24.

———. *The Rooster's Egg.* Cambridge, MA: Harvard University Press, 1995.

Williams, Vernon. *Rethinking Race.* Lexington, KY: University Press of Kentucky, 1996.

Williamson, C. "Prejudices and Generalizations," *International Journal of Moral Social Studies* 2 (Summer 1987): 95–104.

Williamson, Joel. *The Crucible of Race—Black White Relations in the American South Since Emancipation.* New York: Oxford University Press, 1984.

Willis, David. "Racial Justice and the Limits of American Liberalism," *Journal of Religious Ethics* 6 (Fall 1978): 187–220.

Wilson, Clint. *Black Journalists in Paradox: Historical Perspectives and Current Dilemmas.* Westport, CT: Greenwood, 1991.

Wilson, Edward O. *On Human Nature.* Cambridge, MA: Harvard University Press, 1978.

———. *Sociobiology: The New Synthesis.* Cambridge, MA: Harvard University Press, 1975.

Wilson, Edward O., and W. L. Brown. "The Subspecies Concept and Its Taxonomic Application," *Systematic Zoology* 2 (1953): 97—111.

Wilson, William Julius. *The Decling Significance of Race.* 2d ed.

———. *Sociology and the Public Agenda.* Newbury Park, CA: Sage Publications, 1993.

———. *The Truly Disadvantaged: The Inner City, the Underclass, and Public Policy.* Chicago, IL: University Press of Chicago, 1987.

Windsor, Philip, ed., *Reason and History: Or Only a History of Reason?* Ann Arbor, MI: The University of Michigan Press 1990.

Wistrich, Robert. *Antisemitism: The Longest Haired.* New York: Pantheon, 1992.

Wolpe, H. "Capitalism and Cheap Labor Power in South Africa: From Segregation to Aparthied," *Economy and Society* 1 (1972): 425–56.

Woodmansee, J. J., and S. W. Cook. "Dimensions of Verbal Racial Attitudes: Their Identification and Measurement," *Journal of Personality and Social Psychology* 7 (1967): 240–50.

Wriggins, Jennifer. "Rape, Racism, and the Law," *Harvard Women's Law Journal* 6 (1983): 103–41.

Wright, W. R. *Café con leche: Race, Class, and National Image in Venezuela.* Austin, TX: University of Texas Press, 1990.

Wuthnow, R. "Anti-Semitism and Stereotyping," *In the Eye of the Beholder.* New York: Praeger, 1982.

Yamatani, Hide, and Gary Koeske. "Strategies for Examining Racial Discrimination Patterns: Limits of the Classical Validation Method," *Journal of Social Service Research* 8:1 (Fall 1984): 49–60.

Yang, Kun. *Min tsu yu min tsu hsueh.* Chen tu: Ssu-chuan min tsu chu pan she, 1983.

Young, Iris M. *Justice and the Politics of Difference.* Princeton, NJ: Princeton University Press, 1990.

Zegeye, Abebe, R. Cohen, and Y. G. Muthien, eds. *Repression and Resistance: Insider Accounts of Apartheid.* London: Hans Zell Publishers, 1990.

Zack, Naomi. *American Mixed Race.* Lanham, MA: Rowman and Littlefield, 1995.

———. *Race and Mixed Race.* Philadelphia, PA: Temple University Press, 1993.

Zubaida, Sami, ed. Race and Racialism. London: Tavistock, 1970.

Authors

K. Anthony Appiah, Professor of Afro-American Studies and Philosophy at Harvard University, is author of *Assertions and Conditionals, In My Fathers House*, and co-author with Amy Gutman of *Color Conscious*.

Etienne Balibar, Professor of Philosophy, University of Paris I (Pantheon-Sorbonne), is author *Philosophy of Marx; On the Dictatorship of the Proletariat;* and *Masses, Classes, Ideas*, and is co-author with Immanuel Wallerstein of *Race, Nation, Class* and co-author with Louis Althusser of *Reading "Capital."*

Martin Barker, who teaches in the Department of Philosophy, Bristol Polytechnic, England, is author of *The New Racism* and co-editor with Anne Beezer of *Readings into Cultural Studies*.

Ruth Benedict (1887–1948) was a noted Columbia University anthropologist and author of such field-defining works as *Race, Science, and Politics* and *Patterns of Culture*.

Claudia Card is Professor of Philosophy at the University of Winconsin, where she also has teaching affiliations with Women's Studies and Environmental Studies. She is author of *The Unnatural Lottery: Character and Moral Luck* and *Lesbian Choices*, and is the editor of *Feminist Ethics, Adventures in Lesbian Philosophy*, and *On Feminist Ethics and Politics*.

George M. Frederickson is Edgar E. Robertson Professor of United States History at Stanford University, and author of *The Inner Civil War, White Supremacy, The Black Image in the White Mind,* and *The Arrogance of Race.*

Jorge L. A. Garcia, Professor of Philosophy at Rutgers University, New Jersey, is author of *Ontology.*

David T. Goldberg, Chair, School of Justice Studies at Arizona State University, is author of *Racist Culture, Anatomy of Racism, Multiculturalism,* and *Jewish Identity.*

Lewis R. Gordon, who teaches in Africana Studies and in the Department of Religion at Brown University, is author of *Existence in Black, Franz Fanon,* and *Bad Faith and Antiblack Racism.*

Colette Guillaumin, French intellectual and activist, is author of *L'Idéologie raciste; Sexe, race et pratique; Bruler l'idéoloque raciste;* and *Racism, Sexism, Power, and Ideology.*

Antonio Sergio Alfredo Guimarães is Adjunct Professor of Sociology at the Universidade Federal da Bahia in Salvador, Brazil. He has been a research fellow at the CNPq (Brazilian Research Foundation) and is an editor of *Revista Afro-Asia.* He is also the author of numerous studies on industrial relations in Brazil.

Leonard Harris, Professor of Philosophy at Purdue University, is editor of *Philosophy Born of Struggle* and *Philosophy of Alain Locke,* and co-editor with Abebe Zegeye and Julia Maxted of *Exploitation and Exclusion.*

Philip Kitcher, Professor of Philosophy at the University of California, San Diego, is author of *Lives to Come, Abusing Science, Advancement of Science,* and *Vaulting Ambition.*

Joel Kotkin is Senior Fellow with the Center for the New West in Colorado and international Fellow at the Pepperdine University School of Business and Management. He is author of *Tribes* and co-author of *The Third Century.*

Alain Locke (1886–1954), a noted initiator of the Harlem Renaissance, was Professor of Philosophy at Howard University, editor of *The New Negro,* co-editor with Bernhard J. Stern of *When Peoples Meet,* and author of *Philosophy of Alain Locke* and *Race Contacts and Interracial Relations.*

Albert G. Mosley, Professor of Philosophy at Ohio University, is editor of *African Philosophy* and co-author with Nicholas Capaldi of *Affirmative Action*.

John A. Rex, Research Professor on Ethnic Relations (1984–1990), emeritus, and former Associate Director of the Centre for Research on Ethnic Relations (1974–1990) at the University of Warwick, is the author of numerous books, among them: *Ethnic Identity and Ethnic Organization in Britain, The Ghetto and the Underclass, Race and Ethnicity, Colonial Immigrants in a British City,* and *Social Conflict.*

Paula Rothenberg, who teaches at William Paterson College in New Jersey, is author of *Feminist Frameworks, Race, Class and Gender in the United States* and *Racism and Sexism.*

Pierre-André Taguieff teaches at the Sorbonne in Paris, and is author of *La force du préjugé: Essai sur le racisme et ses doublés, Face au racisme, Racisme: République menancée,* and *Les fins de l'antiracisme.*

Gerald Torres, Professor of Law at the University of Texas, is consultant to the U.S. Attorney General.

Pierre L. van den Berghe, Emeritus, University of Washington, and Center for Advanced Studies in the Behavioral Sciences at Stanford University, is author of *Race and Racism: A Comparative Perspective, Ethnic Phenomenon, Race and Ethnicity, Man in Society: A Biosocial View, State Violence and Ethnicity,* and *Race and Ethnicity in Africa.*

David A. Washbrook, Lecturer in History at the University of Warwick, is author of *The Emergence of Provincial Politics* and co-author with C. J. Baker of *South India: Political Institutions and Political Change.*

Index

479

480

India, 171; formation, 191; struggle, 196, 442

Class racism, 201–12; examples, 204, 209

Clothes, as markers, 224–26

Code words, defined by Michael Omi and Howard Winant, 288; example of, 288–89

Color: prejudice as distinct from race, 47–48; somatic norm image, 67; prejudice, 315, 319; differentiated from discrimination, 315; distinction, 315; as natural, 320; and race, 320–22; as criterion for objective groups, 320; in Brazil, 322; consciousness, 262; preferences, 412

Colonialism, 347, 438

Colored: as a different race, 223; Creoles, 97, 324–26. *See also* Color

Communitarianism, 303–304

Community, defined by social, 46, 299, 357

Concept, defined, 17; of racism, 47

Consciousness, 349, 355; false, 384; liberated, 448

Conservationists, and race, 111–14; and preservation, 217, 449

Construction, 216; of difference, 281, 289; nature of 282, 290; racial, 282, 283; gender, 282–84, 286, 291; reconstruction of, 282, 285–87, 291; in United States, 282; categories of, 282; as metaphysical, 283; as natural, 283–84; process of, 284; as a matter of degree, 285; descriptive use of, 285; liberal paradigm, 286–87; as moral deficiency, 289–91; gender as race, 291–92; example of, 292; deconstruction of, 293; created by racism and sexism, 294; ideological and political advocacy of, 303–304; as wealth, 304; blackness as social construction, 227; morally odious, 439; as cautionary tales, 446

Constructivism: defined, 44; strengths and weaknesses of, 443; examples of racism, 446

Conversos, 263–64

Critical theory, 147–48

Culture, and determinism, 62; markers, 68; inheritance, 91; cultural goods, 216–18; and reciprocity, 218; danger of mixing, 245

Darwinism, 173, 175, 206, 274; natural selection and race, 274–75; neo-Darwinism, 237–38, 248; defined, 238; and aggression,

241–42; and civilization, 248; and sociobiology, 249; Tory ideology as neo-Darwinism, 237

Dawkins, Richard, 249

Davenport, Charles B., 88–89

Democracy, as solution to racism, 47

Deontology, 386

De-culturalize, defined, 362

Determinism, 228; endogenous, 228, 234

Difference, extremes, 98, 238; and race, 270–71

Differentialist discourse, 302. *See also* Racism

Discrimination, 152, 383, 401; types, 152–55; 383; utility maximizing, 383, 399; higher order, 401; not racist, 408; reverse, 425. *See also* Color, Racism

Domination, 217; in male behavior, 248; and baboons, 248, 233

Du Bois, W. E. B., 75, 257; definition of race, 257; non-racist use of race, 257; race consciousness, 258

Durkheim, Emile, and sociology, 305

Dysteleological, 442

Ego schema, 58

Eliminativism, about race, 87; claims of, 98, 101–102; rejection of, 104

Equality, 45, 217, 361; and postmodernism, 362

Endogamy, defined, 59–61, 417

Entitlement, 385

Environment: normal, natural, artificial, 246; and neo-Darwinian, 246; men as changer of, 247; and ethnology, 246; and social behavior, 246, 448

Essences, and genes, 275

Essentialist, 273

Ethnic status, communialism, 166; ascription of, 334–35; limitation of, 336; affected by power, 337

Ethnicity: irrepressible nature, 50; and race, 51; defined by Pierre van den Berghe, 52; instrumentalist, 53; defined, 53; circumstantialist, 53; ethnism and ethny defined, 57; endogamy, 59–61; exogamy, 59; ethnies and inbreeding, 61; as shared experience, 62; as kin selection, 62; markers, 64, 68–69; as determined by, 62; markers, 64, 259, 261, 263; defined by Kitcher, 107; and boundary, 144; and theories of race, 182; concept of, 122, 161; politics of, 182, 183–84, 189; zero sum game, 184; rejec-